THE NATIONAL INSTITUTE OF
ECONOMIC AND SOCIAL RESEARCH

Economic and Social Studies
XIX

THE ANTITRUST LAWS
OF THE U.S.A.

The National Institute of Economic and Social Research is an independent, non-profit-making body, founded in 1938. It has as its aim the promotion of realistic research, particularly in the field of economics. It conducts research by its own research staff and in co-operation with the universities and other academic bodies. The results of the work done under the Institute's auspices are published in several series, and a list of its publications up to the present time will be found at the end of this volume.

THE
ANTITRUST LAWS
OF THE
UNITED STATES OF
AMERICA

A Study of Competition Enforced by Law

BY

A. D. NEALE

WITH A FOREWORD BY
ABE FORTAS

SECOND EDITION

CAMBRIDGE
AT THE UNIVERSITY PRESS
1970

Published by the Syndics of the Cambridge University Press
Bentley House, 200 Euston Road, London N.W.1
American Branch: 32 East 57th Street, New York 22, N.Y.10022

Library of Congress Catalogue Number: 73–92251

Standard Book Number: 521 07657 9

First edition 1960

Printed in Great Britain
at the University Printing House, Cambridge
(Brooke Crutchley, University Printer)

FOREWORD

The institution of antitrust in the United States has long been regarded as peculiarly a native product, like our popular music. Strangers to our culture, exposed to the gyrations and massive impact of antitrust, have generally responded with bewilderment and disbelief. At most, they have dimly perceived the shape and power of antitrust. They have seen it as a remarkable compound of law, economic philosophy, cultural commitment and social religion. But the mechanics and the dynamics of this peculiar institution have been largely beyond the ken of the foreigner.

A. D. Neale, a British civil servant, is the exception to this generality. He has mastered the strange language of this peculiar American institution, and he has penetrated to the heart of its meaning. His purpose in studying American antitrust was to write an account of its actual working for the benefit of British businessmen and lawyers, but his accomplishment surpasses this objective. He has set down a solid analysis and a highly perceptive evaluation of American antitrust from which Americans themselves will derive much profit.

I know of no other single volume which covers the entire field of antitrust so comprehensively and so well. In about 500 pages, Mr Neale sharply analyses the case law and the statutes in each area of antitrust. He has an instinct for the jugular of a case. He senses the difference between a ripple and a current in the vast stream of the law, and he is able, with remarkable sensitivity, to trace the particulars of antitrust development to their abiding source: to America's 'distrust of all sources of unchecked power'; to our ambivalent attitude towards 'big business', which he aptly sums up as our 'romantic view of the achievements and efficiency of large industrial organizations', coupled with our 'suspicious view of their power'.

Antitrust in the United States is not, in the conventional sense, a set of laws by which men may guide their conduct. It is rather a general, sometimes conflicting, statement of articles of faith and economic philosophy, which takes specific form as the courts and governmental agencies apply its generalities to the facts of individual cases in the economic and ideological setting of the time. It is for this reason that both knowledge of past decisions and a sense of the animating theory of antitrust are essential to understanding. In Mr Neale's short book, American as well as British businessmen, lawyers and economists will find a sound guide through the wilderness of antitrust precedents, and a perceptive index to its philosophy.

ABE FORTAS

Washington, November 1959

CONTENTS

PREFACE TO THE SECOND EDITION

The generous reception accorded to this book, particularly in the United States, has led to a continuing demand which has so far been met by reprinting the original text. By 1966, however, it had become clear that, if it was to continue to be useful to students, a new edition had to be prepared. New antitrust law is being made all the time in the courts and each year brings a crop of important decisions. In particular, when the original text was completed, the appellate courts had hardly begun to hand down decisions under section 7 of the Clayton Act, and the treatment of the law on acquisitions and mergers was therefore so summary as to be of little value.

At this time I was fortunate to meet Mr Dan G. Goyder, an English solicitor who had just completed a study of the subject including the latest case material. He has been largely responsible for the selection and exposition of the leading cases which have occurred since the original text was written, and I am greatly indebted to him for the skill and clarity with which he has fitted this new material into the original structure of the book. The opportunity has also been taken in the new edition to revise and shorten Part II to take account of the considerable changes in the climate of thought and the many additions to the literature which have occurred since 1960.

We are both indebted to Mr Matthew Nimetz and Mr Ronald Lewis, who have kindly undertaken the task of reading the proofs of the new edition and have offered valuable comments and corrections. We are also indebted to the officers and staff of the National Institute for making arrangements for publication of the new edition, and in particular to Mrs Gillian Barlow for her devoted work on the index and proofs.

A.D.N.

NATIONAL INSTITUTE OF ECONOMIC
AND SOCIAL RESEARCH
September 1969

[xii]

PREFACE TO THE FIRST EDITION

I believe there is room on this side of the Atlantic for a book about the antitrust laws of the United States. Increased activity by United Kingdom business in the United States market and increased contacts with American firms have drawn more British companies into uncomfortable proximity with antitrust litigation, and the beginnings of a corpus of case law under the Restrictive Trade Practices Act of 1956 may make it useful and interesting to have available the means for comparing the United Kingdom decisions, as they appear, with the established lines of antitrust doctrine.

The opportunity to enlarge on an initial interest in this topic came to me as a result of the privilege of being awarded a Commonwealth Fund Fellowship in 1952, and I must record my debt to the officers of the Fund for their help in facilitating my programme of study in the United States and for many personal kindnesses.

While I was in Washington I was kindly given working space in the Federal Trade Commission and received every assistance from the Commission's Librarian. I was greatly helped and encouraged by the friendly interest and willingness to discuss their work of officials both in the Federal Trade Commission and the Department of Justice, who are too numerous to be acknowledged individually. I must, however, record my special indebtedness to Professor Corwin D. Edwards, at that time head of the Bureau of Industrial Economics in the Commission, who guided me at the outset and has subsequently read substantial parts of the manuscript and made many illuminating comments and corrections; and to Mr Sigmund Timberg, formerly a Special Assistant to the Attorney General in the Antitrust Division of the Department of Justice, who has, with the greatest kindness and tolerance, read nearly all the draft and suggested many improvements. I must also thank Mr George E. Frost of Chicago, who kindly read and gave me good advice about the chapter on the patent cases. For whatever errors and misjudgments remain, I am, of course, solely responsible.

The writing of the book would not have been possible without the generous help of my employers, the Board of Trade, in allowing me to be seconded to the National Institute of Economic and Social Research for a period sufficient to enable the bulk of the drafting to be done. This in turn was made possible by a grant received from the Government under the Conditional Aid Scheme for the use of counterpart funds derived from United States economic aid which I acknowledge with gratitude. As a public servant I must make it clear that all the judgments expressed in the book are entirely personal and in no way represent the views of the Board of Trade or of H.M. Government generally.

The National Institute of Economic and Social Research made available to me their facilities, and the officers of the Institute have shown me much kindness, besides relieving me of the administrative chores of publication. I must mention my particular gratitude to Miss Alison Clarke, who took charge so efficiently of the tasks of preparing the manuscript and reading the proofs, and to Miss Janet Telfer, who did the bulk of the typing.

A.D.N.

NATIONAL INSTITUTE OF ECONOMIC
AND SOCIAL RESEARCH

April 1960

INTRODUCTION

BACKGROUND AND DEFINITIONS: THE AIM AND SCOPE OF ANTITRUST

1. *Object of the study*

The antitrust laws of the United States of America are unique in scope of content and rigour of enforcement. In no other country is there such an elaborate and comprehensive body of law dealing with monopolies and restrictive business practices. At the same time it is widely conceded that the United States is pre-eminent in the power and drive of her industry and commerce. It is natural, therefore, to infer some connexion between economic success and the existence of this special body of law.

Connexion is, of course, more than conjunction; *post hoc* is not always *propter hoc*. Even the most ardent of American 'trust busters' would hardly claim that these laws are the sole or even the main cause of their country's high place in economic achievement. But many well qualified persons in the United States do, in fact, believe that the antitrust laws make an important contribution to economic health; other countries have frequently been enjoined by spokesmen of the United States, both official and unofficial, to introduce similar laws and, as it is often put, 'enjoy the benefits of competition'.

It is a mistake to think that outsiders are invariably wrong about what is good for us, so that this strongly held American opinion is at least a good reason for getting to know something about the antitrust laws and the way they work.

There are other reasons besides urging from outside for interest in the subject. The performance of the British economy is by common consent a more critical matter in these days than formerly. Short-comings, whether real or fancied, arouse a lively concern; and the effect of restrictive business practices on efficiency is one of the topics most often discussed. Successive legislative measures in Britain since the Second World War have reflected a consensus of opinion that private arrangements which suppress competition may go too far and require to be checked.[1] Competition between firms is, after all,

---

[1] In the United Kingdom jurisdiction over such arrangements has been divided between (*a*) the Monopolies Commission, an administrative body which investigates companies, industries and mergers under the provisions of the Monopolies and Restrictive Practices (Enquiry and Control) Acts of 1948 and 1953 as amended by the Monopolies and Mergers Act, 1965, and (*b*) the Restrictive Practices Court, which rules on the validity of restrictive trading agreements and resale price maintenance schemes, within the framework of the Restrictive Trade Practices Acts, 1956 and 1968, and the Resale Prices Act, 1964: these Acts contain a presumption that such restrictions work against the public interest.

accounted a principal virtue of private economic activity, operating as a stimulus to improved methods and as a safeguard against indifference to the wishes of consumers. It would seem inconsistent, therefore, to allow competition to be freely impaired, even eliminated, by private agreements between firms or by the acquisition of private monopoly power.

Even if it is accepted that there may be situations in which, for example, rationalization of production in larger units should be promoted and competition may justifiably be lessened or restrained, it seems questionable whether the job of deciding which these situations are and what form of restraint to adopt should be left to those upon whom competition is expected to exercise a salutary influence. Yet all this raises large questions. Who else is fitted to decide the proper occasions for limiting competition? By what criteria are these decisions to be made? By what legal or administrative processes are they to be enforced?

Answers to some of these questions are being worked out in our own way within the framework of the successive post-war statutes. But the existence across the Atlantic of a well established system of law which purports to be a comprehensive and successful solution of the problem still claims attention. It would not be difficult to find people who would warmly advocate introducing similar laws and processes of enforcement into this country; others are to be found who would believe just as strongly that such a policy would be disastrous here. Yet others would express a cynical view: how can these laws make much difference when great corporations like General Motors, Standard Oil of New Jersey, du Pont and others appear to enjoy without hindrance assets greater than those of many a sovereign state? Which view of the matter is to be believed? The object of this book is to provide an account of the actual working of the antitrust laws, so that the American approach to the subject may be fairly assessed and weighed against our own and other methods.

2. *The main provisions of the Sherman Act, Clayton Act and Federal Trade Commission Act; the means of enforcement*

The substantive provisions of the antitrust laws are few and brief; they are contained in seven sections taken from three statutes—the Sherman Act of 1890 and the Clayton Act and Federal Trade Commission Act of 1914. The two latter statutes have been amended in important ways by subsequent measures which will be mentioned below. There are some other minor laws, for example in connexion with resale price maintenance (see Chapter X) and with imported goods, but these three Acts contain the essentials of the system.

The *Sherman Act* of 1890 contains two main prohibitions:

Section 1. 'Every contract, combination in the form of trust or otherwise, or conspiracy, in restraint of trade or commerce among the several States or with foreign nations, is hereby declared to be illegal. . . .'

Section 2. 'Every person who shall monopolize, or attempt to monopolize, or combine or conspire with any other person or persons to monopolize any part of the trade or commerce among the several States, or with foreign nations, shall be deemed guilty of a misdemeanour. . .'

The *Clayton Act* of 1914 declares illegal four specified types of restrictive or monopolistic practice. They are in brief:

(a) price discrimination (section 2),
(b) exclusive-dealing and tying contracts (section 3),
(c) acquisitions of competing companies (section 7),
(d) interlocking directorates (section 8).

All these sections are qualified by provisos (some more elaborately defined than others) to the general effect that the practice concerned becomes unlawful only when its 'effect may be to substantially lessen competition or tend to create a monopoly'. The section dealing with price discrimination was revised in the Robinson-Patman Act of 1936 and that dealing with acquisitions in the Celler-Kefauver Act of 1950.[1]

The *Federal Trade Commission Act* of 1914 is concerned largely with the setting up of the Commission and the mechanics of its operation. Section 5 of the Act, however, contains one important substantive provision, which reads (as amended by the Wheeler-Lea Act of 1938) as follows: 'Unfair methods of competition in commerce and unfair or deceptive acts or practices in commerce are hereby declared illegal.'

The prohibitions of the Sherman Act create criminal offences punishable by fines and even imprisonment. Their enforcement, like that of any other criminal law, is a police function and is directed by the United States Department of Justice. The Sherman Act, however, also charges the Department of Justice with the duty of instituting proceedings in equity to prevent and restrain violations of the law. The significance of this is that a federal court may translate the general terms of the Act into a set of detailed injunctions regulating the future conduct of businesses found to be in violation of the law, and may even order the dissolution of such businesses or divest them of subsidiary

---

[1] It will be convenient to defer quotation in full of the provisions of the Clayton Act and its amendments to the chapters dealing with the case law under these statutes (see Chapters VII, VIII and IX).

parts, where these measures are found to be necessary to prevent continuing violations. From the point of view of maintaining competition these measures of equity relief have been more important to the Department of Justice than criminal penalties. Much of the Sherman Act case law therefore consists of suits in equity; civil and criminal actions are sometimes taken concurrently or in quick succession.[1]

The Department of Justice may also institute civil proceedings under the Clayton Act, but this is a shared responsibility because section 11 of that Act vests in the Federal Trade Commission the authority to enforce compliance with its provisions. The substantive provisions of the Clayton Act do not create criminal offences and the Commission has no criminal jurisdiction: it is an administrative agency with quasi-judicial powers entitled to conduct hearings in respect to suspected violations of the law and, if violations are found, to issue 'cease and desist' orders against further infringement. The Commission's 'cease and desist' order under the Clayton Act is subject to review by appellate courts, and is broadly equivalent to a trial court's equity decree in civil proceedings under the Sherman Act.

The Federal Trade Commission is also charged with securing compliance with the general ban on 'unfair methods of competition' in section 5 of the Federal Trade Commission Act.[2] This Act, like the Clayton Act, does not create criminal offences, but section 5 is of great importance, because the courts have ruled that the phrase 'unfair methods of competition' covers conduct that would also violate the Sherman Act and consequently that the Commission may exercise jurisdiction over what could equally well be Sherman Act cases. It will thus be found in the case law that many proceedings that are, in all but name, Sherman Act cases are taken by the Federal Trade Commission. Indeed, although it is established in principle that some forms of restrictive conduct may be 'unfair methods of competition' without 'assuming the proportions' of Sherman Act violations, it is rare in practice to come across instances; section 5 thus adds comparatively little to substantive antitrust law.[3]

---

[1] The various procedures and the considerations determining the choice between civil and criminal suits are described below, Chapter XIII.

[2] Many 'unfair or deceptive acts or practices in commerce', such as misleading advertisements, the use of lotteries for sales promotion and so forth, are covered by section 5 but not subject to the Sherman Act: these practices, however, are rather outside the sphere of antitrust law proper.

[3] '. . . although all conduct violative of the Sherman Act may. . . come within the unfair trade practice prohibitions of the Trade Commission Act, the converse is not necessarily true. It has long been recognized that there are many unfair methods of competition that do not assume the proportions of Sherman Act violations. . .' Supreme Court opinion in *Federal Trade Commission* v. *Cement Institute* (1948). The Commission has, however, made increasing use of section 5 to enable it to attack practices which, on technical jurisdictional grounds, cannot be attacked under the Clayton or Robinson-Patman Act, but which are

The enforcement of the antitrust laws does not depend exclusively on the Department of Justice and the Federal Trade Commission. The Sherman and Clayton Acts permit any private person who suffers damage as a result of violations to sue offenders and recover 'threefold the damages by him sustained'. A number of the cases described below will be 'treble-damage' actions of this kind. No action for damages is available under the Federal Trade Commission Act.[1]

3. *Sectors of the economy with legislative exemptions from antitrust laws: labour, public utilities, agriculture; financial and professional services partially immune*

The content of the antitrust laws is not fully described without some mention of exemptions from the statutes. The Sherman Act is all-embracing in its terms, so that any exception must be specified in amending legislation. This is important in itself, since it means that a majority in Congress has to be persuaded before any part of the economy can be insulated from these laws. A number of important exemptions have, however, been enacted.[2]

There is first a broad exemption for *labour*. Cases against restrictive behaviour by labour unions were successfully prosecuted under the Sherman Act before 1914, but section 6 of the Clayton Act declared 'that the labor of a human being is not a commodity or article of commerce'. Later legislation[3] has reinforced this position and the antitrust laws do not now apply to the activities of trade unions directed to promoting the interests of their members. This rule holds even when the union action is bound to impair business competition, so long as the union is pursuing its own rightful objectives and is not acting in collusion with employers. For example, a strong union may be able to prevent the products of a non-union factory from reaching the market or to keep goods from low-wage areas out of high-wage areas. The economic effects of such action may be much the same as those of a

in pari materia with the prohibitions of those statutes. Thus, under the Robinson-Patman Act it is illegal for a supplier to discriminate in various ways among purchasers of his products, but not illegal for the purchasers to induce certain favours, e.g. a promotional allowance, from the supplier; but the Commission has interpreted section 5 as entitling it to declare that such a purchaser has violated the antitrust laws (*Grand Union Co.* v. *Federal Trade Commission* (Second Circuit Court of Appeals, 1962),.

[1] This is because the Federal Trade Commission Act is not technically one of the 'antitrust laws' enumerated in section 1 of the Clayton Act; it is, however, an integral and essential part of the canon of antitrust law for ordinary purposes.

[2] Professors C. Kaysen and D. F. Turner in *Antitrust Policy*, Harvard University Press, 1959, estimate that 18·4% of American national income originates in sectors of the economy exempt from antitrust laws. Chapter VI of the *Report of the Attorney General's National Committee to Study the Antitrust Laws*, U.S. Government Printing Office, Washington, 1955, contains a detailed account of exemptions.   [3] In particular the Norris-La Guardia Act of 1932.

trade boycott or price fixing arrangement but no antitrust action will lie against the union: 'So long as a union acts in its self-interest and does not combine with non-labor groups, the licit and illicit . . . are not to be distinguished by any judgment regarding the wisdom or unwisdom, the rightness or wrongness, the selfishness or unselfishness of the end to which the particular union activities are the means.'[1]

The law, however, still bites on situations where trade unions and groups of employers conspire together to suppress or eliminate competition. In other words, businessmen are not entitled to take advantage of the relative immunity of labour and suborn the union, perhaps in consideration of a wage increase, to carry out restrictive schemes that they cannot legally operate themselves. Cases in which collusion between employers and unions is alleged are not infrequent; even so, some commentators believe that a serious loophole is left, as the community of interest between employers and unions may at times be so close that collusion is either unnecessary or of so informal a nature that its occurrence cannot be proved.[2]

Public utilities are largely exempt in practice from the laws. The power, transport and communications industries, though mostly carried on by private business, are subject to supervision by special regulatory commissions such as the Federal Power Commission, Federal Communications Commission, Interstate Commerce Commission, Federal Maritime Commission and Civil Aeronautics Board. It is accepted by the courts that the supervisory powers conferred by statute on these commissions give them prior jurisdiction in matters that might otherwise be litigated under the antitrust laws. Those who complain about discrimination or other restrictive behaviour on the part of power or transport concerns must therefore seek a remedy in the first place through administrative action by the appropriate commission. So long as the decisions made by the commissions are within their statutory powers, their prior jurisdiction is in practice controlling. Moreover, rate fixing agreements between steamship lines, airlines and railroads have been relieved by statute from antitrust action where the agree-

---

[1] Supreme Court opinion in *United States* v. *Hutcheson et al.* (1941).

[2] In *Local 189* v. *Jewel Tea Company* and *United Mine Workers* v. *Pennington et al.* (1965), the Supreme Court ruled that, even if the agreement at issue is intimately related to the union's legitimate area of concern, i.e. wages, hours and working conditions, the exemption does not automatically apply; the courts must consider whether the relationship of the agreement to the union's objective is sufficiently 'direct and immediate'. In general a union can, in law, have a direct and immediate interest only in restricting the commercial freedom of its immediate employer, and not in restraining the freedom of itself or such employer in relationships with third parties. *Jewel Tea* (which concerned the hours during which fresh meat should be on sale to the public in Chicago supermarkets) was, however, the first case for over twenty-five years in which the Supreme Court upheld a union-management bargain challenged under the antitrust laws.

ments are approved by the appropriate commission. In some situations
—the case law on this topic is complex—a residual field for antitrust
action may remain open;[1] but in general the Congress has not thought
it appropriate that there should be free competition in the field of
utilities and it is assumed that the commissions will use their statutory
powers to safeguard the public interest against undue restrictiveness.

Agricultural marketing over a wide range of products is also substantially insulated from the antitrust laws.[2] The Clayton Act declared
that nothing contained in the antitrust laws should be construed to
forbid the operation of agricultural or horticultural organizations conducted for mutual help and having legitimate objects. Later legislation
—the Capper-Volstead Act of 1922 and the Co-operative Marketing
Act of 1926—has extended and elaborated this general exemption for
agricultural co-operatives. Growers and even processors may join
together to market their products, and it is left to the Secretary of
Agriculture to prevent them from unduly enhancing prices. A similar
exemption operates for fishermen's co-operatives. Here again a residual
field for antitrust action remains open and there have been cases in
which predatory activities of co-operatives, outside the scope of their
legitimate objectives and directed to excluding the competition of
outsiders, have been successfully challenged in the courts. But a complete
monopoly in a market may be lawfully built up if the only means
adopted are co-operative buying and selling.[3]

Insurance and banking services are in part immune from the laws.
For a long time it was supposed that insurance was not within the
scope of the Sherman Act on the ground that it was not commerce.
In 1944 the Supreme Court upset this idea[4] and held that restrictive
agreements between insurance companies could violate the Act. In
1945, however, legislation was passed which granted insurers a mora-
torium against antitrust action until 1948, and provided that thereafter
the antitrust laws should apply only to the extent that the business of
insurance was not regulated by State law. Since all the States have
in fact introduced regulatory statutes, the scope for federal antitrust

---

[1] In *S.S.W.* v. *Air Transport Association* (1951) it was held that '[in] each case brought
against a regulated company under the antitrust laws, the subject matter or remedy afforded
by the regulatory statute are compared with that of the antitrust laws. If the latter either
covers subject matter outside the scope of the Commission's power or provides a remedy
which the Commission may not give, then they remain in effect to that limited extent.'

[2] This passage refers to private marketing agreements. There are also, of course, price
support schemes for the major crops in the United States and governmental marketing
programmes which insulate farmers from free competition.

[3] See the *Report of the Attorney General's National Committee*, pp. 307–11. An important
decision subsequent to that *Report* is *United States* v. *Maryland and Virginia Milk Producers'
Association* (Supreme Court, 1960).

[4] *United States* v. *South-Eastern Underwriters Association.*

action is now limited to situations not covered by these statutes. Boycotts and other coercive agreements between insurance companies would, however, still violate the Sherman Act, and mergers between them are within the reach of the Clayton Act. Co-operation between banks over lending policies and interest rates is accorded some immunity from antitrust action under the Federal Reserve Act of 1913; but this immunity is by no means complete and successful cases have been brought by the Government against restrictive commercial practices by banks.[1]

The question whether *other services and professions* are vulnerable to antitrust action is again a matter of defining the words 'trade and commerce' and is answerable only by reference to the case law; there is no general exemption for services and professions as such. The Supreme Court confirmed in 1954 a thirty-year-old rule that the business of putting on professional baseball games was sport and not commerce, but has since refused to extend this exemption to boxing, football and theatrical promotions.[2] In 1950 real estate brokers were held to be infringing the law by fixing prices for their services.[3] And in *United States* v. *American Medical Association* (Supreme Court, 1943) it was held that action taken by the Association to deny the services of doctors and hospital facilities to a group health scheme in Washington, D.C. was a conspiracy in restraint of trade. It has also been held by the Supreme Court (*Silver* v. *New York Stock Exchange*, 1963) that, even where a private association has a statutory right to regulate its members, it remains subject to the antitrust laws if it performs actions outside the scope of its proper jurisdiction.[4] Rules of conduct for professional bodies in connexion with the maintenance of ethical standards, even though they might have restrictive aspects, would probably not be challenged—it is not perhaps surprising that the legal profession seems

[1] An example is *United States* v. *Investors' Diversified Services et al.* (settled by a consent decree in 1954) in which it was alleged that a number of banks and insurance companies had conspired *inter alia* to require persons taking out mortgages on property from members of the 'ring' to insure the property through other members. Also, recent legislation makes it clear that the Justice Department may challenge a bank merger under the Clayton Act despite prior approval of the merger by a regulatory agency.

[2] The baseball case was *Toolson* v. *New York Yankees*: those on boxing, football and the theatre were *United States* v. *International Boxing Club of New York*, *Radovich* v. *National Football League* and *United States* v. *Lee Shubert*, respectively. The Attorney General's National Committee to Study the Antitrust Laws considered the *Toolson* decision a special and rather unorthodox application of the doctrine of *stare decisis* and of doubtful authority for any other art or sport (see the Committee's *Report*, pp. 63–4). In 1961 Congress enacted a special law to allow clubs which were members of a league engaged in professional team sports to pool their individual television rights for sale by the league as a package.

[3] *United States* v. *National Association of Real Estate Boards* (Supreme Court).

[4] The New York Stock Exchange was empowered by statute to control the dealings of its members with non-members, but this did not extend to instructing members to cut off all communications with a non-member securities dealer without allowing him any hearing.

to have been immune—but in general it appears that the commercial aspects even of the learned professions may come within the scope of the Sherman Act.

4. *Exemptions for certain practices: resale price maintenance; export agreements; wholly intra-State activities*

Apart from insulating certain sectors of the economy, such as labour, agriculture and public utilities, from antitrust action, Congress has also passed measures from time to time which exempt certain types of restrictive practice. The outstanding example of this kind of exemption is the practice of resale price maintenance, which manufacturers of branded goods have been specifically permitted by statute to enforce on their retailers. The story of the legal vicissitudes affecting this practice over the years will be given in Chapter X below.

Another example is the Webb-Pomerene Act of 1918, which allows American exporters to act together in export markets in ways that would otherwise violate the Sherman Act, for example, by arranging to avoid undercutting one another's prices. This exemption is supervised by the Federal Trade Commission and is subject to the proviso that agreements made under it must not raise prices or otherwise restrain trade in the United States, nor injure independent American exporters who prefer not to be parties to them. As will appear in Chapter XII below, the exemption does not entitle United States firms to participate in international cartel agreements.

Apart from these specific exemptions, the antitrust policy may sometimes be overborne or modified by other policies with conflicting aims.[1] The outstanding example occurred in the great depression when the legislation embodying President Roosevelt's 'National Recovery Program' involved a virtual suspension of the antitrust policy and industries were brought together under government auspices to devise measures for steadying price movements. While it is worth remembering that the policy was thus abandoned at a time of crisis, it must also be noted that the experiment was shortlived and subsequently much criticized. Less sweeping arrangements have been made when United States industry has had to be mobilized to meet external danger; necessary measures of industrial co-operation have then been indemnified against antitrust action, subject to safeguarding procedures in which the antitrust authorities have been joined.

State policies, such as conservation measures, may also override

[1] For an excellent discussion of the relationship between antitrust and other governmental policies see M. S. Massel, *Competition and Monopoly*, Brookings Institution, Washington, D.C., 1962, especially Chapters 1–3.

antitrust policy. For example, the Texas Railroad Commission, like similar bodies elsewhere, limits the amount of crude oil that may be extracted in any period from the Texas oilfields. This is primarily a conservation measure, since uncontrolled extraction may wastefully exhaust reserves. But within the limits set by the need for conservation, the amounts to be extracted are in practice calculated by reference to estimates of demand at the going price. This practice seems likely to affect the level of crude oil prices, a result which, in an industry not subject to this form of regulation, might well be challenged under the Sherman Act.

Finally, antitrust is a federal policy and can apply only to the extent that federal authority will carry. The constitution of the United States enumerates the powers surrendered by the several States to the federal Government and the so-called 'commerce clause' applies only to trade between the States and with foreign nations; commerce of a purely local nature must be regulated, if at all, by the government of the State concerned. This limitation is nowadays not so stringent in practice as it may appear. So far as the Sherman Act is concerned, wholly local restraints of trade are actionable so long as some actual or threatened, direct or indirect effect on interstate commerce is shown.[1] For example, a complaint that sugar refiners in California agreed on the price to be paid for sugar beet grown in California was held by the Supreme Court to state a cause of action under the Sherman Act on the ground that sugar made from the beet would eventually pass into interstate commerce.[2] As Mr Justice Jackson once put it: 'If it is interstate commerce that feels the pinch, it does not matter how local the operation which applies the squeeze.' Conversely, a local monopoly, such as that of a newspaper in a single town, can be brought within the Act by virtue of the transactions in interstate trade—purchases of newsprint, subscriptions to nation-wide agency services and so forth— by which it carries on business.[3]

Nevertheless there may be some purely local trade, and there is a great volume of business having local *and* national aspects, over which both federal and State authorities may exercise jurisdiction. The several States differ widely in their own approach to monopoly and restraint of trade. Some States, like Texas, have and enforce antitrust laws of a rigour comparable to that of the federal statutes; others have relatively

---

[1] The Clayton Act and Federal Trade Commission Act apply to practices occurring 'in commerce', i.e. in the course of interstate trade, and it is generally supposed that this is a narrower criterion than that adopted by the courts for the Sherman Act.

[2] *Mandeville Island Farms* v. *American Crystal Sugar Company* (1948). In *United States* v. *Pennsylvania Refuse Removal Association* (Eastern District Court, Pennsylvania, 1965) a conspiracy among Pennsylvania refuse collectors was held to fall within the jurisdiction of federal antitrust law, because some of the refuse was eventually disposed of over State lines into New Jersey!

[3] See *United States* v. *Lorain Journal Company* described below, in Chapter V, pp. 128–9.

little legislation or quite meagre means of enforcement. State antitrust activity is, however, increasing, especially to combat 'bid rigging' and price fixing in connexion with the supply of products to departments and agencies of the State itself. State courts, furthermore, have applied State antitrust laws not only to strictly local matters, but also to agreements and practices affecting more than one State which have a substantial local effect.[1] In some areas of the United States local restrictive arrangements are carried on without much hindrance. A majority of States even have legislation enforcing licensing and registration schemes which govern entry into various trades and occupations. Such schemes often extend beyond the professions proper to such trades as barbering and dry cleaning; and when they involve elaborate regulations and, as sometimes happens, are administered largely by established practitioners of the trade concerned, they may lead to restrictions of entry and even pricing arrangements of a kind which, if they were private restrictions in interstate commerce, would certainly fall foul of the Sherman Act.

5. *The origins and historical development of antitrust: the antecedent common-law rules; early enforcement; change of emphasis after 1914*

The object of this book is to present an up-to-date picture of the working of antitrust;[2] but a brief sketch of its historical origins may help the perspective of the picture. Although lawyers sometimes imply that the law stands majestic and immutable in a naughty world, courts are not in practice immune from the changing currents of social, economic and political thought. Different courts facing different problems at different times have in fact made different distinctions and brought now more, now less within the class of restraints of trade. Antitrust, like any human institution, has known periods of quiet and periods of energy, tediums, crises and climacterics. There is evidence that the aim and scope of the antitrust policy have changed a good deal since the passing of the Sherman Act, and may easily change some more in the future.

The impetus behind the movement for the earliest legislation gathered strength during the 1870s and 1880s. Already half a century before

[1] See 'Symposium on State Antitrust Laws', *American Bar Association, Antitrust Section, Proceedings,* vol. 29, 1965, pp. 255–300.

[2] Antitrust—it will be convenient hereafter to use this portmanteau word to stand for the composite made up of the statutes, the case law, and the policy and processes of administration—does not, of course, deal only with 'trusts'. A 'trust' in the strict sense was a particular technique for extending financial control over a number of enterprises. When the Sherman Act was passed in 1890 the 'trust' was already becoming outmoded; new laws of incorporation in certain States, the first of which was the New Jersey Holding Company Act of 1899, were enabling use to be made of the more flexible device of the holding company.

this a deep-rooted political tradition against concentrations of private power had forced the break-up of the central bank of the United States. After the Civil War, the railways with their privileges, charters and subsidies became the main object of suspicion and hostility. Many bodies with revealing names like 'The National Anti-Monopoly Cheap Freight Railway League' sprang up. The source of this hostility was primarily the farming community, and in the down-swings of the trade cycle an economic spur goaded their inherent political susceptibilities.

The farmers could not fail to mark the contrast between the rapidly falling prices which they received for their produce and the relatively 'sticky' prices of the goods they needed to buy. The farmer lost both as buyer and seller. 'Just as the price which the farmer received for the commodities he sold seemed to him to be fixed by those to whom he sold, so also he felt that the price of his supplies was fixed by those from whom he bought.'[1] The explanation was found in the 'trusts' or monopolies which were being built up in a number of consumer goods industries—fuel oil, sugar, matches, linseed oil, whisky and others. Reports of the secret rebates which the trusts obtained from the already unpopular railways added to the resentment against them. The farmers, together with the small businessmen, many of whom had been bankrupted by the rough methods of the trust builders, now directed their hostility against these new concentrations of industrial power, and against the eastern financiers who were believed to call the tune for the railways and the business trusts alike. Professors Stocking and Watkins quote a contemporary writer as saying: 'Indeed, the public mind has begun to assume a state of apprehension, almost amounting to alarm, regarding the evil economic and social tendencies of these organizations. The social atmosphere seems to be surcharged with an indefinite, but almost inexpressible fear of trusts.'[2]

The farmers were better endowed with political influence than economic strength, and organizations like the National Grange and the National Farmers' Alliance insistently demanded some control of the railways and of monopolies in general. The Congress outlawed rate discrimination by the railways in the Interstate Commerce Act of 1887. By 1888 both major parties had anti-monopoly planks in their platforms and the Republican Fifty-first Congress determined to legislate. The result was the Sherman Act of 1890.

A great deal is written in the United States about what was in the minds of the authors and sponsors of the Sherman Act, and it is not always easy to trace a clear and consistent story, as different schools of

[1] Solon J. Buck, *The Granger Movement*, Harvard University Press, 1913.
[2] George Gunton, writing in 1888, quoted by G. W. Stocking and M. W. Watkins, *Monopoly and Free Enterprise*, Twentieth Century Fund, New York, 1951.

thought about what antitrust ought to be tend to seek support for their views in selected quotations from contemporary writings and speeches.[1] It is pretty clear, however, that the paramount aim of the politicians of the day was the simple one of meeting the public demand for action against the trusts. The political sentiment of the grassroots against concentrations of power as such bulked large in the manner of presentation. 'If we will not endure a king as a political power, we should not endure a king over the production, transportation, and sale of any of the necessaries of life,' said Senator Sherman.

Although the American ideal of unfettered economic opportunity and the view that has been called 'Social Darwinism' were all part of the atmosphere of the period, there is little evidence that Sherman and the others had any idea of imposing an economist's model of competition on American industry. They did not consult the economists of the time; and even if they had done so, they would have found little support for any such course. The American Economic Association had been founded in 1886 as a protest against *laissez faire* economics, and one of its leading figures, J. B. Clark, had written of combinations in 1887:

Combinations have their roots in the nature of social industry and are normal in their origin, their development and their practical working. They are neither to be deprecated by scientists nor suppressed by legislators. They are the result of an evolution, and are the happy outcome of a competition so abnormal that the continuance of it would have meant widespread ruin. A successful attempt to suppress them by law would involve the reversion of industrial systems to a cast-off type, the renewal of abuses from which society has escaped by a step in development.

The economists of the day wanted to retain the advantages of both combination and competition. Sherman himself made it clear that the courts would be expected to distinguish between 'lawful combinations in aid of production and unlawful combinations to prevent competition and in restraint of trade. . . . It is the unlawful combination, tested by the rules of common law and human experience, that is aimed at by this bill.'

The phrase 'tested by the rules of common law' is the key. The American senators of the period, as of most periods, were nearly all professional lawyers. When they finally settled for the present wording of the Sherman Act with its blanket prohibition of restraint of trade, they assumed that they were carrying into statute law various distinctions

[1] I am much indebted in what follows to Mr William L. Letwin's paper, 'Congress and the Sherman Antitrust Law: 1887–1890', *University of Chicago Law Review*, vol. 23, no. 2, Winter 1956, p. 221, and to a further paper, on the 'Early History of the Sherman Act', which Mr Letwin delivered to the University of Chicago Law School Antitrust Seminar in June 1953 and kindly made available to me.

between lawful and unlawful restraints and combinations that the
courts had already made in common law and would continue to make.
'Restraint of trade', in other words, was a term of art from the beginning. Senator Hoar, one of the leading sponsors of the Act, said later:
'It was believed that the phrase "in restraint of trade" had a technical
and well understood meaning in the law. It was not thought that it
included every restraint of trade, whether healthy or injurious.'[1] It
seems likely that many of the senators believed that the courts would
strike down the rough and 'unfair' competitive methods of the big
trusts and loosen their exclusive hold on their industries, but would
not prevent consolidations aimed at more efficient large-scale production, nor even in every case restrictive agreements designed to avoid
'destructive' competition.[2]

Just what the 'rules of common law' were on restraint of trade, and
what distinctions were made between lawful and unlawful combinations is, however, a matter of dispute. Different lines of cases from
different courts can lead to different conclusions. Professor Milton
Handler warns us that 'the failure to recognize that the "common
law" is but a metaphorical expression and that there are as many
common laws as there are independent judicial systems has been the
principal cause of confusion'.[3] The English common law, for example,
was already well along the road which led to upholding almost any
restrictive combination whose participants could show that they had
some common economic interest and that they were not motivated by
sheer malice towards third parties.[4] Few American courts went this
far; the prevailing trend, according to Handler, was hostile to restrictive
arrangements between competitors even when it was urged that they
were necessary to put an end to 'ruinous' competition. He agrees,
however, that some courts upheld agreements to mitigate competition,
particularly when the participants were not dominant in their industry.
Letwin holds that the courts were becoming increasingly amenable in
this respect in the years leading up to the Sherman Act and that many
judges were sympathetic to the view that competition could become

[1] This quotation is a good example of how the term 'restraint of trade' may be used first
as a term of art and then as a description in the same breath.

[2] Mr Letwin records that Senator Hoar advised a group of wire manufacturers that a
proposed price fixing and profit sharing agreement designed to avoid destructive competition
would probably not violate the Act.

[3] Milton Handler, *A Study of the Construction and Enforcement of the Federal Antitrust Laws*,
(United States Temporary National Economic Committee, Monograph 38), U.S. Government Printing Office, Washington, 1941, p. 4.

[4] The leading English cases of the period are *Nordenfelt* v. *Maxim Nordenfelt Guns and
Ammunition Company* (1894) and *Mogul Steamship Company* v. *McGregor* (1892). Another article
by Mr Letwin ('The English Common Law Concerning Monopolies', *University of Chicago
Law Review*, vol. 21, no. 3, Spring 1954, p. 355) provides an admirable short outline of the
relevant English law.

excessive. Thus, while the Sherman Act may properly be said to have embodied the common law of restraint of trade in statutory form, there was at the outset more than one line along which the law might develop.

It was rather in the administration of law than in its content that the Sherman Act was a revolutionary new departure. First, it put teeth into the law of restraint of trade. Most common-law actions on the subject arose when one party to a restrictive contract sought to enforce it against another party. The most that a court could do in such a case was to declare the contract void and unenforceable because of its restrictive features. This did nothing to stop people making such contracts; whereas the Sherman Act made them a crime punishable by fines and even imprisonment, and thus brought against the trusts the threat of federal police action. The Act also required and empowered the federal law officers to institute equity proceedings against violations on behalf of the public at large. The legal risks facing monopolists and combinations thus became much more imposing than previously, when there was only the remote chance that their actions might be challenged as *ultra vires*, or the even remoter one that a private individual would be bold enough and rich enough to start an action for damages against them.

Secondly, by bringing all combinations and conspiracies in restraint of trade within the ban and prohibiting monopolization, the Act made it clear that the means by which restraint of trade was brought about was a matter of indifference to the law. Whether the trick was done by a legal contract or some looser form of agreement, by the formation of a trust or a holding company or simply by sheer aggregation of market power, the Act was still to apply.[1] This was important because, at common law, private litigation was much less likely to be effective, or indeed to arise at all, when the restraint was caused by concentration of business power than when it arose directly from the terms of a contract.

These two points tend to confirm the impression that the paramount aim of the Sherman Act at the start was to meet the public demand that the Federal Government should 'do something about the trusts'. The Act was concerned with bringing the administration and enforcement of pre-existing law within the domain of executive responsibility, rather than with interfering in the judicial role of deciding what constituted unlawful restraint of trade.

This impression is strengthened, too, by the early history of the

---

[1] Although now seen by hindsight to be implicit in the statute, some of these points had of course to be settled by the courts. For example, the question whether a combination carried out by means of a holding company could be caught under the Act was not settled until the Supreme Court's decision in the *Northern Securities* case in 1903.

enforcement of the Act. Indeed, the mere passage of the Act seems to have taken the heat off the topic, and for a considerable period next to nothing was done in Washington to secure forceful administration. It seems to have been thought that the prestige of the Act in itself, coupled with the provision for private, treble-damage actions and industry's supposed fear of publicity, would make it largely self-enforcing. No extra funds were voted to the Department of Justice for the tasks of enforcement until 1903. Very few cases were initiated by the Government, but, even so, six of the first seven were lost in the courts, including cases against the whisky and sugar trusts.[1]

The Supreme Court decision of 1895 in *United States* v. *E. C. Knight* (the sugar trust) even threatened for a time to make the Act a dead letter so far as manufacturing monopolies were concerned. It was held that, in so far as the trust's monopoly of sugar refining was concentrated in the State of Pennsylvania, it had not been shown to involve a direct restraint on interstate commerce. Yet this decision was apparently accepted with equanimity by the Attorney General of the day.[2] Despite all the setbacks, however, which were offset by little except one or two successful cases against railway rate fixing, Senator Hoar felt able to say in the Senate in 1903 that the Act 'has accomplished more, I believe, than was expected of it when it passed'.

The year 1903 ushered in a much more active period under the administrations of Theodore Roosevelt and Taft. Indeed, the Supreme Court decision of that year in the *Northern Securities* case, in which a railway merger organized by famous and powerful eastern financiers was successfully challenged by the administration amid great publicity, caught the public imagination and helped greatly to establish antitrust as a popular institution. By the end of the Roosevelt/Taft period, after the famous *Oil* and *Tobacco* cases of 1911 had laid a new and firm foundation for the development of case law under the Sherman Act, and by the time the Democratic Congress of 1914 had passed the Clayton and Federal Trade Commission Acts, antitrust was emerging as something much closer to a positive policy of maintaining competition.[3]

---

[1] Much information on this topic is to be found in Hans B. Thorelli's well documented study of the origins and early history of antitrust, *The Federal Antitrust Policy*, Norstedt, Stockholm; Allen and Unwin, London, 1954. Mr Thorelli shows, for example, that of the twenty-three cases brought by the Government up to 1903, only six were inititated by the Department of Justice, and of those six, significantly enough, four were against labour unions and the other two—the *Northern Securities* and *Beef trust* cases—came right at the end of the period. It appears that before this the bringing of cases depended on keen United States attorneys in the field.

[2] It was for all practical purposes reversed by the Supreme Court's decision in 1899 in the *Addyston Pipe* case.

[3] A brief account of the aims of Congress in passing these measures is given below at the beginning of Chapter VII.

This evolution was still spasmodic. For a long period after the First World War there was little new development, antitrust administration was not notably vigorous and some important decisions even seemed to retreat from positions established before 1918. A new burgeoning of antitrust came in the later 1930s when Thurman Arnold headed the Antitrust Division, and the years since 1945 up to the present (with perhaps a slight relaxation in the early 1950s) have been without question the most exuberant in antitrust history.

In short, antitrust has changed with the years. On the face of it the founders of antitrust (and the courts which dealt with the early cases) were thinking mainly in terms of the flagrantly anti-competitive activities of the trusts. The harm done by these activities could be recognized at sight and by the political rumpus they caused; it did not have to be deduced from economic theory, and the desire to put a stop to it did not involve a commitment to any particular economic doctrine. The subsequent development may be described as a change of emphasis, whereby antitrust comes to be seen much more as a positive instrument of economic policy. The Sherman Act is taken to embody the assumption, as Chief Justice Stone once put it, 'that the public interest is best protected from the evils of monopoly and price control by the maintenance of competition'. Economic theory is believed to have established a presumption that any impairment of competition is harmful, and those concerned with enforcing antitrust come to take this presumption as their rule of thumb.

This change of emphasis from a negative (literally 'anti-trust') approach to a positive ('maintaining competition') aim—it is difficult to define more precisely—has exerted a recognizable influence, particularly in the most recent period, on the development of the case law and the choice of suitable remedies. With the negative approach the tendency will be to compare the minor restraints of trade with the worst, and they may come fairly well out of the comparison: with a positive aim, even minor impairments of competition will tend to be compared with some ideal model that it is hoped to achieve, and will look worse in consequence. In various subtle ways the change of emphasis will shift the margin between what is and what is not acceptable.

The extent to which antitrust can ever become a thoroughgoing pursuit of competition for its own sake is nevertheless limited. In the first place the statutes are proscriptive, not prescriptive. Businessmen cannot be made to compete, but only restrained from impairing competition. Secondly, political pressures, such as that in favour of the protection of 'small business' in the United States, cut across the main theme and, as will be seen, influence the statutes and their interpretation at many points, sometimes in ways adverse to the aim of promoting competition. Thirdly, the courts must preserve a keen and cautious sense of what is practicable, for on this the public credit of the law ultimately depends: the case law will show many examples in which the pursuit of more strenuous competition is tempered by judicial realism.[1]

From the sum of these elements a first approximation to a definition of the aim and scope of modern antitrust may be derived for use as a rough guide to the case law. Antitrust seeks, so far as is practicable, to maintain competition against private efforts to impair its vigour, fairness and effectiveness. If this is a more comprehensive aim than that of the founders, and if antitrust in recent years has looked a good deal different from anything that Senators Sherman and Hoar envisaged in 1890, it does not follow, of course, that antitrust has 'gone wrong'. Second thoughts are sometimes best, and the origins of things are not moral imperatives by which to judge their later development. The common law of restraint of trade in the United States would have developed along one line or another had there been no Sherman Act, and it is more realistic to see the case law under the Act as a development than to try to set it against some absolute standard of what was law before the Act was passed.

By the same token, however, the strenuous period since 1945 may appear on a longer time-scale as an abnormal one. The emphasis could change again. Periods of advance and periods of consolidation in antitrust may continue to succeed each other as the industrial development of the United States changes in response to economic needs.

6. *Definitions; restraint of trade*

Subject to the exemptions explained earlier, the production and distribution of all goods and services which enter into the interstate commerce of the United States are subject to the general prohibition of 'restraint of trade' which is the essence of antitrust. It is clear from the statutes that this prohibition covers all forms of 'restraint of trade' whether the restriction arises from contracts or agreements to which businessmen voluntarily engage themselves, or whether it results from the acquisition of monopoly power by a single firm. But what exactly is 'restraint of trade'?

As has been shown in the historical section above, 'restraint of trade' is a legal term of art, deriving its meaning from the current decisions and constructions making up the particular body of law in which it appears. A seventeenth-century English lawyer, for example, would have

---

[1] This point comes out particularly in the choice of remedies imposed by the courts in cases of monopolizing—see below, Chapter XIV.

defined it by reference to quite different decisions from those that would be quoted by a Supreme Court judge in the United States today. In other words, the logic of the term is not that of a description, like 'expansion of trade' or 'trade depression', but rather that of a term like 'offside' in football which you cannot use appropriately until you know whether you are dealing with Rugby, Association, American or Australian football, and until you are provided with the current rule book for the code in question and are familiar with the construction put on the rules by the best referees. Thus, where antitrust is concerned, nothing less than the whole body of case law constitutes the definition of 'restraint of trade'; it can be given, if at all, at the end of the book but not at the beginning.

It is important to have this point firmly established at the outset, because in practice we all—lawyers and non-lawyers alike—tend to have in our minds a broad idea of what we mean by such terms as 'restraint of trade' and to use them in a correspondingly loose sense. It sometimes happens indeed that such a term is used both as a term of art and as a broad description more or less in the same breath, and this can give rise to confusion.[1]

Even the layman's broad idea of restraint of trade will no doubt take account of some of the distinctions known to the law. Taken literally the phrase seems to cover any restriction on the freedom of traders to make whatever bargains they please. But many laws restrict freedom of bargaining—laws against fraud or adulteration, laws dealing with trademarks, or regulating hours of business or credit terms—yet would not normally be regarded as restraints of trade. It is obvious, perhaps, to exclude legislative and governmental regulation from our idea of restraint of trade but there are also trade customs, such as conventional forms of contract and nomenclature, accepted gradings of size and quality, and so forth, which in practice restrict the range of possible bargains but which (so long as they are not operated so as to exclude bona fide competitors from the market) are normally seen not as restraints of trade but as ground rules which on the whole facilitate trade.

But any brief definition still falls far short of the legal content of 'restraint of trade'. If it were applied to actual cases, it would be found that the notion of preventing competition had to be further defined in its turn and this would raise difficult questions of degree and intention. What is the position, for example, if some types of business behaviour (or structure) limit competition in one way, but increase it in another?

---

[1] See above, p. 14. Subject to these points, a broad definition of restraint of trade might be that it consists of action by private businessmen to prevent some form of competition from operating in the market.

As different cases exemplifying different facts come along, new and careful distinctions will have to be made: it will be necessary to 'draw the line somewhere' when conflicting considerations arise. So it is that, though the Sherman Act in terms is an unqualified prohibition of *every* restraint of trade, the courts in the United States have been engaged ever since 1890 in deciding case by case exactly what the law proscribes. No broad definition can really unlock the meaning of the statute: the danger is to suppose that the bold words of the law ignore the need for refinements or distinctions. In fact, seeing how antitrust really works is a matter of seeing just what distinctions are made and why; this is why a survey of the case law must come before any attempt to assess the value of antitrust.

7. The rule of reason; the views of Chief Justice Taft and Chief Justice White compared

It is, of course, the province of the courts to make the distinctions and draw the lines by which the generality of the term 'restraint of trade' is tamed to the infinite variety of particular facts. As Chief Justice Hughes said in a famous opinion: 'The Sherman Act, as a charter of freedom, has a generality and adaptability comparable to that found to be desirable in constitutional provisions.' These words point clearly enough to the importance of judicial interpretation in dealing with so broad a concept as restraint of trade.[1] The same obviously applies to the phrase in the Clayton Act 'where the effect may be to substantially lessen competition' and to the words 'unfair methods of competition' in the Federal Trade Commission Act. How much is 'substantially'? What is 'unfair'? There are certain legal principles and rules of interpretation which the courts apply to these problems and which need some introduction in general terms before being displayed in action in the cases themselves.

First there is the so-called 'rule of reason', which, as the guiding principle of Sherman Act construction, is as difficult to define at the outset as 'restraint of trade' and for much the same reasons. It is difficult partly because the application of the rule is revealed only through the case law, and partly because it is not an absolute and unvarying standard but has been applied, now more broadly, now more narrowly, as different courts have faced different problems at different times. The scope accorded to the rule of reason at any time

---

[1] Judge Learned Hand has said about the task of a judge called upon to interpret constitutional provisions: 'The words he must construe are empty vessels into which he can put nearly anything he will.' Mr Justice Holmes once struck a somewhat similar note in a letter to Sir Frederick Pollock: 'The prophecies of what the courts will do in fact, and nothing more pretentious, are what I mean by the law.'

is indeed the measure of the permissible degree of judicial discretion in interpreting the Sherman Act and in particular the term 'restraint of trade'. A need for some interpretation has always been apparent: indeed, this is implicit in the use of any term of art. Argument arises about the proper limits of judicial discretion.

Some functions of the judiciary in interpreting the statutes are straightforward and uncontroversial. The courts must, for example, consider in the first place whether a contract or agreement exists and, if so, whether it is 'in restraint of trade' at all in any meaningful sense of the term. A distinction was noted above between restraints which altogether prevent some form of competition and those which, though in some way restricting the range of possible bargains, are meant to regulate rather than impede the competitive process. Sometimes there are borderline cases in which there could be argument as to whether an agreement was central or merely incidental to the free play of competition—destructive or merely regulatory. This borderline has to be marked out by applying commonsense to the facts of the particular case.

A well known antitrust suit illustrates the point. In 1918 the Department of Justice brought an action against the Board of Trade of the City of Chicago—the great grain exchange of the Middle West—on the ground that its method of operation involved price fixing.[1] The facts were that both spot and future sales of grain were made in public auction sessions on each business day that the exchange operated. A great many sales of grain already in transit or ready for shipment to Chicago from the country dealers and farmers were, however, made after the end of the daily session. Purchasers made their offers by mail or telegraph subject to acceptance before the beginning of the next morning's business session. The exchange made a rule that its members should make no purchase or offer in this way except at the price ruling at the end of the day's business session. This, said the Government, was clearly a price fixing practice. Between 2 p.m. on Monday and 9.30 a.m. on Tuesday no free bargains could be made; each member had bound himself to bid only at the final Monday price. The Supreme Court threw out this case, largely on the basis of the argument for the defence that the rule was in no way intended to prevent competition or control prices but simply to serve the convenience of the trade.

Mr Justice Brandeis, in giving judgment for the defendant, pointed out the essential distinction:

The case was rested upon the bald proposition, that a rule or agreement, by which men occupying positions of strength in any branch of trade fixed prices at which they would buy or sell during an important part of the

[1] *United States* v. *Chicago Board of Trade* (Supreme Court, 1918).

business day, is an illegal restraint of trade under the Antitrust Law. But the legality of an agreement or regulation cannot be determined by so simple a test as whether it restrains competition. Every agreement concerning trade, every regulation of trade restrains. To bind, to restrain, is of their very essence. The true test of legality is whether the restraint imposed is such as merely regulates and perhaps thereby promotes competition or whether it is such as may suppress or even destroy competition. To determine that question the Court must ordinarily consider the facts peculiar to the business to which the restraint is applied . . . the nature of the restraint and its effect, actual or probable.

The difference between preventing competition and merely regulating some matter incidental to competition is a difference in kind; there are also differences in degree that call for the exercise of discretion. There is a sense in which any one bargain excludes others: when a bargain is sealed, the competition for that particular portion of trade is at an end. It would be a *reductio ad absurdum* to call trade itself restraint of trade; yet some types of bargains may preclude a great deal of potential competition. When a large buyer, whose requirements are an important part of the total demand for a commodity, places an order for his next few weeks' supplies, no great problem arises; but suppose he contracts to take his whole requirements from a single supplier for a year or for five years? Suppose he goes further and undertakes in consideration of favourable terms not to buy from any other supplier? Suppose he obtains a controlling interest in the stock of the supplier's business? Obviously there may come a point when competitive opportunities in the market for the commodity concerned have notably diminished. Similarly with horizontal integration. A man with two bakeries in Chicago buys another in Gary and there is no problem. By and by, however, he acquires more bakeries and yet more until the observer has very real doubts whether the bread trade in the area is competitive. Somewhere along the way comes the question whether this firm's newest acquisition is to be regarded as an attempt to monopolize.

The point of all these problems is that the line between quite ordinary everyday transactions and those that may come within the definition of restraint of trade is not clearly marked: the one may merge almost imperceptibly into the other. At one end of the scale a *de minimis* rule may be appropriately applied: at the other the existence of meaningful restraint of trade may be clear. The courts will have to 'draw a line' somewhere in between.

The questions arising in these illustrations of the judicial function are practical and factual. Is there really an agreement? If so, is it to any meaningful extent restrictive? All courts have to answer questions of this type and 'judicial discretion' may seem a misleadingly high-flown way of referring to the process: reason clearly enters into the matter, but nobody would have laid down a special rule of reason to describe so obvious a part of the judicial function. This notion probably owes its origin, historically, to a further category of cases in which an element of true discretion is present—the category of 'ancillary' restraints of trade.

Sometimes a deliberate undertaking not to compete appears to be a reasonable, even essential, element in transactions. The owner of a small workshop or retail business may wish to sell it and move to another district. The goodwill he has built up is a valuable asset of the business which a would-be buyer expects to have to pay for and hopes to profit by. If the seller, having taken good money for the good-will, were immediately to set up in another shop next door, the buyer would regard himself as swindled. It is common in such a case for the contract of sale to include a restrictive covenant by which the seller binds himself not to compete against the buyer. In common-law cases restraints of trade of this type (which were known as 'ancillary' restraints because the restriction was incidental or ancillary to some legitimate object) had long been regarded as legitimate before the Sherman Act was passed, so long as the restriction involved was reasonably adapted to its purpose and did not offer the buyer excessive protection or keep the seller out of too wide an area for too long a time. This rule recognized that unless such conditions could legally be attached to the sale of properties, legitimate business dealings might be hindered and sellers might be unable to recover the fair value of their assets.

At one time the courts commonly used the term 'partial' of restraints of trade in which the restrictive covenant was limited as to time and place, and 'partial' restraints were contrasted with 'general' restraints which embodied no such limitation. Later the courts began to divide the class of ancillary restraints between those where the restriction was 'reasonable' (in relation to a legitimate main purpose) and those which were 'unreasonable'—a distinction which genuinely called for the exercise of discretion, even though its scope was narrow and controlled by numerous precedents. Judge Taft, in his famous opinion for the Sixth Circuit Court of Appeals in the *Addyston Pipe* case (1898), traced the development of these distinctions and held that, apart from reasonable ancillary restraints, the common law had condemned all restraints of trade. 'Where the sole object of both parties in making the contract . . . is merely to restrain competition, and enhance or maintain prices, it would seem that there was nothing to justify or excuse the restraint, that it would necessarily have a tendency to monopoly and therefore be void.' Thus Congress, following the common law, had left no room in the statute for judicial discretion in the case of direct, non-ancillary restraints.[1] The distinction between reasonable and unreasonable restraints was not to apply to price fixing, boycotting and suchlike directly restrictive agreements.

A similar view of the law was taken by the majority of the Supreme Court in two important decisions condemning a rate fixing association of railroads[2] and a merger of competing railroads by means of a holding company.[3] But Mr Justice White dissented from both these decisions because he believed that judicial discretion should not be confined within the narrow field of ancillary restraints. His argument was later developed into the famous *Standard Oil* opinion of 1911 by which (as Chief Justice) he established the authority of the rule of reason.

White agreed that the Sherman Act used the term 'restraint of trade' as a term of art deriving its content from the common law. But his account of the common-law background differed markedly from Judge Taft's. In his view the common law applied a 'standard of reason' and was opposed only to 'undue' restraints of trade. In a survey of the legal history he suggested that the law had always been concerned with the harmful effects of monopolies and not with their mere existence:[4] restraint of trade, he believed, had come to be treated as amounting to monopoly when it was found to have the same harmful effects. 'Undue' restraint of trade or 'unreasonably restrictive' business behaviour, broadly speaking, was that which of its nature, or by dint of evidence that its purpose was aggressive and exploitative, would be expected to lead to such evils as enhanced prices.[5] Chief Justice White's own summary, though prolix, brings out this point strongly:

Without going into detail, and but very briefly surveying the whole field, it may be with accuracy said that the dread of enhancement of prices and of other wrongs which it was thought would flow from the undue limitation on competitive conditions caused by contracts or other acts of individuals or corporations led, as a matter of public policy, to the prohibition or treating

---

[1] This does not mean, of course, that Judge Taft would have jibbed at the type of distinction made in the *Chicago Board of Trade* case or at the use of a *de minimis* rule in appropriate cases. He probably took it for granted that judges should be discriminating in these ways.

[2] *United States* v. *Trans-Missouri Freight Association* (1897).

[3] *Northern Securities Company* v. *United States* (1903).

[4] The common law, as White explained, had also been very much concerned with the individual's right to pursue his chosen trade; but this aspect of the matter is not central to the present argument.

[5] The words 'of its nature' here—'from the nature or character of the contract', as White had it—cover the case where the necessary effect of the contract or restrictive agreement would be to raise prices, so that the passage amounts to saying that 'undue' restraint of trade is that which necessarily produces or is intended to produce enhanced prices. High prices are used here, as by White, to typify or symbolize the 'evils' of monopoly: he realized, of course, that there were other evils, and himself mentioned limitation of output and deterioration of quality.

as illegal of all contracts or acts which were unreasonably restrictive of competitive conditions, either from the nature or character of the contract or act, or where the surrounding circumstances were such as to justify the conclusion that they had not been entered into or performed with the legitimate purpose of reasonably forwarding personal interest and developing trade, but, on the contrary, were such as to give rise to the inference or presumption that they had been entered into or done with the intent to do wrong to the general public and to limit the right of individuals, thus restraining the free flow of commerce and tending to bring about the evils such as enhancement of prices which were considered to be against public policy.

In the light of this opinion, White's earlier dissents in the railway cases show that he did not find in the facts of those cases any necessary tendency of the agreements in question to raise prices or otherwise harm the public interest, nor any intention on the part of the companies to exploit the public; hence they were not 'undue' restraints of trade. It was justifiable for railway companies to try to save themselves by a merger or by rate fixing agreements from suffering heavy losses as a result of 'cut-throat' competition.

The view of the law which emerges from Chief Justice White's opinions reflects a familiar, commonsense view of the monopoly problem. It is important to note that monopoly and restraint of trade are not condemned, on this view, *only* when ill effects, such as unduly high prices, can be shown to result. White was quite prepared to infer the probability of harmful effects from evidence of aggressive purpose: when businessmen aggressively seek market power by suppressing competition, the law must protect the public interest. On the other hand, he would not infer injury to the public interest on *a priori* grounds from the mere fact that competition was impaired. For not all impairment of competition is aggressive in purpose. This view attaches special importance to purpose and does not equate the policy of the Sherman Act with that of maintaining competition for its own sake.[1] On this view of the law the rule of reason requires a discriminating judgment of restraints of trade by reference to their necessary effects on the public interest or their evident purpose.[2]

[1] Mr Justice Holmes, who also dissented from the result in *Northern Securities Company* v. *United States*, made this point explicitly. After quoting the words of the Sherman Act, he said: 'Much trouble is made by substituting other phrases assumed to be equivalent, which then are reasoned from as if they were in the Act. The Court below argued as if maintaining competition were the expressed object of the Act. The Act says nothing about competition. I stick to the exact words used.'

[2] Chief Justice White's summary in the *Tobacco* case is perhaps his clearest statement of this point: 'Applying the rule of reason to the construction of the statute, it was held in the Standard Oil case that, as the words "restraint of trade" at common law and in the law of this country at the time of the adoption of the antitrust Act only embraced acts or contracts or agreements or combinations which operated to the prejudice of the public interest by unduly restricting competition, or unduly obstructing the due course of trade, or which,

The opposing views of White and Taft about the limits of judicial discretion have each found support in the subsequent literature and case law, and it is hard to sum up *the* 'rule of reason' without apparent paradox. White's classic opinions brought the phrase 'rule of reason' into everyday use by lower courts and writers of textbooks: Taft does not seem to have used the phrase, yet his view of the law has prevailed on the issue that divided them and, in so far as White believed that defensive restrictions of competition might be justifiable, the later development of the case law has belied him.

Too much can be made of the practical differences between the two views. Although he did not admit any formal limitation on the courts' discretion, White's view does not imply that competition may be restrained with impunity so long as some plausible argument in terms of economic and social advantage can be advanced for the restraint. He would not have admitted defence arguments based on business expediency (for example, on the need for high profits to finance research and investment) or on the general unwisdom of any State interference with business, once he was satisfied that he was dealing with an 'undue' —a predatory or inevitably price enhancing—restraint of trade.[1] He might well have been more amenable than Taft, however, to a defence that denied any injury to the public and claimed some defensive justification, such as the danger of 'cut-throat' competition, for the restrictive arrangement.

In modern antitrust there is no appeal to the rule of reason on the ground that a restrictive combination or agreement is intended only to mitigate a state of competition that has become abnormal or undesirable. Direct restraints are illegal *per se*, as Taft's view required. Nowadays it is more accurate to regard the rule of reason as directed to winnowing out the restraints which are merely ancillary or incidental to competition, or which do not affect competition to a significant degree, than to regard it as directed to deciding when a restraint is 'undue' in White's sense.[2] Nevertheless, some modern literature has

either because of their inherent nature or effect, or because of the evident purpose of the Acts, etc., injuriously restrained trade, the words as used in the statute were designed to have and did have but a like significance.'

[1] He made this point clearly in both the *Oil* and *Tobacco* cases. Once it was established, he said, that contracts or agreements 'were clearly restraints of trade within the purview of the statute, they could not be taken out of that category by indulging in general reasoning as to the expediency or non-expediency of having made the contracts, or the wisdom or want of wisdom of the statute which prohibited their being made'. There is no evidence that White, any more than Taft, would have approved of deciding cases by reference to an assessment of economic advantage in the light of the latest theory.

[2] At this point we are concerned, of course, only with what the rule of reason is, not with what it ought to be. There has been much discussion in the United States of 'revitalizing' the rule of reason by adopting the test of 'workable' or 'effective' competition. This is discussed below, in Part II, Chapter XV.

sought to reconcile this subsequent case law with White's theory.[1] It will be best to revert to this matter when the issue can be judged in the light of the case law (see below, Chapter XV, pp. 438–9). It would not be surprising, however, if there had been a change of emphasis since White first defined the rule of reason; indeed, such a change would be in line with a general development in antitrust policy, by which, as the historical outline above has shown, modern antitrust has come to rely, much more than the founders of the policy would have done, on a presumption that any significant impairment of competition is harmful.

8. Per se *rules*

From the rule of reason, which is essentially a rule of construction, we turn to what are known as '*per se*' rules, which are rules of evidence. Once it becomes a rule of thumb that any significant impairment of competition is harmful (and therefore constitutes 'restraint of trade' within the meaning of the Sherman Act), many antitrust judgments become simple matters of fact. A price fixing agreement, for example, is never an 'ancillary' restraint of trade and normally leaves no question of degree or intent to be decided. Any question as to the harm it does or is intended to do is answered by the general presumption. No further question arises. This situation is expressed by the proposition that price fixing is illegal *per se*.

The significance of judicial rulings that certain restrictive practices are illegal *per se* is evidentiary. The prosecution has only to prove as a matter of fact that price fixing has occurred and judgment must follow. The defence can argue that the prices were not really fixed—for example, that an observed uniformity of prices was due to the normal interplay of economic forces and not to any illegal agreement—but cannot bring evidence to show that, though there was an agreement, the public came to no harm or that the industry was concerned only to avoid an intolerable situation. The defence, in other words, must not challenge the presumption in favour of competition: as to any practice

[1] The reader should compare the account of the rule of reason given in the *Report of the Attorney General's National Committee to Study the Antitrust Laws*—particularly the summary, on p. 11, of Chief Justice White's doctrine. The great authority of the Committee is lent to the view that White's teaching is itself the basis of current doctrine; that the rule of reason 'permits the courts to decide whether conduct is *significantly and unreasonably* [author's italics] anti-competitive in character or effect' but does not enable a restrictive arrangement to be justified by reference, for example, to risks of 'cut-throat' competition. It does not seem easy to reconcile this last proposition with White's dissents in the *Railway* cases (unless those dissents are treated as relevant only to the special case of railways as public utilities). White's doctrine and the current one come to the same thing if it is believed—as modern supporters of antitrust usually do believe—that any conduct that is *significantly anti-competitive* is *ipso facto* unreasonable in White's sense. There still seems room for doubt, however, as to whether White believed this.

that is illegal *per se*, the courts will, as a rule of evidence, exclude defence submissions of this kind. In addition to price fixing, such practices as collective boycotts, market sharing and certain restrictive practices involving patents are nowadays regarded as illegal *per se*.

Indeed, it may be said that every restrictive practice that significantly impairs competition is illegal *per se* in modern antitrust; evidence challenging the desirability of unimpaired competition is scarcely ever admissible. When the courts have agreed in recent years that a practice is not illegal *per se*, this has not meant that they were prepared to judge each instance of the practice by reference to its effect on the public interest; it has meant only that the practice might not in every instance have a significant effect on competition at all. (It might, for example, be one of those practices which proceed by differences of degree from normal, innocuous trading to serious restraint of trade or monopoly.) This is clearly what is meant, for example, by saying that vertical integration is not illegal *per se*.[1]

In speaking of practices that are illegal *per se*, however, one must not define a given practice too broadly. An abstract term like 'price fixing' covers a multitude of different factual situations. It is always possible to find or invent a set of facts to which the term 'price fixing' might be applicable but which, as a matter of commonsense, would not be included in the class of significant restraints of trade. The *Chicago Board of Trade* case is an illustration of this. Similarly, a 'price fixing' agreement between a small baker in London and another in Edinburgh (if any agreement so pointless were ever made) presumably would not be illegal because it would not affect competition at all. This is a matter of semantics: you might say of these examples either that they were not 'really' price fixing at all, or that they were price fixing but not significant restraints of trade. Using the words in the second way and defining price fixing (or any other practice) broadly, no practice is ever quite illegal *per se*: but this is only a verbal inconsistency.

It will be seen that there is no substantive inconsistency between *per se* rules and the rule of reason in its modern guise. In some of the literature it is suggested that these two principles are in conflict; but conflict would arise only if the rule of reason involved a distinction between good and bad, justifiable and unjustifiable restraints of trade. But in modern antitrust, as we have seen, the rule of reason invokes the exercise of discretion only on what are ultimately questions of fact. Some borderline questions of fact are, however, very complex and difficult, and it is useful to note at the outset the judicial axiom, often repeated in the cases, 'that under the Sherman Act matters of form must

---

[1] See the analysis of the Supreme Court's opinion in *United States* v. *Columbia Steel Company*, below, Chapter V.

always be subordinated to matters of substance'. This axiom is in effect a warning from the courts themselves not to be too legalistic in the interpretation of antitrust. The substance is the interference with competition; when this is established, the courts are often inclined, as the cases will show, to be cavalier in their treatment of formal matters— the forms, for example, of agreements or combinations or price formulas —and impatient of defences relying on formal ingenuities.

The rule of reason and *per se* rules are relevant mainly to the Sherman Act. The Clayton Act introduces explicitly a test of effect on competition—'where the effect may be to substantially lessen competition or tend to create a monopoly'. Though in a sense this phrase is a built-in rule of reason for the Clayton Act—some Congressmen in 1914 would have left its prohibitions unqualified—it still needs interpretation. Does 'may be' mean 'will probably be' or 'might conceivably be'? It will be noted that the Clayton Act involves an element of prediction, whereas under the Sherman Act some actual effect on competition must be shown, or else an intention to bring about such an effect. The treatment by the courts of these and many other points of interpretation can be shown only in the cases themselves.

9. *Plan of the study*

Part 1 of this book consists of a description of the more important antitrust case law. Starting with Sherman Act cases against restrictive agreements among competitors, the description proceeds with the treatment of monopolization under section 2 of that Act and so to the specific monopolistic practices dealt with by the Clayton Act and problems affecting the distribution of goods by the manufacturer, including resale price maintenance. Additional chapters then deal separately with the special issues arising in cases concerned with patents and international cartel agreements respectively. Finally there are chapters on the administration of antitrust, describing the functions and methods of the Antitrust Division of the Department of Justice and the Federal Trade Commission, their procedure for enforcing the law, and the penalties and remedies that the courts may impose.

As has been foreshadowed in the preceding section, the important cases are largely concerned with borderline questions of law and fact. Seeing how antitrust 'really' works is mostly a matter of accurately locating these borderlines; this involves understanding what the case was for shifting the borderline further forward or back, and what were the reasons that led the judges to decide to locate it where in fact it is. As with most political and administrative problems, a good case can usually be made out for both sides: there is no simple clash of powers of light against powers of darkness, but sensible and sincere men arguing by reasonable analogy from one situation to the next and reaching different conclusions.

Generally speaking, it will be convenient in each chapter to establish first the clear and flagrant antitrust offences, and then illustrate a kind of 'declension' down the legal scale as more and more doubt about the nature of supposed offences creeps in, until the court is faced with one of the difficult borderline problems. The reader may identify himself, if he will, with the law enforcement officer who, believing whole-heartedly in antitrust as the means of maintaining competition, feels that his job would not be done if he did not persuade the courts to bring within the class of unlawful activities just that next variant which may be seen as a loophole for evading the spirit and purpose of the law. What is the use, he may ask himself, of all the effort that goes into prosecuting such and such a case if the businessman is to be allowed to get away with so and so? Alternatively, the reader may see himself as the businessman who, unconvinced of the relevance of the theoretical advantages of competition to his immediate practical problems, strives to retain as much freedom as possible to make his own decisions: to him the 'declension' down the legal scale will show just what types of behaviour will certainly fall foul of the law, then what it may be possible to 'get away with' at the borderline, and finally what it should be safe to do.[1]

In proceeding from the clear and flagrant cases down the legal scale, it is inevitable that the most space must be given to the borderline cases, in which the issues are often intricate and fascinating. It takes only a few lines to establish the illegality of overt price fixing agreements, whereas the problems that arise when the use of basing-point price formulas is coupled with a 'price leadership' situation may take several paragraphs or pages to expound. This creates a great difficulty as regards keeping things in proportion and it is necessary to put the reader on his guard against getting a distorted impression of antitrust from this cause. Whereas the borderline cases are often the most interesting and are important from the point of view of defining antitrust doctrines, they are by no means the most important quantitatively, or as a measure of the success of antitrust as a policy. It is worth remembering that there are probably thirty or forty straightforward price fixing cases in the records for every one that involves new ingenuities in the analysis of the concepts of 'conspiracy' or 'intent'.

---

[1] It had better be stated—*ex abundanti cautela*—that this is no invitation to regard this book as a safe conduct through antitrust territory; any business reader who really is operating near the borderlines of antitrust needs a good lawyer. It is a sure bet that the facts in his case will not exactly correspond to any described here—and nobody ever yet insured against antitrust risks for the price of this book.

The descriptive chapters of Part I will mostly avoid criticism; the aim will be to set out the law as it stands. Part of the task will be to elucidate the arguments which have swayed the courts in making the law what it is, and there will be no point in disguising the fact that some are better arguments than others. Another part of the task will be to point out in each chapter the decisions which have gone furthest in pushing the 'maintaining competition' doctrine to an extreme and which are, so to say, the high-water marks of the antitrust tide; there will also be low-tide marks to record, and it will be proper to point out the implications of both ebb and flow. But all these matters will be recorded, so far as possible, as facts and data, without taking sides for or against any particular trend.

Assessment and appraisal will be kept for Part II of the book, which will seek to answer two main questions. The first question is whether antitrust has been a success on its own assumptions. Given that this body of law, whatever was thought at the time of its origin, is now taken to represent the policy that private barriers to competition should be removed, how far does it succeed in its aim? Is scepticism based on the bigness of 'big business' in the United States justified? The second is the broader question of whether antitrust is, after all, the right answer to restraint of trade. How far are those who enjoin the rest of the world to adopt a Sherman Act, and those who would regard a Sherman Act on their doorstep as disastrous, justified in their respective hopes and fears?

PART I

THE CONTENT AND ADMINISTRATION
OF ANTITRUST

CHAPTER I

AGREEMENTS BETWEEN COMPETITORS
I. PRICE FIXING

1. *Section 1 of the Sherman Act and restrictive trade agreements*

Danger lies in restraint of trade because the result of suppressing or limiting competition may be to build up a position of power in a market. People in a position of power in a market can make the terms of bargains more favourable to themselves and less favourable to others than they would otherwise be. There are two obvious ways of achieving market power. One way is for the sellers (or buyers) to band together and exert their joint power by agreements instead of competing one against the other. The other way is for a single firm to achieve by itself a dominant position in the market, in other words to monopolize it.[1] Section 1 of the Sherman Act deals with restraint of trade arising from agreement or combination; section 2 deals with monopolization. This description of antitrust case law begins with the law under section 1 concerning agreements between competitors.

There are also two main ways of exerting power in a market. The first is to use it to influence prices directly; in the case of sellers, to raise prices above the level that would otherwise be reached or, as it may sometimes be regarded, to prevent their falling below a level that those concerned think fair. The second is to use it to exclude competitors from the market, thus consolidating or extending the original degree of market power. Power over prices and power to exclude competitors have always been regarded as the earmarks of monopoly and restraint of trade. The use of market power to exclude competitors is in a sense secondary, since its aim is to consolidate a strategic position; ultimately the object of market strategy is to gain some control over price. (Control does not necessarily mean exploitation, of course, for the stability of price and profit levels is often regarded in practice as more important

---

[1] Monopoly means dominance by a seller. Dominance by a buyer is technically called 'monopsony'; but in antitrust the words 'monopoly' and 'monopolization' are taken to cover dominance on either side of the market.

than short-term maximizing of gains.) Certainly the law has always attached predominant importance to restraints of trade which directly influence prices, even to the extent of dealing with other forms of restriction, such as output restriction, largely in terms of their effect on price. It will be apt, therefore, to start with those agreements between competitors which seek directly to affect prices.

2. *Price agreements: the* per se *rule against price fixing developed in the* Addyston Pipe, Trenton Potteries *and* Socony-Vacuum *cases; the* Appalachian Coals *case distinguished*

Agreements between independent firms to fix a common price for their products violate section 1 of the Sherman Act. This was made clear in some of the earliest cases. For example, in *United States* v. *Addyston Pipe and Steel Company,*[1] decided by the Sixth Circuit Court of Appeals in 1898, part of the charge was that six manufacturers of cast-iron pipe made an agreement whereby in many southern and western States the prices of pipe for all six were fixed by a central agency. Evidence showed that these prices were set just low enough to keep eastern manufacturers out of the area, and that the public were deprived of the lower prices that might have resulted if the local factories had competed among themselves. It was said in defence of the agreement that the fixed prices were reasonable, and many affidavits from buyers to this effect were produced. The defendants, however, lost the case. The Court said about the level of the prices: 'We do not think the issue an important one, because, as already stated, we do not think that in common law there is any question of reasonableness open to the courts with reference to such a contract. Its tendency was certainly to give defendants the power to charge unreasonable prices had they chosen to do so.' These words clearly foreshadow the opinion of Mr (later Chief) Justice Stone in the *Trenton Potteries* case in which it was established that price fixing was illegal *per se*.

United States v. *Trenton Potteries Company* (1927) is the leading case on price fixing. Prices of vitreous pottery for bathrooms and lavatories were fixed by the Sanitary Potters' Association, whose members were responsible for over 80 % of the national output. The defence was that the prices fixed were reasonable and worked no injury to the public. Mr Justice Stone's rebuttal of this defence is a classic statement of antitrust doctrine:

That only those restraints upon interstate commerce which are unreasonable are prohibited by the Sherman Law was the rule laid down by the opinions

---

[1] Since this description of antitrust is intended for the general reader rather than for the law student, citations of cases mentioned will not be given in footnotes. An alphabetical list of the cases with a note on sources appears on p. 511.

of this Court in the *Standard Oil* and *Tobacco* cases. But it does not follow that agreements to fix or maintain prices are reasonable restraints and therefore permitted by the statute, merely because the prices themselves are reasonable.... Whether this type of restraint is reasonable or not must be judged, in part at least, in the light of its effect on competition, for whatever difference of opinion there may be among economists as to the social and economic desirability of an unrestrained competitive system, it cannot be doubted that the Sherman Law and the judicial decisions interpreting it are based upon the assumption that the public interest is best protected from the evils of monopoly and price control by the maintenance of competition. The aim and result of every price fixing agreement, if effective, is the elimination of one form of competition. The power to fix prices, whether reasonably exercised or not, involves power to control the market and to fix arbitrary and unreasonable prices. The reasonable price fixed today may through economic and business changes become the unreasonable price of tomorrow. Once established, it may be maintained unchanged because of the absence of competition.... Agreements which create such potential power may well be held in themselves unreasonable or unlawful restraints, without the necessity of minute inquiry whether a particular price is reasonable or unreasonable.

In other words, price fixing is illegal *per se*: no evidence of the reasonableness of the prices fixed need be heard by courts or submitted to juries. The emphasis in Stone's argument is laid on the effect of price fixing on competition: by eliminating price competition the members of the association obtained a position of power in the market which might be used arbitrarily. Deliberately to seek such power is an offence regardless of whether its exploitation in any particular period can be proved.

This argument derives from early antitrust authority. Chief Justice White in 1911 had pointed to the deliberate drive for market power of the oil and tobacco trusts as the earmark of their offences, and contrasted it with what he called 'normal methods of industrial development'. A price fixing combination would not appear as a 'normal method' simply because of an assertion that the prices were reasonable. White would probably have taken Stone's point that the reasonable price fixed today may become the unreasonable price of tomorrow; and the courts at all times would, in any case, have disclaimed any competence to judge whether a particular price was reasonable.[1]

On the other hand, as the *Railway* cases mentioned in the Introduction suggest, White might well have given weight to a defence based on the need to avoid losses resulting from cut-throat competition. If he were convinced that the purpose of a price agreement was defensive

---

[1] It is noteworthy that by contrast the Restrictive Practices Court in the United Kingdom does not appear to be afraid of making such judgments, e.g. in the *Permanent Magnets* case (1962).

rather than aggressive, he would probably not condemn it as an 'undue' restraint. The argument that fixed prices are reasonable and therefore innocuous is not the same thing as the argument that the purpose of the price fixing is primarily defensive, and Stone's opinion in the *Trenton Potteries* case did not deal explicitly with the question whether price fixing might be justified as a defence measure.

Any possible doubt on this score was laid by the Supreme Court in *United States* v. *Socony-Vacuum Oil Company* (1940), when a defence based on the claim that 'weak selling' of petrol needed to be checked was rejected in the strongest terms. This case is also important as illustrating that collusive activities directed to controlling output of a commodity and only consequentially affecting prices are treated by the courts as equivalent to price fixing.[1]

The story behind the *Socony-Vacuum* case began in the depressed period of the early 1930s. The discovery of new oilfields in Texas worsened a situation in which demand generally was falling. The small, independent producers of crude oil and the small refiners ran into difficulties and, when they badly needed cash, petrol was put on the market at 'give away' prices. While the National Industrial Recovery Act (N.R.A.) was in force, administrative arrangements were made to deal with this situation, and to get what was called 'distress gasoline' on to the market in an orderly fashion, so as to stabilize the price level. In 1935 the legislation under which these measures were taken was declared unconstitutional. Nevertheless, the major oil interests continued on their own account to operate various measures for preventing, as they saw it, the bottom falling out of the market. What happened, broadly speaking, was that the major companies bought the surpluses of the small companies; although this meant that the major companies had to reduce sales of their own oil, it gave them the opportunity of influencing the marketing of petrol in such a way as to keep retail prices fairly stable.

The Department of Justice attacked these arrangements under the Sherman Act, and the Supreme Court in due course held that the weakness of the market due to the depression was of no account in determining the legal issues. Nor was it regarded as relevant that the United States Government itself had so recently been prepared to limit

---

[1] This development was foreshadowed in *United States* v. *Patten* (1912) when heavy forward buying of cotton on the New York Exchange by a group of speculators was condemned as an attempt to push up prices elsewhere. A more modern example is *United States* v. *American Smelting and Refining Company* (Southern District Court of New York, 1960) in which an agreement between competing lead producers, under which one acted as the exclusive sales agent for the other in the eastern half of the United States, was struck down, *inter alia*, on the grounds that it had, in the circumstances, an indirect effect on the market price of lead as well as a direct effect on the total output of the industry.

price competition in emergency conditions. Since there was abundant evidence, in the view of the Supreme Court, that the combination aimed at raising the level of prices and had in fact done so, the offence was clear. It did not matter that the major oil companies had no express agreement to sell petrol at specified prices in the spot markets, nor indeed that they still had to face competition from independent refineries in those markets.

Mr Justice Douglas summarized the position in the following terms:

The fact that sales on the spot markets were still governed by some competition is of no consequence. For it is indisputable that that competition was restricted through the removal by respondents of a part of the supply which, but for the buying programs, would have been a factor in determining the going prices on these markets.... The whole scheme was carefully planned and executed to the end that distress gasoline would not overhang the markets and depress them at any time.... Prices rose, and jobbers and consumers in the Mid-Western area paid more for their gasoline than they would have paid but for the conspiracy. Competition was not eliminated from the markets; but it was clearly curtailed.

He then dealt explicitly with the argument that the arrangements were defensive in purpose, intended only to remedy 'competitive evils'.

Ruinous competition, financial disaster, evils of price cutting and the like appear throughout our history as ostensible justifications for price fixing. If the so-called competitive abuses were to be appraised here, the reasonableness of prices would necessarily become an issue in every price fixing case. In that event the Sherman Act would soon be emasculated; its philosophy would be supplanted by one which is wholly alien to a system of free competition.... Any combination which tampers with price structures is engaged in an unlawful activity. Even though the members of the price fixing group were in no position to control the market, to the extent that they raised, lowered or stabilized prices, they would be directly interfering with the free play of market forces. The Act places all such schemes beyond the pale and protects that vital part of our economy against any degree of interference. Congress has not left with us the determination of whether or not particular price fixing schemes are wise or unwise, healthy or destructive.

The industry's argument that they were only trying to tackle the problem of 'distress gasoline' and that they did not have power enough in the market to set an arbitrary and non-competitive price for their petrol, even if they wanted to, was equally unavailing. Even the restricted aim of stabilizing prices—placing a floor under the market—involved what Douglas called 'market manipulation': 'And market manipulation in its various manifestations is implicitly an artificial stimulus applied to (or at times a brake on) market prices, a force which distorts those prices, a factor which prevents the determination of those prices by free competition alone.'

In rebutting the argument that the industry had not power enough for aggressive price fixing, Justice Douglas went so far as to say in a footnote that effective power is not a necessary element in the offence of conspiracy to fix prices. The offence is simply the conspiracy, which is illegal 'though no overt act is shown, though it is not established that the conspirators had the means available for the accomplishment of their objective'. He also observed that the amount of commerce involved in a price fixing agreement was not material, 'since section 1 of the Act brands as illegal the character of the restraint, not the amount of commerce affected'.

These remarks need careful handling. It might appear that on this argument Douglas would even condemn the hypothetical price fixing agreement, mentioned in the introductory chapter, between two small bakers in London and Edinburgh. Such an agreement would not have the power to affect the market price of bread and would involve only a minute amount of trade: but Douglas says that these points are immaterial. It would be a mistake, however, to interpret his argument as excluding altogether a sensible *de minimis* rule. The agreement of the two small bakers would scarcely be condemned as a conspiracy in restraint of trade if it were incapable of having any significant effect on competition at all.

The point is, however, that in the real world wholly impotent agreements do not get made. Mr Justice Douglas's argument rests on the assumption that, in practice, businessmen will not go to the trouble of making agreements unless they expect and intend to affect market conditions. In the normal case an agreement between competitors is purposive more or less by definition; and once the element of purpose is present, then the rest of the argument follows. The people concerned may not succeed in altering the market price; they may indeed be without power to do so; but they cannot deny being in a conspiracy to restrain trade. Certainly it is settled law that an agreement effecting a partial interference with price competition is as much an offence as one which, as in the *Trenton Potteries* case, eliminates it altogether. The dictum that the amount of commerce affected is immaterial to the legality of an agreement challenged under section 1 is frequently quoted; it is well to bear in mind, therefore, that this is so only on the assumption that the agreement reveals, *per se*, an intent to restrain trade.[1]

---

[1] Even the two small bakers might well be condemned if it could be shown that they *specifically* intended to raise prices, however remote their chance of doing so. The offence then would be analogous to that of 'attempting to monopolize'. See below, Chapter IV, pp. 94–5, in which the law as to 'intent' is examined.

The *Socony-Vacuum* case disposed of any distinction between aggressive and defensive price fixing: it is now settled law that no amount of distress or depression can justify trade agreements to suppress price competition or indeed to 'tamper' in any way with the free working of the price mechanism. It also removed any residual doubts on this score left by the famous case of *Appalachian Coals* v. *United States* (Supreme Court, 1933).

This case also dealt with conditions arising from a depressed market. The defendants were 137 producers of bituminous coal in the Appalachian region. Together they produced something like 60 % of the soft coal in their area. In the years of depression, 'distress coal', just like the 'distress gasoline' in the *Socony-Vacuum* case, was brought unprofitably on to the market, depressing prices. To meet this situation the defendant producers made plans to set up a joint selling agency to act as exclusive selling agent for all of them and get the best prices it could. This plan had not gone fully into effect when the case was brought.[1]

Clearly this story is rather similar in its outline to that of the *Socony-Vacuum* case. But the Supreme Court took a different view of it. Chief Justice Hughes held that the provisions of the Sherman Act did not make impossible 'the adoption of reasonable measures to protect it [commerce] from injurious and destructive practices and to promote competition upon a sound basis'. He laid great stress on the 'deplorable condition' of the industry and on the fact that various State authorities were as much concerned as the industry itself, in view of the problems created by unemployment and general distress, to find some cure for the weakness of the market. The Court endorsed the conclusion 'that defendants were engaged in a fair open endeavour to aid the industry in a measurable recovery from its plight'.

The Court noted that no attempt was made to limit output and that the coal from the Appalachian area had to be sold in other parts of the country in competition with coal from other areas. It could not be supposed that the selling agency would come anywhere near setting the prices of coal in the consuming markets. In other words, this was not price fixing because the prices were not fixed. 'Putting an end to injurious practices, and the consequent improvement of the competitive position of a group of producers, may be entirely consonant with the public interest, where the group must still meet effective competition in a fair market and neither seeks nor is able to effect a domination of prices.' On these grounds the case against the coal producers was dismissed. But it is important to note that the Court retained jurisdiction of the matter so as to be in a position to interfere if the actual operation

---

[1] As matters turned out, it was not needed. First under N.R.A. and later under the bituminous coal legislation, prices were fixed by governmental agencies.

of the scheme proved to be an undue restraint of trade. 'If it should appear that the plan is used to the impairment of fair competitive opportunities, the decision upon the present record should not preclude the Government from seeking the remedy which would be suited to such a set of facts.' It may be doubted whether the result of the *Appalachian Coals* case is wholly consistent with the law as it emerged in the *Socony-Vacuum* case. It is true that there are quite important differences in the facts of the two cases; in particular, the coal scheme did not involve an organized withholding of substantial supplies from the market, and no evidence could be given of its effect on prices because the case was brought before the plan went into operation. Nevertheless, it is hard to see how the plan, if it was to be of any value to the coal producers, could have amounted to much less than a combination intended to 'tamper' with price structures. It is tempting to look to the different composition of the Supreme Court and the different economic circumstances of 1933 as against 1940 for part of the explanation.

It is worth noting, however, that Mr Justice Douglas himself did not overrule the *Appalachian Coals* decision in 1940 but distinguished the two cases. 'Unlike the plan in the instant case [*Socony-Vacuum*] the plan in the *Appalachian Coals* case was not designed to operate *vis-à-vis* the general consuming market and to fix the price in that market. Furthermore, the effect, if any, of that plan on prices was not only wholly incidental but also highly conjectural. For the plan had not then been put into operation.' From this it would appear that the *Coals* decision retains some legal authority; it would be generally agreed nowadays, however, that it is authority for little beyond the exact circumstances peculiar to that case. The prudent businessman will take the *Socony-Vacuum* opinion as his guide.

Price fixing agreements, then, are illegal *per se*: no defence resting on claims that the prices fixed are reasonable, or on evidence that price competition in an industry is excessive and ruinous, will succeed. Agreements directed to controlling the flow of surplus supplies into the market so as to stabilize prices will be regarded as 'tampering' with free price movements and hence as equivalent to price fixing. These basic rules cover the bulk of the cases; and straightforward charges of price fixing probably account for the majority of all antitrust cases every year.

These rules, like all such rules in antitrust, are not to be escaped by legal sophistry: they cover all the variants that may be introduced into the form of agreements or the method of price fixing. The law deals with substance, not form. Many devices intended to disguise the fact of agreement have been tried, as some of the cases to be described below will show, without eluding the courts' definition of what constitutes 'conspiracy' under the Sherman Act. It is no easier to camouflage the method. Thus actual prices may be specified in dollars and cents or only minimum prices specified or only a formula agreed by which to calculate prices—any method is price fixing.[1] Agreements as to tenders to be submitted for particular contracts are, of course, covered, and not only when bids are identical, but also when it is arranged that a particular firm shall put in the winning bid while others put in fictitious bids at higher prices. Agreements among buyers count equally with agreements among sellers.

3. *Price filing and 'open competition' cases:* American Column and Lumber; Linseed Oil; Maple Flooring; Sugar Institute; *recent cases*

Price fixing agreements throw up few borderline questions of law. By definition they are never merely incidental to competition nor ancillary to legitimate transactions. Moreover, differences of degree hardly ever have to be considered, since agreements that might escape under a *de minimis* rule are not in practice made. There is nothing, in short, for the modern rule of reason to bite on. This, indeed, is what is meant by saying that price fixing is illegal '*per se*'.

Antitrust cases against price fixing, however, sometimes involve difficult borderline questions of fact. Nearly all these questions turn on the point whether in fact any agreement exists. It will be remembered that the offence under section 1 of the Sherman Act is not simply the absence of vigorous price competition. The offence that has to be proved is the existence of an agreement—a contract or conspiracy—relating to prices. Whether or not there is an agreement is a question of fact and in some circumstances it may be a very difficult fact to elicit. Difficulties arise in particular when industries engage in activities which are in themselves legitimate but which may also be used to disguise or facilitate collusion. A trade association may, for example, collect and circulate statistics relating to the current production, stocks, sales and prices of member firms. Sometimes it is agreed that member firms will file all price changes with the association so that all competitors may know what they are up against; it may even be agreed that price changes will not be put into effect until there has been time for all members to be notified. Similarly, bids for competitive tenders may be filed with a central agency. Trade associations may also promote uniform methods of cost accounting and collect and circulate figures of current labour and

---

[1] Even maximum price fixing is apparently illegal. In *Kiefer-Stewart Company* v. *Seagram and Sons* (Supreme Court, 1951), it was decided that joint action by a group of affiliated distillers to ensure that their wholesalers did not exceed a specified resale price for liquor was an illegal price fixing conspiracy. The plaintiff recovered nearly $1 million 'treble damages' in this case. To similar effect is the case of *Albrecht* v. *Herald Company* (Supreme Court, 1968).

material costs, together with average or 'standard' figures for overhead costs in the industry.

On the one hand, it must clearly be legitimate for businessmen to seek to be well informed about market conditions. Knowledge of relevant data can hardly be thought incompatible with freedom of decision; and the economic theory of competition does not require decisions to be made in the dark.[1] Some trade association services have obvious educative value; cost accounting methods in small businesses, for example, are often primitive, and outside help in this field may well be desirable in the interests of efficiency.

On the other hand, it is clear that these activities may be used to facilitate collusion between firms. At trade association meetings a general understanding may develop that production should be cut back when stocks reach a given proportion of current sales, and the circulation of the relevant figures may be the means of giving effect to this understanding. When price changes or bids for contracts are filed with a central body, especially when it is agreed to leave a waiting period before making the change or bid, the opportunity exists for pressure to be put on the firm that would reduce prices or make a particularly low bid to think again. Advice about cost accounting may amount to prescribing formulas that ensure uniform prices or at least set a minimum price.

In sum, these activities may make it a great deal easier for firms in an industry collusively to avoid price competition without going to the extent of making express agreements about particular prices. When elaborate interchanges of information are found going together with uniformity and inflexibility of prices, it is not surprising that the law enforcing agencies, acting on the belief that price competition ought to occur, become suspicious of concealed collusion. A number of antitrust cases reflect situations of this kind, and the problem for the courts is to decide whether there is in fact an agreement or conspiracy to limit price competition.

American Column and Lumber Company v. *United States* (Supreme Court, 1921) concerned an association of hardwood manufacturers who adopted what was known as an 'open competition' plan. This plan was avowedly based on the proposition that 'knowledge regarding prices actually made is all that is necessary to keep prices at reasonably stable and normal levels'. Participation in the plan was optional, but in practice 90 % of member firms, accounting for about one-third of the national output of hardwood, took part in it. The participants were required to let the secretary of the association have daily reports of all

---

[1] On the contrary, the theory of 'perfect competition' requires all sellers and buyers to have complete and instantaneous knowledge of all the bargains occurring in the market.

their sales and deliveries, with copies of invoices, and monthly reports of production and stocks. Each member had also to file a price list every month, and the association employed inspectors to check up on the grades of timber offered by the members, so that the price lists should be comparable. The secretary of the association in turn sent out periodical reports to the members, showing what sales had been made at what prices and summarizing the various price lists. Meanwhile there were periodic meetings of members in different areas at which prices and output policies were discussed. There was evidence to show that at these meetings members were encouraged to adjust their price and output policies to the general aim of keeping the industry profitable and given expert advice designed to avoid weak selling through overproduction. Many quotations from letters and speeches at meetings were produced to illustrate the forcefulness of the warnings against too much output.

The Supreme Court condemned these arrangements. Although no specific agreement to restrict output or fix prices was proved, the Court found that:

The fundamental purpose of the plan was to procure 'harmonious' individual action among a large number of naturally competing dealers with respect to the volume of production and prices, without having any specific agreements with respect to them, and to rely for maintenance of concerted action in both respects, not upon fines and forfeitures as in earlier days, but upon what experience has shown to be the more potent and dependable restraints of business honour and social penalties—cautiously reinforced by many and elaborate reports, which would promptly expose to his associates any disposition in any member to deviate from the tacit understanding that all were to act together....

The Court concluded that the conduct of the defendants was not that of competitors but '...clearly that of men united in an agreement, express or implied, to act together and pursue a common purpose under a common guide'. This was not a new form of competition, as the trade claimed, but an old form of combination in restraint of trade.

Nevertheless, the issue was a close one; Mr Justice Brandeis, for example, dissented from the majority view on the grounds that there was no coercion and that the information gathered by the association was not kept secret from the public. He argued that the Sherman Act did not require that business rivals should compete blindly and without the aid of relevant trade information. He found no evidence of uniformity of prices; and if prices had sometimes been higher than they otherwise would have been because well informed sellers avoided weak selling, that in itself was no offence. The expert warnings against overproduction were meant to curb the greed of the sellers rather than to exploit the consumers. Finally, he feared that if the industry were not allowed to 'rationalize competition' it would go in for consolidation by mergers, with real monopoly as the outcome.

A similar result was reached in *United States* v. *American Linseed Oil Company* (Supreme Court, 1923). This case involved much the same sort of scheme. It appears that there was particularly strong evidence of pressure on the participants to keep in line. Attendance at monthly meetings was mandatory, and 'at the regular meetings the conditions in the industry were discussed and members were "put on the carpet" and subjected to searching inquiry as to their transactions'. The Supreme Court found that the manifest purpose of the arrangements was to evade the Sherman Act. 'We are not called upon to say just when or how far competitors may reveal to each other the details of their affairs. In the absence of a purpose to monopolize, or the compulsions that result from contract or agreement, the individual certainly may exercise great freedom; but concerted action through combination presents a wholly different problem, and is forbidden when the necessary tendency is to destroy the kind of competition to which the public has long looked for protection.'

In 1925, however, two associations with somewhat similar arrangements were found by the Supreme Court not to have violated the Sherman Act. *Maple Flooring Manufacturers' Association* v. *United States*[1] concerned an association of twenty-two manufacturers of hardwood flooring. The association worked out, from information supplied by members, the average of members' costs for all dimensions and grades of flooring and circulated these figures together with booklets showing the freight rates from a base point to several thousand possible consuming centres. Summaries of all sales, prices and stocks were regularly circulated and there were meetings to exchange views on the industry's problems. But evidence was given that, at any rate after the decision in the *Linseed Oil* case, no discussion of prices took place at the association's meetings. It was found that members' prices were not uniform and that on the whole they were lower rather than higher than those of manufacturers outside the association. 'Both by the articles of association and in actual practice, members have been left free to sell their products at any price they choose and to conduct their business as they please.'

The Supreme Court observed that 'competition does not become less free merely because the conduct of commercial operations becomes more intelligent through the free distribution of knowledge of all the essential

[1] The other case in 1925 was *Cement Manufacturers' Protective Association* v. *United States*, which the Government again lost. Cement prices were found to change frequently and their uniformity was attributed by the Supreme Court to the necessity for competing sellers of a homogeneous product to meet price changes promptly. Also, the exchange of information was found necessary to prevent fraud by purchasers in this particular commercial context.

factors entering into the commercial transaction'. In the earlier cases, according to the Court, trade associations had been found to violate the law not because they had combined to gather and distribute trade information but because the Court in each case had been able to infer from the facts 'that concerted action had resulted or would necessarily result in tending arbitrarily to lessen production or increase prices'. In the *Flooring* case the majority of the Court did not feel that the evidence pointing to collusion was persuasive. This result is sometimes attributed by those in a position to know to defective pleading on the part of the government lawyers, who are said to have relied too complacently on the analogy with the earlier cases and to have neglected to deploy their evidence of collusion convincingly. However this may be, the case shows that in situations of this type the courts require any inference of collusion to be solidly established.

The Government won the next important case, *The Sugar Institute* v. *United States* (Supreme Court, 1936), which has certain special features. In the 1920s competition in the sugar industry was intense because of a buyers' market caused by chronic overproduction. Sugar being a standard product, competition centred on price, and business was fought for with secret rebates and other discriminatory concessions. The Supreme Court accepted the lower Court's finding that 'the industry was in a demoralized state which called for remedial measures'. In 1929 the refiners formed the Sugar Institute to administer a so-called 'code of ethics' for the industry.

The Institute circulated statistics of production, stocks and deliveries to members in elaborate detail, and in this respect the plan was similar to the 'open competition' schemes of earlier cases. It was already the custom of the trade that refiners publicly announced impending price changes or 'moves', allowing a period of grace in the case of price advances, so that buyers should have an opportunity to purchase at the old price. This form of 'price filing' meant that any price reduction would be promptly met, while any proposal to advance the price would have to be withdrawn unless all the refiners were ready to follow suit. The special feature of the 'code of ethics' was that it constituted an agreement among the refiners that, once any of them announced a price, he would stick to it and not make secret concessions from it. There was no agreement as to the prices announced: each refiner was free to announce changes as often as he liked.

What the Supreme Court condemned in this case was the agreement not to deviate from the announced prices. Among the factors taken into account was the difference in trading conditions before and after the formation of the Institute. It was found that the frequency of price changes declined and that there was 'a marked increase in margin and a substantial increase in profits despite a concededly large excess capacity'. Moreover, changes in the price of refined sugar were found to follow changes in the price of raw sugar less closely than before.

Chief Justice Hughes expressed the view that not all concerted action by an industry to improve trading conditions violated the law. 'Voluntary action to end abuses and to foster fair competitive opportunities in the public interest may be more effective than legal processes. And co-operative endeavour may appropriately have wider objectives than merely the removal of evils which are infractions of positive law. Nor does the fact that the correction of abuses may tend to stabilize a business, or to produce fairer price levels, require that abuses should go uncorrected or that an effort to correct them should for that reason alone be stamped as an unreasonable restraint of trade.' Specifically, the price filing practice of the sugar refiners was not found unreasonable, and the circulation of detailed statistics of production, sales and stocks was allowed to continue, provided that the figures were made available to buyers and sellers equally. What had to be given up was the agreement among refiners to stand by their announced prices: 'The unreasonable restraints which defendants imposed lay not in advance announcements, but in the steps taken to secure adherence, without deviation, to prices and terms thus announced. It was that concerted undertaking which cut off opportunities for variation in the course of competition, however fair and appropriate they might be.'

Notwithstanding the rigour of antitrust enforcement generally in later years and the fact that many cases on the lines of the lumber, linseed oil and sugar plans have been successfully prosecuted, some courts have continued to absolve defendants in cases in which the element of agreement over prices is not firmly established. *Tag Manufacturers' Institute* v. *Federal Trade Commission*[1] (First Circuit Court of Appeals) in 1949, for example, concerned an elaborate price filing scheme covering labelling tags. But the agreement between the members of the Institute expressly provided that there was no obligation on any member to adhere to his price list and evidence was given of a considerable amount of 'off list' selling. Although the Federal Trade Commission still found that substantial uniformity of prices existed and pointed to collusion, the appeal Court reversed this decision on the ground that the inference was not solidly enough based.[2]

An important element in these cases is whether the information supplied by the members of the association to each other is kept

[1] In recent years many cases of this type have been brought under section 5 of the Federal Trade Commission Act instead of under the Sherman Act.

[2] The case was not appealed to the Supreme Court. As with the *Flooring* case, mentioned above, it has been suggested that defects in the handling of the case before the Commission affected this result.

confidential, or is also made available to purchasers and the general public. In the *Tag Manufacturers* case every invoice sent by the members of the association to buyers of their products stated that the statistics submitted to the association were available at its head office to any interested persons. Kaysen and Turner[1] identify confidentiality of price information as one of several factors which distinguish undesirable price reporting systems from those which are at least on their face unobjectionable. Among other factors which they list as suspicious are the identification of individual buyers and sellers in each reported transaction, the opening of competitors' books to one another, and the reporting of transactions and examination of information without any time lag.[2]

On the other hand, the dissemination of cost accounting methods, though a possible vehicle for price fixing, may well be justified if the emphasis is on the calculation and proper attribution of fixed and variable costs rather than merely on the level of mark-ups to be adopted. Thus, in 1953, the Commission itself dismissed a case against an association of vitrified-china manufacturers supplying hotel ware.[3] The association consisted of seven firms with widely differing costs of manufacture. Accountants were employed to make a study for the purpose of arriving at an average or standard figure for the various elements of manufacturing costs; as a result of this study all seven manufacturers adopted a common 'basic list' of prices for the various lines. The Commission took into account, however, that the prices paid by the hotels were made up by adding to the 'basic list' prices various supplements for special features as well as packaging and freight costs; these additions varied between the seven manufacturers, so the final prices that the customers actually paid were not the same. Hence there was no uniformity and, in the Commission's view, no antitrust offence.

4. *The detection of collusion in pricing; pricing in conditions of oligopoly*

What comes out of this line of price filing and 'open competition' cases? Many of the decisions are close and it is tempting to regard the different results from rather similar sets of facts as reflecting inconsistency and vacillation among the courts. And indeed there may be an element of luck in some of these cases—a flash of well timed ingenuity by a particular advocate, a failure of penetration by a particular judge. But it would be unwise to give too much weight to this factor. Brief summaries of the facts, even a full record of the court proceedings, are in no

---

[1] Kaysen and Turner, *Antitrust Policy*, pp. 150–2.

[2] The case of *United States* v. *Container Corporation of America* (Supreme Court, 1969) adopted this reasoning and held illegal exchanges of information about pending bids to specific customers.

[3] *The matter of the Vitrified China Association* (Federal Trade Commission Docket 5719).

way equivalent to the actual hearings at which the court can observe the demeanour of witnesses and find an inference strengthened or weakened by subtleties of inflexion or evasion.

The job of detecting collusive price fixing amid legitimate inter-changes of information about business conditions and intentions seems to be done on the whole with realism and good sense. The cases show, first, that collusive price fixing, like any other violation of law, may be established by circumstantial evidence: direct evidence of an express agreement is not needed. If this were otherwise, evasion would obviously be too easy.

There are in practice two main lines of argument by which a circum-stantial proof of collusive price fixing may be built up; sometimes both lines may be used in the same case. One starts from the existence of an agreement—any trade association activity reflects an agreement of some kind—and seeks to show that the agreement, even though not expressly concerned with price fixing, necessarily involves a significant restriction of price competition. In the *Sugar* case, for example, there was an express agreement among the refiners that each would adhere without deviation to the prices he announced. Although each was free to vary the announced price as he wished, it was held that this agreement necessarily restrained an important type of price competition.

The alternative line of argument starts from the absence of price competition and seeks to show that this state of affairs could not be maintained without collusion. This type of argument was successful in the *Lumber* case when the Court inferred agreement from the behaviour of the parties. For this second line of argument various types of evidence are important. Uniformity of prices among ostensible competitors is only the starting point. It is usually important to show that uniformity is maintained when diversity would be expected. It impresses the courts more, for example, when prices are shown to go up simultaneously than when a price reduction is promptly met. It may be shown too that price changes become markedly less frequent after an 'open competition' scheme is introduced than before, or that prices become much less respon-sive to changes in raw-material costs. (Both these tests were used in the *Sugar* case.) The question whether deviations from list prices are rare or frequent will be of interest. Even more important will be evidence of any action taken by an industry when deviations do occur. Are they ignored or endured in the same way as changes in the weather? Or do they, on the other hand, become a matter of industry-wide concern—the subject of meetings, exhortations, even organized sanctions?

It is often argued on the defence side that uniformity of prices is an unfair test of collusion, since in any market the prices of different sellers are made uniform by normal competitive pressures. But in practice uniformity at a particular moment is never relied upon, and when all the evidence of price behaviour over a period is aggregated, the matter of drawing an inference of collusion is seldom so complex or arbitrary as skilled defence counsel may make it appear. It is the kind of thing about which reasonable men with no axe to grind would often be able to agree.

As the *Maple Flooring* case and the later *Tag* case show, moreover, the burden rests on the prosecution to build up such a case that the inference of collusion becomes virtually inescapable. Collusion means in this context a real 'meeting of the minds' in a common endeavour to suppress or limit price competition; moreover, it is implied that the plan or understanding can be relied upon with reasonable confidence by the participants. The individual firm, in other words, must be under some fairly effective inhibition as regards 'breaking the price line' when the temptation to do so is apparently strong.

Conversely, when the members of a trade group are genuinely left free in their pricing decisions and do in practice exercise their own discretion, collusion cannot be inferred and no antitrust offence can be established. And this is so even when interchanges of information have some dampening effect on price competition. As Mr Justice Brandeis put it in his dissent in the *Lumber* case: 'But there is nothing in the Sherman Law to indicate that Congress intended to condemn co-operative action in the exchange of information, merely because prophecy resulting from comment on the data collected may lead, for a period, to higher market prices.' If all that happens is that the firms in an industry, having become better informed as a result of exchanges of information, act 'oligopolistically'[1]—that is to say, avoid price reductions on the theory that these would be immediately met and would result only in reducing the revenue of all firms in the industry— the necessary element of collusion or conspiracy is lacking.

To distinguish between informed oligopoly and collusion as the cause of damped-down price competition is the most difficult task that the courts have to face in this field, given that they must give due weight to normal legal safeguards in favour of the defendant and yet avoid being deceived by merely specious arguments. It would not be claimed that they never make a mistake in this task. Indeed, the distinction is not always hard and fast; one can imagine situations in which it would be genuinely difficult even for the businessman himself to say whether he was acting from individual prudence or under the suasion of a common understanding. Inevitably the courts are criticized from both sides.

---

[1] The term 'oligopoly' describes a market in which the sellers are few enough for sensible market strategy to require that the probable reactions of competitors to changes in price and output be taken into account. In practice this is a very typical market situation in modern industry and trade.

Many people in industry in the United States would hold that the courts are at times too readily persuaded of collusion, and that they give too little weight to the good reasons which prudent and well informed businessmen often have—independently of any agreement—for not upsetting the going price. It may perhaps be that the courts are not always so rigorous in their handling of circumstantial evidence in price fixing cases as they would be in matters of major crime. It is a very human tendency in law to make the evidence fit the crime no less than the punishment; evidence good enough to secure a conviction for a minor motoring offence would often be found wanting in a murder trial. To this extent the complaint may have some substance. But there is little evidence that injustice to defendants is other than extremely rare, and the *Flooring* and *Tag* cases show that the prosecution case must be solidly based.

On the other hand, fears are sometimes expressed by antitrust supporters that it is too easy to get away with tacit collusion in avoiding price competition, and it is possible that among very small groups this is sometimes successful. But again it can hardly be frequent. In many trades, price schedules are so complicated—with different grades of product, functional and quantity discounts, freight charges and so forth—that competitive variation is bound to break out at one point or another unless the mere desire of individual sellers for price stability is reinforced by some actively collusive arrangements. Certainly the risks involved in deliberately exploiting the borderline between collusion and oligopoly in order to evade the law are formidable. If collusion really occurs, attempts to suppress evidence of it in an industry of any size are not likely to succeed. Some at least of the participants will surely keep damaging material on files to be presented to the court in due course by government counsel. Moreover, any firm which has to be subjected to any degree of pressure to abide by an understanding about price competition is a potential prosecution witness.[1] It must be noted, too, that if an attempt at evasion is made and fails, the court may use its equity powers to prevent even innocent interchanges of information from being carried on in the future.[2]

[1] To the extent that successful antitrust enforcement in the past has conditioned businessmen (and their advisers) to keep files clear of damaging material, to keep tabs on potential witnesses and so forth, the authorities have necessarily been forced to rely more and more on circumstantial evidence. Thus, antitrust supporters might contend that the efforts of the authorities to get somewhat indirect evidence of collusion accepted by the courts are, to some extent, a reaction to sophisticated business efforts to avoid straightforward types of agreement and the provision of clear-cut evidence.

[2] It is established that otherwise lawful activities may be prohibited in court decrees in antitrust cases if they have been abused for the purpose of evading the law. Consider the following injunction in a consent decree entered into by the National Association of Printers' Roller Manufacturers. Injunctions in these terms have been frequently imposed.

'The defendants are jointly and severally enjoined and restrained from collecting or

Thus the safest rule for the businessman is to assume that the courts will most of the time get at the truth. If he really has entered into a common understanding with his competitors, the courts will probably find it out and the reckoning will be unpleasant. If he is acting independently, even though he is well informed in an oligopoly situation and takes account of the probable reactions of his competitors, the courts will not simply invent collusion where there is no evidence to support it. And it must be stressed once more that cases which are exactly poised on the borderline are extremely infrequent as compared with those that are straightforward. Given that the law requires a line to be drawn between collusion and oligopoly in situations where price competition appears to lack vigour, it seems likely that the courts get the right answer as often as can be expected of any human institution.

The wider question remains of whether this borderline makes sense in the context of the policy of maintaining competition. Is the legal immunity of non-collusive oligopoly a serious loophole in antitrust? Does the dampening effect on price fluctuations, which occurs when well informed sellers recognize the interdependence of their decisions, frustrate the general policy? Does 'pure' oligopoly occur very often in practice? These are essentially questions of assessment and appraisal, and, as such, must be deferred to Part II, below. Certainly some zealots in antitrust faith see these points as weaknesses in the system and as a problem to be tackled. This view has led to attempts to stretch the legal meaning of 'conspiracy', and some cases illustrating such attempts and their treatment in the courts will be described below (Chapter III).

5. *Price leadership*

This chapter may suitably end with a brief note on 'price leadership' situations. Price leadership raises no new point of principle. In a trade where the sellers are kept fully and promptly informed about the price decisions of their rivals, it may happen, as has been seen, that price fluctuations will be damped down because of prudent individual calculation and without collusion. In a price leadership situation this result occurs not because of the mutual canniness of more or less equal competitors, but because one seller has a predominant position which others, if they are prudent, will not see fit to challenge. If a small local manufacturer of, say, paint wishes to keep his position in the market, he may

---

compiling and disseminating or communicating among themselves or to any manufacturer of printers' rollers or to or from any trade association or other central agency for such manufacturers except in connection with a bona fide purchase or sale of printers' rollers by any such defendant, any information or statistics relating to prices, discounts, terms or conditions of sale, or costs or elements of costs in connexion with the manufacture, sale or distribution of printers' rollers....'

well think it wise to accept the going price of the large mass producer. He may know that if he should start a challenge by competing in price and begin to extend his market, he could easily be swamped by the powerful competitor. Where competitors are very unequal in power and resources, uniformity of prices may well occur without any collusion. Price leadership is a special case of oligopoly.

It is clear that where the evidence in a case establishes no more than the existence of a price leadership situation, neither the leader nor the followers will be found to have violated the antitrust laws. It may be, of course, that the dominance of the price leader will be found on other grounds to result from monopolization, and a case under section 2 of the Sherman Act may then be brought. Alternatively, it may prove on investigation that as a result of collusion there has been a conscious allocation of initiative in price matters to a particular firm. A spurious 'price leadership' situation would be a possible device for evading the law, and solid evidence of an understanding between firms to abide by the price decisions of an appointed leader would be enough to establish a case of illegal conspiracy under section 1 of the Act. But evidence based solely on uniformity of prices would, as before, be insufficient to sustain the case. As it was put in a frequently quoted sentence from the opinion of the Supreme Court in *United States* v. *International Harvester Company* (1927): 'The fact that competitors may see proper, in the exercise of their own judgment, to follow the prices of another manufacturer does not establish any suppression of competition nor show any sinister domination.'

Once again the question may be raised whether the legal immunity of genuine price leadership situations seriously frustrates the policy of maintaining competition. As in the case of oligopoly generally, the answer will depend in part on the frequency with which genuine price leadership situations occur and on the extent to which they are likely to be stable and lasting. These too are questions which must be raised later in the book in the context of assessing the success and value of the antitrust policy.

NOTE ON DELIVERED-PRICE SYSTEMS

The problem of detecting whether or not an agreement about prices exists may be particularly difficult in the case of industries in which delivered prices are the rule. A number of further illustrations of this problem can in fact be drawn from the cases involving 'basing-point' systems and other forms of delivered prices. To have added these illustrations to the body of the chapter would have made for a serious unbalance of its contents, giving far too much space to the borderline cases and far too little to the arguments in the *Trenton Potteries* and *Socony-Vacuum* cases, which are much more

3

important in terms of the number of cases decided by reference to them. On the other hand, so much is written in the United States about the legality of delivered-price systems that this topic cannot simply be ignored. This supplement to Chapter I will therefore cover the ground for those who are interested in the application of antitrust to delivered-pricing arrangements, and the reader who is content with the main issues may safely skip it.

The problem presented by delivered-price systems is basically the same as that outlined in the body of the chapter: indeed, the *Flooring* and *Cement* cases of 1925 involved delivered prices, though this aspect was not stressed at the time. The special difficulty of detecting agreements in respect of delivered prices is that of determining whether the businessmen concerned are actively in collusion or are just passively but independently deciding their prices by reference to well established formulas. Some description of different types of delivered pricing may be needed to show how the problem arises.

In industries producing goods which are of light weight in relation to their value, and particularly when there are factories in several different parts of the country, the cost of delivery to consumers is not a significant element in price. Tubes of toothpaste or packets of cigarettes, for example, can be packed up so that many thousands of units of the product are transported in quite small and light containers. The cost of transporting them works out at such a small fraction of the price per unit in the shop that the way in which transport costs are paid for is not of much importance.

When, however, a product is very heavy in relation to its value, delivery charges become important. A ton of cement or steel girders at the works will be worth only a tiny fraction of a ton of cigarettes, but the cost of getting that ton to a user will be just as great. In some industries where the factories tend to be concentrated around sources of raw materials or power, very long hauls may be needed to get the product to consumers. In such cases it is out of the question for the manufacturer to absorb the cost of delivery in his general structure of costs; delivery may even cost more than the product. Various possibilities are then open to him.

He may sell only from his factory, quoting an '*ex works*' or an '*f.o.b. mill*' *price*. Then the cost of delivery will fall to the purchaser and the total amount paid by the purchaser to get the goods where he wants to use them will be the factory or mill price plus the actual cost of delivery. In this example no question of a delivered price arises. The purchaser pays two separate bills, one to the manufacturer and one to the railway or other transporter. But the same (f.o.b. mill) method of pricing could be followed if the manufacturer took charge of delivery: the only difference would be that he would now pay the railway charges and recover them from the purchaser. In some industries it has become the custom for manufacturers or producers to take charge of delivery in this way and to quote delivered prices.

If the manufacturer is some distance removed from a main centre of production, he may think it wise, while still shipping direct from his works, to quote a delivered price made up of his mill price and the cost of delivery from the main centre. This will enable him to keep his prices in line with those of his competitors at the centre itself. A manufacturer twenty miles out of Birmingham would find it difficult to get orders for delivery in or beyond the city if he insisted on adding to his delivered prices the cost of getting his product into the centre of Birmingham. In order to compete, he would have to meet or absorb this extra cost. Sometimes he would get a bit back, however, because his local customers (and customers away from the town but nearer to him than to the factories at the centre) would be prepared to pay a price based on the cost of delivery from the centre. They could not get a better price by transferring their custom elsewhere.

This method of quoting prices is called a '*single basing-point*' system. The use of a basing-point means, as we have seen, that a seller away from the base has to absorb some of the freight costs when he sells at the base (i.e. he does not get back from the purchaser the whole of what it costs him to deliver the goods); but he can compensate himself by charging his local customers the full cost of delivery from the base (i.e. he charges them more than it costs him to deliver). Pricing by reference to a single basing-point was the rule in the American steel industry for a long period. Far more steel was produced in the Pittsburgh area than anywhere else, and Pittsburgh was made the single basing-point, so that 'Pittsburgh plus' prices were generally quoted even by steel makers as far away from the centre as Chicago.

Where there are a number of main centres of production, a single basing-point becomes unrealistic and impracticable. Competition among the various firms at any centre will keep the price there well below that at which a manufacturer from a distant centre can afford to sell after footing the bill for delivery from one centre to the other. Hence prices tend to be based separately on each of the centres, though a manufacturer a short way out from one of the centres may still find it convenient, as before, to quote prices based on delivery from the centre.

If a product is made both at Birmingham and Glasgow, both towns being main centres and basing-points, a manufacturer in the Birmingham area will expect to be able to get plenty of orders from London, but will not expect to be able to sell in Scotland, because the cost of delivery from Birmingham to Edinburgh or Perth will be much heavier than the cost from Glasgow. Somewhere between Birmingham and Glasgow, however, will be an area where the freight costs are roughly equal. Here manufacturers from both centres will compete for orders. If the manufacturer near Birmingham was going through a difficult period and badly needed orders to keep his plant employed, he might well find it worth while to try to get orders in the area rather nearer to Glasgow than to Birmingham. But he could not expect customers in this area to pay more than the price they would pay to a manufacturer in the Glasgow area. In such a case he would have to quote a 'Glasgow plus' delivered price and face the fact that he would not be compensated for the full cost of delivering from Birmingham.

When manufacturers, whether in main centres of production or at some remove from them, base their delivered prices on the going prices at the nearest centre to the point of delivery plus the cost of delivery from that centre, you have what is known as a '*multiple basing-point*' system. This is much the same as the so-called '*freight equalization*' method whereby the

3-2

manufacturer who wants orders in an area nearer to a competitor undertakes to charge only as much for delivery as his competitor will charge.

It would, of course, be theoretically possible for a manufacturer even of heavy products to charge the same to all customers, no matter where delivery was made. He would then have to average out the costs of long and short hauls. This method—*averaged delivered prices*—however, would entail special difficulties. For one thing it would make him unpopular with some of his customers. A customer at Wolverhampton only a mile or two from the Birmingham works might well wonder why he was asked to pay as much as a customer at Glasgow or Penzance, in effect having to subsidize customers at a greater distance than himself from the works. A last possible method would be to divide the total area to be served into arbitrary zones—for example, circles of a radius of 50 miles, 100 miles, 150 miles and so on away from the works—and then keep the delivered price uniform to all customers within any particular zone.[1] This method—*zone-averaged delivered prices*—would probably run into similar difficulties, though perhaps not in such an acute form.

We must now look at these various methods of pricing from the point of view of those enforcing antitrust. Let us assume that, as in the 'open competition' cases described in the body of the chapter, a trade association has organized some form of 'price filing' arrangement and that the members are kept fully informed of current trading conditions. As in those cases, evidence that price movements are 'sticky' and uniform as between competing sellers may lead to a suspicion of concealed collusion. As the heavy materials, for which delivered pricing is usual, are often homogeneous in character—one steel girder is very like another—uniformity of prices as between rival sellers at any particular time is only to be expected and in itself may be of little significance.[2] Competitive variation might be expected to break out, however, in the matter of delivery; in a vigorously competitive situation producers might be found seeking out specially cheap forms of transport in order to invade a wider market. But in many industries in which delivered pricing is the rule, this type of variation does not seem to occur in practice. Among the information circulated by trade associations may be compilations of current rail freight rates from the centres of production (or basing-points) to many hundreds of consuming centres, or of averaged freight costs throughout a zone served by a producing centre. In other words, each producer may be put in possession of a formula by reference to which a going price for each point of delivery may be calculated.

When the antitrust authorities find that a basing-point or other formula is adhered to without deviation throughout an industry, the system of delivered

---

[1] An interesting British example of a zoning arrangement is described in the Ministry of Works, *Report of the Committee on Cement Costs*, H.M. Stationery Office, London, 1947.

[2] The argument that uniformity of prices arises out of the homogeneous nature of the product may be double-edged. In the *Cement* case (see pp. 61–2) there was evidence of considerable quality differences between sellers. The fact that these differences were not reflected in price differences (together with evidence that the industry sought to ignore or deny them) was one of the pointers to collusion.

prices may fall under the suspicion, together with the rest of the paraphernalia of 'open competition', of serving as a cloak for collusion in the avoidance of price competition. This is especially the case when, as sometimes happens, it is a 'rule' in the industry that only delivered prices are quoted and suppliers refuse to allow their customers to buy 'ex works' and collect the goods in their own transport.[1] A number of cases have attacked the legality of delivered-price systems.

Sometimes the detection and proof of collusion in these cases appear fairly straightforward. Let us consider, first, the situation that arises when *averaged delivered prices* are charged over the whole country or by zones. It is clear in the first place that, where there are a number of producers scattered over the area, there must be some agreement or understanding that all will use the method of averaging the delivery costs to different customers; otherwise one would expect some at least of the producers to try to keep their local markets to themselves by refraining from loading the price in those markets with a share of the delivery costs to more distant customers. Conceivably there might be an agreement to use the averaging method without any further agreement as to the actual prices to be charged; but in a concrete case it is often hard to explain the facts without some further agreement. Each seller would presumably have a different list of customers scattered over the zone and not all sellers would be delivering from the same place. Thus it would be any odds that average costs of delivery would differ significantly from seller to seller; and if the prices of different firms were nevertheless identical at each delivery point, some artificial influence at work would be strongly indicated.

So indeed it has appeared to the courts. *Federal Trade Commission* v. *Fort Howard Paper Company* (Seventh Circuit Court of Appeals, 1946) involved a zone pricing system operated by manufacturers of crêpe paper. The main selling zone was the whole of the country east of the Mississippi, but two manufacturers were in Wisconsin only just east of the river while others were located in eastern States. Yet all sold at any point in the zone at the same price; moreover, all added the same differential for sales west of the river, even though some towns to the west were only spitting distance from Wisconsin but well over a thousand miles from the Atlantic. 'The existence of substantial similarity in delivered prices to zoned territories having identical zone price differentials by six manufacturers located at different places, was not a happenstance,' was the vivid conclusion of Judge Kerner, who made much of the point that, while manufacturers might naturally be expected to match any lower price of a competitor that they found in a given area, it was odd that they always matched higher prices than they needed for normal profits. 'We are unable to comprehend a manufacturer's disdain of a natural

---

[1] The point should not be ignored that collection by customers may in practice prove a rather high-cost method of effecting delivery so far as the seller is concerned. The customer's truck may turn up at any odd time and his order for various quantities of different grades of the product in question may involve a disproportionate use of the time of clerks and dispatchers. Nevertheless, these troubles can often be overcome by good organization, and the refusal by suppliers to allow customers to collect *on any condition* may well be persuasive evidence of a restrictive scheme.

advantage, utilizing the same to gain local business, unless he were indoc-
trinated with the belief (or forced by superior economic competitors to align
himself to concerted action of identical delivered prices) that elimination of
all competition was economically preferable.'

A similar result was reached in the more recent case of *In the matter of the
National Lead Company* (Federal Trade Commission, 1953). The National Lead
Company was said to be a strong 'price leader' in the paint industry, and it
was urged (by, among others, a dissenting member of the Commission itself)
that the smaller firms, in following exactly the zoning scheme of National
Lead, were acting simply as rational individuals: if they beat the National
Lead prices, even in areas where they had the strongest advantages of location, National Lead might retaliate in such strength that they could not
survive. Nevertheless, the majority of the Commission found that the zonal
price uniformity was so artificial in view of the relative geographical positions
of the firms that an inference of some element of collusion was irresistible.[1]

At the other extreme the *single basing-point* method of pricing heavy commodities may also yield fairly straightforward signs of collusion. As we have
seen, where there is a single main centre of production, it may be no more
than a matter of convenience for individual firms a few miles out from the
centre to base their delivered prices at distant points on the cost of delivery
from the centre. So long as single basing-point pricing meant only that a few
firms scattered around the outskirts of a big centre were acting in this way,
it would probably cause little concern. But if a number of producers at a
substantial distance from a main centre consistently take it as a basing-point
for sales in their own immediate area, suspicions can hardly fail to be aroused.
Given, for example, that Pittsburgh was the main centre of the steel industry,
a single mill fifty or so miles away might follow the Pittsburgh lead in most of
its pricing without causing surprise. But when a whole group of steel makers
in and around Chicago, nearer five hundred miles away, all used the Pittsburgh base, questions were bound to be asked. Surely some among the Chicago
steel makers would see fit to exploit the advantage of having the rich Mid-
West market near at hand and would sell in that market without adding to
their prices the heavy freight charges from Pittsburgh which, of course, they
never incurred? Surely if there were not some element of collusion which
prevented the Chicago makers from competing among themselves, Chicago
would have become established as a separate base in a multiple basing-point
system?[2]

A single basing-point system so operated as to lead to a strong inference of
collusion was an important issue in *Federal Trade Commission* v. *United States*

---

[1] The Seventh Circuit Court of Appeals upheld the Commission in 1955, finding that it
was not 'conscious parallelism' but price identity in zones without regard to shipping costs
that made the system so 'arbitrary and artificial' as to reject the inference of innocent
behaviour.

[2] A case was in fact brought against 'Pittsburgh plus' pricing of steel by the Federal
Trade Commission in 1924 but it was based on the element of price discrimination involved
in the system and so is not on all fours with the other cases described here. Its immediate
result was that the steel industry increased the number of basing-points in use.

Maltsters' Association (Seventh Circuit Court of Appeals, 1945). The eighteen maltsters in the Association were mostly located in the State of Wisconsin or in Chicago, but there were three plants in Buffalo and others in eastern States. As in the 'open competition' cases, the Association operated elaborate price filing arrangements; any change of prices by any maltster was immediately reported to all the members. Evidence was given of instances when an increase of price by one member was at once followed by the others; and it was found that malt prices remained unchanged over periods when the price of barley fluctuated considerably. Thus a price fixing conspiracy might perhaps have been inferred, on the authority of the *Lumber* and *Sugar* cases, without reference to the question of delivered prices. The Commission noted, however, that delivered prices were calculated so that in effect Chicago was taken as a single basing-point, despite the scattered locations of the producers, and the Circuit Court of Appeals upheld the Commission's finding that the use of this system was an essential part of the arrangements for keeping prices uniform. 'The fact that petitioners utilized a system which enabled them to deliver malt at every point of destination at exactly the same price is a persuasive circumstance in itself. Especially is this so when it is considered that petitioners' plants are located in four different States....'

In short, it seems probable that, given a fairly large trading area with a considerable number of sellers, averaged delivered prices throughout a zone, or prices related to a single basing-point which produced a high degree of price uniformity over a period, would nearly always require and betray an element of collusion. The element of collusion has been found a good deal more elusive, however, in the case of '*multiple basing-point*' or '*freight equalization*' schemes and most of the argument on this topic in the United States has raged about these methods.

On the face of it, *multiple basing-point* pricing is a normal and natural development. Each main centre of production becomes a basing-point and the sellers located there are in effect charging 'f.o.b. mill' prices. We have noted already how the odd firm at some distance from a centre will probably find it sensible to quote delivered prices which include freight costs from the centre instead of from its own works; and there seems nothing untoward about this. Also, we have seen that a firm located in or near one centre of production may, when badly needing orders, invade the area served by another centre at the cost of absorbing some of the freight costs in order to compete. The Birmingham firm will sometimes seek orders in areas nearer to Glasgow than to Birmingham, despite the fact that it cannot expect to recover the full delivery cost, rather than have its plant idle. And this too seems a quite normal and competitive kind of business behaviour.[1]

---

[1] Some American economists object to any departure from 'f.o.b. mill' pricing: they would say that the firm in need of orders should compete by reducing its price at the base, thus bringing down the general level of prices. This view is well represented by Professor Frank Fetter, 'Exit Basing Point Pricing', *American Economic Review*, vol. 38, no. 5, December 1948, p. 815. For the more moderate view that *sporadic* raids into the territory of other producers by means of 'freight absorption' should not be discouraged, see Corwin D. Edwards, 'The Effect of Recent Basing Point Decisions upon Business Practices', *American*

The position of a producer who is well away from any centre of production sometimes injects intellectual confusion into the problem, but largely because it is misconceived. A firm located somewhere between two main centres of production—a 'non-base mill' in the jargon of this subject—will naturally be able to command in its own locality a price equal to the delivered price of the producers at the nearest centres. (For example, if the Birmingham base price and the Glasgow base price are both 100 and freight costs from both centres to Middlesbrough are 20, Birmingham and Glasgow producers will compete for orders in Middlesbrough at a delivered price of 120. A lone producer in Middlesbrough itself will also be able to charge 120, and will have no incentive not to do so as long as business is buoyant.) If the non-base firm wants to sell outside its immediate locality, however, it will have to meet the delivered prices charged by producers selling from the nearest centre. It will endeavour, if possible, to spread its sales away from the centre so as to keep its advantages of location. But it may have to seek orders in the area towards the centre: in which case, the further towards the centre it goes in search of orders, the lower will be the delivered prices it has to meet. The non-base firm in fact can get the biggest price right on its doorstep and may be found selling at lower prices at a distance, even though sales at a distance involve freight costs which local sales avoid. (For example, the lone supplier in Middlesbrough can get 120 locally though no freight costs are incurred. Half-way to Glasgow or Birmingham he can get only 110—the going 'Glasgow plus' or 'Birmingham plus' price—though these sales incur 10 units of freight cost; so his net receipts from these sales will be 100 as against 120 from local sales).

The fact that individual firms away from main centres of production may obtain windfall profits from local sales in this way owing to their favourable location has at times confused the issue. This type of windfall profit has been called 'phantom freight'—the suggestion being that the price is improperly loaded with freight costs that are not incurred—and some commentators (and even some courts) have rather uncritically assumed that 'phantom freight' is in itself a sign of antitrust sin.[1] It is true that where a number of producers

---

Economic Review, vol. 38, no. 5, December 1948, p. 828. Professor Edwards makes it clear, however, that *systematic* price matching by means of freight absorption induces wasteful cross-hauling and is therefore economically objectionable. A good summary of the legal and economic issues is Carl Kaysen's 'Basing Point Pricing and Public Policy', *Quarterly Journal of Economics*, vol. 63, no. 3, August 1949, p. 289.

[1] This probably results from a confusion between a 'fair' price and an 'economic' price. There is a tendency to believe that a businessman should not charge more than a 'fair price', this being a price that covers his costs and affords a modest profit. Hence the windfall profit of the non-base mill comes into instinctive disfavour. But this, though a respectable view, springs from the very opposite economic tradition from that which is supposed to lie behind antitrust. Under the system of free competitive bargaining, for which antitrust stands, price is supposed to be 'given' by the structure of the market and not to require decisions or ethical fiddle-faddle from the bargainers. The economic man will take the highest price he can get, and windfall profit due to a favourable location is a beneficent force attracting new supplies to the area. However, the 'fair price' philosophy still persists: a cynic might say that according to some antitrust authorities the poor businessman should accept the 'economic' price when it hurts but not exceed a 'fair' price when the market is in his favour.

with a substantial local market all charge 'phantom freight' (i.e. all base their prices on a distant basing-point, as in the example of the Chicago steel makers given above) this will probably be persuasive evidence of collusion and 'not a happenstance'.[1] But the individual non-base mill may have good reasons for accepting the going price set by the nearest base and no valid reason for upsetting it. It is obviously not economically improper to exploit a favourable location: indeed, economists would want it to be exploited in order to attract new producers to the area. On the other hand, if the competitors at the base are big and powerful, it may be suicide for a small non-base firm to upset their going price in his area: this may be the surest way to attract heavy retaliation.

Thus, on the face of it, there need be nothing artificial about the behaviour of the various participants in an industry in which delivered prices are calculated by reference to multiple basing-points: this type of price structure might be a natural development. This conclusion has respectable authority among economists. Professor Corwin Edwards, for example, has written: 'I have been able to convince myself...that it is possible for a basing-point structure to arise as a mere matter of competitive interaction without collusion. Wherever most of an industry's output comes from one important centre of production and new lesser concerns appear in outlying markets, it is reasonable to expect that they, for a time, will base their prices on the prices they find. Thus, you will get what is in practice a price structure based upon the central point of production.'[2] It does not follow, of course, that basing-point systems are typically built up in practice without artificial aids. Professor Edwards goes on to say that, if there are merely competitive influences at work, a basing-point structure will be inherently unstable: more and more sources of supply will become bases on their own account and the structure will approximate more and more to 'f.o.b. mill' pricing in which every mill or factory is its own base.

It is indeed the stability, together with the systematic nature, of certain multiple basing-point price schemes that has attracted the suspicious attention of the antitrust authorities. To them the picture is one of an exact uniformity of the delivered prices of numerous sellers from different locations at any of several thousand possible destinations; and this uniformity persists despite many changes in freight rates and other costs. It is precisely this persistent stability, and not the individual firms' adoption of basing-points as such, that raises the issue of collusion.

An industry which finds itself under suspicion of collusive price fixing by means of a multiple basing-point system will, of course, lay great stress in its defence on the way in which, as outlined above, this type of price structure may be a spontaneous and natural development. As in the 'open competition' cases, too, it will be argued that it can be no crime for the businessmen concerned to be in possession of essential trade information such as current base

---

[1] In this example the offence is the collusion and not the 'phantom freight' as such.

[2] Corwin D. Edwards and others, 'Comments and Discussion' in *Robinson-Patman Act Symposium for 1947*, Commerce Clearing House, Chicago, 1947, pp. 57–58.

prices and freight rates, and it will be urged that rational and well informed businessmen will naturally seek off their own bat to avoid weak selling or cut-throat competition and hence that stable conditions can be fully explained without collusion. But this argument takes a good deal for granted. It is not impossible that, in a very small industry or in one in which the restraining force of price leadership was strong, the individual decisions of businessmen, given their reluctance to start a 'price war' or challenge an entrenched leader, might add up to a stable system with long-maintained price uniformities. But in practice, in an industry of any size, long-term stability seems most unlikely to be achieved without being helped along by collusion.

There are a number of reasons why this should be so. Chiefly it is because of the complexity of the arrangements that are needed for real stability. There are often different grades of the product, different discount rates for different quantities or for different classes of customer, different routes by which delivery may be made. All these differences create possibilities of error which alone may be enough, in the absence of collusion, to upset the desired uniformity. Moreover, the temptation to make secret concessions is very strong except in boom periods, so that, apart from those who are just not good at reading their freight rate books accurately, there will be those whose errors develop a surprising degree of system. When this happens, the other participants have either to reconcile themselves to a breakdown in stable conditions or there will be meetings, exhortations and pressures as signs and tokens of incipient collusion. Many collusive schemes are found to have been organized at a time when the granting of secret rebates and other concessions has reached a stage hardly distinguishable from the dreaded 'price war'.

One of the hardest points to explain on the theory that stability may develop naturally is the absence of competition between different modes of transport. A customer sited on a canal may know that delivery by barge is much cheaper than by rail and ask for shipment by barge in the expectation of having the saving passed on to him in the delivered price. Another customer may want to pick up his supplies in his own lorries and again expect a price advantage. But if real stability is to be maintained, these special methods of delivery will either have to be refused or the expected price advantage will have to be withheld from the customer. Either way the element of 'phantom freight' seems very obtrusive and unfair, and always makes customers (and judges) cross. A general refusal by suppliers to use other than rail delivery or to adjust the delivered price for cheaper means of transport has been a feature of some of the schemes attacked under antitrust and has been found persuasive evidence of collusion.[1]

Apart from these reasons why stability without collusion is difficult in practice to maintain, there are, of course, many reasons why 'organized' or collusive stability will be preferred by industry if it can be managed. When a small supplier refuses to allow a good customer the benefit of cheap freight

---

[1] Accordingly it has been found that the most effective relief measure is usually to require suppliers to give customers an option as to method of delivery.

by barge, he may genuinely and of his own volition wish to avoid upsetting a 'going price'. But it will be a good deal easier for him—as a matter of presentation—and will protect him against the customer's suspicion of profiteering or discrimination, if he can attribute his refusal to the workings of the 'National Federation Fair Price Scheme' rather than to his own free choice. Similarly, if he is nervous of the effects of challenging a powerful 'price leader', he will be anxious to avoid breaking the going price by pure error in the complex calculations of discounts, freight rates and so on: again it will be easier for him if his association issues clear directives as to the 'proper' prices to be charged. In general the mutual confidence of members of an industry in each other's will and ability to maintain stable conditions will be altogether firmer for a modicum of organization than if it relies merely on a 'natural' tendency to stability. Mutual confidence may also be severely strained at times when price changes are unavoidable unless some understanding is developed regarding the allocation of initiative in making changes.[1]

In practice, then, long-term stability of prices in a multiple basing-point system is improbable without collusion; and collusion can rarely go on without leaving traces. And so the American courts have found. The Seventh Circuit Court of Appeals, for example, upheld the Federal Trade Commission in *Federal Trade Commission* v. *Milk and Ice Cream Can Institute* in 1946. Prices of cans had been uniform at each delivery point for substantial periods by virtue of freight equalization. A customer in St Paul purchased cans at the same delivered price whether they came from St Paul itself or Chicago. 'Just how such an unnatural situation could be brought about by members of an industry without a plan or agreement is difficult, if not impossible, to visualize,' said Judge Major; and the Court held, in effect, that the uniformity of prices must have been the result of the activities of the Institute.

Much the most important case on this topic is *Federal Trade Commission* v. *Cement Institute*, decided by the Supreme Court in 1948. The Court of Appeals in 1946 had failed to find convincing evidence in the 100,000 pages of record to sustain the Commission's findings of illegal collusion, partly perhaps because it was widely felt at the time that the legality of the industry's multiple basing-point scheme should be tested in the Supreme Court. But the Supreme Court had no doubt about it. As Mr Justice Black put it:

The Commission's findings of fact set out at great length and with painstaking detail numerous concerted activities carried on in order to make the multiple basing-point system work in such a way that competition in quality, price and terms of sale of cement would be non-existent, and that uniform prices, job contracts, discounts, and terms of sale would be continuously maintained.... Among the collective methods used to accomplish these purposes, according to the findings, were boycotts; discharge of unco-operative employees; organized opposition to the erection of new cement plants; selling cement in a recalcitrant price cutter's sale territory

---

[1] Professor Corwin D. Edwards, formerly chief economist of the Federal Trade Commission, has observed that the heart of a basing-point conspiracy lies precisely in this 'allocation of initiative' by which in any given area only the base mill (or mills) has any influence in bringing about price changes, and non-base suppliers and those from outside the area simply follow the lead of the base.

at a price so low that the recalcitrant was forced to adhere to the established basing-point prices; discouraging the shipment of cement by truck or barge; and preparing and distributing freight rate books, which provided respondents with similar figures to use as actual or 'phantom' freight factors, thus guaranteeing that their delivered prices...would be identical on all sales, whether made to individual purchasers under open bids or to governmental agencies under sealed bids.

Later he summed up as follows: 'It seems impossible to conceive that anyone reading these findings in their entirety could doubt that the Commission found that respondents collectively maintained a multiple basing-point delivered price system for the purpose of suppressing competition in cement sales. The findings are sufficient. The contention that they were not is without substance.'

The lesson of the delivered-pricing cases is in the end very much the same as that of the 'open competition' cases described in the body of the chapter. These cases have been concerned essentially with the occurrence of collusive price fixing and not with the merits of basing-point pricing as such; not with the individual use of a price formula, but with the collective espousal of the formula as the basis of systematic price stability. As with the previous cases, the businessman should assume that, by and large, the courts will detect collusion when it is present and not invent it when it is not. Sometimes the dicta of the courts seem open to criticism, more perhaps than their decisions; 'phantom freight', for example, sometimes seems to be automatically regarded as a form of cheating, whereas for a small non-base firm, afraid of challenging a powerful 'price leader', it may result from prudent, individual decision. On the whole, however, it is difficult after reading the records to believe that the courts' decisions in this field have been unjust. Where collusion has been found, most reasonable men would find it hard to explain the facts without it.

The antitrust authorities have encountered a further problem with delivered pricing, especially multiple basing-point systems. Although, as has been shown, it is difficult for such a system to produce long-term price stability without providing evidence of collusion, nevertheless, once in smooth operation, very little obtrusive collusion may be needed to keep it going. Having succeeded in the courts, therefore, the authorities have been faced with the problem of effectively putting a stop to these systems and preventing their becoming tacitly re-established. This has appeared to require some sanction against the individual firm. In one case this sanction was found in what seemed to be a substantial extension of previous doctrines of conspiracy or collusion. This issue will be considered below (Chapter III). In other cases a legal hold over the individual firm has been sought through the law against price discrimination, and it has been alleged that the individual use of delivered-pricing methods—other than 'f.o.b. mill' pricing—necessarily involves illegal discrimination. This is a quite separate issue from that of collusion and it will be dealt with below (Chapter IX) in a supplementary note on the Robinson-Patman Act.

CHAPTER II

AGREEMENTS BETWEEN COMPETITORS II. EXCLUDING COMPETITORS AND SHARING MARKETS

1. *Agreements other than price agreements*

Not all restraint of trade is directed to influencing the level of prices. While the ultimate aim of market strategy is to obtain favourable terms in bargaining, the immediate objective of many restrictive agreements is to build up or maintain or enhance a position of power in the market. Power in the market is, of course, a necessary condition of effective action even for those whose purpose in limiting competition is defensive and directed to stabilizing a situation in which competition is believed to be excessive. Whether the intention is defensive or exploitative, the classic prescription for improving a bargaining position is to exclude competitors from the market and confine the available trade so far as possible to a manageable number of participants. This chapter will deal first with those agreements between competitors which seek in various ways to regulate entry into the market or to keep out of the market those outside a favoured group.

The amount of competition in a market may also be reduced by agreements between competitors to keep out of each other's way. When a market is divisible, whether geographically by areas, functionally by classes of customers, technically by types of product or in other ways, some suppliers may agree to confine themselves to a particular selling area or class of customers or technical field in return for undertakings from others not to compete in that part of the market. These market sharing agreements will be considered in the second part of the chapter. They have the same aim as exclusionary agreements—to improve the bargaining position of the participants by reducing the amount of competition; the difference is that market sharing agreements seek this result from a voluntary division of effort among the participants, whereas in exclusionary agreements all the participants band together to resist encroachments from outsiders.

A link between these exclusionary and market sharing agreements and direct price fixing agreements is provided by agreements to limit output of a commodity or the amount of it coming into the market. There is an obvious sense in which restrictions of output or sales come into the class of restraints of trade designed to enhance bargaining power. Such restrictions reduce the amount of competition in the market by removing a part of the supply. The effect of restrictions of output or sales on prices is, however, very direct. For this reason, and because the law has always looked to effect on price levels as the surest criterion of illegal restraint of trade, it has usually been found best in antitrust enforcement to attack output restrictions as a form of price manipulation. The *Socony-Vacuum* case, for example, is always quoted as a leading case in the field of price fixing, though it rests, as was seen in Chapter I, on the planned removal of 'surplus' quantities of petrol from the market. The result is that antitrust case law contains hardly any cases in which output restriction as such is the central issue. There can, however, be little doubt that collusive arrangements to limit the amount of a product reaching the market are illegal *per se* under section 1 of the Sherman Act and would be so found even if no evidence of concomitant effects on prices could be produced, which is unlikely.[1]

It can, of course, happen that direct restrictions of price competition, restrictions of output, arrangements to divide a market and exclude new competitors are all found together in one set of trade agreements. The separate elements are here dealt with seriatim for ease of exposition and not because they do not in practice commonly co-exist.

2. *Collective exclusive-dealing agreements: the* Standard Sanitary *case*

The most comprehensive aim of exclusionary agreements is to pre-empt a market completely for the participating group and keep outsiders away. Some of the most impressive examples of agreements with this aim are to be found in situations where the exclusionary device is control over patents, and the leading cases in this field will be described below (Chapter XI). Other cases in later chapters will show how powerful individual firms or small groups in an industry have sometimes succeeded in excluding or greatly hindering competitors by pre-empting sources of supply of vital materials or by tying essential channels of distribution exclusively to themselves. Where large groups are concerned, it is usually necessary for agreements to be made between associations of traders at different market levels if outside firms are to be effectively impeded. An association of wholesalers, for example, even though their total share of a trade is very large, can do little by themselves to exclude new entrants; but if they can make an agreement with an equally dominant group of manufacturers whereby no non-participating wholesaler will be supplied, the exclusionary effect may

---

[1] In 1969 the Justice Department filed a complaint against automobile manufacturers alleging a conspiracy to inhibit research and development in anti-pollution devices.

be strong. The manufacturers will probably require on their side of the bargain that the wholesalers do not distribute the goods of any manufacturer outside the participating group, and in this way the competition of non-participating manufacturers will also be hindered. The power and advantage of agreements of this kind often arise from their reciprocity. They are known as *collective exclusive-dealing agreements* and they violate section 1 of the Sherman Act just as much as price fixing agreements.

From an early stage in the enforcement of the Sherman Act there have been cases involving large groups or associations which have sought in this way to pre-empt or foreclose markets. As early as 1903, in *Montague and Company* v. *Lowry* (Supreme Court), an agreement whereby a group of wholesalers undertook to obtain supplies of tiles only from a particular group of manufacturers, and the manufacturers agreed in turn to distribute their goods only through the group of wholesalers, was found repugnant to the Sherman Act. Another early case may be mentioned here, even though it involved patents, as setting the tone for this line of decisions. This was *Standard Sanitary Manufacturing Company* v. *United States* in 1912, in which again associations of manufacturers and dealers made agreements by which the dealings of each group were to be confined to the other. These agreements were also condemned by the Supreme Court: 'The agreements in the case at bar combined the manufacturers and jobbers of enamelled ware very much to the same purpose and results as the association of manufacturers and dealers in tiles combined them in *Montague and Company* v. *Lowry* . . . which combination was condemned by this Court as offending the Sherman law. The added element of the patent in this case at bar cannot confer immunity from a like condemnation.'

It may be taken as an established rule of antitrust that all agreements between trade associations or groups at different levels of the market—for example, between manufacturers and wholesalers, wholesalers and retailers, jobbers and contractors—whereby the flow of supplies (or orders) from one of the groups is confined to members of the other, are illegal *per se*. Nor is it a question only of the flow of supplies; agreements whereby only firms within the participating associations can obtain certain favourable terms of trade, such as special discounts and rebates, fall under the same ban. In the most general terms the rule is that any collective arrangements under which supplies (or orders to supply) or preferential terms and conditions of sale (or of purchase) are confined to an exclusive group of firms, whether this group is defined by a formula or enumerated in a list, and whether or not it is co-extensive with the membership of a particular trade association, are restraints of trade within the prohibition of section 1 of the Sherman Act.

Thus, while it may be unobjectionable for an individual supplier of, say, building materials to grant 'functional discounts' of different amounts to different types of distributor and user, it is never permitted for these arrangements to be formalized into trade-association agreements under which the persons entitled to receive a particular level of discount are determined collectively.[1] All the 'classification'[2] agreements which are so commonly found in building materials and other industries in many parts of the world are in this way offensive to the Sherman Act.

Since collective exclusive-dealing agreements are regarded as illegal *per se*, the courts will not accept, any more than with price fixing agreements, defence arguments resting on alleged social or economic advantages of limiting competition. Nor does the share of the output of a product that is controlled by the participating groups have to reach some given percentage, so long as a significant effect on competition is produced or intended. In practice no agreement is likely to escape the law on the ground that its effect on competition is negligible, since exclusive-dealing agreements are not easy to organize or negotiate, and businessmen are unlikely to go to the trouble of making agreements that have no effect.

3. *'Bottleneck' agreements which deny scarce facilities to competitors:* Associated Press

While exclusive-dealing agreements between two groups at different levels of the market are usually necessary if either group is to be able effectively to exclude or impede outsiders, this is not invariably so. Sometimes it happens that one group alone has sufficient command over some essential commodity or facility in its industry or trade to be able to impede new entrants. These are so-called 'bottleneck' situations in which those who wish to pursue a trade must be able to use some specific facility and those who own or control it can in practice prevent new entry. Classic 'bottleneck' situations have arisen in the transport industries; the only accessible site for a railway or bus terminal in a city, for example, comes under the control of established concerns, and new entrants must either be allowed to share the facilities or fail. Cases of monopolies based on 'bottleneck' facilities will be illustrated below (Chapter V).

[1] It is possible for the individual supplier who grants 'functional discounts' to come up against certain difficulties with the Robinson-Patman (price discrimination) Act; this matter is considered below, Chapter IX.

[2] These are arrangements under which the various types of traders in and users of a material are classified for discount purposes so that a particular class, e.g. building contractors, cannot obtain from the manufacturers such a favourable discount rate as a 'higher' class, e.g. builders' merchants, even though individual contractors may be able to buy in comparable qualities and to perform for themselves the functions of the merchant. See, for example, the Monopolies and Restrictive Practices Commission's *Report on the Supply of Cast Iron Rainwater Goods*, H.M. Stationery Office, London, 1951, Chapters 10 and 11.

Sometimes large groups of competitors are able by agreement to exert a control of this type. The Sherman Act requires that where facilities cannot practicably be duplicated by would-be competitors, those in possession of them must allow them to be shared on fair terms. It is illegal restraint of trade to foreclose the scarce facility. A leading case is *Associated Press* v. *United States* (Supreme Court, 1945).

Associated Press is a news gathering agency to which at the time of the case more than 1,200 newspapers subscribed. Among the by-laws of the organization, to which the subscribers consented to be bound and which were enforceable by heavy fines, were such rules as that no member firm should sell news from its own area to any agency or publisher other than Associated Press, nor make any news supplied by Associated Press available to any non-member in advance of publication. In this way the rules secured that membership of Associated Press was a pre-requisite to obtaining any news supplied either by Associated Press itself or by any one of its individual subscribers. Much turned, therefore, on the ease with which newcomers could be admitted to the association. It was found that the board of directors of Associated Press were bound by the by-laws not to elect any new applicant who would directly compete as a newspaper publisher with an established member, except after reference to a meeting of the association. At such a meeting it was necessary for the new applicant to receive a majority vote of the established members. The applicant had also to relinquish any exclusive rights he might have to news from other sources and make available all the news he obtained himself to the association and its members. Finally, to secure election, the new applicant was required to pay the association 10% of the total payments that had been made in the whole period since 1900 by any directly competing newspaper which was an established member of the association.[1] No such difficulties were made about the admission of a non-competing applicant.

From this evidence the Supreme Court formed the view that the association, by systematically stacking the cards in favour of its established members, seriously limited the opportunity for any new newspaper to enter into competition where Associated Press members were already publishing. The requirements of the law were stated as follows: 'The Sherman Act was specifically intended to prohibit independent businesses from becoming "associates" in a common plan which is bound to reduce their competitors' opportunity to buy or sell the things in which the groups compete. Victory of a member of such a combination over its business rivals achieved by such collective means cannot, consistently with the Sherman Act or with practical, everyday

---

[1] For a new applicant proposing to compete in New York, this 'entrance fee' would have amounted to over a million dollars.

knowledge, be attributed to individual "enterprise and sagacity"; such hampering of business rivals can only be attributed to that which really makes it possible—the collective power of an unlawful combination.'

It was argued in defence of the Associated Press that there were other news agencies from which new entrants might draw their news. Indeed, some papers were shown to have got along for years without Associated Press news. But it was found that morning papers having in total 96 % of the whole morning newspaper circulation in the United States took the Associated Press news service. The Court held that in any event the Sherman Act did not require that a product or service should be 'indispensable' to be an instrument of restraint of trade. 'Most monopolies, like most patents, give control over only some of the means of production for which there is a substitute; the possessor enjoys an advantage over his competitors, but he can seldom shut them out altogether.' Associated Press was collectively organized to secure competitive advantages for members over non-members and, as such, was in restraint of trade, even though the non-members were not necessarily prevented altogether from competing. In its decree the Court prohibited Associated Press from continuing to operate by-laws under which new membership could be unreasonably restricted.

The *Associated Press* case is a clear guide to this aspect of the law. It shows that for refusal of entry into an association to constitute illegal restraint of trade there must be some important facility—sometimes a virtual 'bottleneck'—in the association's control, such that, by keeping it exclusive to themselves, the members of the association impose a real handicap on would-be competitors.[1] This handicap need not be fatal; the facility need not be 'indispensable': it is enough that the association's exclusive hold on the scarce resource confers significant competitive advantages on members as against outsiders. An interesting example of this was *International Boxing Club of New York* v. *United States*, in which the Supreme Court ruled in 1959 that the respondents, who had been found to have monopolized championship boxing promotions in the United States, must for the next five years offer leases of all the stadiums which they controlled to other promoters at a fair and reasonable rental, to be determined by the Court if the parties could not agree. Finally, it is no defence that the members have built up a facility—such as the Associated Press news service—for themselves; new entrants must still be allowed to share it on reasonable terms unless it is practicable for them to compete without it.

In this field there is clearly some scope for the rule of reason. Some-

---

[1] In industries where the main competitors have cross-licensed important patents, the resulting 'patent pool' may be a facility which cannot legally be kept exclusively for the original contributors: examples are given below, Chapter XI.

times it is only fair that the newcomer should pay rather more for a facility than those who have invested in it over a long period. How much more is reasonable? Sometimes, as in the *Associated Press* case, the new-comer can find facilities of a sort elsewhere than in the association; but they may be far inferior. How much worse must the inferior ones be to make it illegal to keep the better ones exclusive? These are questions which the courts have to answer by reference to 'the facts peculiar to the business' in each case. What they are really trying to get at is the actual competitive situation; and, once again, the prudent businessman who wants to steer clear of antitrust trouble should reckon that if his association's exclusiveness really does harm the newcomer or outsider, then the courts will discover the harm and penalize it. But they will not simply infer injury where it does not exist from the sheer fact of exclusive-ness.

Certainly there are many types of exclusive association that do not offend the law. Small retailers or farmers, for example, may decide to band together in co-operative buying schemes, and there is normally no obligation on them to make these schemes open to those who may be unpopular or unco-operative, for it is assumed that there will be plentiful sources of supply open to outside firms. Many voluntary grading or 'standards' schemes have an element of exclusiveness in that the associa-tion's grade or certification mark may be applied to goods only by those who subscribe to the scheme and manufacture in accordance with the agreed standards. Here again there is nothing in the exclusiveness as such to offend the law. The organizers of such schemes, however, must always be on their guard to see that they are not misused so as to confer com-petitive advantages on a favoured group.

The danger may be illustrated by a series of charges brought by the Department of Justice in 1940 and 1941 against associations in the lumber industry, and settled by consent decree.[1] These associations had organized schemes for standardizing lumber in terms of grades, sizes and so forth, and had encouraged the application of a mark which would give consumers some assurance that their purchases met acceptable standards. The Government's charges alleged that these arrangements were used to handicap non-members of the associations; that, for example, non-members could not obtain the mark except at heavy cost, or that the inspectorate set up by the association to see that lumber bearing the mark met the prescribed specification adopted a more rigorous standard for non-members than for members. Moreover, it was contended that the associations had induced many federal and local

---

[1] *United States* v. *Southern Pine Association* (District Court of Arkansas, 1940); *United States* v. *Western Pine Association* (District Court of Washington, 1941); *United States* v. *West Coast Lumbermen's Association* (District Court of Washington, 1941).

authorities to specify grade marked lumber in their building codes, so that non-members who were denied access to the grade mark were virtually excluded from an important sector of the market. The consent decrees[1] accepted by both sides and endorsed by the Court prohibited various devices which made the grading schemes injurious to competitors but have in no way prevented the schemes as such from being implemented.

There have also been a number of cases concerning the tobacco growing industry of the south eastern United States, in which the tobacco growers of a certain area imposed restrictions on the daily selling time of newly built warehouses in the area, usually by reference to the proportion of their floor space to the total floor space of all tobacco warehouses in the district (regardless of whether these were suitable for the auction of tobacco or not). Whereas, by analogy with the *Chicago Board of Trade* case, it would be lawful for the local association to arrange selling times for local warehouses in order to allow potential buyers the widest possible range of choice, it was clearly not lawful for them to use their power to restrict competition by artificial restrictions on selling time allowed to growers entering the tobacco market for the first time or expanding their existing capacity: see for example, *Rogers* v. *Douglas Tobacco Board of Trade* (Fifth Circuit Court of Appeals, 1957). The Federal Trade Commission have also brought a number of cases against such practices.

4. *Collective boycott agreements:* Fashion Originators Guild

The exclusionary agreements so far considered rely in the main on the negative power of a group not to admit new members; the favoured group is defined or listed and the difficulty for the outsider is that of getting enrolled on the exclusive list. Competitors may, of course, also be excluded from the market by the positive action of a dominant group in placing their names on a 'black list'. Whether a favoured or 'white' list is compiled, or certain names are 'blacklisted', is a matter of the convenience and purpose of those who wish to limit competition. In operating an exclusive-dealing agreement it is usually necessary for the participants to know the names of all those in the favoured groups and it would be cumbersome to blacklist all the firms outside. A black list or boycott, on the other hand, is more convenient when the exclusion is a form of sanction imposed by the dominant group against former members who are in disfavour for breaking agreements or some other cause. The black list or 'stop list', for example, is a favourite device (in countries where it is lawful) for enforcing resale price maintenance

---

[1] Consent decrees and other procedures for settling cases are described below, Chapter XIII.

agreements; the 'price cutter' who is blacklisted is unable to obtain further supplies from manufacturers or wholesalers taking part in the scheme.

White lists and black lists are simply two sides of the same coin and there is no legal difference under antitrust. Hence collective boycott arrangements are illegal *per se* under section 1 of the Sherman Act in the same way as collective exclusive-dealing agreements; and this fact has the familiar consequence that no defence of the boycott on social or economic grounds—on the ground, for example, of the alleged unfair or unethical practices of those boycotted—will succeed in the courts. Even a boycott or refusal to deal on the part of a single powerful firm may sometimes be an illegal monopolistic act under antitrust, and illustrations of this will be given below (Chapter V). Where large groups are concerned, as with exclusive-dealing agreements, a successful boycott often requires groups at different levels of the market to combine. Retailers alone, for example, cannot normally discipline the price cutting backsliders among them by a black list unless they have an agreement with a group of suppliers to withhold goods from those listed.

Some boycotts are, however, unilateral, and an early case well illustrates this type. In *Eastern State Lumber Dealers' Association* v. *United States* (Supreme Court, 1914) the systematic circulation by a retailers' trade association of the names of wholesalers who sold directly to the public was condemned under the Sherman Act. In this case, as in many of the price fixing cases, no express agreement was found; on the face of it each retailer was left free to act as he saw fit. But the Court felt able to draw the inference that the plan was intended to induce the members of the association to boycott the wholesalers on the black list.

In 1930 in *Paramount Famous Lasky Corporation* v. *United States* (Supreme Court) a group of producers and distributors of motion pictures had agreed among themselves to adopt a standard form of contract with exhibitors. This form of contract provided for disputes to go to arbitration; but in the event of any failure by an exhibitor to arbitrate or comply with an arbitration award, all the members of the group agreed to take common punitive action against the offender. It was contended that these arrangements were needed to protect the industry against undesirable practices and were quite reasonable in relation to this aim. But this claim was rejected by the Court as irrelevant. 'It may be that arbitration is well adapted to the needs of the motion picture industry; but when, under the guise of arbitration, parties enter into unusual arrangements which unreasonably suppress normal competition, their action becomes illegal. The prohibitions of the statute cannot "be evaded by good motives. The law is its own measure of right and wrong, of what it permits, or forbids, and the judgment of the courts cannot be set up against it in a supposed accommodation of its policy with the good intention of parties and, it may be, of some good results.'''

This last point—that to have a good reason for joint action against undesirable practices is not enough to justify a boycott—was hammered home by the Supreme Court in *Fashion Originators Guild* v. *Federal Trade Commission* in 1941—a case brought under section 5 of the Federal Trade Commission Act instead of under the Sherman Act. The Guild—an association of textile manufacturers—had made an agreement with an association of garment manufacturers under which the latter undertook not to use or deal in textiles copied by 'pirate' manufacturers from designs by members of the textile group. The garment manufacturers further agreed that they would not sell their goods to retailers who did not also fall in with this ban on pirated designs. It was strongly urged that design piracy was doing harm to the public and getting the trade generally a bad name. It seemed only reasonable, said the defence, that the trade should defend itself against this unethical practice. In this they relied on the words of Chief Justice Hughes in the *Sugar* case to the effect that the provisions of the Sherman Act 'do not prevent the adoption of reasonable means to protect interstate commerce from destructive or injurious practices and to permit competition upon a sound basis. Voluntary action to end abuses and to foster fair competitive opportunities in the public interest may be more effective than legal processes.'

Mr Justice Black, speaking for the Supreme Court, rejected these arguments. He noted that the Fashion Originators Guild had an elaborate system of private tribunals to determine whether a given garment was in fact a pirated copy of a member's design. Retailers who had sold pirated designs were all indexed and any sale to them made the seller subject to heavy fines. He found, moreover, that apart from defending members against the 'pirates' the Guild was responsible for other restrictions, such as prohibiting members from retail advertising, regulating their discounts, prohibiting them from selling through retailers who traded from private houses, and so on.

As to the argument that the Guild's boycott agreement was reasonable and necessary to protect the industry against pirated designs, the Court sustained the Federal Trade Commission, which had declined even to hear evidence on the point, on the ground that the boycott was illegal *per se*. Mr Justice Black stated the law as follows: 'The reasonableness of the methods pursued by the combination to accomplish its unlawful object is no more material than would be the reasonableness of the prices fixed by unlawful combination. . . . Nor can the unlawful combination be justified upon the argument that systematic copying of dress designs is itself tortious. . . . Even if copying were an acknowledged tort under the law of every State, that situation would not justify petitioners in combining together to regulate and restrain interstate commerce in violation of federal law.'

This case makes it abundantly clear that a collective boycott in the United States is not to be justified by any claim, however striking, that the state of an industry requires some sanction to be available against businesses guilty of unethical practices. Those concerned may seek a remedy at common law or persuade the legislature to enact a suitable regulatory statute, but they must not take the law into their own hands. Any form of collective sanctions to sustain a restrictive scheme is *a fortiori* anathema under antitrust.[1] Nor can a boycott be justified as resulting from a private quarrel which has little or no effect on the public interest. This was affirmed by a unanimous Supreme Court in *Klor's Inc.* v. *Broadway-Hale Stores Inc.* (1959). Klor's was a small electrical appliance retailer in San Francisco, which stood next door to a store of one of its competitors, Broadway-Hale. Klor claimed that Broadway-Hale and a number of national manufacturers of television sets and other electrical appliances had jointly conspired to cut off its supplies, resulting in severe loss of profits. The lower courts had upheld the defendants, who had not denied the allegations but claimed that the controversy was a 'purely private quarrel' between competitors which gave no right of action to Klor's. There were hundreds of other retailers in the district who sold all the varieties of electrical appliances, including those from which Klor's had been excluded. The public, therefore, could not have suffered any detriment. Mr Justice Black for the Court ruled that in such a case the victim of a boycott does not need to prove that the boycott has injured the public in some way; it is enough that he himself has been injured. The 'collective boycott' is not to be tolerated, he said, merely because the victim is just one merchant whose business is so small that his destruction means little to the economy.

Even where there may be normal commercial grounds for selecting distributors, the decision must be a genuinely unilateral one. In cases involving the enforcement of resale price maintenance policies[2] the courts have taken a very strict view of the meaning of 'unilateral'. In *United States* v. *General Motors* (Supreme Court, 1966) it was made clear that if, for example, a decision to cut off supplies from a dealer is taken by a manufacturer at the request of third parties, such as other dealers, the courts will not be slow to find evidence of a 'conspiracy' to boycott. In this case Chevrolets were being sold in Los Angeles by discount stores at less than regular retail prices, and the local dealers' association

---

[1] Thus even though resale price maintenance is now legalized for the individual manufacturer, any attempt to enforce it collectively remains an offence against the Sherman Act.

[2] See Chapter X below, notably *United States* v. *Parke, Davis & Co* (Supreme Court, 1960).

sought General Motors' assistance in applying pressure on those of its dealers who dealt with the discount stores. General Motors accordingly wrote to all the dealers stating that sales to discount stores constituted a violation of their selling agreement and obtained promises from them not to deal with the discount stores in future. General Motors was, on these facts, adjudged by the Supreme Court to have taken part in a conspiracy with the complaining dealers to boycott offending dealers in order to put an end to the practice complained of, and to have used the assistance of its co-conspirators to check on whether promises to discontinue the practice were honoured. As Mr Justice Fortas put it:

What resulted was a fabric interwoven by many strands of joint action to eliminate the discounters from participation in the market, to inhibit the free choice of franchised dealers to select their own methods of trade and to provide multi-lateral surveillance and enforcement. This process for achieving and enforcing the desired objective can by no stretch of the imagination be described as 'unilateral' or merely 'parallel'.

Collective boycott, like price fixing, leaves little scope for the rule of reason. A boycott can hardly be incidental to competition or ancillary to some legitimate transaction. Nor does it often raise questions of degree: if it were 'only a little' boycott, it would not be worth organizing. But, again like price fixing, collective boycott may face the courts with difficult borderline matters of fact which turn on the question whether an agreement or conspiracy to withhold supplies from a firm really exists.

There is, however, one big difference from the situation in price fixing cases; it is far less likely that a boycott agreement can be tacitly reached and implemented. This is for the obvious reason that a boycott by definition has a victim. Concealed price collusion by means of an 'open competition' plan may possibly escape detection because all those who know about it are presumably in favour of it; it does harm, if at all, only to the unorganized and inarticulate body of consumers. Everybody with experience in administering any form of antitrust law knows that the complaints reaching enforcement agencies rarely come from the general public. They come almost invariably from businessmen who are suffering from some exclusionary practice—not getting supplies, or not getting some discount or rebate obtained by their competitors. Whatever else they may do, the victims of a boycott do not usually remain silent. Thus collusion in this field is more difficult to conceal. Each partner to the boycott agreement has had to give the victim some reason for not supplying him, and the accumulated evidence may well point to collusion even in the absence of an express agreement. The *Lumber Dealers* case outlined above is an illustration.

Yet there may still be cases in which the courts have difficulty in deciding whether the facts can be plausibly explained only by an illegal boycott agreement. Sometimes an alternative explanation is obvious. A wholesaler has his supplies cut off by a number of leading manufacturers: but all that has happened is that they have had an adverse report from a credit rating agency and each in his individual wisdom thinks it best to drop the account. It could not easily be maintained that the circulation of credit information by a bona fide agency was part of a boycott plan, nor that the manufacturers' reactions to it, even if the situation was 'common knowledge' in the trade, were conspiratorial. On the other hand, the circulation of the names of price cutters followed by withholding of supplies might be very persuasive of collusion. Sometimes, however, the problem may be more difficult. There may be sound commercial reasons for not doing business with a particular type of customer, and if all the main firms in an industry take this view of a particular trader, the result will be very like that of a boycott. But, except sometimes for a monopoly, it is not illegal for individual suppliers to choose their customers or refuse to direct their trade to channels that seem to them commercially unsound.

The kind of situation which can arise is well illustrated from the motion picture industry. In a small town there may be two cinemas, one of them large and luxurious in the main square and the other a back-street 'flea pit'. It is not surprising that all the main producers and distributors choose the former for the first showing of their best pictures. But this is an extreme difference: the two cinemas may be much more alike in their facilities. Suppose now that there has been a long history in the industry of restrictive agreements among the film producers and distributors, directed to favouring powerful chains of cinemas or cinemas owned directly by the producers and thereby excluding or impeding the small independent exhibitor. It can readily be seen that the courts may have real difficulty in a particular case in deciding whether the refusal of several large distributors to let a given cinema have the first showing of their 'big hits' is to be attributed to a set of reasonable and independent commercial decisions or to the effects of illegal agreement. Exactly this situation has in fact occurred and some of the resulting litigation has raised very complex questions of what constitutes illegal agreement. Since these cases are some of the best available material for illustrating attempts to extend the legal meaning of conspiracy, they must, however, be deferred to the next chapter, which will be concerned with that issue.

5. *Agreements for dividing or sharing markets:*
Addyston Pipe

We turn next from the coercive type of agreement for lessening competition, by which the participants try either to force competitors out of
a market by a boycott or resist their entry into it by exclusive dealing
and other devices, to the voluntary type, in which competitors agree to
keep out of each other's way by confining themselves to allotted parts
of the market. Market sharing may sometimes be a direct substitute for
price fixing, since it may be found easier and more workable to divide
up the market than to agree about the prices to be charged. Market
sharing is another practice which, unless insignificant in scope and
effect, is illegal *per se* under section 1 of the Sherman Act.

This rule, like the similar rule in the matter of price fixing, has its
origin in *United States* v. *Addyston Pipe and Steel Company* in 1898. The six
manufacturers of cast-iron pipe divided the total territory in which they
traded into three categories of market. The largest part was the so-called
'pay territory' in which the prices they all charged were fixed by a
board. There was also a 'free territory' in which there were no restrictions; this was in practice the territory where they could not avoid competing with manufacturers from outside their area. Finally there were
the so-called 'reserved cities'. These were cities allocated by agreement
to particular members of the association. This last category reflected a
market sharing agreement, giving particular firms a monopoly in their
own area. It was condemned by the Court as part of the total plan, but
there is little doubt that the market sharing agreement standing alone
would have been found repugnant to the Sherman Act.

Later cases have firmly established the rule,[1] but many of those which
would best illustrate it are concerned with market sharing in licences
granted under patents. Because of the special considerations introduced
by patent rights, these cases will be considered below (Chapter XI).
Other such agreements are a characteristic feature of international cartel
arrangements, and these too come within the subject matter of a later
chapter. Often international agreements are themselves based on exchanges of patent rights and technical information.

There are a number of ways in which a market may be divided, and
consequently a number of variants in the form of market sharing. The
most obvious way is to divide the market territorially, as in the *Addyston
Pipe* case. This way is common in international agreements; the manufacturers in a particular country are granted exclusive rights to sell their
product within that country and agree in return not to sell it in the

---

[1] The prohibition of horizontal market division was reaffirmed in *United States* v. *Sealy, Inc.*
(Supreme Court, 1967), see pp. 220–1 below.

countries of the other participants. Sometimes there are further agreements reserving specified parts of the outside world for particular groups of manufacturers.

Markets may also be divided by reference to classes of customers, even particular customers or particular transactions. It may be agreed that certain customers or classes of customers will be approached for their orders only by certain specified firms in an association, in return for which other classes of customers are reserved for other members. The basis may even be the individual transaction. For example, when contracting jobs or supply requirements are opened by public authorities to tender, it may happen that an association will arrange for bids to be first made to it and for the job or order then to be allocated to some particular member according to a prearranged formula. In such cases it is not uncommon to find that only the firm to which the contract has been allotted by the association makes a genuine bid, while the others either do not bid at all or put in fictitious bids at higher prices. These allocation schemes may or may not go together with the payment, by the favoured firms, of sums of money which are used to compensate firms not obtaining a prearranged share of the total business.

A market may simply be divided quantitatively, that is by reference to the quantities or percentage shares to be supplied by each participant in an agreement. The firms taking part in the agreement negotiate market shares, based either on some yardstick of past performance or simply on what each can get by bargaining power. Schemes of this kind are usually not so much substitutes for as concomitant to price fixing. When it is believed by a trade association that price levels need to be sustained by an agreement to avoid overproduction and weak selling, it is often difficult to reach agreement about whose production and selling effort shall be cut back. Unless the members have great confidence in one another, there will be fears that some 'fly' characters in the trade will evade their fair share of the cut-back and continue to market their full output, profiting meanwhile from whatever improvement in prices results from the restraint of their colleagues. To avoid this outcome, it may be agreed that members shall do no more than maintain their previous percentage shares of the total trade. This type of agreement is sometimes coupled with arrangements whereby any firm which exceeds its 'quota' is required to make a money payment into a pool from which any firm which falls below its 'quota' will be compensated.

Agreements of this kind are the obverse of those in which competitors agree to keep out of each other's way in order to improve each other's bargaining position; quota schemes are devices by which competitors agree not to take action that would worsen each other's bargaining position. As with pure output restrictions, they are most likely to be considered by the courts as agreements to manipulate price levels: but there is no doubt that a quota agreement in itself violates section 1 of the Sherman Act.

Lastly, markets may be divided by reference to technical factors. It may be provided that particular firms will concentrate on certain specified end-uses of a given material or on a particular manufacturing process while other firms concentrate on other end-uses or processes. Agreements of this kind have been found to exist in complicated technical fields, such as the chemical industries.

Every variant of market sharing is illegal under section 1 of the Sherman Act, so long as it has a significant restrictive effect on competition. It is, of course, possible that a set of facts could be found or invented such that it could be brought under the head of market sharing but not regarded as showing a significant restraint of trade, just as in the *Chicago Board of Trade* case a set of facts which could be called price fixing was found insignificant.[1] In this sense the rule of reason would come into play. Agreements to divide a technical field purely for purposes of research so as to avoid wasteful overlapping of effort might be regarded, for example, as promoting rather than impeding the free flow of commerce and hence as not an 'undue' restraint of trade.[2]

Market sharing agreements produce the usual crop of borderline questions of fact when it may be difficult to distinguish collusion from independent but parallel decisions. When certain firms are found not to be selling in particular markets, are there sound commercial reasons for it or is there evidence from which collusion may be inferred? When markets are divided as a result of patent agreements, a borderline may have to be defined between legitimate conditions attaching to patent licences and restrictions going beyond the scope of the patent grant. These conditions will best be explored, however, in the later chapters dealing with patents and international cartels.

[1] A market sharing agreement may be regarded as an agreement on the part of a firm or firms not to compete in a given market. As was noted in the introductory chapter, an agreement by a seller of a business not to compete against the buyer, so long as the estoppel is reasonably limited in time and space, may be regarded as merely 'ancillary' to a legitimate transaction and hence as a 'reasonable' restraint of trade. In this sense agreements not to compete in a given market are not illegal *per se*.

[2] American lawyers have pointed out to me that such agreements might or might not be 'safe': even in this example great care would have to be taken to ensure that the agreement could not be interpreted as significantly reducing competition between the participants.

CHAPTER III

AGREEMENTS BETWEEN COMPETITORS
III. AGREEMENTS AMONG SMALL GROUPS

1. *Collusion and oligopoly; the law of conspiracy in antitrust*

In Chapter I it was shown that all price fixing agreements between competitors, including agreements designed to 'manipulate' price levels by keeping surplus supplies off the market, are illegal *per se* under the Sherman Act, so long as they have, or are meant to have, a significant effect on competition. Most cases reaching the courts are in practice straightforward, so that the *Trenton Potteries* case, for example, is an adequate model for settling them. But sometimes, as was seen, difficult borderline questions of fact arise. If businessmen are fully informed of all the factors in the market situation, may it not happen that they independently and quite rationally refrain from cutting each other's throats, so that an absence of price competition is explained without postulating agreement or conspiracy? How is this situation, which is beyond the reach of the law,[1] to be distinguished from that which arises from illegal agreement? The 'open competition' and basing-point cases illustrating this point showed, however, that it is very difficult, at least for large groups of competitors, to avoid price competition without to some extent 'organizing' the requisite mutual restraint; in practice, collusion is often present and, if present, is usually detected. But it still seemed possible that among small groups of competitors an absence of price competition might escape legal penalty, either because it arose from a genuinely 'oligopolistic' mutual restraint or because, if there were a common understanding among the group, it might be successfully concealed.

Chapter II reached much the same point in respect to agreements between competitors to exclude outsiders from the market, or to divide the market and avoid competition among themselves. Once again the majority of cases are in practice straightforward and easily decided by reference to such precedents as the *Addyston Pipe* case or that of the *Fashion Originators Guild*. Once again there comes a point at which borderline questions of fact have to be determined. If the major companies in the motion picture industry all decline to have their

---

[1] 'The defendants cannot be ordered to compete, but they properly can be forbidden to give directions or to make arrangements not to compete': Mr Justice Holmes in *Swift and Company* v. *United States* (1905).

films shown in a particular cinema, is this the result of a set of independent decisions reached on genuine commercial grounds, or is it the
result of an illegal agreement designed to hamper the small exhibitor
and favour the powerful cinema chain or the subsidiary, exhibiting
interests of the major companies themselves? Is there a danger that
the second situation may successfully ape the first?

All these borderline questions point to the existence of a margin of
possible inefficiency in antitrust, a chance for 'getting away with' restrictive behaviour. It is understandable that convinced champions of
the antitrust policy would like to eliminate this margin. Their efforts
to this end raise two quite separate issues. The first is simply that of
the efficiency of the courts in getting at the truth. Are the courts readily
deceived by efforts to conceal collusion? Do many illegal conspiracies in
practice go undetected and unpunished? It is, of course, entirely proper
that law enforcing authorities should seek to eliminate sheer error in dispensing justice. But, as is suggested in the previous chapters, it does not
seem likely that errors are frequent. In any event, error is a factor that
may cut both ways, and it is a respectable tradition of the law that those
on trial should receive the benefit of the doubt, lest the innocent suffer.

The second and much more important issue is that of the legal
definition of conspiracy. Some of those who seek the maximum
effectiveness of antitrust are concerned not only to eliminate error but
also to break free from restrictive definitions of such terms as 'conspiracy' or 'agreement' when these appear to place uncompetitive
situations beyond the reach of the law. Antitrust, they argue, is intended
to maintain a state of lively competitiveness in American commerce;
situations in which competition is lacking or stagnant are therefore a
matter for reproach; all such situations require remedy, and the law
should be so written as to make this possible. At the extreme the view
is held that oligopolistic behaviour, which has the effect of limiting
competition, ought to be regarded as a form of collusion and that
powerful firms following parallel courses of action with restrictive effect
should be deemed conspirators. Some commentators go so far as to
claim that the law already requires these conclusions, not merely that
it ought to require them.[1]

In recent years views of this type have attained a good deal of
influence, certainly in the selection and presentation of cases by the
enforcement agencies and to some degree in the judgments handed
down by the courts. In this chapter the discussion of restrictive agreements between competitors will be concluded by an examination of
some cases in which the limits of the legal meaning of 'conspiracy' have
been probed and, as some think, stretched.

[1] An outline of this view is given below, Chapter VI, pp. 174–5.

As a starting point we may take two propositions about the law of conspiracy under antitrust that would not be seriously disputed. First, as has been seen already, an agreement or conspiracy in restraint of trade may be proved by circumstantial evidence. No express agreement, let alone an agreement in writing, between the parties has to be produced in court for a case to succeed, so long as a chain of evidence can be built up for which the only plausible explanation is a common understanding or plan. Even those who feel most strongly about improper extensions of legal doctrine in antitrust would accept that this is settled law and could hardly be otherwise. Secondly, it is clear on the other hand that antitrust knows no doctrine of 'constructive conspiracy'; that is to say, the existence of a restrictive agreement cannot be proved simply by showing that the effects usually associated with such an agreement have occurred. It is not enough to show that prices have been uniform and unchanged, or that no new entrants have appeared in an industry for ten years, and invite the court to jump directly to a conclusion of conspiracy. The most ardent trust buster would in turn accept this as settled law. Within the limits of what may count as circumstantial evidence without being mere construction, there is, however, plenty of room for subtle minds to manoeuvre.

The underlying issue is what, at the minimum, constitutes that 'meeting of the minds' which must be directly or circumstantially established; what degree of mutual knowledge and confidence among businessmen amounts to a common understanding and hence, if there is a restrictive effect on competition, to an illegal conspiracy within the meaning of the Sherman Act? The precise location of this legal boundary is of the highest importance for assessing the impact of antitrust on American business. Many industries in the United States are oligopolistic in the sense that three or four big firms are responsible for the great bulk of the output. These firms exist of necessity in a state of lively mutual awareness. If—to take an extreme hypothesis—this type of mutual awareness were in itself enough to constitute illegal conspiracy when coupled with restrictive effects on competition, a huge sector of American business would be in legal jeopardy.[1]

The cases chosen to illustrate this chapter deal particularly with situations in which a number of firms act in the same way, and the questions are raised whether their parallel courses result from collusion or from some other cause, and how the correct explanation can be established. It should be mentioned here, however, that these questions at the margin of the law of conspiracy are not the only ones that the

---

[1] This is not so far-fetched as it may seem. The theory that oligopoly should be illegal *per se* has not lacked sponsors. This is why the debate about antitrust and 'big business' has raged so furiously in the United States in recent years.

general problem of the impact of antitrust on oligopoly raises. It is also possible to approach the legality of concentrated industries through the law of monopolization, and the questions raised by this alternative approach will be considered below (Chapter VI).

2. *The motion picture industry as an example: the* Interstate Circuit *and* Paramount *cases;* Milgram v. Loew's; Theatre Enterprises v. Paramount Film Distributing

The motion picture industry in the United States, as already mentioned, has provided the courts with some difficult exercises in distinguishing mere similarity of action on the part of major companies from collusion between them. This has come about because there are sound commercial reasons for not treating all cinemas alike and, at the same time, there are the usual incentives for powerful companies and groups to extend their sway over the industry (particularly over its exhibiting side) and to adopt restrictive and exclusionary tactics in the process.

The commercial aspect of the matter is clear enough. Cinemas differ greatly in size, amenity, location and 'pulling power' in general. The film producers and distributors, with expensive investments to recoup, are naturally going to see that their best pictures are shown to advantage and they are 'choosy' about their customers. The usual practice is to seek an important cinema for the first run of a big picture in a given area; the public will, of course, pay higher prices to see it while it is new than later on. Lesser cinemas will be offered the picture for second or subsequent runs according to their pulling power. A period of time or 'clearance' is left between the first and second runs (and between subsequent runs), so as to give the public a greater incentive to pay a higher admission charge to see it early on; in turn, the cinemas showing the first run will pay a larger fee than those showing later runs. There is a pedantic sense in which this procedure is in itself 'monopolistic', for the first run of a picture is a natural monopoly. But the rule of reason allows that the producer of a picture is entitled to try to maximize his takings by normal commercial methods, and it is clear that this method obtains more revenue than would one in which the picture was released simultaneously to all the cinemas that wanted it.[1]

At the same time the structure of the industry is one that lends itself to exclusionary practices. The production of pictures is largely confined to a handful of major companies, most of which are closely integrated with distributing companies. These large producer-distributor groups have had substantial interests in cinema ownership, controlling the

---

[1] In any case, only a limited number of copies of a film can be made if prohibitive expense is to be avoided.

best cinemas in many areas. Many other cinemas are owned by large circuits which are the most powerful customers of the producers and distributors. It is understandable that, when choices have to be made regarding the showing of films, the producer-distributor groups will favour cinemas in which they are financially involved, or cinemas owned by large circuits whose disfavour they cannot afford. Sometimes ordinary commercial prudence and these special interests coincide: the producer owned or circuit cinema is the obvious choice for an important first run. But this is not always so: it may be found that an independently owned cinema of first-class amenity is consistently refused first runs in favour of circuit cinemas of lesser attraction. The antitrust authorities have indeed alleged from time to time that the buying power of the large circuits, and the control over supply exerted by the major distributors in collusion, have been used to exclude small exhibitors from the cream of the market, and over the years the industry has had many antitrust charges to defend.

One type of charge may be illustrated by *Interstate Circuit* v. *United States*—a case which reached the Supreme Court in 1939 and contributed to the development of the law on conspiracy. There were two groups of defendants: first, eight distributors of motion pictures; secondly, two large cinema circuits operating in Texas and New Mexico. These two companies were affiliated and run by the same people. The Interstate Circuit had an almost complete monopoly of first run theatres in six Texas cities. The Consolidated Circuit operated in various cities of the Rio Grande Valley and elsewhere, and in most of the leading cities had no competition for first runs.

What happened was that, in 1934, the manager of both circuits sent a letter to each of the eight major distributors demanding that they should set a minimum admission price for subsequent runs of those pictures which the two circuits took for first runs. The second demand was that these pictures should not later be exhibited as part of double-feature programmes. The object of these demands was clearly to increase the drawing power of first runs and reduce the attraction to the public of being able to see the pictures later at other cinemas in long programmes at low prices. Each distributor knew from the wording of the letter that these demands had been made to all the others. There followed a series of conferences between the circuits and representatives of the distributors as a result of which the demands were met. The Government charged that this was an illegal conspiracy to exclude competitors.

There was, of course, no express agreement among the distributors and this was one of the first cases in which conspiracy was inferred from a course of conduct. The Supreme Court held that, since each

4

distributor knew that the plan had been put to all the others, there was an effective 'meeting of the minds'. Mr Justice Stone described the situation as follows:

Each was aware that all were in active competition and that without substantially unanimous action with respect to the restrictions for any given territory there was risk of a substantial loss of the business and goodwill of the subsequent-run and independent exhibitors, but that with it there was the prospect of increased profits. There was, therefore, strong motive for concerted action, full advantage of which was taken by Interstate and Consolidated in presenting their demands to all in a single document. . . . It taxes credulity to believe that the several distributors would, in the circumstances, have accepted and put into operation with substantial unanimity such far-reaching changes in their business methods without some understanding that all were to join, and we reject as beyond the range of probability that it was the result of mere chance.

The Court noted that the industry's 'bigwigs' had not been called as witnesses to rebut the inference of collusion: 'The failure, under the circumstances, to call as witnesses those officers who did have authority to act for the distributors and who were in a position to know whether they had acted in pursuance of an agreement is itself persuasive that their testimony, if given, would have been unfavourable to appellants. The production of weak evidence when strong is available can lead only to the conclusion that the strong would have been adverse.'

This case presents a new context in which illegal conspiracy may arise, namely, one in which a restrictive plan is presented to a number of separate parties from outside and is then adhered to by each in the knowledge that all the others will also adhere. It is this feature that has made the case a jumping-off point for later attempts to expand the notion of conspiracy. Mr Justice Stone's words, however, clearly show that in his view the Court was doing no more than infer collusion from circumstantial evidence.

In the 1940s the Government brought several more cases against the industry. A number were directed against large circuits which were charged with monopolizing or attempting to monopolize the exhibiting side of the business in their areas.[1] Certain of these cases will be referred to below in the chapters dealing with section 2 of the Sherman Act. Then came *United States* v. *Paramount Pictures* (Supreme Court, 1948), in which the defendants were the major producing and distributing companies; this famous case is one of those to be used in a later chapter to illustrate a direct legal attack on an oligopoly situation. The Government won all these major cases, and the result was that a large

---

[1] *United States* v. *Crescent Amusement Company* (Supreme Court, 1944); *United States* v. *Griffith* (Supreme Court, 1948); *United States* v. *Schine Chain Theatre* (Supreme Court, 1948).

number of private actions were then started by exhibitors, who sued various of the distributors for treble damages on the ground that they had lost profits and suffered other injury as a result of the exclusionary practices shown up by the *Paramount* and other cases.[1] Scores of these treble-damage actions, which have been going on ever since 1948, have been brought: they have involved, in total, claims for hundreds of millions of dollars of damages, quite apart from mountainous legal costs, and have constituted a serious financial burden on the industry.

Some of these cases have raised, in an acutely difficult form, the problem of distinguishing a situation in which a group of large firms acts on parallel lines because of a common plan, from one in which their parallel behaviour is fully explained by ordinary commercial considerations. The cases usually involve the complaint that first-run showings are denied to cinemas which in point of amenity are regarded by their owners as fully competitive. Complaints of this kind have been brought to court by aggrieved exhibitors at every point in the scale, from those who really are competitive to those with no sensible claim on commercial grounds. All have the psychological advantage of being Davids up against Goliath, and all can point to the history of illegal exclusionary plans revealed by the government cases. Thus the courts have needed a nice discrimination, and the advocates have had every opportunity for deploying new theories about the nature of conspiracy.

Milgram v. *Loew's* (Third Circuit Court of Appeals, 1951) goes furthest in purporting to develop the law of conspiracy. It was held in this case that the consistent refusal of the major distributors to grant first runs to an independent 'drive-in'[2] theatre was due to collusion, and could not be accounted for on the argument that the distributing firms were each independently making commercial decisions on their merits. It was strongly urged that each company had in fact the best of reasons for its refusal: drive-in theatres are seasonal in operation, at the mercy of the weather, limited to car owning patrons and away from city centres. Moreover, it was claimed that each distributor had acted in ignorance of what the others did. The trial court judge had found this last testimony 'incredible' and, having weighed the evidence of what he called 'consciously parallel practices', had concluded that a finding of conspiracy was warranted. 'In practical effect, consciously parallel business practices have taken the place of the conception of meeting of the minds which some of the earlier cases emphasized. Present concert of action, further proof of actual agreement among the

---

[1] The use that may be made of government suits in evidence in treble-damage actions and other procedural aspects of private antitrust litigation are described below, Chapter XIII.

[2] English readers may wish to know that a 'drive-in' is in effect a large car park with a cinema screen at one end. People watch the film from their cars. In rural and suburban areas in the long American summer, this is a convenient and popular form of cinema.

defendants is unnecessary, and it then becomes the duty of the Court to evaluate all the evidence in the setting of the case at hand, and to determine whether a finding of conspiracy to violate the Act is warranted.'

The Court of Appeals felt unable to say that the judge was in error: '. . . In this modern era of increasing subtleties, it is rare indeed for a conspiracy to be proved by direct evidence. There is no dispute over the proposition that circumstantial evidence will sustain a finding of conspiracy. . . . Uniform participation by competitors in a particular system of doing business, where each is aware of the others' activities, the effect of which is restraint of interstate commerce, is sufficient to establish an unlawful conspiracy under the statutes before us.'

The Court of Appeals did, however, feel it necessary to hedge some-what on the judge's statement that conscious parallelism had 'taken the place' of meeting of the minds as the criterion of conspiracy. (One of the three appeal judges went further and entered a vigorous dissent.) Their opinion goes on to say: 'This does not mean, however, that in every case mere consciously parallel business practices are sufficient evidence in themselves, from which a court may infer concerted action.' Their suggestion seems to have been that evidence of parallel action should transfer the burden of proof to the defendants 'to explain away the inference of joint action'. In the case before them, they did not feel that this burden had been discharged.

A counterblast to this line of argument occurred in *Fanchon and Marco* v. *Paramount Pictures*, which was tried in California before Judge Yankwich, also in 1951.[1] The main complaint was again the denial of first runs by the major distributors, this time to a modern cinema in a suburban area of Los Angeles. Judge Yankwich noted that the preference of distributors for one cinema rather than another was an inescapable feature of the industry. He then defined the legal issues as follows:

So he who claims to have been injured by such preference must show (a) that the preference was the result of concert of action between the defendants, (b) that it was unreasonable and not based upon the various factors which courts have considered as reasonable considerations entering into the determination . . . and (c) that he has been injured by such action.

As to the manner of proof, the courts have adopted a liberal attitude, and have permitted inferences of *joint* action to be drawn from parallel action. But, regardless of burden of proof, in the last analysis the trier of facts must be satisfied that the practices which the plaintiff claims to have injured him were the result of joint action.

---

[1] The judgment in favour of the defendants was confirmed by the Ninth Circuit Court of Appeals in August 1954. The reader who wishes to delve further into the problems dealt with in this chapter cannot do better than read in full Judge Yankwich's careful and distinguished analysis of this case in 100 Fed. Supp. 84 or *Commerce Clearing House Trade Cases*, Chicago, 1950–51, 62,909.

In the case before him, Judge Yankwich felt that the facts were fully explained by normal business decisions of the individual distributors, and that their separate actions, in having their pictures exhibited in cinemas which seemed to give them the best chance of good financial results, were reasonable in relation to the peculiar conditions of the industry. 'No parallelism conscious or unconscious can overcome a finding of reasonableness.' Here we have the rule of reason introduced to show that, since some cinemas owing to the nature of the industry, are bound to be preferred to other cinemas, the mere fact that preferences are granted—even in parallel by a number of large suppliers— does not necessarily indicate a conspiracy to restrain trade.

It is evident that these two cases reflect very different views of the law on the part of the different courts concerned. Such a situation requires authoritative settlement by the Supreme Court. This was forthcoming in *Theatre Enterprises* v. *Paramount Film Distributing Corporation*, decided in 1954. In this case the Supreme Court accepted evidence to the effect that the denial of first runs to a suburban cinema in Baltimore arose out of similar but independent decisions by the various distributors for sound commercial reasons. Mr Justice Clark stated the law as follows: 'To be sure business behavior is admissible circumstantial evidence from which the fact finder may infer agreement. . . . But this Court has never held that proof of parallel business behavior conclusively establishes agreement, or, phrased differently, that such behavior constitutes a Sherman Act offence. . . . "Conscious parallelism" has not yet read conspiracy out of the Sherman Act entirely.' The *Fanchon and Marco* case has thus turned out to be better law than *Milgram* v. *Loew's*.[1]

From this decision it is clear that the attempt to extend the meaning of 'conspiracy' to cover parallel courses of action—an attempt intended to enable antitrust to be brought to bear more easily on oligopoly situations—has failed. It is interesting to trace the steps in the argument and see where it went wrong. Mr Justice Stone in the *Interstate Circuit* case certainly spoke of the mutual awareness of the parties as an essential element in the case: but this was common knowledge of a plan. 'It was enough', he said, 'that, knowing that concerted action was contemplated and invited, the distributors gave their adherence to the scheme and participated in it.' The Court of Appeals in *Milgram* v. *Loew's* replaced the word 'scheme' by the ambiguous word 'system'; to them it was enough that the distributors were mutually aware of their 'uniform participation . . . in a particular system of doing business', though the Court still thought of their conclusion as an

---

[1] This does not, of course, mean that *Milgram* v. *Loew's* was necessarily a bad decision; the facts might have been found compelling even on Judge Yankwich's view of the law.

inference of joint action from parallel action. And whereas Stone had merely commented on the failure of the defendants to produce strong evidence to rebut an inference of joint action, the Court of Appeals spoke firmly of the burden on defendants to explain away their parallel actions. Finally, the trial judge in *Milgram* v. *Loew's* spoke of consciously parallel practices as having 'taken the place' of meeting of the minds as the criterion for conspiracy; in other words, as the substance of and not merely as evidence for the offence.

Here we see the screw that holds the concept of conspiracy in place being loosened, thread by thread, until Mr Justice Clark's common-sense screwdriver tightens it up again in the *Theatre Enterprises* case. The root of the trouble is ambiguity in the use of apparently simple terms like 'know' and 'mutual awareness'. (The lawyers need not feel ashamed of this: the philosophers have had the same trouble these three thousand years.) Whenever there is a plan, there is mutual awareness among the participants; but it does not follow that whenever there is mutual awareness, there is a plan. A plan implies some assurance of reliable action in the future; its breakdown will usually be a matter for reproach between the parties. 'Conscious parallelism of action' is without this quasi-moral element. The actions of others may be highly predictable, as when a number of firms refuse to deal with a bad credit risk, or the film distributors refuse first runs to a 'flea pit'; but an unforeseen action is regarded as a fact, like a change in the weather, and not as a betrayal, like a change of allegiance.

The law now seems pretty clear on this topic. A genuine 'meeting of the minds' is still required for conspiracy. Moreover, in the last resort, it is still for the prosecutor or plaintiff to prove: a burden rests on the defence only in the sense that the best way of defending oneself against circumstantial evidence is always to produce a plausible alternative explanation of the facts. Parallel courses of action on the part of powerful firms have no substantive significance in law: they are significant only as evidence, which may be more or less powerful according to circumstances, of a common understanding. In so far as economic theories of oligopoly postulate merely a state of mutual awareness among the parties, such that each takes account of the other's reactions, this state does not fall within the legal meaning of 'conspiracy'. Even though such a state of affairs has restrictive effects on competition, it is beyond the reach of the law of conspiracy, so long as the additional bond of a common understanding is lacking.[1]

---

[1] This topic is well covered in an article by Professor Milton Handler, 'Contract, Combination and Conspiracy', *A.B.A. Antitrust Section, Proceedings*, vol. 3, 1953, p. 58. Later cases, notably *Parke, Davis* and *Albrecht* suggest that less common purpose need be shown to establish an illegal 'combination' than a 'conspiracy' under section 1 of the Sherman Act.

3. '*Conscious parallelism of action*': *the* Triangle Conduit *case*

The phrase 'conscious parallelism of action' had actually been invented in 1948 in a statement issued by the Federal Trade Commission in connexion with a price fixing case involving a multiple basing-point system of delivered prices. As a sequel to the previous section it is worth while to review this further application of the concept of parallelism.

It has been noted above[1] that, even though the Federal Trade Commission in the post-war years won a number of cases against price fixing agreements that were carried on by means of delivered-price systems, it was feared that these might prove Pyrrhic victories, since these systems, once established, might persist without leaving much trace of fresh collusion. Some sanction against the individual firm seemed to be required if tacit collusion was to be effectively prevented.

This situation is not uncommon in the administration of antitrust. The usual way of meeting it[2] is for the Commission or the court in their order or decree to impose on the participants in an illegal scheme a series of injunctions against all activities—even activities not in themselves illegal—that might enable the restrictive effects of the conspiracy to be carried on. In the delivered-pricing cases, however, the Commission's lawyers sought a more direct sanction against the individual firm. In a number of cases the firms concerned were not charged only with taking part in a conspiracy, but there was a second charge alleging that, apart from the conspiracy, they were individually guilty of illegal discrimination.[3]

In one important case, however, the Commission's second charge did not rely on the Robinson-Patman Act but was brought under section 5 of the Federal Trade Commission Act. This was *Triangle Conduit and Cable Company* v. *Federal Trade Commission* (Seventh Circuit Court of Appeals, 1948), in which it was charged that the members of the Rigid Steel Conduit Association, quite apart from the conspiracy, individually violated section 5 'through their concurrent use of a formula method of making delivered-price quotations with the knowledge that each did likewise, with the result that price competition between and among them was unreasonably restrained'.

This charge was clearly directed against consciously parallel business action on the part of competitors. Such a charge might be used in any situation in which, without any sign of a common understanding, firms

---

[1] See the supplement to Chapter I, p. 62.

[2] The powers of the Commission and the courts to impose remedies in antitrust cases are examined below, Chapters XIII and XIV.

[3] This aspect of the matter is dealt with below, supplement to Chapter IX.

were found to be following the pricing decisions of a powerful leader or refraining from making price changes because of their expectations about the reactions of their rivals in an oligopolistic market. The word 'knowledge' in this charge refers simply to knowledge of fact— that is the fact that other suppliers were for the time being using a particular formula; it is not implied that each firm knew of a mutual obligation to use the formula.

Since this charge was brought under section 5 of the Federal Trade Commission Act, it did not directly involve the law of conspiracy, for 'unfair methods of competition' under this section may be the methods of individual firms. This, however, would give little comfort to the business world, for if it became an offence under section 5 for individual firms to act on lines consciously parallel with those of their rivals, a strict definition of 'conspiracy' under the Sherman Act would no longer avail them; they would be out of the Sherman Act frying pan into the Federal Trade Commission Act fire. There was, therefore, great anxiety in business circles when the Commission's decision on this charge went against the members of Rigid Steel Conduit Association and was upheld on appeal by the Seventh Circuit Court of Appeals.

The Court of Appeals found authority in the Supreme Court's opinion in the *Cement* case for the view that 'individual conduct . . . which falls short of being a Sherman Act violation may as a matter of law constitute an "unfair method of competition" prohibited by the Trade Commission Act. A major purpose of that Act . . . was to enable the Commission to restrain practices as "unfair" which, although not yet having grown into Sherman Act dimensions, would most likely do so if left unrestrained. The Commission and the courts were to determine what conduct, even though it might then be short of a Sherman Act violation, was an "unfair method of competition".'

The Court went on to describe the conduct of members of the association in using the basing-point system in the following terms: 'Each knows that by using it he will be able to quote identical delivered prices and thus present a condition of matched prices under which purchasers are isolated and deprived of choice among sellers so far as price advantage is concerned. . . . Each seller consciously intends not to attempt the exclusion of any competition from his natural freight-advantage territory by reducing his price, and in effect invites the others to share the available business at matched prices in his natural market in return for a reciprocal invitation. . . . We cannot say that the Commission was wrong in concluding that the individual use of the basing-point method as here used does constitute an unfair method of competition.'

Shortly after this the Federal Trade Commission sought to explain their view of the law in a public statement of policy.[1] In a paragraph describing the situation in the *Rigid steel conduit* case the statement ran:

It would have been possible to describe this state of facts as a price conspiracy on the principle that, when a number of enterprises follow a parallel course of action in the knowledge and contemplation of the fact that all are acting alike, they have, in effect, formed an agreement. Instead of phrasing its charge in this way, the Commission chose to rely on the obvious fact that the economic effect of identical prices achieved through conscious parallel action is the same as that of similar prices achieved through overt collusion, and, for this reason, the Commission treated the conscious parallelism of action as violation of the Federal Trade Commission Act. Should the Supreme Court sustain the Commission's view, the effect will be to simplify proof in basing-point cases, but to expose to proceedings under the Federal Trade Commission Act only courses of action which might be regarded as collusive or destructive of price competition.

Like *Milgram* v. *Loew's*, this case and the ensuing statement represent a high point of influence of those among the enforcers of antitrust who would have the law bite on uncompetitive situations without being restricted by rigid legal concepts. (Note how courses of action that are 'destructive of price competition' are regarded in this statement as actionable *per se* and not only when they are also collusive.) It must be noted that the *Rigid steel conduit* case has not subsequently been overruled by the Supreme Court.[2] Nevertheless, it is pretty clear that its influence has waned. It must be remembered that a conspiracy had been properly established in the *Rigid steel conduit* case and that the second charge was essentially directed to preventing its revival. So far as the case has authority, it probably means only that the Commission, after a conspiracy has been proved, may bring a charge under section 5 of the Federal Trade Commission Act as an alternative means of preventing individual firms from tacitly carrying on in a manner consistent with the continuance of the conspiracy. It does not appear that the Commission is prepared to follow the logic of their second charge to the extent of prosecuting cases in which individual sellers simply follow the lead of more powerful competitors where no agreement or conspiracy is ever established. This impression is borne out by evidence given on behalf of the Commission to congressional committees and certainly, in the years that have passed since the decision, no attempt has been made to press its logic to this point.[3]

---

[1] *Statement of Federal Trade Commission Policy towards Geographic Pricing Practices for Staff Information and Guidance*, issued 12 October 1948. This document is valuable source material for those who wish to go more deeply into the legality of delivered-pricing systems.

[2] The Supreme Court declined to review the case when application for *certiorari* was made.

[3] There have, of course, been many changes since 1948 in the membership of the Commission.

CHAPTER IV

MONOPOLIZATION
I. THE CRITERIA FOR OFFENCES UNDER SECTION 2 OF THE SHERMAN ACT

1. Section 2 of the Sherman Act: monopoly and monopolizing; the legal meaning of 'intent'; the significance of the remedies to be achieved

The previous chapters have dealt with restraints of trade proceeding out of agreement or combination between competitors: the position of power in the market which is achieved by combination is typically used to influence the level of prices or to exclude competitors from the market. Sometimes a position of power in the market is achieved by a single firm which thereby becomes capable of producing the same economic effects as a combination. Section 2 of the Sherman Act is designed to bring this type of situation within the scope of antitrust. 'Every person who shall monopolize, or attempt to monopolize, or combine or conspire with any person or persons to monopolize any part of the trade or commerce among the several States, or with foreign nations, shall be deemed guilty of a misdemeanour. . . .' In this and the two subsequent chapters the case law under section 2 will be examined.

There are a number of important differences between the considerations that the courts must have in mind in section 2 cases and those which have been shown to apply to section 1. Perhaps the most important is the broader scope for the rule of reason under section 2; monopoly as such is not and cannot be illegal *per se*. The reason for this is obvious. The first firm to bring a new product on to the market is inevitably a monopolist for a time, but it would be ludicrous to charge it with a criminal offence against the system of free competition. A town of 25,000 people may be unable to support more than one newspaper; here again it would be absurd to regard the publisher's monopoly as criminal. Then, too, it is always possible in a competitive system that a firm, by its sheer efficiency, will—for a time at least—win the competition; in terms of business folklore it may simply have 'made a better mousetrap' and attracted all or nearly all the demand for mousetraps. This must surely be counted a success of the competitive system, not an assault upon it.

This point is recognized in the wording of section 2 itself—by the use of the active verb 'monopolize'; the Act does not prohibit 'monopoly'. To monopolize is not simply to possess a monopoly: the word implies some positive drive, apart from sheer competitive skills, to seize and exert power in the market. The same point has been expressed in judicial statements in the form that a monopoly which is 'merely thrust upon' an enterprise is not illegal. The job of the courts under section 2 of the Sherman Act is to isolate and define the elements of positive drive that constitute monopolizing.

The next point that the courts have to watch is the application (and the limitations) of the apparently straightforward analogy between monopolizing and forming a restrictive agreement or combination. It is tempting to suppose that one might derive the law under section 2 simply by translating the various legal rules about restrictive agreements into rules of conduct for the single dominant firm. Since, for example, it is illegal for a combination to raise prices or make exclusive-dealing or boycott arrangements, so 'monopolizing' might be said to occur when a dominant firm raises prices or excludes competitors. A lot of the time these translations turn out near enough right, but the analogy always needs careful handling and at times breaks down.

Several instances of the faulty use of this analogy will appear below. Meanwhile the difficulty may be conveniently illustrated by reference to price fixing. Every agreement between competitors to fix prices is illegal *per se* and it is of no consequence under section 1 of the Sherman Act whether or not the prices fixed are reasonable. The offence is the agreement not to compete in price. If one tries to apply this rule to a single dominant firm—that is, a firm enjoying by itself as much power in the market as is created by an agreement between competitors—the analogy breaks down. Such a firm must sell at some price, and the price it 'fixes' will not be a price arrived at by competition. Going by the analogy, one should conclude that a monopolist is inescapably guilty of illegal price fixing. But this cannot be right: such a rule would catch the involuntary monopolist and make monopoly illegal *per se*.

The reason why the analogy leads to a false conclusion on this point is that it ignores the vital element of the intent or purpose lying behind the achievement of market power. The purpose of those who achieve market power by combining or agreeing together scarcely needs stating and in consequence can largely be ignored in the case law under section 1. Unless the parties intend to limit competition, there is no point in their meeting and negotiating and finally agreeing: and, in any case, their restrictive purpose is normally made manifest in the content of their agreement. It may be an agreement to avoid price competition or to divide the market or to impede new entrants, but an agreement for no purpose would be meaningless.

All this is different in the case of a single firm which achieves a position of market power. The achievement does not necessarily reflect a purpose on the part of the firm to seize and exert power; the power may have been 'thrust upon' it by economic necessity or it may simply have accrued to it by virtue of a normal exercise of competitive skills. Moreover, there is no equivalent in the case of a single firm to the content of a restrictive agreement; once such a firm enjoys a position of power in the market, the question whether its power will be exploited to enhance prices or exclude competitors is not to be answered by reference to the terms of an agreement—since no agreement exists—but only by examining the intent or purpose of those who control its policies. Thus the principal task of the courts under section 2 of the Sherman Act in seeking to isolate the element of positive drive which constitutes monopolizing is to identify the intent of the firm.

Since the nature of a firm's intent or purpose plays so large a part in the law of monopolization, it is necessary to digress briefly at this point in order to consider what is normal legal doctrine on the subject of criminal 'intent'. The traditional analysis has it that there are two elements in a crime—the wicked deed (*actus reus*) and the guilty mind (*mens rea*); *mens rea*, which is in effect criminal intent, is held to be indispensable to the notion of most types of crime. This analysis, which springs from an ancient logic, might suggest that, having detected a murder, the enforcer of law must then search for some additional 'substance' in the mind of the murderer before a conviction of crime can be obtained. But this is misleading.

In legal practice the search for the criminal intent is normally cut short by applying the rule that a man is to be held responsible for the natural consequences of his acts. 'He who wills the means wills the end.' Thus the commission of the act is in most cases sufficient witness to the intent. The need to show *mens rea* has in practice a mainly negative significance; it enables an accused person to plead in his defence that because of some special factor, such as infancy, insanity or duress, he was not responsible for his act and thus lacking in criminal intent.[1]

In antitrust law these same principles apply. A firm's intent may be made manifest by its particular acts or by its general course of action. When a firm in a position of power has exploited the public by charging excessive prices, or has driven small competitors out of business, there is no need to look further for its intent to monopolize. Even without particular, identifiable acts of exploitation or predation, a firm's general course of policy and behaviour may be such as to give rise to an inference of monopolistic intent. This was established as early as 1905 in *Swift and Company* v. *United States* when Mr Justice Holmes pointed

---

[1] See P. H. Nowell-Smith, *Ethics*, Penguin Books, Harmondsworth, 1954, p. 292: 'A man is held to have *mens rea*, and therefore to be guilty, if the *actus reus* is proved, *unless* there are certain specific conditions which preclude a verdict of guilty.'

out that a general allegation of intent and purpose to monopolize might 'colour and apply to' all the specific charges and that the Court had to look at the plan or policy as a whole. 'It is suggested that the several acts charged are lawful. . . . But they are bound together as the parts of a single plan. The plan may make the parts unlawful.'

Thus in cases of monopolization, as in criminal law generally, the prosecutor is not expected to prove a specific criminal intent as something distinct from the behaviour of the accused firm. The only exception to this rule arises when the charge is one of 'attempting to monopolize'. This charge presupposes that the firm concerned has not yet achieved a position of power in the market but is trying to build up such a position. Being without power to exploit or exclude, such a firm must be shown to have a specific intent to achieve these results. This rule too was clearly stated by Mr Justice Holmes in the *Swift* case.[1]

Finally, by way of preamble, a further big difference must be noted in the problems facing the courts in section 2 cases as compared with those arising under section 1. This difference relates to the matter of remedies. A successful prosecution of a restrictive agreement simply puts a stop to the agreement. If the case is a criminal one, fines or even prison sentences are imposed and the parties presumably will not risk repeating the offence. In a civil case the equity powers of the court may be used to decree detailed injunctions against specific practices of the parties. Either way, the firms concerned still exist and have only to modify their conduct.

In a case of monopolization, on the other hand, the exaction of a criminal penalty may have no significant effect on the situation. The maximum fine permitted by law may impose no financial burden whatever on a rich monopoly; and, in any case, no deterrent against repeating the offence will have any meaning when the offence is monopolizing. For if an industry has been successfully monopolized, there is no need to repeat the offence. Consequently, it is normal for the antitrust authorities when bringing charges under section 2 to rely on a civil action (either alone or in conjunction with a criminal suit), and to try to persuade the court of equity to decree the dissolution or break-up of the monopoly concern. The court is then faced with the responsibility not of merely telling businessmen to stop a given practice, but of actually ordering them to dismember the existing structure of their industry. Such action may have far-reaching, indeed unforeseeable

---

[1] 'Where acts are not sufficient in themselves to produce a result which the law seeks to prevent—for instance, the monopoly—but require further acts in addition to the mere forces of nature to bring that result to pass, an intent to bring it to pass is necessary in order to produce a dangerous probability that it will happen. . . . But when that intent and the consequent dangerous probability exist, this statute . . . directs itself against that dangerous probability as well as against the completed result.'

economic repercussions stretching beyond the business concerned to the well being of the nation as a whole. It is small wonder, then, that the courts may be inclined to tread warily in this field.

To sum up, the legal task of the courts under section 2 of the Sherman Act is to apply the rule of reason to a diagnosis of the intent of firms which achieve a monopoly position. In carrying out this task they are subject to the stringent discipline that is imposed by the knowledge that weighty economic consequences are involved in their decisions. The remainder of this chapter will show how the process has worked out in the principal cases.

2. *Early cases:* Northern Securities; Union Pacific

Some of the earliest monopoly cases in the record lay down the rule that, when independent firms combine together to form a monopoly, this in itself is enough to establish that element of positive drive towards market power that constitutes monopolizing.[1] It is irrelevant in such a case that the power, once obtained, is not used to exploit the consumer nor even that it may serve a useful economic purpose. Railway mergers were the subject of these early cases.

Northern Securities Company v. *United States* was decided by the Supreme Court in 1903. Two competing railroads running across the north western States from the Great Lakes to the Pacific Coast were brought under unified financial control by the formation of a holding company. Although both railways had other competitors along some parts of the route, the Supreme Court held that this was a case of monopolization and ordered that the holding company be dissolved and the two railroads returned to separate ownership. Mr Justice Harlan said in his opinion: 'The mere existence of such a combination and the power acquired by the holding company as its trustee constituted a menace to, and a restraint upon, that freedom of commerce which Congress intended to recognize and protect, and which the public is entitled to have protected.' He noted that, if the merger were not dissolved, all the advantages that should accrue to the public from competition between the two lines would be lost.

This was a close decision of five judges against four, and Mr Justice Holmes led the dissent. He pointed out that the Act said nothing about competition and, in his view, did not look to maintaining every existing piece of competition. He clearly attached more importance to the question whether the combination prevented some third party from competing, than to the question whether the absence of competition

[1] These cases were brought under section 1 of the Sherman Act but their interest lies in their contribution to the analysis of monopolizing.

between the two existing railroads would have some adverse impact on the public as consumers. Holmes was, however, in the minority and the law has taken its tone from the majority decision. It will be noted that the case in no way turned upon evidence of abuses of monopoly power in the form of predatory or discriminatory practices.

Other railway cases later on resulted in similar decisions. In *United States* v. *Union Pacific Railroad Company* in 1913 the acquisition by the Union Pacific of large stockholdings in competing railroads, especially in Southern Pacific, came under attack. Again the Supreme Court condemned the merger. Mr Justice Day said: ('The consolidation of two great competing systems of railroad engaged in interstate commerce, by a transfer to one of a dominating stock interest in the other, creates a combination which restrains interstate commerce within the meaning of the statute, because, in destroying or greatly abridging the free operation of competition theretofore existing, it tends to higher rates. . . . Nor does it make any difference that rates for the time being may not be raised and much money [may] be spent in improvements after the combination is effected. It is the scope of such combinations and their power to suppress or stifle competition or create monopoly which determines the applicability of the Act.'[1])

3. *The* Standard Oil *case of 1911*

The line of cases from which the definition of monopolization has proceeded for industries of a more general character than the railways starts from the two great seminal trials which reached the Supreme Court in 1911—*Standard Oil Company of New Jersey* v. *United States* and *United States* v. *American Tobacco Company*. The oil and tobacco 'trusts' were the first of major importance that antitrust, twenty years after its foundation, managed to strike down.

The evidence before the Court in the *Standard Oil* case told how the Rockefeller family and others, who had previously operated as separate partnerships, had organized the Standard Oil Company of Ohio. In the period between 1870 and 1882 this concern acquired nearly all the oil refineries in Cleveland and many others elsewhere and gained control of the oil pipelines from the eastern oilfields to the refineries. Eventually the group dominated the industry, controlling some 90% of trade in refined products, and was able to set the price both of crude and of refined petroleum. Evidence was given that the combination, by

---

[1] A number of other cases in this line of authority might be cited. In particular there were cases at the same period dealing with amalgamations between railroads and anthracite mining companies. These cases—*United States* v. *Reading Company* and others—will be more aptly used to illustrate points below, Chapter VI.

obtaining heavily preferential rates and rebates from the railroads, had forced smaller competitors either to join it or go out of business. In 1882 a trust in the strict sense was formed, and the trustees arranged for the ownership of the various properties coming under the trust agreement to be transferred to the Standard Oil Companies of New York, New Jersey, Pennsylvania and Ohio. Subsequently, after anti-trust litigation in the State of Ohio, the trust device was replaced by a holding company—Standard Oil of New Jersey—which assumed financial control of the whole conglomeration of interests. The record of the group's operations was rich in predatory practices such as local price cutting, using bogus independent concerns as 'fighting companies' and many others.

The Supreme Court was in effect making the first serious attempt to give meaning to section 2 of the Sherman Act. Hence Chief Justice White, after the famous passage in which he expounded the rule of reason, sought to get clear certain initial conceptions and definitions. He outlined a historical theory according to which certain activities of individual firms that had the same harmful results as restraint of trade, particularly the raising of prices, had come to be equated with restraint of trade. He defined this class of individual activities as those 'of such a character as to give rise to the inference or presumption that they had been entered into or done with the intent to do wrong to the general public. . . .'

Whereas section 1 of the Sherman Act dealt generally with restraints of trade proceeding from contracts, combinations or conspiracies, section 2 was intended 'to make sure that by no possible guise could the public policy embodied in the 1st Section be frustrated or evaded'. The word 'monopolize' covered every individual activity bringing about restraint of trade. White then summed up the meaning of section 2 as follows: '. . . the 2nd Section seeks, if possible, to make the prohibitions of the Act all the more complete and perfect by embracing all attempts to reach the end prohibited by the 1st Section: that is, restraints of trade, by any attempt to monopolize, or monopoliza-tion thereof, even although the acts by which such results are attempted to be brought about or are brought about be not embraced within the general enumeration of the 1st Section.'

In the same passage the rule was laid down that the words 'any part of trade or commerce' were both geographic and distributive in their meaning, applying not only to any territorial section of the United States but also to 'any one of the classes of things forming a part of trade'.

Applying these principles to the record of Standard Oil, White stated his main conclusion as follows: '. . . the unification of power and control over petroleum and its products, which was the inevitable result of the combining in the New Jersey corporation . . . of the stocks of so many other corporations . . . gives rise in and of itself, in the absence of countervailing circumstances, to say the least, to the prima facie presumption of intent and purpose to maintain the dominancy over the oil industry. . . .' He stressed that this power had not been built up 'as a result of normal methods of industrial develop-ment, but by new means of combination which were resorted to in order that greater power might be added. . . .' The whole record demonstrated 'the purpose of excluding others from the trade, and thus centralizing in the combination a perpetual control of the movements of petroleum and its products in the channels of interstate commerce'.

White's next point was that this prima facie presumption of intent to restrain trade was '. . . made conclusive by considering (1) the conduct of the persons or corporations who were mainly instrumental in bringing about the extension of power in the New Jersey corporation before the consummation of that result . . .; (2) the proof as to what was done under those agreements . . . the modes in which the power invested in that corporation has been exerted, and the results which have arisen from it.'

He made it clear, in other words, that he was considering the methods adopted by the combination to obtain power and the uses made of the power 'solely as an aid for discovering intent and purpose'.

In sum, White found himself 'irresistibly driven to the conclusion that the very genius for commercial development and organization which it would seem was manifested from the beginning soon begot an intent and purpose to exclude others, which was frequently manifested by acts and dealings wholly inconsistent with the theory that they were made with the single conception of advancing the development of business power by usual methods, but which, on the contrary, neces-sarily involved the intent to drive others from the field and to exclude them from their right to trade, and thus accomplish the mastery which was the end in view'.

These quotations bring out clearly the two fundamental points of law implicit in section 2 of the Sherman Act. First, Chief Justice White saw the need to distinguish the positive drive of monopolization from the sheer fact of monopoly, and he did this by contrasting the history of Standard Oil with what he called 'normal methods of industrial development'. He implied that market power which simply accrued from normal methods—by 'making a better mousetrap'—would not have been unlawful. Secondly, he saw that the true indicator of the requisite element of positive drive was the 'intent and purpose' of the company to exclude competitors and secure dominant power. This purpose he detected from the record of the company's course of action and policy as a whole, and he saw the company's particular acts of exploitation and predation not as the substance of their offence but as further evidence confirming and fortifying his conclusion as to their purpose.

It will be noted that White did not have to decide whether the charge of monopolization would have been sustained in the absence of the evidence of competitors who had actually been driven out of existence; for the record was replete with evidence of this kind. The argument about the bearing of the law on 'unexerted power' was to be left to a later stage. By stressing as the hallmarks of the crime of monopolization, first, the existence of market power and, secondly, the purpose underlying the acquisition and deployment of that power, White had laid a solid foundation for the next steps in that argument.

4. *Cases between 1911 and 1945:* United Shoe Machinery;
United States Steel

Curiously enough, more than thirty years were to pass before the main lines of the argument were taken further by Judge Learned Hand in the *ALCOA* case. The intervening period is worth sketching briefly as an interesting illustration of the vicissitudes of antitrust.

The oil and tobacco 'trusts' were both ordered to be broken up as a result of the judgments of 1911.[1] In the *Oil* case, for example, it was decreed that the stock held by the New Jersey holding company should be transferred back to the various operating concerns, which should thereafter be run as separate businesses. The immediate aftermath of these two cases was a small but important crop of government successes. The du Pont group of explosives manufacturers was split into three parts. The Eastman Kodak company was found to have monopolized the manufacture and sale of photographic apparatus and supplies; and the glucose and farm machinery monopolies were also successfully prosecuted.

For the most part the law as stated in these cases followed closely the lines laid down by Chief Justice White and little new was added. Some of the points made by Judge Learned Hand, who tried the case of *United States* v. *Corn Products Refining Company* (1916), are, however, of interest. Among the matters brought in evidence against this company was its sporadic and selective use of violent price cutting (sometimes in its own name, sometimes through secret agents and bogus inde-

---

[1] The tobacco case—*United States* v. *American Tobacco Company*—is not described here because the statements of law by Chief Justice White in that case add little to those already quoted from the *Oil* case.

pendent concerns) to harm its competitors. Judge Learned Hand, in reviewing this evidence, did not take the position that this 'unfair competition' was in itself a proof of illegal monopolizing: on the contrary, he held that evidence of intent was needed to show whether its low prices were merely a tactical device and not likely to be of long-run benefit to the consumers. Pointing out that the statute took a long-term view of competition and that most of the devices of 'unfair competition' condemned by the courts contained a sporadic element, he added:

It is on this account that the intent of the combination so often appears in the cases as the determinating [sic] factor in illegality. It is not because unfair competition is a crime, but only because a monopolistic intent is the clearest evidence that the competition attempted is shown to be temporary and local, and that there is on this account a reasonable expectation that it will be succeeded by competition which the newcomer might well be able to meet had his development been all the while left unimpeded. If that temporary or local competition were not coupled with such an intent, if there were honest grounds for supposing that it would or could remain to the permanent advantage of the consumer, the public would have no ground to complain, so long as the organization of industry remains on a competitive basis.

Hand is here saying that the purpose of a dominant firm is more important legally than its actual competitive behaviour; and his reason is that cut-throat competition, no matter how vigorous and no matter how much business failure it causes, is of benefit to the public so long as it is competition between equals and therefore continuous. These observations mark the high point of judicial commitment to the positive policy of promoting competition until Judge Hand himself took up the story again in 1945.

After the First World War a reaction set in. Two important cases lost by the Government seemed to set strict limits to what could be done under section 2 of the Sherman Act; and in any case the tone of anti-trust administration became notably less vigorous in the inter-war years and less concerned about the economic and social dangers of business power.

The first of the two unsuccessful cases—*United States* v. *United Shoe Machinery Company of New Jersey* (Supreme Court, 1918)—may be seen as an exercise in distinguishing 'normal methods of industrial development' from the positive drive for power that constitutes monopolizing. The amalgamation which had created this company was not so much a merger of competing companies as of companies which each produced one or more machines needed in the manufacture of shoes, but not on the whole the same machines. Testimony on the point was conflicting to some degree, but the lower Court had found that the companies were not in competition at the time of their union in the United Shoe Machinery Company (U.S.M.). Thus the process of consolidation was not comparable to that which in the railway merger cases had been found to violate the Act.

The Government claimed that after the formation of U.S.M. there had been a course of action, consisting of acquiring competing companies, which on the analogy of the *Oil* and *Tobacco* cases was enough to show the necessary intent and purpose to secure dominant power. The Supreme Court, however, did not look to the cumulative force of the fifty or more acquisitions but considered each separately and accepted defence arguments that in the main they were 'justified by the exigencies or conveniences of the situation'. The size to which the business had expanded was held to be 'the result and cause of efficiency' that was beneficial to the shoe manufacturers.

The Supreme Court also held that the use made by U.S.M. of its many patents had not gone beyond the legitimate rights of patent holders. The Government claimed that the company's practice of refusing to sell its patented machines but only allowing them to be held on leases, subject to various restrictive provisions, was another element in a course of action showing an intent to dominate the industry. These leases required, for example, that once a shoe manufacturer had a machine from U.S.M., he should use no competitive machine of the same type and should obtain from U.S.M. any auxiliary machine he needed. The Court took the view that these conditions too were properly based on patent rights; the method of leasing machines simply continued the practice of the various constituent companies before the merger and had real advantages for the users, particularly in respect of the service which was available to keep the machines properly maintained. Besides, the shoe manufacturers, if they did not like the conditions attaching to the leases, were free to find machines elsewhere.

In sum, the Supreme Court took the view that this was a record of 'normal industrial development'—a valid example of a 'better mousetrap' situation. The lower Court had refused to find that the shoe manufacturers had been coerced into installing U.S.M. machines, and Mr Justice McKenna endorsed this view: 'The installations could have had no other incentive than the excellence of the machines and the advantage of their use, the conditions imposed having adequate compensation and not [being] offensive to the letter or policy of the law.' It is noteworthy that in this judgment the evidence is nowhere analysed in terms of its tendency to show an intent or purpose on the part of the company to dominate the industry; the leasing and other practices of U.S.M. are considered instead from the standpoint of determining whether they are in themselves illegal. It is probably this gap in the argument that makes the case doubtful authority in the light of later developments.[1] However this may be, the Government lost the case, though only four justices constituted the majority in the Supreme Court, three dissenting and two taking no part in the case.

The second case in which the Government was unsuccessful was *United States* v. *United States Steel Corporation*, decided by the Supreme Court in 1920, again by a four to three vote with two justices taking no part. Like the oil and tobacco 'trusts', United States Steel was a holding company with financial control over a large number of operating concerns. The way in which this financial consolidation was carried out, culminating in the dramatic meeting of Andrew Carnegie and J. P. Morgan, is a well known episode of industrial history and need not be recounted here. Although the figures involved were enormous in absolute magnitude,[2] the power of United States Steel in the market was never comparable (over the whole range of its products) to that of the oil or tobacco 'trusts'. It has been estimated that it controlled over 50% of national steel output at its foundation in 1901, rather less than 50% at the time of the case, and no more than a third in the period 1937–46. Although the case and some of the Supreme Court's dicta in it have sometimes been given a wider significance, it was really decided on the question of fact—whether United States Steel had effective power in the market.

Rightly or wrongly the majority in the Supreme Court took the view that the company never achieved a position of power. A trial Court of four judges, though disagreeing on their reasons, had come unanimously to this conclusion. Two thought that the aim of the consolidation had always been to integrate and rationalize production rather than to control the market; the other two thought that it had started out as an attempt to monopolize but that power to control prices had never been achieved. The Government sought to show that the company exercised a coercive form of price leadership, but the company brought two hundred of its customers and dealers as witnesses to rebut this contention, while the Government argued it on theoretical grounds and put up an unfortunate 'teacher of economics' whom Mr Justice McKenna derided:

. . . In a case of this importance we should have something surer for judgment than speculation, something more than a deduction. . . . We

---

[1] It will be seen later in this chapter that the Government subsequently brought and won another monopolization case against U.S.M.

[2] Even in the 1930s, when United States Steel was estimated to control only about one-third of the steel output of the United States, its manufacturing capacity was more than twice that of the entire British steel industry. See Clair Wilcox, *Competition and Monopoly in American Industry*, (United States Temporary National Economic Committee, Monograph 21), U.S. Government Printing Office, Washington, 1941, p. 120.

magnify the testimony by its consideration. Against it competitors, dealers and customers of the corporation testify in multitude that no adventitious interference was employed to either fix or maintain prices, and that they were constant or varied according to natural conditions. . . . The situation is indeed singular, and we may wonder at it, wonder that the despotism of the corporation, so baneful to the world in the representation of the Government, did not produce protesting victims.[1]

Justice McKenna even used the argument that evidence of collusive price fixing, in which United States Steel was said to have taken the lead, told in favour of the defence, for collusion would have been unnecessary if United States Steel alone had had effective power. And if the Government had wanted to bring a conspiracy charge, they should have joined United States Steel's competitors in it as accomplices and not represented them as victims.

Nor could the Government bring evidence of the use of market power to drive out competitors by price cutting, discrimination or other forms of 'unfair competition'. The record was one of buying out, not driving out, competitors.

Faced by their failure to carry the Court with them in their proof of United States Steel's possession of market power, the Government's correct legal course should have been to establish an 'attempt to monopolize', and for this, as has been seen, a showing of a 'specific intent' to achieve power and hence of the 'dangerous probability' of monopoly would have been required.[2] Whether or not this could have succeeded it is now profitless to speculate, though Mr Justice Day in his dissenting opinion pointed to the type of evidence that might have been used, for example, the purchase by the group of competing concerns at prices so inflated that they could be explained only as 'capitalizing the anticipated fruits of combination'.

In practice, however, the government lawyers regarded United States Steel's power in the market as so palpable that they relied solely on the argument that power obtained by financial merger was illegal.[3] Thus,

[1] Economic historians have not found it altogether 'singular' that the smaller steel makers who attended the famous 'Gary dinners' were unavailable as hostile witnesses against United States Steel.

[2] See the quotation from Mr Justice Holmes in *Swift and Company* v. *United States* in the footnote to p. 95 above.

[3] Moreover, this argument was stated in a rather misleading way: 'The combination embodied in the corporation unduly restrains competition by its necessary effect, and therefore is unlawful regardless of purpose.' What this means is that monopoly power obtained by financial merger (as in the *Railway* cases) is *ipso facto* deliberately acquired; 'intent' in the lawyer's sense is already established, so that the firm's 'purpose' in the sense of what it proposes to do with the power when it has got it becomes irrelevant. But it looks as if it means that purpose is altogether irrelevant to the law under section 2, and this is wrong. The form of the Government's argument may well be part of the reason why the Supreme Court in turn ignored the question of 'intent' in this case.

when the majority of the Supreme Court refused to believe that United States Steel possessed effective power, the Government was bound to lose the case.

Mr Justice McKenna in his statement of the law took the position that, since market power had not been shown to exist, the case was an attack on the sheer size of United States Steel as a business unit; and he laid down the indisputable rule that 'the law does not make mere size an offence'. Some of his other dicta, however, are not good law. For example, his way of saying that United States Steel, since they were without effective power, could not have violated the Sherman Act was as follows: '. . . it is against monopoly that the statute is directed; not against an expectation of it, but against its realization, and it is certain that it was not realized.'

This statement is true in the sense that monopoly power must exist before the question of monopolizing arises; but taken literally it offends against the basic principle of section 2 of the Act that it prohibits monopolizing and not monopoly. Moreover, he went on to say: '. . . the law does not make . . . the existence of unexerted power an offence. It . . . requires overt acts and trusts in its prohibition of them and its power to repress or punish them.' Since the majority in the Court did not believe that United States Steel had power at all, it was unnecessary in this case to speculate whether the power they did not have would have been an offence had it been unexerted. It is a truism that monopoly power is no offence if it is not only unexerted but non-existent. But if it exists, the question whether its exertion is indispensable to an offence requires consideration, as will be seen below, of the intent of those who wield it.

Nevertheless, the Court's dictum in the *Steel* case to the effect that only monopoly power expressed through overt acts of aggression is an offence was influential throughout the inter-war years, and hardly any new government cases were brought under section 2 for almost two decades.

5. ALCOA

Since the Second World War there has been another crop of successful government cases under section 2 of the Sherman Act,[1] and the law has been developed largely by returning to and extending the lines laid down by Chief Justice White in 1911. It will be remembered that White insisted on 'intent and purpose' as the main test for deciding whether monopoly power had been built up or was being deployed with the 'drive' that distinguishes monopolizing from mere monopoly.

---

[1] Some of the most important have concerned monopolies built up by aggregating patents: these cases are considered below, Chapter XI.

Moreover, he used an important though negative test of this purposive drive—namely, whether the record of the concern in question could be explained as 'advancing the development of business power by usual methods'.

Starting out from this base, the courts in the later cases have been concerned with two main issues. First, they have settled the question, which White did not reach, whether the necessary 'intent and purpose' can be proved only by overt acts of exploitation or predation, as the dictum in the *Steel* case suggested. Must a monopolist have actually driven competitors out of business or fleeced the public before his monopolizing purpose is disclosed? This is essentially a question of law and logic. It has been settled, as might have been expected *a priori*, that an intent to monopolize does not necessarily require the corpses of its victims to betray it; once settled, this rule is unlikely to be reversed.

Secondly, the courts have asked themselves how wide a departure from 'normal methods of industrial development' must be shown to disclose an intent to monopolize. It is legitimate to 'make a better mousetrap', using all the skill, foresight and energy at your command, even though monopoly power accrues; but if skill and energy are reinforced with business stratagems that are directed to competitive advantage and power rather than to productive efficiency as such, there comes a point where unlawful purpose is revealed. The root of the matter is just how much stratagem is within reason and at what point it becomes an intent to monopolize. Is this firm simply doing the best job it can of making mousetraps or is it really out for power?[1] These are not in the end questions of law but of fact. The court as finder of fact, or the jury, must answer them as best they can in the light of the evidence available in each particular case.

They are often very difficult questions and the answers are inescapably controversial, for a sharp line cannot always be drawn between skilful and energetic competition on one side and business aggression on the other; competitiveness can hardly be devoid of stratagem. The real reason why some of the recent judgments in monopolization cases have caused criticism and controversy is indeed the fear of business people that 'normal methods of industrial development' have now been given so narrow a definition that a powerful firm has positively to 'pull its punches' to avoid giving an impression of unlawful intent.

Of the cases that illustrate these two issues the first in time and in importance is *United States* v. *Aluminum Company of America (ALCOA)*. The case was decided in 1945 by the Second Circuit Court of Appeals,

---

[1] Or, as Judge Wyzanski expressed the issue in *United States* v. *Grinnell Corp.* (District Court of Massachusetts, 1964), 'Was growth in response to external grasp, or to internal grit?'

acting exceptionally as a court of last resort, and the opinion was written by Judge Learned Hand.

ALCOA had originally enjoyed sole control in the United States over the production of aluminium by virtue of patent rights. Some of the background evidence in the case referred to various measures taken in advance by the company to maintain and secure its dominant position when the patent rights expired in 1909. For example, it had made many contracts with electric-power companies for the supply of the great amounts of electricity needed for the manufacturing process, and had included in those contracts covenants binding the companies not to supply power to anyone else for the manufacture of aluminium. The early history also showed that the company had been in trouble with antitrust because of cartel agreements with foreign producers, by which imports of aluminium into the United States were either not made at all or were permitted only under restrictions. Although, as will be seen, Judge Hand went out of his way to rest his argument on later happenings, it is well to remember that this background evidence was all part of the case and was bound to affect the question of whether the story was one of 'normal methods of industrial development'.

The first question for Judge Hand to decide was whether ALCOA had in fact a position of power in the market. By the period immediately before the Second World War, ALCOA was producing 90% of the virgin ingot aluminium used in the United States. This figure ignored the fact that substantial amounts of secondary aluminium (that is, metal reclaimed from scrap) came on the market and set a limit to the price of virgin ingot. ALCOA supplied only about 64% of virgin and secondary metal combined. A good deal of argument has raged on this account about the correctness of taking the 90% figure as a measure of market power. Judge Hand argued that, despite the secondary, ALCOA could still largely determine the supply of the metal in the market, since the amounts of secondary available would be a function of its own previous output of virgin metal and, in deciding its current output, it could take into account both the current availability of scrap and the effect of that output on the future availability of scrap; these calculations might well be inaccurate, but even a substantial margin of inaccuracy would not dispel its considerable influence over total supply. It was also argued that the free availability of imported metal (which accounted for the odd 10% of virgin ingot) set a limit to ALCOA's control over price. On this point Judge Hand pointed out that the tariff and transport costs borne by imported metal gave the company a margin for manoeuvre in its price policy: the availability of imports, like that of secondary metal, might indeed put a 'ceiling' on ALCOA's prices, but being subject to a ceiling is not at all the same thing as being without power in the market. A six-foot man in an eight-foot room is subject to a ceiling, but he can still reach higher than a dwarf.

In sum, though certain of Judge Hand's arguments on this topic may be disputable, it is hard to believe that any fair and neutral arbiter could resist the conclusion that ALCOA had an effective position of power in the American market for aluminium.[1]

Having decided that ALCOA was indeed in a position of power, Judge Hand turned to the argument that the power had not been abused. An important part of the defence case was that, even if ALCOA had a monopoly, it had not been maintained by unlawful means; its power had not been exerted to exploit consumers or exclude competitors, and hence, according to the *Steel* case, it did not violate the Sherman Act.

The main defence point under this head arose out of the claim that secondary and imported ingot set limits to ALCOA's prices. Not only were these limits operative, it was argued, but in fact ALCOA's prices and profits had never been unreasonable. It was found that over the whole lifetime of the company the net return on capital invested had been only about 10%, and Judge Hand himself agreed that this was not 'exorbitant'; albeit he pointed out that this rate of profit on the business as a whole (which included a vast trade in the competitive field of fabricated aluminium) did not necessarily apply to ingot production, and he also made the shrewd economic point that 'the mere fact that a producer having command of the domestic market has not been able to make more than a "fair" profit is not evidence that "fair" profit could not have been made at lower prices'.

Judge Hand proceeded to show, however, that as a matter of law the reasonableness of ALCOA's prices and profits was irrelevant to the charge of monopolization.[2] In his argument he made use of the analogy with restrictive agreements, such as price fixing agreements, which are

[1] Judge Hand himself seems to have confused the issue somewhat by his dictum that 90% control of output 'is enough to constitute a monopoly; it is doubtful whether 60 or 64% would be enough: and certainly 33% is not'. This statement seems to make his argument for ignoring secondary aluminium central to the case, for the secondary precisely accounted for the difference between 90% and 64%. But, as will be shown later in the chapter, it is doubtful whether the law has ever required or even found satisfactory a purely arithmetical measure of market power.

[2] Judge Hand preceded his statement of the law with a characteristic statement of social philosophy which, though not strictly germane to the argument, is interesting as harking back to the basic political tradition of antitrust—namely, a dislike of concentrations of private power despite their economic advantages. 'It is possible, because of its indirect social and moral effect, to prefer a system of small producers, each dependent for his success upon his own skill and character, to one in which the great mass of those engaged must accept the direction of the few. These considerations which we have suggested only as possible purposes of the Act, we think the decisions prove to have been in fact its purpose.' Later he again spoke of the purpose of the Act to preserve 'for its own sake and in spite of possible cost' an industrial structure of small competing units.

condemned as illegal *per se* under section 1 of the Sherman Act. The reasonableness of the prices fixed under such agreements is irrelevant to the offence because the agreement to limit competition, being a purposive means of achieving power in the market, is in itself illegal restraint of trade. As Mr Justice Stone had put it in the *Trenton Potteries* case: 'The power to fix prices, whether reasonably exercised or not, involves power to control the market and to fix arbitrary and unreasonable prices.' Hand pointed out that a monopoly has the same power to fix prices as the parties to an agreement and must indeed 'fix' prices whenever it sells. As he put it, 'the power and its exercise must needs coalesce'. In the case of a monopoly, as in that of an agreement, it is the creation of market power that constitutes the restraint of trade, regardless of whether the power is subsequently found to have been used reasonably or unreasonably.

The analogy with restrictive agreements is here used correctly, for Hand does not attempt to draw the mistaken conclusion that monopoly power is illegal *per se*. All he is saying, in this part of his opinion, is that monopoly power must be, among other things, a power to fix prices and, as such, cannot be saved, any more than restrictive agreements, by arguments of reasonableness or social advantage. He goes on immediately to make the necessary distinction between possessing monopoly power and monopolizing. 'It does not follow because ALCOA had such a monopoly that it monopolized the ingot market. It may not have achieved monopoly: monopoly may have been thrust upon it.'

Judge Hand then entered upon his famous and original analysis of the element of 'positive drive' that turns the mere possession of monopoly power into the offence of monopolizing. He showed first that, if the origin of the ALCOA monopoly had been a combination of existing smelters, through the setting up, for example, of a holding company exerting financial control over a number of previously competing concerns, then it would certainly have monopolized. The *Railway* cases mentioned at the beginning of this chapter were sufficient authority for this.

But there might be ways of acquiring monopoly power which would not show the necessary element of positive drive. Judge Hand listed some of the possibilities:

Persons may unwittingly find themselves in possession of a monopoly, automatically so to say; that is, without having intended either to put an end to existing competition, or to prevent competition from arising when none had existed; they may become monopolists by force of accident. . . . A market may, for example, be so limited that it is impossible to produce at all and meet the cost of production except by a plant large enough to supply the whole demand. Or there may be changes in taste or in cost which drive out all but one purveyor. A single producer may be the survivor out of a group of active competitors, merely by virtue of his superior skill, foresight and industry.

On this last point Judge Hand seems to have agreed (though using a form of words that did not quite commit him) that it would be wrong and unfair to attach the crime of monopolizing to sheer industrial success: 'In such cases a strong argument can be made that, although the result may expose the public to the evils of monopoly, the Act does not mean to condemn the resultant of those very forces which it is its prime object to foster: *finis opus coronat*. The successful competitor must not be turned upon when he wins.'

Judge Hand held, however, that it would be wrong to interpret ALCOA's position as that of a 'passive beneficiary of a monopoly, following upon an involuntary elimination of competitors by automatically operative economic forces'. Going back to the exclusive contracts and other aggressive tactics of the early days and sketching the later development of the company, he concluded that its 'continued and undisturbed control did not fall undesigned into ALCOA's lap; obviously it could not have done so. It could only have resulted, as it did result, from a persistent determination to maintain the control, with which it found itself vested in 1912.'

Then comes the passage which constitutes the core of his opinion:

We need charge it with no moral derelictions after 1912; we may assume that all it claims for itself is true. The only question is whether it falls within the exception established in favor of those who do not seek, but cannot avoid, the control of a market. It seems to us that that question scarcely survives its statement. It was not inevitable that it should always anticipate increases in the demand for ingot and be prepared to supply them. Nothing compelled it to keep doubling and redoubling its capacity before others entered the field. It insists that it never excluded competitors; but we can think of no more effective exclusion than progressively to embrace each new opportunity as it opened, and to face every newcomer with new capacity already geared into a great organization, having the advantage of experience, trade connections and the elite of personnel. Only in case we interpret 'exclusion' as limited to manoeuvres not honestly industrial, but actuated solely by a desire to prevent competition, can such a course, indefatigably pursued, be deemed not 'exclusionary'. So to limit it would in our judgment emasculate the Act; would permit just such consolidations as it was designed to prevent.[1]

---

[1] It is of some interest to note that the main ground on which economic writers have condemned the aluminium monopoly has been precisely that ALCOA consistently failed to embrace opportunities for expansion, and so underestimated the demand for the metal that the United States was woefully short of productive capacity at the outset of both world wars.

Finally Judge Hand noted that his finding of ALCOA's 'persistent determination' to maintain its monopoly was a sufficient showing of intent. 'In order to fall within section 2, the monopolist must have both the power to monopolize, and the intent to monopolize. To read the passage as demanding any "specific" intent makes nonsense of it, for no monopolist monopolizes unconscious of what he is doing. So here, ALCOA meant to keep, and did keep, that complete and exclusive hold upon the ingot market with which it started. That was to "monopolize" that market, however innocently it otherwise proceeded.' The Government had won its case.[1]

It is worth noting how closely the structure of Judge Hand's legal argument in this case follows that of Chief Justice White's opinion in the *Standard Oil* case. First, the existence of market power is established: secondly, an inquiry is made into the 'intent and purpose' lying behind the acquisition and deployment of that power. White does not reach the question whether the actual exercise of power in acts of aggression or exploitation is necessary to the offence. Hand reaches it and decides that, given an intent to retain power, it is irrelevant whether its actual use is reasonable or not. Both judges emerge finally with a negative test of the purposive drive that constitutes monopolizing.

The important difference in content between the two opinions—a difference that measures the development of the law between 1911 and 1945—is the difference between these tests. To White, monopolizing means a departure from 'normal methods of industrial development'. To Hand, it means any activity more positive than that of one who 'does not seek but cannot avoid' the control of a market, one who is a 'passive beneficiary' of monopoly power or has had monopoly power 'thrust upon' him. This test is, of course, far stricter and harder to escape than White's, for there is much business activity which would qualify as 'normal' but which, if it led to the creation or maintenance of a monopoly, could hardly be called 'unavoidable'. In effect, Judge Hand's test puts the onus on the defendant to show that he simply cannot help having monopoly power: to any extent that he reaches out to grasp or strives actively to hold his leading place, he is denied the right to claim that he has no unlawful intent.

The important issue that remains is the size of the gap left open for innocent monopoly by Judge Hand's statement of the law. By the test of the *ALCOA* case this gap is small indeed. On the one hand Judge Hand allows that the monopolist may be legally safe if he is the sole

---

[1] The problem of finding a suitable remedy for the situation was not immediately gone into because the war had brought substantial changes in the structure of the industry. For the outcome, as it emerged from Judge Knox's opinion on relief measures, see below, Chapter XIV.

survivor of a group of active competitors merely by virtue of his skill, foresight and industry. On the other hand he is guilty of the criminal offence of monopolizing if, by progressively embracing each new opportunity as it opens, he dampens the spirits of potential competitors. Even though the seeing and taking of opportunities of expansion are matters of skill and foresight—certainly they are 'normal' and 'honestly industrial' business methods—they may yet disclose a monopolistic intent, according to Judge Hand's opinion, if they are clearly exclusionary in effect. An extreme interpretation of this view would impute illegal intent to a firm with monopoly power even on account of its very efficiency, if exclusionary effects were shown to result. Judge Hand's opinion is clearly one of the high-water marks of antitrust and it may be that the tide will recede—at least from extreme interpretations of his meaning.[1]

6. *Other cases since 1945:* American Tobacco; Griffith *and* Schine; United Shoe Machinery; *the* Cellophane *case*

The cases since 1945 have not on the whole brought further developments in the law, and Judge Learned Hand's *ALCOA* opinion remains the most radical statement of recent doctrine. Some of the later cases, however, contain useful material for clarifying particular points of law.

Immediately after ALCOA came *American Tobacco Company* v. *United States* (Supreme Court, 1946)—a case to be used below (Chapter VI) to illustrate the law of 'conspiracy to monopolize' but which must be noted here because in it the Supreme Court, with no dissentients, took occasion to endorse the main points of law in Judge Hand's *ALCOA* opinion.[2] Mr Justice Burton's opinion also put beyond doubt the rule that proof of the actual exercise of monopoly power to exclude competitors or charge excessive prices is not required for a showing of monopolization: 'A correct interpretation of the statute and of the authorities makes it the crime of monopolizing, under section 2 of the Sherman Act, for parties . . . to acquire or maintain the power to exclude competitors from any part of the trade or commerce among the several States or with foreign nations, provided they also have such a power that they are able . . . to exclude actual or potential competition from the field and provided they have the intent and purpose to exercise that power. . . . Neither proof of exertion of the power to

---

[1] See Judge Leahy's dicta in the *Cellophane* case, below, p. 124.

[2] Although the Supreme Court quoted at length from the opinion, it is noteworthy that neither the passage about 'embracing each new opportunity' nor the statement that the purpose of antitrust was to preserve an industrial structure of small units was specifically endorsed.

exclude nor proof of actual exclusion of existing or potential competition is essential to sustain a charge of monopolization. . . .'

Some cases dealing with regional monopolies on the exhibiting side of the motion picture industry further illustrate the question of the bearing of exclusionary activities by a powerful group on the offence of monopolizing. In *United States* v. *Crescent Amusement Company* (Supreme Court, 1944) a powerful group of affiliated exhibitors had been charged with blatantly using their buying power to eliminate smaller competitors.

For example, the defendants would insist that a distributor give them monopoly rights in towns where they had competition, or else defendants would not give the distributor any business in the closed towns where they had no competition. The competitor not being able to renew his contract for films would frequently go out of business or come to terms and sell out to the combination with an agreement not to compete for a term of years. The mere threat would at times be sufficient and cause the competitor to sell out to the combination 'because his mule was scared'.

In such a case there was no legal difficulty about finding a violation of section 2 of the Sherman Act, because these were overt exclusionary acts which in themselves constituted illegal restraint of trade. It has always been obvious that for one having monopoly power to exert it by means of restraints of trade that would be illegal under section 1 must necessarily constitute illegal monopolizing under section 2 of the Act.

In two cases decided by the Supreme Court in 1948—*United States* v. *Griffith* and *United States* v. *Schine Chain Theatres*—the matter was rather more complicated. It must be noted that the monopoly power derived from owning the only cinema in a small town is in a real sense inescapable or 'thrust upon' the owner. Hence in these cases the element of purposive drive needed for a showing of monopolization could not lie in the way in which the monopoly position had been acquired, but only in the way in which the power had been used. It was not, however, contended that the Griffith or Schine circuits of cinemas had made blatantly exclusionary arrangements like those in the *Crescent Amusement* case. The suggestion was that, by negotiating in bulk with the distributors for all their cinemas, they still in practice secured competitive advantages in 'open' towns owing to the leverage of their monopoly power in 'closed' towns. Merely negotiating for the circuits as a whole was clearly not in itself illegal restraint of trade; but was it evidence of a purpose to exclude competition and hence of monopolizing?

Mr Justice Douglas held that it was. In the *Griffith* case he set out the situation in the following terms:

A man with the monopoly of the theatres in any one town . . . need not be as crass as the exhibitors in *United States* v. *Crescent Amusement Company*, in order to make his monopoly effective in his competitive situations. Though he makes no threat to withhold the business of his closed or monopoly towns unless the distributors give him the exclusive film rights in the towns where he has competitors, the effect is likely to be the same where the two are joined. When the buying power of the entire circuit is used to negotiate films for his competitive as well as his closed towns, he is using monopoly power to expand his empire. And even if we assume that a specific intent to accomplish that result is absent, he is chargeable in legal contemplation with that purpose since the end-result is the necessary and direct consequence of what he did.

In other words, the general conduct of the defendants' business in these cases was capable of disclosing and did disclose an intent to exercise monopoly power; and by the rule laid down in the 1946 *Tobacco* case the conjunction of power and the intent to exercise it was in itself a violation of section 2. As Justice Douglas put it: 'It follows . . . that the use of monopoly power, however lawfully acquired, to foreclose competition, to gain a competitive advantage, or to destroy a competitor is unlawful.'

Like some parts of Judge Hand's *ALCOA* opinion, this result raises the question whether the possessor of monopoly power can ever in practice be legally safe. The Crescent Amusement circuit had been 'crass' in flagrantly deploying its monopoly power in certain towns to gain advantages over competitors in other towns. The Griffith and Schine circuits avoided this 'crassness', yet did not avoid illegality by simply combining 'open' and 'closed' towns in one transaction. From this it would appear that to be legally safe a circuit ought to instruct the individual managers of its cinemas to deal separately with the film distributors. Yet even then might it not be said that the distributors would inevitably take account of the buying power of the circuit as a whole and would tend to be more chary of offending a member of a large organization than of overriding the wishes of a small independent cinema owner? This method might be less 'crass' still; but would it altogether exorcize the inescapable fact of the influence in the market-place of the large organization? These cases illustrate very well the difficulty that antitrust has in setting bounds to the use of the market power of large concerns, without going to the other extreme and making it next to impossible for such concerns to conduct their business at once efficiently and lawfully.

One later case is outstanding in giving a full conspectus of the issues arising under section 2 of the Sherman Act and clarifying what might be called the post-Hand state of the law. This is *United States* v. *United Shoe Machinery Corporation* which was tried by Judge Wyzanski in the District Court of Massachusetts in 1953.[1] The case is also particularly interesting in that it enables the modern legal treatment of the issues to be directly compared with that adopted by the Supreme Court in the earlier case against the company (see above, pp. 101–3).

The facts presented to the Court in 1953 were in most essentials unchanged from those considered thirty-five years earlier when the company was cleared of the charge of monopolization. U.S.M. was found to supply somewhere between 75 and 85% of the machines used in the boot and shoe industry, although there was no tariff on imported machines and almost every industrial process could be carried out on machines made by other companies. Only U.S.M., however, produced a full line of all the necessary equipment. It was shown that it spent some three million dollars a year on research and that 95% of the patents it held were attributable to its own research staff. For a long time past it had made no important acquisitions of businesses, inventions or patent rights from outside.

The company still followed its traditional practice of never selling but only leasing its machines. The common form of lease had a ten-year term and required that so long as work was available the machine would be worked to capacity. If the hirer wanted to return the machine before the end of the ten-year term, a charge was made that tapered off from a considerable sum in the earlier stages to an insignificant amount by the end of the term. If he was returning it in order to replace it, he paid less if he took another U.S.M. machine in replacement than if he switched to another manufacturer's machine. There were no separate charges for U.S.M. repair and maintenance services, with the result that there were no independent servicing firms and it became essential for any rival manufacturer to offer service on a similar scale.

One new aspect of the situation was that in one particular field relating to the new 'cement' process of manufacture—a recently established firm, Compo, had achieved something approaching equality with U.S.M. as a supplier of machines. It was shown that U.S.M. adjusted its hiring charges so that it obtained higher returns on those machines which had no effective competition than on the machines for which there were readily available substitutes such as the Compo machines.

Judge Wyzanski took as his starting point the most straightforward test of illegal monopolization—namely the acquisition or exercise of

---

[1] The Supreme Court affirmed Judge Wyzanski's judgment and decree against the company in May 1954. Any reader who wishes to delve more fully into the law of monopolization should certainly study Judge Wyzanski's admirable opinion at length in 110 Fed. Supp. 295, or *Commerce Clearing House Trade Cases*, Chicago, 1952–3, 67,436. The case is also the subject of a valuable monograph by Carl Kaysen, *United States* v. *United Shoe Machinery Corporation* (Harvard Economic Studies, 99), Harvard University Press, 1956.

monopoly power by means that would in themselves be illegal restraints of trade (for example, the 'crass' exclusionary acts of the *Crescent Amusement* case). Clearly U.S.M. could not be condemned on this test. The 1918 case had established rightly or wrongly that the original mergers forming U.S.M. did not constitute illegal acquisition of market power. Moreover, a Clayton Act case in 1922 had condemned certain tying clauses in the leases then used by U.S.M. and it had to be assumed that their recent leases took account of that judgment. These matters were *res judicata*.

Thus, at one extreme, U.S.M. might have been but in fact could not be condemned as having monopolized by dint of outright restraints of trade. At the other extreme the company might again be found to have achieved its dominant position purely by superior skill and foresight; the case might be a valid example of a 'better mousetrap' situation, such as had been regarded by everybody, from the senators who wrote the Sherman Act to Judge Learned Hand himself, as beyond the reach of the law. Judge Wyzanski showed, however, that there was a middle ground between these extremes and defined it in very clear terms: 'the intermediate case where the causes of an enterprise's success were neither common-law restraints of trade, nor the skill with which the business was conducted, but rather some practice which without being predatory, abusive, or coercive was in economic effect exclusionary'. He would have to decide the case on this middle ground, which, as he showed, was exactly the ground covered by Mr Justice Douglas in the *Griffith* case and Judge Learned Hand in the *ALCOA* case.

Mr Justice Douglas had found in the behaviour of the large cinema circuits an exclusionary purpose which, coupled with their power, was enough to establish monopolization. 'The least that this conclusion means', said Wyzanski, 'is that it is a violation of section 2 for one having effective control of the market to use, or plan to use, any exclusionary practice, even though it is not a technical restraint of trade.' Judge Learned Hand had gone further still by attributing a purpose to exclude competition to any monopolist who could not show that his monopoly was 'thrust upon' him or that it was due, in Wyzanski's words, 'solely to defendant's ability, economies of scale, research, natural advantages, and adaptation to inevitable economic laws'.

Judge Wyzanski found it unnecessary to choose between the tests laid down by Douglas and Hand, since he thought the result in the *U.S.M.* case would be the same on either test. The question he had to answer was whether U.S.M. had simply made a 'better mousetrap' or whether its conduct was in some degree purposefully exclusionary. In large part this came down to a question of the effect on its rivals of its leasing system. On the one hand the leasing system was popular with the shoe industry and U.S.M.'s few competitors imitated it. The service given by the company was excellent and machinery costs accounted for less than 2% of the wholesale prices charged by the average shoe manufacturer. On the other hand, the leases were so drawn as to fortify U.S.M.'s position as against its competitors. The ten-year term, the return charges, the full-capacity clause—all this constituted, as Wyzanski put it, a 'magnetic tie' making it that much harder for competitors to break into the market. The differences in hire charges between the various machines, according to the degree of competition with which they were faced, also presented a real difficulty to a would-be competitor.

Wyzanski recognized that these leasing practices were in one sense 'normal methods of industrial development'; yet, as he stated in his main conclusion: '. . . they are not practices which can be properly described as the inevitable consequences of ability, natural forces, or law. . . . They are contracts, arrangements and policies which, instead of encouraging competition based on pure merit, further the dominance of a particular firm. In this sense they are unnatural barriers: they unnecessarily exclude actual and potential competition: they restrict a free market. While the law allows many enterprises to use such practices, the Sherman Act is now construed by superior courts to forbid the continuance of effective market control based in part upon such practices.'

On these grounds the Government's case against the machinery monopoly was upheld. It was also found that U.S.M. had achieved a monopoly in various minor supplies, such as nails and tacks, because of their dominant position in the machinery field. This minor matter was an offence on any ground: 'An enterprise that by monopolizing one field secures dominant power in another field has monopolized the second field in violation of Section 2 of the Sherman Act.'[1]

Like Judge Hand in the *ALCOA* case, Judge Wyzanski was drawn at length into an expression of economic philosophy. As against U.S.M.'s claims for the social advantage of their research programmes (which he found irrelevant to the legal issues), he pointed to the achievements of the Compo firm in securing equality with U.S.M. in a new field. 'This experience illustrates the familiar truth that one of the dangers of extraordinary experience is that those who have it may fall into grooves created by their own expertness. They refuse to believe

---

[1] This does not mean that a company which enjoys a 'lawful' monopoly in one market cannot enter into another market making use of the profits earned in the first market, but it must not use that monopoly in any way as economic leverage in the newly entered market. See for example *Union Leader Corporation* v. *Newspapers of New England Inc.* (First Circuit Court of Appeals, 1960).

that hurdles which they have learned from experience are insurmount-able can in fact be overcome by fresh, independent minds.' He pointed out that what looks to be a progressive policy on the part of a monopoly may, in fact, be less venturesome than one which responds to the spur of competition: 'Industrial advance may indeed be in inverse proportion to economic power; for creativity in business, as in other areas, is best nourished by multiple centres of activity, each following its unique pattern and developing its own *esprit de corps* to respond to the challenge of competition.'

Having found that U.S.M. had monopolized the shoe machinery industry within the meaning of the Sherman Act, Judge Wyzanski nevertheless refused the Government's request for a decree dividing the company into three separate parts. He ordered merely that the leases should be purged of their restrictive features, and that the ten-year term should be shortened; that all the machines were to be offered for sale if the customers wished to buy; that the minor monopoly in various supplies, like tacks and nails, should be divested from the main business; that U.S.M. should no longer have exclusive distributorships for other shoe supplies; and that U.S.M.'s patents should be licensed to any applicant on payment of reasonable royalties.[1]

To complete this account of the principal post-war cases it is of interest to come to one which the Government lost. This is *United States* v. *E.I. du Pont de Nemours and Company* tried by Judge Leahy in the District Court of Delaware in December 1953. The complaint was that du Pont had monopolized trade in cellophane—one of the vast range of products the company turned out.

Judge Leahy felt unable even to take the first essential step and find that du Pont had an effective position of power in the market. The defence argued that no separate market for cellophane could be distinguished from the market for flexible packaging materials as a whole and there was a great deal of evidence, which the Court accepted, to the effect that users of packaging materials exercised an effective choice among different types of material with varying qualities at different prices. Cellophane was in fact among the higher-priced materials and accounted for less than 20% of the whole field. As Judge Leahy summed it up: 'Shifts of business have been proved. It has been proved in every major end-use; du Pont cellophane has lost and gained actual paying customers, as a result of cost and quality judgments by these customers. It has been proved these gains and losses are substantial.' The Judge, however, declined to be drawn into

---

[1] The strongly practical tone of Judge Wyzanski's opinion on remedies is interesting and will be considered further in Chapter XIV, below. A subsequent Supreme Court decision suggested that divestiture of shoe machinery assets would be appropriate, and under a later consent decree U.S.M. agreed to divest enough to reduce its market share to about 33%.

a subtle economic argument on the question whether cellophane was a separate product or 'part of commerce'; for the purposes of the law there was simply a question of fact to be decided—whether du Pont had effective market power. 'Market control or lack of market control are ultimate facts. They are determined by fact finding processes, and on the basis of knowledge and analysis of all competitive factors which bear on a seller's power to raise prices, or to exclude competition.' Judge Leahy found that in practice du Pont's prices had to respond to competitive pressures, and that it exerted no exclusive patents or other means of excluding competitors from the manufacture of cellophane itself, let alone from that of competing materials. In fact, other companies making cellophane were expanding. He concluded: 'Facts, in large part uncontested, demonstrate du Pont cellophane is sold under such intense competitive conditions, acquisition of market control or monopoly power is a practical impossibility.'

Since he found that du Pont had no effective market power, there was no need for Judge Leahy to reach the question whether its 75% share of cellophane output had been built up or maintained by methods that disclosed an intent to monopolize. Nevertheless, he did in fact analyse the evidence of the company's business practices in relation to this question and found under each head—patent licensing, pricing, distribution and other policies—that the company had adopted fair and normal business practices. Anyway, the case was a valid example of a 'better mousetrap' situation: 'I am able, after critical examination of the record, to determine du Pont's position is the result of research, business skill and competitive activity. . . . Its "monopoly" was "thrust upon" it within the true meaning of the decisions. . . .'

The Supreme Court upheld Judge Leahy's decision, but only by the narrow majority of four to three. The essence of the majority opinion was that the extent of the cross-elasticity of demand for cellophane and other wrapping materials was crucial, so that the relevant market was in those products that had reasonable interchangeability with cellophane for the purposes for which they were produced, considering price, use and technical qualities. They agreed with Judge Leahy that du Pont's control over the price of cellophane was in practice very limited, as it was interchangeable with many rival packaging materials for most end-uses. The minority of three claimed, however, that the argument of 'reasonable interchangeability' was no more than a re-statement of the theory of inter-industry competition, and that cellophane alone constituted a separate sub-market which du Pont could be shown to have 'monopolized'.

7. *Recapitulation of the law of section 2: the importance of 'intent'*

By way of epilogue a brief recapitulation of the critical points in the argument seems to be needed if only to serve as a pointer to the issues which are still fluid and which will continue to engage the minds of the courts and the commentators in the future.

First, something more should be said about the initial decision that has to be made in each case; namely, whether the firm concerned possesses effective market power. How is its power measured and how is the relevant market defined? It was noted above that Judge Learned Hand in the *ALCOA* case gave a rough arithmetical answer to the former question; 90% of aluminium output certainly meant monopoly power, 64% was doubtful, and 33% clearly insufficient. But it is doubtful whether any formula of this kind is really of value. The courts (including Judge Hand himself) have preferred a strictly practical approach to the question. Instead of trying to decide, on economic or other grounds, whether 50% or 75% is the right figure to measure dominant power, they have looked to questions of fact; for example, whether those who might have wanted to enter the industry or increase their share of the market could be prevented from so doing, or whether the suspected monopolist was able to set his own price on his product without too much regard to competition.[1]

It is not, of course, supposed that the monopolist's power will be absolute and unlimited. As was seen above (Chapter II), the exclusive character of membership in Associated Press did not make it absolutely impossible for outsiders to produce a newspaper: but it made it much more difficult, and this was enough to condemn the scheme. Similarly, Judge Hand admitted that both secondary and imported ingot set limits to ALCOA's prices but the company still owed to its power a comfortable margin for manoeuvre in pricing policy. On the other hand, Judge Leahy found that for all du Pont's 75% share of cellophane output, the market in which it sold was acutely sensitive to price changes and the company could not be said to possess significant market power.

These considerations, which Judge Leahy summed up in the words 'market control or lack of market control are ultimate facts', also answer the question about defining the market. A great deal has been written by economists about the potential competition of substitutes that the monopolist always has to face. The point that they make is obvious enough. There is no absolute monopoly in the real world, short of a monopoly of everything. If golf-clubs became

---

[1] As Judge Taft put it in the *Addyston Pipe* case: 'The most cogent evidence that they had this power is the fact, everywhere apparent in the record, that they exercised it.'

impossibly expensive, more men would take up bowls; if all sports goods became impossibly expensive, they would ride bicycles or read books. The scale of 'substitutability' of products is nowhere markedly discontinuous. ALCOA's prices would, in the last resort, be kept in check by the competition of tin plate and magnesium no less than by that of secondary and imported aluminium.

But the courts, in practice, do not allow themselves to be bewildered by recondite economic concepts such as 'substitutability'; they simply ask whether a firm before them has attempted to build up or to use its power to raise prices or exclude competitors. If there is evidence of such conduct, they take it for granted that the firm sees real gains to be made by it: in other words, that there is a market worth monopolizing. It may be true that ALCOA's power was in some degree limited by the availability of tin plate or magnesium; but unless there was some margin of advantage to them, why did their course of action demonstrate (assuming that the Court was right in holding that it did demonstrate) an intent on their part to maintain their dominance and ward off competitors from their own particular field? In other words, the courts will take as the market, for the purposes of deciding cases, just that market which the concern itself takes for its field of activity: if a firm shows an intent to exclude competition from that field, it will be assumed that the field sufficiently describes a market—for otherwise what would be the point of the effort to exclude? Evidence of intent to exclude is the vital pointer not only to the danger of restraint of trade that lies in market power but also to the very existence of that power itself. On this point one may well surmise that the lawyers have shown a shrewder grasp of the real world than the economists.

Next, a last look at the argument about 'unexerted power' is in order, because those in the United States who regard the law under section 2 of the Sherman Act as having gone too far in recent years frequently attack the idea that a charge of monopolizing should be sustainable in the absence of evidence that monopoly power has actually been exerted to the detriment of consumers or competitors. Some commentators profess indeed that this idea never was in the law in the sensible old days of the *Standard Oil* case. The argument is usually put in the form that Chief Justice White required outright restraints of trade from his monopolists. One commentator puts it thus: 'So in the days of Standard Oil, the lawyer called upon to defend a client charged with being a monopolist was able to give his client some idea of the elements of that crime. . . . Power acquired as a result of or used to effect an unreasonable restraint of trade was recognizable.'[1] It seems reasonably

[1] H. Templeton Brown, 'Monopoly—the 1953 Model', in *Lectures on federal antitrust laws: 1953*, Michigan University Law School, 1953.

clear that this view, though frequently stated and influential, ought in logic to be, and in practice probably is, a lost cause.[1]

In the first place a careful reading of Chief Justice White's opinion in *Standard Oil* does not confirm the view that in his mind monopolistic purpose was only to be disclosed by acts of combination or aggression that would in themselves be illegal restraints of trade. On the contrary, there is every indication that he recognized that monopoly power, when purposefully directed, in itself constituted restraint of trade. He spoke indeed 'of the practical evolution by which monopoly . . . came to be spoken of as, and to be indeed synonymous with, restraint of trade'. And this is only logical, for restraint of trade means limiting competition, not what happens after or because competition is restricted. White's insistence on 'intent and purpose' as the crux of the argument and his treatment of the plentiful evidence of predatory acts in the *Oil* case 'solely as an aid for discovering intent and purpose' seem clearly consistent with the modern view as expressed in the *ALCOA* and *American Tobacco* cases.

But, furthermore, the even older authority of Mr Justice Holmes in the *Swift* case had already laid down that business practices lawful in themselves might yet be seen as contributory to a plan or purpose to monopolize; and this is little different from Mr Justice Douglas's treatment of circuit negotiation in the *Griffith* case. The most decisive point of all lies in what would be entailed if monopolization did after all require overt acts of predation or exploitation. The monopolist having the power and the intent to exclude competitors would then be legally safe until it could be shown that the prices he charged were 'unreasonable' or that competitors had actually gone out of business. Yet nothing in antitrust is more firmly settled than that a purposive restrictive agreement between competitors—whether to fix prices or for exclusive dealing—is illegal, regardless of any showing of excessive prices or bankrupt businesses. It cannot be reasonably supposed that so great an asymmetry between section 1 and section 2 of the Sherman Act was intended by its authors or would be tenable in practice.

Power and intent, as White's early analysis foreshadowed, are the only indispensable indicators of monopolizing. And it follows that the truly controversial matter—on which each case finally turns—is what test to adopt to establish an intent to monopolize. Overt acts of exploitation and predation are, of course, one such test and the least disputable. But they are not the only test: the crux of the argument is what is the

---

[1] This is not, of course, to say that a law which condemns monopoly power (when coupled with unlawful purpose) regardless of its exertion is a good thing: this is a matter of assessment for Part II of the book. I mean only that section 2 of the Sherman Act cannot logically escape this position.

minimum test. Something other than 'normal methods of industrial development', said White: something other than the conduct of one 'who does not seek but cannot avoid the control of a market', said Learned Hand.

In the end there is no truly legal test at all, for monopolistic intent, like monopoly power, is an 'ultimate fact'—a question for a jury. It is one of those things of which people say: 'I can't really define it but I know it when I see it.' And indeed it is probably true that juries, and even judges, would get the right answer far more often than not, even though they might well give different accounts of how they arrived at it.[1] Not but what the question—whether a firm is really out for monopoly or is simply making the best mousetrap it can—may at times be very hard to answer, for in the real world motives are often mixed. When the mousetrap producer—by an exclusive contract or by buying financial control—pre-empts an important source of timber or steel wire, is his aim the 'honestly industrial' one of securing a smooth flow of supplies and so enabling an improved production plan to operate, or is he really intent on making things difficult for actual and potential competitors? Quite possibly a bit of each; and that is why the diagnosis of monopolistic purpose under section 2 of the Sherman Act must be subject to the rule of reason. For a modicum of stratagem is to be found in the cleanest fighter's strategy: the question is how much is reasonable.

Certain of the dicta—rather than the statements of law or the decision—in the *ALCOA* case do appear to go to an extreme in suggesting that monopoly power can be innocent only when it is literally 'unavoidable', only when its possessor is a 'passive beneficiary'. (Certainly a mixture of motives is not good enough under the rule of *ALCOA*: where 'honestly industrial' aims and exclusionary aims—or effects—go together, the latter prevail legally.) This may be taken to mean that anything done by a businessman to further his own interests—however reasonable and normal—may subsequently be adduced as proof of monopolistic purpose if in fact monopoly power accrues to him. The government lawyers have in fact taken just this line in some recent cases. In the *Cellophane* case, for example, they contended that only monopoly power which was thrust upon a defendant 'through circumstances beyond his control' was defensible. Judge Leahy, however, held that this was a distortion of Judge Hand's meaning. He recalled that Judge Hand himself had included the

---

[1] This is a point of some importance. You might, for example, disagree strongly with what Judge Learned Hand said as to the considerations that convinced him of ALCOA's monopolistic intent. You would, however, be most unwise to assume from this that, if you had been trying the case and had heard all the evidence, you would have reached a different conclusion.

producer who wins the competitive race 'merely by virtue of his superior skill, foresight and industry' among those who have monopoly 'thrust upon' them. The Supreme Court in the 1946 *Tobacco* case had also included in this class the producer who makes 'a new discovery or an original entry into a new field'. As Judge Leahy put it:

A position achieved by 'superior skill, foresight and industry' or one resulting from 'a new discovery or an original entry into a new field' cannot be achieved through circumstances beyond the defendant's control. Intense research activity, market development and expansion of production capacity were a necessary part of du Pont's development of cellophane. The Sherman Act was not intended to discourage these things. . . . The position taken by plaintiff—the existence of monopoly power standing alone is condemned under the Act, unless thrust upon a defendant by 'circumstances beyond his control'—has no substance as a matter of business reality.

The *Cellophane* case may therefore have heralded the beginnings of a judicial reaction against a too literal interpretation of Judge Hand's 'inevitability' test and perhaps a return to something more akin to Chief Justice White's test of 'normal methods of industrial development'.

The way in which judges and juries[1] answer the question of whether a firm's conduct betrays an intent to monopolize is indeed likely to change somewhat from period to period. The same set of acts will appear in a somewhat different light according to the esteem or lack of it in which 'big business' is held for the time being in the public mind, or according to whether the current standard of what constitutes fair and normal business conduct favours a robust or a nervous view of competition. The test laid down by the judges will necessarily reflect the attitudes of their time.

At all times, however, there has been and will be a large pragmatic element in the decisions. Faced with assessing a firm's power to exclude and its will to exclude, the courts in practice tend to spread their risk of error by looking to the product of the two, such that the more there is of the one, the less there need be of the other, to constitute an offence. Thus, where the firm's power is so great that its very existence tends to act as a barrier against competition, relatively slender indications of an intent or will to exclude, as in the *ALCOA* and *U.S.M.* cases, may be persuasive.[2] Conversely, if a firm's conduct is blatantly

---

[1] The reader may be mystified by the frequent references in this chapter to judges answering what are essentially jury questions. The reason is that most big monopoly trials are civil actions in which the Government complains to a court of equity and seeks relief. In such cases the court is the finder of fact. Even in criminal suits under antitrust it is not uncommon for the defendant as a matter of convenience to waive his right to trial by jury.

[2] It should be noted that Judge Wyzanski in *United States* v. *Grinnell Corp.* (District Court of Massachusetts, 1964) held that the possession of a very high market percentage by the defendant should itself be regarded as a presumption of monopolization. The defendant

predatory, the courts may readily be convinced that it enjoys significant power in some meaningfully defined market.[1] There must always, however, be some admixture of the two elements: monopoly power alone, in the absence of any behaviour that betrays illegal intent, is no offence; and rough business tactics alone cannot be condemned without some evidence of market power.[2] Simple cases, like the *Oil* and *Tobacco* cases of 1911, in which market power and predatory behaviour are both present in high degree, naturally tend to be rarer as time goes on. It is where the evidence is of some but not overwhelming power, and of some but not unequivocally aggressive tactics, that good judgment is particularly required by the courts.

Thus the test of illegal intent is likely to vary with the degree of danger that the courts see in the alleged monopolist's power as well as with historical shifts in economic and social beliefs. Intent is assessed in the light of power. As to whether the inescapable subjective element in all this makes for good law or for too much uncertainty; whether a more objective test is possible or desirable; whether the effects of section 2 of the Sherman Act on American business have been healthy or otherwise—these questions are matters of appraisal and assessment in Part II, below.

himself would then have the burden of proving that his market position was achieved by legitimate methods. The Supreme Court, in upholding Judge Wyzanski's finding that the defendants, manufacturers of fire and burglar alarms, had violated section 2, refused to approve or reject this view, since the evidence showed that the defendants were 'conscious monopolists'. No other court has yet followed Judge Wyzanski's lead, but it might be a mistake to assume that the Supreme Court will never adopt his reasoning.

[1] See the *Klearflax* case below, Chapter V, pp. 131–2.

[2] In 1967 however, the Department of Justice filed suit claiming an illegal *attempt* to monopolize by a company with less than 5 % of the relevant market. The conduct relied upon was the practice of reciprocity, and a count under section 1 of the Sherman Act was included in the complaint (*United States* v. *General Tire & Rubber Co.*, Northern District Court of Ohio, 1967).

MONOPOLIZATION
II. MONOPOLISTIC PRACTICES

1. *Definition of monopolistic practices*

The previous chapter has dealt with the quite small number of cases in the history of antitrust in which the United States Department of Justice has sought to break the dominant hold obtained by a single firm over a whole industry. Such cases are naturally taken first because they exhibit the law of monopolization comprehensively in all its aspects. Section 2 of the Sherman Act may also be used, however, with more limited objectives.

As has been seen, the element of purposive drive that constitutes monopolization may appear in the way monopoly power is acquired and held or in the way it is used. If unlawful purpose is shown in getting and keeping dominant power, it is immaterial whether the power is actually exerted; and if it is unlawfully exerted—with the purpose or effect of raising prices or excluding competitors from the market—it is immaterial that it may have been lawfully acquired or merely 'thrust upon' its possessor. Many cases brought under section 2 deal with particular practices that powerful firms may adopt in building up or maintaining or exerting their power. These may be called monopolistic practices and they broadly correspond to the restrictive practices adopted by agreement between competitors that were considered above (Chapter II).

In this chapter the main lines of cases of this type will be illustrated. In the first part of the chapter the emphasis will be on ways in which a legitimately acquired or 'inescapable' monopoly may run the risk of a charge of monopolizing by the use made of its power. The latter part will consider the law as it relates to various ways in which firms may augment their power in the market—for example, by acquiring competing businesses (horizontal integration), by acquiring their own sources of supply of materials or their own distributive outlets (vertical integration), or by entering into various types of exclusive contract with suppliers or distributors. It will be seen that the cases on this second topic form a link between the big monopoly cases and the case law under the Clayton Act relating to restrictive behaviour on the part of individual concerns which have not necessarily achieved monopoly power.

2. *'Bottleneck' monopolies:* Terminal Railroad of St Louis;
Lorain Journal; Times-Picayune. *Boycotts by monopolies:* Eastman
Kodak *v.* Southern Photo Materials; *the* Klearflax *case*

Monopoly power may be 'thrust upon' a firm as a result of purely physical or technical circumstances. An interesting line of cases illustrates the attitude of antitrust to what have been called 'neck of the bottle' monopolies of this kind.

The classic case of a 'bottleneck' monopoly problem is *United States v. Terminal Railroad Association of St Louis* (1912). The city of St Louis happens to be so sited on a series of hills that it can be approached from the west only by a narrow valley. All railroads coming from the west must use this route, and when the railways were constructed it was seen to be impracticable for each company to have its own separate terminal facilities. In 1889 several railroads joined in constructing terminal facilities and set up a jointly owned company, the Terminal Railroad Association of St Louis, to run them. The Government brought a civil action against this company under the Sherman Act, on the ground that its operation suppressed competition.

The Supreme Court, applying the rule of reason, took the view that the unification of the terminal facilities was not in itself an illegal combination in restraint of trade. In a normal case a number of railroads getting together in a joint enterprise for this purpose would be unlikely to run up against the law; for if they made the terms on which other railroads could use the facilities too onerous, those concerned could simply construct their own terminus elsewhere in the city.

The physical situation in St Louis, however, was such that this option could not in practice be exercised. The Supreme Court held that although the group's monopoly power was legitimately acquired, it was incumbent on them, as a matter of law, not to use this power oppressively. The contract setting up the joint company had stipulated that railroads outside the proprietary group might only be admitted 'to joint use of said terminal system on unanimous consent, but not otherwise, of the Directors of the first party, and on payment of such consideration as they may determine'. In other words, the proprietary group had retained a power of veto and a power to discriminate in the matter of charges against any newcomers who might wish, and in the circumstances require, to use the facilities. These conditions in the contract were held to violate the Sherman Act, and the Court directed that the joint company be reorganized so as to permit non-proprietary companies to make proper and equal use of the facilities on terms that were reasonable and non-discriminatory.

Some rather similar situations have occurred in later cases. *Gamco v.*

Providence Fruit and Produce Building (First Circuit Court of Appeals, 1952) concerned a fruit and vegetable market in Providence, Rhode Island. The market was constructed by a subsidiary company of the New Haven Railroad and was subsequently leased to Providence Fruit and Produce Building Incorporated, a company in which the stock was mostly held by local wholesalers. Practically all the local trade in fruit and vegetables was centred in the building, which was thus a kind of 'neck of the bottle' monopoly. One of the proprietary wholesalers, Gamco, got into financial difficulties and they amalgamated with another wholesaler to whom they transferred their stock in the market building. This was said to be an infringement of a covenant in Gamco's lease and they were told to quit the building. Since their exclusion from the facilities of the market was found to impose a considerable competitive handicap on Gamco, it was held by the Circuit Court of Appeals that this exclusionary action constituted an abuse of monopoly power.

Where, as here, a business group, understandably susceptible to the temptations of exploiting its natural advantages against competitors, prohibits one previously acceptable from hawking his wares beside them any longer at the very moment of his affiliation with a potentially lower-priced outsider, they may be called upon for a necessary explanation. The conjunction of power and motive to exclude, with an exclusion not immediately and patently justified by reasonable business requirements, establishes a prima facie case of the purpose to monopolize.

The defendants in this case had not shown any good reason for the exclusion and consequently the Court awarded Gamco equitable relief: '. . . The plaintiff should be accorded space in the building as a tenant on terms similar to those accorded others, at once if available without dispossessing innocent parties, otherwise as soon as available.'

Monopoly may also be 'thrust upon' a concern for economic reasons, as where, for example, a market is large enough to support only one firm. This situation is not uncommon in the production of newspapers in the United States, where there are many towns that cannot support more than one paper. Cases of the misuse of monopoly power have arisen in this field.

In *United States* v. *Lorain Journal Company* (Supreme Court, 1951), the newspaper concerned had a circulation of only about 20,000 copies but even so was thought to reach 99% of all families in the city of Lorain, Ohio. It was clear that the town could not support a rival paper; it could, however, support a radio station and one was set up in 1948. The radio station derived most of its income from local and national advertising, in getting which it was in direct competition with the *Lorain Journal*. The Government alleged that, as soon as the radio station was set up, the *Lorain Journal* made it a condition of accepting advertisements in the paper that the advertiser should not advertise over the local radio; moreover, they took care to monitor the radio programmes to identify the businesses advertising by radio.

Although both the paper and the radio station operated in one small locality in the State of Ohio, the contention that interstate commerce was not affected was rejected by the Supreme Court on the ground that the dissemination of national news broadcasts and national advertising was part of interstate commerce. The Court found that the newspaper publisher was illegally seeking to maintain its local advertising monopoly; even though the newspaper monopoly had been 'thrust upon' the company, it was an offence against section 2 of the Sherman Act to use the power it gave in this way. In effect the newspaper was trying to force the local advertisers to boycott the radio station, and this in itself was an attempt to exclude a competitor. The fact that the radio station had not been put out of business altogether, at least by the time the case was brought, was irrelevant, since the course of action showed a quite specific purpose on the part of the newspaper to destroy threatened competition. Thus the Government won the case and the Court handed down a decree prohibiting the *Lorain Journal* from refusing to publish advertisements for the reason that the advertiser also supported the radio station.

Another important case on this topic is *Times-Picayune Publishing Company* v. *United States* (Supreme Court, 1953). In this case the Government's complaint was about the exclusion of the competition not of a radio station but of another newspaper. The Times-Picayune company is the leading newspaper publisher in New Orleans, producing both morning and evening papers, *The Times-Picayune* and *The States* respectively. It had no competitors in the morning, but there was at that time a rival evening paper, *The Item*. The company sold its advertising on a so-called 'unit plan', whereby the advertiser had to take space in both the morning and evening papers. (Evidence was given that before the 'unit plan' was introduced, fewer than half of the advertisers in the morning paper also bought space in the evening.) Since the advertiser had to take space in *The States* if he was to reach the morning paper readers through *The Times-Picayune*, the unit plan made it less likely on the face of it that he would buy space in *The Item*. The Government contended that this was an illegal misuse of the Times-Picayune's monopoly of morning papers.

The Government lost this case by a five to four decision of the Supreme Court. The four judges in the dissenting minority would have condemned the company on the ground that it enjoyed a 'monopoly' of access to morning readers and had used the power of this monopoly to 'tie up' the advertisers who wanted to reach the evening readers. On this analysis the analogy with the *Lorain Journal* case would have been close. The majority, however, took another view of the relevant market. Adding together the advertising 'line-age' that appeared in all three New Orleans daily newspapers, they found that *The Times-Picayune* (the morning paper) accounted for only 40%, and this did not seem to them enough to constitute a dominant position. In other words, it did not seem to be a case in which leverage obtained by dominance in one market was used to hamper a competitor in a second market, for they did not agree that the readers of morning newspapers and the readers of evening newspapers were to be regarded as separate markets from the point of view of the advertisers.

While this particular argument seems artificial to the point of being hardly defensible,[1] the decision may be seen as an interesting application of the rule of reason. What seems to have weighed most with the majority was evidence that the unit plan of selling advertising space had been adopted by many newspaper publishers for sound business reasons, in particular 'as a competitive weapon in the rivalry for national advertising accounts'. Indeed, at the time when the publisher of *The Item* also produced a morning paper, it too had used a unit plan; and when both companies used the unit plan, the Times-Picayune company had gone ahead of its rival rather more quickly, if anything, than subsequently. Meanwhile *The Item* still flourished and 1950 was actually its record year for both circulation and advertising. In other words, there was little to show that the unit plan was a factor seriously impairing *The Item*'s competitive strength. And if there was an element of stratagem in the Times-Picayune's policy, it was no more than a reasonable response to business conditions. Lastly, *The Item* had not in fact been driven out of business,[2] so that if an 'attempt to monopolize' was to be proved against Times-Picayune, there would need to be a showing of 'specific intent'. As Mr Justice Clark put it: 'Since we have viewed that step [the unit plan] as predominantly motivated by legitimate business aims, this record cannot bear out the specific intent essential to sustain an attempt to monopolize under section 2.'

[1] Professors J. B. Dirlam and A. E. Kahn, in their book *Fair Competition: the Law and Economics of Anti-trust Policy*, Cornell University Press, 1954, have brilliantly exposed the errors of this curious argument. In particular they point out that by taking all advertising line-age as the relevant market, the Court was lumping together the 'tying' with the 'tied' product: in reality it was *The Times-Picayune*'s 100% control of the morning market that provided the leverage in the evening market, just as in *Griffith* and *Schine* the cinema chains' 100% share of 'closed' towns provided leverage in 'open' towns. Dirlam and Kahn also point out that if *The Item* had ceased publication, *The Times-Picayune* still could not have gained more than 50% of total advertising line-age because of the unit plan itself: in this light their actual 40% share looks substantial.

[2] It is an interesting postcript to this case that *The Item* went out of business by selling to *The Times-Picayune* in July 1958.

Despite the fact that the *Times-Picayune* case was lost by the Government,[1] the lesson of the 'bottleneck' cases in general is clear enough. They establish that if you have dominant power in the market, no matter how innocently and inescapably you came by it, you are obliged under antitrust to take the greatest care not to 'throw it about'. If a rival comes into the field, you must avoid doing anything by way of 'tying up' your established suppliers or customers so that he cannot obtain equal access to them. If your monopoly consists of some physical facility like a rail or bus terminus or a market building, you must even take your new rival in and share the facility with him without discrimination, unless it is clear that he is physically able to obtain or construct equivalent facilities for himself. As in the *Associated Press* case,[2] the facility in question does not have to be indispensable for its denial to a rival to constitute a misuse of monopoly power. It is enough that the denial imposes a real competitive handicap on him. The only way to defend business activity which is prima facie exclusionary is, as in the case of the Times-Picayune unit plan, to show that it is on merits a reasonable and normal response to conditions, and also that it has neither the effect nor the purpose of driving out or seriously impeding a competitor.

As a footnote to this section it must also be noted that a refusal by a dominant firm to trade with a small firm, whether as supplier or buyer, may be regarded in effect as a one-man boycott and hence as a misuse of market power. A good illustration is *Eastman Kodak Company of New York* v. *Southern Photo Materials Company* (Supreme Court, 1927). Southern Photo Materials was a wholesaler of photographic materials in Georgia. For a long time it dealt in Eastman Kodak goods, but when Eastman Kodak acquired control of competing wholesalers in Georgia (and incidentally attempted unsuccessfully to buy out Southern Photo Materials), further supplies were refused except at retail prices. In the trial Court a jury had decided that the refusal 'was in furtherance of a purpose to monopolize and constituted an actionable wrong' and treble damages were awarded against Eastman Kodak. The Supreme Court upheld this result.

Another interesting case is *United States* v. *Klearflax Linen Looms* (1945). Klearflax was the only manufacturer of a particular type of linen rug. One of its distributors successfully underbid it for a government contract and, when Klearflax found out about this, it refused to supply the distributor with the rugs needed to fulfil the contract. It also reduced the distributor to the status of a jobber, which meant trading at a

---

[1] It seems likely that this decision can stand for little beyond the particular set of facts in question.

[2] Outlined above, Chapter II, pp. 67 ff.

lower discount level. A District Court held that these punitive measures violated section 2 of the Sherman Act, in that they showed a purpose 'to monopolize the sale of linen rugs in the line of commerce involved in the government contract business'.

This is incidentally an excellent example of a court's practical outlook on what constitutes a separate 'market' or 'line of commerce'. Linen rugs are only one type of rug, and rugs are only one type of floor-covering. The economist might well place the product in the middle of a continuous series of substitutes and wonder how the concept of monopoly could sensibly apply. The answer is that the Court was not interested in the theoretical question of whether these particular linen rugs constituted a separate product which could be monopolized. The Court saw only that a public authority had wanted a consignment of these rugs, and that the firm which made the lowest bid to supply them had been ousted from its competitive opportunity by the power of the manufacturer. Thus the 'market' in this case was simply that market which Klearflax had gone after. Had the public authority been interested in some other type of floorcovering, there would have been no point in the predatory use made by Klearflax of its control of the product. Since it took predatory action, it must have thought it worth-while; there must have been something worth fighting for, and that was market enough for the purpose of the case.

It is clear that in condemning these one-man boycotts the courts must have particular regard to intent and purpose. It would be another faulty use of the analogy between restrictive agreements and the behaviour of single powerful firms to argue that, because a boycott agreement is illegal *per se*, therefore any refusal by a dominant firm to trade must also be illegal *per se*. In this form the analogy once again suppresses the vital element of intent. A collective boycott agreement is purposely restrictive more or less by definition: but this is not the case with a single firm's refusal to trade. In one sense a huge business like Eastman Kodak is always 'boycotting'; in so far as it buys from (or sells to) X, it may be unable to buy also from (or sell to) Y. There may be many sound business reasons for such a firm to change its supplier of some material or to drop an account among its dealers. It would be an obviously impossible position if a dominant firm were put under an obligation to deal with all who wished to trade with it. The courts have recognized this in practice, and it is when normal business reasons cannot plausibly be offered as an explanation for refusing to deal and when, on the contrary, there is evidence of a purpose to sup-press smaller rivals, as in the cases quoted above, that the individual refusal to deal becomes actionable as a misuse of monopoly power. Nevertheless, the powerful firm undoubtedly has to exercise the greatest caution, as the law stands, about cutting off a dealer or taking its business away from an established supplier; this is particularly the case when the firm has integrated backwards or forwards and has its own distributing or supplying subsidiaries, for in such a case it is only too easy for the refusal to deal to appear, rightly or wrongly, as a purposive exclusion of competition with the subsidiary companies.

3. *Monopoly and price discrimination: the* A. & P. *case*

The next case to consider forms a link between the two different aspects of the subject matter treated in this chapter. This is *United States* v. *The New York Great Atlantic and Pacific Tea Company* (Seventh Circuit Court of Appeals, 1949). The Government was here attacking both the misuse of the company's market power directly to injure its retail competitors, and the arrangements it was able to make with its suppliers to augment its power in retail markets. The means by which the company deployed its power on both the selling and buying sides of the market was price discrimination, and the case also forms a link, therefore, with the case law under the Robinson-Patman Act. As will appear below (Chapter IX) the Robinson-Patman Act is antitrust's normal weapon against price discrimination, but the *A. & P.* case shows that this practice may also be the basis of monopolistic offences under section 2 of the Sherman Act.

The defendant in this criminal case was the holding company controlling the large group of concerns making up the A. & P. food chain. This is a vertically integrated group, incorporating manufacturers, processors, brokers and retailers; but retail trade is its main concern and at the time of trial it operated some 5,800 stores all over the United States. It was never suggested that A. & P. had anything approaching a monopoly in the retailing of food generally. A. & P. is only one of a number of large chains which compete with great numbers of independent shops in every area, and its share of retail food sales has never exceeded 20% in any substantial part of the United States, let alone over the country as a whole.

The contention was, however, that A. & P.'s vast scale of operations gave it effective power in many different markets. On the selling side there were many shopping centres in the United States where the local A. & P. dominated the grocery trade, and there was some evidence that local grocers had been put out of business by what the Court called 'the lethal competition put upon them by A. & P. when armed with its monopoly power'. It was said that A. & P. aimed at different rates of return from its stores according to the degree of competition they had to face: 'If Area X is having a tough experience competitionwise, or the area looks prospective in which to increase the volume of business, the gross profit percentage in this area is lowered. This lowers the price at which goods may be sold and the volume increases at the expense of somebody. Sometimes the gross profit rate is fixed so low that the store runs below the cost of operation.' This selective variation of price levels was held to be one of the ways in which A. & P. misused its power.[1] The Court based its conclusion on this topic partly on the view that the group could afford to reduce its returns in the competitive areas only if it were doing very nicely elsewhere. 'There must inevitably be a compensation somewhere in the system for a loss somewhere else, as the overall policy of the group is to earn $7 per share per annum on its stock.'

But the essence of the case lay in A. & P.'s practices on the buying side. The general complaint was that the group exploited its buying power to insist on lower prices than those available to its competitors. Evidence was presented of various means that it adopted to this end. Suppliers who would not 'play' were said, for example, to be placed on a private black list or faced with the threat that the group would go into the manufacturing business in competition with them.

At one time suppliers were required to make a 5% brokerage payment to A. & P.'s own buying agents, but the brokerage provisions of the Robinson-Patman Act eventually made this illegal. Thereafter the group insisted that suppliers reduce their prices by the amount of the previous brokerage and this reduction was said to be an extra discount granted to A. & P. solely by virtue of its market power. Under the Robinson-Patman Act any such discount must be justified by a showing that it reflects only the cost savings resulting from the buying method or the large quantities purchased, and the defence claimed that the discounts met this test. The Court held, however, that the discounts obtained by A. & P. were larger than any cost savings justified. 'One cannot escape the conclusion, on the very substantial evidence here, as one follows the devious manipulations of A. & P. to get price advantages, that it succeeded in obtaining preferential discounts not by force of its large purchasing power and the buying advantage which goes therewith, but through its abuse of that power by the threats to boycott suppliers and place them on its individual black list, and by threats to go into the manufacturing and processing business itself, since it already possessed a considerable establishment and experience that would enable it to get quickly and successfully into such business if a recalcitrant supplier, processor or manufacturer did not yield.'

[1] For the way in which this practice has been treated in Robinson-Patman Act cases, see below, Chapter IX, pp. 248–9.

Another part of the story dealt with a subsidiary of the group known as the Atlantic Commission Company (ACCO). This company had the dual function of acting as buyer of fruit, vegetables and produce for A. & P. and as a broker in transactions with the rest of the trade.[1] ACCO was indeed the largest broker in the field. Because of the Robinson-Patman Act it could not, after 1936, take brokerage from suppliers for the merchandise it passed on to A. & P. But it was alleged that, through ACCO, A. & P. got the best of the merchandise at the lowest prices and other kinds of preferential treatment. For example, while taking the normal discounts for cash buying (by which the buyer of perishable foods usually assumes considerable risks), A. & P., through ACCO, got a guarantee from suppliers that all deliveries would be of the top grade. This guarantee was not open to ACCO's other customers. Another device was for ACCO to get perishable foods delivered to A. & P. without accepting any obligation to purchase until their arrival. At this point a 'take it or leave it' offer could be made, and A. & P. were thus protected if prices fell between the time of shipment and the time of arrival.

But the main charge was again that ACCO was a means for profiting by discrimination. 'When ACCO purchased in the open market for A. & P., even though it paid the market price, it always came out with an advantage not only in the quality of merchandise but in price. Supose an item was selling in the market at 100, ACCO could buy it for A. & P. and have its choice of quality at 95. The balance of the trade could buy at 100 and pay ACCO a 5% brokerage. Thus, the price to A. & P. was 95 and to A. & P.'s competitors 105.'

Throughout his opinion Judge Minton laid much stress on the point that profits made by ACCO as a broker accrued to the A. & P. group. 'From this evidence, we see that ACCO collected brokerage from the trade which increased the price to A. & P. competitors, and the brokerage went into A. & P. coffers to increase its competitive advantage.' He argued that the profits of the manufacturing companies owned by the group were similarly 'available' to enable the group to lower their retail prices to the disadvantage of smaller competitors. Indeed, he went on to add up all the profits made by ACCO and the manufacturing companies, together with all the preferential discounts and allowances made to the group, and to show that 90% of the group's total profits came from these sources, leaving only 10% as the profit from the vast chain of retail stores.

---

[1] There was evidence that ACCO took brokerage commission both from suppliers of produce and from buyers (other than A. & P.) and generally of what the District Court described as 'odorous, unjustified transactions'. See Dirlam and Kahn, *Fair Competition*, p. 79.

This seemed to the Court to confirm the proposition that the concessions squeezed out of suppliers were used to finance predatory competition in the retail field to the harm of small, independent retailers. 'With this large fund accumulated at the buying and supplying level and allocated to the advantage of low cost of merchandise at the retail or selling level, A. & P.'s enormous power or advantage over competitors emerges more clearly when we consider the evidence on the retail level. Here the price advantage A. & P. has enjoyed through the coercive use of its power enables it to undersell its competitors and to pick and choose the locations in which the price advantage shall be used.'

So Judge Minton came to his conclusions of law. First, A. & P.'s private black list of suppliers who declined to make the concessions demanded was, he said, 'a boycott, and in and of itself a violation of the Sherman Act'. Secondly, the evidence led inescapably to the conclusion that A. & P. 'was encouraging its suppliers to violate the Robinson-Patman Act'. Finally: 'With the concessions on the buying level acquired by the predatory application of its massed purchasing power, A. & P. was enabled to pressure its competitors on the selling level even to the extent of selling below cost and making up the loss in areas where competitive conditions were more favourable. The inevitable consequence of this whole business pattern is to create a chain reaction of ever increasing selling volume and ever increasing requirements and hence purchasing power for A. & P., and for its competitors hardships not produced by competitive forces and, conceivably, ultimate extinction. Under all the cases this is a result which sections 1 and 2 of the Sherman Act were designed to circumvent.'

Thus A. & P. was found guilty of the criminal charges laid against it and fines were imposed. The Government later brought a civil action in order to obtain equity relief including the dissolution of the group into a number of smaller companies. In 1954 this action was settled by a consent decree under which, among other things, the ACCO subsidiary had to be divorced from the group or dissolved and the group was forbidden to aggregate the requirements of all its stores for the purpose of getting specially high rates of discount. But no dissolution of the retail business into smaller parts was ordered.

Some of the dicta in Judge Minton's opinion directed to the economics of the case have been severely criticized.[1] It has been pointed out, for example, that the profits made by ACCO from the brokerage business and by the group's manufacturing subsidiaries represented, at least in

[1] See, for example, Professor Morris Adelman's article 'Integration and Antitrust Policy', *Harvard Law Review*, vol. 63, part 1, November 1949, p. 27. Another article by the same writer, 'The A. & P. Case: A Study in Applied Economic Theory', *Quarterly Journal of Economics*, vol. 63, no. 2, May 1949, p. 238, challenges the economic conceptions underlying the Government's brief in the case.

part, a legitimate return on the group's investment in these activities. Hence it was wrong to imply that it cost the group nothing to apply these funds to reducing retail prices. (The reductions, of course, could still be predatory whatever the source of the funds that financed them.) There has also been criticism of the calculation by which Judge Minton concluded that when the market price of produce was 100, A. & P., buying through ACCO, got it for 95 while other retailers paid 105. A. & P.'s competitors were free to use or not to use ACCO or any other broker as they pleased. The fact that they chose to employ brokers at a cost to them of 5% suggests that they found it paid to do so; and the fact that ACCO became the biggest broker in the field suggests that the trade generally liked its service. Nor is the fact that a broker as large as ACCO could buy at 95 particularly surprising, since they performed a valuable jobbing service for the suppliers. Finally, the fact that ACCO could buy at 95 did not mean that A. & P. was getting the merchandise for 95, since the services for which ACCO charged 5% to other people still had to be carried out to get the goods into A. & P.'s individual stores, and it is clearly false to assume that these services cost nothing in an integrated business. The critics conclude that the gap between 95 and 105 gives a quite misleading impression of A. & P.'s cost advantage, and add, moreover, that such gap as would remain after more refined calculation might reflect no more than the genuine economies which the A. & P. group gained by integration, which ought to be encouraged.

Indeed, the general complaint of critics of this case is, in brief, that the Department of Justice and the courts alike failed to maintain a clear distinction between competitive advantages, which A. & P. created by initiative and efficiency, and 'unfair' advantages, which they were alleged to obtain by abuses of market power. The Court came near, it is suggested, to holding that it is 'unfair' *per se* for an integrated organization like A. & P. to enjoy competitive advantages of any kind. But, while there may well be grounds for criticism of some of the things that the government briefs and the courts said, it is a different matter to complain that the result of the case was unjust. A. & P. itself, after all, did not exercise their right to petition the Supreme Court for a writ of *certiorari*.

The truth probably is that the company's aims and motives were mixed, directed certainly to improving the efficiency of its service but also to making life difficult for its competitors; and, as already noted, a mixture of motives is not good enough under the Sherman Act. Neither the trial Court which heard all the evidence at first hand, nor the Court of Appeals which reviewed it, had any difficulty in deciding that A. & P. had market power and exerted it in a course of conduct that betrayed an intent to exclude competition.[1] The law of the case does not therefore go beyond the rules set out in Chapter IV, though it may not perhaps be one of those in which market power or predatory behaviour is most clearly marked. The critics of the case may still raise the question of whether a large business concern that wishes to compete vigorously and effectively, yet within the rules, can in practice ensure its legal safety within the fine lines drawn by Judge Minton in this opinion. Can such a firm never exert its countervailing power against a supplier by threatening to manufacture itself, or meet vigorous competition in a particular area with lower than normal prices? And if not, will not the consumer lose rather than gain by the inhibition? But these questions verge on the task of assessment and must therefore be deferred to a later chapter.

4. *Mergers and acquisitions:* Columbia Steel

We turn now to those monopolistic practices which aim at building up or augmenting market power. One way to create a monopoly is by the consolidation of previously competing companies. Two leading concerns, for example, may amalgamate, or a company with, say, a 40% share of output in its industry and only limited power in the market may set about buying up its smaller competitors to the point where effective power is established. Horizontal integration of this kind may be a method of monopolizing under section 2 of the Sherman Act.

The line of railway merger cases described early in Chapter IV, for example, showed that the creation of monopoly power by bringing competing companies under the unified financial control of a trust or holding company was a sure way to infringe the Act. But not all acquisitions result in monopoly power. In 1921, for example, *Geddes* v. *Anaconda Copper Mining Company* (Supreme Court) dealt with a situation in which Anaconda, controlling some 22% of the domestic output of copper, acquired another small copper company. It was decided that this relatively small proportion did not give Anaconda monopoly power; consequently there was no violation of the Act. These two extreme examples point the way to another of the borderline problems of antitrust, namely how to distinguish between those acquisitions and mergers which are legitimate and those which amount to a sufficient build-up of power to constitute monopolizing. The cases brought under the Sherman Act form a link with section 7 of the Clayton Act, under which any acquisition of a competing company is illegal 'where the effect may be to substantially lessen competition . . .'.

---

[1] See the analysis of the District Court opinion given by Dirlam and Kahn, *Fair Competition*, pp. 78–80.

A leading case in which the borderline under the law of the Sherman Act was explored is *United States* v. *Columbia Steel Company* (Supreme Court, 1948). This was a case in which the Government sought to bar the United States Steel Corporation from purchasing the assets of an independent steel maker on the Pacific coast on the grounds that the acquisition would restrain competition and that it was an attempt by the United States Steel group to monopolize the market in certain fabricated steel products.

The facts in this case involved both horizontal and vertical integration, which it will be desirable to consider separately when we come to the legal issues. The United States Steel Corporation and its subsidiaries mainly produce rolled-steel products in semi-manufactured form— about one-third of the total United States output. They also make finished products in heavy structural steel but they do not fabricate from steel plate. Thus they use some of their 'semis' themselves and also sell vast quantities to other fabricators. Columbia Steel is their main subsidiary in the Pacific coast area, producing 'semis' and acting as selling agent for the group's other rolled-steel subsidiaries and for its structural-steel business.

During the Second World War the United States Government had set up a steel rolling plant in Geneva, Utah, which had been operated for the Government by United States Steel. After the war the Government set about disposing of such plants to private industry; and although United States Steel at first decided not to bid for the Geneva plant, the Government solicited a bid from them and eventually, in June 1946, sold it to them.

The proposed sale was submitted to the Attorney General and cleared by him as not offensive to the Sherman Act. The acquisition of the Geneva plant would, it was calculated, raise United States Steel's ingot capacity only from 31.4% to 32.7% of national capacity, and the group had previously had a much higher percentage of capacity than this.[1] (It will be remembered that it was about 50% at the time of the 1920 case against United States Steel.)

United States Steel arranged to set up a cold-reduction mill at Pittsburg, California, to gear in with the Geneva output. In the negotiations for the Geneva plant they had said nothing about fabricating facilities to provide a market for the hot-rolled and cold-rolled 'semis' coming from the Geneva and Pittsburg plants, and the Government evidently supposed that the operation of these plants would encourage new independent fabricators to set up in the Pacific area.

---

[1] According to United States Steel's own figure, however, it gave them 51% of the ingot capacity of the far western States.

Meanwhile, the Consolidated Steel Corporation had been in contact with a number of big steel producers with a view to disposing of its business. This was a purely fabricating business, producing structural-steel and plate products from rolled 'semis' which it brought in. Its total requirement for 'semis' represented less than $\frac{1}{2}\%$ of annual national consumption and only about 3% of the 'semis' used in the eleven far western States. By defining the 'market' as consisting of just those kinds of rolled 'semis'—plates and shapes—that Consolidated in fact used, it could be shown that their requirements were 13% of the western market. United States Steel had all along wanted fabricating facilities in the west (other big groups, including Bethlehem, had them) and had considered erecting plants. On investigation they found that it would be cheaper to buy the Consolidated plant than build a new plant. This they proceeded to do in December 1946.

The Government now brought suit under the Sherman Act against this additional acquisition, partly on the theory that Consolidated would become tied to the United States Steel group for its supply of rolled 'semis', so that competition, which would otherwise have taken place between United States Steel and other steel makers for Consolidated's business, would be eliminated. This line of attack was directed against the element of vertical integration in the situation, and we shall consider it below as part of the line of cases dealing with that subject.

The Government also launched a two-pronged attack against the acquisition considered as a measure of horizontal integration. It was, they claimed, an offence under section 1 of the Sherman Act, because the elimination of existing competition between the United States Steel group and Consolidated as producers of structural steel and pipe was an illegal restraint of trade. Also, viewed in the light of many previous acquisitions by the group, it was an attempt to monopolize the western market for structural steel and pipe.

The strongest evidence put in by the Government in support of these charges was that in 1946 United States Steel took 13% of the orders for structural steel in the western market and Consolidated took 11%, so that the merger would bring 24% under the group's control. Against this the defence argued that, with the new ingot capacity available in the west, United States Steel's eastern fabricating plants would become less able to compete, because of heavy freight costs, against local fabricators of structural steel in the west. Moreover, the types of structural steel made by United States Steel and Consolidated only partly overlapped; much of their output was non-competitive. Similar points were made in respect of steel pipe.

The trial Court had found on this evidence, and the Supreme Court agreed, that the amount of competition eliminated was too small to involve a significant restraint of trade. It had been argued that the sheer magnitude of the business at stake should be decisive, but Mr Justice Reed said: 'In determining what constitutes unreasonable restraint we do not think the dollar volume is in itself of compelling significance; we look rather to the percentage of business controlled, the strength of the remaining competition, whether the action springs from business requirements or purpose to monopolize, the probable development of the industry, consumer demands and other characteristics of the market.'

The Government based its case of monopolization on the same facts. The Supreme Court pointed out, however, that, since United States Steel clearly had not achieved monopoly power in the western market, the relevant charge must be that of 'attempting to monopolize' and this required a showing of 'specific intent' to monopolize; the Government had relied merely on general inferences from United States Steel's previous acquisitions. Anyway, the Government had been directly involved in the much larger acquisitions of the Geneva and Pittsburg plants without raising any objection; and it seemed unlikely that objection would have been raised if United States Steel had built their own fabricating plant instead of buying Consolidated. Mr Justice Reed concluded that it was much more plausible to interpret the latest acquisition as reflecting a 'normal business purpose' than as showing a specific intent to monopolize. Commenting on the general issue of United States Steel's position in the industry, he added: 'Its size is impressive. Size has significance also in an appraisal of alleged violations of the Sherman Act. But the steel industry is also of impressive size and the welcome westward extension of that industry requires that the existing companies go into production there or abandon that market to other organizations.'

Thus the application of the Sherman Act to horizontal mergers inevitably involves the courts in the exercise of the rule of reason to decide 'where to draw the line'. Taking the most unfavourable view of the figures, the most that could be said of this acquisition (qua horizontal merger) was that 24% of some kinds of structural steel would be brought under United States Steel's control in the western market. This degree of consolidation in the market could not confer power over price nor did it tend to exclude competition. Accordingly the Court found that, since United States Steel neither sought nor obtained monopoly power, the acquisition did not violate the Sherman Act. It could not be compared, for example, with the early railway mergers, in which the only substantial competitors were brought under unified financial control.

In 1950 (partly because of the decision in Columbia Steel) section 7 of the Clayton Act was revised and stiffened by the Celler-Kefauver Act and most cases dealing with horizontal integration have subsequently been dealt with under that section (see Chapter VII below). Following the enactment of the Bank Mergers Act of 1960, however, it was believed (wrongly, as it later turned out) that if commercial banking mergers had received approval from the Comptroller of the Currency under that Act the Clayton Act did not apply. Accordingly the Department of Justice, when it decided in 1961 to challenge the merger between the First National Bank and Trust Company of Lexington ('First National') and the Security Trust Company of Lexington ('Security Trust') brought suit under sections 1 and 2 of the Sherman Act.

First National at the date of the merger had been the largest bank in Fayette County, Kentucky (the relevant geographic market) and Security Trust the fourth largest, and the new bank formed as a result of the combination was larger than all the other banks in the market put together. The trust departments of the banks were the two largest in the county, controlling over 90% of all trust assets deposited with all banks in the county. The Supreme Court found that the merging companies were 'major competitive factors' in the relevant market, and that the elimination of significant competition between them violated section 1 of the Sherman Act.

On this occasion the early railroad merger cases were cited in support of the Court's decision, as were the criteria for judging Sherman Act merger cases used by Mr Justice Reed in *Columbia Steel*. Justices Harlan and Stewart in a dissenting opinion, however, felt that the Court's opinion amounted to 'a presumption that in the antitrust field good things are usually, if not always, in small packages'. Questioning whether the railroad cases had any relevance to the present facts, they pointed out that in *Columbia Steel* the proposition that control by one competitor over another necessarily violated the Sherman Act had not found favour with the Court. Of the criteria referred to by Mr Justice Reed only the figures of the dollar volume and the percentage of business control could be said to tell against the banks, and there was nothing in the findings of the trial Court pertinent to the effect of the merger on competition, the probable development of the industry, consumer demands and other market characteristics which would support the Court's finding. The decision was tantamount to saying that the merger was bad because the merged banks would be 'big'.

Nevertheless, the principles enunciated by the *Lexington* case were subsequently applied in another bank merger case, *United States* v.

Manufacturers Hanover Trust Company (Southern District Court of New York, 1965). Manufacturers Trust Company was a bank specializing in retail accounts, that is small and medium-size accounts, catering to the mass needs of the general public and small business. It had arranged a merger with the Hanover Bank, largely a 'wholesale' bank dealing with large corporations, government bodies, financial institutions and wealthy individuals, and the merger had actually been consummated when Department of Justice brought suit against it under section 1 of the Sherman Act.

After an exhaustive consideration of the characteristics of both the local and national markets, Judge MacMahon found that there was a direct relationship between the number of branches operated by a bank and its market share of retail accounts, and that the merger would result in control by the combined bank of over 20% of the branch banking offices in the metropolitan New York area, and in a concentration of over 80% of those offices in the hands of the five largest banks in the area. The permanent elimination of the significant competition formerly existing between major companies was itself, under the rule in *Lexington Bank*, enough to make the merger a violation of section 1 of the Sherman Act.

5. *Vertical integration:* Yellow Cab; Columbia Steel

The *Columbia Steel* case also raised the question whether vertical integration might not be a monopolistic device for augmenting and consolidating a powerful firm's hold on the market. One of the Government's charges was that United States Steel, as a dominant supplier of rolled-steel 'semis', was illegally restraining trade in acquiring the business of a substantial user of 'semis', because the result would be that the user (Consolidated) would in future take all its requirements of 'semis' from United States Steel and that that part of the market for 'semis' would thus be foreclosed to United States Steel's competitors.[1]

The idea that vertical integration might in itself be a monopolistic practice is a recent development in antitrust; no case prior to the Second World War could be said to turn on this particular question. It came into prominence in a Supreme Court opinion written in 1947 by Mr Justice Murphy in *United States* v. *Yellow Cab Company*. It must be noted that this opinion was not given after a trial of the issues in that particular case—indeed the Government eventually lost the case—but was

---

[1] This charge, like several more in the rest of this chapter, was actually brought under section 1 of the Sherman Act against a contract in restraint of trade. This does not, of course, alter the fact that its legal content belongs more to the field of monopolizing than to that of restrictive agreements.

directed to quashing a decision of a lower Court summarily dismissing the charges on the ground that the Government had made out no case for the defence to answer. The opinion dealt therefore in general terms with the legal issues presented by vertical integration.

The case concerned a company called the Checker Cab Manufacturing Corporation (C.C.M.) which manufactured taxicabs and a group of affiliated companies which ran taxicabs in various cities. The group eventually won control of over 80% of the cabs operating in Chicago and high percentages in three other big towns. There was an agreement that the operating companies would purchase cabs only from the manufacturing company. The Government took the view that this agreement illegally foreclosed a large market for cabs. In towns where the operating companies had a dominant position, other manufacturers of cabs found a closed market. Meanwhile the operating companies in the group were not taking advantage of competition between the manufacturers of cabs.

Mr Justice Murphy's first premise in applying the Sherman Act to this situation was that unreasonable restraints of trade were outlawed by section 1 regardless of the amount of the commerce affected. Secondly, section 2 made it unlawful to monopolize 'any part' of interstate commerce and did not specify how large a part must be affected. As he put it: 'It is enough if some appreciable part of interstate commerce is the subject of a monopoly, a restraint or a conspiracy.'

The supply of replacements for a fleet of some 5,000 taxicabs in four cities was, he said, 'an appreciable amount of commerce under any standard'. Thus the Government did not need to prove that the manufacturing company had a monopoly by reference to all the taxicabs in the United States. 'By excluding all cab manufacturers other than C.C.M. from that part of the market represented by the cab operating companies under their control, the appellees effectively limit the outlets through which cabs may be sold in interstate commerce.' Mr Justice Murphy also took the point that the agreement might restrain trade by preventing the operating companies from buying cabs in a free competitive market.

He then turned to the legal significance of the fact that the parties to the restrictive contract were affiliated companies. On this point he said: 'The fact that these restraints occur in a setting described by the appellees as a vertically integrated enterprise does not necessarily remove the ban of the Sherman Act. The test of illegality under the Act is the presence or absence of an unreasonable restraint on interstate commerce. Such a restraint may result as readily from a conspiracy among those who are affiliated or integrated under a common ownership as from a conspiracy among those who are otherwise independent. Similarly, any affiliation or integration flowing from an illegal conspiracy cannot insulate the conspirators from the sanctions which Congress has imposed.'

He concluded that if the Government showed that the integration of the manufacturing with the operating companies was a calculated and purposive plan to restrain or build up monopoly power, it would involve a plain violation of the Act. When the case came to trial, however, the trial Court found, and the Supreme Court later agreed, that the relationship between C.C.M. and the operating companies was not in fact a deliberate plan to restrain trade or monopolize; it was also held that the purchases of C.C.M. cabs were not made under compulsion but as a matter of business judgment having regard to their suitability.

Nevertheless, Mr Justice Murphy's opinion had indicated that other examples of vertical integration might be vulnerable and great interest was therefore aroused by this aspect of the *Columbia Steel* case. It will be remembered that Consolidated needed for its fabricating business less than $\frac{1}{2}\%$ of the total national output of rolled 'semis', about 3% of the total amount going to the eleven western states and about 13% of the supply of 'plates' and 'shapes' in that area. The Government argued that the acquisition of Consolidated by the United States Steel group would in effect reserve this portion of the market for 'semis' exclusively to the group and that this was illegal. Mr Justice Murphy's opinion in the *Yellow Cab* case was taken by the Government to mean that 'it is illegal *per se* for a manufacturer to pre-empt any market for his goods through vertical integration provided that an appreciable amount of interstate commerce is involved'.

The Supreme Court, by a five to four decision, threw out the Government's case. Mr Justice Reed accepted the proposition that the amount of commerce involved is immaterial in the case of any restraint of trade, such as price fixing, which is illegal *per se*; but he would not include exclusive-dealing arrangements between the parts of a vertically integrated concern in the class of *per se* restraints. It was necessary, he said, to consider the effect of the integration 'on the opportunities of other competitor producers to market their rolled steel'. The *Yellow Cab* case had not ruled that vertical integration was illegal *per se* but only that integration did not exonerate a concern if an unreasonable restraint of trade had occurred.

Nothing in the Yellow Cab case supports the theory that all exclusive-dealing arrangements are illegal *per se*. A subsidiary will in all probability deal only with its parents for goods the parent can furnish. That fact, however, does not make the acquisition invalid. . . . The legality of the acquisition by United States Steel . . . of Consolidated depends not merely upon the fact of that acquired control but also on many other factors. Exclusive dealings for rolled steel between Consolidated and United States Steel, brought about by vertical integration or otherwise, are not illegal, at any rate until the effect of such control is to unreasonably restrict the opportunities of competitors to market their product. . . . It seems clear to us that vertical integration, as such without more, cannot be held violative of the Sherman Act. It is an indefinite term without explicit meaning; . . . the extent of permissible integration must be governed, as other factors in Sherman Act violations, by the other circumstances of individual cases.

Finally Mr Justice Reed noted that economic and technological factors might make vertical integration essential in some industries, and it was not the job of antitrust, in his view, to impede the process:

It is not for courts to determine the course of the nation's economic development. Economists may recommend, the legislative and executive branches may chart legal courses by which the competitive forces of business can seek to reduce costs and increase production so that a higher standard of living may be available to all. The evils and dangers of monopoly and attempts to monopolize that grow out of size and efforts to eliminate others from markets, large or small, have caused Congress and the Executive to regulate commerce and trade in many respects. But no direction has appeared of a public policy that forbids, *per se*, an extension of facilities of an existing company to meet the needs of new markets of a community, whether that community is nation-wide or country-wide.

Mr Justice Reed was here using a test of legality that is recognizably in the tradition of Chief Justice White's 'normal methods of industrial development'. The law on vertical integration, as on all these monopolization problems, comes back in the end to the intent and purpose of the parties. Where the purpose is to exclude competition or create monopoly power, vertical integration may be vulnerable like any other device;[1] where it is a reasonable step to take on its commercial merits and the remaining competition appears effective, vertical integration as such is unlikely to fall foul of the law.

In taking Mr Justice Murphy's opinion in *Yellow Cab* to mean that all measures of vertical integration which foreclosed 'an appreciable amount of commerce' were illegal *per se*, the government lawyers were

---

[1] Among the particular practices found unlawful in the *ALCOA* case, for example, was that of selling ingot aluminium at a relatively high price while selling fabricated aluminium at a relatively low price: in this way, while obtaining a good return on their investment in the business as a whole, ALCOA could make things difficult for competitors in the fabricating field. But it must be noted that the harm of the practice did not depend on vertical integration as such so much as on ALCOA's monopoly of ingot, the price of which they could have raised whether or not they themselves had an interest in fabricating. Since the practice was only a consequence of the control of the price of ingot, as Judge Hand put it, 'perhaps it ought not to be considered as a separate wrong'.

once again neglecting the vital element of intent, though Mr Justice Murphy himself had made it clear that the case turned on whether there was a 'calculated plan' to restrain trade, and the Government finally lost it on that issue. This part of the Government's argument is indeed another example of the faulty use of the analogy between monopolistic practices and restrictive agreements, an analogy which is always vitiated unless careful track is kept of the element of intent. It is true enough that the amount of commerce involved in restraint of trade is immaterial when the element of intent or purpose is clearly established, as it usually is, for example, when people go to the trouble of negotiating a restrictive agreement. Similarly, the amount of commerce involved in an illegal monopolistic practice may be very tiny so long as an exclusionary purpose is clear: this is shown, for example, by the *Klearflax* boycott case described above in which the 'part of commerce' in question was a single contract for a particular type of rug.[1] When, however, business behaviour can be readily explained by normal commercial motives, then the amount of commerce affected, the strength of the competition in the market and the other factors mentioned by Mr Justice Reed become relevant to the question of fact—whether the intent or the necessary effect of the behaviour is to hamper or exclude competitors.

Vertical integration is clearly a type of business behaviour that may have legitimate commercial motives: many concerns go in for it when they have no prospect or intention of dominating their industry or excluding competitors from the market. A concern may wish to acquire a source of raw material or of some essential component in order to secure itself against interruptions in supply in times of brisk demand; a manufacturer may wish to have his own retail shops to ensure that there will be some steady distributive outlet for his product when trade generally is bad. Measures of this kind may aim at stability and security rather than dominance: moreover, once some firms in an industry start them, it may be risky for others not to follow suit. It is not unusual or unhealthy to find a number of vertically integrated concerns competing briskly one against the other.

Those who took the Government's part in the *Columbia Steel* case, however, had another shot in their locker and a more difficult one to ward off. They appealed to the rule that illegal intent may always be demonstrated by the necessary effect of what is done, for 'he who wills the means, wills the end'. In other words, however much United States

---

[1] See above, pp. 131–2, also below, Chapter VI, pp. 156 ff, and 171–2, the *Automobile finance* and *National City Lines* cases. It is now established law that the words 'any part of the trade or commerce . . .' in section 2 of the Sherman Act may stand for the trade of a single large customer if it is an appreciable amount of commerce and if the evidence of exclusionary purpose is clear.

Steel may have thought in terms of legitimate commercial development, the plain fact, according to this view, was that their acquisition of Consolidated would in practice hamper competition. This view was best stated by Mr Justice Douglas, who wrote the angry dissent of the minority in the Supreme Court:

It is, of course, immaterial that a purpose or intent to achieve the result may not have been present. The holding of the cases . . . is that the requisite purpose or intent is present if monopoly or restraint of trade results as a direct and necessary consequence of what was done. We need not hold that vertical integration is *per se* unlawful in order to strike down what is accomplished here. . . .

Approval of this acquisition . . . makes dim the prospects that the western steel industry will be free from the control of the eastern giants. United States Steel, now that it owns the Geneva plant, has over 51 % of the rolled steel or ingot capacity of the Pacific coast area. This acquisition gives it unquestioned domination there and protects it against growth of the independents in that developing region. That alone is sufficient to condemn the purchase.[1]

On this view the sheer volume of business foreclosed by the acquisition could not be ignored. As Mr Justice Douglas put it: 'The competitive purchases by Consolidated are over $5,000,000 a year. I do not see how it is possible to say that $5,000,000 of commerce is immaterial. It plainly is not *de minimis*. . . . If it is not insubstantial as a market for United States Steel, it certainly is not from the point of view of the struggling western units of the steel industry.'

The content of these quotations amounts virtually to the doctrine that such large concentrations of business power as United States Steel must be illegal, because the necessary consequence of organizing industry in such large units must be to make things difficult for small independent producers. And if this is a necessary consequence, it is enough to establish illegal intent for the purpose of the law, for no big business could have grown so big unconscious of what it was doing. Justice Douglas's dissent in *Columbia Steel* is no doubt a possible logical extension of some of Judge Learned Hand's dicta in the *ALCOA* case— that progressively to embrace each new opportunity, for example, may be a sign of an intent to exclude.

There is a sense indeed in which this doctrine is but the 'logical

[1] It is interesting to note that these legal observations had been preceded by a statement of social philosophy very similar to that of Judge Learned Hand in the *ALCOA* case. 'Industrial power should be decentralized. It should be scattered into many hands so that the fortunes of the people will not be dependent on the whim or caprice, the political prejudices, the emotional stability of a few self-appointed men. The fact that they are not vicious men but respectable or social-minded is irrelevant. That is the philosophy and the command of the Sherman Act. It is founded on a theory of hostility to the concentration in private hands of power so great that only a government of the people should have it.'

conclusion' of much that has gone before in the law of monopolizing. But this is just the kind of 'logical conclusion' that the sensible Anglo-Saxon tradition of law and administration knows well how to avoid. Perhaps it is not impossible that, if and when there is another upsurge of radical sentiment in antitrust administration, this line of thought may be resumed and carried further. Meanwhile it is well to remember that Mr Justice Douglas's opinion was a dissent and that Mr Justice Reed's majority opinion stated the law.

As the law stands, it is clear that the courts will not in practice infer monopolistic intent from the mere fact that a given industrial structure is hard for small firms to penetrate. When considering whether a measure of vertical integration is monopolistic, they will look to the strength and prospects of the firm's actual competitors, not to the notional problems of hypothetical small competitors.

So too in *Columbia Steel*, the majority of the Supreme Court accepted the real world as they found it, with the American steel industry consisting of a small group of huge integrated concerns and a larger number of smaller, more specialized businesses on the periphery. This structure reflects economic and technological factors which inevitably restrict entry into the steel industry: this is a fact of life, and it would be quite unrealistic to attribute the difficulty of the would-be new entrant to one particular measure of vertical integration. Nor is the structure inconsistent with the existence of genuine competition between United States Steel and such lesser giants as Bethlehem and Republic. Given that some of these large competitors had already established integrated steel plants in the far west, the majority of the Supreme Court could not see anything particularly unreasonable or monopolistic in United States Steel's acquiring a fabricating plant which, measured by its consumption of raw material, accounted for some 3% of regional output; and this at a time when United States Steel's fabricating plants in the east were being priced out of the western market because of the west's newly acquired self-sufficiency in ingot production. Certainly, to have barred this particular acquisition would have done nothing to transform the steel industry into a model structure of small producers.[1]

In short, the courts will apply the rule of reason to the question of whether vertical acquisitions are monopolistic devices within the condemnation of the Sherman Act. This will mean judging each case in relation to the actual competitive situation rather than with an eye to some ideal but economically unrealistic structure.[2] For 'it is not for the

---

[1] However, under the present standards of the Clayton Act, discussed in Chapter VII below, courts would be likely to bar the acquisition on the ground that doing so might preserve the opportunity for eventual de-concentration of the steel industry.

[2] See Mr Justice Douglas's summary of the law relating to vertical integration quoted below, Chapter VI, pp. 169–70.

courts to determine the course of the nation's economic development'.
This is where the notion of 'effective competition' comes in—the
idea that antitrust judgments should be based on the types of competition actually operating in a modern economy and not on textbook
models.[1]

Vertical integration is often difficult for antitrust to handle just
because industries consisting of a small number of integrated firms
may certainly pose severe obstacles to the competition of new entrants
while yet exhibiting vigorous competitiveness in other ways. It looks
logical to argue that a given structure must either be competitive or
not; then, by showing that small firms or new entrants are impeded,
to conclude that it is not competitive and carry on from there. As
with so many arguments of this form, the logic is spurious, because it
neglects the possibility that situations may be competitive in some ways
and not in others. It happens that this possibility is the reality over the
greater part of a modern, industrial economy: and this is one reason
why antitrust is such a difficult subject.

6. *Exclusive-dealing and tying contracts:* American Can

The last subject to consider in this chapter is that of contractual
arrangements which have much the same effects and motives as vertical
integration. A firm which wishes (legitimately) to secure a source of
supply or a steady distributive outlet or which plans (monopolistically)
to foreclose a market against its competitors may achieve its end by
bringing the resources in question under its direct ownership by
vertical integration. But this is not always necessary or convenient.
Similar results may often be achieved by entering into exclusive
contracts with suppliers or distributors, and these contracts too may
fall foul of the Sherman Act.

Broadly speaking, there are three types of contract that may come
into question. These are:

(a) *exclusive-dealing contracts* whereby a firm agrees with a supplier or
distributor that the latter will not supply to or distribute for any
other firm;

(b) *requirements contracts* whereby users or distributors of the firm's
product undertake to obtain from it their total requirements of
the product over a period;

(c) *tying contracts* whereby the firm undertakes to supply a given
product only on condition that the users or distributors will also
obtain from it some other product.

---

[1] The theory that antitrust is or ought to be concerned with something called 'effective
competition' is considered below, Part II.

These types of contracts are also the target of section 3 of the Clayton Act, and the main discussion of the law relating to them must await Chapter VIII, which will also consider the ticklish question of how the standard of proof required under the Clayton Act differs from that which is needed to sustain a Sherman Act case. In this chapter one or two important cases that have been brought under the Sherman Act must be noted.

It is, of course, clear that exclusive agreements of these kinds between trade associations are illegal *per se* under section 1 of the Sherman Act; this is for the familiar reason that the very existence of a collective agreement is normally sufficient witness to a restrictive purpose. It is clear, too, that for any firm which unmistakably possesses monopoly power to make such an agreement is an illegal misuse of that power, on a par, for example, with the practices disclosed in the *Lorain Journal* and other cases mentioned at the beginning of this chapter. This is true whether the possessor of monopoly power gets the benefits of integration by entering into exclusive contracts or by obtaining control through ownership.[1] The cases considered here, however, do not fall into these straightforward categories but concern the use of exclusive contracts to augment or consolidate a position of power.

The issues are perhaps best illustrated in *United States* v. *American Can Company* (District Court of California, 1949). This company was the largest manufacturer in the United States of the tins used for canning fruit and other foodstuffs. Measured by the tin plate it used, its share of the output of tins in 1946 was over 40%. The other great company in this field, Continental Can Company, had another 30% of the output and together they sold in 1946 some 86% of all tins entering the market. (Their share of sales is higher than their share of output because there are firms producing tins solely for their own use.) In some large areas of the United States, American Can has the only factories available to serve the needs of local packers.

American Can also manufactures the closing machines which are the other essential equipment of the canning industry. In 1946, American made over 50% of these machines and Continental made another 36%. American normally refused to sell the closing machines, which, with few exceptions, were leased to the users. The rental was low (it was claimed that it did not cover costs) and originally the leases had required that the lessee should not use the machines 'for any purpose except therewith to close cans which the lessee shall have bought from

---

[1] In 1943, for example, the Pullman concern was ordered to dispose either of its operating company—running Pullman coaches on railways—or of its manufacturing company which built the coaches. It was found that Pullman's 100% operating monopoly, coupled with exclusive-dealing arrangements between the operating and manufacturing sides of the business, was a violation of section 2 of the Sherman Act.

the lessor'. This provision had later been eliminated from the leases but the Government claimed that the tying provision had been kept alive in the negotiation of contracts, and that in practice American would lease the machines only to customers who entered into requirements contracts for tins. The trial Court accepted the Government's case on this point and found that the leases infringed section 3 of the Clayton Act.

Much of the evidence concerned the long-term requirements contracts under which American supplied the canners with tins. These contracts usually ran concurrently with the leases for closing machines and the standard term was five years. They covered 'the sale by the supplier and the purchase by the user of all the containers specified in the contract which the user shall require for his actual use in his operations in all specified points in the United States . . .'. It was charged that by thus combining the leases for the machines and the requirements contracts for the tins, American was able to ensure that its customers in the canning industry were tied to it for substantial periods. There was additional evidence to the effect that American made important concessions to the largest canners in order to pre-empt their custom. The Government argued that these arrangements withdrew a large share of the market for tins from competition.

The Court, for technical reasons, dismissed the cases against the five-year requirements contracts under the Clayton Act. It found, however, that these contracts violated both sections of the Sherman Act, because they unreasonably restrained trade and resulted in the monopolization of the market. Judge Harris was careful to point out that requirements contracts were not to be regarded as illegal *per se*. He took account of evidence that some form of requirements contract was a matter of great convenience to both sides of the industry. The canners had to be assured of a constantly available supply of tins to meet the seasonal nature of their operations; and American could produce more economically if they had some assurance of a steady market. He concluded that the trouble about the requirements contracts was their long term of five years: 'It is only fair to conclude after a careful review of the evidence that a contract for a period of one year would permit competitive influences to operate at the expiration of said period of time and the vice which is now present in the five-year requirements contracts would be removed.'

Both the condemnation of this firm under the Sherman Act and the permission accorded to it in the Court's decree to enter into requirements contracts of one year's duration are of great interest as an application of the rule of reason. Given American Can's powerful hold on the market, the five-year requirements contracts (coupled with the practice of only leasing the closing machines) appeared to the Court to be not so much a 'normal method of industrial development' as a calculated device for making the market more difficult for competitors to invade. At the same time there were sensible commercial reasons for some assurance to the supplier of steady orders and to the user of readily available supplies. The one-year requirements contract was a compromise intended to take account of reasonable business needs without unduly obstructing competition; a new supplier canvassing for orders could now get a chance at yearly intervals of capturing American Can's customers.[1]

The *American Can* case turned on requirements contracts, though tying arrangements were also an element in it. At the beginning of the next chapter two cases will be given in which tying contracts and exclusive-dealing contracts were respectively the central feature.[2] In all these cases some form of exclusive contract has been condemned as unreasonably restricting competition. It is of interest that for a moderately powerful firm—a firm with, say, a 40% share of its market but still having to meet considerable competition—it seems to be more dangerous legally to seek the advantages of integration through these types of contract than by tighter knit arrangements. This is so even where the contract or understanding is between affiliated companies or parent and subsidiary. As has been seen in the *Columbia Steel* case, the courts will be reluctant (at least under the Sherman Act[3]) to bar such a firm from purchasing outright the business of a supplier or customer unless the monopolistic purpose is clear. Curiously enough, the safest course of all is for the firm to start its own supplying or distributing business from its own resources as a new division or department within the same corporate structure, though this is the tightest form of integration of all.[4] It is obvious that a greater volume of 'exclusive dealing' goes on between the various departments of large integrated companies than in any other way, yet antitrust does not call these intra-corporate arrangements into question: indeed, it would be quite impracticable to do so, for it would involve holding that different servants of the same company could be co-conspirators, so that all businesses of any size and complexity would be conspiracies in the eyes of the law. In practice integrated companies do not come up against

---

[1] The decree under which the company now operates further provides that contracts for cans shall be negotiated on the basis of individual canning plants, and also that new contracts shall be negotiated at a different time of the year from the leases for the closing machines.

[2] *United States* v. *General Motors Corporation; Federal Trade Commission* v. *Motion Picture Advertising Company.*

[3] Vertical acquisitions may also fall foul of section 7 of the Clayton Act: see below, Chapter VII.

[4] It has been pointed out to me that this method may nevertheless be regarded as less restrictive than some, because it brings new resources into the industry instead of taking existing independent resources under a unified control.

the law until there are grounds for a full-scale charge of monopolization, as in the *ALCOA* case.

Thus if, for example, a large metal smelter feeds its fabricating plant with ingot from its own mill, the 'exclusive' transactions involved will not be challenged unless the company as a whole is vulnerable to a charge of monopolizing. But if its business at a given moment is confined to smelting, it may be vulnerable if it buys a fabricating plant. That plant's demand for ingot, it will be argued, will thereby be withdrawn from competition between smelters. As the *Columbia Steel* case showed, however, such a charge may well fail if the smelter concerned has powerful integrated competitors and competition remains effective. But if the smelter were to make an exclusive-dealing or requirements contract with a fabricator which had the effect of tying up the fabricator's demand for five years, this would very likely be found to violate the Sherman Act and would certainly infringe section 3 of the Clayton Act.

This curious situation runs counter to the usual axiom of antitrust that 'substance not form' is what concerns the law. In fact, similar economic effects may attract very different legal consequences according to the form of structure within which they appear. There are a number of reasons why this situation has come about. One is the existence of the Clayton Act, which reflects a congressional purpose to prohibit contractual forms of integration. Another is the fact that exclusive contracts, unlike intra-corporate arrangements, impose obligations on third parties and often run along with some degree of coercion which in itself offends the moral sense of the courts. A third is that prohibiting exclusive contracts does not upset any industrial structure—a result that judges with little technical knowledge are understandably nervous about[1]—but appears only to increase freedom of choice: after all, the canners who patronize American Can are fully entitled to renew their contracts every year with that company, but it seems to be an advance that they may now freely decide the question instead of being tied for five years. How far all this makes sense as a matter of economic and social policy is another matter of appraisal for Part II, below: it is worth noting here that this kind of difficulty in being fully consistent is very likely to occur in any form of legal or administrative assault on the problems of restraint of trade and monopoly.

---

[1] If a business which has once been vertically integrated is ordered to 'disintegrate', i.e. divest itself of one part of the industrial process, real diseconomies may result; moreover, the original vertical expansion will have involved investment in which risks of ownership were undertaken in good faith, and courts will usually require more persuasion that they should upset the whole expectation on which the investment was based than when they are faced merely with condemning a particular contract.

CHAPTER VI

MONOPOLIZATION
III. SECTION 2 OF THE SHERMAN ACT AND OLIGOPOLY SITUATIONS

1. *Antitrust and oligopoly*

In Chapter III above the outline of the law under section 1 of the
Sherman Act, dealing with restrictive agreements between competitors,
was rounded off by a description of various attempts that have been
made to bring this part of the law to bear against so-called 'oligopoly'
situations—those in which a few firms are responsible for much the
greater part of an industry's output. In the same way this chapter must
complete the story of the law of monopolization by showing how it too
may be applied to oligopoly situations.

The broad conclusion of Chapter III was that the attempt to extend
the legal meaning of 'conspiracy' under section 1 to cover so-called
'conscious parallelism of action' has so far failed. Those who see highly
concentrated, 'oligopoly' industries as a reproach to antitrust would
like the law to treat as conspiracy any situation in which a few leading
firms seem to abridge their internecine competition by mutual reaction,
or to adopt (with restrictive effect) parallel courses of action in their
dealings with others; but the courts have held that a true 'meeting of
the minds' is still an essential element in conspiracy, and also that 'no
parallelism conscious or unconscious can overcome a finding of reasonableness'. So long as this is the law, it is probable that some oligopoly
situations in which competition is not notably vigorous will escape
antitrust action, even though, as has been seen, the courts have
developed acute organs for smelling out a 'meeting of the minds' from
circumstantial evidence.

The champions of antitrust action against oligopoly, however, have
more than one string to their bow. Section 2 of the Sherman Act, for
example, is directed against 'conspiracy to monopolize' as well as
monopolizing by a single firm. Might not 'conspiracy' in this context
be given a broader scope than under section 1? The leading cases on
this topic will be considered later in this chapter. Then again, might
not some strands of the legal doctrine on monopolizing be extended, so
that in an industry dominated by a few large firms each individually
might be held to have monopolized its segment of the market or to be
guilty of monopolistic practices?

[155]

There is at least one respect in which the enforcing authorities have made progress—if it be progress—along these lines. This development follows directly from the line of cases broached at the end of the last chapter. It seems clear from the case law that when exclusive contracts and tying arrangements of various kinds are challenged under the Sherman Act, a more serious view will be taken if a number of powerful firms in a concentrated industry enter into such arrangements in parallel than if one isolated firm in a less concentrated industry does so. The issues will be seen more clearly in the following section.

2. *Monopolistic practices in conditions of oligopoly:* Automobile finance cases; Motion Picture Advertising

The first important case was *United States* v. *General Motors Corporation* (Seventh Circuit Court of Appeals, 1941). Although this case was brought as a criminal suit under section 1 of the Sherman Act, it clearly comes within the field of monopolistic practices.

General Motors distributed their vehicles through the General Motors Sales Corporation (G.M.S.C.). Another subsidiary, General Motors Acceptance Corporation (G.M.A.C.), which was set up in 1919, was in the business of financing trade in automobiles. The Government charged that General Motors were in a conspiracy with G.M.S.C. and G.M.A.C. to secure all the financing business in respect of General Motors' cars for G.M.A.C. and to exclude any competing finance companies who tried to get a share of it. This was done partly by inducements, but it was alleged that G.M.S.C. also resorted to coercion against dealers who were not using or did not promise to use G.M.A.C. for financing sales. In some cases they might refuse altogether to sell cars to a dealer unless he used G.M.A.C.; or they might delay delivery of cars to recalcitrant dealers or threaten dealers with cancellation of their agency agreements. In general it was said to be unhealthy for a dealer not to co-operate, even though he might lose sales from customers who wanted to use other finance companies or who were refused credit by G.M.A.C.

General Motors' answer to all this was, broadly speaking, that there were some very shady people in the financing business. They said that G.M.A.C. was run solely to promote sales of cars, and to protect General Motors' goodwill against undesirable financial practices. It was claimed that G.M.A.C.'s rates and terms were fully competitive and that they gave better service than their competitors. In short, the practice was a reasonable one on its commercial merits.

The Court of Appeals rejected this defence on the ground that, if G.M.A.C. was the best finance company to use, the dealers and the public would use it anyway. They accepted the jury finding that there was a conspiracy between General Motors and its subsidiaries by which they 'made use of their monopoly over the supply of General Motors' cars to force G.M.A.C. on dealer-purchasers and retail purchasers of General Motors' cars, in effect tying the G.M.A.C. finance conditions and restrictions to the wholesale purchase and retail sale of General Motors' cars'. In the view of the Court such a conspiracy clearly violated section 1 of the Sherman Act, 'for it operates to force un-reasonable terms and conditions upon independent traders, and to impose control restrictions upon their trading—coercive conduct which unnecessarily burdens the interstate trade and commerce in their product and unduly limits their liberty to do business in the interstate markets'.

Here then was a case of a tying arrangement or 'package deal', not unlike the tying element in the *American Can* case in which it was found that leases for closing machines were in practice made conditional on the lessee's use of the lessor's tins. As such, particularly as it involved coercion of third parties, it is not very remarkable that it constituted an antitrust offence; certainly in the Clayton Act case law, as will be seen below (Chapter VIII), there are numerous parallels in which firms as powerful or less so than General Motors have been in trouble through tying devices of various kinds.

Nevertheless, the *General Motors* case has noteworthy features of its own. It was an innovation at the time, for example, to bring the facts within the condemnation of section 1 of the Sherman Act by holding that a parent company and its subsidiaries could conspire together. As Judge Kerner put it:

Clearly a vertical combination or combination of non-competitors may conspire to restrain unreasonably the interstate trade and commerce of third parties and thereby subject themselves to the prohibitions of the Sherman Act. . . . Nor can the appellants enjoy the benefits of separate corporate identity and escape the consequences of an illegal combination in restraint of trade by insisting that they are in effect a single trader. The test of illegality under the Sherman Act is not so much the particular form of business organization effected, as it is the presence or absence of restraint of trade and commerce.[1]

---

[1] See the quotation from Mr Justice Murphy's opinion in the *Yellow Cab* case at Chapter V above, p. 144. See also Chapter I above, footnote to p. 40, on *Kiefer-Stewart Company* v. *Seagram and Sons* as another instance of a holding that a parent and subsidiary companies can conspire together. A good deal has been written about the apparent artificiality of the idea that financially linked companies should be regarded as conspiring if they follow centrally controlled policies. The current state of the law was summed up at p. 34 of the *Report of the Attorney General's National Committee to Study the Antitrust Laws*. It was briefly that concerted action between affiliated companies may violate section 1 of the Sherman Act if its purpose (or effect) is 'coercion of or unreasonable restraint on the trade of strangers to those acting in concert'. But, according to the Committee, no violation occurs if the affiliates merely accept mutual restrictions, e.g. agree on the prices they will charge; the Committee criticized complaints brought by the Federal Trade Commission against affiliated liquor distillers for fixing prices within the corporate family.

It was also interesting, as foreshadowing more recent doctrine on the question of what may constitute a separate 'part of commerce' for the purpose of the law, that the Court found no difficulty in deciding that it was enough that the General Motors organization was restraining trade in its own product: the tying arrangements, of course, affected trade only in General Motors cars, not the trade in cars generally. Indeed, the Court several times voiced its concern at the fact that the restraint of trade 'tended to reduce the supply of General Motors' cars in the channels of trade'. Judge Kerner said at another point: 'The trade in General Motors' cars was suppressed entirely in instances where dealer-purchasers and retail purchasers would not or could not use G.M.A.C.' Thus the theory was that General Motors and its subsidiaries were in league to place obstacles in the way of selling General Motors' cars; and the Court found this theory plausible in the belief that the real object was to increase profits from financing: 'Sometimes it is good business to sacrifice car sales in order to increase the sale of a complementary product or service.'

But the real importance of the case lies in what happened afterwards. Having won the criminal case, the Department of Justice in due course started a civil action against General Motors for equity relief. This case was eventually settled by a consent decree under which the company undertook to abide by many detailed regulations enjoining them not to put any pressure on dealers to use G.M.A.C. and requiring them to give equal facilities to all bona fide finance companies.[1] Civil actions had already been started against the Ford and Chrysler companies, and they in turn consented to be bound by exactly similar injunctions.

Thus the Government had successfully proceeded on the basis that all three leading firms in the 'oligopolistic' automobile industry could separately be held to be at variance with the Sherman Act in tying the business of financing car sales to that of selling the cars. Each one of the three, in other words, was regarded as restraining trade in its own segment of the market, though there was, of course, no question of their working together in this or any other respect. This is particularly interesting in the case of the Chrysler company, which, as the smallest of the three, could not affect more than a quite small proportion of the

---

[1] It is interesting to note that the consent decrees in these cases contained elaborate provisions for registering finance companies subject to their undertaking to comply with rules of good financial conduct and fair dealing. A finance company refusing this undertaking or breaking the rules could in effect be 'struck off'. This was an attempt by the Government to meet the point that the manufacturers had set up their finance companies in order to protect themselves against shady financial practices. But one cannot help wondering whether, if the manufacturers had got together and organized a register of finance companies for themselves, this would not have constituted an illegal boycott under the rule of *Fashion Originators Guild*.

car trade as a whole by adopting tying arrangements. Had Chrysler's practices alone been considered in the context of a less concentrated industry, it might have seemed doubtful whether any case would lie against them—at any rate under the Sherman Act.[1] But as one of the 'big three' in the car industry, Chrysler were in practice seen as part of a general picture of restrictiveness in the field of car financing.

This important addition to antitrust doctrine which was implicit in the *Car finance* cases was brought out into the open in *Federal Trade Commission* v. *Motion Picture Advertising Company* (Supreme Court, 1953). This company produces and distributes advertising films. Many of its contracts with exhibitors relating to the showing of these films contained a provision that the cinema owner would not show any advertising films produced by other companies. M.P.A., the biggest company in the industry, had exclusive contracts of this type with about 40% of the cinemas in its area of operation. The contracts ran for varying periods up to five years, though the normal period was one year only. A case was brought under section 5 of the Federal Trade Commission Act,[2] and the Commission found that the exclusive contracts were unduly restrictive so as to amount to an 'unfair method of competition'. Obviously influenced by the result in the *American Can* case, the Commission ordered that no contract of more than one year's duration should be entered into.

Mr Justice Douglas, speaking for the Supreme Court when the case was appealed, made much of the fact that, if M.P.A. were taken together with three other companies which used similar types of contract, the exclusive-dealing arrangements for advertising films covered about 75% of the cinemas that used such films.[3] There was no suggestion that the four big companies in the industry were acting in concert. But Mr Justice Douglas, in upholding the Commission's conclusion, put the issue as follows: 'Due to the exclusive contracts, respondent and the three other major companies have foreclosed to competitors 75% of all available outlets for this business throughout the United States. It is, we think, plain from the Commission's findings that a device which has sewed up a market so tightly for the benefit of a few falls within the prohibitions of the Sherman Act and is therefore an unfair method of competition within the meaning of section 5(a) of the Federal Trade Commission Act.'

[1] The cases dealing with 'tie-ins' under the Clayton Act are considered below, Chapter VIII.
[2] For technical reasons the form of the contracts did not fall within the wording of section 3 of the Clayton Act.
[3] This figure includes all the exclusive contracts. Those of more than one year's duration —which were all that the Commission condemned—were a much smaller proportion. Even M.P.A.'s longer-term contracts 'tied up' only 15% of the cinemas that show advertising films.

This reference to the Sherman Act is the more important for being gratuitous, since the practice in question might have been held to be an unfair method of competition without being an offence against the Sherman Act.[1] Justice Douglas was in fact holding explicitly that an individual company's restrictive conduct—in this case, exclusive-dealing contracts—might come within the condemnation of the Sherman Act because of its place in a context in which a few firms, though not in collusion, had the industry 'buttoned up'. The smallest of the four firms had made exclusive contracts of more than one year's duration with a little over 1% of the cinemas showing advertising films; yet it came under the ban no less than M.P.A.

Mr Justice Frankfurter wrote a vigorous dissenting opinion against this ruling. As he put it:

There is no reliance here on conspiracy or on concerted action to foreclose the market, a charge that would, of course, warrant action under the Sherman law. Indeed, we must assume that respondent and the other three companies are complying with an earlier order of the Commission directed at concerted action. . . . While the existence of the other exclusive contracts is, of course, not irrelevant in a market analysis . . . this Court has never decided that they may, in the absence of conspiracy, be aggregated to support a charge of Sherman law violation.

Justice Frankfurter, indeed, would have sent the case back to the Commission for reconsideration on the ground that advertising films were a minute part of the cinema business and the number of exclusive contracts of more than a year's duration was small; since there was some evidence that the inititative for the exclusive contracts came at least as much from the exhibitors as from the film producers, it might turn out, according to the rule of reason, that no significant restraint of trade was involved at all.

But this is a minority view: Mr Justice Douglas was speaking for a majority of seven to two in the Supreme Court. It seems now to be settled law that where exclusive contracts and other types of tying device are concerned, the restraint of trade is to be judged from the point of view of the small or new competitor trying to make his way in the industry. Thus, where similar tying devices are adopted by a number of leading firms, the courts will tend nowadays to look to their aggregate effect in foreclosing the market against outside competition. This, however, is a position which the courts seem to have arrived at empirically, as a matter of practice rather than by a decision of principle. Hence it would be unsafe to assume that the principle

---

[1] As has been seen, all offences against the Sherman Act may be treated as unfair methods of competition under section 5 of the Federal Trade Commission Act, but the reverse does not follow and is not in fact true.

involved, which could clearly have far-reaching implications for the legal treatment of oligopoly situations, will in practice be extended over a wide range of such situations. The legal outlook in this respect will be considered more fully at the end of this chapter; for the moment, it is important to note that this line of cases has been concerned with exclusive contracts and tying devices and nothing more.

3. *Conspiracy to monopolize: the* Reading *case*

It might be expected that charges of 'conspiracy to monopolize' under section 2 of the Sherman Act would be one of the main ways in which the antitrust authorities would try to reach 'oligopoly' situations—those in which an industry is dominated by a small number of powerful concerns. In practice the number of cases brought under this head is small, for even where the economic effects of an oligopoly structure are thought to be restrictive, it is not necessarily the fact that the firms concerned have 'conspired' in the legal sense to produce them; or if it is strongly suspected that they have conspired—by a true 'meeting of the minds'—to monopolize the industry, it may be exceedingly difficult to prove it.

There may, of course, be blatant cases of conspiracy to monopolize, differing from cases of conspiracy in restraint of trade only in the number of firms concerned and the compactness of their arrangements.[1] The few recorded cases prior to the Second World War are indeed of this kind. One such case is of interest here because it leads on to an early example of the way in which the courts, as a practical matter, may judge an individual firm's conduct in the light of the total effect on competition of the conduct of a group.

This is *United States* v. *Reading Company* (Supreme Court, 1912). The story of the case concerns the anthracite industry of the United States. The country's principal hard-coal seams are in northern Pennsylvania and, since there are no navigable rivers to the east, rail transport is essential to get the coal to the eastern markets. At one time there was fierce competition between the railways serving the coalfield, and a number of them saw the advantage of acquiring financial control of anthracite companies so as to tie a certain amount of the traffic to their routes. Eventually the greater part of the industry was in the hands of vertically integrated railroad-cum-mining companies and, as the evidence showed, competition between them gave way to collusion.

The Government charged the leading companies with conspiracy to

---

[1] Since a conspiracy to monopolize is unlikely to get far without showing itself also as a conspiracy to restrain trade, it is usual for cases of this type to involve concurrent charges under both sections of the Act.

gain complete control of the anthracite. It was said, for example, that they put a stop to a scheme for building a competing railway by setting up a holding company to buy out the leading 'independent' coal producers who backed the scheme; that they collectively arranged contracts on standard terms for the purchase of the whole output of the remaining independent coal producers. By these means they effectively controlled almost all the anthracite reaching, distributing points for eastern markets and were thus able to control prices in those markets. The evidence of collusion was strong and the Government won the case.

This was straightforward. What is of special interest here is that the Government went on to bring civil actions (under section 2 of the Sherman Act) against the two largest integrated companies individually,[1] and succeeded in getting the courts to order the railway companies to divest themselves of their anthracite holdings in each case. The Reading Company was a holding company controlling two important railroads as well as mines responsible for some 33% of anthracite output. The anthracite interests of the Lehigh Valley Company accounted for only about 17% of output. It is, of course, very unlikely that the Government would have succeeded in monopolization cases against these companies had they not been considered in the context of the earlier conspiracy case; the Reading Company's 33%, let alone the Lehigh Valley Company's 17%, of anthracite output would not ordinarily have been enough to establish that they possessed effective power in the market.[2] Clearly the Supreme Court, as a body of practical men, looked at the power (and the purpose) of these companies in the light of the picture presented by the industry as a whole; in this sense the *Reading* case may be seen as a forerunner of the *Automobile finance* and *M.P.A.* cases described earlier in the chapter.

4. American Tobacco; Paramount

There are two important post-war cases that explore the law of 'conspiracy to monopolize'—the *American Tobacco* case and the *Paramount* case.

American Tobacco Company v. *United States* (Supreme Court, 1946) involved the three leading manufacturers of cigarettes, the American Tobacco Company ('Lucky Strike'), Liggett and Myers ('Chesterfield') and R. J. Reynolds ('Camel'). Each company faced charges both of conspiracy to restrain trade under section 1 of the Sherman Act and of monopolization and conspiracy to monopolize under section 2.

[1] *United States* v. *Reading Company* (Supreme Court, 1920); *United States* v. *Lehigh Valley Railroad Company* (Supreme Court, 1920).

[2] Curiously enough, the *Reading* case of 1920 was decided by the Supreme Court only a few days after their decision in the *United States Steel* case. It will be recalled that United States Steel's 50% share of steel output was not regarded as giving that company effective market power.

It was found that the big three produced 90% of all American cigarettes in 1931, but the percentage had dropped to 68% in 1939. No other company had ever produced more than 10% of the total. Evidence was given of the huge assets of the three companies and of their tremendous advertising expenditures, which the Supreme Court described as 'a widely published warning that these companies possess and know how to use a powerful offensive and defensive weapon against new competition. New competition dare not enter such a field, unless it be well supported by comparable national advertising.'

Much of the evidence in the case dealt with the buying practices of the companies. The big three took between 50% and 80% of the domestic crop of flue cured tobacco and between 60% and 80% of the crop of burley tobacco. Because the tobacco crop is perishable in the hands of the farmers, it must all be sold in the year it is grown. The method of sale is by auction markets in the growing areas. Evidence was given that each of the big three refused to make purchases at these auctions unless the other two were also represented, and the Government alleged that each company gave careful instructions to its buyers before each auction as to the limits of the prices they could offer. The suggestion was that the same price ceilings were set for each of the big buyers. Even when one of the big three did not want a particular batch of tobacco, their representative entered the bidding in order to see that the price went up to the understood ceiling. As Mr Justice Burton put it: 'The petitioners were not so much concerned with the price they paid for the leaf tobacco as that each should pay the same price for the same grade and that none should secure any advantage in purchasing tobacco. . . . The prices which were set as top prices by petitioners, or by the first of them to purchase on the market, became, with few exceptions, the top prices prevailing on those markets.'

It was also alleged that when certain manufacturers began to make lower-priced, '10 cent' cigarettes in competition with the big three, each of the big three simultaneously began to make large purchases of the cheaper tobaccos which the competing manufacturers would want. The Government claimed that these purchases were intended to deprive the independent makers of cheap cigarettes of their raw material, or alternatively to raise the price of the cheaper tobaccos to a point where the cheaper cigarettes would become unprofitable. Mr Justice Burton commented: 'No explanation was offered as to how or where this tobacco was used by the petitioners. The compositions of their respective brands of cigarettes calling for the use of more expensive tobaccos remained unchanged during this period. . . .'

The rest of the evidence was on the selling side. It was shown that whereas price competition had been marked prior to 1923, the prices charged by the big three to wholesale distributors of cigarettes were substantially identical between 1923 and 1928 and had been absolutely identical from 1928 until the case was brought. Since 1928, only seven price changes had been made and all were identical in amount. In each case the change was first announced by Reynolds, and the other two companies then conformed.

The most spectacular and influential part of the evidence dealt with the depression year 1931, when tobacco prices dropped to the lowest point for twenty-five years and other manufacturing costs were low. Mr Justice Burton summarized what happened as follows:

On June 23, 1931, Reynolds, without previous notification or warning to the trade or public, raised the list price of Camel cigarettes, constituting its leading cigarette brand, from $6.40 to $6.85 a thousand. The same day, American increased the list price for Lucky Strike cigarettes, its leading brand, and Liggett the price for Chesterfield cigarettes, its leading brand, to the identical price of $6.85 a thousand. No economic justification for this raise was demonstrated. The president of Reynolds stated that it was 'to express our own courage for the future and our own confidence in our industry'.

It is interesting to note that at least one of the other companies—Liggett—thought the price advance at such a time was a mistake, but gave evidence that they felt bound to follow it as otherwise 'the other companies would have greater resources to spend in advertising and this would put Chesterfield cigarettes at a competitive disadvantage'. Although the increased retail prices resulting from these price advances led to a loss in volume of sales, the profits of the big three in 1932 (of all years) were more than $100 million and the year was one of the three best (up to that time) in the history of the industry.

At the same period, however, the 10-cent brands of cigarettes were beginning to attract the public. Between 1931 and 1932 sales of these cheap cigarettes multiplied many times, rising from 0·28% of total sales in June 1931 to 22·78% in November 1932. The big three then reacted to this threat and reduced their wholesale prices by just under 20% in two cuts, from $6.85 to $5.50. By May 1933, sales of 10-cent brands had dropped again to 6·43% of total sales and, the threat having been warded off, the big three increased their prices again in January 1934 to $6.10 a thousand. Mr Justice Burton noted: 'During the period when the list price of $5.50 a thousand was in effect, Camels and Lucky Strikes were being sold at a loss by Reynolds and American. Liggett at the same time was forced to curtail all of its normal activities and cut its differential to the bone in order to sell at those prices. The petitioners in 1937 again increased the list prices of their above-named brands to $6.25 a thousand and in July 1940 to $6·53 a thousand.'

There was evidence also of strenuous efforts by the big three to induce the retailers to sell their major brands at no more than 13 cents, in order to keep a differential of no more than 3 cents above the 10-cent brands. 'In addition to the use of these inducements, petitioners also used threats and penalties to enforce compliance with their retail price program, removed dealers from the direct lists, cancelled arrangements for window advertising, changed credit terms with a resulting handicap to recalcitrant dealers, discontinued cash allowances for advertising, refused to make deals giving free goods, and made use of price cutters to whom they granted advantageous privileges, to drive down retail prices where a parity or price equalization was not maintained by dealers between the brands of petitioners, or where the dealers refused to maintain the 3-cent differential between the 10-cent and the leading brands of petitioners' cigarettes.'

The question has been much discussed whether the evidence in this case, of which only a few salient points have been outlined here, should have been persuasive of conspiracy. Some commentators, in particular some economists, have seen the story as typical of what they would expect to happen, given the kind of oligopoly structure that obtains in the cigarette industry. They point out, for example, that, given the mutual awareness indispensable to the leading firms in such an industry, it is not surprising that they take care not to bid up raw tobacco prices against each other; also that a 'follow my leader' technique in making price changes is readily explicable without any express agreement. Even the fact that there was apparently a marked change in the conduct of the industry after 1923 may be explained on the basis that it takes time and experience for oligopolists to learn what the economists expect of them.

Themselves convinced that the story is a prize exemplar of the economic theory of oligopoly, these commentators have tended to ascribe a greater legal significance to this case than it will bear. Thus Professor W. H. Nicholls has written:[1] 'The *Tobacco* case is clearly a legal milestone in the social control of oligopoly. By permitting the inference of illegal conspiracy from detailed similarity of behaviour ... the courts have at last brought oligopolistic industries within the reach of successful prosecution under the antitrust laws.' It is true, of course, as Professor Nicholls points out, that there was no evidence of an express agreement and that conspiracy was inferred from wholly circumstantial evidence: but this is no more than was done twenty

[1] William H. Nicholls, 'The Tobacco Case of 1946', *American Economic Review*, vol. 39, no. 3, May 1949, p. 296.

years before in the price filing cases.[1] When he goes on to say, 'Thus, the *Tobacco* case brought the basic assumption of modern oligopoly theory squarely before the courts. In finding in the facts a reasonable basis for the jury's inference of unlawful conspiracy, the Court of Appeals accepted the practical implications of that assumption; namely, that a few dominant firms will, perhaps independently and purely as a matter of self-interest, evolve non-aggressive patterns of behavior . . .', he is attributing to the Court and the jury more economics than they would own: what the jury found and the Court confirmed was precisely that the conduct of the firms could not be accounted independent action. Rightly or wrongly, the Kentucky jury felt able to infer a true 'meeting of the minds' from the evidence, and the case really adds nothing new to the law of conspiracy. This is confirmed by Mr Justice Burton's summary of this aspect of the case: 'The essential combination or conspiracy in violation of the Sherman Act may be found in a course of dealings or other circumstances as well as in any exchange of words . . . Where the circumstances are such as to warrant a jury in finding that the conspirators had a unity of purpose or a common design and understanding, or a meeting of minds in an unlawful agreement, the conclusion that a conspiracy is established is justified.'

Fundamentally the *Paramount* case—*United States* v. *Paramount Pictures* (Supreme Court, 1948)—makes a more radical approach to the problem of a concentrated industry. The defendants in this case were five major concerns which produce motion pictures and distribute them through subsidiaries—Paramount, Loew's, R.K.O., Warner Brothers and Twentieth Century Fox; two smaller concerns of the same integrated type, Columbia and Universal; and finally, United Artists Corporation, which is purely a distributor. The five major producer-distributors owned or controlled many cinemas of their own. The charge that the producing companies had together monopolized the making of motion pictures was not substantiated, and the Supreme Court dealt only with charges of conspiracy to restrain and monopolize trade in the distribution and exhibition of pictures, and with charges against the distributors individually of entering into restrictive contracts.

Mr Justice Douglas, speaking for the Supreme Court, seemed almost perfunctory about endorsing the trial Court's findings of conspiracy. It had been found, for example, that the major distributors had conspired to set 'substantially uniform minimum prices' for admission to cinemas in the copyright licensing agreements under which exhibitors showed their pictures. There was no express agreement among the distributors

---

[1] See above, Chapter I, pp. 40 ff.

about admission prices;[1] it was, as Douglas put it, 'inferred from the pattern of price fixing disclosed in the record. We think there is adequate foundation for it too. It is not necessary to find an express agreement in order to find a conspiracy. It is enough that a concert of action is contemplated and that the defendants conformed to the arrangement. . . . That was shown here.'

Similarly it had been found that the defendant distributors, in deciding on the clearance period to be left between the first runs of a picture and subsequent runs, did not look just to the commercial factors that justify the clearance practice[2] but imposed clearances that at times discriminated unreasonably between one exhibitor and another. In effect, a uniform and conventional system for granting runs and clearances, which all the major firms followed, had grown up in the industry. Mr Justice Douglas, however, did not review the evidence pointing to a 'meeting of the minds' on this subject. He stated simply: 'The evidence is ample to support the finding . . . that the defendants either participated in evolving this uniform system of clearances, or acquiesced in it and so furthered its existence. That evidence, like the evidence on the price fixing phase of the case, is therefore adequate to support the finding of a conspiracy to restrain trade by imposing unreasonable clearances.'[3]

These two practices—horizontal price fixing and imposing unreasonable clearances—were the only ones which were brought even formally under the head of a general conspiracy between the defendants. Certain of the defendants had made arrangements under which they operated cinemas as a joint venture (sometimes associating independent firms of exhibitors with them) and shared the profits according to prearranged percentages; and these arrangements were condemned as agreements in restraint of trade. For the rest, the practices reviewed by Mr Justice Douglas mainly consisted of different forms of tying contract which the distributors severally adopted in dealing with independent exhibitors.

For example, the Court took exception to the so-called 'formula deals' of two major distributors: these were licensing arrangements with large circuits whereby the distributor took as his fee a specified percentage of the total sum earned by a popular picture over the whole

[1] There were express agreements between individual distributors and exhibitors—analogous to resale price maintenance agreements; these were also condemned, and it was held that the distributor's copyright in the picture did not entitle him to set a common or minimum admission price for competing cinemas.

[2] See above, Chapter III, p. 82.

[3] To 'participate in evolving' a system or to 'acquiesce' in a system and so 'further its existence' are tests that seem to fall well short of a 'meeting of the minds'. By these tests might not Beethoven, Brahms and Sibelius be held co-conspirators in the business of writing symphonies?

circuit. The operators of the circuit were left to make their own arrangements as regards the rental to be paid by and the run allotted to particular cinemas. This form of contract was found restrictive because it tied the pictures to the large circuits and gave no opportunity for other theatre owners to bid for them. So-called 'master agreements' were on the same pattern, though usually confined to only part of a circuit, and these were found unlawful in the same way as 'devices for stifling competition and diverting the cream of the business to the large operators'.

Equally, contracts or 'franchises' which licensed large numbers of pictures in one contract, sometimes covering more than one season, were suspect because they might be misused to reserve a distributor's best pictures to favoured exhibitors and so discriminate against the small independents. Another practice was 'block booking',[1] which consisted of putting a number of pictures into a batch so that the exhibitor had to take the whole batch or none at all. This is a form of 'package deal', similar in principle to the tying of car finance to car sales, and it too was found illegal; exhibitors might contract for a batch of films if they wished, but should not be obliged to take a batch as a condition of getting a popular feature. Finally, various other devices were found to discriminate against small exhibitors in favour of large circuits and cinemas affiliated to the distributors.

The condemnation of the various tying devices adopted by the individual distributors would seem to be analogous to that in the *Car finance* and *Motion Picture Advertising* cases; and, as in those cases, the Court clearly looked to the cumulative effect on freedom of competition in the industry of the parallel use of these devices by all the leading companies. Mr Justice Douglas, speaking for a unanimous Supreme Court,[2] nowhere made any clear distinction between these practices and those as to which conspiracy had been found: indeed he gave the impression of considering them all as contributory to the general conspiracy. The trial Court had reached the conclusion that the companies could not be held individually or collectively to have monopolized the exhibiting of pictures and had therefore considered that it would be adequate, by way of remedy, to order the companies to give up the various restrictive practices and to require that a system of competitive bidding for each picture individually should be introduced. Mr Justice Douglas, who regarded competitive bidding as an

---

[1] For a later Supreme Court case involving this practice, see *United States* v. *Loew's Inc.* (1962), discussed in Chapter VIII below (pp. 214–15).

[2] Mr Justice Frankfurter dissented on the question of relief measures and Mr Justice Jackson took no part in the case: but there were no dissents as to the substantive law by which the defendants were condemned.

impracticable and undesirable remedy,[1] held that there might well be
good grounds for a finding of 'conspiracy to monopolize' and he
remitted the matter to the trial Court so that 'a new start on this phase
of the case may be made . . .'; the object of this decision was to
enable the trial Court to order the divestiture of the exhibiting interests
of the companies (instead of decreeing the competitive-bidding system)
if indeed monopolization was established.

Thus Mr Justice Douglas spoke in terms of a general conspiracy
among the defendants: 'It is clear, so far as the five majors are concerned, that the aim of the conspiracy was exclusionary, i.e. it was
designed to strengthen their hold on the exhibition field. In other words
the conspiracy had monopoly in exhibition as one of its goals. . . .'
He proceeded to outline the argument by which a case of monopolization might be established. 'A conspiracy to effect a monopoly through
restraints of trade' was the starting point of this argument: in other
words he took it for granted that this much at least had been established. Then it became necessary to look at the results of this conspiracy. Monopolization might be proved without any showing of a
nation-wide monopoly of exhibiting; for 'it is the relationship of the
unreasonable restraints of trade to the position of the defendants in the
exhibition field (and more particularly in the first-run phase of that
business) that is of first importance on the divestiture phase of these
cases.' Thus, the trial Court should consider whether the defendants
had monopoly power over some 'appreciable part' of commerce—for
example, over the first-run cinemas of the country as a whole or even the
'first-run field in the ninety-two largest cities of the country, or . . . the
first-run field in separate localities'. (Justice Douglas had already noted
earlier in his argument that 'in the ninety-two cities of the country with
populations over 100,000 at least 70% of all the first-run theaters are
affiliated with one or more of the five majors'. He now stressed again that
'the first-run field, which constitutes the cream of the exhibition business,
is the core of the present cases'.) If monopoly power were indeed found
to exist in some 'appreciable part' of commerce, and if it had come
about 'as a necessary consequence of what was done' (that is, the
restrictive practices), then there would be no need to show any specific
intent to monopolize on the part of the defendants.

Mr Justice Douglas also considered the effect on the situation of the
vertical integration of producing, distributing and exhibiting as shown
by the major companies. Vertical integration, he said, was not illegal
per se; it must be judged by the power it creates and the purpose with
which it is conceived. '. . . it runs afoul of the Sherman Act if it was

---

[1] Mr Justice Douglas's observations on the choice of appropriate remedies are an important
contribution to that topic and his opinion will be referred to again below, Chapter XIV.

a calculated scheme to gain control over an appreciable segment of the market and to restrain or suppress competition, rather than an expansion to meet legitimate business needs.' The power created by vertical integration must be measured in relation to '. . . the nature of the market to be served . . . and the leverage on the market which the particular vertical integration creates or makes possible'. This was another matter that the trial Court was instructed to reconsider.

In the event, the trial Court, on the remand of the case, found that the divestiture of the cinema owning interests of the distributors was justified and so ordered. In many small cities particular defendants had an effective monopoly position in exhibiting, because it was found that in practice the major companies mostly 'kept out of each other's way'. The picture in the ninety-two cities with over 100,000 population was not dissimilar; although no agreement to divide markets was found, the business practices of the defendants effectively limited competition between them. '. . . the geographical distribution became a part of a system in which competition was largely absent and the status of which was maintained by fixed runs, clearances and prices, by pooling agreements and joint ownerships among the major defendants, and by cross-licensing which made it necessary that they should work together.'

The trial Court was not satisfied that the vertical integration of the various companies had come about as a calculated scheme to control the market; but the fact that they were vertically integrated had 'powerfully aided' their conspiracy. 'Such a situation has made the vertical integrations active aids to the conspiracy and has rendered them in this particular case illegal, however innocent they might be in other situations.' Finally, the Court found that a conspiracy to monopolize was adequately established. 'In respect to monopoly power we think it existed in this case. As we have shown, the defendants were all working together. There was a horizontal conspiracy as to price fixing, runs and clearances. The vertical integration aided such a conspiracy at all points. In these circumstances the defendants must be viewed collectively rather than independently as to the power which they exercise over the market by their theatre holdings. . . .'[1]

---

[1] It will be noted that the trial Court rested the conspiracy only on those practices—price fixing and imposing unreasonable runs and clearances—in respect of which there had been formal findings of conspiracy; it did not include as part of the conspiracy the various 'tying' devices practised by the distributors severally.

5. National City Lines; du Pont

Two cases in which conspiracies to monopolize of a rather different kind have been alleged must also be included in this chapter. These cases deal with situations in which powerful firms extend their financial interests into wider and wider industrial fields; it has been alleged that in such situations the power and influence of the firm (or group of firms) in any one market is continually reinforcing and being reinforced by its power in other markets, so that opportunities for small competitors are reduced over a wide industrial front.

An aspect of this problem is illustrated by *United States* v. *National City Lines* (Seventh Circuit Court of Appeals, 1951). In this criminal case a group of suppliers of essential requirements for motor transport were charged with conspiracy to monopolize 'certain portions of interstate commerce': namely, the requirements of a number of affiliated bus companies for the commodities they supplied. Among the defendants were the Firestone Tire and Rubber Company, General Motors and two of the biggest oil companies—Phillips and Standard Oil of California.

The story was that the group of suppliers had agreed to furnish capital to three bus companies—National City Lines, Pacific City Lines and American City Lines—on the understanding that these companies would then look to the suppliers for their requirements of tyres, petrol, buses and so on. The capital provided by the suppliers would be used to purchase financial interests in, or outright control of, local transport systems in various parts of the United States; these systems too would then become substantially exclusive markets for the suppliers. By the time the Government brought its case the three affiliated bus companies operated between them forty-six transport systems in sixteen different States. It was alleged that there were other agreements, such that the National and Pacific companies would not enter into any new contract for supplies from suppliers outside the defendant group without the express permission of the latter, and that they would not dispose of their interest in any bus operating company without requiring the purchaser to assume the same obligations as respects supplies.

The Court of Appeals found that there was no serious dispute about the existence of agreements between the defendant suppliers and the bus companies, each of which had entered into ten-year requirements contracts for all their buses, tyres and tubes, petrol and oil. The Court also accepted findings of fact to the effect that National City Lines had obtained a great deal of capital from the suppliers for purchasing transport systems where streetcars (*anglice* trams) were being supplanted by buses, and that the provision of capital always went together with agreements to make requirements contracts.

The defence rested essentially on the contention that, even if there were arrangements to pre-empt the particular market represented by the bus companies' requirements, these requirements were not a separable part of the total market. They insisted that the indictment had not charged monopolization of the sale of petrol or buses in any particular area of the United States, nor even in a particular city, but only of sales to a particular customer. The Court of Appeals rejected this argument on the ground, for which Mr Justice Murphy's opinion in the *Yellow Cab* case gave authority, that the requirements of public transport systems in some forty-five cities amounted to 'a substantial segment of interstate commerce'.

The story was indeed similar in outline to that of the *Yellow Cab* case in a number of respects; but there were also marked differences. In particular the suppliers concerned—firms like General Motors and Standard Oil of California—were much more potent influences in their own fields than was the Checker Cab Manufacturing Company. Thus their financial entry into the bus operating business, coupled with the requirements contracts, no doubt seemed more likely to restrict competitive opportunities in that market. The Court of Appeals found that there was ample evidence to support the jury's finding that the various defendants had acted in concert and that, since the inevitable consequence of their arrangements was to exclude competitors from a substantial market, they could not escape having attributed to them the requisite 'intent and purpose' to monopolize that market. Thus this situation was found to reflect a 'calculated plan' to pre-empt a market: the Government won the case and substantial fines were imposed.[1]

United States v. *E.I. du Pont de Nemours and Company* (originally decided in the United States District Court for the Northern District of Illinois, December 1954) is also an important illustration of the problem that arises when powerful firms in a number of different industries (though individually in an oligopoly rather than a monopoly position in their own fields) are so interconnected financially that their mutual relationship may be thought to present serious barriers to competitors over a wide front. In this case the Government complained in effect that vast stock interests held by the du Pont company (and by members of the du Pont family as individuals) in the General Motors Corporation and in the United States Rubber Company necessarily 'tied up' a huge volume of trade between them, so that competitive opportunities in the

---

[1] The Supreme Court refused to review the case. The Government subsequently brought civil proceedings in order to secure equity reliefs against the defendants.

many fields covered by these companies were reduced; in the Government's view the financial connexions between the companies amounted to a conspiracy to restrain and monopolize a large volume of trade.

The trial Court dismissed the Government's charges. While the evidence showed that the du Pont company and family had made enormous investments in General Motors and United States Rubber, and had taken part as important stockholders in the selection of key officials of those companies and in the formulation of high-level policy, it was not shown to the satisfaction of the Court that these mutual relations had influenced the course of trade between the three concerns. Judge La Buy's broad conclusion was that du Pont's status in General Motors and United States Rubber resulted in 'consultation and conference but not domination' and it was said to be 'conjectural' whether, if it ever came to a showdown, the voice of du Pont would have carried against that of the management and other interests concerned in those companies.

Meanwhile, though it was conceded that General Motors was a huge customer for du Pont's synthetic fabrics and finishes and that United States Rubber was its main supplier of tyres, Judge La Buy found no evidence that General Motors was in any way 'tied' to du Pont in matters of trading; indeed, he accepted evidence to the effect that they decided these matters on their commercial merits and not infrequently went to other suppliers for products that du Pont had to sell. 'When read as a whole the record supports a finding, and the Court so finds, that there has not been, nor is there at present, a conspiracy to restrain or to monopolize trade and no limitation or restraint upon General Motors' freedom to deal freely and fully with competitors of du Pont and United States Rubber, no limitation or restraint upon the freedom of General Motors to deal with its chemical discoveries, no restraint or monopolization of the General Motors market and no restraint or monopolization of the trade and commerce between du Pont and United States Rubber.' On appeal the Supreme Court held that the du Pont holdings in General Motors violated section 7 of the Clayton Act without ruling on the Sherman Act aspects of the case. A discussion of the problem of devising a suitable remedy in this case is contained in Chapter XIV below. Similar issues have arisen under section 7 of the Clayton Act and mergers have been prohibited on the grounds that 'they would lead to reciprocity in trading, and thereby the foreclosure of other companies from part of the market.'[1]

---

[1] See Chapter VII below, especially pp. 191–4.

6. *Recapitulation of the law of section 2 as applying to oligopoly situations*

How then does the law stand with regard to the oligopoly—the concentrated industry in which a handful of large firms dominate the scene?

In the first place it seems to be the better opinion that antitrust will not succeed in eliminating such restrictive effects as may result from this type of industrial structure by broadening the legal meaning of 'conspiracy'. As was seen above (Chapter III), mere similarity of action in pricing policy and other matters will not be enough—particularly since Mr Justice Clark's opinion in the *Theatre Enterprises* case—to sustain a case under section 1 of the Sherman Act. There must be evidence of substance from which a genuine 'meeting of the minds' in a common understanding or plan may be inferred. It now appears that this holds true also in respect to charges of 'conspiracy to monopolize' under section 2. Rightly or wrongly, a jury, properly instructed as to the law, found that a common understanding had been established in the *Tobacco* case. Even in the *Paramount* case—which perhaps exhibits a more relaxed view of 'conspiracy' than any other in the record—the trial Court as finder of fact ultimately rested its finding of 'conspiracy to monopolize' on the prior conspiracy between the distributors to fix minimum admission prices in cinemas, and to impose unreasonable runs and clearances.

It is true that some commentators of authority take the other view. They hold in effect that the Sherman Act is concerned solely with unreasonable restraint of trade and that the courts will not much concern themselves with the label attached to the means by which the restraint is brought about. Thus one writer has it that a finding of conspiracy may be simply 'a shorthand device for saying that two or more persons have violated the Sherman Act by combining to produce an unreasonable restraint of trade'.[1] It is claimed that the Sherman Act itself in condemning 'any combination in the form of trust or otherwise . . . in restraint of trade' is authority for this view, and that a situation such as that in the *Tobacco* case is more accurately described as an 'otherwise form of combination' than as a conspiracy in the dictionary or common-law sense. The essence of this view is summed up in the proposition: 'If what they do produces a demonstrably unreasonable effect on competition, the requirement that they do so in combina-

---

[1] The quotations in this paragraph are taken from a paper, 'Conspiracy and Conspire—What do these Words Mean in Sherman Act Decisions?', delivered by Mr Robert L. Wright to the University of Chicago Law School Antitrust Seminar in 1953. This paper has not been published and I am indebted to Mr Wright for making available a copy and permitting me to make use of it here.

tion seems to be satisfied if each understands what the other is doing and the intended result.'[1]

A powerful case can be made for this view. The negative aspect of the argument is indeed unassailable. If they are not convinced that trade is significantly restrained, the courts will not find an antitrust offence even though the element of conspiracy or agreement is palpable. 'No parallelism whether conscious or unconscious can overcome a finding of reasonableness,' said Judge Yankwich; and indeed an outright agreement, as the *Appalachian Coals* case witnesses, may escape condemnation if competition is not in practice effectively restrained by it. But it does not follow that, wherever competition *is* effectively restrained, the courts will be able to impute to the parties concerned some form of illegal combination or conspiracy so as to bring the matter within the condemnation of section 1 of the Sherman Act. It is this proposition that the weight of authority disclaims; it appears implausible, too, in the light of the time and effort spent by the government prosecutors in the cases in establishing, directly or by inference, just that element of agreement that is said to be unnecessary.

This whole discussion may, of course, be academic. It may be that in practice the leading firms in a concentrated industry (given that their output is genuinely overlapping and competitive) cannot for long damp down the competition between them without giving rise to evidence of a common understanding sufficient to condemn them. This view too has informed support. It is, of course, a matter of appraising the law rather than describing it to say how true this may be, and the attempt must be deferred to Part II, below. But this view in any case does not deal with the problem—if it be a problem—that a concentrated or oligopoly industry, even when the leading firms are competing among themselves, may still present barriers to the competition of new entrants and small firms generally. In other words, such an industry, though competitive in some ways, may be restrictive in others. Those who want to bring antitrust to bear on oligopoly often seem to have this problem in mind at least as much as the problem of competition between the oligopolists themselves.

This leads on to another powerful reason why section 1 of the Sherman Act is unlikely to serve their purpose. The obvious remedy when a restrictive agreement is condemned under section 1 is to prohibit the parties from continuing to work to the agreement and to insist

---

[1] This sentence might be taken as simply defining a 'common understanding'. If each 'understands' by dint of an understanding, it is not far from the orthodox view. But if each 'understands' only in the sense of 'recognizes' or 'appreciates' without the slightest hint of reciprocal obligation, it goes beyond what is settled law. A similar ambiguity arises from the words 'intended result': if restraint of trade is really the *common* intent of the parties, then there is a true conspiracy.

that they make their commercial decisions wholly independently. But if those economists are right who say that the very existence of an oligopoly structure will result in damping down competition, and if those lawyers are right who say that the damping down of competition is in itself enough to constitute an offence, whether or not the legal label of 'conspiracy' can strictly be applied, then successful prosecutions under section 1 will not in any case put matters right. It is no good telling the businessman to stop conspiring if all that is meant by 'conspiring' is reacting intelligently to the situation in which he finds himself. How can he make decisions independently if the very structure of his industry makes him and his main rivals interdependent?

This point has not escaped those who want antitrust to crack oligopoly. They see clearly enough that to put matters right (from their standpoint) means altering the structure itself. In other words, they would hope to persuade the courts to order the dissolution of the leading firms in a concentrated industry—to break up the 'big three' or 'big four' in an oligopoly into a medium-sized nine or twelve. But even if the courts, against the weight of authority, were prepared to treat the concept of conspiracy elastically, it seems very doubtful that they would ever adopt the drastic remedy of dissolution in a case that turned on an extreme legal interpretation.[1]

For these reasons—because the concept of conspiracy seems unlikely to be stretched any further, and because, even if it were, the remedy of dissolution would probably not be applied—it may well be that in future the attack on oligopoly will be based not on imputing conspiracy to the firms concerned, but on law derived from cases against monopolizing under section 2 of the Sherman Act.

It is not difficult to see how a powerful argument might be constructed from various of the doctrines and dicta outlined in the last three chapters. The *Motion Picture Advertising* case shows the way. There was no suggestion in that case of collusion, yet the exclusive contracts of the four leading companies were viewed by the Supreme Court in the light of their cumulative effect on actual and potential competition. The contracts of the four, added together, 'tied up' 75% of the users of advertising films (even this figure of 75% was reached only by including the contracts of one year's duration that the Federal Trade Commission was prepared to allow), and the Supreme Court thought it was 'plain . . . that a device which has sewed up a market so tightly for the benefit of the few falls within the prohibitions of the Sherman Act'.

---

[1] It is noteworthy in this connexion that, although the Government won the *Tobacco* case in 1946 having convinced a jury that there was a genuine 'conspiracy to monopolize', no civil case to seek the dissolution of the major companies has ever been proceeded with.

It is true that this decision dealt only with a particular monopolistic practice, not with monopolizing as such. The *Car finance* case also dealt with tying devices and, as far back as 1941, one of the arguments used against General Motors was that the group were 'monopolizing' the financing of their own cars. Presumably, in the civil cases subsequently brought against Ford and Chrysler, the same argument could have been advanced about them and their cars. There seems to be no legal difficulty about bringing three or four cases of monopolizing simultaneously in the same industry. Since the *Car finance* case, too, the so-called 'parts of commerce' doctrine has developed considerably. From the *Yellow Cab* opinion and the *National City Lines* decision it seems clear that the trade done in a commodity by any large group of affiliated companies can constitute 'an appreciable part of commerce' for the purposes of section 2 of the Sherman Act. And 'it is illegal *per se* to foreclose an appreciable part of commerce'.

It may be objected that these examples still have to do with foreclosing a market by means of exclusive-dealing or coercive tying arrangements or vertical integration. But might it not be argued that the method by which an appreciable segment of commerce is foreclosed or monopolized cannot be decisive, since the Sherman Act looks to substance, not to form? Provided that the three or four leading firms in an industry were each found to have shown some element of purposive drive to get and keep their oligopoly position (in other words, provided that they could not claim it was merely 'thrust upon them'), could they not each individually be charged with monopolizing their own segment of the market? There would be no difficulty about establishing intent and purpose, for evidence would be brought to show that an industry sewn up so tightly for the benefit of three or four firms necessarily reduces competitive opportunities. What could be more exclusionary in effect than for each of the three leading firms in a concentrated industry progressively to embrace each new opportunity in its own segment of the market and face every newcomer with new capacity already geared into one of the three great organizations? He who wills the means wills the end, and no oligopolist oligopolizes unconscious of what he is doing.

This argument is at present, of course, a fiction constructed for purposes of illustration: no major case, so far as the record shows up to date, has been fought by the Government on this theory. Yet one may wonder if Judge Learned Hand or Mr Justice Douglas would find serious flaws in it; and one may conjecture that it is an attack on these lines that the concentrated industries have to fear rather than any further attempt to broaden the concept of conspiracy.

CHAPTER VII

THE CLAYTON ACT
I. INTRODUCTION; MERGERS AND ACQUISITIONS

1. *Origins and aims of the Clayton Act*

The previous chapters have dealt almost entirely with the case law under the Sherman Act, though a few cases under the Federal Trade Commission Act have been mentioned. We turn now to the Clayton Act, which was passed in 1914.[1]

The evidence given in the big cases in the period leading up to this legislation—particularly the *Oil* and *Tobacco* cases—had shown certain recurrent ways in which the monopoly power of the 'trusts' was built up. They had secretly gained control of ostensibly independent companies by acquiring stock and voting it through holding companies; they had 'tied up' important sources of supply or channels of distribution through various types of exclusive contract; they had brought to heel inconvenient competitors by local price cutting campaigns, often carried on through 'fighting companies'. The feeling grew that it ought to be possible to prohibit these trust building or monopolizing devices specifically: the hope was that, given such a prohibition, no new 'trusts' of the Standard Oil type would appear and the Sherman Act would meanwhile secure the break-up of those already in being. The preamble to the original Clayton bill explained that its purpose was:

to prohibit certain trade practices which . . . singly and in themselves are not covered by the [Sherman Act] . . . and thus to arrest the creation of trusts, conspiracies and monopolies in their incipiency and before consummation.

There were, however, two opposed theories of how this should be done. In the House of Representatives, the favoured plan was to specify the devices in question—acquisition of stock in competing companies, exclusive dealing, and price discrimination or local price cutting—and make them straightforward criminal offences. Thus exclusive dealing was to be prohibited without qualification; price discrimination was to

---

[1] I have been greatly helped in these pages by Mr Breck P. McAllister's brief but very clear account of the legislative history of the Clayton Act in his paper, 'Where the Effect may be to Substantially Lessen Competition or Tend to Create a Monopoly', *A.B.A. Antitrust Section, Proceedings*, vol. 3, 1953, p. 124.

be an offence when accompanied by an intent to injure a competitor; and stock acquisitions were to be banned when their effect was substantially to lessen competition. This theory reflected in part a desire to make the antitrust laws clearer and to leave the businessman less excuse for pleading uncertainty as to what he could and could not lawfully do. There were at that time complaints, as there have always been before and since, that the broad terms of the Sherman Act (and the differing standards of the courts in applying the rule of reason) left too much open to doubt. President Wilson himself had called for legislation 'in such terms as will practically eliminate uncertainty'.

The majority in the Senate, on the other hand, believed that the prophylactic work of 'nipping in the bud' attempts to build up monopoly power should be left to the newly created Federal Trade Commission, which was to be an expert body capable of assessing the competitive effects likely to result from the various dodges that powerful firms might adopt in their quest for market power. Consequently they introduced into the measure setting up the Federal Trade Commission a general declaration that 'unfair methods of competition' were unlawful.[1] It was assumed that these words would cover the specific practices which the House was aiming to prohibit in the Clayton bill.

It was argued in favour of this method of proceeding that it would be at once more efficacious and more selective than specific prohibitions: more efficacious, because any list of specific offences might be found later not to cover some new device that the ingenious monopolist might hit upon; more selective, in that unqualified (or barely qualified) prohibitions might restrict the activities of those who had the best chance of competing against the giants. Much was made in the debates of the point that what was 'unfair' competition on the part of a powerful firm against small rivals might very well be 'fair' when used by the small against the powerful. Nobody should worry, for example, if a small oil company, attempting to get a footing in the market, secured steady distributive outlets through exclusive contracts or if it infiltrated into a major company's territory by price cutting. Yet the proposed unqualified ban on exclusive dealing, and that on price discrimination with intent to injure a competitor, would bite on large and small alike.

The Senate, on this theory, would have done without a Clayton Act altogether, and did indeed delete the prohibitions of price discrimination and exclusive dealing from the House's bill. Eventually a compromise was reached between the two Houses, under which the specific prohibitions were retained in the Clayton Act but in a form that simply declared these practices unlawful and did not make them criminal offences. At the same time the qualifying phrase, 'where the effect may

---

[1] Section 5 of the Federal Trade Commission Act.

be to substantially lessen competition or tend to create a monopoly', was inserted in each main provision. It seems that the school of thought in favour of specific prohibitions was satisfied with getting the illegality of exclusive dealing, price discrimination and stock acquisitions spelled out in the Act, and felt that this declaration of congressional condemnation of such practices would give the Federal Trade Commission unmistakable authority to deal with them effectively. The other school of thought accepted the compromise because it avoided new criminal offences, and because it was felt that the qualifying clause would enable the Commission to be flexible and discriminating in their enforcement of the measure.

The compromise did not do much, however, to reduce the businessman's uncertainty about what the law required of him. The qualifying clause was in effect a rule of reason for the Clayton Act, and all would now depend on the view taken by the Federal Trade Commission and the courts of what constituted a 'substantial' lessening of competition. Moreover, the words 'may be' in the qualifying clause introduced an element of prophecy into the matter; they were in a sense a mortgage taken out against the expected economic expertise of the Commission. The plaintiff would not be required to prove that the practice complained of had already seriously impaired competition (though, of course, if he could prove this, it would be decisive), nor that those responsible for the practice specifically intended to effect a substantial lessening of competition, though they had not yet done so. It would be enough for him to show a threat or potential whence a substantial lessening of competition in the future might be expected; and this showing the respondent would have to rebut. This element of looking into the future was perhaps indispensable, given the lawmakers' hope of catching the process of monopolizing 'in its incipiency', and given their abandonment of the proposal to make specified practices illegal *per se*. But it could hardly make things easier for the businessman; and so the old issue between a clear law and a flexible law remains unresolved.

2. *Original section 7 of the Clayton Act; the 1950 Celler-Kefauver Act amendments*

Section 7 of the Clayton Act is a development in more specific form of an aspect of the law on monopolization under the Sherman Act; for example the *Columbia Steel* case, in which the question was raised whether the acquisition of competing companies witnessed to a purposive drive for monopoly power.

Originally section 7 was referred to as the 'holding company' section, and the lawmakers in 1914 seem to have envisaged it as a means of preventing important concerns in any industry from growing into 'trusts' by buying up stock in competing concerns and exercising industry-wide control through a holding company. They worded the main provision as follows:

That no corporation engaged in commerce shall acquire, directly or indirectly, the whole or any part of the stock or other share capital of another corporation engaged also in commerce, where the effect of such acquisition may be to substantially lessen competition between the corporation whose stock is so acquired and the corporation making the acquisition, or to restrain such commerce in any section or community, or tend to create a monopoly in any line of commerce.

Further provisions made it clear that the prohibition extended to the acquisition of stock in a number of companies such that competition between all those acquired might be substantially lessened, but that it did not apply to purchases of stock purely for investment nor to the formation of subsidiary companies intended to carry on the legitimate business of the parent company. It will be noted also that the wording of the section did not cover the acquisition of the physical assets of a competing company.

In the course of time, because of loopholes in the formulation of these provisions and the manner in which the courts interpreted them, the section came to be regarded as ineffective. On its face the wording covered any case in which the acquiring and the acquired companies were direct competitors. The courts, however, were inclined to look for a substantial effect on competition in the industry at large, and dismissed cases in which the business of the acquiring and acquired companies was largely done in different markets or in which, though competition between the acquiring and acquired concerns was eliminated, there was evidence of strong competition from outside the group.[1]

As acquisitions of the physical assets of a competitor were not covered by the section, mergers could still continue on a large scale.[2] In *United States* v. *Celanese Corporation of America* (Southern District Court of New York, 1950) it was held that 'a merger with another company . . . does not constitute an indirect acquisition of stock, although it is an acquisition of the property represented by the stock, and although an acquisition of stock may be incidental to the merger'. The Court explained that the original purpose of section 7 had been

[1] The leading case on this topic is *International Shoe Company* v. *Federal Trade Commission* (Supreme Court, 1930). *United States* v. *Republic Steel Corporation* (District Court of Ohio, 1935) is also important.

[2] 'Merger' is used here in its American sense, that is the consolidation of the assets of two or more companies into a single corporate body.

'to prevent the secret holding of stock by one company while the captive company was held out to the public as a competitor'. An open and outright merger did not, therefore, come within the rationale of the section. Even earlier it had been decided that, where a company illegally acquired stock in a competing concern and then, before the Federal Trade Commission issued a 'cease and desist' order against the acquisition, used the stock to obtain control of the physical assets, it could not subsequently be ordered to disgorge the physical assets. Only if the Commission acted before the physical assets had been acquired, could it prevent a company that illegally acquired stock from proceeding to get control of the assets.[1] This loophole in itself was enough to emasculate the prohibition.

In 1950 the Congress, in the Celler-Kefauver Act, made another attempt to draft effective provisions. This time it clearly intended to check mergers of all kinds and not merely secret stock holdings. By this Act the main provision of section 7 of the Clayton Act was revised to read as follows:

No corporation engaged in commerce shall acquire, directly or indirectly, the whole or any part of the stock or other share capital and no corporation subject to the jurisdiction of the Federal Trade Commission shall acquire the whole or any part of the assets of another corporation engaged also in commerce, where, in any line of commerce in any section of the country, the effect of such acquisition may be substantially to lessen competition or to tend to create a monopoly.

As before, the section does not apply to purchases of stock purely for investment nor to the formation of legitimate subsidiary companies. This revision was calculated to close the loophole by which mergers could previously be accomplished by purchases of assets, whether or not these purchases were brought about through illegally held stock. The words 'part of the assets' have indeed been held to cover even the purchase of a single trademark by one company from another.[2]

Supreme Court decisions on the interpretation of the revised section 7 have made it clear that the section now bites not only on 'horizontal'

---

[1] *Swift and Company* v. *Federal Trade Commission* (Supreme Court, 1926). Mr Justice McReynolds said: 'When the Commission institutes a proceeding based upon the holding of stock contrary to section 7 of the Clayton Act, its power is limited . . . to an order requiring the guilty person to cease and desist from such violation, effectually to divest itself of the stock and make no further use of it. The Act has no application to ownership of a competitor's property and business obtained prior to any action by the Commission, even though this was brought about through stock unlawfully held.' This ruling was followed in *Arrow-Hart and Hegeman Electric Company* v. *Federal Trade Commission* (Supreme Court, 1934).

[2] The acquisition by Lever Brothers from Monsanto Chemical Company of the trademark 'all' relating to detergents: *United States* v. *Lever Brothers Company* (Southern District Court of New York, 1963).

mergers between competitors in the same markets, but also on the 'vertical' merger between firms in a supplier and customer relationship, and on the 'conglomerate' merger between firms in unrelated markets. In the years since the passage of the revised section, a large number of cases under it have come before the Supreme Court, and it is noteworthy that the Department of Justice and Federal Trade Commission have not yet lost a case at this level.[1] In considering how the Supreme Court has developed the interpretation of section 7 it will be convenient first to consider cases involving mergers with horizontal or vertical aspects, and to postpone the treatment of conglomerate mergers, which raise rather special considerations, to a later section.

3. *Supreme Court treatment of horizontal and vertical mergers:* Brown Shoe; Philadelphia National Bank; Continental Can; Von's Grocery

Twelve years had elapsed from the passage of the revised section 7 before the Supreme Court handed down its first full-length decision in which the legislative history and substantive content of the section were analysed and applied to the facts of a particular merger. The case in which this was done was *Brown Shoe Company v. United States* (Supreme Court, 1962). During these twelve years decisions of the District Courts in cases brought by the Department of Justice, and decisions of the Federal Trade Commission, had indicated that the new section would undoubtedly serve to prevent further acquisitions by companies already dominant in their relevant markets, at least of their leading competitors. Thus, for example, in 1958 the proposed merger between Bethlehem Steel Corporation and Youngstown Sheet and Tube Company, who at the time ranked as the second and sixth largest steel companies in the United States, was enjoined by the District Court for the Southern District of New York on the grounds that competition in an already oligopolistic market would be still further lessened by the elimination of one of the largest companies in the industry. But many questions arising on the interpretation of the section remained unanswered, and the full potential of the section was not yet completely appreciated.

The merger at issue in the *Brown Shoe* case was that between the Brown Shoe Company and the G. R. Kinney Company, both of which were manufacturers and retailers of shoes. There were, therefore, both horizontal and vertical aspects to the merger. Brown was the fourth largest manufacturer, though with only 4% of the total United States market, and the third largest retailer of shoes, of both its own and other manufacture, with a 6% market share. Kinney was the twelfth largest

---

[1] Except for the second hearing in the Supreme Court of the *Penn-Olin* case (see pp. 198–9), when that Court affirmed by a four to four vote the result of the retrial in the District Court which found for the defendants.

manufacturer, producing only 0·5% of total output, but as a retailer it ranked eighth in the country with just under 2% of total sales. Before the merger Kinney retail shops had obtained 20% of their total supplies from Kinney factories and none from Brown's factories; after the merger they still only took 20% of their supplies from factories formerly owned by Kinney and 8% from factories owned by Brown.

The District Court for the Eastern District of Missouri had held that the merger of the manufacturing operations was not significant enough to violate section 7, and the Department of Justice did not appeal against this decision. The Supreme Court did, however, uphold the District Court's findings that the merger would violate the section with regard to both its vertical aspect and its horizontal effect on retail trade. Chief Justice Warren, in rendering the Court's decision, emphasized that the intention of Congress had been to check the rising tide of concentration in the American economy by arresting mergers at a stage where the trend to a lessening of competition in a particular line of commerce was still in its incipiency. The Sherman Act had proved inadequate for this purpose (this was a clear reference to *Columbia Steel*), and the concern of the new section 7 was therefore to be with the probabilities of substantial damage to competition, rather than with any proof that such damage was inevitable. Congress had provided no definitive quantitative or qualititative test for determining the meaning of a substantial lessening of competition, but had plainly indicated that each merger had to be seen in the context of its particular industry. The factors to be considered included, first, whether the merger was to take place in an industry not yet concentrated; secondly, whether that industry had seen a recent trend towards domination by a few market leaders or had remained fairly consistent in its distribution of market shares among participating companies; and, thirdly, whether there was easy access to markets by suppliers and to suppliers by buyers, or whether substantial business was foreclosed to competition. A fourth relevant factor was whether new entry to the industry was possible without undue difficulty.

In applying these tests Chief Justice Warren noted that the District Court had found significant trends in the shoe industry: an increase in the number of retail outlets controlled by shoe manufacturers, who were supplying an ever increasing percentage of their own retail requirements, and a decrease in the number of companies manufacturing shoes. He dealt first with the vertical aspects of the merger, and emphasized that an important consideration was the percentage of the relevant market which it would foreclose. This percentage share would not normally be determinative in itself, unless of either monopoly or *de minimis* proportions, and it was therefore necessary in addition to consider the various economic and historical factors relating to the industry. These included the trends towards concentration and manufacturer-retailer integration referred to above, and Brown's undoubted object to supply as large a share as possible of the shoes sold by the Kinney retail outlets, thereby foreclosing them from the purchase of shoes made by other manufacturers. After defining the relevant lines of commerce as being men's, women's and children's shoes, and the geographic market as the entire United States, he concluded:

...the shoe industry is being subjected to just such a cumulative series of vertical mergers which, if left unchecked, will be likely substantially to lessen competition.

Turning to the horizontal aspects of the merger, the Court again considered its effect against the background of the way the shoe business had developed in the past and likely future trends. The Court noted that the parties had failed to demonstrate any 'mitigating factors', such as that they were companies which required to merge in order to compete more effectively with other powerful companies in the market. It gave weight to the finding that in the relevant geographic sub-markets, which could properly be treated as the appropriate 'section of the country', the combined market share of the two companies would exceed 20% in many cities, and would thereby place the new company at a strong competitive advantage over most of its rivals. In striking down this aspect also of the merger, Chief Justice Warren commented:

Some of the results of large integrated or chain operations are beneficial to consumers. Their expansion is not rendered unlawful by the mere fact that small independent stores may be adversely affected. It is competition, not competitors, which the Act protects. We cannot fail to recognize Congress's desire to promote competition through the protection of viable small locally owned businesses. Congress appreciated that occasional higher costs and prices might result from the maintenance of fragmented industries and markets. It resolved these competing considerations in favour of decentralization. We must give effect to that decision.

The *Brown Shoe* decision appeared at the time to mean that the principal criterion in assessing a merger was to be its 'qualitative substantiality', that is its overall impact on the competitive process in the particular industry, rather than merely its 'quantitative substantiality' —the size and market share of the companies involved. In the following year, however, the judgment of the Supreme Court in *United States* v. *Philadelphia National Bank* (1963) seemed in its turn to throw doubt on this assumption. This case concerned a proposed merger between the Philadelphia National Bank and Girard Trust Corn Exchange Bank, whose shares of the commercial banking market within the four-county area in and around Philadelphia (adjudged the relevant geographical market) were 22% and 15% respectively. They were the second and third largest banks within the area, the largest having 23% of the market. Thus, in approximate terms, before the merger the 'top two' held 45% of the market, the 'top three' 60%, and the 'top four' about 70%. After it the corresponding figures would have been 60%, 70% and 78%. The decisive passage in the Supreme Court's opinion was as follows:

Specifically we think that a merger which produces a firm controlling an undue percentage share of the relevant market and results in a significant increase in the concentration of firms in that market is so inherently likely to lessen competition substantially that it must be enjoined in the absence of evidence clearly showing that the merger is not likely to have such anti-competitive effects.) . . . Such a test lightens the burden of proving illegality only with respect to mergers whose size makes them inherently suspect in the light of Congress's design in section 7 to prevent undue concentration. Furthermore the test is fully consonant with economic theory. . . .

The Court's five to two decision on the merits of the case went on to state that, even if it accepted certain evidence advanced by the banks to the effect that their combined market share did not exceed 30%, this percentage was still large enough to justify the inference drawn by the Court. In an interesting footnote it pointed out that 'scholarly opinion' had suggested 20% or 25% as a suitable figure at which such an inference could begin to be drawn.[1]

As authority for this approach, the majority of the Court relied on statements in the legislative history of the revised section 7 that the tests of illegality under it were intended to be similar to those which the Court had used in interpreting the same language in other sections of the Clayton Act. They pointed out that in *Standard Stations* (discussed in Chapter VIII below and decided under section 3 of the Act), the defendant, whose exclusive-dealing arrangements had been held illegal, had accounted for 23% of the sales in the relevant market and, together with the six other leading firms in the market, had accounted for 65% of such sales. In *Federal Trade Commission* v. *Motion Picture Advertisers* (above, Chapter VI), the exclusive arrangements there held illegal were carried on by the four leading companies in the industry with about 75% of the market. These figures were therefore held to be 'highly suggestive' in the context of the merger between the two Philadelphia banks, especially as integration by merger was inherently more suspect than integration by contract because of the permanence of its effect.

[1] Thus Kaysen and Turner, for example, had suggested 20%: *Antitrust Policy*, p. 99.

The banks also argued that Philadelphia needed a bank of the size contemplated by the merger in order to be able to compete with the large New York City banks in making major industrial loans. The Court's treatment of this argument was curt.

We are clear however that a merger the effect of which 'may be substantially to lessen competition' is not saved because, on some ultimate reckoning of social or economic debits and credits, it may be deemed beneficial. A value choice of such magnitude is beyond the ordinary limits of judicial competence, and in any event has been made for us already, by Congress when it enacted the amended section 7. Congress determined to preserve our traditionally competitive economy. It therefore proscribed anti-competitive mergers, the benign and the malignant, fully aware, we must assume, that some price might have to be paid.

In effect, therefore, the Supreme Court was now saying that the *Brown Shoe* approach of examining each merger in the context of its particular effect on the competitive process in the relevant market did not apply, or at least could be shortcircuited by a purely quantitative test, where the combined market shares of the two companies involved, and of the other leading companies in the relevant market, reached the levels of the *Philadelphia National Bank* case.

In the following year, 1964, the Supreme Court had occasion to apply its *Philadelphia National Bank* reasoning in two other cases brought by the Department of Justice, in which the legality of the mergers between the Aluminum Company of America (ALCOA) and the Rome Cable Company, and between the Continental Can Company and Hazel Atlas Glass Company, were challenged.[1] In the *Continental Can* case the majority of the Court found that the relevant market was glass and metal containers throughout the entire United States, of which market Continental held approximately 22% and Hazel Atlas 3%, being the second and sixth largest firms respectively. Their resulting combined market share was said to approach that held presumptively bad in the *Philadelphia National Bank* case. Furthermore, besides reducing the number of significant competitors in the market from five to four, the merger would, if permitted, engender a much broader anti-competitive effect by triggering other mergers by companies seeking the same advantages as those sought in this case by Continental. Elaborate proof of market structure, market behaviour and probable anti-competitive effects was not required in cases where the merger was of the size to be inherently suspect.

The judgment in the *ALCOA* case followed a similar pattern. Mr

---

[1] Both cases turned very largely on the definition of the 'relevant market' to be adopted, and this aspect of the *Continental Can* case is dealt with in section 5 of this chapter.

Justice Douglas for the majority of the Court stressed that ALCOA was a leading force in the highly concentrated markets of aluminium and copper manufacture, which were dominated by a few large companies but were also served by a small and diminishing group of independent, non-integrated manufacturers. Entry into the market was difficult and the establishment in recent years of new competition in the industry had only come about through federal intervention. Although Rome only held 1·3% of the relevant cable market, compared with ALCOA's 27·8%, it was an aggressive competitor which had pioneered new developments in aluminium insulation and had an active and effective research and sales organization ('the prototype of the small independent that Congress sought to preserve by section 7'). In the context of an oligopolistic market, it should be protected in order that the tendency to oligopoly might be halted and even reversed. Mr Justice Harlan entered a vehement dissent, calling the majority opinion 'an abrupt and unwise departure from established antitrust law'. The main ground of his disagreement was with the majority's finding as to the relevant market, but he also alleged that the majority decision meant that all mergers between two large companies in related industries were presumptively unlawful. He claimed that the majority had failed to recognize that, where the allegation was that competition between two distinct industries would be threatened, the 'short cut' market share approach was inappropriate.

Mr Justice Harlan (together with Mr Justice Stewart) was also to dissent sharply in a subsequent case, *United States* v. *Von's Grocery Company* (1966). Here the central issue was not, however, the relevant market (for this was clearly the retail grocery business in the Los Angeles area) but whether the facts found by the District Court entitled the Supreme Court to rule that there was, within this market, a trend towards concentration. The merger challenged was that between Von's Grocery Company and its competitor, Shopping Bag Food Stores. Von's had the third largest retail sales in the area (4·7%), Shopping Bag had the sixth largest (4·2%). The four largest companies had 24% of the market, the eight largest had 41% and the twelve largest had 49%; whereas ten years previously the corresponding percentages had been 26%, 34% and 39%. The number of single-store grocers had dropped in the same period from approximately 5,300 to 3,800, and nine of the top twenty chains had acquired an aggregate of at least 120 stores from their smaller competitors. Against the background of this 'threatening trend to concentration' the merger of Von's and Shopping Bag was characterized as 'the case of two already powerful companies merging in a way which makes them even more powerful than they were before'. Mr Justice Black continued, in giving the majority opinion:

If ever such a merger would not violate section 7, certainly it does when it takes place in a market characterized by a long and continuous trend towards fewer and fewer owner-competitors, which is exactly the sort of trend which Congress, with power to do so, declared must be arrested.

Mr Justice White delivered a brief concurring opinion, in which he expressly dissociated himself from purporting to hold that, in any industry exhibiting a decided trend towards concentration, any merger between competing firms violates section 7 unless saved by the 'failing company' doctrine. He preferred to base his agreement with the majority on the ground that, where the eight leading companies in a market have over 40% of that market, any merger by or (*a fortiori*) between them is 'vulnerable' in the absence of some special proof to the contrary.

The really sharp criticism, however, of the majority opinion came in the minority opinion of Justices Stewart and Harlan. In a powerfully reasoned analysis, they accused the majority of laying down a startling *per se* rule, contrary not only to previous Supreme Court decisions, but also to the language and legislative history of section 7, as well as economic reality. The majority had apparently adopted the fallacy that competition is necessarily reduced when the number of competitors has declined, whereas the fact was that the structure of the Los Angeles grocery market was not in any meaningful sense threatened by concentration; on the contrary, the continuing population explosion offered a surfeit of business opportunities for stores of all kinds. The decline in the number of single-store owners was the natural result of the demise of the 'Mom and Pop grocery store' and the advance in the growth of the modern supermarkets (often themselves only one, two or three-store operations). The dynamism and vitality of competition during the decade under review, and the lack of barriers to entry, were typified by the fact that during that time alone 173 new chains had made their appearance and 119 had gone out of existence. After further analysis of the record, and criticism of the failure of the majority to demonstrate that the increment in market share obtained by the merging firms gave them any increase at all in market power, the dissent concluded with a warning that the decision might well in the long run harm competition, by deterring potential entrants who might reasonably fear being unable to sell out at some future date if they should wish to do so.

It is hardly surprising that the spokesmen of big business, taking their cue from this judicial dissent, have also freely expressed their criticisms of the *Von's Grocery* decision. They claim that its effect is virtually to prohibit the acquisition by any substantial company of any other company in competition with it on the horizontal level; and in this context 'substantial' by the test of *Von's Grocery* may be a company with a 5% share of a local market. It may indeed be that the case will come to be regarded as the high-water mark of judicial interpretation of section 7: the final step in a process that, to quote one leading practitioner, 'has seen reasonable probability become possibility; possibility become prediction; prediction become presumption of competitive effect'.[1]

Certainly the tests used in this case seem a far cry from that of intent to monopolize under section 2 of the Sherman Act, or even from those that might be apt for determining whether the use of acquisitions might disclose such an intent 'in its incipiency'. Much weight has clearly been given to the desire of Congress in the 1950 legislation to promote decentralization and, in Chief Justice Warren's words, 'the protection of viable small locally owned businesses'.

On the other hand it is noteworthy that the areas of commerce covered by this line of cases have not in general been such as to draw the attention of the courts, as might happen in major manufacturing industries, to defences based on the economic case for a larger scale of operations than one party to a merger seemed likely to attain on its own, or on the possible desirability in a fairly concentrated industry for two of the smaller firms to merge in order to provide more effective competition against the giants. Much of the manufacturing industry of the United States is, of course, a great deal more highly concentrated in oligopolistic structures than the grocery business in Los Angeles and had become so well before the Celler-Kefauver Act was passed.

Clearly this Act and the subsequent case law are likely to act as a powerful deterrent against further concentration in any industry, but it might be premature to assume that the tests of 'qualitative substantiality' propounded by Chief Justice Warren would not enable the courts to take account of defences related to very different economic and industrial contexts from those of *Brown Shoe* or *Von's Grocery*. What may, perhaps, be doubted is whether economic theory, once the courts were to depart from the fairly simple presumptions of these cases, would permit the economic consequences of a merger to be identified with the precision needed for a confident judgment.[2]

Meanwhile the essence of the rule in *Von's Grocery* is, first, the identification of a market—as still relatively unconcentrated but with a detectable tendency in that direction—and, second, the presumption that a merger between competitors in that market (other than of *de minimis* size) will hasten that trend. The antitrust authorities have evidently taken the view that in the long run this approach will protect com-

---

[1] *A.B.A. Antitrust Section, Proceedings*, vol. 27, 1965, p. 115.

[2] See for a discussion of this point, D. C. Bok, 'Section 7 of the Clayton Act and the Merging of Law and Economics', in *Harvard Law Review*, vol. 74, 1960, p. 226. Dean Bok concludes that presumptive rules in the field are therefore to be favoured.

petition better than a full economic inquiry into each merger. This does not, however, apply to the same extent to conglomerate mergers.[1]

4. *Supreme Court treatment of conglomerate mergers:* Consolidated Foods; Clorox

Any doubts remaining over the applicability of section 7 to conglomerate mergers were removed by dicta of the Supreme Court in *Brown Shoe*; and a number of cases have since been brought by both the Federal Trade Commission and the Department of Justice against such mergers. They fall into two major classes: (*a*) 'Product extension', in which a company in one product market acquires a company operating in another unrelated market, for example a hardware chain in New York acquiring an electronics firm in Boston; (*b*) 'Market extension', in which a company operating in one or more geographic markets acquires a company operating in a similar product market in a separate geographic area, for example a hardware chain in New York acquiring another hardware firm in Boston.

The first case of a conglomerate merger to come before the Supreme Court was *Federal Trade Commission* v. *Consolidated Foods* (1965). The Federal Trade Commission had found that Consolidated, a large company which processed foods and sold them both wholesale and retail, had violated section 7 by its purchase of Gentry Inc., a company engaged in the production of dehydrated onion and garlic, on the ground that the acquisition would enable Consolidated to indulge in the practice of 'reciprocity'. By this was meant that Consolidated would make plain to its own suppliers, over many of whom it would, as a large and powerful company, have some economic leverage, that in return for Consolidated's purchases from them they would be expected to make purchases of dehydrated onion or garlic from Gentry. The other manufacturers of dehydrated onion and garlic might in this way be foreclosed from competing with Gentry for a part of this business.

The Seventh Circuit Court, in reversing the Commission's decision, had relied largely on ten years of post-acquisition experience,[2] which indicated that, while Gentry's share of the dehydrated onion market had increased by 7%, its share of the garlic market had decreased by 12%. For the Supreme Court, Mr Justice Douglas ruled that not much weight should be accorded to the post-acquisition evidence, because section 7 deals in terms of probabilities at the date of the acquisition and because such

---

[1] The Department of Justice issued, in 1968, 'Merger Guidelines' setting out the analysis which it will undertake in examining mergers under section 7 of the Clayton Act, and informing the business community and the legal profession of those mergers which the Department will consider clearly unlawful. These 'Guidelines', which generally reflect the underlying case law, are interesting in their detail and are reprinted as an appendix (see p. 494 ff.).

[2] The actual merger had taken place as long ago as 1951.

evidence, particularly during litigation, can be significantly manipulated by the defendant. Reciprocity was one of the 'congeries' of practices at which the antitrust laws were aimed: a threatened withdrawal of orders from suppliers if they ceased to buy products of an affiliate, or a conditioning of future purchases on the placing of such orders, was without doubt an anti-competitive practice. A merger would not violate section 7 merely because it made reciprocal buying possible, but a finding by the Federal Trade Commission of the substantial probability that this practice would follow the acquisition of a company commanding a substantial share of the market should, as in this case, be respected. Justices Harlan and Stewart delivered separate, but concurring, opinions.[1]

The practice of reciprocity has played a part in other cases brought under section 7. In *United States* v. *General Dynamics Corporation* (Southern District Court of New York, 1966), Judge Cannella refused to dismiss a Department of Justice action under this section challenging the acquisition by General Dynamics, one of the country's leading defence contractors (with net sales in 1957 of over 1·5 billion dollars), of Liquid Carbonic Corporation, the nation's largest domestic producer of carbon dioxide. The Judge ruled that the motive of the acquisition had been the opportunity for reciprocal trading, and that a special sales programme had been set up to take advantage of it. He went on to add that agreements which resulted in this practice would themselves be in breach of section 1 of the Sherman Act, since they involved a not insubstantial amount of commerce and were designed to foreclose competitors of Liquid Carbonic Corporation from the market.

Federal Trade Commission v. *The Procter & Gamble Co.* (Supreme Court, 1967) was the second conglomerate merger case to reach that Court. This concerned a product extension merger between Procter and Gamble, the country's leading producer of soap and detergent products, and Clorox Chemical Company, manufacturers of the leading brand of household liquid bleach. As in the *Consolidated Foods* case, the Court reversed a Court of Appeals decision that the Commission's prohibition of the merger should be overruled. The grounds relied on by the Court of Appeals had been post-acquisition evidence showing that Clorox's competitors in the household liquid bleach market suffered no loss of business following the merger; nor was there any evidence that Procter had intended to indulge in predatory practices.

The opinion of the majority of the Supreme Court was delivered by Mr Justice Douglas. He began by pointing out that before the merger Clorox (whose total assets were about $12 million) had 49% of the national market for household liquid bleach, with a dominant sales

---

[1] In a complaint brought by the Department of Justice against a merger between International Telephone and Telegraph Company and the Canteen Corporation, a major charge is that reciprocity is *likely*—not that either company has practised it in the past, or has specific intentions to do so.

position in nearly every major region of the country. Its nearest rival had 15%, and the 'top six' together 80% of the market. The remaining 20% was divided among 200 small producers. Since all liquid bleach is chemically identical, heavy advertising to create 'product differentiation' in the mind of the consumer was vital. Procter on the other hand was a huge manufacturer of low-priced household products, notably soaps, detergents and cleansing powders, with over 50% of the nation's packaged detergent market alone. Its total assets were over five hundred million dollars and its expenditure on advertising the largest in the country. Acquisition of a liquid bleach company was a natural 'product extension' move for Procter because the product would be sold through the same outlets as its existing main products and similarly required massive 'pre-selling' by advertising.

Against this background Mr Justice Douglas had little difficulty in finding that the merger would be likely to have substantial anti-competitive effects. The substitution in the liquid bleach market of the powerful Procter, in place of the smaller, but already dominant, Clorox, would undoubtedly dissuade smaller firms in the market from active price competition with Procter. Entry barriers would be raised because the volume discounts that Procter could obtain for its own advertising would be placed at the disposal of Clorox; and if any competitors in the future did attempt to enter the liquid bleach market, Procter could, at least temporarily, use its profits from other markets for a massive increase in sales promotion and advertisements to support Clorox in resisting the attack.[1] Further, prior to the merger Procter had itself been the most likely entrant to the market; and the mere possibility of its own entry (now removed) had had a beneficial effect on the competitive attitudes of the firms in that market.

Once again Mr Justice Harlan delivered a notable separate, though on this occasion concurring, opinion. As in *Von's Grocery* he expressed his disapproval of the majority's summary of the relevant competitive situation, and called for a 'more refined analysis' in place of their '*res ipsa loquitur*' approach. He said that lower courts had obviously been troubled in recent, conglomerate merger cases by the lack of authoritative criteria for their assessment, and it was incumbent upon the Court to embark upon the formulation of such standards, which the majority had made no effort to do. He himself offered four main guides for the assessment of such mergers:

First the decision can rest on analysis of market structure without resort to evidence of post-merger anti-competitive behaviour. Second, the operation of the pre-merger market must be understood as the foundation of successful analysis. The responsible agency may presume that the market operates

[1] This is graphically described as the 'deep pocket' or 'war chest' theory.

in accord with generally accepted principles of economic theory, but the presumption must be open to the challenge of alternative operational formulations. Third, if it is reasonably probable that there will be a change in market structure which will allow the exercise of substantially greater market power, then a prima facie case has been made out under section 7. Fourth, where a case against a merger rests on the probability of increased market power, merging companies may attempt to prove that there are countervailing economies reasonably probable which should be weighed against the adverse effects.

Applying these tests to the facts of the case, he agreed with the findings of the Commission that the merger would enhance the power of Clorox over prices in the relevant market, which, on the basis of the market shares of the leading firms and in the absence of any more cogent explanation put forward by the defendant, he would deem oligopolistic. He was less impressed by the argument that the mere existence of Procter as a potential entrant to the market would be sure to increase competition in that market, pointing out that the threat of potential competition merely affected the range over which pricing power extended and did not compel any more vigorous striving within the market nor advance any other social goal which Congress might have been said to have favoured in enacting section 7.

The case law on conglomerate mergers is not yet very extensive, and it may therefore be premature to attempt a comprehensive assessment of how the courts will treat them. It is clear that market share percentages are of less prima facie significance here than in horizontal and vertical mergers, and in their place it seems likely that the courts will choose certain significant factual issues as guides to their decisions. Professor Turner[1] has identified and analysed a number of these issues. Prominent among them are the effects of the merger on the behaviour of the other firms in the market, and also whether the size of the new entrant (as in the *Clorox* case) is so proportionally large that the existing firms in the market will be frightened off normal price competition. The risk of predatory pricing and 'reciprocity' should also be taken into account, but is of less central significance.[2]

5. *The relevant market in merger cases; its product and geographic dimensions:* Brown Shoe; Continental Can; Pabst Brewing

Section 7 forbids those mergers whose effect may be substantially to lessen competition or tend to create a monopoly 'in any line of com-

---

[1] D. F. Turner, 'Conglomerate Mergers and Section 7 of the Clayton Act', *Harvard Law Review*, vol. 78, 1965, p. 1313.

[2] Since *Clorox* the Department of Justice has pressed a stepped-up attack on conglomerate mergers, in the light of a substantial increase in their numbers. Cases have already been brought and new legislation is being considered by Congress.

merce in any section of the country'. In every case brought under the section, therefore, a finding must be made as to both the 'line of commerce' and the 'section of the country', that is on the relevant market or markets concerned. It will already be clear from the summary given above of some of the leading cases decided under section 7 that market definition can be crucial to the final outcome of the case.

It is normally the 'line of commerce', the product market, which causes the greatest difficulties. This problem is, of course, not confined to section 7 cases, since it also arises in connexion with section 2 of the Sherman Act. The decision, for example, of the Supreme Court in the *Cellophane* case turned very largely on the finding that the relevant market was the flexible packaging industry as a whole and not merely the cellophane industry. The broad principles to guide the courts in establishing the product market were laid down by Chief Justice Warren in the leading case of *Brown Shoe*.

The outer boundaries of a product market are determined by the reasonable interchangeability of use or the cross-elasticity of demand between the product itself and substitutes for it. However, within this broad market, well defined submarkets may exist which, in themselves, constitute product markets for antitrust purposes. . . . The boundaries of such a submarket may be determined by examining such practical indicia as industry or public recognition of the submarket as a separate economic entity, the product's peculiar characteristics and uses, unique production facilities, distinct customers, distinct prices, sensitivity to price changes and specialized vendors. Because section 7 of the Clayton Act prohibits any merger which may substantially lessen competition in any line of commerce, it is necessary to examine the effects of a merger in each such economically significant submarket to determine if there is a reasonable probability that the merger will substantially lessen competition. . . .

Applying these tests to the facts before him, the Chief Justice concluded that, with respect to both the horizontal and vertical aspects of the merger, the relevant lines of commerce were men's, women's and children's shoes respectively. Each of these product lines was recognized as distinct by the public, was manufactured in separate factories, had characteristics rendering it generally non-competitive with the others, and was directed towards a distinct class of customer. Brown argued that the relevant markets should be broken down still further into high, medium and low-price varieties of each of the three classes of shoe, and that the category of children's shoes should be spread into three further sub-markets (namely infants' shoes, misses' and children's shoes, and youths' and boys' shoes). These refinements were, however, dismissed by the Court as 'unrealistic' and 'impractical'.

The appropriate product market can, of course, be quite straightforward. In *Philadelphia National Bank* it was the provision of the normal range of commercial banking services; in *Von's Grocery* it was the retail grocery business. But equally it can be extremely hard to locate, and perhaps the outstanding recent example of this is the *Continental Can* case, which was discussed earlier in this chapter. It will be recalled that Continental was a very large manufacturer of metal containers, and Hazel Atlas Glass Company was a very large producer of glass containers. The defendants conceded, and the District Court found, that the metal container and glass container industries were each relevant 'lines of commerce', and that beer containers (both glass bottles and cans) also constituted a distinct sub-market. On the other hand the District Court ruled that the Government's proposed 'packaging industry' market was far too wide, and rejected a number of other sub-markets put forward by the Government (including, for example, containers for the canning industry, the toiletries and cosmetics industry, and the drug industry) because they had the common defect of including disparate and non-interchangeable containers for different end-uses within a single category, and failed to satisfy any of the *Brown Shoe* indicia referred to above.

The majority of the Supreme Court, however, took a quite different view. Mr Justice White found on the facts 'a rather general confrontation between metal and glass containers and competition between them for the same end-uses which is insistent, continuous, effective and quantity-wise very substantial'. He conceded that glass and metal containers have different characteristics which might disqualify one or the other from particular uses, and that for various reasons many users of glass or cans could not switch at will from one kind of container to another. But, nevertheless, he reiterated that there was sufficient inter-industry competition to justify treating 'glass and metal containers' as a sub-market within the larger packaging-industry classification. Justices Harlan and Stewart, however, agreed with the District Court in their dissenting opinion and said that the majority view read the '"line of commerce" element out of section 7, destroying its usefulness as an aid to analysis'.

The interpretation of 'any section of the country' has in general presented fewer problems. *Brown Shoe* laid down that the geographic market must be one which both corresponds to the commercial realities of the industry and is economically significant. In *Philadelphia National Bank* the problem was defined as finding the location of 'where, within the area of competitive overlap, the effect of the merger on competition will be direct and immediate'. Economic barriers to entry (such as transport costs) around certain areas and administrative or statutory regulation or recognition of definite geographical areas as separate markets are relevant. Further, just as a product sub-market may have significance as the 'proper line of commerce', so may a geographic sub-market be considered the appropriate 'section of the country'. Often the United States as a whole, the national market, is obviously appropriate, as in *Continental Can* and in connexion with the vertical aspects of *Brown Shoe*. Alternatively the market may be regional or local. In *United States* v. *Pabst Brewing Company* (Supreme Court, 1966) the opinion of the majority would seem to indicate that identification of the particular geographic area need not be as exact as had previously been thought, and that it may suffice merely to show that competition may be substantially lessened somewhere in the United States without necessarily having to delineate the section by 'metes and bounds as a surveyor would lay off a plot of ground'. This approach parallels the more relaxed attitude to product definition to be found in *Continental Can*. On the facts, the majority held in *Pabst* that the effect of the proposed merger between Pabst and the Blatz Brewing Company would be substantially to lessen competition in the United States, as well as in the three-state area of Wisconsin, Michigan and Illinois, and in Wisconsin itself.

While agreeing on the record that the merger would have those effects in one or other of the markets, four members of the Court nevertheless disagreed with relaxing the definition of the geographic market. Mr Justice White confined his concurrence with the majority to the finding that the merger might have the prescribed effects in the nation as a whole; Mr Justice Fortas stated that it was the Government's duty to prove the 'section of the country', both because it was the express mandate of the section and because without it neither the analysis nor the result of the cases would be of acceptable quality. Justices Harlan and Stewart also reiterated their belief that the accurate delineation of the geographic market was inherent in the section. Admittedly no designation of area could be perfect, for all geographic markets are to some extent interconnected, and over time any barrier could disappear owing to structural or technological changes in the industry. Thus, for example, the geographic market for perishable foods had been considerably widened by the introduction of refrigeration. But they felt that the tests laid down in *Brown Shoe* and other cases decided by the Supreme Court had established a flexible and workable approach to the resolution of the market problem. In view of the sharp difference of opinion within the Supreme Court, it may be too early to assume that the Government's task of establishing definite product and geographic markets affected by the merger under challenge will be substantially eliminated.

6. *Joint ventures and potential competition:* Penn-Olin;
El Paso; Beatrice Foods

One interesting question on which the Supreme Court had not pronounced before *United States* v. *Penn-Olin* in 1964 was whether section 7
applied to joint ventures. Prior to this case it had been possible to
argue that, if two companies formed a joint subsidiary to carry on a
business of any kind, this would not of itself constitute a violation of
section 7, since the joint subsidiary would not be 'engaged also in
commerce' at the date of its formation. Sections 1 and 2 of the Sherman
Act alone would be available for an attack on the joint venture as a
restraint of trade. In *Penn-Olin*, however, seven members of the Supreme
Court held that a corporation which is formed or acquired specifically
to engage in interstate commerce is covered by the section, even if it
does not commence to be so occupied prior to such formation or
acquisition.

Pennsalt Chemicals Corporation and Olin-Mathieson Chemical
Corporation had formed their joint subsidiary, Penn-Olin, to produce
and sell sodium chlorate in the south eastern United States. At the
time of the formation over 90% of the market in the south eastern area
of the country was held by two companies, Hooker and American
Potash, and the remaining small percentage was produced by Pennsalt
in Oregon and sold on an exclusive basis by Olin-Mathieson. With an
increase in demand in that area for sodium chlorate, a joint entry into
the production field by the construction of a plant in the South East
seemed a sensible move, although both Pennsalt and Olin had at
different times in the past considered their own independent entry into
production in the South East. The District Court ruled that the Government had failed to establish a reasonable probability that both companies would have entered the south eastern sodium chlorate market
but for the joint venture, and that the formation of the joint company
was not likely to lessen competition substantially in the area.

The Supreme Court, however, held that a finding should have been
made by the District Court as to the reasonable probability that either
one of the corporations would have entered the market by building a
plant, while the other would have remained a substantial potential competitor. If this question were to be answered affirmatively on remand to
the District Court, that Court would then have to consider whether the
joint venture would itself be likely substantially to lessen competition.[1]
Mr Justice Clark noted the following criteria for their assistance:

[1] On remand the District Court found, however, that this question should be answered in
the negative for both companies, so that the application of Mr Justice Clark's criteria to the
joint venture was not necessary, and the Supreme Court affirmed this factual finding.

The number and power of the competitors in the relevant market; the background of their growth; the power of the joint venturers; the relationship of their lines of commerce; competition existing between them and the power of each in dealing with the competitors of the other; the setting in which the joint venture was created; the reasons and necessities for its existence; the joint venture's line of commerce and the relationship thereof to that of its parents; the adaptability of its line of commerce to non-competitive practices; the potential power of the joint venture in the relevant market; and appraisal of what the competition in the relevant market would have been if one of the joint venturers had entered it alone instead of through Penn-Olin; the effect, in the event of this occurrence, of the other joint venturer's potential competition; and such other factors as might indicate potential risk to competition in the relevant market.

It is interesting to compare this approach of the courts with that of Kaysen and Turner[1], who recognize that joint ventures offer the possibility both of benefit and of harm to the competitive process and suggest that the seriousness of the risk depends on the following considerations. Do the joint venture or the joint ventures individually or collectively possess market power? Are the joint venturers themselves competitors? Is the product of the joint venture closely related to those produced by the joint venturers? They would deem joint ventures presumptively lawful if neither the joint venture nor its participants (individually or collectively) nor the venture plus participants has substantial market power, and there is no close relationship between the product of the venture and any of the products of the participants.

Penn-Olin illustrates also, in a rather special context, the significance that the existence of potential competition may have on the quality of competition within a market. But the significance of potential competition is by no means limited to joint ventures. In *United States* v. *El Paso Natural Gas Company* (Supreme Court, 1964), it was held that the acquisition by El Paso of the Pacific Northwest Pipeline Corporation violated section 7 even though at the time of the acquisition Pacific Northwest did not supply the relevant market at all, which was the production, transportation and sale of natural gas in California. Entry into this market was controlled by the Federal Power Commission which had to approve all sale contracts. Once the successful supplier had been approved in respect of a fixed quantity of gas per day, and had built its pipeline, that part of the market was withdrawn from competition for the duration of the agreement. At the time of the acquisition El Paso was the sole supplier of natural gas from out of State, but there was evidence that it regarded Pacific Northwest as a dangerous competitor in the future supply of California's requirements for natural

[1] *Antitrust Policy*, pp. 136 ff.

gas over and above the daily quantity which El Paso currently supplied. Although Pacific Northwest had been unsuccessful in the past in obtaining a foothold in the California market, there was little doubt that it had the resources and managerial skills to do so in the future. The case was eventually settled by a consent judgment under which El Paso agreed to divest itself of Pacific Northwest and to organize a new, independent gas pipeline company capable of competing in the industry. Future acquisition by El Paso of any natural gas transmission properties in the United States was prohibited for ten years, unless the prior approval of the Government or Court was obtained.[1]

'Potential competition' has also been a relevant factor in Federal Trade Commission cases. In *Federal Trade Commission* v. *The Procter & Gamble Co.*, as we have seen, Mr Justice Harlan considered at some length the effect on competition of the removal of Procter and Gamble as a potential competitor in the household liquid bleach market. Again, in *Beatrice Foods*, a 1965 case, the Commission considered the significance of potential competition in a rather different context. The mergers challenged by the Commission were market extension mergers, between Beatrice, the third largest national dairy company in terms of total annual sales, and numerous small local dairy companies. After noting the formidable trend in the industry towards concentration, Commissioner Elman for the Commission stated that the concepts of actual and potential competition were not completely interchangeable. Potential competition might tend to keep prices in a concentrated market down to levels that would discourage new entry; but prices low enough to dissuade a firm trying to force its way into a new market (always a risky venture) might be substantially higher than those that would prevail if there was vigorous competition among the sellers already there. Nor would the behaviour of the dominant firms in the market be greatly influenced merely by the possibility of future new entry, if the size of the new entrant and the state of the market made it appear unlikely that the firm could offer any real challenge to the principal firms in the market. Furthermore, if there were a great number of potential entrants, the elimination of only one of them would probably have no significant effect on the conduct of firms already engaged in the market. Nevertheless, in the circumstances, the numerous acquisitions by Beatrice violated section 7.

[1] Supreme Court litigation concerning the terms of the consent judgment continued in *Cascade Natural Gas Company* v. *El Paso Natural Gas Company* (1967) and *Utah Public Service Commission* v. *El Paso Natural Gas Company* (1969).

7. Section 8 of the Clayton Act and interlocking directorates

As a footnote to this chapter, section 8 of the Clayton Act should be mentioned briefly. The main provision of this section reads as follows:

. . . no person at the same time shall be a director in any two or more corporations, any one of which has capital, surplus, and undivided profits aggregating more than $1 million, engaged in whole or in part in commerce . . . if such corporations are or shall have been theretofore, by virtue of their business or location or operation, competitors, so that the elimination of competition by agreement between them would constitute a violation of any of the provisions of any of the antitrust laws.[1]

This prohibition of interlocking directorates seems to have been aimed at restrictions of competition which may come about if ostensibly competing companies are, in reality, controlled by the same set of people. The very existence of such a statute no doubt cuts down the extent of interlocking directorates to some degree. The lawyers advising large companies will prevent their clients from flagrant infringement as a matter of legal prudence. However, this section of the Clayton Act has been difficult for the Government to enforce. No case reached the Supreme Court until 1953, almost thirty years after the law reached the statute book. This case—*United States* v. *W. T. Grant Company*—illustrates some of the difficulties.

It concerned a member of an investment firm who was at the same time a director of three pairs of competing companies in the field of large-scale distribution. As soon as the complaints were filed, this director resigned from the boards of one of each pair of companies and the defendants then moved to dismiss the case on the ground that the actions were 'moot'. (Some district courts had accepted this type of claim as a good defence to such actions.) The Supreme Court made it clear that the mere voluntary cessation of illegal conduct could not make a case moot, that is, deprive the courts of the power to hear and adjudicate on the charge. The case would be moot only if the defendants could show that there was no reasonable expectation that the offence would be repeated. On the other hand, in order for the Government to secure an injunction against a continuation of the offence, it must show positively 'that there exists some cognizable danger of recurrent violation, something more than the mere possibility which serves to keep the case alive'.

Since then the tendency of the district courts has been to refuse to declare such cases moot. Thus in *United States* v. *Newmont Mining Corporation* (Southern District Court of New York, 1964), Judge Bryan

---

[1] There are separate provisions dealing with interlocking directorates among banks, and between common carriers and their suppliers, but there is not space to pursue the subject.

refused to grant summary judgments in favour of individual defendants on the grounds that their resignations of challenged directorships and promises not to serve again as directors of those companies were insufficient in all the circumstances. Among the circumstances were that a series of similar violations by the same defendants was alleged, that the corporate defendant was charged under section 7 as well as section 8 of the Act, and that one of the ex-directors had continued his relationship with the company after his resignation in the ill defined status of 'financial adviser'. *Grant's* case was distinguished as having held merely that 'the Supreme Court would not interfere with the discretion exercised by the District Court in the absence of a showing that there was no reasonable basis for its exercise'. A similar result was reached in the same Court in the following year, in *Treves* v. *Servel Inc.*, when Judge Feinberg ruled that, in spite of defendant's contentions that the proposed merger of the two corporations concerned had been abandoned, and the forbidden relationships ended, the defendants had not sustained the heavy burden of showing that there was no reasonable expectation that the wrong would be repeated.

In a third case from the same Court, *Paramount Pictures* v. *Baldwin-Montrose Chemical Company* (1966), Judge Palmier decided that the section applied only to horizontal relationships, that is to those between companies performing similar functions in the production or sale of comparable goods and services, but not to companies whose competitive relationship was only *de minimis* or merely potential.[1]

The defects of the section are many. Thus a person may be an executive employee of one company and a director of its competitor,[2] and partners in a single banking or financial house can serve on the boards of competing companies. Thus, if there is an underlying intention of two companies to have their policies run in parallel, the secretary or financial adviser can be made a director of the other without penalty. It has been suggested that the Federal Trade Commission may have to make use of their residual powers under section 5 of the Federal Trade Commission Act to stop up the loopholes, if experience shows this to be necessary.

---

[1] Subsequently, however, a number of directors, who each served on the boards of two companies, both selling tyres and other car accessories but through different retail distributors, resigned voluntarily when informed by the Department of Justice that a suit for an injunction would be brought.

[2] A common provision in consent decrees on the other hand is that no person shall be 'an officer, director, or executive employee' of both of two named companies.

CHAPTER VIII

THE CLAYTON ACT
II. EXCLUSIVE DEALING AND TYING CONTRACTS

1. *Section 3 of the Clayton Act and exclusive dealing:* Standard Fashion *v.* Magrane-Houston *and other cases*

In the latter part of Chapter V above (and continuing into Chapter VI) it was shown that, first, vertical integration by outright ownership and, secondly, various contractual forms of integration which foreclose a market against competitors may offend against the Sherman Act. Vertical integration may be unreasonable restraint of trade or may constitute an attempt to monopolize if it is not 'an expansion to meet legitimate business needs' in an effectively competitive context, but is rather 'a calculated scheme to gain control over an appreciable segment of the market and to restrain or suppress competition'. Equally, various types of exclusive contract, as in the *American Can* case, may be deemed unlawful restraint of trade when a dominant firm is involved and when the contracts go so far beyond reasonable business needs as to have the necessary effect, or disclose a clear intention, of suppressing competition. In the *Motion Picture Advertising* case it was found that the exclusive-dealing contracts of a number of leading firms in an industry might be considered cumulatively, even in the absence of collusion, and an offence ascribed to each firm because of the aggregate effect of their practices in suppressing competition.[1]

Even if such agreements do not violate the Sherman Act, however, they may well be declared unlawful under section 3 of the Clayton Act, which reads as follows:

It shall be unlawful for any person engaged in commerce, in the course of such commerce, to lease or make a sale or contract for sale of goods, wares, merchandise, machinery, supplies, or other commodities, whether patented or unpatented for use, consumption or resale . . . or fix a price charged therefor, or discount from, or rebate upon, such price, on the condition, agreement or understanding that the lessee or purchaser thereof shall not use or deal in the goods, wares, merchandise, machinery, supplies, or other commodity of a competitor or competitors of the lessor or seller where the

---

[1] See above, Chapter VI, pp. 159 ff. The *Motion Picture Advertising* case was brought under section 5 of the Federal Trade Commission Act. Certain dicta of Mr Justice Douglas's opinion imply that the offences proved under that Act would also have stood as offences under the Sherman Act.

effect of such lease, sale or contract for sale or such condition, agreement
or understanding may be to substantially lessen competition or tend to create
a monopoly in any line of commerce.

One of the first important cases on this section was *Standard Fashion
Company* v. *Magrane-Houston Company* (Supreme Court, 1922). A manufacturer of paper patterns for women's clothing had entered into
contracts with retailers under which the retailer, who agreed to buy
substantial quantities of patterns and keep a considerable stock, also
undertook 'not to sell or permit to be sold on its premises during the
term of the contract any other make of patterns'. Although the contract
was dressed up as one of agency, the goods were in fact sold to the
retailer, and the Court regarded the transaction as a sale. The only
remaining question was whether the effect of the contracts might be
'to substantially lessen competition or tend to create a monopoly'.

Mr Justice Day, speaking for the Supreme Court, based his opinion
on the proposition that 'the Clayton Act sought to reach the agreements
embraced within its sphere in their incipiency'. He analysed the
meaning of the qualifying clause as follows: 'We do not think that the
purpose in using the word "may" was to prohibit the mere possibility
of the consequence described. It was intended to prevent such agreements as would, under the circumstances disclosed, probably lessen competition, or create an actual tendency to monopoly. That it was not
intended to reach every remote lessening of competition is shown in the
requirement that such lessening must be substantial.'

He found that Standard Fashion already controlled almost 40% of
all the pattern agencies in the United States; and if they were allowed
to maintain and extend the system of exclusive contracts, they might
well increase their hold on the industry. Consequently the test of the
Clayton Act was fulfilled and Standard Fashion had infringed the law.

Other cases showed, however, that exclusive-dealing arrangements
did not infringe the Clayton Act if the effect on competition was too
remote to be substantial, or if the transaction was in the form of a bona
fide agency arrangement. In *Pearsall Butter Company* v. *Federal Trade
Commission* (Seventh Circuit Court of Appeals, 1923), a manufacturer
of margarine, whose share of the total output of margarine in the United
States was little more than 1%, appointed an exclusive wholesale dealer
for a specified territory and the dealer agreed to sell only that manufacturer's margarine. Although the form of this agreement was on all
fours with that in the *Standard Fashion* case, it was held that the
manufacturer was not in any sense an important factor in the trade, and
that this arrangement, therefore, could not have a substantial effect on
competition.

2. *Requirements contracts: the* Standard Stations *and*
Tampa Electric *cases*

There is, of course, a wide gap between the Standard Fashion Company
with its 40% hold on its industry and the Pearsall Butter Company
with less than 1%. Where lies the borderline between these extremes?

This question has been exhaustively considered in two very well
known decisions, *Standard Oil Company of California and Standard Stations*
v. *United States* (Supreme Court, 1949) and *Tampa Electric Company* v.
Nashville Coal Company (Supreme Court, 1961). Mr Justice Frankfurter's
opinion in the *Standard Stations* case is a landmark in the law on this
subject.

The Standard Oil Company of California is the largest refiner and
supplier of petrol in the western States—Arizona, California, Idaho,
Nevada, Oregon, Utah and Washington. The channel of distribution
to the consumer is divided between its own service stations and independent filling stations. In 1946 its total sales in the area amounted to
23% of all the petrol sold. Its own filling stations accounted for about
7% and its sales to independent filling stations about the same. (The
balance of the 23% was sold to industrial users.) It had six major
competitors who between them supplied about 42% of the petrol
sold by retail as against Standard's nearly 14%. Seventy other
small refiners were also engaged in the business. All the other main
companies used the same sort of contracts with their distributors as
Standard.

These were exclusive-supply contracts. Standard had entered into
such contracts with nearly 6,000 independent filling stations—16% of
the filling stations in the area—and sold nearly $60 million worth of
petrol through these stations in 1947. Under these exclusive-supply
contracts the independent dealer undertook to purchase from Standard
all his requirements of one or more products; by far the greater number
concerned petrol and other oil products only. Most of the contracts
were renewed from year to year, but some were for longer terms. The
question was whether these contracts tended seriously to reduce competition or create a monopoly, given that they affected rather less than
7% of the petrol sold in the area (14% of that sold by retail) and that
many of Standard's competitors used the same methods.

Mr Justice Frankfurter reviewed the cases under section 3 of the
Clayton Act which had come before the Supreme Court. The best
parallel was the *Standard Fashion* case mentioned above. There it had
been possible to show that the supplier was dominant to the extent of a
40% hold on its industry. However, in a case dealing with contracts
tying the supply of salt to the use of patented machines—*International*

Salt Company v. *United States*[1]—the Supreme Court had condemned the contracts simply on the basis that the volume of business foreclosed was not insignificant or insubstantial. (The International Salt Company was the largest producer of salt for industrial purposes in the United States.) Mr Justice Frankfurter considered whether tying contracts, of the type found in the *International Salt* case, were inherently more restrictive than requirements contracts. If they were, this might explain why a rather looser test of their effect on competition had been adopted. He found indeed that tying contracts 'serve hardly any purpose beyond the suppression of competition' and that this could not be said of requirements contracts. As he put it: 'Requirements contracts, on the other hand, may well be of economic advantage to buyers as well as to sellers, and thus indirectly of advantage to the consuming public. In the case of the buyer they may assure supply, afford protection against rises in price, enable long-term planning on the basis of known costs, and obviate the expense and risk of storage in the quantity necessary for a commodity having a fluctuating demand. From the seller's point of view, requirements contracts may make possible a substantial reduction of selling expenses, give protection against price fluctuations, and—of particular advantage to a newcomer to the field to whom it is important to know what capital expenditures are justified—offer the possibility of a predictable market.'[2]

This argument seemed likely to lead to rejecting a purely quantitative test of the effect of Standard's requirements contracts on competition. The Supreme Court might have looked to Standard's hold on the retail petrol market and to the situation of their competitors in the industry, and might have considered whether Standard's contracts were not serving normal business needs rather than suppressing competition. Mr Justice Frankfurter, however, thought that the courts would get into difficulty if they attempted a refined economic analysis on these lines. Granted that Standard alone did not dominate the market and that their competitive position had not improved as a result of the requirements contracts, nevertheless a full economic analysis would have to consider such questions as whether, in the absence of the requirements contracts, Standard's position might not have deteriorated. He continued: 'Moreover, to demand that bare inference be supported by evidence as to what would have happened but for the adoption of the practice that was in fact adopted, or to require firm prediction of an increase of competition as a probable result of ordering the abandon-

---

[1] See below, Chapter XI, in which a number of cases involving patented machines or processes as the 'tying' device are described.

[2] It will be noted that this argument closely follows that of the Court in the *American Can* case (above, Chapter V, pp. 151 ff.), where it was held that requirements contracts of one year's duration were permissible, but that those with a five-year term were unduly restrictive.

ment of the practice, would be a standard of proof if not virtually impossible to meet, at least most ill suited for ascertainment by courts.' In other words, since the courts were not qualified to make predictions about effects on competition, they had better hold on to a relatively straightforward quantitative test in terms of the amount of business foreclosed by the restrictive contracts.

Thus, despite all the factors pointing to a rule of reason based on economic considerations, Mr Justice Frankfurter decided that Standard's requirements contracts came within the condemnation of the Clayton Act. 'We conclude, therefore, that the qualifying clause of section 3 is satisfied by proof that competition has been foreclosed in a substantial share in the line of commerce affected. It cannot be gainsaid that observance by a dealer of his requirements contract with Standard does effectively foreclose whatever opportunity there might be for competing suppliers to attract his patronage, and it is clear that the affected proportion of retail sales of petroleum products is substantial.'

This was a decision of five Justices against four in the Supreme Court, and Mr Justice Douglas's opinion is interesting in pointing out that Standard's answer to the decision might well be to adopt further measures of vertical integration. They might control filling stations by some form of agency agreement, or they might add to the large numbers of outlets that they already owned. A considerable increase in concentration of control over petrol distribution might come about in these ways without incurring much danger, as the law stood, of charges of monopolization. Mr Justice Douglas was for leaving well alone. 'The requirements contract which is displaced is relatively innocuous as compared with the virile growth of monopoly power which the court encourages.'[1] Mr Justice Frankfurter, who had foreseen this argument, had expressed the majority view that so broad a decision of policy between one system of distribution and another was not an issue for the Court to decide. They were concerned only with the specific issue of an offence against section 3 of the Clayton Act.

The decision in *Standard Stations* led to a wide ranging debate over its significance as a guide in deciding future cases. One theory was that the decisive element was the cumulative effect on small and new refiners in the industry of the use of the exclusive arrangements with

---

[1] It is interesting to compare Mr Justice Douglas's dissent in the *Columbia Steel* case (above, Chapter V, pp. 139 ff.). There he was protesting against allowing a giant concern to acquire ownership of an important customer. Here, quite consistently, he argues against prohibiting exclusive contracts and perhaps giving Standard an incentive to add to its ownership of filling stations. He, in other words, would make the law tougher against integration by ownership and looser against integration by contract. The majority in each case—and hence the law—took the opposite course, probably because the practical difficulties of banning certain types of contracts are so much less than those of upsetting industrial structures.

distributors by a number of major companies.[1] In this it may simply have been the precursor of the *Motion Picture Advertising* decision. Another explanation was that no 'dominant' company should be allowed to use its market power to impose full requirements contracts as a condition of sale on dealers lacking reasonable alternatives to do business on a non-exclusive basis, where competitors were seriously handicapped as a result.[2] A third explanation was that any large supplier of a commodity like petrol, even if his share of the market was well below a figure indicating dominance, and even with many competitors operating in the same way, should be unable to enter into such exclusive agreements with his distributors if the total amount of business which he did each year had a large number of noughts after the initial figure. The general uncertainty led to the lower federal Courts treating the decision in a correspondingly mixed fashion, some applying it reasonably strictly but others sidestepping its effects.

The subsequent decision in *Tampa Electric* did not expressly overrule *Standard Stations*, but it significantly modified some of the more restrictive interpretations of the circumstances in which exclusive-dealing arrangements would be allowed. The plaintiff, a Florida public utility producing electricity, made plans to expand its output by constructing additional generating plant. For the first two units of the new plant it decided to try coal (although every other Florida generating plant at the time used oil) and contracted with Nashville for its expected requirements. The agreement embraced the total requirements of fuel for the first two units, not less than 250 thousand tons per unit per year, for a period of twenty years. In order to equip these first two units to burn coal Tampa spent three million dollars more than the cost of constructing oil burning units and Nashville spent seven and a half million dollars preparing themselves to perform delivery.

Before any coal was delivered, however, Nashville declined to perform the contract on the ground that it was illegal under the antitrust laws, and Tampa brought suit for a declaration that the contract was both valid and enforceable. The Supreme Court found that the relevant market was not merely Florida, nor Florida and Georgia combined, but was rather the wider area in which Nashville and the seven hundred other coal producers in the south eastern United States effectively competed. This area covered parts of Pennsylvania, Virginia, West Virginia, Kentucky, Tennessee, Alabama, Ohio and Illinois.

---

[1] The *Standard Stations* decision was followed later in another oil case, *United States* v. *Richfield Oil Corporation* (District Court of California, 1951). This case involved similar issues but Richfield's share of the western market for petrol was considerably smaller than that of Standard. They had contracts with rather under 3,000 filling stations as against Standard's nearly 6,000, but were nevertheless found to be infringing section 3.

[2] See Dirlam and Kahn, *Fair Competition*, pp. 100-1.

After an examination of production statistics the Court concluded that the proportionate volume of the total relevant production as to which the challenged contract pre-empted competition was less than one per cent, which was described as 'a quite insubstantial amount'. A more accurate figure, even assuming pre-emption to the extent of the maximum requirements of Tampa, would be $0 \cdot 77\%$. Requirements contracts were not illegal *per se*; to be illegal they must have a tendency to work a substantial, not merely remote, lessening of competition in the relevant competitive market. Mr Justice Clark, speaking for the majority of the Supreme Court, elaborated the meaning of 'substantiality' as follows:

> To determine substantiality in a given case, it is necessary to weigh the probable effect of the contract on the relevant area of effective competition, taking into account the relative strengths of the parties, the proportionate volume of commerce involved in relation to the total volume of commerce in the relevant market area, and the probable immediate and future effects which pre-emption of that share of the market might have on effective competition therein. It follows that a mere showing that the contract itself involves a substantial number of dollars is ordinarily of little consequence.

The Court distinguished earlier cases on a number of grounds. In this case there was no seller with a dominant position in the market, as in *Standard Fashion*, nor were there myriad outlets with substantial sales volume coupled with an industry-wide practice of relying upon exclusive contracts, as in *Standard Stations*. On the contrary, the requirements contract in this case was of the type which might well be of economic advantage to the buyer as well as the seller, for it could assure the buyer of a steady source of supply, while for the seller it offered a substantial reduction in selling expenses, protection against price fluctuations and the possibility of a predictable market. In the case of public utilities, the public interest in a steady supply of fuel meant that the twenty-year period of the contract, though long, could not be said to be unreasonable.

As Dean Bok[1] has pointed out, the strength of the *Tampa* case is its creation of a doctrinal base flexible enough to avoid the uncompromising prohibitions of *Standard Stations*; its weakness the vagueness of that base. The manufacturer wishing to make use of exclusive-dealing arrangements is probably unlikely to obtain much more practical help in the generalized principles of *Tampa* than he would have done from Mr Justice Frankfurter's opinion in *Standard Stations*. The problem of finding the borderline between *Standard Fashion* and *Pearsall Butter* still remains.

---

[1] I must acknowledge my debt to Dean Bok for his comprehensive account of the *Tampa Electric* case in 'The Tampa Electric Case and the problem of exclusive arrangements under the Clayton Act', *Supreme Court Review 1961* (University of Chicago) p. 267.

Sometimes there are special factors. In *United States* v. *J. I. Case Company* (District Court of Minnesota, 1951) a manufacturer of farm machinery having about a 7% share of the United States market was alleged to have aimed at getting its dealers to handle its goods exclusively. It was not contended by the Government that the company's contracts with the dealers contained any express restriction, but it made one-year supply contracts, and there was evidence of oral conditions of sale whereby the dealers were not to handle other goods and of refusals by the company to make or renew contracts with those who would not accept these conditions. This case failed, and it seems that a mixture of various factors led to this result—the fact that the Case company was by no means the largest in its field, the absence of evidence that other manufacturers were unable to find dealers for their goods, the fact that no express restrictions were written into its contracts and, in particular, the fact that many of the dealers clearly preferred to deal in one manufacturer's line. The Court said:

. . . a mutual arrangement between the farm machinery manufacturer and its dealer that it is for the best interest of both for the latter to handle a full line of the manufacturer's output, without any competitive restriction imposed upon the dealer, is not violative of any law. Apparently, most dealers in the farm machinery industry normally prefer to handle the full line of the farm machinery manufacturer which they represent. So far as the evidence indicates herein, the full-line dealerships of Case mean nothing more than that the pattern of the industry has been followed by mutual agreements between the manufacturer and the dealers. The handling by a dealer of a few items of several full-line manufacturers might tend to discourage competition rather than stimulate it.

Thus, evidence that the arrangement is not an involuntary one, imposed by the seller on the buyer, may save it from illegality.

Dean Bok suggests, however, at least two other situations where section 3 should not be invoked, namely where new outlets can be found by competitors without any difficulty, or where the manufacturer making use of the exclusive arrangements has entirely trained his own dealers. The Federal Trade Commission has, however, decided two cases, *Dictograph Products* v. *Federal Trade Commission* (upheld in Second Circuit Court of Appeals, 1956) and *Mytinger and Casselbery Inc.* v. *Federal Trade Commission* (upheld in District of Columbia Court of Appeals, 1962) which appear to hold that, even in those circumstances, such agreements would be deemed in breach of section 3 if the percentage of the relevant market affected was substantial. *Dictograph* was, of course, decided prior to *Tampa Electric*, but the appeal in *Mytinger* came afterwards. In *Mytinger* the exclusive-dealing arrangements were between the country's largest supplier of vitamin products and a large number of door-to-door 'distributors', who were not, however, employees of the company but independent contractors. Evidence showed that these distributors were easily obtained and were trained entirely by the manufacturer. The foreclosure affected 61·5% of the market if the line of commerce was taken as the vitamin concentrates sold solely through the door-to-door method, 34·6% if the market was taken as vitamins and mineral combination preparations marketed through all types of retail outlets, or 8·6% if it included all vitamin concentrates sold through all types of outlet. The Commission found that all three markets were separate lines of commerce, but the Court of Appeals viewed each of the percentages as substantial and therefore as justifying a finding of a substantial lessening of competition, regardless of which was chosen as the relevant market. One judge, however, dissented, on the grounds that the vitamins sold through all types of outlet were the relevant market, and that 8·6% was not a substantial foreclosure in the special circumstances of this case because of the ease with which new distributors could be obtained and the particular nature of the product.

Another suggestion of Dean Bok's is that such arrangements should be permitted where it is not a reasonable commercial proposition for a manufacturer to enter into a market without having the assurance of outlets able to bind themselves to sell his products alone. In this situation the encouragement of new entry by allowing such arrangements could be argued to outweigh any possible lessening of competition by the denial to other suppliers of those exclusive distributors. Once, however, the new entrant had established himself in the market, there would come a point at which his exclusive distributorship arrangement would be deemed to become a violation of section 3 of the Clayton Act, and would no longer be allowed. The manufacturer should also not overlook that section 5 of the Federal Trade Commission Act may be invoked by the Commission against exclusive distributorship arrangements on the grounds that these may constitute 'unfair trade practices'. Under the Clayton Act injury to competition has to be shown before such arrangements can be declared unlawful, but in *Federal Trade Commission* v. *Brown Shoe Company* (1966) the Supreme Court held that under the Federal Trade Commission Act no proof of a competitive injury was required, and that the Commission had broad powers to declare practices 'unfair' which conflicted with the basic policies of the Sherman and Clayton Acts even though such practices might not constitute a violation of those laws.

3. *Tying contracts: the early* Gratz *case*; Northern Pacific Railway;
Loew's Inc.; Jerrold Electronics *and* Dehydrating Process

Exclusive dealing, as prohibited by section 3 of the Clayton Act, may
take another form. In the cases considered so far there has either been
an express condition against handling a rival's product or a requirements contract tying the customer to a single supplier for substantial
periods. The 'tying' involved in this type of exclusive dealing is a tying
of customers to a particular supplier. It will be noted that the wording
of section 3 of the Clayton Act also covers situations in which one
commodity is tied to another if the effect is to foreclose trade in the
'tied' product.[1]

The manufacturer of a machine, for example, may say to the customer
that, so long as this machine is used, he must use with it exclusively some
other product of the manufacturer. The *American Can* case dealt in part
with a charge that canners who hired that company's closing machines
had in practice to buy its tins. The *Car finance* case[2] dealt with a plan
to make dealers in a manufacturer's cars use its subsidiary company's
financial services. Thus, as with the other lines of cases under section 3,
some instances of this practice (which goes by the name of 'tying
contracts' and is sometimes referred to as 'full-line forcing'[3]) have
already been found to violate the Sherman Act. Many more instances
occur in which the tying product is a patented machine or even a
licence to practise a process patent, and the case law on this subject
will be outlined below (Chapter XI).

Where a dealer obtains a product or machine from only one source,
the effect of tying another product to the supply or hire of that product
or machine will be the same as that of forcing the dealer into an
exclusive-dealing or requirements contract for the tied product.
Situations of this kind are the most likely to infringe the Clayton Act.
Thus in the *Standard Stations* case, for example, many of the dealers who
entered into requirements contracts with Standard for petrol were also
persuaded to contract for their total requirements of tyres, tubes,
batteries and other products; and this was one of the things which the
Court found illegal about the arrangements.

In the earlier years of antitrust the courts were not always so sure
of the restrictive effect of such contracts, particularly where it had
been a 'custom of the trade' to sell different products in combination.
An early case—*Federal Trade Commission* v. *Gratz* (Supreme Court, 1920)

[1] For an authoritative and detailed account of the subject matter of this section see D. F.
Turner, 'The Validity of Tying Arrangements under the Antitrust Laws', *Harvard Law
Review*, vol. 72, 1958, p. 50.   [2] See above, Chapter VI, pp. 156 ff.
[3] 'Full-line forcing' is used more specifically when the manufacturer seeks to have his
dealers carry the whole range of his products.

—dealt with the question of whether a selling agent, who represented a manufacturer of jute bagging for cotton baling and also a manufacturer of steel ties to secure the bales, ought to be allowed to insist that any customer buying bagging or ties should take corresponding quantities of each. This case was brought under section 5 of the Federal Trade Commission Act and raised the question of whether it was for the Federal Trade Commission or the courts to lay down what constituted 'unfair methods of competition'. Even though the two manufacturers for whom Gratz acted as sole agents were pretty well dominant in the supply of steel ties and bagging respectively, the majority of the Supreme Court said that this particular tying arrangement was 'never heretofore regarded as opposed to good morals because characterized by bad faith, fraud . . . or as against public policy because of a dangerous tendency unduly to hinder competition'. Thus they held that the Commission were wrong to regard it as an unfair method of competition. Mr Justice Brandeis, however, though he did not think that the practice was illegal *per se*—'a method of competition fair among equals may be very unfair if applied where there is inequality of resources'—thought that the Commission had sufficient evidence on which to condemn the particular arrangements in the case. Subsequent case law has, however, limited very severely the circumstances in which tying arrangements can be justified.

In the *Times-Picayune* case (see above, Chapter V, pp. 129–31) Mr Justice Clark had made the following distinctions between the test of legality under the Sherman Act and under the Clayton Act:

From the 'tying' cases a perceptible pattern of illegality emerges: when the seller enjoys a monopolistic position in the market for the 'tying' product or if a substantial volume of commerce in the 'tied' product is restrained, a tying arrangement violates the narrower standards expressed in section 3 of the Clayton Act because from either factor the requisite potential lessening of competition is inferred. And because for even a lawful monopolist it is 'unreasonable *per se* to foreclose competitors from any substantial market' a tying arrangement is banned by section 1 of the Sherman Act wherever both conditions are met.

Provided that the person imposing the tie-in has sufficient economic power with respect to the tying product to restrain free competition in the market for the tied product to some degree, and a not 'insubstantial' amount of interstate commerce is affected, tying contracts will almost certainly now be held illegal, under whichever Act the action is brought.[1] This summary of the present position is taken from

---

[1] Section 3 of the Clayton Act is, however, inapplicable to tying contracts for the sale of land, or when the tying item is the provision of services, rather than of 'goods, wares, merchandise, machinery, supplies or other commodities. . .', whereas the Sherman Act applies

the leading case of *United States* v. *Northern Pacific Railway Company* (Supreme Court, 1958). The Northern Pacific Railway had, in the late nineteenth century, been granted by Congress approximately forty million acres of land in the North West in return for its construction of a railway line from Lake Superior to the Pacific Coast. Over the years most of this land had been sold or leased out subject to the terms of a 'preferential routing' clause, under which the purchaser or lessee was obliged to ship over Northern Pacific's lines all commodities produced or manufactured on his land. Mr Justice Black, for the majority, pointed out that the tying agreement served little or no legitimate business purpose, foreclosed competing suppliers from an open market in the tied product and prevented buyers from exercising a free choice. Northern Pacific clearly possessed economic leverage over those who had purchased or leased land from it, because the land contained natural resources essential to their businesses.

Northern Pacific put forward two main defences: first it claimed that an earlier Supreme Court decision on tying[1] was not an authority on this occasion because the tying product in the earlier case had been patented; but the Court ruled that the case was authoritative, regardless of whether patents were involved or not. Second, it claimed that the purchasers or lessees had always been free to ship by alternative routes if these could be shown to be cheaper than Northern Pacific's lines. This argument was also rejected on the ground that Northern Pacific had no right to prevent its competitors from competing on equal terms with it.

Northern Pacific was followed shortly afterwards by a case concerned with a practice already mentioned in Chapter VI (p. 168), namely 'block booking' in the cinema industry. In *United States* v. *Loew's Inc.* (Supreme Court, 1962), the defendants held the rights to a large number of old films, in which several television networks were interested. The networks would naturally have preferred to purchase only the better films, but were told that they could have these only if they accepted, at the same time, a number that they found less attractive.[2] No allegations of conspiracy or collusion were made against the defendants, nor any claim of monopolization or attempt to monopolize; the case turned solely on the legality of each defendant's insistence upon selling popular films only as part of a 'package deal'.

to every kind of contract. The Supreme Court has held illegal under the Sherman Act contracts tying the sale of land and prefabricated housing materials to the provision of a service, in this case financial credit. (*Fortner Enterprises Inc.* v. *United States Steel Corporation*, 1969).

[1] *International Salt Company* v. *United States* (Supreme Court, 1947), which is discussed in Chapter XI below. This was the case in which the Court first promulgated the rule that 'it is unreasonable *per se* to foreclose competitors from any substantial market'.

[2] Thus, for example, to obtain 'The Man who Came to Dinner' one network was required to purchase *inter alia* both 'Gorilla Man' and 'Tugboat Annie Sails Again'.

Referring to the standard of illegality laid down in *Northern Pacific*, Mr Justice Goldberg said that 'sufficient economic power' over the tying product could be inferred either from its desirability to consumers or from uniqueness in its attributes. Accordingly, it should seldom be necessary in such cases to embark upon a full-scale factual enquiry into the scope of the relevant market for the tying product or the seller's percentage share of that market. As twenty-five contracts were involved, comprising payments ranging from about $60,000 to over $2,500,000, the requirement that a 'not insubstantial amount' of interstate commerce be affected was easily met.

It would, however, be wrong to infer that tying agreements are never upheld by the courts, and it may be helpful to conclude this section by referring to some of the cases in which such restrictions have been upheld as based on 'proper business reasons'. One of the grounds on which they have been upheld is that the tied product is so closely integrated with the tying product that the seller's goodwill may be damaged if the products of other manufacturers are used in the place of the tied product. The defendant in *United States* v. *Jerrold Electronics Corporation* (Eastern District Court of Pennsylvania, 1960[1]) was a pioneer in the early 1950s in the provision of community television antennae systems, and had installed more than 75% of the systems in operation throughout the country. At the beginning, the equipment installed was not fully proven and of a highly sensitive nature, and Jerrold were afraid that if inexperienced purchasers of the equipment were allowed to carry out their own maintenance the systems might break down and earn an unjustifiably bad reputation for Jerrold's equipment. The Court found that 'a wave of system failures at the start would have greatly retarded, if not destroyed, this new industry and would have been disastrous for Jerrold'. It was relevant that Jerrold was a relatively small company, without the resources of some of its large competitors in the same field. Accordingly, Jerrold's requirement that purchasers of its antennae systems purchase also its maintenance services was justified under the rule of reason and since an injustice would be done by the blind acceptance of a *per se* rule of illegality. On the other hand, while the Court was satisfied that the tie-in was reasonable at the beginning, it held that it would cease to be reasonable at a certain stage in the development of the business, once the technical requirements of the system were more widely understood and individual failures would no longer materially prejudice the future of the whole industry.

A somewhat analogous situation was found in *Dehydrating Process Company* v. *A. O. Smith Corporation* (First Circuit Court of Appeals, 1961). Smith, the defendant, was a manufacturer of storage equipment,

---

[1] Subsequently the Supreme Court summarily affirmed this decision.

including a patented glass-lined silo with a slippery inside lining, and a patented silo unloader. For several years it had sold the silos and unloaders separately, but had received a large number of complaints that its unloaders did not work properly in conjunction with silos manufactured by other companies, which apparently did not have correct mechanical tolerances, or sufficiently slippery inside surfaces. Accordingly, to placate customers it had to take back some of these unloaders, and eventually refused to sell them unless they were to be installed with silos of its own manufacture. In this private treble-damage action the First Circuit Court affirmed the direction by the District Court of a verdict for the defendant, on the grounds that the defendant was entitled to require that its unloaders should be used only in conjunction with silos of certain specifications corresponding to those of its manufacture (as laid down in *International Salt*, see Chapter XI below, p. 327), and the plaintiff had failed to show that any other manufacturer's silos would fulfil these specifications.

4. *Problems of distribution; unilateral refusal to deal*

The provisions of the Clayton Act dealing with requirements contracts, tying contracts and other forms of exclusive arrangement have an important impact on the methods used by manufacturers to secure the distribution of their products. A manufacturer with a product to sell always has the problem of finding a system of distribution for that product which will make possible the largest possible volume of sales. He can, of course, arrange to set up his own retail stores and sell direct to the public; in this case, as the retail selling will be done under his control, no agreements will be needed to govern the conditions under which the goods will be sold, and neither section 1 of the Sherman Act nor section 3 of the Clayton Act can become relevant. On the other hand, manufacturers often do not wish to have the trouble and expense of setting up a distribution system of their own, as this will involve tying up a large amount of capital (which could probably be more profitably invested in other ways) in a retail business of which they may not have had much experience. It is therefore normal for manufacturers to sell their goods to distributors, who in turn will resell either direct to the public or, acting as wholesalers, to retail dealers who will effect the final sale to the public.

Let us therefore suppose that a manufacturer has chosen a distributor, and agrees to supply him with his products for resale. The law traditionally respects the parties' freedom of contract, including the right of the manufacturer at any time to say, 'I now exercise my freedom to refuse to deal with you any more'. This was established in *United*

States v. *Colgate and Company* (Supreme Court, 1919)[1] in which Colgate were charged with having violated the Sherman Act by refusing to sell to certain retailers, who had declined to abide by its prescribed resale prices, and in having announced publicly that it would not supply any retailers who adopted this attitude. Where the refusal to deal is simply and solely a unilateral refusal it cannot be treated as an infringement of the antitrust laws.

The firm which refuses to deal must, of course, also be in an effective position of power for any antitrust offence to arise. There is no suggestion that the mere refusal by any ordinary supplier to deal with a particular distributor would be a significant restraint of trade. This was established in *Federal Trade Commission* v. *Raymond Brothers and Clarke* (Supreme Court, 1924). In this case a wholesale grocer had put it to a manufacturer that he should not supply another wholesaler who was in the practice of making direct retail sales. The wholesaler said, in effect, that, if the manufacturer went on supplying the wholesaler-retailer, he would take his business elsewhere. Neither the manufacturer nor the wholesaler was in any sense dominant in the grocery trade and the wholesaler's threat to withdraw his custom was upheld as simply an exercise of the individual's normal freedom to deal with whom he chose, though the Court made it clear that it would certainly have been an offence had the same type of threat been made in concert by a group of firms or by a single firm with dominant power in the market.[2]

In *Nelson Radio and Supply Company* v. *Motorola* (Fifth Circuit Court of Appeals, 1952) the plaintiff sought treble damages on the ground that Motorola, a manufacturer of communications equipment, had refused to renew his franchise and reappoint him as a dealer when he had refused to sell only products made by Motorola. The Court (in a two to one decision) dismissed the complaint for failure to state a cause of action and argued that, whether or not the renewed franchise with its restrictive condition would have violated the Clayton Act, the plaintiff could not recover damages on the basis of a mere refusal to supply. 'There is nothing whatever in the Act to suggest that it covers a situation where the manufacturer refuses to make a sale or enter into a contract, and it has been stated time and again that a manufacturer has the

---

[1] *Colgate*, and the cases decided subsequently which have rendered it largely ineffective in connexion with the maintenance of resale prices, are discussed in Chapter X.

[2] A later case—*Fargo Glass and Paint Company* v. *Globe American Corporation* (Seventh Circuit Court of Appeals, 1953)—makes the same point. A manufacturer of gas ranges making less than 1% of the national output of ranges made an agreement with a big distributor under which the distributor acquired a financial interest in the manufacturer and contracted to take its entire output. As a result various small dealers who had provisionally undertaken to distribute the ranges could not be supplied by the manufacturer. It was held that this situation did not disclose any monopoly position nor any intent to monopolize.

unquestioned right to refuse to deal with anyone for reasons sufficient to itself. . . . There is a real difference between the act of refusing to deal and the execution of a contract which prevents a person from dealing with another. The plaintiff has not been injured as the result of a contract, either express or implied, which sought to prevent him from dealing in the goods of any competitor of the defendant.'

Again, in *Hudson Sales Corporation* v. *Waldrip* (Fifth Circuit Court of Appeals, 1954) it was found by the same Court that Hudson, one of the smaller automobile manufacturers, was within its right to refuse to renew a dealer's contract on the ground that the dealer could not and did not give Hudson's product adequate representation so long as his selling effort was dispersed over a number of makes. Hudson's action, in the Court's view, was taken for sound business reasons and not in pursuance of a policy that violated the antitrust laws.

The manufacturer would, however, be ill advised to rely too much on these cases. The difficulty is that a unilateral refusal to deal normally takes place against a background of a distribution system which imposes restrictions on all the dealers involved. If the unilateral refusal is part of a larger scheme or arrangement which is itself a violation of the antitrust laws, it will be no defence to a treble-damage action for the manufacturer to point out that contractually he was entitled to refuse to continue to supply, or to cancel or refuse renewal of a franchise with an individual dealer.[1]

Thus, in *Osborn* v. *Sinclair Refining Company* (Fourth Circuit Court of Appeals, 1960), Sinclair were found to have engaged in an unlawful tying agreement under which Osborn, as the lessee of their filling station, had to purchase certain minimum quantities of tyres, batteries, and accessories from Goodyear Tyre and Rubber Company, in addition to supplies of petrol from Sinclair. Osborn apparently failed to purchase enough Goodyear products, and Sinclair terminated his lease and supply agreement. On these facts Chief Judge Sobeloff ruled that Osborn was entitled to treble damages for any loss incurred by him as a result of the illegal tie-in and the consequent termination of his lease and supply agreement, stating that 'if a seller, who is not a mono-polist and who does not act in concert with co-conspirators, neverthe-less is able to coerce buyers into arrangements for fixing prices or other unlawful arrangements, and the seller could refuse to deal with buyers unwilling to adhere to such arrangements without answering for the resulting loss, the effectiveness of treble-damage suits as an enforcement measure would be to a great extent nullified'.

The Ninth Circuit Court, voting two to one, came to an identical

---

[1] The strict criteria adopted by the courts as regards what constitutes a 'unilateral' decision were shown in *United States* v. *General Motors*, see Chapter II above, pp. 73-4.

conclusion in *Lessig* v. *Tidewater Oil Company* (1964),[1] where the lessee of a filling station had his lease terminated in similar circumstances. The majority of the Court reaffirmed that, where a plaintiff can show that the defendant has caused him loss by refusing to deal with him unless he becomes a party to an agreement that would violate the antitrust laws (whether the Sherman or Clayton Acts), then the plaintiff may recover treble damages for such loss.

It appears, therefore, that once a manufacturer has selected a dealer he will be unable subsequently, without risking a treble-damage action, to drop him merely because he refuses to comply with the manufacturer's policy in any particular respect, unless that policy is one which in all the circumstances does not constitute a violation of the antitrust laws.[2] Thus in the *Hudson* case, for example, it would not have been contrary to the antitrust laws for Hudson to have required its dealers not to sell competing products, given that Hudson was one of the smallest car manufacturers. On the other hand, under the rule in *Standard Stations*, a similar requirement by one of the major car manufacturers might well have been held to violate the antitrust laws and a refusal to deal (or continue dealing) based on such a policy could have led to a successful treble-damage action. It is also worth mentioning one specific statute, the Automobile Dealers Franchise Act of 1956, which entitles a car dealer to sue any car manufacturer who fails to act in good faith in connexion with the termination, cancellation or non-renewal of his franchise. It is open to the manufacturer, however, to produce evidence that the dealer has himself not acted in good faith, and that its own action was thereby justified. In nearly all the cases to date this defence has been successful. The Act only applies, however, to the sale of vehicles, and congressional attempts to widen its scope to dealers in other industries have not yet succeeded.

5. *Territorial and other restrictions imposed on distributors* · Sealy; White Motor; Snap-On Tool *and* Sandura; Schwinn

When a manufacturer wishes to appoint dealers to sell his products, he may well feel it appropriate to allow each of them freedom within a certain area from competition in the sale of his products—freedom from 'intra-brand' competition—in order to encourage them to promote these products more vigorously in competition with rival makes—in 'inter-brand' competition. To effect this it will be necessary to

[1] In this case the Supreme Court was asked to grant *certiorari*, but refused.
[2] It has also been held that the fact that the dealer has begun a treble-damage action against the manufacturer is of itself not sufficient justification for the manufacturer to refuse further supplies: *Bergen Drug Company* v. *Parke, Davis and Company* (Third Circuit Court of Appeals, 1962).

insert in all dealer agreements provisions under which the manufacturer agrees not to appoint any other dealers within the defined area, and under which the dealer agrees not to sell the product outside this area, or in default to pay a penalty to the dealer in whose area the offending sale is made. A further restriction, commonly coupled with such territorial restrictions, but inherently quite separable from them, is to restrict dealers from selling goods to certain classes of customer.

The antitrust laws, however, considerably limit the use which may be made of such restrictions. It should be noted that restrictions of this kind are unaffected by section 3 of the Clayton Act, because the dealer is not restricted in his freedom to deal with any of the manufacturer's rivals, but only in his freedom to compete with fellow dealers (territorial restrictions), or with the manufacturer himself (customer restrictions).[1] Cases instituted by the Department of Justice against these restrictions have therefore been brought under section 1 of the Sherman Act, but might also be brought under section 5 of the Federal Trade Commission Act.

We have already seen (in Chapter II, pp. 76 ff.) that a horizontal market sharing agreement involving significant restraint on competition is illegal *per se*. Thus, if it can be shown that the division of territories between the dealers has been imposed on the manufacturer as the result of concerted action between the dealers, it will be illegal. In *United States* v. *Sealy Inc.* (Supreme Court, 1967) the defendant was a company engaged in licensing manufacturers of bedding products to sell them under the Sealey name and trademark within certain defined territorial areas. The shareholders in the company were about thirty small bedding manufacturers and the directors of the company were also stockholders or their nominees. The Court held that the relationship between Sealy Inc. and its licensees could not be described as genuinely 'vertical', and that Sealy Inc. was the instrument of the licensees for the purpose of allocating territories between them. There was a further ground for striking down the territorial restrictions. The District Court had found that these did not exist in isolation, but were combined with an effective system of resale price maintenance policed by Sealy Inc. Even if the territorial restrictions could have been shown to have been imposed by Sealy Inc. on the licensees, rather than initially agreed by the licensees *inter se*, they would still have been condemned as part of 'an aggregation of trade restraints'. Referring to *Timken Roller Bearing Company* v. *United States*,[2] Mr Justice Fortas emphasized that the illegal price fixing agreement tainted the whole distribution system so

---

[1] Section 3 speaks only of restrictions affecting competitors of the seller and does not apply to restrictions affecting merely the seller himself or competitors of the buyer.
[2] See Chapter XII, pp. 346 ff.

that there could be no scope for a rule-of-reason enquiry into the business, or economic justification of the restrictions or their effect on the market.

The position of genuinely vertical territorial allocations was for a long time in doubt.[1] The Department of Justice had taken the view since 1948 that such agreements were illegal *per se*, and a large number of consent decrees had been negotiated under which defendants had agreed not to indulge in any such practices. However, in *United States* v. *White Motor Company* (1963) the Supreme Court admitted that it did not know whether such territorial allocations should be illegal *per se* and reversed a District Court verdict giving summary judgment in favour of the Government in order that the District Court could hold a full trial taking account of the commercial effects of such allocations.

The facts of the case were that White had entered into agreements with its distributors and dealers that the latter would sell White trucks only to persons having a place of business or purchasing headquarters within their assigned territories, and in default would pay a sum of money, commonly known as a 'profit passover', to the distributor or dealer in whose territory such truck was first registered. Three members of the Supreme Court (Chief Justice Warren and Justices Clark and Black) would have condemned the restriction as a *per se* violation without the necessity for a full hearing at the District Court level.[2]

Shortly afterwards two separate Circuit Courts of Appeals ruled that territorial restrictions should be assessed in the light of the rule of reason, and upheld particular schemes of sales territory allocation which had been challenged by the Federal Trade Commission. In *Snap-On Tool Corporation* v. *Federal Trade Commission* (Seventh Circuit Court of Appeals, 1963) a manufacturer of mechanics' handtools for the automotive and aircraft industries had appointed dealers for the sale of these tools, who were given exclusive selling areas. In reversing the Commission's finding of illegality, the Court of Appeals stated that the restrictions had no anti-competitive implications, there being over eighty competing manufacturers in the same industry, and it being shown that within an eighteen-month period the defendant had had a turnover of several hundred dealers, which indicated the difficulties involved in building up a distribution system. It also ruled that lack of exclusiveness in these circumstances would make it very difficult for the dealers to retain regular contact with customers for the purpose of extending credit, collecting instalment payments, replacing defective goods, collecting rentals and making warehouse facilities available.

[1] I must acknowledge my debt to an article by Mr Sigmund Timberg, 'Territorial Exclusives', in *A.B.A. Antitrust Section, Proceedings*, vol. 29, 1965, p. 233.

[2] In the event White agreed to a consent judgment, under which it became bound not to retain any exclusive territorial agreements, and so the full trial at District Court level was never held.

The Sixth Circuit Court also rendered a decision to much the same effect a few months later in *Federal Trade Commission* v. *Sandura Company* (1964). Territories were allocated to its dealers by Sandura, a small manufacturer of vinyl floorcoverings. The Court found that Sandura had been losing ground to the larger companies in the industry, and had lost many of its distributors in the past because of product failures. As an inducement to new dealers, therefore, and to ensure that they were willing to carry out local advertising it needed to be able to offer closed territories. The Court felt that, without the closed territories, Sandura would probably not have been able to remain in the vinyl floorcovering business at all and the restrictions were therefore reasonable.

These last two cases must now, however, be regarded as of doubtful authority, for in *United States* v. *Arnold, Schwinn* (Supreme Court, 1967) the Supreme Court has ruled that where a manufacturer sells products to its distributors subject to territorial restrictions upon resale, this is a *per se* violation of the Sherman Act, provided that the manufacturer has parted with 'title, dominion and risk' in the goods to the distributor. Schwinn had, in 1951, some 22·5% of the United States bicycle market, though by 1961 its share had fallen to 12·8%. Its products were distributed to the public in two main ways: first, by sale to its wholesale distributors throughout the country who resold to a large number of franchised retailers; secondly, by direct sale to the franchised retailer combined with a payment of commission to the wholesaler placing the order on the retailer's behalf (the so-called 'Schwinn Plan'). The wholesale distributors and retailers were free to deal with other makers of bicycles, as they commonly did, but were restricted as to the class of persons to whom they could resell. Distributors were not allowed to sell to retailers outside their own exclusive territory. Retailers were not allowed to sell to other unfranchised retailers, but only to consumers.

The Department of Justice had originally alleged that Schwinn had fixed the prices at which the distributors and dealers resold, but this claim was rejected by the District Court without appeal by the Department. The fundamental question before the Supreme Court was therefore the illegality of a vertical territorial restriction on distributors, and the Court's answer was that such restrictions were illegal *per se* if title, dominion and risk in the goods had passed to the distributor. On the other hand, it would not be appropriate to prohibit *per se* the practice of franchising, namely the designation of specified distributors and retailers as the channels through which the manufacturer, whilst retaining ownership of the goods, could distribute them to the public.

Where title, dominion and risk are retained by the manufacturer and 'the position and function of the dealer in question is in fact indistinguishable from that of an agent or salesman of the manufacturer', a territorial restriction will only violate section 1 if it is an unreasonable restraint of competition. On the facts of this case there were no grounds for concluding that, when Schwinn retained title to the goods, there was any such restraint. The relevant factors included that the distributors and retailers were free to handle competing makes of bicycle, of which there was no shortage, that Schwinn had adopted its distribution programme when it had less than one-seventh of the total market, and that there were powerful competitors with access to large-scale advertising and promotion and a wide choice of retail outlets.

The Supreme Court also dealt with the issue of customer restriction. Was it permissible for Schwinn's franchised distributors to be restricted from selling to persons other than franchised retailers or for Schwinn's retailers to be prevented from selling to other, unfranchised, bicycle retailers? The answer was in the negative. This too was a restriction in support of which no substantive justification, economic or legal, could be advanced. This view had perhaps already been foreshadowed by the concurring opinion of Mr Justice Brennan in the *White Motor* case, when he said:

Customer restrictions . . . present a problem quite distinct from that of territorial limitations . . . customer restraints would seem inherently the more dangerous of the two for they serve to suppress all competition between manufacturer and distributor for the custom of the most desirable accounts. At the same time they seem to lack any of the countervailing tendencies to foster competition between brands which may accompany the territorial limitations. . . . The crucial question to me is whether in any meaningful sense the distributors but for the restrictions would compete with the manufacturer for the reserved outlets. If they could, but are prevented from doing so only by the restrictions, then in the absence of some justification neither presented nor suggested by this record, their invalidity would seem to be apparent. . . . If on the other hand it turns out that as a practical matter the restricted dealers could neither fill the orders nor service the fleets of . . . customers, then the District Court might conclude that because there would otherwise be no meaningful competition, the restrictive agreements do no more than codify the economically obvious.

In summary, then, the manufacturer who wishes to place territorial restrictions on the resale of his goods has but two alternatives. He can adopt his own variant of the 'Schwinn Plan' and place such restrictions only on those, acting as his employees or agents, who do not actually receive title to the goods. (This is analogous to what under the *General Electric* case of 1926 has for over forty years been permitted in connexion with the maintenance of resale prices.[1]) The alternative is one expressly

[1] See Chapter X, p. 281.

permitted by a large number of consent decrees, under which no exclusive territories are allotted but the manufacturer chooses his distributors and dealers and designates geographical areas in which they have primary responsibility for sales, though no penalty can be exacted from them for sales outside these areas. Failure, however, of a distributor or dealer to represent the manufacturer adequately within his particular area would, of course, entitle the manufacturer, under the rule in *Colgate*, to come to a unilateral decision to terminate the franchise.

CHAPTER IX

THE CLAYTON ACT
III. PRICE DISCRIMINATION

1. Section 2 of the Clayton Act before 1936;
the Robinson-Patman Act amendments to section 2;
the legal issues raised by the Robinson-Patman Act

The practice of price discrimination was made unlawful by section 2 of the Clayton Act. It is clear that what the 1914 Congress had in mind when enacting this section was the vigorous local price cutting that some of the big 'trusts' had been found to adopt as a weapon against inconvenient competitors. With its huge resources the trust could cheerfully face a period of selling well below cost in a selected area where, for example, an obstinate 'independent' was refusing to sell out, or where an impudent new entrant was making inroads into the local market. It was not uncommon for small concerns to be put out of business by predatory price cutting of this kind. In short, the competition which the Congress regarded as threatened by price discrimination was that between the discriminating supplier and his competitors; they were not much concerned with the effect of discrimination on the supplier's customers.

It was realized that not every difference in price was discriminatory; that, for example, a bulk buyer might properly get more favourable terms than one who bought in penny numbers. There was also a strong desire not to penalize the small firm which found it necessary to lower its price in a particular area or to a particular customer in order to meet a price offered by a powerful competitor. The lawmakers tried to meet these points in a proviso to the general prohibition.[1]

It was found in practice that the proviso made the section very difficult to enforce. By exempting from the ban 'discrimination in price ... on account of differences in the ... quantity of the commodity

---

[1] The original section 2 of the Clayton Act read as follows: 'That it shall be unlawful for any person engaged in commerce, in the course of such commerce, either directly or indirectly, to discriminate in price between different purchasers of commodities, which commodities are sold for use, consumption, or resale...where the effect of such discrimination may be to substantially lessen competition or tend to create a monopoly in any line of commerce: *Provided*, that nothing herein contained shall prevent discrimination in price between purchasers of commodities on account of differences in the grade, quality, or quantity of the commodity sold, or that makes only due allowance for differences in the cost of selling or transportation, or discrimination in price in the same or different commodities made in good faith to meet competition. . . .'

sold', the lawmakers left open a wide escape route.[1] Differences in the quantities sold could nearly always be adduced as an explanation of different prices, and the courts were not disposed to look too closely at the question of whether the difference in quantity could really be said to account for or justify the whole of the difference in price.

Moreover, when attempts were made to bring cases against price discrimination which injured competition among the supplier's customers (rather than the competition between him and rival suppliers), the courts for a long time declined to find any infringement of the Act. Going by the legislative history rather than by the wording of the section, they held that the ban was directed only against discrimination which injured competition at the supplier's level—so-called 'first-line' competition.[2] This particular ruling was reversed by the Supreme Court in 1929,[3] but by then it was widely believed that section 2 was more or less of a dead letter. Between 1914 and 1936, when the Robinson-Patman Act was passed, very few cases were successfully brought under the section.

In the depressed years of the early 1930s a strong pressure was built up for revising and strengthening the law against price discrimination. The rise of the chain stores—particularly in the food trades—and the advantages they appeared to enjoy in the intense price competition generated by the slump were seen as an important factor in the plight of small retail business. The small traders were convinced that the big chains used their buying power coercively to wring from the suppliers substantial price advantages which were quite out of line with any cost savings arising from large-scale buying. A Federal Trade Commission report on the trading methods of the retail chains lent colour to this belief and in 1936 the Congress passed the Robinson-Patman Act. The effect of this Act was to replace section 2 of the Clayton Act by a much more elaborate set of provisions designed to prevent the powerful buyer from obtaining undue favours from suppliers.

Thus the motives of the legislators in 1936 were quite different from those underlying the original section 2 in 1914. The emphasis was no longer on the unfair tactics of the supplier who used local price cutting monopolistically to exclude competitors from his markets (though, as will be seen, the revised law still bites on this practice); attention was now focused on the powerful buyer who, by agreement with the supplier or by putting pressure on him, was able to secure unjustifiable competi-

[1] It will be noted that in the 1914 version this part of the proviso was not qualified by the words 'that makes only due allowance for': in other words, it was not clear that differences in quantity were to be taken as justifying discrimination only to the extent that they involved savings in cost.

[2] The leading case is *Mennen Company* v. *Federal Trade Commission* (Second Circuit Court of Appeals, 1923).   [3] *Van Camp and Sons* v. *American Can Company* (1929).

tive advantages as against the small trader. The intention of the legislators in due course became the guiding light of the courts and they
too turned their attention in the case law from a concern for the
competitors of the discriminating supplier to a concern for equal
treatment for his customers.

The main provisions of the Robinson-Patman Act, whose enforcement
the cases described in this chapter will illustrate, are as follows:[1]

Section 2 (a). That it shall be unlawful for any person engaged in commerce, in the course of such commerce, either directly or indirectly, to
discriminate in price between different purchasers of commodities of like
grade and quality, where either or any of the purchasers involved in such
discrimination are in commerce, where such commodities are sold for use,
consumption, or resale . . . and where the effect of such discrimination may
be substantially to lessen competition or tend to create a monopoly in any
line of commerce, or to injure, destroy, or prevent competition with any
person who either grants or knowingly receives the benefit of such discrimination, or with customers of either of them:

Provided, That nothing herein contained shall prevent differentials which
make only due allowance for differences in the cost of manufacture, sale, or
delivery resulting from the differing methods or quantities in which such
commodities are to such purchasers sold or delivered:

Provided, however, That the Federal Trade Commission may, after due
investigation and hearing to all interested parties, fix and establish quantity
limits, and revise the same as it finds necessary, as to particular commodities
or classes of commodities, where it finds that available purchasers in greater
quantities are so few as to render differentials on account thereof unjustly
discriminatory or promotive of monopoly in any line of commerce; and the
foregoing shall then not be construed to permit differentials based on differences in quantities greater than those so fixed and established . . .

(b) Upon proof being made, at any hearing on a complaint under this
section, that there has been discrimination in price or services or facilities
furnished, the burden of rebutting the prima facie case thus made by
showing justification shall be upon the person charged with a violation of
this section, and unless justification shall be affirmatively shown, the Commission is authorised to issue an order terminating the discrimination:

Provided, however, That nothing herein contained shall prevent a seller
rebutting the prima facie case thus made by showing that his lower price or
the furnishing of services or facilities to any purchaser or purchasers was
made in good faith to meet an equally low price of a competitor, or the
services or facilities furnished by a competitor . . .

(f) That it shall be unlawful for any person engaged in commerce, in the
course of such commerce, knowingly to induce or receive a discrimination
in price which is prohibited by this section.

[1] The provisions quoted here were embodied in section 1 of the Robinson-Patman Act
but are always referred to as section '2(a)', '2(f)', etc. of the Clayton Act as amended.

Two additional provisos of section 2(a) have been omitted as not being essential to an understanding of the topic.[1] Subsections 2(c), 2(d) and 2(e) are omitted at this point, because they really contain a new piece of legislation rather than a mere amendment of the old, and will be considered separately below. Section 3 of the Robinson-Patman Act is also a separate law for separate consideration.

Before proceeding to the illustrative cases it may be useful to set out in broad terms the main questions which these provisions raise for the litigants and the courts. First, it is for the plaintiff or enforcing authority to establish that goods 'of like grade and quality'[2] have been sold to different purchasers at different prices and that the effect of this may be substantially injurious to competition. The Robinson-Patman Act wording makes it clear that the competition in question is not solely that between the supplier and other suppliers ('first-line', or 'primary line', competition); it may be competition between the favoured customer and his trade rivals ('second-line', or 'secondary line', competition); it may even be competition between customers of the favoured customer (for example, retailers who get supplies from a favoured wholesaler) and their competitors ('third-line' competition).[3] The courts have to decide whether the price difference is likely to have a serious effect on competition at any of these levels.

A showing of a price difference that has the requisite effect on competition constitutes a prima facie case under the Act. But the defendant may show that the price difference was due to differences in cost arising from different quantities sold or different methods of delivery and hence that it was, so to say, a difference without a discrimination. In contrast to the original section 2, he must now show that the difference of price made 'only due allowance' for the difference of cost. In other words, he cannot justify a difference in price of a shilling (dime) by reference to a difference in cost of sixpence (nickel). The

[1] They are in fact saving clauses making it clear (a) that the prohibition is not intended to affect a supplier's normal right to choose his own customers and (b) that price changes caused by the deterioration of perishable goods, obsolescence and so forth are not actionable.

[2] A discussion of the problems that may arise from these words will be found at pp. 156–9 of the *Report of the Attorney General's National Committee*. Suppose a manufacturer sells a well known branded line to the ordinary retailer at a standard price and also sells the same thing unbranded to mail order houses or chain stores at a lower price. Can he defend himself against a charge of price discrimination on the ground that the goods are 'different' in the public mind? In *Federal Trade Commission* v. *Borden Co.* (Supreme Court, 1965) the Court accepted the Commission's 'longstanding interpretation' of section 2 in ruling that milk sold under Borden's own label was of 'like grade and quality' with chemically identical milk sold under private labels, saying that labels alone did not differentiate products for the purpose of determining grade and quality. A defendant may, however, still be able to show that the price differential could not substantially injure competition because, for example, milk sold under both labels was available to all purchasers, or alternatively that it could be cost justified.

[3] Competitive injury has even been found at the 'fourth-line' level in *Perkins* v. *Standard Oil Company* (District Court of California, 1969).

question for the courts is what evidence to accept as a satisfactory showing of 'cost justification'.

The defendant may also escape, as under the old section 2, by showing that his lower price to a favoured customer was charged 'in good faith to meet an equally low price of a competitor'. There are problems here both as to the procedural significance of this proviso, which is placed separately in section 2(b), and as to what in substance is a proof of 'good faith'.

Finally, a new feature of the Robinson-Patman Act was that, instead of biting solely on the discriminating supplier, it extended the prohibition to buyers. Subsection 2(f) makes it unlawful 'knowingly to induce or receive a discrimination in price which is prohibited by this section'—that is, by subsection 2(a).[1] The problem here is to decide whether the buyer who induces price favours can properly be asked to bear the onus of proving that the lower price he receives is 'cost justified' or otherwise defensible.

The Robinson-Patman revision of section 2 of the Clayton Act, whatever its other failings, has at least given rise to plenty of cases; but since many of these have been disposed of by consent order and other informal processes, the legal principles now regarded as applicable have been established in relatively few litigated cases. This fact, together with the origin of the Robinson-Patman Act in the National Industrial Recovery Act period, when the 'rescue' of small business from depression was much in mind and antitrust principles had been partially set aside, should be remembered as the main lines of cases are reviewed in the remainder of this chapter.

2. *Section 2(a) and discrimination in favour of large buyers: the* Morton
Salt *case. The test of injury to competition under section 2(a)*

Since the clear intention of Congress in the Robinson-Patman Act was to ensure that the law should prevent large buyers like the chain stores from being unduly favoured by their suppliers, it is curious to find that cases illustrating this type of situation do not bulk particularly large in the records. A good deal of the case law, as will be seen, has been concerned, almost in the spirit of 'art for art's sake', with developing the legal implications of the wording of the Act—implications which were probably unforeseen to a great extent by the legislators. However, it is right to consider first the cases which best illustrate the main

[1] It is not clear whether subsection 2(f) applies to recipients of benefits from violations of subsections 2(d) and 2(e). The issue is probably of academic interest only, since it has been held that the Federal Trade Commission can proceed against such recipients under the provisions of section 5 of the Federal Trade Commission Act as an 'unfair trading practice': *Grand Union Company* v. *Federal Trade Commission* (Second Circuit Court of Appeals, 1962).

purpose of the legislation. A convenient starting point is *Federal Trade Commission* v. *Morton Salt* (Supreme Court, 1948).

Morton Salt is one of the largest manufacturers of branded table salt in the United States. It sells salt partly through wholesalers, who supply the greater part of the retail trade, but also direct to large retailers like the chain stores. It was shown that it charged different prices for different quantities. The highest price for its best brand was charged to those who bought less than a carload. Those who bought a carload got a 10-cent discount (just over 6%) off this price. This was purely a quantity discount. The higher rates of discount were not given in respect of the quantities purchased at any one time but in respect of total purchases made over a year. Those who bought five thousand cases or more in a year were given a $12\frac{1}{2}$% discount from the top price, and those who bought fifty thousand cases or more in a year got nearly a 15% discount. It was found that only five companies—five large chain stores—had ever bought enough in a year to get the top rate of discount. The suggestion was that, as a result of this concession, these companies could sell the salt over the counter at a price below that at which small retailers could buy it from wholesalers, let alone sell it. The discount picture varied for other brands and there was some evidence of other types of discriminatory concession, but this was the main burden of the case.

The *Morton Salt* case raised in clear-cut terms the two main issues implicit in section 2(a) of the Act: what constitutes in law a serious threat to competition between buyers, and what evidence of cost savings will be needed to justify a schedule of differential discounts? On the first of these questions Mr Justice Black's opinion for the Supreme Court was a landmark. He pointed out that, as in the other sections of the Clayton Act, the words 'where the effect may be substantially to lessen competition . . .' do not require a showing of actual impairment of competition in the past: they involve an element of prediction, of assessing what the effect on competition would be if the challenged practice were allowed to go on. But whereas, ever since the opinion of Mr Justice Day in the *Standard Fashion* case under section 3 of the Act,[1] the courts had spoken of this assessment as one of a 'reasonable probability' of injury to competition, Mr Justice Black now reduced the requirement to one of showing a 'reasonable possibility'.

This change of wording, though it drew a sharp dissent from Justices Jackson and Frankfurter and caused much flurry at the time, was probably more important as a symbol of a new judicial approach than as a point of legal substance. The really significant thing was the *a priori* form of Mr Justice Black's argument. 'Here the Commission found what

---

[1] See above, Chapter VIII, p. 204.

would appear to be obvious, that the competitive opportunities of store merchants were injured when they had to pay respondent substantially more for their goods than their competitors had to pay. The findings are adequate.' This looks very much like saying that price discrimination, where 'substantial', necessarily involves injury to competition; that the danger to competition may simply be deduced from the fact of discrimination and need not be investigated.

Mr Justice Black found that the different prices charged by Morton Salt had been enough to produce differences in the retail price of salt in different types of shop. The Commission had heard many witnesses and had evidence to show that small retailers had in practice suffered damage. In face of this evidence it was irrelevant to argue that, since sales of salt were a very small part of the total business of a grocer's shop, there could be no serious impairment of competition. 'Congress intended to protect a merchant from competitive injury attributable to discriminatory prices on any or all goods in interstate commerce, whether the particular goods constituted a major or minor portion of his stock. Since a grocery store consists of many comparatively small articles, there is no possible way effectively to protect a grocer from discriminatory prices except by applying the prohibitions of the Act to each individual article in the store.'

Along these lines the case might well have been decided in the same way but without so sweeping a judicial commitment. Mr Justice Jackson, who dissented, would himself have condemned some of the discounts in question. The top rates, granted to a handful of firms on the basis of aggregate annual purchases, seemed to him clearly discriminatory: that they would injure competition was probable, not merely possible.[1] Nevertheless, Mr Justice Black ended, as he had begun, with the *a priori* argument which, as Mr Justice Jackson complained, meant that 'no quantity discount is valid if the Commission chooses to say it is not'. This version of the argument ran as follows: 'It would greatly handicap effective enforcement of the Act to require testimony to show that which we believe to be self-evident, namely, that there is a reasonable possibility that competition may be adversely affected by a practice under which manufacturers and producers sell their goods to some customers substantially cheaper than they sell like goods to the competitors of these customers. This showing, in itself, is sufficient to justify our conclusion that the Commission's findings of injury to competition were adequately supported by evidence.'

The key phrase here is 'substantially cheaper'. Mr Justice Black was

---

[1] The 6% carload discount was a different matter, for there was evidence that 99% of all Morton Salt's customers qualified for this discount and its threat to competition seemed negligible to the dissenting Justices.

ready to hear evidence on whether the difference in price, as between big and small customers, was 'substantial'—for example, whether it was large enough, in relation to the size of the distributor's margin as a whole and of the price change that would induce buyers to shift, to affect their volume of business. But having found that the price difference was 'substantial' in this sense, he would take it for granted without further evidence that there would be substantial injury to competition. The point is very like that in the decisions on requirements contracts, where Mr Justice Frankfurter held, in effect, that evidence of exclusive contracts covering a substantial slice of the business was enough, without more, to allow it to be inferred that a substantial injury to competition was probable. In these decisions both Justices Black and Frankfurter illustrated the historic preference of courts for basing themselves on ascertainable fact rather than on such arguable matters as the analysis of states of competition.

A case in which the price differences in question did not appear to the Court substantial enough for a finding of injury was *Federal Trade Commission* v. *Minneapolis-Honeywell Regulator Company* (Seventh Circuit Court of Appeals, 1951). The goods in this case were thermostats for oil burners. The Court held that the price of the thermostat was only one of a number of elements in the price of the oil burners as a whole, and observed that competition was thriving both between Minneapolis-Honeywell and its rival makers of thermostats and between dealers in oil burners. 'Where the controls were used in the manufacture of burners, the cost of which was determined by many other factors . . . it cannot be said that discriminatory price differentials substantially injure competition or that there is any reasonable probability or even possibility that they will do so.'[1] It must be admitted, of course, that this case, in which differential discounts for a component in an expensive installation were challenged, dealt with a very different situation from that in *Morton Salt*, where the price differences affected retail prices of a staple food. Nevertheless, it shows that the duty of the courts to assess competitive effects in the context of the particular case is not as dead as some critics of Mr Justice Black's *a priori* argument have feared.

The Federal Trade Commission, too, just as it has done in the fields of exclusive dealing and acquisitions, has often asserted its expertise in assessing competitive effects and its resolve to use it, and in this direction has received fairly general support from the Courts of Appeals. In *Federal Trade Commission* v. *Foremost Dairies Inc.* (Fifth Circuit Court of Appeals, 1965), the Court ruled that 'it must defer to the Commission the task of drawing the inference of probable injury to competitors so

---

[1] The Federal Trade Commission's appeal to the Supreme Court against this decision was lost on a technicality over the protest of Mr Justice Black.

long as that inference is supported by a reasonable quantum of evidence in the record'. In this case, where a large dairy company was charged with selling milk at different prices (so that *inter alia* one favoured retailer received cash rebates of over $7,500 on total milk purchases of $150,000 in an eighteen-month period), the Commission had said that if a substantial price differential had been sustained over a significant period of time in a business where profit margins were low and competition keen, it was proper to infer that injury was possible to competition with the favoured purchaser.

The Commission has also elaborated the criteria for determining whether injury has occurred to first-line competition. In another case involving sales of milk by a dairy, the Chairman of the Commission stated that it was 'the Commission's opinion that a finding of possible substantial competitive injury on the seller level is warranted in the absence of predation where the evidence shows significant diversion of business from the discriminator's competitors to the discriminator, or diminishing profits to competitors resulting either from the diversion of business or from the necessity of meeting the discriminator's lower prices, provided that these immediate actual effects portend either a financial crippling of those competitors, a possibility of an anticompetitive concentration of business in larger sellers, or a significant reduction in the number of sellers in the market. In such a situation the finding of possible competitive injury is not bottomed solely upon the fact that there has been or may continue to be diversion of business or loss of profits. Instead the emphasis is placed upon the reasonably foreseeable results of the diversion or loss of profits.'

At least one Circuit Court of Appeals[1] has, however, taken the view that *Morton Salt* (which was concerned specifically with second-line injury) has no application to first-line injury, and that accordingly the test for determining the likelihood of injured competition should be a showing that the defendant has indulged in 'a course of conduct calculated to injure rivals and harm competition generally'. It seems clear from statements by the Commission referred to above and from the cases that the inquiry in a first-line injury case has to be more extensive than in a second-line case. But the view of the Fifth Circuit Court in this matter would seem to involve a very strained interpretation of the word 'may' in the statute, nor is there anything in the wording of the Act to justify such a distinction between primary and secondary line injury. Indeed, in *Federal Trade Commission* v. *Anheuser-Busch Inc.* (1960), the Supreme Court had reaffirmed that the Act was aimed equally at the prevention of first-line, second-line and third-line injury.

Much of this argument has centred on the question of whether

[1] The Fifth Circuit Court in *Borden Co.* v. *Federal Trade Commission* (1964).

the Commission and the courts have not too readily accepted injury to competitors as equivalent to injury to competition. This line of inquiry, however, is probably sterile. It is true that in practice the evidence available to the authorities invariably pertains to injury to competitors, so that the distinction between the two concepts readily tends to be blurred or neglected. But there is little evidence from the decisions (despite certain of the dicta) that injury to particular competitors is enough to establish illegality, though injury to classes of competitors may be. The more important distinction, as noted above, is between analysing competitive effects, with all the economic argumentation that this implies, and relying on Mr Justice Black's equation of a substantial price difference with a sufficient likelihood of a substantial injury to competition, for the purposes of the statute.

3. *Cost justification:* Minneapolis-Honeywell; American Can *v.* Bruce's Juices; American Can *v.* Russellville Canning

The second big issue raised by the *Morton Salt* case was that of 'cost justification'. Morton Salt might still have escaped the charge had they been able to show that their various discounts made 'only due allowance' for reduced costs of selling to the larger customers. The case established that the onus in this respect was on them, and it is clear that the burden of proof is a heavy one. Where a pure quantity discount, like Morton Salt's carload discount, is in question, it may be comparatively straightforward to produce costings to show economies of bulk delivery. Direct costs, such as freight and packaging costs, can be calculated for carload deliveries and for penny-number deliveries, and a reasonable (though not necessarily exact) estimate of the difference can be obtained.

It is otherwise with discounts or rebates granted in respect of aggregate purchases over a period. Some of the savings that are supposed to arise from dealing with big customers are pretty questionable; some, though probably real, are imponderable; others are variable. One chain store which takes 50,000 cases of salt a year may require only a few large deliveries to central points: another may insist on frequent small deliveries to individual stores. How far is the supplier entitled to average out these costs? Most businessmen would believe that it was worth paying something to retain a large account in order to gain the secure backing for a planned flow of output that large regular orders will give him. But how does the businessman demonstrate in shillings and pence to a hostile critic that the discount he allows in consideration of this additional security makes 'only due allowance for differences in the cost of manufacture' resulting from the differing 'quantities sold'?

Should advertising costs be allotted *pro rata* over total sales to all customers? Or should there be some reduction in the allocation to those big organizations which advertise widely themselves? When the supplier sells more than one product, the situation gets still more complicated. How, for example, should his indirect costs be allocated to each line? All cost accountants know that the answer to this question comes from making arbitrary (though none the less sensible) decisions; there is no 'right answer', as to a child's sum.[1]

These questions make it clear that if the Federal Trade Commission and the courts were to require a sufficiently stringent standard of proof from the businessman who has to show cost justification for his price differences, aggregate discounts could hardly survive as a business practice. At times it has seemed to the business world that the Robinson-Patman Act would have just this result. In practice, however, it seems that a 'rule of reason' on this topic is being gradually worked out.

In the *Morton Salt* case itself the defendant company seems to have made very little attempt to produce chapter and verse to justify its discount levels. In the *Minneapolis-Honeywell* case a cost study was produced and the Commission accepted the justification for the smaller rates of discount on aggregate purchases but not for the larger discounts granted to the biggest buyers. But more light is thrown on the attitude of the courts to this problem by two private suits brought against the American Can Company.

This company granted discounts on a scale ranging from 1% to 5% to customers whose annual purchases of tins exceeded $500,000; those who spent $7 million annually got the top rate, but those who spent less than $500,000 got nothing. In *American Can Company* v. *Bruce's Juices* (1951), a Florida canner, whose purchases ran to about $350,000 a year, complained that these discounts were discriminatory and could not be justified by differences of cost. It was said, for example, that large customers were allowed to pool their purchases for different plants in different parts of the country for the purpose of claiming the aggregate discount; yet it could hardly cost American Can less to supply three plants in, say, Florida, California and Hawaii, if they were under the same ownership, than it would have cost had they all been separate companies. Since the cost of tins was an important element in total costs of canning and the trade in canned fruit juices was highly competitive, Bruce's Juices claimed that these discriminations did serious injury to their competitive position.

---

[1] The wording of the cost justification proviso to section 2(a), restricting it to 'differences in the cost of manufacture, sale and delivery resulting from the differing methods or quantities in which such commodities are . . . sold or delivered', was intended by Congress to prevent claims of cost justification from being based on differential allocations of overhead costs.

The Fifth Circuit Court of Appeals upheld Bruce's Juices. The discount schedule was found to be 'tainted with the inherent vice of too broad averaging, as a result of which it favoured a few large customers at the expense of a multitude of small buyers. . . .' It was no good saying that each level of discount was 'open to all' and therefore not unfair: the high level of purchases needed to qualify for discount meant that the discounts were 'open to all' only in the same sense as is the Ritz Hotel. As the Court put it: 'Any discount system, such as here, which arbitrarily excludes 98% of the customers involved from qualifying for any discount whatever imposes a heavy burden on its proponent to justify its continued existence. This burden defendant has here signally failed to meet.' Bruce's Juices were awarded $180,000 as treble damages together with the costs of the action.

On the other hand, in *American Can Company* v. *Russellville Canning Company* (1951), on much the same evidence about the discount structure, the Eighth Circuit Court of Appeals took a more lenient view of the burden of cost justification. This Court did not think that a schedule of discounts had to be shown to be accurately related to costs at all points, but only to have been adopted in good faith after some reasonable study of costs. 'If a manufacturer granting quantity discounts is required to establish and continuously maintain a cost accounting system which will record the expenses incurred in selling to every individual customer, and all of the data which the plaintiff deems essential, the burden, expense and assumption of risk involved would seem to preclude the granting of quantity discounts, at least until the approval of the plan by the Federal Trade Commission had been secured.' The Court did not think that Congress had intended such a result. Given that a cost study had been carefully made over a period and showed that the aggregate discounts reflected 'with substantial accuracy' differences in selling costs as between classes of customers, the plan met the test of good faith. To probe into the justification for granting discounts to individual customers within each class, and to refine the requirements in other ways, was to apply too rigid a standard.

Such differing views of how strictly the businessman should be required to justify differences of price by reference to costs continue to worry the business community and cause controversy in the United States. It is, however, becoming accepted that to require a standard of proof so strict as to exclude almost any plan for graduated aggregate discounts would go beyond the intention of Congress. On the other hand, it is still the case that some genuine and reasonably thorough study of costs has to be made and followed if the Federal Trade Commission and the courts are to be satisfied. In this connexion the criticism (in the *Bruce's Juices* case) of too broad averaging has certainly to be taken into account. It is not enough simply to compare average costs with net prices for each level of discount. This point was among those made by the Supreme Court in another case involving the Borden Dairy chain, *United States* v. *Borden* (1962), which is the leading case on this defence. Here Borden had put all the stores in the A. and P. and Jewel chains in one class, and all independent stores into another class divided into four brackets based on their volume of purchases. Borden based its cost justification defence on an analysis of its average cost of similar sales to each of the four groups of independent stores. The costs taken into account were wages, transport, and losses on bad debts and returned milk. The Court, however, by a seven to one majority, found this defence unconvincing since it 'not only failed to show that the economies relied upon were isolated within the favored class but affirmatively revealed that members of the classes utilized were substantially unlike in the cost saving aspects considered'. On the other hand its general attitude towards the use of cost justification as a defence was not unlike that of the Eighth Circuit Court of Appeals in *American Can Company* v. *Russellville Canning Company*. Mr Justice Clark pointed out that the Government had never sought to establish that discrepancies in price between any two purchasers must always be individually justified, since this would in effect have amounted to elimination of the defence altogether. On the other hand, price differentials could not be based on arbitrary classifications or even those which were representative of a numerical majority of their individual members. A balance had to be found by the use of sufficiently homogeneous classes to make the averaging of the cost of dealing within that group a valid and reasonable indicator of the cost of dealing with any of its individual members.

4. *Section 2(b) and meeting competition 'in good faith':* Standard Oil of Indiana; Tri-Valley; Sun Oil

So much for the defence of 'cost justification'. What now of the other main line of defence—that of justifying your lower price to a particular customer on the ground that you were simply meeting 'in good faith' an equally low price offered by your competitor?

The leading case on this topic is *Standard Oil Company (Indiana)* v. *Federal Trade Commission* (Supreme Court, 1951). Standard of Indiana sold petrol partly through large jobbers or wholesalers and partly by direct delivery to filling stations. The jobbers naturally took larger quantities than the individual retailers. They had bulk storage in which they could take as much as a tank-car load (8,000–12,000 gallons) at a time. Filling stations normally took a tank-wagon load (700–800

gallons). Standard sold to the jobbers at prices which worked out at
1½ cents per gallon less than the prices to filling stations. It was contended that as a result the jobbers were able to get the petrol to their
own retailer customers at prices below the tank-wagon prices paid by
Standard's direct retailer customers. This, said the Federal Trade
Commission, resulted 'in injuring, destroying and preventing competition between said favored dealers and retailer dealers in respondent's
gasolene and other major brands of gasolene'.

Standard first tried to show that the difference of 1½ cents per gallon
between the tank-car and tank-wagon prices reflected a difference of
costs, but they were unable to make good this defence. The Commission
challenged it on the ground that motor transport from Standard's
storage points to individual filling stations was often just as cheap as the
rail transport which took the tank-cars to the jobbers. Figures were
produced and argued about and the conclusion reached was that, though
there might be some difference, Standard could not make good the claim
that there was any consistent difference of as much as 1½ cents a gallon.

The Supreme Court was concerned only with Standard's second line
of defence. This defence rested on evidence that in the highly competitive oil industry other refiners were constantly trying to get the business
of the four favoured jobbers, and were offering them lower prices than
Standard's tank-wagon price. Standard claimed that, in order to retain
these customers, they had to offer a tank-car price as low as that offered
by their competitors.

The Commission had rejected this argument out of hand without
hearing the evidence. They ruled as a matter of law that section 2(b)
of the Robinson-Patman Act did not make the meeting of competition
an absolute defence to a charge of price discrimination; they interpreted
the section as merely requiring them to 'weigh the potentially injurious
effect of a seller's price reduction upon competition at all lower levels
against its beneficial effect in permitting the seller to meet competition
at its own level'.

This point of legal construction is too recondite for discussion here.[1]
In any case it is now of only academic interest, for the Supreme Court
decided that meeting competition in good faith should constitute an
absolute defence. Whatever the merits of the legal arguments, this
decision, as so often with Supreme Court decisions, was clearly more
in tune with informed opinion of the requirements of public policy than
was the alternative view.

[1] To an outside observer the most sensitive of the legal arguments seemed to point in the
direction of making some distinction between the legal status of the straightforward saving
clauses in section 2(a) of the Act and the qualified form of proviso in section 2(b). This
would suggest that there was a good deal in the Federal Trade Commission's view of the
matter.

Mr Justice Burton, speaking for the majority of the Supreme Court, said:

The heart of our national economic policy long has been faith in the value of competition. . . . We need not now reconcile, in its entirety, the economic theory which underlies the Robinson-Patman Act with that of the Sherman and Clayton Acts. It is enough to say that Congress did not seek by the Robinson-Patman Act either to abolish competition or so radically to curtail it that a seller would have no substantial right of self-defence against a price raid by a competitor. For example, if a large customer requests his seller to meet a temptingly lower price offered to him by one of his seller's competitors, the seller may well find it essential, as a matter of business survival, to meet that price rather than to lose the customer. It might be that this customer is the seller's only available market for the major portion of the seller's product, and that the loss of this customer would result in forcing a much higher unit cost and higher sales price upon the seller's other customers. There is nothing to show a congressional purpose, in such a situation, to compel the seller to choose only between ruinously cutting its prices to all its customers to match the price offered to one, or refusing to meet the competition and then ruinously raising its prices to its remaining customers to cover increased unit costs. There is, on the other hand, plain language and established practice which permits a seller, through section 2 (b), to retain a customer by realistically meeting in good faith the price offered to that customer, without necessarily changing the seller's price to its other customers.

The Supreme Court ordered the Commission to reconsider the case and take evidence on the question of whether Standard of Indiana had in fact adopted their policy in good faith to meet competition. But the good commonsense of Mr Justice Burton's opinion did not end the matter; more trouble lay concealed. It was one thing for Standard to win the right to use this defence: it was another to prove it.

On the second round of the case the majority of the Commission declined to accept the claim that the policy was adopted in good faith. They felt that Standard was simply following a conventional system of regarding purchasers of more than two million gallons in a year as 'entitled' to an arbitrary price concession. This brought out a very real difficulty. If it was simply a historical fact about the trade that the big oil refiners fought for the biggest accounts with discriminatory price concessions, the 'good faith' of each company would surely need strict examination. The object of the Act would be frustrated if each oil company were enabled to discriminate with impunity by simply pointing to the discrimination of the others. Competitive law breaking could hardly be the same thing as claiming exemption from the law in good faith.[1]

---

[1] See *Federal Trade Commission* v. *Staley Manufacturing Company* (pp. 264–5 below), in which it was ruled that a defendant cannot plead that he is meeting the illegal price of a competitor.

On the other hand, if the requirement of good faith was to be given weight, it must mean that a company using this defence ought to have satisfied itself in some way that the prices it was meeting were themselves lawful. The majority of the Federal Trade Commission indeed took this line. The burden, they said, should be on Standard, in making good its defence, to show that it was meeting lawful prices, not just emulating other discriminators. Two Commissioners who dissented from this view felt that this was an impossible burden to place on a company which, as they pointed out, had already lost three important wholesale customers. Apparently the company had either to stand by and lose still more customers or else, in order to establish its good faith, set itself up as a court of law to assess the legality of its competitors' prices; and this without having detailed knowledge of its competitors' business and without the right to call for evidence.[1]

The difficulty of this issue was shown by the narrow split when the case again reached the Supreme Court. Five members, a bare majority, held that the use by Standard of two prices, the lower of which could be obtained by any of the four favoured jobbers when they threatened to switch to other 'pirating' competitors, was legal as a response to individual competitive situations. The minority of four, however, held that a pricing system which was itself arbitrary, both as regards cost and function, could never constitute a good-faith meeting of competition. The requirement of 'good faith' on the part of those who use the 'meeting competition' defence seems to be at once necessary to prevent evasion and next to impossible to demonstrate. In the interest of competition among suppliers it seems reasonable that any one competitor should be free to match the selling policies of his rivals. But it is evident that competition among distributors could be distorted—and the whole purpose of the Act stultified—if the meeting of a rival's price were a complete defence for the supplier against a charge of discrimination. Ideally, perhaps, the legal test should be the balance of advantage arrived at after weighing the different effects on competition on both sides of the market. But different economists and judges of equal qualification and integrity might well strike such a balance differently, and with such a test the law might be even more uncertain in its incidence than at present.

Since the *Standard Oil of Indiana* decision there have been indications of a trend towards, or at least a search for, some kind of rule of reason on this issue. The Federal Trade Commission has stated in the case of the *Continental Baking Company* (1963) that a good-faith defence is intended

---

[1] There is also the point that too much inquiry into a rival's price decisions may arouse suspicions under the Sherman Act—a real possibility, though one that seems to have been played up for rather more than it is worth in American controversy on this issue.

as 'a flexible and pragmatic, not technical or doctrinaire concept', embodying the standard of the prudent businessman responding fairly to what he reasonably believes is a situation of competitive necessity. In that case the application of this test was comparatively straightforward. The defendant had begun to grant discounts only after its market position had been impaired by discounts granted by its competitors for many years. Its own discounts were highly selective, applicable only where verified cases had occurred of its customers' having received discounts from its competitors and never exceeding in amount the discount granted by such competitors.

But in other cases the requirements of proof imposed upon defendants by the majority of the Commission would seem to accord more with the spirit of the minority rather than the majority of the Supreme Court in the second *Standard Oil* case. Thus in a case—*Tri-Valley Packing Association* (1962)—involving the prices charged by Californian canners for fruits and vegetables to different classes of buyers in San Francisco, the majority of the Commission ruled that the defendant must show at least the existence of circumstances which would lead a reasonable person to believe that the lower prices it was meeting were lawful. Commissioner Elman, on the other hand, preferred the reverse test, that the defence should be available unless the seller had knowledge of facts which would indicate to a reasonable and prudent businessman that his competitor's lower price was probably unlawful. The Commission has divided similarly in other cases involving this defence.[1] It is noteworthy that the Attorney General's Committee adopted a view similar to that of Commissioner Elman, namely that a seller should be deemed to have met a lawful price unless he knew or had reason to believe that it was unlawful.

However, another recommendation of that Committee was that the defence should be available not only to enable a supplier to cut prices defensively in order to retain his existing customers, but also to enable him to attempt to woo a competitor's customers by matching his (lawful) prices. The majority of the Commission had taken the tradi- tional view that defensive cuts only were permissible, the view adopted by the Second Circuit Court. Commissioner Elman and the Seventh Circuit Court have, however, taken the view that nothing in the *Standard Oil of Indiana* case requires such a restriction on the defence, and that in a fluid and competitive market a seller cannot distinguish between 'his' customers and those who 'belong' to some other supplier. Only the Supreme Court can now resolve this conflict. But in all cases the reduction must be a conscious effort to meet competition.

One issue which the Supreme Court has resolved is whether the defence applies to competition being met by the supplier's customer

[1] E.g. *American Oil Company* (1962), reversed on other grounds by the Seventh Circuit Court.

rather than by the supplier himself. The facts of *Federal Trade Commission v. Sun Oil Company* (1963) were that a price war had broken out among competing petrol stations in Jacksonville, Florida. A petrol station selling one of the lesser known brands of petrol, Super Test, had cut its prices; Sun, a petrol refiner and wholesaler, accordingly gave one of its dealers across the road a reduced price on his supplies in order to allow him to compete. The Supreme Court laid down, overruling the Fifth Circuit Court of Appeals, that the phrase in section 2, an 'equally low price of a competitor', referred only to the price of the competitor who grants, and not to that of the buyer who receives, the discriminatory price cut. To allow the defence to be expanded in this way would encourage price rigidity, because it would reduce the incentive for suppliers to alter their pricing policies and would discourage the enterprising retailer from making reductions on his own account. It would, however, have been different had Sun obtained evidence that the Super Test dealer had received price cuts from his own supplier, or that he was himself an integrated supplier-retailer. Upon remand the Hearing Examiner found that in fact at the relevant time the Super Test dealer had received price reductions from its own supplier, but that Sun had not known of this at the time when it had initiated its own reductions, so that it could not shelter behind the 'meeting competition' defence.

This was not the end of the *Sun Oil* saga. Instead of confirming the findings of the Hearing Examiner the Commission determined that to issue a 'cease and desist' order against Sun Oil would not provide a complete or effective solution to the pricing problems of the petrol industry. It accordingly dismissed the case, as it had already done with four other similar cases against other petrol companies. It stated that the use of Robinson-Patman Act charges against individual companies was not necessarily the best way of ensuring the smooth working of the competitive process in the industry, given both the very large number of cases that might have to be brought to achieve an effective enforcement of the law, and the need for more information as to the working of the industry. The Commission accordingly set in hand industry-wide investigations into its pricing problems in an effort to put matters on a better footing.

5. *Section 2(f) and cases against those inducing or receiving illegal discrimination:* Automatic Canteen

Although Congress in passing the Robinson-Patman Act was exercised about the coercive use of buying power, the main provisions of the Act still strike against the supplier who grants the discrimination rather than against the buyer who benefits from it. This seems a little hard, like punishing a child for giving a toy away to a bully; especially so when there is so much difficulty about establishing the supplier's defences of 'cost justification' and 'meeting competition'. But Congress also included in the Act a provision directed expressly against the big buyer who presses his suppliers to grant discriminatory price concessions. This is subsection 2(f), which makes it unlawful for any person 'knowingly to induce or receive a discrimination in price which is prohibited by this Section'. How does this direct attack on the coercive buyer fare in the courts?

The leading case is *Automatic Canteen Company of America* v. *Federal Trade Commission* (Supreme Court, 1953).[1] This company not only leases vending machines for sweets but is also a large wholesale supplier of sweets to go in the machines and a correspondingly large buyer of sweets from manufacturers. The Federal Trade Commission alleged that Automatic Canteen put great pressure on these manufacturers to give it special price concessions. It was said that the company negotiated for supplies by quoting a price which it thought the manufacturers should be able to meet. This was often a price substantially lower than other wholesalers were getting. The manufacturer was told of the savings he might enjoy in supplying such a large buyer as Automatic Canteen. But, according to the Commission, no inquiry was made by the company into the question of whether the manufacturer who accepted its prices would make cost savings to the extent necessary to justify them in comparison with his prices to other buyers.

The case turned on construing the words of the subsection. The offence is 'knowingly' to induce a prohibited discrimination; a prohibited discrimination, as we have seen, is a price difference which may injure competition and which cannot be saved by either the 'cost justification' or the 'meeting competition' defence. When a case is brought against a supplier, the onus lies on him to establish one or other of these defences. The *Automatic Canteen* case raised the question of where the onus of proof should lie when the defendant is a large buyer.

The buyer who positively seeks price concessions and receives them is clearly in the position of having 'knowingly' induced differential prices; he must, therefore, rely for his defence on the proposition that the differential was not an illegal discrimination. But the factors that may save it from being a prohibited discrimination are the supplier's cost savings or his good faith in meeting competition.

It seems quite unfair, on the face of it, that the buyer who receives the concession should have to go to court and offer proof of these intimate matters of his supplier's business. How can he produce in the

---

[1] The case also involved charges under section 3 of the Clayton Act.

9   N A L

court, for example, the detailed cost schedules which will be needed to prove cost justification? On the other hand, if this burden is not placed on him, how will the Federal Trade Commission ever be able to bring home a case? It would seem easy enough for the buyer to keep himself in a state of calculated ignorance of his supplier's affairs so that the Commission could never say that he had induced a discrimination which he knew to be unlawful.[1]

The Supreme Court had to decide in effect where the burden of proof should lie. The Federal Trade Commission did not produce evidence that the price concessions received by Automatic Canteen were greater than any cost savings could justify. They stood squarely on the ground that their job was to make out a prima facie case by showing a price difference and the requisite threat to competition; thereafter, as under section 2(a), the onus was on the company to show that the discrimination involved was not a prohibited discrimination. Their buyers were experts in the trade and it was up to them to get to know whether the concessions they sought and received were justified. The defence stood on the other line. In their view the company would have violated the section only if, as well as knowing that they were being given a concession, they knew that the concession constituted a prohibited discrimination; and it was up to the Commission to prove that this was known to the company. All in fact turned on the construction of the word 'knowingly' in its context.

The Supreme Court, as always, was more concerned with the broad and practical equities of the issue than with purely legal subtleties. Mr Justice Frankfurter, speaking for a majority of six Justices against three, upheld the defence case and rejected the Commission's. While agreeing readily that the wording of the statute was 'ambiguous' and 'infelicitous', he thought that the word 'knowingly' in section 2(f) must refer in part to knowledge of the illegality of the concession; otherwise any buyer who received a concession might be charged with an offence, even though utterly ignorant of the seller's costs. He concluded, therefore, 'that a buyer is not liable under section 2(f) if the lower prices he induces are either within one of the seller's defences such as the cost justification or not known by him not to be within one of those defences'.

As to the onus of proof, Mr Justice Frankfurter pointed out that the reason for putting the onus on the supplier—in cases under section 2(a) —was precisely that he 'has at his peculiar command the cost and other record data by which to justify such discriminations'. This was not true of the buyer. Indeed, Frankfurter had commented sharply at the

---

[1] The dilemma is very similar to that raised by the 'meeting competition' defence. To require the big buyer to satisfy himself about his supplier's costs seems on the one hand an impossible burden; on the other hand, not to require it seems likely to open a way for evasion.

beginning of his opinion on the stringency of the Commission's requirements for the cost justification defence and had pointed out what a heavy burden they would place on the buyer. He concluded: 'We think the fact that the buyer does not have the required information, and for good reason should not be required to obtain it, has controlling importance in striking the balance in this case; . . . we think we must disregard whatever contrary indications may be drawn from a merely literal reading of the language Congress has used.'

The effect of this judgment is apparently to leave it to the Federal Trade Commission in future cases to prove the negative of Mr Justice Frankfurter's double-negative proposition—that a price concession was not known by the defendant not to be within one or other of the seller's defences. This might mean that the Commission must prove that the defendant *knew* that it was not a justifiable concession; alternatively, it might mean that the Commission need prove only that the defendant did not *know* that it was a legitimate concession to make. In the rarefied intellectual atmosphere in which Robinson-Patman litigation is nowadays carried on this could be quite a difference, and it may be that this Supreme Court decision will be found no less ambiguous than the statute.

Mr Justice Frankfurter himself did not think he had placed an 'undue administrative burden' on the Commission. Section 2(f) would in his view still bite on a buyer who, 'knowing full well that there was little likelihood of a defence for the seller, nevertheless proceeded to exert pressure for lower prices'. He went on to define the Commission's task in prosecuting cases:

The Commission need only to show, to establish its prima facie case, that the buyer knew that the methods by which he was served and quantities in which he purchased were the same as in the case of his competitor. If the methods or quantities differ, the Commission must only show that such differences could not give rise to sufficient savings in the cost of manufacture, sale or delivery to justify the price differential, and that the buyer, knowing these were the only differences, should have known that they could not give rise to sufficient cost savings. The showing, of course, will depend, to some extent, on the size of the discrepancy between cost differential and price differential, so that the two questions are not isolated. A showing that the cost differences are very small compared with the price differential, and could not reasonably have been thought to justify the price difference, should be sufficient.[1]

---

[1] Perhaps the best piece of advice that Mr Justice Frankfurter gave to the Commission was that they might 'in many instances find it not inconvenient to join the offending seller in the proceedings'. If the seller who granted the concession were charged under section 2(a) at the same time as the buyer who induced it was charged under section 2(f), the onus would be on him to produce the figures relating to cost justification. Some observers thought that the Commission were tactically at fault in not bringing the main suppliers of candy into the *Automatic Canteen Company* case. But of course suppliers are under no obligation to raise a cost defence.

Mr Justice Frankfurter's view has been justified by subsequent events. In spite of the *Automatic Canteen* decision the Commission has succeeded in winning a number of subsequent cases under section 2(f). Many of them have been concerned with the supply to jobbers of replacement parts for cars. Typically these jobbers are small businessmen who operate in a keenly competitive market, and whose competitors include large chain stores, oil companies, and car dealers. In order to strengthen their bargaining position they form themselves into co-operatives, and the charge brought against them has been that they knowingly induced the suppliers of parts to give these co-operatives a discount not available to other independent jobbers. Their typical defence has been that the Commission have not succeeded in proving, in accordance with the requirements of *Automatic Canteen*, that the jobbers knew that the suppliers could not justify preferential prices under either the 'cost justification' or the 'meeting competition' defence. But the counterargument, which on the evidence has generally prevailed, particularly at the Court of Appeals level, has been that the jobbers knew very well that the prices they were paying through their co-operative were substantially lower than prices paid by non-member jobbers, that their orders and shipments were handled in exactly the same way, and that there were no savings in connexion with the granting of credit, so that the cost justification argument was inapplicable. As for the meeting-competition defence, the co-operatives were formed not for the purpose of persuading suppliers to meet the lower prices of other suppliers, but to enable the member jobbers to obtain jointly a benefit from suppliers which individually they could not obtain.

In *Federal Trade Commission* v. *General Auto Supplies* (Seventh Circuit Court, 1965) the facts were rather more involved, but once again the Commission prevailed. In this case over fifty jobbers in Georgia had formed a limited partnership to purchase parts at a discount not available to them individually, but the partnership also performed many of the functions of a warehouse distributor, such as running a warehouse and purchasing some parts for resale to non-member jobbers. At the end of each year the jobber members received a dividend in proportion to the purchases made through the partnership during that period. Looking at the substance rather than the form of the operation, the Court had no difficulty in finding that the real purpose of the operation was to obtain discriminatory discounts for the member jobbers, as only 6% of the warehouse business involved actual purchase and resale to non-member jobbers. The 'indirect purchasers' who could be held to have knowingly induced the discriminatory prices were the jobbers themselves.

While the logic of these decisions is understandable, given the conceptual framework of the Act, it is extremely questionable whether it makes economic sense to deny these small businesses the opportunity to compete with their larger competitors in this way. This thought may well have been in the mind of a member of the Court of Appeals in another case involving a co-operative of car-part jobbers when he said that, if the result was to entrench further the large competitor in the market, 'the result, if bad economics or bad social policy, is for Congress to change. Until that is done, one caught in the middle cannot, to ward off his huge and overpowering rival, injure even unwittingly a smaller one.'[1]

6. *Price discrimination as a weapon in the competition between suppliers: the* Anheuser-Busch, Atlas Building *and* Sam H. Moss *cases;* Balian Ice Cream *v.* Arden Farms

Although the bulk of the case law under the Robinson-Patman Act focuses on the harm that price discrimination may do to competition between powerful and less powerful buyers, there are still cases in which the contention is that a supplier uses price discrimination as a weapon against his own competitors. *Federal Trade Commission* v. *Anheuser-Busch Inc.* (Supreme Court, 1960) reaffirmed that for a supplier to make sales at different prices to customers even in different areas and not in competition with each other is as much 'price discrimination' as when the customers are in direct competition. In that case the defendant, a leading national brewer, had for many years sold its Budweiser brand of beer at a price considerably higher than the locally brewed beers in the St Louis area. In 1954, however, it reduced the price of Budweiser in St Louis alone without making corresponding reductions in its other markets. The Court ruled that a 'price discrimination' means merely a 'price difference', and remanded the case to the Seventh Circuit Court for a determination of whether any injury to competition in the relevant market could be proved.[2]

The Seventh Circuit Court found in the *Anheuser-Busch* case that the motives for the price cutting by the defendants were not predatory or vindictive, but many of the cases illustrating this aspect of the law have been concerned with local price cutting in an attempt to dispose of inconvenient competitors, though they are a far cry from the predatory competition and 'fighting companies' of the trusts. A case which is perhaps the nearest post-war approach to trust building by local price cutting was *Atlas Building Products Co.* v. *Diamond Block and Gravel Co.* (Tenth Circuit Court of Appeals, 1959). The plaintiff, a manufacturer of cinder

---

[1] *Federal Trade Commission* v. *Mid-South Distributors* (Fifth Circuit Court of Appeals, 1961).

[2] The Seventh Circuit Court found on remand that no actual or potential injury to competition had occurred in the St Louis market.

concrete blocks in Las Cruces, New Mexico, brought a treble-damage action against the defendant, who manufactured the same products in El Paso, Texas, alleging that the price quoted by the defendant was 23·1 cents per block in El Paso, where it had a virtual monopoly of the market, but in Las Cruces it was only 20 cents per block in order to put the plaintiff out of business. The Court upheld the jury verdict that the plaintiff was entitled to treble damages in respect of his financial loss attributable to this predatory price cutting.

In *Sam H. Moss* v. *Federal Trade Commission* (Second Circuit Court of Appeals, 1945) a supplier of rubber stamps was alleged to have gone after business by canvassing possible customers and undertaking to supply them at lower prices than they could get elsewhere. In effect he simply bid low enough in each case to get the business. It was held that this type of competitive behaviour is banned by the Robinson-Patman Act, since it cannot be said that offers of this kind are made in good faith to meet competition. Moss took no trouble, it was said, to find out what his competitors' prices were and could not, therefore, show that he had not undercut them rather than 'met' them.

This case stands as a warning that special price offers designed to attract particular customers are always likely to be vulnerable under the Robinson-Patman Act. It must, of course, be shown that the discriminatory concessions may substantially injure competition. In practice this requirement probably means that a powerful firm is much more vulnerable in this respect than a small firm. If Joe Bloggs landed a soap contract under the noses of Lever or Colgate, the chances are that nobody would care whether the price he quoted was lower than his usual price. If Lever or Colgate undercut their usual prices to take business away from Joe Bloggs, a serious injury to competition would probably be assumed. Joe Bloggs would very soon go out of business and the dominance of the giants would be to that extent consolidated. As the law stands, the small man is probably pretty safe in initiating selective price cutting to get business away from the big. The big fellow must not start the game; once it is started, he may play for a draw but not go all out for a win.

Two other private suits illustrate the delicate balance that has to be maintained by the courts between preventing concerns from competing 'unfairly' by price discrimination and preventing them from competing at all. In *Balian Ice Cream Company* v. *Arden Farms Company* (District Court of California, 1952) the defendant was a large manufacturer and supplier of ice-cream in the western States which had substantially reduced its prices in Los Angeles and elsewhere in California as compared with its price in the other States where it carried on business. The plaintiffs—various local manufacturers and suppliers of ice-cream in California—claimed that this was predatory price discrimination designed to drive competitors from the Californian market.

The case was lost in the trial Court. Judge Yankwich found that the Californian market for ice-cream was highly competitive and that the local manufacturers were fighting for custom and using all manner of special inducements and concessions to get it. 'What we are, in reality, asked to do, under the guise of encouraging competition, is to freeze a certain pattern of price discrimination until the others in the industry get ready to make it more universal.' Arden, in fact, had been losing business continuously from 1946 until they made their price cut in November 1949. In 1950, after the price cut, their sales were slightly lower than before, whereas the plaintiffs, so far from being forced out of the market, maintained their sales at a steady level.

Judge Yankwich drew authority from Mr Justice Burton's opinion in the *Standard Oil of Indiana* case[1] for the proposition that in meeting competition in a discriminatory situation a supplier is justified in reducing his price in the locality concerned.[2] 'Reason and good sense warrant the conclusion that such course is sound legally, as well as economically.' He went on: 'To repeat—the object of the antitrust laws is to encourage competition. Lawful price differentiation is a legitimate means for achieving the result. It becomes illegal only when it is tainted by the purpose of unreasonably restraining trade or commerce or attempting to destroy competition or a competitor, thus substantially lessening competition. . . .'

This was in effect a 'rule of reason' approach to the problem, and Judge Yankwich finally spelled out the tests of reasonableness in this type of situation: 'It is apparent that the price reduction here (a) was long in contemplation; (b) it bore a realistic relation to previous changes by others in the field, either in the locality or elsewhere; (c) it corresponded to factors relating to cost of production and demand for the article, and the continuous shrinkage of Arden's custom—all of which, after long and mature consideration, called for the reduction. These are legitimate criteria for legal price reduction.'[3]

On the other hand—in *L. L. Moore* v. *Mead's Fine Bread Company* (Supreme Court, 1954)—the Supreme Court upheld the plaintiff's suit. Moore was a small baker in Santa Rosa, New Mexico; there was evidence that he persuaded the local shopkeepers to deal exclusively in his bread and not buy any from firms outside the town. Mead, a

---

[1] Quoted above, p. 239.

[2] He also held by way of dictum that Mr Justice Burton's words sanctioned a seller's underbidding a competitor to retain a particular customer. It is doubtful if this would be generally accepted.

[3] Judge Yankwich's decision in this case was upheld by the Ninth Circuit Court of Appeals in 1955.

substantial bakery concern in New Mexico and Texas, regarded this situation as a boycott and replied by slashing the wholesale price of its bread in Santa Rosa (but nowhere else) by half. In about six months Moore was forced to close his business.

In this instance the commercial situation which had arisen in Santa Rosa was not regarded as justifying Mead's price discrimination. Mr Justice Douglas quoted a ruling from an earlier case that 'the alleged illegal conduct of petitioner . . . could not legalize the unlawful [activity of] respondents nor immunize them against liability to those they injured'.[1] Thus the use of price discrimination as a competitive weapon is strictly circumscribed. In some circumstances, if the *Arden Farms* case is good law, you may fight to hold your position: but even when provoked, you run serious legal risks if you counter attack so vigorously that competitors are eliminated.

7. *Functional discounts under the Robinson-Patman Act:* the Ruberoid *case;* Standard Oil of Indiana; *the* Bird *and* Kraft-Phenix *cases; the* Sparking plug *case*

The previous sections of this chapter have sketched the main issues arising in Robinson-Patman Act case law. There remain some interesting applications of the law: applications to trading situations which would not normally be thought of as discriminatory and which the sponsors of the Act probably never envisaged as coming within its scope. The most important topic under this head is the bearing of the Act on ordinary trade or 'functional' discounts.[2]

The commonest type of trade discount is that which a manufacturer grants to a wholesaler. The wholesaler's place in the chain of distribution comes from the fact that he carries out important and specialized functions which the manufacturer does not choose or is not able to organize for himself. The cost of performing these functions and the wholesaler's profit have to be paid for. Consequently the manufacturer will sell his goods to the wholesaler at a lower price than that at which he would sell to retailers if he dealt with them directly. In many trades the manufacturer will quote as the 'list price' of his product the price

[1] The main question decided by the Supreme Court was whether a local struggle of this kind involved interstate commerce. The 'price war' between Moore and Mead took place in one small town in New Mexico. But it was held that since a company operating in interstate trade and drawing its resources from such trade was the beneficiary of the illegal price cutting, its local activities were 'in commerce' for the purposes of the statute. If this were not so, 'interstate business could grow . . . with impunity at the expense of local merchants. . . . The profits made in interstate activities would underwrite the losses of local price cutting campaigns.'

[2] Another such topic—the bearing of the Act on the individual supplier's use of delivered prices—is considered in a supplementary note to this chapter.

that he expects the public to pay in the shop. Then the price which the retailer pays for the product and the price at which the manufacturer will sell it to the wholesaler can be expressed in terms of discounts from the list price. Retailers, for example, might buy the goods at $33\frac{1}{3}\%$ 'off list' and wholesalers at a discount of 45%.

In some trades there are more complex discount schedules. Building materials, for example, may be sold by the manufacturer both to merchants who carry out wholesaling functions and to large builders and contractors for use in construction projects. The merchants will resell not only to retailers but to small builders, plumbers and other tradesmen, and even to the general public. The manufacturer in such a trade may compile a whole schedule of discounts from the list price for the various classes of people who use or resell the goods.[1]

All this is common trade practice, and nobody is surprised that a wholesaler buys goods more cheaply than a retailer and a retailer more cheaply than a housewife. But when a supplier sells a product to customers at different discount levels—when, for example, a manufacturer sells partly through wholesalers but also direct to retailers, or when a builder's merchant sells to both plumbers and members of the public—he is selling goods of like grade and quality to different customers at different prices. This is why the practice may become entangled in the provisions of the Robinson-Patman Act.

In most instances there is no problem because there can be no question of an adverse effect on competition. A wholesaler and a retailer are normally performing different functions in different markets and not competing against each other; the builder's merchant is not in competition with the construction company. Some types of situation can, however, cause trouble. One such comprises situations in which a single concern straddles two or more trade functions. There are firms, for example, which conduct a wholesaling business but also have retail shops of their own; there are large contractors which also run a merchant's business in building materials. Is the manufacturer to grant the wholesaler-cum-retailer the wholesale or the retail discount?

Commonsense suggests that he will grant the wholesale discount. It may be assumed that such a firm will buy in the quantities typical of wholesalers and, from the manufacturer's standpoint, it will perform

---

[1] The extent to which all these discounts are strictly functional is questionable. The contractor who installs a bath in a home is performing in part a retail function. It is obviously impossible to say that his discount accurately reflects the cost of his partial retail function as compared with the retailer who sells but does not install. There are elements of status and goodwill, group pressures and a high degree of conventionality in the figures adopted in a trade. Collective agreements about discount levels and the 'classification' of those entitled to receive them are likely, of course, to violate the Sherman Act (see above, Chapter II, p. 65). In this chapter it is assumed that the individual supplier acts independently.

wholesaling functions not only for the goods it resells to the retail trade but also for those which subsequently pass to its own shops. Moreover, such a firm will expect to get the wholesale discount and the manufacturer will not be surprised if by refusing it he loses the account.

But the authorities enforcing the Robinson-Patman Act may see the situation from another angle. The wholesaler-cum-retailer is none the less a retailer and in competition with other retailers. If he is given the wholesale discount on the goods he sells by retail, he will in effect be getting a preferential price as against his competitors. Goods of like grade and quality will be reaching different purchasers at different prices and there may be an adverse effect on competition. Thus the situation is prima facie within the scope of the Act. It could be argued, moreover, that if the Act were not enforced against this situation, the way would be wide open for evasion; for nothing would then prevent the chain stores from setting up wholesale businesses to supply their shops and taking the wholesale discount on all their purchases. But what Congress clearly intended by the Act was that the chains should not get preferential prices unless they could be cost justified.

The authorities have indeed taken this argument to the courts, in the well known case of *Federal Trade Commission* v. *Ruberoid Company* (Supreme Court, 1952). Ruberoid is an important manufacturer of asbestos and asphalt roofing materials, selling to three different types of trader—wholesalers, retailers and 'applicators'—at different prices or discount levels. ('Applicators' are roofing contractors who use the product for their contract work.) The evidence showed, among other things, that one purchaser whose main business was 'applicating' also acted as a wholesaler, reselling substantial quantities to other applicators. Another was mainly a wholesaler but also did some contract work. It was said, too, that lively competition existed between applicators and retailers; the applicator resold the material to the general public like an ordinary retailer, the only difference being that he sold some labour as well.

Ruberoid simply made the best determination it could as to the appropriate discount level for any particular customer and then granted that level of discount on all his purchases. The Federal Trade Commission held that this practice involved a danger of substantial injury to competition and so constituted illegal price discrimination. If the wholesaler-applicator got the wholesale discount, the competition between him and the ordinary applicators was no longer fair and square; in so far as an applicator was regarded as retailing, his applicator discount gave him improper competitive advantages over the ordinary retailer, and so on. The Commission said in effect that the designation given to any particular firm was to be disregarded and ordered Ruberoid to give equal treatment to firms which in fact competed with one another in the resale of the product. The Supreme Court endorsed this result: 'We think the order is . . . reasonably related to the facts shown by the evidence, and within the broad discretion which the Commission possesses in determining remedies.'

It seems to be generally accepted that the teaching of the *Ruberoid* and other cases is that traders who in fact compete at any level must be granted the same level of discount, except so far as differences may be cost justified.[1] How, then, can the manufacturer compensate the wholesaler-cum-retailer for his wholesaling functions? The lawyer's textbook solution to this problem prescribes charging two different prices to a customer with two different trade functions. The wholesaler-cum-retailer should be invoiced separately at different net prices for the goods he takes for each function.

While this solution seems to have the sanction of the law,[2] it is difficult to regard it as satisfactory. For one thing it creates yet another situation in which the legality of the supplier's price policy depends on the good faith of a third party whom he cannot and should not control. Apparently the supplier, when selling to a wholesaler-retailer, should require a certified return to be made by his customer showing which of the goods were resold by wholesale and which were retailed; he should then adjust the discounts accordingly. But is he to accept the customer's return at its face value or must he attempt to check it in some way? The customer has an obvious incentive to 'chisel', but it is the supplier who runs the legal risk. A court might find that a wholesaler-retailer had in fact taken the wholesale discount on goods he retailed, so that competition between him and other retailers was injured. Then, once again, the question would arise whether the supplier 'ought to have known' of the deception. It can hardly be good law when so much turns on what the accused 'ought to have known' about the activities of third parties.

There is a more important reason why this solution is unsatisfactory. The wholesaler-retailer may—indeed almost certainly does—perform wholesaling functions in respect of the goods which he later sells by retail in his own shops. A rule which insists that he should get the

---

[1] Even before the Robinson-Patman Act a court had ruled that it was the character of a trader's selling, not his buying, which marked him as wholesaler or retailer: *Mennen Company* v. *Federal Trade Commission* (1923). It is interesting to note that at that time the Commission was attacking a manufacturer for *not* granting a wholesale discount to a retailers' co-operative buying concern: it urged that no discount based on a buyer's label as 'wholesaler' or 'retailer' should be permitted. The Court held that the supplier could, if he wished, sell at the same price to the wholesaler and the retail co-operative but was not obliged to by virtue of their buying in similar quantities.

[2] This was confirmed in the *Sparking plug* case described below, pp. 257 ff.

wholesale discount only on goods which he resells to the trade takes no account of this. And this is economically perverse.[1]

The supporter of the Robinson-Patman Act will argue that the integrated distributor has no cause for complaint because nothing prevents his receiving low prices that are cost justified. But the point at issue here exposes a serious shortcoming in the exemption for cost justified concessions. The cost savings that may justify a lower price under this proviso to the Act are solely the supplier's cost savings. But cost savings are also made in an integrated wholesale-retail business— indeed they are one of the main reasons for integration. Since the integrated distributor cannot, as the law stands, obtain the wholesaler's functional discount on goods which pass to his own retail outlets— even though he performs wholesale functions as respects these goods— his internal economies are wasted and cannot be passed on to the consumer. Worse than that, when he receives only the retailer's discount, he will have to meet the cost of the wholesale functions he performs out of his own pocket. So the law may act as a positive disincentive against seeking economies of integration.[2] This is one of the aspects of the Robinson-Patman Act which have led some economists to describe it as a law for promoting price discrimination—discrimination against the efficient integrated firm and in favour of the small retailer.

So much for the difficulty that arises when functional discounts are granted to firms that straddle two or more trade functions. There is also a problem when a supplier sells partly through wholesalers and partly direct to retailers, acting for the sales to retailers as his own wholesaler. In this situation he will normally grant the wholesaler a better discount than his direct retail customers. This looks innocuous enough: but if it happens that retailers buying the goods from his wholesalers can get a better price than the retailers who buy direct, the authorities may see a danger to third-line competition.[3]

[1] This difficulty might perhaps be overcome if the wholesaler-retailer completely segregated his wholesale business in a separate company and resold goods to his own retail business on the same terms as to other retailers. But this might dissipate some of the economies of integration besides creating taxation problems. Also there would be no guarantee that the courts would not condemn such an arrangement as a 'fiction' designed for evasion: for antitrust deals with substance, not form.

[2] It is arguable that distribution costs borne by the wholesaler-retailer could be adduced in defence as a rebuttal of the proof of injury, i.e. that if a 5 cent extra expenditure by the distributor could be shown, this should rebut the contention that a 5 cent price advantage granted by the supplier could cause injury to competition. But this might be a chancy business because the defendant is usually the supplier but the facts for this defence would be in the hands of the distributor.

[3] In the words of section 2(a) of the Act, the effect of the price difference (that is, between the supplier's wholesaler and retailer customers) 'may be . . . to injure . . . competition with any person who either grants or knowingly receives the benefit of such discrimination, *or with customers of either of them*'. 'Third-line' competition is that in which the customers of the discriminatory supplier or the favoured buyer are involved.

This is what happened in the *Standard Oil of Indiana* case (see above, pp. 237 ff.); Standard's jobber (wholesaler) customers got the higher tank-car discount while its direct retailer customers got only the tank-wagon discount. It was found that some of the retailers supplied by the jobbers bought petrol cheaper than retailers supplied by Standard direct; this was the ground on which Standard's arrangements were found to threaten competition.

The interesting thing is the method adopted by the Federal Trade Commission in its 'cease and desist' order to remedy the danger to competition. The order prohibits Standard from selling petrol 'to any retailer at a price known by respondent to be higher than the price at which any wholesaler-purchaser is reselling such gasoline to any retailer who competes with such direct retailer-customer of respondent, when respondent is selling to such wholesaler at a price lower than respondent's price to such direct retailer-customer'.

This order means that, so long as Standard sells at different prices to jobbers and retailers, it must see to it that its own price to retailers is the same as the jobbers' price to retailers. It is in effect an order under which Standard must impose a rigid system of resale price maintenance on its wholesalers.[1] This result is the more fantastic because of the fact that the Federal Trade Commission has strenuously opposed the legislation legalizing resale price maintenance.[2] If the Commission's view in this respect should prevail at some future time, and if the federal and State laws allowing resale price maintenance were repealed, Standard might find itself in the dock for destroying competition between its wholesalers by maintaining prices: and it would be maintaining these prices in pursuance of the Commission's order as a means of avoiding injury to competition among the retailers!

The odd thing is that it should be thought necessary to worry about third-line competition in this context, for one might suppose that this would be a self-correcting problem. If retailers find that they can get Standard's petrol cheaper from jobbers than from Standard, they will surely switch their custom to the jobbers until such time as Standard brings its own price in line or squeezes the jobbers' margin? The case illustrates the way in which a law designed to secure that large retail organizations should not get undue concessions may come to be interpreted to mean that something is wrong unless all retailers buy goods at exactly the same price—a very different matter.

Standard would have one other legal recourse in the situation

---

[1] The alternative would be for Standard simply to follow the wholesalers' prices. But, apart from the fact that Standard might well dislike having its price to retailers fixed for it, this would be no answer if different wholesalers charged different prices to retailers.

[2] In particular the McGuire Act of 1952: this legislation is described in Chapter X.

outlined above—namely to sell to jobbers and retailers at exactly the same price. Ignoring the commercial impracticality of this course, it is curious that this should be lawful, since it would necessarily affect third-line competition even more seriously than Standard's alleged discrimination. Retailers who purchased from wholesalers would then be at a permanent disadvantage compared with those who bought direct. Yet as long ago as 1937 (*In the matter of Bird and Son*) it was established that there was nothing unlawful in sales by a manufacturer of floorcoverings to wholesalers and retail mail order houses at the same price. This is because the law does not detect price discrimination in the absence of a price difference (the advice of economists notwithstanding).

From this rule it follows that the law never *requires* the granting of functional discounts (for example, charging wholesalers less than retailers) even though their absence may injure third-line competition. There is, however, an important qualification to the rule of the *Bird* case. A manufacturer who charges the same price to wholesalers and retailers must not lay down the prices (or discounts) that are to apply to the wholesalers' sales to retailers. It has been held by the Federal Trade Commission (*In the matter of the Kraft-Phenix Cheese Corporation*, 1937) that a manufacturer who himself solicits the custom of retailers and determines their buying prices should be regarded as dealing directly with the retailers for the purpose of the Act. 'A retailer is none the less a purchaser because he buys indirectly if, as here, the manufacturer deals with him directly in promoting the sale of his products and exercises control over the terms upon which he buys.'

Curiouser and curiouser! If the manufacturer charges wholesalers less than direct retail customers, as in the *Standard* case, he must take care to see that the wholesalers' resale price to their retail customers is kept in line with his own. Otherwise there may be an effect on third-line competition such that his lower price to wholesalers will be unlawfully discriminatory. But if he charges wholesalers and retailers the same price—which, according to the law, cannot be discriminatory —he must take care *not* to influence the wholesalers' price to retailers. Otherwise he will be regarded as accepting responsibility for that price and hence for the fact that it will necessarily be higher than his own price to retailers.

One last problem of differential discounts must be noted: it arises when a product is sold to manufacturers for use in new equipment at a lower price than to wholesalers who distribute it for use in repairs and replacements. This is the case, for example, with sparking plugs, and the Federal Trade Commission has brought charges of illegal discrimination against all three leading manufacturers of plugs. The issues are best illustrated by *In the matter of the Champion Spark Plug Company* (1953).

This company had sold sparking plugs to the Ford Company for new cars at 6 cents each, and for resale through their sales and service organization as replacement parts at 22 cents each. Champion's price for replacement plugs to wholesalers supplying the service trade generally was 26 cents.[1]

On these facts the enforcement staff of the Federal Trade Commission mounted an attack on the proposition that a dual-function buyer, like Ford, may safely be charged two different prices according to the use made of the goods. It was contended that the 'real' price paid by Ford was the weighted average of the two prices and that this was 16½ cents. As this price was higher than that charged to other manufacturers who bought only for new cars and lower than that charged to other wholesalers for the replacement trade, it necessarily involved discrimination between competing purchasers.[2]

Had this argument succeeded, it would—as it was intended to do—have finally scotched functional discounts in all trades where there are firms that straddle two or more functions. The averaging argument could be used against any dual-function firm, so that a wholesaler-retailer, for example, could get no price concession at all by virtue of its wholesaling functions but only a 'cost justified' concession. The Commission, however, rejected this argument; it was held that Champion's two categories of sale to Ford were in distinct markets and that the price differential could have no adverse effect on competition between buyers.

It was also argued that the 6-cent price of plugs for new equipment was so low that it prevented other manufacturers of plugs, especially new entrants, from getting a share of the new equipment business. Since the harm alleged by this line of argument was to first-line competition among makers of plugs, it did not matter that the 6-cent and 22-cent plugs were sold in different markets: it was still price discrimination which injured competition, as in the *Atlas Building Products* case.[3] On this issue the Commission, while accepting in principle that an especially low functional price might be unlawful because of its

---

[1] The difference between 22 cents and 26 cents was the basis of successful charges, but these raised no new legal issues and will be ignored here.

[2] While using the 16½-cent figure as the 'price' to compare with the price paid by other wholesalers, the enforcement staff still used the 6-cent 'price' as the basis of a contention that the supplier discriminated in favour of Ford and against other manufacturers.

[3] In the *Atlas Building Products* case the discriminating sellers had picked out a particular geographic division of the market for predatory price cutting: the contention here was that Champion had picked out a particular functional division of the market from which would-be competitors could be excluded by low prices.

adverse effect on first-line competition, held that the burden of showing such an effect in the particular case had not been sustained.

This was an interesting decision. The main reason why a firm like Champion quotes such a favourable price to Ford is probably the ever present threat that such a customer may decide to make his own plugs if he is dissatisfied with the price or quality of outside supplies. (General Motors, for example, do make their own plugs.) Thus, although a very low price for new-equipment plugs may well present a serious obstacle to a new entrant into the sparking plug industry—for the newcomer cannot match such a price until he has a huge output and cannot get the output until he has captured some new-equipment business—it does not follow that the competitive situation would be improved by declaring the low price illegal. Had the Federal Trade Commission interpreted the Robinson-Patman Act to require new-equipment and replacement plugs to be sold at the same price, they might have helped small manufacturers of plugs to compete successfully against Champion; on the other hand, they might merely have caused all the giant car firms to manufacture plugs for themselves and have dished the independent plug manufacturers for good and all.[1] In the complex real world the choices facing those who want to promote competition are often of this kind.

8. *Quantity limit rules; the brokerage provisions; subsections 2 (d) and 2 (e) and advertising allowances; section 3 of the Robinson-Patman Act*

There is still a great deal more to the Robinson-Patman Act, which could well be given a book to itself.[2] The quantity limit rules will first be considered. The cost justification proviso to subsection 2(a) of the Act is itself subject to a qualifying proviso under which the Federal Trade Commission may set quantity limits beyond which even cost justified, quantity discounts may not be granted to large buyers; the Commission may do this 'where it finds that available purchasers in greater quantities are so few as to render differentials on account thereof unjustly discriminatory or promotive of monopoly in any line of commerce'. This wording is curious in itself, for the rest of subsection 2(a) is based on the assumption that what makes a price difference 'unjustly discriminatory' is precisely that it cannot be justified by cost savings. The words 'promotive of monopoly' are probably the true test. The provision pre-

---

[1] Indeed, in a case challenging a merger between Ford and the Autolite Company, a non-integrated, sparking plug manufacturer, one of Ford's defences—all of which were unsuccessful—was precisely that competition was not impaired because, without the merger, Ford would begin producing its own sparking plugs.

[2] There is indeed an admirable book on the Act by Professor Corwin D. Edwards, *The Price Discrimination Law*, Brookings Institution, Washington, 1959.

sumably aims at the buyer who is so large that, if he were given the full advantage of the cost savings resulting from his huge purchases, he would be able to undersell all his competitors and achieve a position of monopoly; it requires that such a buyer be discriminated against in that some part of the cost savings he creates may not be passed on to him.[1]

Cases that genuinely meet this prescription must be rare indeed. One case that the Federal Trade Commission has dealt with under the provision concerns the tyre industry, in which it was found that only sixty-three distributors out of nearly 50,000 qualified for the manufacturers' highest rates of aggregate annual discount. These sixty-three firms between them bought rather less than 30% of the tyres and tubes going to the replacement trade in 1947. The Commission found, however, that this situation was 'promotive of monopoly' and ordered that the 'quantity limit' for discounts should be a carload quantity (of 20,000 pounds weight) when ordered and delivered at one time. This order in effect banned all aggregate annual discounts in the tyre trade. The Court of Appeals for the District of Columbia held the order invalid, however, on the ground that the Commission had not made the finding required under the section, namely that available purchasers for quantities greater than a 20,000-pound carload were so few as to render differentials given for such amounts either 'unjustly discriminatory' or 'promotive of monopoly'.

Subsection 2(c) of the Act makes it unlawful for a buyer of goods (or any agent or representative of the buyer) to receive from or to be paid by the supplier any brokerage or other commission 'except for services rendered in connection with the sale or purchase of goods'. This provision closed a loophole through which large buyers might have received favours without breach of subsection 2(a); without it the chain retailers might have been able to set up affiliated buying agents or brokers who would have taken as 'brokerage' precisely those 'undue' concessions that the rest of the Act was meant to prevent. (The part played by ACCO in the *A. & P.* case—see above, Chapter V, pp. 133–8—will be recalled in this context.)

No effect on competition has to be shown under this section, which is in effect a *per se* rule. For many years the words 'except for services rendered' were strictly interpreted to mean only that the seller (or buyer) might compensate his own agent for services rendered but not the agent of the other party. In cases commencing with *Federal Trade Commission* v. *Henry Broch and Company* (Supreme Court, 1962), however,

---

[1] The Senate Committee which recommended this provision spoke of it as covering economies 'possible only to a very few units of overshadowing size' and suggested that in forgoing the benefits of such economies 'the public is but paying a willing price for its freedom from monopoly control'.

the courts have shown a tendency to accept that in certain circumstances this exception may be interpreted to cover situations where the buyer or his agent has relieved the seller (or vice versa) of functions which he would otherwise perform himself or which represent cost savings to him. This tendency towards a more liberal interpretation of the section is to be welcomed, since section 2(c) has in the past drawn heavy fire from economists, who see it as a bar to making economies by efficiently integrating different distributive functions. It also has curious side effects. One is to produce something like 'closed shop' conditions for independent brokers, who strongly favour it in consequence. Another is that it may bite on attempts by independent retailers to set up co-operative buying organizations in order to match the economies of operation of the large chains, so that a possible exercise of 'countervailing power' may be frustrated.[1]

Subsection 2(d) makes it unlawful for a supplier to make any payment to a buyer in consideration of services or facilities provided in promoting the sale of goods, unless similar payments are made available on 'proportionally equal terms' to other buyers. Subsection 2(e) makes it unlawful for the supplier himself to provide promotional services and facilities to a buyer unless he accords facilities on 'proportionally equal terms' to other buyers. These clauses, like the brokerage clause, are *per se* rules in the sense that no effect on competition need be shown; and they too are designed to stop any loophole whereby, without breach of the main provisions of the Act, large buyers could receive price concessions for services of dubious or merely nominal value, or concessions in the form of services or facilities. Under these clauses, moreover, the cost justification defence is not available. This was confirmed by the Supreme Court in *Federal Trade Commission* v. *Simplicity Pattern Co.* (1959), in which Simplicity was charged with furnishing dress patterns on a consignment basis to department stores, whilst dealing only on a cash basis with small specialist material shops, and with making available to the department stores alone certain display and storage facilities. The 'meeting competition' defence is, however, applicable to those sections as well as to 2(a) and 2(b).

Thus, under subsection 2(d) a manufacturer who pays a large distributor an allowance as a contribution to a local advertising campaign must make some similar allowance available to other distributors who are able and willing to render promotional services. The type of service given need not be of exactly the same kind (clearly the

---

[1] It appears however, that 2(c) may not be violated by a co-operative buying organization, if the organization purchases goods on its own account and makes direct payment to the seller for goods invoiced to it so that there is no buyer-seller relationship between the supplier and the members of the co-operative: *Central Retailer-Owned Grocers, Inc.* v. *Federal Trade Commission* (Seventh Circuit Court of Appeals, 1963).

small retailer cannot go in for expensive newspaper or radio advertising), but the opportunity must be given for some promotional service to be rendered, and the contribution paid by the supplier to the small man must be 'proportionally equal', by reference to the volume of his purchases and the value of the service rendered, to that paid to the big firm. Equally, under subsection 2(e), a manufacturer who provides a big customer with a promotional service, such as sending paid demonstrators of the product to his retail stores, must provide some form of service to smaller distributors: again it need not be a service of the identical kind, which may be impracticable, but it must be 'proportionally equal' in value.

It will be evident that there is much in these provisions to give rise to legal dispute. What constitutes a service or facility? What are 'proportionally equal' terms? As with some other sections of the Act, a tendency on the part of the Federal Trade Commission in the post-war years to hold to the most stringent requirements of the letter of the law seems to have been giving way to an attempt to reach an accommodation between its underlying intention and the practical requirements of the business world. That this accommodation can ever be completely happy is, however, open to doubt.[1]

Finally there is a criminal provision of the Robinson-Patman Act (section 3) by which it is an offence punishable by fines or imprisonment to be a party to discriminatory transactions, or to engage in local price cutting or sell goods at 'unreasonably low prices for' the purpose of destroying competition or eliminating a competitor'. The Supreme Court has so far twice considered this section. In *Nashville Milk Company* v. *Carnation Company* (1958) it ruled by a five to four majority that, on technical grounds, no private plaintiff could bring a treble-damage claim under the section, though of course a claim might well lie on the same facts under section 2(a) of the Robinson-Patman Act. In *United States* v. *National Dairy Products Corporation* (1963), however, the defendants were criminally charged with having violated the statute by selling milk in certain markets at unreasonably low prices, utilizing the advantages of the fact that they operated in a great many geographical locations in order to finance a price war against small dairies in certain towns. The Supreme Court by a majority of six to three held the section constitutional, notwithstanding the vagueness of its proscriptions, since the practice of making unjustifiable sales below cost had for many years been held to violate the Sherman Act, and the

---

[1] An interpretation of section 2(d) may be found in the Commission's decisions dismissing three cases against soap manufacturers (Commerce Clearing House, Chicago, *Trade Regulation Reporter*, para. 11,588); and of section 2(e) in the majority statement of the Commission accompanying the Trade Practice Conference Rules for the Cosmetics and Toilet Preparations Industry (Commerce Clearing House, Chicago, *Trade Regulation Reporter*, vol. 4, para. 41,221.

legislative history of section 3 showed that it was specifically aimed at such predatory sales. On the other hand the Court's opinion was not to be taken to outlaw such sales when made with a legitimate commercial objective, such as the bona fide meeting of competition or clearing stocks of obsolete merchandise, for these would not be 'unreasonably low' prices. Three members of the Court agreed with the District Court that this section was unconstitutional. In subsequent hearings it was held by the Eighth Circuit Court that the meaning of 'below cost' meant 'below fully distributed cost', that is cost of production plus additional allocated delivery, selling and administrative expenses, and not merely 'direct cost'—raw material, processing and container costs only.

*   *   *

There is a real danger that an account of the case law under the Robinson-Patman Act—particularly an account intended primarily for readers outside the United States—will be met with frank unbelief.[1] The idea that a manufacturer may break the law by granting a wholesaler's discount to a wholesaler who also runs retail shops, or by selling goods direct to retailers at a price higher than one of his wholesalers may be charging, or by beating an offer made to an important customer by a rival manufacturer or even by matching that offer unless he is satisfied that his rival can justify his low price by cost savings—all this may simply seem incredible; and not least because the ostensible purpose of the antitrust policy is to preserve a system of free competitive bargaining.

At this stage the reader can only be assured that these things are so. Whether they square with other aspects of the policy of maintaining competition; how it happens that they draw in large measure on the sources of political vitality which sustain that policy; whether and how apparently divergent elements of the general policy can continue to cohabit in harmony the same body of law—these are questions of interpretation and assessment for a later chapter.

NOTE ON PRICE DISCRIMINATION AND DELIVERED-PRICE SYSTEMS

One of the most curious episodes in the administration of the Robinson-Patman Act is its application to basing-point and other delivered-price systems. In the supplementary note in Chapter I above it was shown how delivered-pricing formulas might be an instrument of industry-wide collusion to avoid price competition. A number of cases were described in which the

---

[1] For a witty attack on the inconsistencies of the Act and its case law, see 'Eine kleine juristische Schlummergeschichte' in *Harvard Law Review*, vol. 79, 1965, p. 921.

Federal Trade Commission established price fixing of this type. It was noted that these cases, even when successful, presented an enforcement problem. What was to prevent the individual firms in an industry from continuing tacitly to apply the established formula in their pricing decisions without any further collusion? To prevent evasion of this kind the Commission wanted a sanction against the individual firm.

The fact that an element of price discrimination within the meaning of the Robinson-Patman Act could be detected in some forms of delivered pricing was seized upon as an answer to the problem. In this note, which completes the story begun in the corresponding note to Chapter I, this special application of the Robinson-Patman Act will be examined.

The element of discrimination in delivered pricing arises in the following way. A businessman selling his product 'ex works' or 'f.o.b. mill' charges the same price to all his customers. If he undertakes delivery of the product but still quotes on the basis of 'f.o.b. mill' prices, the amounts paid by his customers will differ, but only to the extent that freight costs vary according to the distance of the customer from the factory. Such differences will in a sense be automatically cost justified.[1] If, however, he departs in any way from 'f.o.b. mill' pricing, this result will no longer follow. Suppose his factory is a few miles away from a main centre of production which he takes as a basing-point. Customers on his doorstep will then pay the base price plus the cost of freight from the base, even though this latter cost is not incurred. Customers at the base will pay just the base price, even though freight costs have been incurred in getting the product from the factory to the base. The differences between the prices paid by the different customers will no longer correspond to differences in freight costs from the factory.

This situation is bound to arise with any basing-point method of pricing, single or multiple, whenever a supplier calculates his delivered price by reference to any base other than his own factory. In other words, basing-point delivered pricing will produce differences in price to which the defence of cost justification will not apply. Such price differences will therefore constitute illegal price discrimination under the Robinson-Patman Act whenever the Federal Trade Commission can find in them the necessary danger to competition and when they cannot be defended as efforts 'in good faith' to meet competition.

The discriminatory aspect of basing-point pricing was first explored in two cases concerning the glucose industry which reached the Supreme Court in 1945. The first was *Corn Products Refining Company* v. *Federal Trade Commission*. Corn Products manufacture glucose or corn syrup; they started in 1910 in the Chicago area, and in 1922 set up another plant in Kansas City. They sold from the Chicago plant 'f.o.b. mill', so that the further customers

---

[1] It is doubtful whether it is strictly correct to say they are cost justified within the meaning of the Robinson-Patman Act. Different costs of delivery due to different distances can hardly be said to result, in the words of the Act, 'from the differing methods in which such commodities are to such purchasers sold or delivered'. But this point is academic, because, if there were any trouble on this score, the supplier selling 'f.o.b. mill' could always bill the freight separately from the goods.

were from Chicago the higher delivered prices they paid. A customer in Kansas City paid the factory price in Chicago plus the freight from Chicago to Kansas City. When Corn Products opened up their new plant in Kansas City, however, they did not make Kansas City a separate base. The customer in Kansas City still paid the 'Chicago plus' price, even though he was getting delivery from the new plant on his doorstep. Customers beyond Kansas City, say in Texas, paid the very considerable cost of having the product shipped all the way from Chicago, even though their supplies came the much shorter distance from Kansas City.

This, said the Federal Trade Commission, constituted illegal price discrimination, favouring customers in the Chicago area as against those supplied from Kansas City. A customer in Kansas City paid $2.49 per hundred pounds for corn syrup: a customer in Chicago paid $2.09. This difference could not be defended by reference to cost savings. And it did harm to competition because confectionery manufacturers who set up in Kansas City were unable to secure and pass on to the public cost advantages which should have accrued from their location. For this reason the system tended to favour established firms against new entrants. 'Manufacturers who pay unearned or phantom freight under petitioners' basing-point system necessarily pay relatively higher costs for their raw material than do those manufacturers whose location with relation to the basing-point is such that they are able to purchase at the base price plus only freight actually paid.' The Supreme Court upheld the Commission's view. Chief Justice Stone ruled that 'petitioner's pricing system results inevitably in systematic price discriminations, since the prices they receive upon deliveries from Kansas City bear relation to factors other than actual costs of product or delivery'. The Court accepted the Commission's judgment that there might be an adverse effect on competition, since the candy manufacturers in different localities were competitors and small differences in raw-material costs were 'enough to divert business from one manufacturer to another'.

Chief Justice Stone, however, rejected the view that the law positively required 'f.o.b. mill' pricing. Congress had considered and rejected a provision having this effect and, in the Court's view, had 'left the legality of [delivered-price] systems to be determined accordingly as they might be within the reach of section 2 (a) . . .'. This ruling left open the possibility that a manufacturer's basing-point pricing might have no adverse effect on competition: it also left open to a manufacturer, who absorbed freight in order to invade a distant market, the defence that his price in that market was quoted 'in good faith' to meet competition.

This last point was the crux of the companion case, *Federal Trade Commission* v. *A. E. Staley Manufacturing Company* (Supreme Court, 1945). Staley is a smaller rival of Corn Products and manufactures glucose in Decatur, Illinois, some two hundred miles from Chicago. Staley, according to the evidence, treated Corn Products' price in any area as the going price. Since their product was competitive, and there was apparently no need to undersell Corn Products to get business, they simply followed this going price, in effect taking Chicago as a single basing-point. Thus when Staley sold glucose in Chicago at the base price, they had to bear or 'absorb' the cost of shipping to Chicago: but when they sold glucose in Decatur at the 'Chicago plus' price, they received this amount of freight cost without incurring it. When they sold elsewhere, they gained whenever the cost of shipping from Decatur was less than the cost of shipping from Chicago, and lost whenever it was more. As in the *Corn Products* case, different customers paid different prices and there was no meaningful sense in which the differences could be cost justified.

Staley's defence to the charge of price discrimination was that they had to meet the competition of Corn Products in each area. When the cost of delivery from Chicago was lower than the cost from Decatur they had to absorb the difference, for they would get no business unless they met the 'Chicago plus' price established by Corn Products. On the other hand, in Decatur itself and in other places where freight from Decatur was less than from Chicago, there was simply no point in going under the Corn Products price, so long at least as business was obtainable at this price.

The Supreme Court rejected this defence. Basically the problem was the same as in the *Standard Oil of Indiana* case (above, pp. 237–40). A business could not be said to be meeting competition 'in good faith' when it simply imitated in detail an illegal pricing system started by a competitor. Chief Justice Stone related this argument specifically to basing-point systems. Had Staley normally sold glucose 'f.o.b. Decatur' and then found that their price in Dallas came out above Corn Products' price in Dallas, they might legitimately have lowered that particular price to meet competition. But Staley, the Court argued, had never attempted to establish their own non-discriminatory price system; on the contrary, they followed the Corn Products price even where they enjoyed an advantage in freight costs over Corn Products. 'They maintained their own prices at the level of their competitors' high prices, based upon the competitors' higher costs of delivery, by including phantom freight in their own delivered prices. . . . Hence it cannot be said that respondents' price discriminations have resulted in "lower" prices to meet equally low prices of a competitor.'

Staley argued against this view that they might have adopted a notional base price in Decatur so high that they would have to 'absorb' freight wherever they sold. But this argument, said the Court, was based on a hypothesis that never existed. 'The systematic adoption of a competitor's prices by including unearned freight in respondent's delivery price or, what amounts to the same thing, the maintenance of a discriminatory and artificially high f.o.b. factory price in order to take advantage of the correspondingly high prices of a competitor, based on its higher costs of delivery, is not sufficient to justify the discrimination, for respondent fails to show, as the statute requires, the establishment of a "lower price" made in good faith to meet the equally low price of a competitor.' The 'meeting competition' defence had failed and the Commission's order against the company was sustained.

The question now arose whether basing-point pricing by an individual seller would be unlawful *per se* whatever the circumstances. Much of the pleading by the Federal Trade Commission's lawyers in the period following the *Glucose* cases suggested that this was their view and that only 'f.o.b. mill' pricing was permissible.[1] Some of the assumptions underlying this contention, however, seem highly questionable.

One point that has been surprisingly neglected in American controversy is the validity of the argument that differential basing-point prices prejudice competition between buyers. Even in the *Glucose* cases, where the buyers were competing candy manufacturers, much was apparently taken for granted on this topic. The candy manufacturers, after all, set up their businesses knowing that glucose was sold at 'Chicago plus' prices and having no reason to expect any change.[2] Some freely chose in consequence to set up in Chicago so as to be near a low-price source of raw material; and this was regarded as evidence of the harm done to competition, for candy manufacturers who freely chose to set up in Kansas City were at a 'disadvantage'. Yet it could be argued equally well that the Commission's insistence on making Corn Products adopt Kansas City as a separate price base could injure competition; for it would upset the expectations of the manufacturers who moved to Chicago and might well lead to their losing business, through no fault of their own, to competitors in Kansas City. While it is true that, as already noted, basing-point pricing tends to favour established manufacturers at or near the base as against new entrants away from the base, it is at least doubtful whether it is a correct procedure to assess injury to competition without reference to what may have been for many years the reasonable expectation of the competitors.

But at least glucose is a raw material entering into a highly competitive manufacturing industry. Many commodities sold at delivered prices go into local distributive channels or to users such as building contractors. It is difficult to see how price differentials between widely spaced localities could affect competition among the buyers of these commodities. It is normal and realistic to regard Edinburgh and London, for example, as separate markets for cement or steel girders.

So, in many instances of the use of basing-point pricing, one would expect an attempt to show injury to competition among buyers to fail, on the ground that the buyers were in separate non-competing markets. This point has at times been lost sight of in the United States, largely, it seems, because of the odium attaching to phantom freight. As was seen above, in the supplementary note to Chapter I,[3] the operator of a 'non-base' mill may have every reason to accept in his own locality the going price set by the nearest base; he will have no cause to forgo the windfall profit or phantom

---

[1] The announced position of the Commission, however, was that it meant by 'price' whatever the term meant in the particular transactions it was examining, and in point of fact in the cement industry and in other basing-point cases the title to the goods passed at the mill even though the term 'delivered price' was used.

[2] No businessman would find it surprising that Corn Products charged what the Kansas City market would bear in the absence of local competition. It must be remembered, too, that 'Chicago plus' pricing went on unchallenged for twenty years before the Commission brought the case.

[3] See above, p. 58.

freight due to his favourable location and he may fear that to cut the
going price will merely invite powerful retaliation. Phantom freight as
such is not a sign of 'unfair competition'[1]: it simply marks the fact that a given
location is economically a separate market.

Yet many people in the United States, among the enforcement agencies,
the courts and Congress alike, have assumed that phantom freight, as a
way of getting 'something for nothing', must be unlawful. And this has
diverted attention from the question of whether different localities may not
be different markets. Thus even Chief Justice Stone, in the passage quoted
above—where he spoke disparagingly of 'the maintenance of a discriminatory and artificially high f.o.b. factory price'—was clearly a victim of the
bias against phantom freight. For how can an f.o.b. factory price be
discriminatory? And what is meant by an 'artificially high' price except
that in an area of freight advantage the seller charges what the market will
bear? Why should it be worse to follow the going price of a leader in a number
of separate local markets, as Staley did, than to do so in a large urban
market?

Some lawyers at one time added greatly to the confusion on this topic by
adopting an expository device that drew special attention to the element of
phantom freight. This was the so-called 'mill nett' theory. It was argued
that common-carrier freight costs were of known amounts for any particular
distance and should not be confused with the amounts charged for the
commodity. In other words, the 'real' price of the commodity was not the
delivered price at all but the amount actually received by the supplier, net
of freight charges. Thus Corn Products received $2.09 a hundred pounds
net for all the glucose manufactured in Chicago and sold at 'Chicago plus'
delivered prices. But in Kansas City the 'Chicago plus' price was $2.49, and
they maintained this price even when they delivered from their local plant
and incurred no freight costs. So the 'mill nett' price in Kansas City was
$2.49 and the difference of 40 cents was said to measure the discrimination
against the Kansas City customer. It also measured the phantom freight
element in the Kansas City price.

This argument makes it a simple matter to equate the discrimination with
the phantom freight. In fact it is a question begging argument. In particular
it simply assumes that all sales, whatever the destination of the goods, are
made in the same market; and this, as has been seen, is far from self-evident.
Secondly, it does violence to the normal meaning of price. It is, of course, a
question of fact whether goods are sold at the destination at a delivered price
or at the factory at an 'ex works' or 'f.o.b.' price. Where the former is the
fact, it is odd to speak of the 'real 'price as something different from what

---

[1] This assumes, of course, that there is no collusion. Where a large number of suppliers
in a rich market all collect phantom freight, this fact will be highly persuasive of collusion
between them. In the steel industry, for example, 'Pittsburgh plus' pricing in Chicago was
not unreasonable when Chicago steel production was far below Chicago demand, but when
Chicago became a surplus producing area, it was hard to justify. One returns always to the
element of monopoly power in pricing, not to phantom freight as such, as the justification
for antitrust action.

the customer pays. The 'mill nett' theory was in effect an attempt to bounce the courts into the belief that only 'f.o.b. mill' pricing was non-discriminatory.

The 'mill nett' argument also implies that differences in cost ought to be reflected in differences in price. Indeed, some contended that this was required by the cost justification proviso to section 2(a).[1] But this is a mistake. The cost justification proviso permits 'only due allowance' to be made for lower costs; a supplier must not reduce a price by a shilling when he only saves sixpence. It clearly does not prevent the supplier from making less than 'due allowance' for a cost saving. (If it did, the Robinson-Patman Act would be an instrument for imposing 'cost plus' pricing on American industry.) In the main line of Robinson-Patman Act cases, for example, all the emphasis is on preventing firms like A. & P. or Automatic Canteen from getting price concessions that are larger than the cost savings produced by their large orders: nobody minds a bit if they get unduly small concessions or no concession at all. Yet if a firm like A. & P. is not given the full benefit of the supplier's savings, it is being charged a 'phantom cost' which is less obvious than, but otherwise on all fours with, phantom freight. It is in general a mistake to argue one way or the other from the cost justification proviso in this field: it is simply inapplicable to delivered-pricing situations.

The view that all basing-point pricing might be vulnerable under the Robinson-Patman Act was at its most influential when the *Cement* case (*Federal Trade Commission* v. *Cement Institute*) came before the Supreme Court in 1948. Some of the argument in Mr Justice Black's opinion bears the marks of this influence. He held for example that '. . . the combined effect of the two [*Glucose*] cases was to forbid the adoption for sales purposes of any basing-point pricing system'. He strongly suggested, too, that the 'meeting competition' defence could never succeed if some of a supplier's delivered prices included an element of phantom freight.

These arguments, however, may be regarded as dicta relevant only to the particular facts, for the *Cement* case did not raise the question of the individual supplier's use of basing-points. The Federal Trade Commission's finding was that the cement firms by adopting *in combination* a multiple basing-point system of delivered prices had brought about systematic price discrimination in violation of the Robinson-Patman Act. Thus, in this particular case, the discrimination charges, no less than the price fixing charges, rested on combination or conspiracy. It is interesting to note, too, that the discrimination was alleged to have injured first-line competition among the suppliers themselves: it was not contended that the buyers of cement were harmed by

[1] '. . . For the life of me, I can't see what Congress meant by making it a substantive defence to the charge of discrimination if you can show due allowance for differences in cost of delivery, unless the statute requires such allowance to be made': W. Wooden, in *Robinson-Patman Act Symposium for 1947*, Commerce Clearing House, Chicago, p. 53. In fairness, it seems likely that those who took this view were thinking purely of common-carrier freight costs and that it just seemed immoral to them to charge for freight something other than what it cost. But this is merely another way of missing the point that a delivered price may be the 'economic' price in a separate market.

the price differences.[1] Furthermore, the Commission's 'cease and desist' order was 'directed solely at concerted, not individual, activity on the part of the respondents'. The various practices listed in the order were prohibited only when they proceeded from a 'planned common course of action'; and both the Commission and the Supreme Court expressly denied that the order would bar an individual supplier from selling cement at delivered prices that produced different 'mill nett' returns, where the low-price sales were made to meet competition in good faith.

The Commission stated later (in 1948) that in the absence of a tendency to monopoly it did not 'regard an effort to get business from a competitor by sporadic price reductions as illegally injurious to that competitor'.[2] In the same statement the 'mill nett' theory was repudiated and it was accepted that 'in geographic price discriminations inferences of injury to competition drawn merely from the existence of price differences between purchasers who compete in some degree would have no sound basis'. The statement suggested that the individual supplier would be in legal jeopardy when his price reductions were not sporadic but 'systematic', as in the *Staley* case. 'It may be presumed that wherever there is an industry-wide pattern of parallel geographic pricing, the claim on the part of one company that it is merely meeting competition will fail. It may also be presumed that this claim will fail where there are phantom freight charges and where formula prices are followed regardless of the existence of competition.'

By the time of a later case—*In the matter of the National Lead Company* (Federal Trade Commission, 1953)—the 'mill nett' argument had been finally buried. The case dealt with lead pigments, and collusive price fixing was inferred from a situation in which a number of manufacturers were found to follow in detail the delivered-pricing arrangements established by the leading firm in the industry—the National Lead Company.[3] This was not a basing-point system but one in which delivered prices were uniform throughout defined zones.

Had the 'mill nett' theory been applied, it could have been held that uniform prices to customers widely dispersed over a large area reflected 'real' differences in price; for it was certain that the 'mill nett' returns of the various manufacturers varied substantially as between customers near at

---

[1] Usually when injury to first-line competition is alleged, the suggestion is that the discriminating supplier is out to ruin competitors by local price cutting. In this unique instance the complaint was that the discrimination aimed at equating the prices of different suppliers and so suppressing competition among them; in other words, they were out not to ruin one another. This shows how artificial the discrimination charge was in the *Cement* case. The Commission had established a price fixing conspiracy aimed at equating prices at all points of sale. It was this that produced as a side effect geographic price differences by individual suppliers. At this point in the argument it seems slightly absurd, at best a work of supererogation, to add that the price differences were discriminatory because they suppressed competition by equating prices. As has already been explained, the reason for the discrimination charges was that the Commission lawyers believed they would not secure adequate remedies on the basis of the collusion charges alone.

[2] *Statement of Federal Trade Commission Policy towards Geographic Pricing Practices for Staff Information and Guidance*, issued 12 October 1948.

[3] See the supplementary note to Chapter I, above, p. 56.

hand and customers at a distance. Thus a customer in the same town as a producer had to pay the 'average' freight cost element in the uniform delivered price—a clear case of phantom freight; a customer at the extremity of a zone, on the other hand, paid only the same amount, so that the supplier 'absorbed' freight in selling to him. Given that some of the customers at different distances from their point of supply were direct competitors, the 'mill nett' differences might have been held to injure competition and so to be unlawful discriminations.

This theory was indeed argued at the initial hearing of the case, but the Commission decided that, in this context at least, the delivered prices were the 'real' prices. '. . . The alleged discriminations occur as a result of differing net prices received by each of the respondents at its factory. Thus, the complaint does not show that the alleged unlawful discriminations as between purchasers located in the same zone occur as a result of differences in actual prices at which the respondents' products are sold.'[1]

The Commission's 'cease and desist' order in the *National Lead* case barred the various manufacturers individually from selling their product '. . . at prices calculated . . . in accordance with a zone delivered-price system for the purpose or with the effect of systematically matching . . . the delivered prices of other sellers . . . and thereby preventing purchasers from finding any advantages in price in dealing with one or more sellers against another'.

This order marks a return to a more direct approach to the problem of preventing tacit collusion. It simply tells National Lead's competitors that they must not 'systematically' follow that company's prices. This is done, rightly or wrongly, on the basis that a price fixing conspiracy has occurred in the industry and that a restriction on the freedom of action of the individual firms is necessary to prevent a recurrence of collusion. Whatever may be thought of the merits of such an order,[2] it gets away from the artificial use of the price discrimination law as a sanction against collusion.

Since the *Glucose* cases, all the delivered-pricing cases have at bottom been cases against collusive price fixing. It seems unlikely that the use of the Robinson-Patman Act to reinforce these cases has been of real advantage in enforcement, and for this reason it may well be abandoned. In the end no legal rule has emerged that prevents the individual supplier from quoting delivered prices by reference to basing-points. In the absence of collusion he may invade the 'natural' markets of other suppliers and by 'absorbing' freight meet the competition of the going price in these markets. Different

---

[1] The price differences between customers in different zones were, however, held to be unlawfully discriminatory. A zoning system entails that two customers on either side of a zonal frontier will pay different prices—sometimes the price 'jump' at the border is substantial—even though they are, relatively speaking, neighbours. The Commission's opinion noted that these differences could not be cost justified but wholly neglected to review the evidence on the question of whether they might 'substantially' lessen competition.

[2] A dissenting Commissioner questioned the good sense and the legal propriety of ordering National Lead's competitors in effect to diverge from that company's prices if it seemed good policy to them individually to follow these. He said it put them 'in a sort of second-class business citizenship'.

prices in different areas, even though the differences do not precisely reflect differences in freight costs, should not normally affect competition between the customers. The individual 'non-base' supplier ought also to be safe in taking advantage of the absence of local competition in his area of freight advantage, though no court has yet taken courage to say so.

It still appears that, as the law stands, the individual supplier may not frankly (and voluntarily) follow the price leadership of a powerful competitor where basing-point delivered prices are adopted. If this is done 'systematically', even though no collusion is shown, he may well fall under the rule of the *Staley* case; and in the absence of some clearer thinking among the courts about the economic realities of such a situation, his defence will probably continue to be prejudiced by the general conviction that phantom freight is a form of theft.

CHAPTER X

RESALE PRICE MAINTENANCE

1. *Definition of resale price maintenance;*
arguments for and against the practice

Resale price maintenance is the practice whereby those who supply goods to traders lay down the prices to be charged on resale and take action to see that these prices are complied with. The typical example is that of the manufacturer of branded goods who prescribes and seeks to enforce the prices at which his goods shall be sold in retail shops.

Resale price maintenance is a curiosity among restrictive practices in that the manufacturers who operate it and the traders who take part in it and support it often have quite different interests to promote. Moreover, the market in price maintained goods often has elements of a competitive situation mixed up with restrictive features in such a way that the resulting effect on the public interest is particularly difficult to determine.

Retail trade is subject, no less than other branches of commerce, to the type of pressures which lead businessmen to desire to mitigate or suppress vigorous price competition. When manufacturers are already willing or can be persuaded to require that their goods be sold in all shops at a common price, the result may approximate to that of a horizontal price fixing agreement among the retailers, who may favour resale price maintenance for this reason. (A horizontal agreement among retailers without the support of suppliers would rarely be effective because of the absence of any sanction against backsliders.)

Resale price maintenance, however, differs in significant ways from horizontal price fixing. For one thing it normally applies only to branded goods. But very few shops sell branded goods exclusively; and it can be argued that the absence of price competition between traders in particular branded lines (intra-brand competition) does not mean in theory or in fact that there will be no price competition between them over their trade as a whole: price competition might be intensified in other lines. Secondly, there are often competing branded lines all of which are price maintained; a particular brand of toothpaste may be sold at the same price at all shops, but at the same time all shops will carry other brands at different prices. It can, therefore, be argued that the consumer has a choice of different brands at different prices and is effectively gaining the benefits of inter-brand competition. Moreover, in almost every trade there is competition from the large retail organizations, mail order houses and so on which sell their own private brands.

It is also important that the manufacturer who makes his goods subject to resale price maintenance does not himself gain directly from the ensuing restriction of competition among retailers. The price he receives for his goods will be the same whether the retailers maintain the prescribed resale price or whether they sell for less. Except where it can be shown that manufacturers adopt the practice only under retail pressure, this is persuasive evidence that the arguments in favour of resale price maintenance are not purely self-interested price fixing arguments.

There is much dispute about the arguments actually used by manufacturers. Many economists, in particular, are eager to tell the manufacturer that he must lose by resale price maintenance. In so far as the practice prevents price competition over a substantial range of retail sales, it must at least raise the prices of some goods in some shops above what they would otherwise be. Economists tend to be very clear that higher prices mean lower sales—this proposition comes on about page 3 of all their textbooks—and that the manufacturer who is misled into maintaining the resale prices of his goods is bound to sell less than he otherwise would. Manufacturers, however, are equally clear, at least in some industries, that they do in practice sell more under a scheme of price maintenance than when each retailer is free to charge what he likes. Since manufacturers spend their lives trying to sell more of their products, it is not necessarily the case that they are wrong and the textbooks right about the best way of going about it.

One of the commonest arguments starts from the point that well advertised branded goods are an apt vehicle for forms of price cutting which are more akin to advertising than to genuine price competition. A retailer who wishes to stagger the local populace with his exceptional bargains will choose a well known branded line for the purpose. It would be no good selling cigarettes at threepence a packet less than the normal price if the cigarettes concerned were put up in plain packets with no manufacturer's name on. They might be excellent cigarettes, but nobody would pay any attention to that. The so-called 'loss leader' must be a popular brand.

Manufacturers often contend that the use of their brands as loss leaders does them no good. The price cutter himself may sell more for a time, but other retailers may fight shy of the brand, and the end-result may be not additional sales in total but a worrying and expensive series of fluctuations in the manufacturer's volume of orders. When a brand is featured here and there for short periods as a loss leader, the unsettling repercussions on the trade at large may persist while local increases in sales may be shortlived.

Manufacturers have other arguments in favour of price maintenance. It is said that sales of durable consumer goods like motor cars, television sets or refrigerators depend in the long run on the provision of satisfactory service after sale by the retailer, and that this service will be provided only if the retailer is assured of a reasonable margin and is not undercut by traders interested only in quick sales. In some trades the manufacturer's support of resale price maintenance is connected with his interest in the existence of shops which will keep substantial stocks of slow-moving merchandise. In the book trade, for example, it is contended that 'good' bookshops carrying a plentiful stock of the less popular works depend on a fair rate of return on best sellers. If chemists and newsagents were permitted to sell just the best sellers at a cut price, the 'good' bookshop would disappear.

None of these arguments is an unqualified intellectual success with critics of resale price maintenance, who point out that the practice usually goes a good deal further than giving reasonable protection against loss leaders or preventing famine among those nourished by 'good' books. The practice typically operates to prevent any price reduction, however genuinely competitive, so that it sometimes seems implausible to suppose that price fixing as such is not one of the main ends in view. The critics contend that even if resale price maintenance may have some value in protecting the manufacturer's goodwill against the loss leader, it does so at the cost of exercising an unhealthy check on competition between different methods of distribution; in short, that the remedy is worse than the disease. They also ask whether the manufacturer's real concern in many cases is not to forestall the probability that intense price competition at the retail level will soon result in pressure on him to reduce his prices. Particularly in industries in which wholesaling, packaging, advertising and other selling costs are high in relation to production costs, the price maintenance system may reduce the risk that new entrants selling a simplified product at a much reduced price will commend themselves to the distributors.

There are other awkward questions which the critics may raise. How widespread would the loss leader practice be in the absence of resale price maintenance? Does not some of the virtue of a loss leader (from the viewpoint of the trader who features it) derive from the very rigidity of the standard, maintained price? Do purchasers of motor cars or television sets really get such a lot of service from the 'authorized dealer' which they do not pay for (often at 'standard' charges) and which there would not always be qualified firms to provide? If readers of scholarly works have to be subsidized, should not some institution like the Arts Council provide the money instead of the readers of detective stories?

This is not the place to attempt to sort out the rights and wrongs of the matter; indeed, it may well be that no generalization will meet the case and that sensible judgments can be made only about particular instances of the practice. What usually happens when fair-minded people with no axe to grind have the arguments put to them is that they find something to be said for both sides. They often conclude that it would be nice to permit resale price maintenance subject to the proviso that it should not be operated unreasonably against a genuinely competitive flexibility of prices, or alternatively that it would be nice to forbid it subject to the proviso that exemptions should be granted when a really good case can be made for it. Judicious recommendations of this kind then become the despair of administrators who are called upon to find legislative formulas and executive techniques to implement the suggested compromise.[1]

The delicate balance of the arguments for and against resale price maintenance has clearly had much to do with the ups and downs in the legal position affecting the practice in the United States.[2] Whether the real aim is to protect the manufacturer's goodwill in his brand or to suppress competition among retailers, whether consumers lose seriously by the absence of price competition between the different types of shops which supply branded goods or whether they are effectively protected by their free choice between competing brands— these and many similar questions have been argued and re-argued in the courts. But the legal vicissitudes probably have had even more to do with the way in which resale price maintenance brings out the underlying ambivalence of antitrust objectives.

As has been seen in other chapters, antitrust is at times concerned with a wholehearted pursuit of the economic advantages attributed to competition; but at other times the emphasis is placed on social objections to the concentration of power in private hands. Over a

---

[1] Another common feature of compromise solutions is to condemn collective boycotts and other arrangements by which prescribed resale prices are enforced. But this too presents its administrative problems, for it is not clear that, where resale price maintenance is a good thing, manufacturers should be forbidden to enforce it effectively; nor that, where it is a bad thing, individual enforcement, which may or may not be effective, should still be permitted. The truth is that collective enforcement is a quite separate issue and has no bearing on the rights and wrongs of price maintenance. In the United States collective enforcement is unconditionally banned by the Sherman Act, and the argument has turned on the rights and wrongs of giving individual manufacturers effective legal means of enforcing resale prices. In Britain, collective enforcement was made illegal by the Restrictive Trade Practices Act of 1956, whereas resale price maintenance by individual manufacturers was legal until the 1964 Resale Prices Act gave the Restrictive Practices Court jurisdiction to decide whether, in particular industries, it was in the public interest for the practice to continue (see below, p. 490).

[2] But the debate has not been purely intellectual. Intense organized pressure from small retailers, originating in depression, has always been present.

large part of the field the suppression of competition and the growth of business power may be roughly identified; and the law which prevents the one is expected to check the other. With resale price maintenance, however, the equation does not hold. More than any other it is the restrictive practice of the small man. Its support comes largely from small shopkeepers, whom it is absurd to see as sinister bearers of over-weening power; indeed, resale price maintenance is often represented as an essential defence mechanism to preserve the small shopkeeper from being swallowed up by the powerful chains.

So it is that many political groups which would yield to none in zeal for 'trust busting' are to be found in the van of the so-called 'fair trade' movement which promotes legislation in favour of resale price maintenance. Many notable individuals have found themselves in the same position. Mr Justice Brandeis, for example, who wrote *The Curse of Bigness*[1] and was a stout supporter of antitrust from the bench and with the pen, nevertheless favoured resale price maintenance, which, he believed, could help small manufacturers to compete against large integrated firms with their own distributive outlets and could also protect them from the coercive power of large mail order and chain distributors. It is not surprising, therefore, that the legal position has often been in dispute and subject to change from time to time and from State to State. In this chapter the ups and downs since the Sherman Act was passed will be outlined and the main features of the current legal position under federal and State laws will be described.

2. *Early decisions under the Sherman Act:* Dr Miles Medical *and other cases*

Early decisions under the Sherman Act held that it was undue restraint of trade and hence illegal for a manufacturer to require his distributors by contract to maintain prescribed retail prices. The leading case was *Dr Miles Medical Company* v. *John D. Park and Sons Company* (Supreme Court, 1911). The Dr Miles company manufactured proprietary medicines under a secret (but not patented) formula and sought in its contracts with wholesalers to prescribe prices for both wholesale and retail sales and to forbid sales to 'cut rate' chemists. When Dr Miles sued a wholesaler for getting supplies of the medicines at cut prices by inducing others to break their contracts, the Supreme Court rejected his case and refused to issue an injunction in his favour. The decision was based on the argument that a manufacturer parts with control over his goods when he sells them and is not entitled to lay down conditions restricting competition in future sales. 'Where commodities have passed into the channels of trade and have been sold by complainant to dealers

[1] L. D. Brandeis, *The Curse of Bigness*, Viking Press, New York, 1934.

at prices satisfactory to complainant, the public is entitled to whatever advantage may be derived from competition in the subsequent traffic.'

Other cases of the period applied the same rule where copyrighted books and patented products were supplied bearing some form of notice which announced a resale price and purported, by virtue of the copyright or patent, to require the maintenance of this price.[1] It became settled law that the holder of a copyright or patent obtained his due reward and exhausted his property rights when he sold the product. Chief Justice Taft put the point clearly in the *General Electric* case of 1926: 'It is well settled . . . that where a patentee makes the patented article, and sells it, he can exercise no future control over what the purchaser may wish to do with the article after his purchase. It has passed beyond the scope of the patentee's rights.'

This principle has been applied even when the patentee-manufacturer supplies a semi-finished product to the distributive trade and the wholesaler or retailer completes the process of manufacture.[2] It has also been applied in important antitrust cases in which resale price maintenance has been only one of a number of restrictive elements. Thus in *Ethyl Gasoline Corporation* v. *United States* (Supreme Court, 1940) the patentee of tetraethyl-lead fluid used in high-performance petrol was found to require all jobbers of petrol containing the patented fluid to be licensed. (The jobbers obtained the petrol from licensed refiners, not from the patentee corporation, which was not itself a refiner.) The jobber licences contained no express conditions with regard to resale prices, but it was found that in practice licences were generally refused to jobbers who cut prices or refused to conform to the marketing policies of the major refiners. As Mr Justice Stone summed it up: '. . . the record leaves no doubt that appellant has made use of its dominant position in the trade to exercise control over prices and marketing policies of jobbers in a sufficient number of cases and with sufficient continuity to make its attitude toward price cutting a pervasive influence in the jobbing trade.' Thus the jobber licences were part of an illegal restrictive scheme. The Court's conclusion of law was put as follows:

---

[1] As to copyright, see *Bobbs-Merril Company* v. *Straus* (Supreme Court, 1908), and as to patents, see *Bauer et Cie* v. *O'Donnell* (Supreme Court, 1913).

[2] *United States* v. *Univis Lens Company* (Supreme Court, 1942). The company supplied blanks for patented bifocal lenses; wholesalers and certain retailers performed under licence the grinding and finishing operations to the optician's prescription. But Chief Justice Stone said: 'The first vending of any article manufactured under a patent puts the article beyond the reach of the monopoly which that patent confers. Whether the licensee sells the patented article in its completed form or sells it before completion for the purpose of enabling the buyer to finish or sell it, he has equally parted with the article, and made it the vehicle for transferring to the buyer ownership of the invention with respect to that article.' Price fixing conditions in the licences issued to distributors were therefore illegal.

Appellant, as patentee, possesses exclusive rights to make and sell the fluid and also the lead-treated motor fuel. By its sales to refiners it relinquishes its exclusive right to use the patented fluid and it relinquishes . . . its exclusive rights to sell the lead-treated fuel by permitting the licensed refiners to manufacture and sell the fuel to [the jobbers]. And by the authorized sales of the fuel by refiners to jobbers the patent monopoly over it is exhausted, and after the sale neither appellant nor the refiners may longer rely on the patents to exercise any control over the price at which the fuel may be resold.

3. *Refusals by manufacturers to supply goods unless resale prices are maintained :*
Colgate; Schrader's Son; Beech Nut; Parke, Davis.
The General Electric *case and distribution through agents*

Another problem that the courts faced in dealing with resale price maintenance under the Sherman Act was that of distinguishing between the enforcement of resale price agreements and the mere refusal of a manufacturer to supply goods to distributors whose marketing practices he disliked.

As we have seen in Chapter VIII above (pp. 216-17), in *United States* v. *Colgate and Company* (Supreme Court, 1919), the Government neither charged nor brought evidence to show that there were contracts or agreements under which traders were bound to maintain the resale prices of Colgate products. But the company was said to have let it be known that it would not supply retailers who did not abide by its prescribed prices and indeed to have refused to sell to some who would not accept this position. It was held that this evidence by itself, without any charge of illegal contracts or agreements, was not enough to state a case of violating the Sherman Act. Mr Justice McReynolds said in his opinion: 'In the absence of any purpose to create or maintain a monopoly, the Act does not restrict the long-recognized right of trader or manufacturer engaged in an entirely private business, freely to exercise his own independent discretion as to parties with whom he will deal. And, of course, he may announce in advance the circumstances under which he will refuse to sell.'

At first sight this decision, especially as elaborated in Mr Justice McReynolds' dictum, seemed to offer a useful way of escape for the manufacturer who wanted to prescribe and maintain resale prices. All he had to do was avoid contracts and rely on refusing supplies to any retailer who would not agree to comply or who did not in fact comply with his prices.[1] This rosy view of the matter, however, overlooked the

---

[1] This, of course, might be difficult where the manufacturer was not in direct touch with the retailer but sold through jobbers or wholesalers; in such a case the wholesalers would have to be got to co-operate, and that would almost certainly involve an illegal boycott agreement.

fact that the *Colgate* decision really dealt only with the sufficiency of a particular indictment. Within a year the Supreme Court was complaining that the *Colgate* case had been 'misconstrued' and was 'distinguishing' it.

Thus in *United States* v. *Schrader's Son Inc.* (Supreme Court, 1920), it was held that, as in other antitrust contexts, an agreement might be inferred from a course of dealing and it was expressly stated that the Court had no intention in the *Colgate* case of overruling the *Dr Miles* decision.[1] The distinction was more elaborately explained in *Federal Trade Commission* v. *Beech Nut Packing Company* (Supreme Court, 1922).

In this case there were no express agreements of the type found in the *Dr Miles* case but the price maintenance scheme was said to depend on the manufacturer's 'tacit understanding with purchasers and prospective purchasers'. The evidence showed that the Beech Nut company had made elaborate arrangements for policing its scheme by obtaining reports of price cutters, placing their names on a private stop list and so forth. In reversing a Circuit Court of Appeals which had regarded the case as covered by the *Colgate* decision, Mr Justice Day, speaking for the Supreme Court, again complained that the decision had been 'misapprehended'. Drawing attention to the *Schrader* and *Frey* cases, he said: 'By these decisions it is settled that in prosecutions under the Sherman Act a trader is not guilty of violating its terms who simply refuses to sell to others, and he may withhold his goods from those who will not sell them at the prices which he fixes for their resale. He may not, consistently with the Act, go beyond the exercise of this right, and by contracts and combinations, express or implied, unduly hinder or obstruct the free and natural flow of commerce in the channels of interstate trade.'

Just how narrow a loophole had been left by *Colgate* was made plain in *United States* v. *Parke, Davis & Co.* (Supreme Court, 1960). Parke, Davis was a national manufacturer of pharmaceutical products, with a long established policy of maintaining prices on its goods. It issued an announcement that it would refuse to deal with drug wholesalers who supplied price cutting retailers, and also specifically notified five wholesalers in areas where price cutting had been prevalent that it would not continue to supply them if they sold Parke, Davis products to such retailers. Each of the five knew that the others had been similarly warned, and agreed to comply with the Parke, Davis policy.

[1] The point of the *Colgate* decision, as Mr Justice McReynolds put it, was that 'the indictment failed to charge that Colgate & Co. made agreements, either express or implied, which undertook to obligate vendees to observe specified resale prices; and it was treated as alleging only recognition of the manufacturer's undoubted right to specify resale prices and refuse to deal with anyone who failed to maintain the same'. See also Mr Justice McReynolds' opinion in *Frey and Son* v. *Cudahy Packing Company* (Supreme Court, 1921).

At the same time each of the price cutting retailers was told that Parke, Davis would cut off supplies to them if they continued to cut prices, and the names of those retailers who refused to co-operate with Parke, Davis were supplied to wholesalers, who refused thereafter to accept their orders. Nevertheless, five retailers still persisted in advertising and selling at discount prices from their existing stocks, and Parke, Davis then decided that the best solution would be to offer to resume supplies to them provided they stopped advertising their discounts. The President of the Dart Drug Company, one of the five retailers, agreed to this proposal. The other four were then told of this agreement and themselves consented to similar terms, provided that Dart also refrained from discount advertising. Discount advertising by the five thereupon stopped and normal supplies were resumed to them both by Parke, Davis and the wholesalers.

The majority of the Supreme Court found on these facts that Parke, Davis had clearly exceeded what was permissible under *Colgate*. Had it merely announced that it would not deal with wholesalers who resold goods at prices below those fixed or in other ways failed to observe company policy and had it then carried out this policy, this would not have violated the Sherman Act. But Parke, Davis had directly approached the individual wholesalers to induce them not to deal with price cutting retailers, had requested individual assurances from retailers that they would not cut prices on Parke, Davis products, and had entered into an agreement with the five price cutting retailers to effect the cessation of discount advertising. The wholesalers and retailers had been thus 'entwined' in Parke, Davis's programme to promote compliance in its price maintenance policy. The legitimate refusal to deal had been used illegally as 'the vehicle to gain the wholesalers' participation in the programme to effectuate the retailers' adherence to the suggested retail prices'.

Mr Justice Harlan, speaking for himself, Mr Justice Frankfurter and Mr Justice Whittaker, dissented and accused the majority of having in substance pronounced the death sentence on *Colgate*. Much the same view of the decision was taken by the Second Circuit Court of Appeals shortly afterwards in *George W. Warner & Company Inc.* v. *Black & Decker Manufacturing Company Inc.* (1960); the Court commented that, although the Supreme Court had left a narrow channel through which a manufacturer might pass, 'the facts would have to be of such Doric simplicity as to be somewhat rare in this day of complex business enterprise'. Since goods are nearly always distributed through wholesalers and other middlemen, it is pretty clear that the manufacturer cannot exercise an effective choice among retailers without some form of organized plan. Even the manufacturer who supplies retailers direct can hardly keep an effective check over their prices without such a plan if his customers are at all numerous. The result is that it would seem next to impossible for a manufacturer of a commodity with nation-wide distribution to police effectively a system of resale price maintenance.

One other loophole was found in the period when the Sherman Act controlled the practice. The General Electric Company organized a system of distributing electric lamps under which the wholesale and retail dealers never purchased or owned the lamps but held and sold them as agents for the company. Under this scheme, it was claimed, the company's instructions to the retail dealers to sell only at specified prices could not run foul of the Sherman Act, for these retail prices were not resale prices: the retailer as the company's agent was making the first sale of the goods.[1]

This claim succeeded: as against the Government's contention that the scheme was simply a colourable device to evade the law, the Supreme Court found 'nothing in the form of the contracts and the practice under them which makes the so-called B and A agents anything more than genuine agents of the company, or the delivery of the stock to each agent anything more than a consignment to the agent for his custody and sale as such'. Chief Justice Taft put the conclusion of law as follows: 'We are of the opinion, therefore, that there is nothing as a matter of principle or in the authorities which requires us to hold that genuine contracts of agency like those before us, however comprehensive as a mass or whole in their effect, are violations of the Anti-Trust Act. The owner of an article patented or otherwise is not violating the common law or the Anti-Trust Act by seeking to dispose of his articles directly to the consumer and fixing the price by which his agents transfer the title from him directly to such consumers.'

As a result of this case, suppliers of goods in a number of different industries adopted schemes under which goods were not sold to their dealers, but were supplied on a consignment basis. This meant that the goods were delivered into the custody of the retailer, who acted as the consignor's agent for the purposes of resale. Title to the goods, however, remained with the consignor[2] until the sale had been completed. Oil companies in particular found this a convenient method of retaining control of the price at which its products were resold, but in recent years even these arrangements have come under attack. In 1963 the Federal Trade Commission adjudged unlawful the consignment arrangements between the Sun Oil Company and its dealers in Norfolk,

---

[1] The detailed working of the scheme is fully described in Chief Justice Taft's opinion in *United States* v. *General Electric Company*, 272 U.S. 476 (1926).

[2] English law would use the terms 'bailor' and 'bailment' rather than 'consignor' and 'consignment' respectively, but this would not make any difference to the legal position.

Virginia, because they were arrived at after discussions between groups of the dealers and Sun on how to deal with the problem of periodic price wars, and therefore constituted 'horizontal as well as vertical' price fixing. A consignment arrangement in this case was said to be no more than 'a device by which the unlawful price fixing arrangement was to be implemented' (*In the matter of Sun Oil Company*, 1963). In the same year consignment arrangements by another oil company, Atlantic, with its dealers in parts of Delaware, Maryland and Virginia were also outlawed on the basis that Atlantic's consignment plan was not 'its regular method of selling', and that 'the shifting back and forth of customers from dealer status to so-called agency status emphasizes that the consignment plan is the device to fix and stabilize prices rather than a good-faith marketing method' (*In the matter of Atlantic Refining Company*, 1963).[1]

It was already clear, therefore, that supplying goods on consignment did not offer a foolproof method of maintaining resale prices and in the following year a private treble-damage suit decided by the Supreme Court (*Simpson* v. *Union Oil Company*) still further undermined the already shaky foundations of *General Electric*. Once again an oil company was involved, and the suit was brought by one of its filling station operators. He had taken a one-year lease on condition that he was to sell on consignment at prices set by Union, and now sought treble damages under the Sherman Act when his lease was not renewed. He claimed that the reason for Union's refusal to renew his lease was that he had sold petrol at less than its fixed price, as he had been unable to sell enough to make a profit at that price. Mr Justice Douglas for the majority admitted that consignment agreements performed a useful function in commerce, and that the arrangement in *General Electric* was somewhat parallel to that adopted by Union. But he said that *General Electric* should be distinguished as applying only to patented goods, and that a consignment agreement used as a 'device' for resale price maintenance (especially as it was being used to cover a vast gasoline distribution system fixing prices through many retail outlets) could be a violation of section 1 of the Sherman Act just as any other kind of agreement. Nor did it make any difference to call the consignment merely an 'agency'. Referring to the Court's holding in *Parke, Davis* that a supplier may not use coercion to maintain resale prices, he said that it made no difference what the coercive device was. Accordingly the case was remanded to the District Court for the assessment of the plaintiff's damages, on the basis that he had suffered an actionable wrong. It seems, therefore, that the two main criteria for making a

---

[1] Subsequent to the Supreme Court decision in *Simpson*, the Commission's findings in *Sun Oil* and *Atlantic* were upheld by the Seventh and Sixth Circuit Courts respectively.

distinction between lawful and unlawful consignment arrangements are whether price restrictions are imposed on consignees who would otherwise be in competition with each other, and whether the consignor has economic leverage over his consignees so that his refusal to deal with them except on the price maintained consignment basis has the required coercive effect on them. It may be that in *Simpson*[1] the fact that the dealer was at risk for any loss or damage to the petrol (other than for 'earthquake, lightning, flood, fire or explosion not caused by his negligence') while it remained in his possession, and was also responsible for payment of all taxes on the petrol other than property taxes, weighed to some degree with the Court. It is of interest that subsequently in *United States* v. *Arnold, Schwinn*[2] the Court declared legitimate territorial restrictions on distributors of goods provided that 'title, dominion and risk' in the goods remained with the manufacturer.

4. *State fair trade Acts; the 'non-signer' clause:*
the Old Dearborn *decision. The Miller-Tydings law:*
Schwegmann Brothers *v.* Calvert Distillers.
The Federal Fair Trade Act of 1952 (the McGuire Act):
Schwegmann Brothers *v.* Eli Lilly

Even before the *Parke, Davis* and *Simpson* cases described above, the state of the law gave little satisfaction to those who wanted effective resale price maintenance in their trades. Few manufacturers could hope to achieve the dainty legal footwork involved in treading the fine line between the *Colgate* and *Beech Nut* decisions; fewer still could operate legally watertight agency schemes of the General Electric type, which in most trades would be cumbersome and inconvenient. Consequently a strong movement developed—especially among associations of small retailers in such trades as proprietary drugs and cosmetics—to achieve legislative recognition for 'fair trade'.[3]

The effort was directed at the State legislatures and had its first success in California in 1931 when a measure was passed which legalized resale price contracts. This was a beginning, but it was soon found that it was still unsatisfactory merely to give the manufacturer of branded goods a legal right to enforce contracts prescribing resale prices. The manufacturer could bring to book the price cutting retailer only when

---

[1] An analysis of the ambiguities of the *Simpson* decision is to be found in J. A. Rahl, 'The Demise of Vertical Price Fixing through Consignment Arrangements' *A.B.A. Antitrust Section, Proceedings*, vol. 29, 1965, p. 216.   [2] See Chapter VIII, pp. 222–3 above.

[3] 'Fair trade' is the term always used for resale price maintenance by supporters of the practice; opponents talk of 'price rings'. Both terms leave a good deal to be desired semantically.

there was a contract directly between them. But an important manufacturer's branded lines may reach many thousands of retail shops
through a variety of channels and it would be an intolerable burden to
seek them all out and negotiate a separate contract with each individual
shopkeeper. (The absence of 'privity of contract' between the manufacturer and his retailers was, of course, one of the main arguments
used in Britain to justify collective measures for enforcing resale prices
before the law was changed in 1956.[1])

To meet this difficulty the California Fair Trade Act was amended in
1933 by the addition of the ingenious and unusual legal device known
as the 'non-signer' clause. This clause provides that, once a resale
price has been prescribed by contract with any distributor, it is unlawful
for any other distributor knowingly to undercut that price.[2]

The essentials of State 'fair trade' statutes are, first, a declaration
that no contract fixing the resale price of a branded article shall be
deemed illegal under any other State law and, secondly, a non-signer
clause. All such laws provide that the price maintained commodity
must be in 'fair and open competition with commodities of the same
general class produced by others', and all make it clear that they do not
legalize horizontal price fixing between manufacturers, wholesalers or
retailers. Some laws (those modelled on the Californian statute) also
legalize contracts by which the manufacturer or other supplier requires
the first purchaser to make resale price contracts in turn with subsequent purchasers. Others, on a later model, go further and legalize
contracts whereby the supplier, in return for an undertaking to maintain
his resale prices, promises the buyer that he will not supply any
retailer who does not agree to maintain them or any wholesaler who
does not require subsequent purchasers to do so. The later laws also
permit action to be taken against retailers who get round the prescribed
prices by making gifts or offering trading stamps or other concessions
in connexion with the sale of price maintained goods. All the laws
contain saving clauses of one kind or another to permit low-price sales
of damaged goods and 'close-out' sales.

At first some State courts found fault with the constitutionality of
'fair trade' laws and the movement to emulate California went slowly.
But in 1936 the Supreme Court upheld the constitutionality of the

---

[1] The Restrictive Trade Practices Act of 1956 provides (section 25) that suppliers may
enforce resale price conditions against persons who subsequently acquire goods from the first
buyer and have notice of the conditions: this is in effect a 'non-signer' clause similar to those
described below. See also p. 490n.

[2] The full wording of the non-signer clause (section 16904) of the Californian statute is
as follows: 'Wilfully and knowingly advertising, offering for sale or selling any commodity
at less than the price stipulated in any contract entered into pursuant to this chapter, whether
the person so advertising, offering for sale or selling is or is not a party to such contract, is
unfair competition and is actionable at the suit of any person damaged thereby.'

California and Illinois Acts and the movement then spread like wildfire. As against ten States with fair trade laws in 1935, there were forty-five in 1941: only Texas, Missouri and Vermont stood out, together with the District of Columbia, which is administered directly by the Federal Government.[1]

There were always some retailers who resented having their selling prices laid down and having to forsake the weapon of price competition. They attacked the constitutionality of fair trade laws on the ground that they unlawfully delegated to private persons the power to dispose of the property of others; it was asserted that when a trader buys goods he acquires an unqualified property right to them, including the right to give them away or sell them at any price he likes. 'Appellants invoke the well settled general principle that the right of the owner of property to fix the price at which he will sell it is an inherent attribute of the property itself and as such is within the protection of the 5th and 14th Amendments.'

When this issue came before the Supreme Court in *Old Dearborn Distributing Company* v. *Seagram Distillers Corporation* (1936), a test case dealing with the Fair Trade Act of Illinois, it was held that the Act, including the non-signer clause, was constitutional. This finding was based on the argument that the primary aim of the statute was to protect the goodwill of the manufacturer or proprietor of the brand name or trademark. Thus, in the view of the Court, retailers who buy branded goods for resale own the goods but 'do not own the mark or the goodwill that the mark symbolizes'. On this theory the manufacturer who requires resale prices to be maintained is not purporting to control the property of others but protecting his own; and the retailer buys the goodwill with the goods and accepts the price condition in accepting the goods. Mr Justice Sutherland put the point as follows:

Section 2 does not deal with the restriction upon the sale of the commodity qua commodity, but with that restriction because the commodity is identified by the trademark, brand or name of the producer or owner. The essence of the statutory violation then consists not in the bare disposition of the commodity but in a forbidden use of the trademark, brand or name in accomplishing such disposition. The primary aim of the law is to protect the property—namely, the goodwill of the producer, which he still owns. The price restriction is adopted as an appropriate means to that perfectly legitimate end, and not as an end in itself.

Appellants here acquired the commodity in question with full knowledge of the then-existing restriction in respect of price. . . . Appellants were not

[1] It is not clear that the State of Vermont, though a 'non-fair trade' State, is 'anti-fair trade', for there is no record of action being taken under other State laws against resale price maintenance.

obliged to buy; and their voluntary acquisition of the property with such knowledge carried with it, upon every principle of fair dealing, assent to the protective restriction. . . .

The *Old Dearborn* decision and the subsequent rapid spread of fair trade laws into forty-five States were substantial victories for the 'fair trade' movement. These State laws, however, could not confer any immunity under federal law, and where interstate commerce was affected resale price maintenance might still run foul of the Sherman Act. The next step, therefore, was to secure a federal Fair Trade Act which would apply to interstate commerce. Bills were introduced into Congress in 1936 and 1937 for this purpose but were strongly opposed by the administration of the time. At the end of the 1937 session, however, the Senate adopted the device of attaching the required amendment of the Sherman Act as a rider to a revenue bill for the District of Columbia. This rider was kept in the bill, for although President Roosevelt denounced it, he was unable to exercise his power of veto without denuding the District of Columbia of necessary funds.

This legislation is commonly known as the Miller-Tydings Act. It amended the Sherman Act by providing that nothing in that Act should

. . . render illegal contracts or agreements prescribing minimum prices for the resale of a [branded] commodity . . . which is in free and open competition with commodities of the same general class produced or distributed by others, when contracts or agreements of that description are lawful as applied to intra-state transactions under any statute . . . now or hereafter in effect in any State . . . in which such resale is to be made, or to which the commodity is to be transported for such resale.

It was also provided that such contracts should not be deemed an unfair method of competition under section 5 of the Federal Trade Commission Act. Like the State laws themselves, the Miller-Tydings Act made it clear that horizontal price fixing agreements between manufacturers, wholesalers or retailers remained unlawful.

This was a further important victory for the supporters of fair trade. The position now seemed to be that resale price maintenance could be enforced by manufacturers even on retailers who did not sign and did not wish to sign specific contracts undertaking to maintain prescribed prices; and this right of enforcement could be exercised in all the forty-five States which had fair trade Acts even in respect of branded goods which entered those States from outside and passed through the channels of interstate commerce. So it was believed from 1937 until May 1951.

The Miller-Tydings law was then tested in the Supreme Court in the case of *Schwegmann Brothers* v. *Calvert Distillers Corporation*. Schwegmann is an independent retailer with a large supermarket in New

Orleans; he had long contended that he was able to sell many branded lines, in particular branded liquor, at prices well below those prescribed by the manufacturers and still make a handsome profit on his large turnover. He steadfastly refused to sign any resale price maintenance contracts and did not see why he should be coerced into price maintenance as a non-signer. When a supplier of branded liquor brought suit to enjoin Schwegmann from selling his product below his prescribed resale prices, the Supreme Court refused to read the non-signer provision into the Miller-Tydings amendment and rejected the suit. As worded, the amendment exempted only 'contracts and agreements' from the general prohibition of the Sherman Act and the majority of the Court would not accept arguments, based on the legislative history, to the effect that Congress had intended the wording to cover enforcement against non-signers.[1]

Mr Justice Douglas's opinion in this case was a strong criticism of the principle of the non-signer clause. In his view it compelled retailers in effect to join in horizontal price fixing. 'Elimination of price competition at the retail level may, of course, lawfully result if a distributor successfully negotiates individual "vertical" agreements with all his retailers. But when retailers are *forced* to abandon price competition, they are driven into a compact in violation of the spirit of the proviso which forbids horizontal price fixing.' Throughout the opinion he laid great stress on the element of compulsion in the non-signer clause, which he saw as different in principle from a freely negotiated contract or agreement between the supplier and the retailer.

They can fix minimum prices pursuant to their contract or agreement with impunity. When they seek, however, to impose price fixing on persons who have not contracted or agreed to the scheme, the situation is vastly different. That is not price fixing by contract or agreement; that is price fixing by compulsion. That is not following the path of consensual agreement; that is resort to coercion.

The *Schwegmann* decision decreed that attempts to force non-signers to abide by prescribed resale prices were not exempt from the Sherman Act. In respect to goods moving in interstate commerce, therefore, the danger that effective resale price maintenance would come up against antitrust action seemed to be renewed and the Department of Justice and the Federal Trade Commission soon let it be known that they would enforce the law strictly against any coercion of non-signers. These events were signalized by some highly publicized price cutting of branded goods by well known department stores in New York and

[1] Three dissenting Justices, led by Mr Justice Frankfurter, held, however, that the congressional purpose was clearly to validate fair trade in interstate commerce and observed that 'we should not substitute our own notion of what Congress should have done'.

elsewhere, and the supporters of resale price maintenance organized themselves to repair the damage. The result was the Federal Fair Trade Act of 1952, known as the McGuire Act, in which the Congress clearly resolved to overrule the *Schwegmann* decision and to put the legality of resale price maintenance beyond doubt. The congressional purpose was indeed firmly set forth in the preamble to this Act. 'It is the purpose of this Act to protect the rights of States under the United States Constitution to regulate their internal affairs and more particularly to enact statutes and laws, and to adopt policies, which authorize contracts and agreements prescribing minimum or stipulated prices for the resale of commodities and to extend the minimum or stipulated prices prescribed by such contracts and agreements to persons who are not parties thereto. It is the further purpose of this Act to permit statutes, laws and public policies to apply to commodities, contracts, agreements and activities in or affecting interstate or foreign commerce.'

The McGuire Act was passed by Congress with such large majorities that President Truman, although advised by the antitrust authorities to veto it, felt unable to do so. In form the Act is an amendment to section 5 of the Federal Trade Commission Act.[1] It repeats the substance of the Miller-Tydings law but adds important new provisions. It applies, for example, to agreements prescribing minimum or stipulated prices, whereas the Miller-Tydings Act applied only to minimum prices. Another new feature is that it applies to agreements by which a supplier requires the first purchaser of his goods to enter into resale price agreements in turn with subsequent purchasers. This provision may enable a manufacturer to transfer to wholesalers a large part of the burden of enforcing resale price contracts. But the vital addition is a provision which specifically overrules the *Schwegmann* decision and extends the exemption from antitrust to cover enforcement of resale prices against non-signers. 'Nothing contained in this Act or in any of the Anti-Trust Acts shall render unlawful the exercise or the enforcement of any right or right of action created by any statute, law, or public policy now or hereafter in effect in any State, Territory, or the District of Columbia, which in substance provides that wilfully and knowingly advertising, offering for sale, or selling any commodity at less than the price or prices prescribed in such contracts or agreements whether the person so advertising, offering for sale, or selling is or is not a party to such a contract or agreement, is unfair competition and is actionable at the suit of any person damaged thereby.'

[1] The Miller-Tydings amendment to the Sherman Act was not repealed and remains on the statute book, though for all practical purposes the McGuire Act is now the relevant measure. However, a task force of scholars and practitioners recommended to Congress in 1969 that the exemption from antitrust of resale price maintenance should be repealed (*Congressional Record*, 91st Cong., 1st Sess., pp. S5642, S5649).

Thus the McGuire Act put the proponents of resale price maintenance on firmer legal ground than ever before. And so far the federal courts have upheld the authority of the Act. A strong challenge to that authority again came from the Schwegmann company, which proceeded, undeterred, to sell the drugs of a pharmaceutical manufacturer named Eli Lilly and Company below the minimum prices established by Lilly in contracts with other retailers. When this manufacturer brought suit to enjoin his company against further price cutting, Schwegmann raised a number of constitutional objections against the Louisiana Fair Trade Act and the McGuire Act.

In *Schwegmann Brothers* v. *Eli Lilly and Company* (Fifth Circuit Court of Appeals, 1953) the case made by Schwegmann was in essence a denial of the rationale of the *Old Dearborn* decision. It was argued that all experience since the case had shown that the real purpose of fair trade was the protection of retailers against cut-throat competition and the loss leader rather than the protection of the manufacturer's goodwill in his brand name. The main pressure on Congress for the McGuire Act, for example, had come from associations of small retailers rather than from the proprietors of branded goods. Moreover, the *Old Dearborn* opinion had regarded the trader who bought branded goods for resale—even though a non-signer—as giving some form of implied assent to the resale price condition running with the goods; whereas Mr Justice Douglas in the *Schwegmann* opinion of 1951 had characterized the enforcement of prescribed resale prices against non-signers as a coercive means of securing what amounted to a horizontal price fixing scheme. If indeed the true purpose and effect of the State law and the McGuire Act were to eliminate price competition among retailers by coercion, it could be argued that the legislation delegated powers of price regulation to private hands and invaded normal property rights without due process of law; all of which would be in direct violation of the American Constitution.

This argument was indeed accepted by one of the three judges of the Fifth Circuit Court of Appeals, Judge Holmes, and clearly expounded in his dissenting opinion.[1] Judge Holmes pointed out that a non-signing retailer, like Schwegmann, could not conceivably be deemed to assent to the fixed resale prices with which he refused to comply and against which he vigorously protested at all times. He showed too how unrealistic was a suggestion in the *Old Dearborn* opinion that the retailer could free himself of the price condition simply by removing the supplier's mark or brand name; this indeed would often be illegal. Judge Holmes challenged the whole theory that retail price

---

[1] This dissent is well worth studying in full. The case is reported in 205 F. 2d. 788 and *Commerce Clearing House Trade Cases*, Chicago, 1952–53, 67,516.

competition was an assault upon the manufacturer's goodwill and held: 'It is a legal, factual and economic impossibility for the owner of tangible personal property to part completely with the possession thereof and yet retain control of the price thereof in perpetuity.'

This, however, was a minority view. The majority held that the fair trade legislation involved no unconstitutional delegation of power, for restrictions imposed on non-signers were not after all the same thing as a horizontal price fixing agreement. And if fair trade protected distributors as well as suppliers, this was a result that legislatures were fully entitled to promote.

The trend of economic practices as tending to show that fair trade Acts are concerned more with the protection of distributors than with the protection of the producer or owner of the trademark are matters, it seems to us, for legislative, not for judicial, consideration. . . . We cannot say that the legislature was not authorized to consider distributors as in a similar position to licensees of a trademark or brand with a direct economic interest in it as regards the sales of the trademarked or branded article. Whether the distributors were to be protected, as well as the manufacturers or trademark owners, was a matter, it seems to us, addressed to legislative discretion and not subject to review by courts. We have no judicial concern with the economic and social wisdom of any feature of the law but solely with its constitutionality.

The Supreme Court, when it came to the pinch, declined to review this decision of the Fifth Circuit Court. This conveys a strong suggestion that the Justices were unwilling again to challenge the clearly expressed view of Congress on the issue of policy involved. When a later case involving the McGuire Act came before the Supreme Court three years afterwards, its constitutionality was not challenged. In *United States* v. *McKesson and Robbins Inc.* (Supreme Court, 1956), however, the Court held that the defendant could not enforce fair trade contracts with independent wholesalers even in fair trade States since it was itself in competition with these wholesalers through its own wholesale division. The McGuire Act was also considered by the Court in a case in which it upheld the constitutionality of the Ohio Fair Trade Act, in *Hudson Distributors* v. *Eli Lilly & Co.* (Supreme Court, 1964). Mr Justice Goldberg confirmed that, where sanctioned by a State fair trade Act, stipulated prices could be enforced by a trademark owner against non-signing retailers, where it had entered into contracts with other retailers which stipulated these prices. He declined, however, to rule on whether a State fair trade Act referring to resale prices set by notice alone, without any 'conventional or express' contract, would be equally valid.

The argument over resale price maintenance in the individual

States still continues. By about the end of 1966 fair trade laws had been declared unconstitutional in all respects in five States (Alabama, Montana, Nebraska, Utah and Wyoming) and had been completely repealed by the legislatures of Kansas and Nevada. In twenty other States courts had held the non-signer clause unconstitutional, and Hawaii had repealed the non-signer clause though retaining the remaining provisions of its fair trade law. Since four other States (Alaska, Texas, Missouri, Vermont) and the District of Columbia had never had fair trade laws, this means that fair trade is enforceable now against contracting parties in approximately thirty-nine states and against non-signers in only about eighteen. (These eighteen, however, cover many of the densely populated, industrial areas of the country.) In States where fair trade Acts have been deemed unconstitutional, the reasons given by the courts for their decisions closely follow those advanced by Judge Holmes in his dissent in *Schwegmann Brothers* v. *Eli Lilly and Company*: that the non-signer clause deprives the non-contracting retailer, without due process of law, of his constitutional right to dispose freely of his property; that the real purpose and effect of the non-signer clause is anti-competitive price fixing rather than protecting the goodwill of branded products and that it therefore improperly delegates a price fixing power to private persons whose pricing decisions are not subject to any form of review nor governed by any legislative standards.

5. *Case law under State fair trade legislation:* Eastman Kodak; McKesson and Robbins. *Legal requirements relating to enforcement of fair trade contracts*

The case law under fair trade legislation is a matter for the specialist, for upwards of fifty separate jurisdictions are involved and the decisions of the courts differ in detail from State to State. The most that can be done here is to attempt a broad summary of the current legal position affecting resale price maintenance and some assessment of the extent to which the law enables the practice to be effectively operated.

As we have seen, the combination of State laws and the McGuire Act enables the manufacturer of branded goods to prescribe resale prices by contract over a large part of the United States—all but the States without fair trade laws and those in which the laws have been held unconstitutional. Moreover, over most of this area—that is, except where the non-signer clause has been held unconstitutional—the manufacturer, having once made a resale price contract with any distributor, has a right of action to prevent distributors generally from undercutting his prescribed resale prices. Where interstate trade is involved, the manufacturer's rights depend on the law of the State in which the resale takes place. A manufacturer in a fair trade State such as New York cannot take legal action to have his prices maintained in a 'non-fair trade' State such as Texas. But the Texan manufacturer has a right of action against price cutters in New York.

The manufacturer may prescribe resale prices for the wholesaler or the retailer or both. He may also make contracts with his wholesalers requiring them to prescribe resale prices at the retail level. Wholesalers or other distributors, when so required or authorized by the owner of the trademark or brand name, are in turn allowed by the laws to prescribe resale prices in contracts and to exercise the right of action against non-signers. Indeed, in some States any vendor of branded goods is allowed to do these things without reference to the manufacturer or brand owner. On the face of it these legal conditions should allow for effective resale price maintenance in most of the populous markets of the United States. Some of the limitations and difficulties involved, however, need a closer look.

A relatively minor limitation is the requirement that 'fair-traded' goods must be 'in free and open competition with commodities of the same general class produced or distributed by others'. This means that the monopolist enjoys no legal sanction for resale price maintenance. The courts, however, have interpreted the words 'general class' broadly and there has been no attempt to prevent patented goods or copyrighted books and gramophone records from being fair-traded simply on the ground that such things have unique or distinctive 'monopoly' characteristics. The Eastman Kodak Company was, however, forbidden to maintain the resale prices of colour film at a time when it was the sole producer of such film, and it was held that colour film could not be placed in the same general class as ordinary black and white film (*Eastman Kodak Company* v. *Federal Trade Commission*, Second Circuit Court of Appeals, 1946). The order was later suspended by the Federal Trade Commission when Ansco colour film came on the market.[1]

A more important problem arises from the proviso in all the State and federal fair trade laws to the effect that horizontal price fixing is still forbidden at all levels. The question has arisen whether an integrated concern which both manufactures branded goods and sells them in part through its own wholesale outlets should be entitled to maintain common resale prices for its own and independent wholesalers. Although the *McKesson and Robbins* case was concerned only with the question of whether an integrated manufacturer-wholesaler could have

---

[1] Later still, in 1954, the company was again enjoined in a consent decree against 'fair trading' colour film, but this decree arose out of a Government complaint under the Sherman Act and the ban on resale price maintenance was presumably negotiated by the Government as a protective measure against monopolization of the industry.

fair trade agreements with independent wholesalers with whom it was in competition, the logic of that decision and of the wording of the McGuire Act[1] mean that a supplier will not be able to rely on that Act to enforce resale price maintenance against his distributors at any level in the chain of distribution if he is himself in business at that level.

The mere existence of the fair trade laws with the non-signer clause does not, of course, make the enforcement of prescribed resale prices an easy matter. Indeed it may be a very troublesome and expensive one. In the first place the price cutter has to be detected. No doubt retailers who abide by the prescribed prices are often eager to let the manufacturer know about backsliders and do so on their own initiative. In this way he may be pretty well informed. It must not be forgotten, however, that any systematic and organized plan for collecting such information—on the old *Beech Nut* model—might well give rise to antitrust action alleging unlawful conspiracy under the Sherman Act. When the manufacturer sells his line through a large number of wholesalers, he may require them by contract to enforce prescribed resale prices and so spread the burden of detecting and preventing price cutting; but their zeal for the task may well vary and he will probably have to provide the main impetus (and meet the bulk of the expense) himself, if he wants the enforcement to be really effective.

When price cutting is detected, it can no doubt often be stopped by warnings and threats of legal action. But the manufacturer has to be ready to take legal action and any large-scale 'fair trader' of branded goods is likely at any time to have a good deal of quite expensive litigation on his hands. Here again he will probably have to bear the brunt himself. Many of his wholesalers may fight shy of the trouble and expense involved. It is true that under the non-signer provisions of State laws the price cutting of fair-traded goods is declared to be 'unfair competition' and 'actionable at the suit of any person damaged thereby'.[2] This means that retailers who abide by the prescribed prices and who may presumably be damaged by losing sales to price cutters are entitled to take legal action on their own initiative. There are indeed a number of recorded cases in which suits brought by retailers have been upheld. The Supreme Courts of Iowa and New York have even held that trade associations of retailers may be proper parties to bring suit. But although the retailer's right of action has been much criticized

---

[1] 'Nothing . . . shall make lawful contracts or agreements providing for the establishment of minimum or stipulated resale prices . . . between manufacturers or between producers, or between wholesalers or between brokers, or between factors, or between retailers or between persons, firms or corporations in competition with each other.'

[2] The manufacturer or owner of the brand name is always deemed to be damaged, within the meaning of the Act, by price cutting, on the theory that the goodwill of his brand suffers. He does not have to prove actual damage.

as tending to make resale price maintenance indistinguishable from horizontal price fixing at the retail level, it seems doubtful whether the burden on the manufacturer is in practice much reduced by it. Few individual retailers are likely to court the trouble and expense of litigation, and even in association their efforts are more likely to be directed to putting pressure on the manufacturer to make his own enforcement effective.

The manufacturer who takes legal action against a price cutter is faced with a considerable burden of proof. The usual form of such action is a suit for an injunction to restrain the party concerned from continuing to undercut the prescribed prices. When an injunction is granted, a repetition of the offence lays the price cutter open to penalties for contempt of court. (Actions for damages for breach of fair trade contracts are rare because of the difficulty of proving the amount of the damage.) In an injunction suit the plaintiff must first show that a valid and current bona fide fair trade contract exists. This need not be (and usually is not) a contract of sale, but it is not enough, for example, for the manufacturer to have attached a notice to his goods announcing that their acceptance constitutes agreement to charge a given resale price. He must also show that the defendant 'wilfully and knowingly' offered for sale or sold the goods below the stipulated price. This involves establishing that the price cutter had notice of the current resale price. This is not always easy in the case of non-signers, particularly when price changes are frequent, but it can often be done by reference to a notice of the 'fair trade' price attached to the invoice for the goods or to the goods themselves.[1]

Apart from establishing these points, the manufacturer may have to meet a variety of defence arguments. As has been seen, the constitutionality of the State law concerned may be challenged and many less radical arguments are heard. Some of the commonest take the line that the operation of resale price maintenance has been in some way unfair or discriminatory as against the trader charged with cutting prices. If, for example, the manufacturers were to prescribe different resale prices for different traders competing in the same market, a defence alleging discrimination would probably succeed, though this does not mean that a manufacturer's fair trade prices need be uniform from coast to coast. If a manufacturer were to allow a wholly owned retail subsidiary to cut prices which he sought to enforce on independent retailers, his enforcement suits might well fail unless it appeared that the subsidiary was separately operated and not in practice an agency of the manufacturer.

---

[1] Such a notice is not of itself a contract; as noted above, there must also be a contract with some retailer, but the notice alone may then suffice as regards the non-signer.

The discrimination issue is most commonly raised in relation to the manufacturer's enforcement policy. In most fair trade contracts the manufacturer undertakes to use 'reasonable diligence' to prevent price cutting. If, therefore, a trader who is sued can show that he has been 'picked upon' while many other instances of price cutting have been ignored, or more generally that the manufacturer's enforcement is so slack that the 'fair price' is not effectively established at all, the case may well fail. The trader may be able to show, for example, that price cutting was so rife that he was forced to cut prices himself to meet competition. The courts of different States have differed a good deal in their attitudes to this kind of defence argument and the courts of the same State have been more or less indulgent from time to time. Generally speaking, however, they do not ask the impossible of the manufacturer; they recognize that he cannot pursue all instances of price cutting simultaneously and that even with diligence he may not catch every case. Thus it is not enough for the defendant simply to be able to point to one or two price cutters who have 'got away with it'. Nevertheless, the manufacturer has got to make a real effort and must not be arbitrary or capricious in his enforcement.

Perhaps the best general statement on the subject was that of the Supreme Court of New York in *Calvert Distillers Corporation* v. *Nussbaum Liquor Store* (1938).[1]

A producer or owner invoking the statute is not required as a matter of law to resort to legal process against every violator . . . before he can enforce a remedy against any one violator. . . . At least where he does not resort to legal action, the producer is required to use reasonable diligence to see to it that none of his products continue to be sold to a retailer who cuts prices after the producer has notice of such violation. In the last analysis it all comes down to a question of whether the producer or owner by his acts or conduct, whether of commission or omission, may be said to have waived or abandoned his rights. . . . He will not be allowed directly or indirectly to discriminate unfairly. In availing himself of the benefits of the statute, he must accept its burdens. . . . The producer cannot act arbitrarily in enforcing observance of fixed prices. There must be a sincere and diligent effort to prevent price cutting of branded products through legal protest if necessary.

But the onus on the manufacturer is greater in States where compliance with the local fair trade legislation is not general. Thus in Ohio, where there has apparently been a widespread break-down in the observance of the local fair trade Act, a State judge ruled,

---

[1] Later decisions in New York, e.g. *National Distillers* v. *R. H. Macy* (New York Supreme Court, 1965) have confirmed that this statement of the manufacturer's obligation is still substantially correct for New York State.

when the *Hudson Distributors* case was remanded to him by the Supreme Court, that the supplier could not enforce its fair trade contracts in Ohio unless it showed a high degree of diligence in the enforcement of this policy. Among the specific requirements upon the supplier were that he must make a definite attempt to convince consumers that it was in their interests to patronize establishments selling at fair trade prices, and must pursue a vigorous unrelenting effort to discover those selling below fixed prices and to get them to abide by the law. Known violators must not continue to receive supplies and must be brought to court at the earliest opportunity. Perhaps not suprisingly, the supplier in that case was held not to have satisfied the onerous requirements laid down by the Court.

Thus the burden on the manufacturer of 'fair-trading' his products is not a negligible one. Given the strongly competitive nature of many American traders, he may well have to face, too, some pretty determined and ingenious attempts at evasion, perhaps by 'phoney' close-out sales, perhaps by mail order selling across State boundaries or from a base in a non-fair trade State. It would, however, be wrong to exaggerate the difficulties or to suggest that resale price maintenance is bound to be ineffective in the United States. The trouble and expense of litigation cut both ways. No doubt they are factors which induce a great many retailers quietly to accept the prescribed prices and others to succumb promptly to warnings. No doubt, too, the acknowledgment by legislatures of a public interest in resale price maintenance strengthens the hands of those who promote the practice. Seeing that the manufacturer has a legal right to enforce his prices, retail trade associations may well feel that it is their public duty to help him by keeping him well supplied with information about price cutters and by exerting strong moral pressures against them on their own account. Probably a good deal of this can be and is done in some trades without attracting the Sherman Act's penalties against collective enforcement.

On balance it seems clear that the device of giving the manufacturer a right of action against non-signers has been of real value to supporters of resale price maintenance in the United States. Almost certainly prescribed resale prices can be more widely and effectively enforced than they would be if, for example, manufacturers were simply left to enforce their prices as best they could by separate contracts with each retailer, or by refusing individually to supply price cutters but without any right of legal action in the absence of a contract. On the other hand, there can be little doubt that resale price maintenance is markedly less effective and widespread in the United States than it is where there is no legal ban against elaborately organized schemes of collective enforcement.

Probably the chief reason for this is that the American law leaves the decision on whether branded goods are to be price maintained up to the individual manufacturer and, as has been seen, puts on him most of the burden of enforcement. While retail trade associations no doubt direct a good deal of propaganda at manufacturers about the desirability of fair trade, there are limits to the pressure they can exert. Any organized boycott of a manufacturer who refused to 'fair-trade' his products would certainly run foul of the Sherman Act, as would any reciprocal exclusive-dealing arrangement between associations of retailers and of fair-trading manufacturers. Equally, an agreement among manufacturers that they would all prescribe and enforce resale prices would clearly constitute illegal restraint of trade even though there was no collusion as to the level of prices to be maintained. These points are important, for the chain of resale price maintenance may prove no stronger than its weakest link. If any important manufacturers in an industry prefer not to operate resale price maintenance, or if they turn a blind eye to price cuts when retail stocks are high, other manufacturers who insist on the full rigours of fair trade may well find themselves at a competitive disadvantage. Enforcement is bound to be weakened also by the fact that the Second Circuit Court has ruled (*General Electric Company* v. *Masters Mail Order Company of Washington, D.C.*, 1957) that a mail order company incorporated in Washington, D.C. (a non-fair trade territory) cannot be enjoined against selling in New York and other fair trade States at below prescribed prices even though this company is a subsidiary of a New York distributor.

6. *State 'unfair sales' legislation*

As a footnote to this chapter some mention must be made of State laws which prohibit the selling of goods 'below cost'. Some thirty of the States have legislation of this kind—usually known as 'unfair sales Acts'. If, as is often claimed, the real purpose of resale price maintenance is to prevent the disruption of normal trade by the loss leader practice, there are obvious attractions in a type of legislation which will prevent the loss leader without making all shopkeepers abide by the same resale price. It is difficult to get agreement on a definition of the loss leader but it would be fairly generally agreed that selling at a loss covers a good deal of what is meant by the term. On the face of it, therefore, laws forbidding such selling might be the best answer to the problem of fair trade.

Unfortunately American experience with laws of this type is not too encouraging, for they bristle with legal and administrative difficulties. Although some of the laws formally apply to all suppliers, including manufacturers, they mainly affect selling by wholesale and retail distributors. One problem is to avoid penalizing legitimate 'below cost' sales, for example, of obsolete or deteriorated goods, or close-out sales of the stock of bankrupt businesses. Sometimes specific exemptions of such sales are written into the laws but the point is also covered by a provision in almost every law to the effect that sales below cost are prohibited only when made for the purpose of diverting trade from competitors or otherwise injuring them.[1] This provision, however, makes for difficulty in enforcing the laws, since the illegal intent is not always easy to prove.[2]

But the biggest problem is that of determining what is 'selling below cost'. Clearly the invoice cost of the goods to the wholesaler or retailer is not enough and sales at cost price in this sense are sales 'below cost'. Most of the laws require that the 'cost of doing business' be added to the invoice cost to arrive at the legal minimum price. This provision, however, brings the courts up against the familiar problem (familiar from the Robinson-Patman Act) of getting satisfactory evidence of business costs. All traders sell a variety of different goods, so that the allocation of their indirect costs among specific items is always open to argument.

In several laws an attempt has been made to shortcircuit this problem by providing that, in the absence of proof of a lower cost, certain statutory percentages shall be added to the invoice cost to arrive at the legal minimum price. Usually 2% has to be added by wholesalers and 6% or 8% by retailers. These mark-ups would, of course, be extremely low for many traders (for example, in the consumer durable field), but are not far from the conventional margins in the United States in some of the food trades in which this type of law has been most used.[3] But the intractable problem remains with this type of law that either the courts must deal with interminable arguments about the allocation of costs, or arbitrary mark-up figures must be used which may be too high for some trades and too low for others.

The result has been in many States that these laws are found too difficult to enforce and become a dead letter. There are a few States where strongly organized bodies of traders succeed in persuading the courts to accept as the 'cost of doing business' the figures shown by their

[1] Only the New Jersey statute is without any provision of this kind and it has been held unconstitutional for that reason. Some State laws bite on sales below cost made with 'the intent or effect' of injuring competitors.

[2] Some courts, however, have gone so far as to take the fact of selling below cost as showing a presumptive intent to injure competitors and have transferred the onus of proof to the defendant.

[3] The grocery trade in the United States often prefers the 'unfair sales' type of legislation to fair trade because, as has been seen, resale price maintenance may unduly restrict the independent retailers as against the chain stores with their private brands.

own cost surveys; where this happens, however, it is only too possible that the legislation will become an instrument for imposing on a whole trade common minimum prices which are well above the loss leader level. In some cases trade associations have even sought to act as the enforcing agency for the minimum prices and the federal antitrust authorities have successfully brought antitrust suits against this kind of activity.[1]

It is perhaps too much to say that the unfair sales Acts tend either to become a dead letter or a racket; but the middle ground is hard to find in the records. It might perhaps be easier to rely in American law on some general precept that selling at excessively low prices should be deemed an 'unfair method of competition'. Indeed, there are one or two cases under section 5 of the Federal Trade Commission Act in which this has been done. But these have been exceptionally flagrant cases in which the tendency to destroy competition and create a monopoly has been well supported by evidence.

[1] See *Food and Grocery Bureau of Southern California* v. *United States* (Ninth Circuit Court of Appeals, 1943).

CHAPTER XI

PATENTS AND ANTITRUST

1. *The United States patent system and the limits set by antitrust to the exercise of patent rights*

The holder of a patent is in a position of monopoly. His monopoly may not be of much economic importance; that will depend on what the patent is for. Often patented articles and components are in competition with other patented or unpatented articles which are close substitutes. But whether the element of monopoly is important or not, every patent is a grant of monopoly power by the state and, as such, is necessarily immune from the prohibitions of antitrust; for if it were a case of illegal monopolization to take out a patent, there would be no point in the patent system. It follows that the antitrust policy is modified in various ways when applied to trade in patented products. Not only the monopoly in the patented article but also certain kinds of restrictive agreement made by the patent holder may be no more than the legitimate exercise of rights inseparable from the grant of the patent.

A United States patent confers on its holder, for a period of seventeen years, the exclusive right to make, use and sell the patented invention.[1] The operative word is 'exclusive', for the inventor, like anybody else, needs no special 'right' to make and sell his goods. The special feature of the patent is a right to exclude others from practising the invention except on the patentee's terms. The patentee may dispose of this right as a form of property.[2] Thus he may sell or assign the patent outright to another person for a lump sum; or he may license another person exclusively to make, use and sell the article in return for royalty payments. Alternatively, he may share the right with others. Thus he may license other people to manufacture and sell the invention while continuing to manufacture and sell it himself. He may license non-exclusively so that a number of other people may make, use and sell the article on payment of royalties; he may license some to make and others to sell. He may define the shares that he licenses in any way he likes.[3] Thus he may in general license others, exclusively or non-

---

[1] The patent claims may describe an article or component part of an article, or they may describe a process of manufacture; in the latter case the right of the patentee is to exclude others from adopting that process.

[2] Mr Justice Holmes spoke of a patent as 'property carried to the highest degree of abstraction—a right *in rem* to exclude, without a physical object or content'.

[3] As Mr George E. Frost has pointed out to me, the right to make normally carries an implied right to sell, and the right to sell an implied right for the buyer to use.

exclusively, to make and sell the article only in a defined territory or only for a specified purpose. For example, an electronic device might be licensed so that the licensee could make and sell it in California but not elsewhere, or for use in aircraft but not for use in television sets.

Many of the arrangements that the patentee may make would clearly violate the antitrust laws were it not for the saving grace of the patent. An arrangement, for example, under which the only manufacturers of a product had exclusive territories assigned to them would normally be illegal market sharing under the rule of the *Addyston Pipe* case, but the patentee may legitimately grant licences having this result.[1]

Antitrust, however, is acutely sensitive to any attempt to carry the exercise of the patent right beyond the point needed to secure a legitimate reward for the invention and to protect it against infringement. Some of the most interesting antitrust cases are concerned with defining the limits of the legitimate exercise of patent rights. There are patents in almost every industry and, if they were regarded simply as convenient pegs on which restrictive arrangements could be loosely hung, a broad sector of industry might escape the discipline of antitrust.

In setting limits to the exercise of patent rights, the courts in recent times have increasingly stressed the point that a patent, though having many of the legal attributes of property, is at the same time a franchise or privilege—a privilege 'conditioned by a public purpose'.[2] On this view the patent is justified by the public interest served by a patent system; the public interest underlies and remains prior to the inventor's interest: it does not require, and indeed does not permit, the inventor to exercise rights going beyond those strictly related to the protection of the invention against appropriation.[3] This chapter will show how the limits have been defined.

[1] As will appear below, however, what is legitimate in this way has been closely restricted by antitrust decisions.

[2] Some ancient cases, for example *Pennock* v. *Dialogue* (Supreme Court, 1829), also stressed the 'public interest' inherent in the patent grant.

[3] The arguments for and against the patent system in general lie outside the scope of this study. So too does any comparative study of the United States code as against others—for example, the English patent laws. It should be noted, however, that the American patent system is unique in that it does not involve any compulsory licensing provisions. This, no doubt, is part of the reason for strict antitrust control of the patent grant and, paradoxically, more 'licences of right' are granted in the United States, as a result of antitrust action, than in the United Kingdom, under the patent law.

2. *Price fixing of patented products:* Bement *v.* National Harrow *and*
the General Electric *case. Limitations of the 'G.E. doctrine':*
the Line Material *case;* New Wrinkle; Masonite; Gypsum.
Price stipulations and challenges to the validity of patents

The first question to consider is how far the patent holder may go in
fixing the price at which the patented article is sold by licensees. The
right to exclude others from making and selling the invention enables
the patentee to keep the trade entirely to himself and he is entitled to
charge whatever the market will bear. Large profits, if they can be
made, will be regarded as a legitimate reward for the invention during
the seventeen-year period of his exclusive right.[1]

If the patentee's own capacity to produce the article is insufficient
to meet the demand for it, he will license one or more other manufacturers to produce it. In this event he will naturally wish to ensure that
his licensees do not sell it at a lower price than that which he has
calculated as the right price to yield the optimum return from the
invention. He will, therefore, make it a condition of his licences that
the licensees shall not charge a lower price than he himself proposes to
charge. Is this a price fixing agreement, illegal under the Sherman
Act, or is it a legitimate condition deriving from the rights conferred
on him by the patent?

The answer from the decided cases has been that it is legitimate in a
simple and straightforward case; but there are pitfalls when the situation is complex. Where all that is involved is that 'A', holding a patent
covering a particular article of manufacture, licenses 'B' to make and
sell that article, he may impose a condition that B shall not charge less
for it than a price he specifies.

This rule was tested very early on in the case law and was upheld in
Bement v. *National Harrow Company* (Supreme Court, 1902). Although
in point of fact this case involved a patent-holding company and might
have been regarded as raising more complex issues had it arisen fifty
years later, it was taken as posing the straightforward question of a
price condition. Mr Justice Peckham stated the rule as follows: 'The
owner of a patented article can, of course, charge such price as he may
choose, and the owner of a patent may assign it or sell the right to
manufacture and sell the article patented, upon the condition that the
assignee shall charge a certain amount for such article.'

The rule was again upheld by the Supreme Court in *United States* v.

---

[1] For a patentee to make an agreement with a licensee under which the latter has to pay
royalties after the expiration of the patents concerned is, however, unlawful *per se*, according
to Mr Justice Douglas, speaking for the majority of the Court, in *Brulotte* v. *Thys Co.* (Supreme
Court, 1964). It would appear, however, that careful drafting could normally ensure that the
consideration required for a new patent licence was payable only during the life of the patent.

General Electric Company in 1926, whence it has come to be known as the 'G.E. doctrine'. The General Electric Company held patents on certain essential components of electric lamps and imposed price stipulations in licences granted to the Westinghouse Company and other manufacturers. Mr Justice Taft squarely put and answered the question.

If the patentee . . . licenses the selling of the articles, may he limit the selling by limiting the method of sale and the price? We think he may do so provided the conditions of sale are normally and reasonably adapted to secure pecuniary reward for the patentee's monopoly. One of the valuable elements of the exclusive right of a patentee is to acquire profit by the price at which the article is sold. The higher the price, the greater the profit, unless it is prohibitory. When the patentee licenses another to make and vend and retains the right to continue to make and vend on his own account, the price at which his licensee will sell will necessarily affect the price at which he can sell his own patented goods. It would seem entirely reasonable that he should say to the licensee, 'Yes, you may make and sell articles under my patent but not so as to destroy the profit that I wish to obtain by making them and selling them myself.' He does not thereby sell outright to the licensee the articles the latter may make and sell or vest absolute ownership in them. He restricts the property and interest the licensee had in the goods he makes and proposes to sell.[1]

Some forty years later in 1965, the Court indeed had a direct opportunity to reverse its earlier decision, in the case of *United States* v. *Huck Manufacturing Company*. Huck owned certain patents essential to the manufacture of lock bolts, which are devices for fastening pieces of metal together, of particular use in the construction of aircraft. Huck licensed another company called Townsend to produce these lock bolts on condition that Townsend did not sell them at less than Huck's own current list prices. The Department of Justice brought a civil action, claiming a conspiracy to restrain trade under the Sherman Act, against both Huck and Townsend, but it was dismissed by the District Court of the Eastern District of Michigan on the grounds *inter alia* that the price restriction in the licence was legal under the *General Electric* doctrine. The Supreme Court, however, split evenly, four against four, largely on a technicality, and therefore, as is customary in such cases, the decision of the lower Court was confirmed without a written opinion from the Supreme Court.[2]

In any case, however, since 1926 the development of the law on this subject is a story of a continual refining—some would say whittling

[1] It was held at the same time that the patent holder was not entitled to control the resale price of patented goods once they had been sold outright to a distributor.
[2] The Department of Justice has, however, announced that it intends to seek to have the 'G.E. doctrine' reversed in an appropriate case.

away—of this doctrine to its bare essentials. The facts may be modified in a number of ways so as to render the straightforward 'G.E. doctrine' inapplicable. In the first place a price stipulation may be made in a patent licence only when the patent covers the actual article manufactured by the licensee, and not merely some part of the product or of an otherwise unpatented assembly. It is not permissible, for example, to license the use of a patented machine and include a condition that unpatented articles made with the machine shall be sold at a price specified by the patentee.[1] This is so even though the machine has no other purpose than to make an improved type of product and though the patentee's main business is manufacturing the product rather than selling or hiring machines. The patent holder may charge what royalty he pleases for the use of the machine but may not protect his trade in the manufactured article directly unless it too is patented.[2]

Judge Knox ruled on this point in *United States* v. *General Electric Company* (Southern District Court of New York, 1948)—the *Carboloy* case—in the following words: 'There can be no justification for fixing the price of an unpatented product. A patentee may not employ his patent to restrain trade beyond the scope of his grant. . . . "The necessities or convenience of the patentee do not justify any use of the monopoly of the patent to create another monopoly." Permissible price control cannot be protected by price control on an unpatented item.' In this case General Electric's subsidiary, Carboloy, had patents for various hard-metal compositions used in the manufacture of tools and dies. The company claimed that it would be unable to maintain the price of the patented carbide component unless it could fix the price for the finished products; but, since most of the finished products were unpatented, this defence failed.

Another way in which the situation may be modified so that the 'G.E. doctrine' no longer applies is through the need to use more than one patented invention in making a product. The complex products of modern industry often require the combining of a number of patented components and techniques. A certain manufacturer may invent a product which temporarily leads the field, and others for a time will make it under licence. But firms compete in technical skills as well as in other ways and one or other of the licensees may soon discover improvements to the original invention. When an improvement patent

---

[1] See *Cummer Graham Company* v. *Straight Side Basket Corporation* (Fifth Circuit Court of Appeals, 1944). It is even doubtful whether the holder of a process patent may lawfully prescribe the price to be charged by a licensee for goods made by the patented process. Different sets of facts have led to different rulings by different courts and the Supreme Court has not decided the question. But in general the recent trend has been to restrict the patent right as closely as possible to what is covered by the patent claim.

[2] This is essentially a rule of patent law rather than of antitrust law: see below, p. 325.

is taken out, neither the original manufacturer nor the inventor of the improvement can get along without regard to the other's interests. The original manufacturer is in a position to prevent the improved article from being made because he may withdraw licences under the basic patent. On the other hand, he cannot himself adopt the improvement without obtaining a licence in turn from its inventor.

This very common situation leads to what is known as cross-licensing. Manufacturer A continues to license the basic patent and manufacturer B licenses A to use the improvement; both of them produce the improved article. Sometimes there is cross-licensing between a large number of firms in an industry and what is known as a patent pool may be formed, with all the manufacturers contributing their inventions to the pool and drawing royalties or paying royalties according to the importance of their contributions. Sometimes it may be open to doubt whether a particular technique is an independent development or infringes earlier patents, and pooling or cross-licensing may be adopted to avoid expensive litigation.

May the holders of cross-licensed patents include price fixing conditions in licences granted to each other or in licences to third parties? Evidently this question presents a difficult choice between the rights of patent holders and the general aims of antitrust policy. On the one hand it seems reasonable that the holder of an improvement patent should be as much entitled as any other patentee to secure the optimum return from his invention by maintaining the price level of the product. Nor is there any obvious reason why the holder of a basic patent should lose his entitlement in this respect, well before the end of the seventeen-year period of the patent grant, just because some other inventor discovers an improvement. By cross-licensing the basic and improvement patents, they are not, after all, acting restrictively but are, on the contrary, ensuring that the full development of the art is available to the public.[1]

On the other hand, if all the leading firms in an industry pool their patented inventions and if all are entitled to take advantage of the 'G.E. doctrine' to enforce minimum prices on their licensees, price competition may be suppressed throughout the industry. Since it is often difficult to be sure whether different patents are 'in interference' (that is, not able to be practised without mutual infringement) or are independent, competing techniques, firms might pool competing methods, for which cross-licensing was not really necessary, in order to show ostensible justification for price fixing.

[1] The case for allowing price stipulations to be made in these circumstances may be found fully deployed in Mr Justice Burton's dissent in *United States* v. *Line Material Company* (Supreme Court, 1948).

How do the courts draw the line between respecting the claims of patent holders and avoiding evasion of the Sherman Act? They have in practice drawn it strongly in favour of antitrust policy and against the patent right. Broadly speaking, they prohibit price stipulations in patent licences whenever patents of different ownership are combined in the manufacture of goods.

The decisive step in this direction was taken in *United States* v. *Line Material Company* (Supreme Court, 1948). The Line Material Company and the Southern States Equipment Corporation were both interested in the manufacture of devices, known as 'drop-out fuse cut-outs', to prevent electric circuits from overloading. The Southern States company owned a basic patent but the article made under it was not commercially satisfactory; Line Material owned a later patent covering an improved version of the basic invention. Since the Line Material patent was subservient to the basic one, neither company could use the advantages of both without some cross-licensing arrangement. 'Only when both patents could be lawfully used by a single maker could the public or the patentees obtain the full benefit of the efficiency and economy of the inventions.'

The two companies proceeded to make a cross-licensing agreement whereby Line Material granted Southern a non-exclusive royalty-free licence under its patent in return for a licence under the Southern patent and the exclusive right to issue sub-licences under that patent. Line Material prescribed that the prices of products made by Southern under the improvement patent should be 'not more favourable to the customer than those established from time to time and followed by the Line Company in making its sales'. Line Material then licensed ten other manufacturers to make the product (sub-licensing at the same time under the Southern patent) and included similar price conditions in these licences.[1] It is worth noting that the product made under these patents had to meet competition with other devices of the same type; it was estimated that they accounted for only 40% of all the cut-outs sold by the manufacturers.

The trial Court considered that these arrangements were legitimately within the saving power of the 'G.E. doctrine'. The Supreme Court, by a five to three majority, took a different view. Mr Justice Reed stressed the primacy of price competition as the object of antitrust policy and the importance of limiting any exception to the rule.[2] Thus

---

[1] The record suggested some degree of collusion among the licensees to espouse the price fixing arrangements, and this may well have been influential with the Court.

[2] Mr Justice Reed's argument on this point is one of the classic statements of the modern antitrust philosophy: 'Whatever may be the evil social effect of cut-throat competition on producers and consumers through the lowering of labor standards and the quality of the produce and the obliteration of the marginal to the benefit of the surviving and low-cost

'the monopoly granted by the patent laws is a statutory exception to this freedom for competition and consistently has been construed as limited to the patent grant'. Mr Justice Reed ruled that the *Line Material* situation differed from that in the *General Electric* case in that price fixing between separate patent owners had a greater effect on competition and was neither expressly nor implicitly authorized by the patent grant.

While the General Electric case holds that a patentee may, under certain conditions, lawfully control the price the licensee of his several patents may charge for the patented device, no case of this Court has construed the patent and anti-monopoly statutes to permit separate owners of separate patents by cross-licences or other arrangements to fix the prices to be charged by them and their licensees for their respective products. Where two or more patentees with competitive, non-infringing patents combine them and fix prices on all devices produced under any of the patents, competition is impeded to a greater degree than where a single patentee fixes prices for his licensees. . . . Even when, as here, the devices are not commercially competitive because the subservient patent cannot be practised without consent of the dominant, the statement holds good. The stimulus to seek competitive inventions is reduced by the mutually advantageous price fixing arrangement. . . . The merging of the benefits of price fixing under the patents restrains trade in violation of the Sherman Act in the same way as would the fixing of prices between producers of non-patentable goods.

Thus the rule of the *Line Material* case is that patent holders competing in the same field must not make any price agreement, even where it is a matter of technological necessity for them to be licensed under each other's patents.

A variant of the *Line Material* situation was found to be equally unlawful in *United States* v. *New Wrinkle* (Supreme Court, 1952). In this case two companies had each developed a product which, when mixed with paints, enamels or varnishes, enabled a hard, wrinkled surface finish to be produced. Each company believed that the other's patents were subservient to its own, but rather than fight it out in the courts they agreed in effect to amalgamate their patents. A holding company—New Wrinkle—was formed to hold both sets of patents; the new company then proceeded to license the two parent companies to make the product. In the course of time some two hundred other

producers, the advantages of competition in opening rewards to management, in encouraging initiative, in giving labor in each industry an opportunity to choose employment conditions and consumers a selection of product and price, have been considered to overbalance the disadvantages. . . . Despite possible advantages to a stable economy from efficient cartels with firm or fixed prices for products, it is crystal clear from the legislative history and accepted judicial interpretations of the Sherman Act that competition in prices is the rule of congressional purpose and that where exceptions are made, Congress should make them.'

manufacturers were licensed to make it and all the licences contained a minimum-price stipulation.

It was contended that New Wrinkle, like any other company holding the patents for a product, should be entitled to secure the best return it could for the inventions, especially as it was not itself a manufacturer and had no other source of revenue than its royalties. But the Supreme Court looked to the substance rather than the form of the arrangement and condemned it. Mr Justice Reed said: 'We see no material difference between the situation in Line Material . . . and the case presented by the allegation of this complaint. An arrangement was made between patent holders to pool their patents and fix prices on the product for themselves and their licensees. The purpose and the result plainly violated the Sherman Act.'[1]

One of the points made by Mr Justice Reed in the *Line Material* case was that multiple licensing under combined patents was persuasive evidence of an intent to restrain trade. Where the courts find that the purpose of licensing arrangements is not so much to secure a legitimate reward for the invention as to suppress competition in an industry, the patent right is no defence against antitrust charges.

The importance of findings as to intent and purpose in this field is illustrated by *United States* v. *Masonite Corporation* (Supreme Court, 1942). In this case a number of firms manufacturing and distributing synthetic hardboard were charged with conspiracy in restraint of trade. Masonite was a manufacturer of hardboard and held a number of patents covering the product and the processes for making it. Another manufacturer, Celotex, also held hardboard patents but was successfully sued by Masonite for infringing the latter's patents. Negotiations followed and Masonite entered into agreements, first with Celotex and subsequently in identical terms with a number of other firms in the industry. Under these agreements Masonite became in practice the sole manufacturer of the product; the other firms, though some still held competing patents, acknowledged the validity of Masonite's basic patents and were appointed Masonite's agents to distribute the product. Masonite fixed the prices and other conditions of sale; the various agents simply took orders in their areas for the product, which was then made by Masonite to the required specification and shipped direct to

---

[1] Further ramifications of this line of cases may be studied in *Westinghouse Electric Corporation* v. *Bulldog Electric Products Company* (Fourth Circuit Court of Appeals, 1950). After the *Line Material* decision was announced, a manufacturer waived the price stipulations it had included in licences it had issued, in much the same way as Line Material, for a combination of its own and other patents. It continued, however, to include price conditions in licences issued wholly under its own patents and was held to be entitled to do so. Judge Parker also ruled in this case that the mere fact that a number of licensees rather than a single licensee were subject to a minimum-price stipulation did not make the 'G.E. doctrine' inapplicable, so long as the price stipulation was within the entitlement of the patent grant.

the customer. The agents were compensated by payment of a commission. Each firm entering into an agreement with Masonite on these lines was said to know, when it signed, that identical agreements were being made between Masonite and the other firms in the industry.

It was contended that Masonite, having by litigation established its position as the holder of dominant patents, was fully entitled to retain the manufacture of the product in its own hands, to make its licences to manufacture (if any) subject to a price stipulation, and to sell the product through agents at whatever price it chose. Mr Justice Douglas, however, did not accept this version of the facts. Pointing out that only the Celotex patents had been found by the courts to infringe Masonite's patents, he held that the arrangements reflected not 'an honest and sincere intent to recognize and exercise the rights belonging to Masonite under its patents' but a clear purpose among competitors to fix prices.

The fact that under the agreements the other firms concerned formally became *del credere* agents of Masonite, merely distributing the product on behalf of the principal, was not allowed to alter the conclusion.

. . . This Court has quite consistently refused to allow the form into which the parties chose to cast the transaction to govern. . . .

. . . when it is clear, as it is in this case, that the marketing systems utilized by means of the *del credere* agency agreements are those of competitors of the patentee and that the purpose is to fix prices at which the competitors may market the product, the device is more an enlargement of the limited patent privilege and a violation of the Sherman Act. . . . So far as the Sherman Act is concerned the result must turn not on the skill with which counsel has manipulated the concepts of sale and 'agency' but on the significance of the business practices in terms of restraint of trade.[1]

This case turned, therefore, on the Supreme Court's finding of fact that the real purpose of the parties was a price fixing conspiracy[2] and not one of accommodating the legitimate rights of a patentee. It did not involve the combination of patents of different ownership but the voluntary abrogation by Masonite's competitors of their patents, partly no doubt in face of Masonite's successful litigation against Celotex, but

[1] It had been found lawful in the 1926 case for the General Electric Company to maintain the prices of electric lamps in the shops by adopting the expedient of appointing the retailers as their agents instead of selling the lamps to them in the usual way. See above, Chapter X p. 281. Mr Justice Douglas was here ruling that this device for maintaining prices would not be accepted where the 'agents' were previously manufacturing competitors of the principal and still his potential competitors.

[2] *United States* v. *Masonite* is also a leading case in the law of conspiracy, for it was held that though the various agreements were made at different times, and though Masonite alone fixed the prices without consultation, each of the parties was 'aware of the fact that its contract was not an isolated transaction but part of a larger arrangement'. There was, therefore, a true understanding or 'meeting of the minds'. This was an extension of the rule laid down in the *Interstate Circuit* case; see above, Chapter III, pp. 83–4.

also, as the Supreme Court held, because of their 'preference for a mutual arrangement for price fixing.'

A similar conclusion was reached in *United States* v. *United States Gypsum Company* (Supreme Court, 1948), which dealt with plasterboard and other products made from gypsum. United States Gypsum had long been the leading firm in the industry and had developed or purchased many patents covering the manufacture of gypsum board. The case dealt with a situation in which all the other principal manufacturers were, by 1937, making the product under licence from United States Gypsum, which fixed prices and terms of sale for the whole industry.

The Government introduced a great deal of evidence, the main lines of which were accepted by the Supreme Court, to show that the process by which this position had been built up was not a straightforward matter of a patentee's issuing licences to others to make and sell the product—on the model required by the 'G.E. doctrine'—but a conscious and concerted plan to bring the industry under a centralized control.[1] As in the *Masonite* case, United States Gypsum had succeeded in some cases of dispute in establishing the primacy of its patents by litigation, but neither the validity of its patents nor the subservience of various competing patents was fought out in the courts in every case. It appeared that the other manufacturers were often prepared to abrogate their claims and accept licences from United States Gypsum in the interests of price stability. Their main concern, which led some of them to stand out for varying lengths of time, was that United States Gypsum's agreements should be industry-wide; they feared that if important manufacturers could remain unlicensed outside the chain of agreements, they themselves would lose business to lower-priced products. There was evidence of meetings and discussions among the firms concerned about this and other problems. However, by 1929 all but two manufacturers were licensed in identical terms under United States Gypsum's patents;[2] by 1937 the chain was complete.

The Government also charged that the licence agreements contained provisions and understandings going beyond the proper exercise of the

---

[1] As in the *Interstate Circuit* and *Masonite* cases, it was held that a number of separate agreements could establish a common understanding. As Mr Justice Reed put it: 'One of the things those two cases establish is the principle that, when a group of competitors enters into a series of separate but similar agreements with competitors or others, a strong inference arises that such agreements are the result of concerted action. That inference is strengthened when contemporaneous declarations indicate that supposedly separate actions are part of a common plan.'

[2] Among the patents licensed in the 1929 agreements was one which one of the outside firms assigned to United States Gypsum as part of the settlement. To this extent the case involved combining patents of different ownership—another variant of the *Line Material* and *New Wrinkle* situation.

patent rights. Thus 'each licensee agreed to pay as royalty a stipulated percentage on the selling of "all plasterboard and gypsum wallboard of every kind" whether or not made by patented processes or embodying product claims'. It was held that this provision was 'strongly indicative of an agreement not to manufacture unpatented board, and the testimony of the witnesses [was] ample to show that there was an understanding, if not a formal agreement, that only patented board would be sold. Such an arrangement in purpose and effect increased the area of the patent monopoly and is invalid.'

Moreover, prices and terms of sale of patented board were said to be prescribed 'in minute detail' and many regulations to ensure price equality at all destinations under a basing-point system were promulgated by periodic issues of a bulletin and enforced by a specially organized subsidiary of United States Gypsum.[1] Later United States Gypsum ordered that the jobbers' discount should be discontinued and it was said that this effectively eliminated a whole class of distributors. All rebates and allowances to customers were forbidden, even including concessions made on other material sold with the patented board. All in all, Mr Justice Reed concluded that:

These licences and bulletins show plainly a conspiracy to violate the Sherman Act. . . . Patents grant no privilege to their owners of organizing the use of those patents to monopolize an industry through price control, through royalties for the patents drawn from patent-free industry products and through regulation of distribution. Here patents have been put to such uses as to collide with the Sherman Act's protection of the public from evil consequences. . . .

The General Electric case . . . gives no support for a patentee acting in concert with all members of an industry, to issue substantially identical licences to all members of the industry under the terms of which the industry is completely regimented, the production of competitive unpatented products suppressed, a class of distributors squeezed out, and prices on unpatented products stabilized.

The two lines of cases illustrated respectively by (a) the *Line Material* and *New Wrinkle* and (b) the *Masonite* and *Gypsum* actions show the main ways in which the courts have checked the possible use of patent rights, under cover of the 'G.E. doctrine', to evade the Sherman Act. As in other branches of antitrust, it will be evident that very delicate borderline questions of fact may arise when differing situations have to be

---

[1] Among other things Mr Justice Reed found that 'specified board sizes and minimum quantities were prescribed, licensees were forbidden to employ commission salesmen without the written consent of the licensor, regulations were prescribed as to the size, quantity and markings of gypsum board used for packing shipments, granting of long-term credit was prohibited, sales on consignment were enjoined and licensees were forbidden to deliver board directly to a building site'.

brought under the rules laid down in these cases. In particular the old question of the price filing cases (see above, Chapter I)—namely, what is satisfactory evidence of an agreement or understanding—may be raised in subtle forms.

In the *Gypsum* case the evidence of a 'planned common course of action' on the part of the firms in the industry to eliminate price competition was strong enough in the event to carry real conviction with the Supreme Court. (The *Gypsum* decision was unanimous.) It is easy to see that very similar facts might reflect genuinely independent conduct by different firms and the borderline could be difficult to draw.

This may be appreciated by putting oneself in the place of a medium-sized manufacturer competing in an industry in which the leading firm has an apparently strong patent position. This firm offers manufacturing licences subject to the licensee's following its prices. Meanwhile, however, there are other firms in the industry with their own patents producing a similar product, perhaps more cheaply than the leader. In this situation one may get to know that the leader regards these other firms as infringing its basic patents and intends to start legal action against them. But one does not know how the litigation will turn out: perhaps the leader's patents are not after all valid. If the leader's patent position is sound, it will no doubt be right to accept a licence on his terms; but if not, it will be commercially unwise to accept his price stipulation because the others may continue to produce a competitive, unlicensed product at a lower price.

In this nasty dilemma it is not unnatural that the manufacturer may go to the leader and say in effect: 'I want to manufacture this product under licence: but I should be much happier about it if I knew that your patents would stand up and that competitors at present unlicensed would in the end have to take licences and abide by your prices.' It is not unnatural that he should confer with others in the same position and see what they think of the prospects. These actions may reflect no more than his own anxieties in a tough problem. Yet when his letter to the leading firm is subsequently found by the Department of Justice in the files and the note of his meeting with other unlicensed firms is produced in court, the effect may be like that of the not so very dissimilar evidence in the *Gypsum* case in the Supreme Court.[1] It may look as if the real object of the firms in the industry is to promote

---

[1] This is not to say that the record in the *Gypsum* case contained no more than the type of predicament set out here. It was evidently persuasive of an industry-wide desire for price fixing under a patent umbrella. A purely unilateral approach to the licensor on the lines suggested might not of itself attract antitrust action. But it is also a good rule to bear in mind that conditions in a patent licence should be for the protection of the patentee, not the licensee.

industry-wide price fixing rather than simply to escape from their own separate dilemmas without expensive patent litigation.

The law as it stands leaves this borderline to be drawn by the good judgment of the courts. In the last few years it has appeared that the courts will tend to give the benefit of any doubt to the public interest in maintaining competition. Thus all transactions in which patent licences are accepted with price stipulations have to be looked at with the greatest care, particularly when it is evident that a large number of firms in the industry are tying themselves by similar agreements to the prices of a major firm.[1]

As a footnote to this section it must be mentioned that there is a further legal hazard in the path of the patent holder who wishes to benefit by the 'G.E. doctrine' and impose a price condition on his licensees. This is the Supreme Court's ruling that, where a price stipulation is included in a patent licence, the licensee is no longer barred (as he normally used to be under patent law) from subsequently challenging the validity of the patent (*Sola Electric Company* v. *Jefferson Electric Company*, Supreme Court, 1942). This rule applies even when the licensee has specifically covenanted not to challenge the validity of the patent and has suggested the price fixing condition himself (*Edward Katzinger Company* v. *Chicago Metallic Manufacturing Company*, Supreme Court, 1947). It applies even though the price stipulation has not been enforced (*MacGregor* v. *Westinghouse Electric and Manufacturing Company*, Supreme Court, 1947). The reason for the rule is that a price stipulation may be founded only on a valid patent; its effect is to place a substantial additional burden on the patentee in prosecuting infringement suits when his licences contain such a stipulation.[2]

3. *Exclusionary and market sharing agreements based on patents:*
National Harrow v. Hench; *the* Standard Sanitary *case
and other early cases;* National Lead; Standard Oil of Indiana

The preceding section may be seen as extending the chapter on price fixing (above, Chapter I) to cover cases involving patent rights. Chapter II, on exclusionary and market sharing agreements, may be similarly extended by applying much the same rules. The individual patentee may legitimately exclude others from making his patented product, or he may share the market by granting another manufacturer an exclusive licence to make and sell it in a given area while he retains

---

[1] It is widely held that as a result of these cases major companies now find the legal risks of attaching price fixing conditions to patent licences to be too great for the benefits received.

[2] The Supreme Court subsequently held that, in general, a licensee under a patent is not estopped from challenging its validity—*Lear Inc.* v. *Adkins* (Supreme Court, 1969).

other areas for himself: so much is inherent in the patent right. But when competing firms combine patents by cross-licensing or pooling, exclusionary or market sharing arrangements will no longer be saved by the patent rights from the prohibition of the Sherman Act. Similarly, on the analogy of the *Masonite* and *Gypsum* cases, evidence that the primary purpose of firms in an industry is to suppress competition rather than merely to accommodate the legitimate rights of patentees will bring them up against the Act.

Some of the basic rules were established in early cases. Thus, in *National Harrow Company* v. *Hench* (Third Circuit Court of Appeals, 1897) it was said: 'The fact that one patentee may possess himself of several patents, and thus increase his monopoly, affords no support for an argument in favor of a combination by several distinct owners of such property to restrain manufacture, control sales and enhance prices. . . . Patentees may compose their differences, as other owners of property may, but they cannot make the occasion an excuse or cloak for the creation of monopolies to the public disadvantage.' Similarly, in *Blount Manufacturing Company* v. *Yale and Towne Manufacturing Company* (District Court of Massachusetts, 1909), in which competing patent owners agreed to confine their trade to their own inventions, to limit improvements, maintain prices and pool profits, it was said: 'A contract whereby the manufacturers of two independent patented inventions agree not to compete in the same commercial field deprives the public of the benefits of competition and creates a restraint of trade which results, not from the granting of letters patent, but from agreement. . . . There is no inconsistency between the proposition that an inventor may withhold his invention from use as he sees fit, and the proposition that he may not make an agreement whereby, for the advantage of a competitor, trade in his potential product is restrained or suppressed.' Thus the patentee may grant an exclusive licence for a given area and respect the licensee's exclusive right by staying out of that area himself, but he may not undertake to refrain from competition in trade not covered by the patent.

Standard Sanitary Manufacturing Company v. *United States* (Supreme Court, 1912), as already mentioned above (Chapter II), made it clear that collective exclusive-dealing arrangements between groups of manufacturers and jobbers were not saved from the Sherman Act by the fact that the products concerned were patented. For, as Mr Justice McKenna put it: 'The agreements clearly . . . transcended what was necessary to protect the use of the patent or the monopoly which the law conferred upon it. They passed to the purpose and accomplished a restraint of trade condemned by the Sherman law.'

More recent cases suggest that any substantial aggregation of patents in a pool, or even by cross-licensing between two leading firms, will be regarded as a 'bottleneck' facility, which, on the analogy of the *Associated Press* case (above, Chapter II), should be made available on reasonable terms to new entrants. Thus, in *United States* v. *National Lead Company* (Supreme Court, 1947), which dealt with the dominant place secured by the National Lead Company and the du Pont company in the titanium pigments industry through, *inter alia*, exclusive cross-licensing of their patents, Mr Justice Burton spoke of the 'proliferation of patents' in the hands of the two companies as 'increasing the difficulty of an attack upon them' and quoted the trial Court's view that 'this exchange between two corporations, who between them controlled the entire market, becomes an instrument of restraint'. Those administering any form of patent pool in the United States at present are normally advised by their lawyers not to withhold a licence on reasonable terms for any of the patents from any responsible applicant.

Other cases have set strict limits to what is permissible in the way of dividing or allocating markets in agreements for cross-licensing patents. The cases which best illustrate this topic, however, concern international cartel agreements and will be considered in the next chapter.

It is important to understand that in all these cases, as in the price fixing cases of the *Line Material* type, it is not the cross-licensing or pooling of patents as such that runs foul of the law. The antitrust offence normally arises from the use made of the pooling or cross-licensing agreement as a vehicle for exclusionary, market sharing, price fixing or other restrictive arrangements that go beyond the entitlement of the patent grant.[1] It is conceded that cross-licensing may be technically necessary and may in itself promote rather than hinder competition.

Some important distinctions on this topic were made by Mr Justice Brandeis in *Standard Oil Company (Indiana)* v. *United States* (Supreme Court, 1931). The case dealt with arrangements made by the holders of patents covering cracking processes for producing petrol. The danger of prolonged litigation about rival patent claims had led the four holders of patents in this field to pool them and divide royalties by agreement.[2] The arrangements did not prevent each patentee from

---

[1] Where the offence charged is monopolization, the sheer aggregation of patents, as distinct from the use made of them, may be important: this aspect of the matter is the subject of the next section.

[2] 'Each primary defendant was released . . . from liability for any past infringement of patents of the others. Each acquired the right to use these patents thereafter in its own process. Each was empowered to extend to independent concerns, licensed under its process, releases from past and immunity from future claims of infringement of patents controlled by the [others]. . . . And each was to share in some fixed proportion the fees received under these multiple licences.'

issuing whatever licences it liked under its own patents and it was found that none of the licences issued imposed any price stipulation or territorial or other restriction.

Mr Justice Brandeis held that the arrangements were justified by the rule of reason: 'An interchange of patent rights and a division of royalties according to the value attributed by the parties to their respective patent claims is frequently necessary if technical advancement is not to be blocked by threatened litigation. If the available advantages are open on reasonable terms to all manufacturers desiring to participate, such interchange may promote rather than restrain competition.'

No evidence was found that the royalties charged were oppressive, nor was it shown that the four patentees effectively dominated the trade in 'cracked' petrol. They and their licensees controlled some 55% of cracking capacity, but there were more than twenty other competing processes; and 'cracked' petrol in any case accounted for only a quarter of the total supply of petrol. Mr Justice Brandeis concluded, therefore, that 'no monopoly of any kind, or restraint of interstate commerce has been effected either by means of the contracts or in some other way'. In the absence of restrictive effects or purposes the patent pooling was legitimate.[1]

4. *Patents and monopolization: the* Hartford-Empire *case;* Besser; Kobe *v.* Dempsey; *the* Hughes Tool *cases*

It will be noted that Mr Justice Brandeis attached importance to the degree of dominance over the industry of the firms which operated the patent pool. Indeed, he said: 'If combining patent owners effectively dominate an industry, the power to fix and maintain royalties is tantamount to the power to fix prices. . . . Where domination exists, a pooling of competing process patents, or an exchange of licences for the purpose of curtailing the manufacture and supply of an unpatented product is beyond the privileges conferred by the patents and constitutes a violation of the Sherman Act. The lawful individual monopolies granted by the patent statutes cannot be unitedly exercised to restrain competition.'

Where large patent holdings are brought under a single control, those responsible may come up against section 2 of the Sherman Act and have to face charges of monopolizing or conspiring to monopolize

---

[1] For a later example of a case where, by contrast, the dominant motive of the parties was held to be exclusionary, see *United States* v. *Singer Manufacturing Company* (Supreme Court, 1963), where the primary motive of Singer in purchasing certain patent rights from European competitors was held to be its desire to be in a strong position to exclude Japanese imports from the United States.

their industry.[1] When a firm or group obtains dominant power by aggregating patents, it may be held to display that purposive drive to get and keep a monopoly position, which, as was shown above (Chapter IV), is the hallmark of the offence of monopolizing. Or the inevitable result of the acquisition and deployment of a great number of patents may be to exclude others from the industry, and it may then be held that this result sufficiently indicates a monopolistic purpose, since 'he who wills the means, wills the end'. The aggregation of competing patents may be seen as analogous in this respect to the financial merger of competing companies, which has long been known as an illegal method of building a position of power. Clearly the monopoly position achieved by the aggregation of formerly competing patents—by purchase or by exclusive cross-licensing with another leading firm— is different in kind from the limited monopoly power bestowed on the inventor himself by the patent grant.

Antitrust's treatment of monopolizing by means of patents may be illustrated by *United States* v. *Hartford-Empire Company* (Supreme Court, 1945). This case dealt with the manufacture of various types of glassware, chiefly bottles and other containers. The situation arose out of the technical advances by which glass blowing became an automatic process. The general charge brought by the Government was that competing glass manufacturers had gradually brought their patents for glassmaking machinery together in a pool under the control of the Hartford-Empire Company, and had used the combined strength of the patents to exclude new entrants from the industry and to control the supply and price of glassware which was not itself a patented product. The Court's findings of fact sustained the charge and showed many instances of the acquisition of patents for purposes of control and of exclusionary licensing policies.[2]

The situation was summarized by Mr Justice Roberts in the Supreme Court as follows:

In summary, the situation brought about in the glass industry, and existing in 1938 was: Hartford, with the technical and financial aid of others in the

---

[1] As Kaysen and Turner point out, 'a large number of patents tend to turn into something larger than the sum of its parts' (*Antitrust Policy*, p. 165). They also draw attention to the interaction of market power and patent practices. Where a company already has a degree of dominance in a market and no comparable rivals, and entry barriers are high, the effect on competition of the accumulation of patents and cross-licensing agreements is at its most serious. On the other hand it is precisely in these situations that the patent as an incentive to invention is least necessary. This is an argument in favour of the concept which Kaysen and Turner advance as a central theme of their book, that the possession of 'unreasonable market power' should itself constitute a civil (not criminal) violation of the antitrust laws.

[2] The complicated story of the negotiations and agreements by which the dominating position was built up may be read in the section of Mr Justice Roberts' opinion devoted to findings of fact: 324 U.S. 570 (1945).

conspiracy, had acquired more than 600 patents. These, with over 100 Corning patents, sixty Owens patents, over seventy Hazel patents and some twelve Lynch patents, had been merged by cross-licensing agreements into a pool which effectively controlled the industry. Production in Corning's field was allocated to Corning, the general container field was allocated to Owens, Hazel, Thatcher, Ball and smaller manufacturers the group agreed should be licensed. The result was that 94% of the glass containers manufactured in this country on feeders and formers were made on machinery licensed under the pooled patents.

The District Court found that invention of glassmaking machinery had been discouraged, that competition in the manufacture and sale or licensing of such machinery had been suppressed, and that the system of restricted licensing had been employed to suppress competition in the manufacture of unpatented glassware and to maintain prices of the manufactured product. The findings are full and adequate and are supported by evidence, much of it contemporary writings of corporate defendants or their officers and agents.

These findings were enough to condemn the defendants on familiar legal grounds under both sections of the Sherman Act. Thus, as in non-patent monopolization cases, the necessary purposive drive that marks an offence under section 2 of the Act may be shown either in the way a position of power is built up (for example, by the purposeful accumulation of patents), or in the way it is exerted. Even where the power is obtained legitimately, as when it arises solely from patents granted for the monopolist's own inventions, the misuse of the patent privilege (for example, to fix prices on unpatented products or enforce other restrictions beyond the protection of the patent grant) may constitute monopolizing.[1] It has also been held in *Walker Process Equipment Inc.* v. *Food Machinery and Chemical Corporation* (Supreme Court, 1965) that the mere enforcement of a patent procured by fraud on the Patent Office would be sufficient grounds for an action under section 2 by the Government or a private party, assuming that all the other elements necessary to establish a section 2 charge were there. It had previously been thought that fraud on the Patent Office could only be alleged as defence to a charge of infringement, but the Supreme Court's ruling means that it can be used as the basis for an affirmative action, or the Government can sue to revoke a fraudulently obtained patent.

Some of the cases deal specifically with the use made of power derived from patent holdings rather than with the build-up of that

---

[1] Detailed analyses of the way in which monopoly power founded on patents may violate section 2 of the Sherman Act may be found in Judge Knox's opinion in *United States* v. *General Electric Company*, 1948 (the *Carboloy* case), 80 Fed. Supp. 989, and in Judge Forman's opinion in *United States* v. *General Electric Company*, 1948 (the *Lamps* case), 82 Fed. Supp. 753.

power.[1] An interesting example is *United States* v. *Besser Manufacturing Company* (Supreme Court, 1952).

The Besser Company is a manufacturer of machines for making concrete blocks. A new type of machinery, patented in 1939, made possible a fully automatic, block making process of great commercial advantage. The two inventors of the machines had licensed a firm named Stearns exclusively under their patents. In 1942 an agreement was reached between the Besser and Stearns companies and the two inventors, whereby both companies obtained exclusive rights to practise the patents and to all future improvements made by the inventors. It was also agreed that the inventors should not issue any other licences without the written consent of both Besser and Stearns, and that all four parties should decide unanimously what infringement suits should be fought. Subsequently Besser secretly purchased a large amount of the stock in the Stearns company and put its own men on the board.

Acting in concert under the 1942 agreement, the parties refused to license other firms and threatened to start infringement suits against any who entered the field. The Government successfully contended that much of this action was directed to 'harassing' competition in order to maintain the monopoly rather than to the legitimate protection of the patents. Evidence was given that under these threats a number of other firms went out of the industry and made over their own patents to Besser. As the trial Court put it, '. . . all felt the persuasion of the Besser arguments. . . . Practically all these men got out of their own business, generally impelled by threats of law suits, being given a job, pressure on customers, or all three, and usually Besser then picked up their patents with a mortgage on the fruits of their genius for years to come.'

This case appears to stand for the rule that it will be regarded as a boycott, and thus as illegal *per se* under the Sherman Act, for patent owners and exclusive licensees to act together to maintain their dominant position by enforcing the patents and refusing further licences. 'It is this combination requiring collective action that primarily invalidates the agreement. We believe it clear that the parties intended this contract to be a means whereby control of the industry could be acquired and competition eliminated.'

Rather similar issues arose in *Kobe* v. *Dempsey Pump Company* (Tenth Circuit Court of Appeals, 1952). This case concerned the manufacture of hydraulic pumps for oil wells. A predecessor of the Kobe Company —'Old Kobe'—was among the first in the field to see the need for an efficient hydraulic pump in the oil industry. Various inventors were experimenting with these pumps without much success. A company

---

[1] These cases may be likened to those in Chapter V above on monopolistic practices as distinct from the full-scale monopolization cases of Chapter IV.

called the Rodless Pump Company had acquired some of the patents arising out of these early experiments. Another inventor, Gage, was having some success and his patents were assigned to a company known as the Alta Vista Hydraulic Company. Old Kobe's own design apparently infringed some of the patents held by Rodless, so Old Kobe and Rodless made a pooling agreement, setting up a patent-holding company, Roko, of which Old Kobe was the sole licensee. Roko later acquired control of the Gage and Alta Vista patents. In this way, in the words of the Court: 'Old Kobe became the sole licensee and manufacturer of hydraulic pumps under the Roko pool, and was free of any threat of competition or patent infringement from any known source after the acquisition of the Gage and Alta Vista patents.' Old Kobe and Roko continued to acquire patents that might affect their business, which so flourished that, by 1948, annual sales were more than $4 million. (In 1944 the Old Kobe Company had been taken over financially by Dresser Industries, and the hydraulic pump part of the business was reorganized as Kobe Inc. but otherwise went on as before.)

Such was the background to the situation that arose in 1947, when an inventor named Dempsey developed a successful pump which aroused great interest at the Tulsa exhibition and threatened to make inroads into Kobe's market. Kobe now served notice that this pump infringed various of its patents (there was evidence that this was done before it had even seen drawings of the pump) and in due course commenced litigation. After filing the action Kobe circularized its most important customers informing them of the impending litigation. It was found that as a result of the suit and the circular the activities of the Dempsey company and its distributor were brought to a standstill.

In defence of the infringement action Dempsey counterclaimed that Kobe had monopolized the industry in violation of the Sherman Act, and sought treble damages. It is of interest that the claim for damages was based on the interruption to Dempsey's business caused by the very act of the patentee in bringing an infringement action. Although one of the Kobe patents was found valid and infringed, it was Kobe's action that failed and Dempsey's that succeeded, damages amounting to half a million dollars being awarded against Kobe.

This result reflected the Court's view that Kobe's course of action had throughout revealed a purposive drive to get and keep a monopoly position.[1] The accumulation of patents under one control, the absence of any licences under the patents, the threat and commencement of an

---

[1] It should be noted that Kobe's hydraulic pump was by no means the only type of pump used in oil drilling, though it was the most suitable for deep wells. As in the *Klearflax Linen Looms* case (see above, Chapter V, pp. 131–2), however, the Court judged whether the case involved monopoly power by the activities of the monopolist rather than by any economic criterion for defining the market for pumps.

infringement action before a technical examination of the Dempsey pump had been made, the implied warning to potential purchasers that use of the new pump might involve infringement—these were some of the facts that led the Court to infer an intent to monopolize. As Judge Pickett put it: 'The facts as hereinbefore detailed are sufficient to support a finding that, although Kobe believed some of its patents were infringed, the real purpose of the infringement action and the incidental activities of Kobe's representatives was to further the existing monopoly and to eliminate Dempsey as a competitor. The infringement action and the related activities, of course, in themselves were not unlawful, and standing alone would not be sufficient to sustain a claim for damages which they may have caused, but when considered with the entire monopolistic scheme which preceded them, we think, as the trial Court did, that they may be considered as having been done to give effect to the unlawful scheme.'

The *Besser* and *Kobe* cases show how stringently the courts have now limited the patent holder's right of protection.[1] The individual patentee may still pursue his legal remedy against infringement. For him it may not be unreasonable to inform customers of pending litigation or take other diligent steps to protect his position. But where competing patents have been accumulated under one firm's control and where these are not freely licensed, the courts may infer a plan to monopolize a segment of commerce; then the very act of enforcing the patents may be seen, as in the *Kobe* case, as a further mark of monopolistic purpose. Or any joint activity between the patentee and exclusive licensees to maintain a privileged position may be seen, as in the *Besser* case, as an illegal boycott.

As in the non-patent monopoly cases, the line between legitimate activities and courses of action that betray an intent to monopolize may be extremely fine. It will be recalled from the end of Chapter IV above, that the existence of monopolistic purpose is ultimately a matter of fact. Just as Judge Hand drew the line somewhere between legitimate competition 'by virtue of superior skill, foresight and industry' and the exclusionary activity of 'progressively embracing each new opportunity as it opened', so, in cases dealing with patent monopolies, the courts must make fine distinctions between activities designed to improve a firm's economic performance and activities aimed at impeding competitors. Indeed, in the patent cases these distinctions are even more subtle, for patents are of their nature exclusionary and a further line has to be drawn between impeding competitors only to the extent inherent in the patent grant and impeding them unnecessarily.

[1] A valuable discussion of these cases will be found in articles by Mr Laurence I. Wood and Mr Marcus A. Hollobaugh in *Lectures on federal antitrust laws: 1953*, Michigan University Law School, 1953.

The equivalent among the patent cases to a 'better mousetrap' issue may be illustrated by *Hughes Tool Company* v. *Ford* (Tenth Circuit Court of Appeals, 1954). The Hughes company had indeed made a 'better rock bit'; rock bits are the key components of rotary drills used in drilling hard rock formations. The efficiency and durability of these bits are important factors in the cost of drilling operations, for the cost of changing the bits may be much more than the cost of the bit itself. The bits, after they have been used, may be retipped so as to prolong their useful life. The production of bits was said to be a highly competitive business and it was common for retipping to be done by firms other than the original manufacturers. Hughes claimed that it found it best to have its bits returned to it for examination and for retipping where practicable. It was contended that Hughes' research staff needed to collect the blunt bits in order to pursue their investigations into the best way of producing a better and more durable tool. Thus from 1942 onwards Hughes adopted the policy of leasing bits (instead of selling them outright) and making it a condition of the lease that the user would surrender them when they had been blunted by use, to be retipped or otherwise used by Hughes.

Ford was one of a number of companies in the business of collecting blunt bits from users and retipping them. Ford in this way got hold of some of Hughes' leased bits; Hughes brought actions against Ford and some other retippers on the ground that the retipping was a reconstruction of Hughes' patented article and, as such, infringed the patent.[1] Ford and the other defendants to these actions made counterclaims, just as Dempsey had done against Kobe, arguing that Hughes' leasing policy was really part of a monopolistic plan to discourage the retipping business and promote sales of new bits, and that Hughes went beyond the entitlement of the patent grant by effectively tying the retipping business to the hire of the bits. The question for the courts was whether Hughes' leases were, as it claimed, an 'honestly industrial' means of competition, designed simply to 'make a better rock bit', or whether, as in the *Kobe* case, the leases and the infringement suits were all part of a course of action that betrayed an intent to monopolize the industry.

How delicate this type of question may be, as the law stands, is shown by the fact that on 1 July 1953 in the Western District of Oklahoma (in *Hughes* v. *Cole*) Judge Vaught found for Hughes, while on 30 June 1953 in the Eastern District of Oklahoma (in *Hughes* v. *Ford*),

---

[1] In patent law a repair to a patented article is not an infringing act, but a reconstruction is. Problems arising from this distinction are fortunately outside the scope of this chapter: all the courts involved in the Hughes litigation seem to have agreed that the retipping was reconstruction. The distinction between repair and reconstruction was also one of the issues before the Supreme Court in the first *Aro* case (pp. 334–5 below).

on precisely similar facts, Judge Wallace held that Hughes had monopolized and not only should be denied relief for infringement but
should pay treble damages to the infringer.[1]

The Circuit Court of Appeals subsequently upheld the judgment in
favour of the Hughes company and reversed that which condemned it.
It accepted evidence that Hughes' leasing practice was devised in the
interests of research towards a better rock bit. It found that the leases
were in no way exclusionary as against other manufacturers of bits.
Unlike Kobe, Hughes had not accumulated for itself the available
patents in the field (since 1935 it had taken out only thirty-eight of
320 patents issued for bits) and had not brought infringement suits
except on patents it had developed itself. In general it had no monopoly
position in the industry except in so far as its lawful rights by virtue
of valid patents gave it the lead in certain types of bits; other companies
were prospering and expanding in other parts of the field. Some evidence that Hughes was accepted as the price leader in the industry was
held not to indicate any illegal understanding. Thus the Hughes
company was held a genuine example of a 'better mousetrap' producer,
entitled to come under the rule that 'the Sherman Act was not directed
against one "who happens by his skill and energy to command a
legitimate monopoly of a business"'.

Since this decision in favour of Hughes comes from the same appeal
Court which condemned Kobe, the two cases may reasonably be seen
as standing on either side of the borderline between legal and illegal
action; and the differences between the facts mark the crucial frontier
points, particularly perhaps the accumulation of all the relevant
patents in the *Kobe* case, the absence in that case of a legitimate alternative explanation for what was done, and the absence in the *Hughes* cases
of infringement suits and threats that could be construed as aiming
merely to 'harass' competitors.

Another 1954 case may similarly mark the safe side of the borderline
which the *Bossor* case transgressed. This is *United States* v. *L. D. Caulk
Company* (District Court of Delaware, 1954), which dealt with an
English invention of an improved dental-impression material. The
American patent was held by a British company which licensed the
Caulk company exclusively under the patent in 1942. Subsequently
Caulk, with the patentee's approval, sub-licensed another firm, Coe.
Caulk and Coe later represented to the patentee that a third firm,
Dental Perfection, though unlicensed, was in fact producing more of
the product than they were. An infringement suit was started against
Dental Perfection and settled in favour of the patentee; then Dental
Perfection also became a sub-licensee of Caulk.

[1] The two cases were in fact tried before Judges Vaught and Wallace sitting together.

Later still both Coe and Dental Perfection complained that yet other firms were infringing the patent without any action being taken, while they were paying substantial royalties. The patentee in its agreement with Caulk had undertaken to prosecute infringement suits 'with reasonable diligence' and there were meetings at which Caulk and the patentee were urged to honour this undertaking. Eventually a test infringement case was successfully brought.

The Government claimed that these facts brought the matter under the rule of the *Besser* case: there was a conspiracy between the patentee and a small number of licensees to enforce the patent by concerted action and maintain their joint monopoly. The trial Court, however, threw out this case. There was, it pointed out, no pooling or joint control of competing patents, nor even, as in the *Besser* case, a contract under which exclusive licensees should have the benefit of all improvements. There was no arrangement under which the existing licensees could jointly determine the patentee's policy with regard to additional licences; Caulk as exclusive licensee had the sole right to sub-license. The concern of the sub-licensees about infringers going scot-free was simply the natural reaction of people paying large sums for something, when they saw others getting it for nothing: it showed no intent to form an illegal boycott. In sum there was no 'combination requiring collective action', which was the crucial matter in the *Besser* case. Judge Rodney summed up the legal position as follows:

I do not find in any actions of the defendants . . . any attempt to mono-polize . . . but only a desire to protect those rights which have been given under [the] patent to the respective parties by the patent laws of the United States or the licences issued pursuant thereto . . .

If, as I believe, the patent laws give to the holder of a valid patent the exclusive rights covered thereby and the further right to grant or not to grant licences for the use thereof by others, then I know of no violation of any law caused by the holder's refusal to grant licences or rights under the patent. This is, of course, based upon the assumption that the option to grant licences or rights is exercised by the holder of the patent or rights and by him alone. He may not, by confederation, combination or conspiracy, unite with others in restraint of trade in connection with his patent.

5. *Patents and violations of the Clayton Act; the distinction between antitrust violation and misuse of patents: some Clayton Act cases*—United Shoe Machinery, *etc.; misuse cases*—Motion Picture Patents v. Universal Film, *the* Carbice *case, etc. The* Mercoid *cases and the doctrine of contributory infringement*

The preceding sections have dealt with patents and the Sherman Act; holders of patents may also violate the Clayton Act, especially the prohibition of tying contracts in section 3 of that Act. A patent may be used as a convenient tying device and it is not uncommon for patentees to insert conditions in licences, particularly for the use of a patented machine or process, bidding the licensee to use, for example, only the patentee's auxiliary machines or other products in the course of practising the patent.

This practice raises two distinct but overlapping legal issues which it is important to keep separate—all the more important because they have not always been clearly distinguished by the courts. In the first place, a tying contract of this kind will be a straightforward violation of section 3 of the Clayton Act if its effect 'may be to substantially lessen competition . . .'. The wording of the section expressly takes in all goods 'whether patented or unpatented'.

Secondly, but as matter of patent law rather than of antitrust law, the courts have held that the inclusion of tying provisions in patent licences may constitute a misuse of patents, in that it lays claim to rights going beyond those legitimately arising from the patent grant. Thus, to tie a licensee, for example, to use an unpatented product in connexion with the operation of a patented machine, is just as improper as to seek to impose a minimum-price condition on an unpatented product made with the machine. The effect of this rule of patent law is that the patentee who includes tying provisions will be denied relief against infringement of the provisions or indeed of the patent itself; for he will come to the court of equity with 'unclean hands' and the court will not hear his complaint. It will be noted that the misuse of patents does not depend, like an offence against the Clayton Act, on whether the improper tying provision may have a substantial effect on competition; since it asserts a right that the courts do not recognize, they will not enforce it even though it has no harmful effect on competition.

Sometimes both these legal issues are raised in the same action. A licensee, for example, may be sued for infringement and may defend the suit on the basis that the conditions infringed constitute a misuse of patents. In some circumstances he may also counterclaim that the patentee is in violation of the Clayton Act and he may ask for treble damages to be awarded. In such a case a clear distinction between the 'misuse' doctrine and the rule of the Clayton Act ought to be preserved. The patentee's suit should fail wherever misuse of the patent is proved, regardless of any effect on competition: but the defendant's counterclaim should succeed only where an offence against the Clayton Act is established and this should involve proof of (actual or potential) injury to competition. The cases outlined in this section will illustrate the two legal issues and show how they intertwine and on occasion become confused.

Some cases are straightforward actions under the Clayton Act. In *United Shoe Machinery Corporation* v. *United States* (Supreme Court, 1922), for example, the Government was simply bringing suit against the company to prevent them from including in their leases of shoe machinery conditions which violated section 3 of that Act. One such condition required, for example, that the leased machinery should not be used in conjunction with machines supplied by other companies. Another was that the lessee of a U.S.M. machine should purchase certain supplies needed in shoe manufacture exclusively from U.S.M. These tying clauses were found to fall squarely within the provisions of section 3 of the Clayton Act and, since U.S.M. had a dominant position in the shoe machinery industry, they were held to have a substantial effect on competition. 'The patent right', said Mr Justice Day, 'confers no privilege to make contracts in themselves illegal and certainly not to make those directly violative of valid statutes of the United States.'

Another case in the same line is *International Business Machines Corporation* v. *United States* (Supreme Court, 1936). The Government brought the suit to prevent I.B.M. (and the other leading company in the business machinery field) from leasing their machines on condition that the lessee should purchase the punched cards used in the machines exclusively from the lessor. The defence in this case relied heavily on the argument that the manufacturer's own cards were specially made for his machines and that other cards might lead to bad performance and hence to loss of goodwill for the machines. It was said, for example, to be 'essential to the successful performance of the leased machines that the cards used in them conform, with relatively minute tolerances, to specifications as to size, thickness and freedom of defects which would affect adversely the electric circuits indispensable to the proper operation of the machines'.

But this defence failed because the Supreme Court held that other people were quite capable of manufacturing suitable cards for use in the machines, as government users had in fact done. Mr Justice Stone put it thus: 'Appellant is not prevented from proclaiming the virtues of its own cards or warning against the danger of using, in its machines, cards which do not conform to the necessary specifications, or even from making its leases conditional upon the use of cards which conform to them. For aught that appears such measures would protect its goodwill, without the creation of a monopoly or resort to the suppression of competition.' I.B.M., however, were not entitled to say that only their cards should be used in their machines and the Court emphasized that this was so whether both machines and cards were patented or whether either or both were unpatented.

International Salt Company v. *United States* (Supreme Court, 1947) illustrates the same point. International Salt is the largest producer of salt for commercial uses in the United States. The case concerned two patented machines: one for dissolving rock salt into a brine used in various industrial processes, the other for injecting salt into canned products during the canning process. The charge was that International Salt's leases for these machines required the lessees to purchase from them all the salt used in operating the machines.

The defence again claimed that the machines ran properly only on salt of high standard, so that it was reasonable to insist that their own salt should be used. As in the *International Business Machines* case, this argument was rejected. Mr Justice Jackson argued similarly to Mr Justice Day: 'But it is not pleaded, nor is it argued, that the machine is allergic to salt of equal quality produced by anyone except International. If others cannot produce salt equal to reasonable specifications for machine use it is one thing; but it is admitted that, at times at least, competitors do offer such a product. They are, however, shut out of the market by a provision that limits it, not in terms of quality, but in terms of a particular vendor. Rules for use of leased machinery must not be disguised restraints of free competition, though they may set reasonable standards which all must meet.' He concluded: 'International Salt has engaged in a restriction of trade for which its patents afford no immunity from the antitrust laws.'[1]

These last three cases—*U.S.M.*, *I.B.M.* and *International Salt*—are typical Clayton Act prosecutions, on all fours with those outlined above in Chapter VIII, and in all of them the effect of the tying contracts on competition was crucial to the court's decision. There is a parallel line of cases—all private actions for patent infringement—in which the courts have considered tying provisions as a misuse of the patent right. In these cases the effect of such provisions on competition has not been the issue, though the public interest in competition has no doubt been a powerful influence on the attitude of the courts.

This line of cases began with *Motion Picture Patents Company* v. *Universal Film Manufacturing Company* (Supreme Court, 1917). The plaintiff held a patent covering parts of the mechanism of cinema projectors; the device was the only satisfactory one then in use. The plaintiff required its licensee, who manufactured projectors under the patent, to sell them subject to the condition that they should be used only to exhibit films made under other patents held by the plaintiff. The licensee accordingly affixed a notice of the required restriction of use to the projectors he

---

[1] In this case an offence against the Sherman Act was found and the Court first promulgated the rule that 'it is unreasonable, *per se*, to foreclose competitors from any substantial market'. See the *Yellow Cab* case, above, Chapter V, pp. 143 ff.

sold. When a cinema subsequently showed other films through one of the patented projectors, the owner and proprietor of the cinema and the producer of the films were all sued for infringing the machine patent.

The Supreme Court threw out the plaintiff's case. The machine patent, it was pointed out, had nothing to do with the materials used with the machine. The patentee had a right to refuse to license the use of the machine altogether, but it did not follow that he could impose any condition he chose on its use, for this would extend the monopoly of the patent beyond its proper scope. As Mr Justice Clarke put it:

We are convinced that the exclusive right granted in every patent must be limited to the invention described in the claims of the patent, and that it is not competent for the owner of the patent, by notice attached to its machine, to, in effect, extend the scope of its patent monopoly by restricting the use of it to materials necessary in its operation, but which are no part of the patented invention. . . . The patent law furnishes no warrant for such a practice, and the cost, inconvenience and annoyance to the public which the opposite conclusion would occasion forbid it.

The Court noted furthermore that the 'opposite conclusion' would in effect enable patentees to fix the prices of unpatented supplies and to 'create a monopoly in the manufacture and use of moving-picture films, wholly outside of the patent in suit. . . .'

This important decision overruled certain previous decisions[1] and set the tone for the modern development of the law on this topic. The next leading case was *Carbice Corporation of America* v. *American Patents Development Corporation* (Supreme Court, 1931). Here the patent claims covered an insulated package or container in which ice-cream or some other foodstuff was packed around a quantity of solid carbon dioxide. The exclusive licensee under the patent was the Dry Ice Corporation, whose business was making and selling solid carbon dioxide—an unpatented material. This company did not make or sell the packages described by the patent claims nor did it formally sub-license the use of the invention. It simply sold its brand of solid carbon dioxide, known as Dry Ice, subject to the conditions that (*a*) Dry Ice should be used only in packages covered by the patent and (*b*) such packages should be refrigerated exclusively with Dry Ice. It was assumed that in this way the company was in effect licensing its customers without royalty to use the invention.

When the Carbice Corporation sold solid carbon dioxide to the Dry

---

[1] Notably *Henry* v. *A. B. Dick Company* (Supreme Court, 1912), in which a patentee had required that its patented duplicating machine should be used only with stencils, paper and ink supplied by it and had successfully sued as an infringer one who used other materials.

Ice company's customers, knowing it would be used in the patented form of package, it was sued as a contributory infringer. But once again the Supreme Court rejected the suit. Given a valid patent, the patentee could properly charge royalties for its use. But, as Mr Justice Brandeis put it, 'It may not exact as the condition of a license that unpatented materials used in connection with the invention shall be purchased only from the licensor; and if it does so, relief against one who supplies such unpatented materials will be denied.' As in the *Motion Picture* case, it was held that the condition which the patentee sought to impose went beyond the legitimate scope of its monopoly.

The rule of the *Motion Picture* and *Carbice* cases has subsequently been applied to many variants of the basic situation. It has been ruled, for example, that the holder of a process patent may not tie the licensing of the patent to the sale of an unpatented material required in the process.[1] Nor may he offer the user of the process the choice between paying a royalty as part of the purchase price of the unpatented material and paying a royalty on the actual use of the process, where the latter royalty is so much higher that it forces the user in practice to purchase the unpatented material from the patentee.[2]

And whereas in the *Carbice* case the unpatented solid carbon dioxide was a staple commodity, it has been held that the rule still applies where the product, though unpatented, is specially designed for use with the patented process. This was the situation in *B.B. Chemical Company* v. *Ellis* (Supreme Court, 1942), where it was contended that it was impracticable for the patentee, Ellis, to obtain any reward for its invention other than by selling to shoe manufacturers the special adhesive compounds required for the patented manufacturing process: it would have been impossible to police the licensing of all manufacturers who used the process. It was also urged that the alleged infringer in this case did not merely offer a suitable product for sale but actively induced manufacturers to use it, knowing that in doing so they would infringe the process patent. Nevertheless, the suit against B.B. Chemical for contributory infringement failed. Mr Justice Stone observed:

. . . In view of petitioner's use of the patent as the means of establishing a limited monopoly in its unpatented materials, . . . we hold that the maintenance of this suit to restrain any form of infringement is contrary to public policy.

The patent monopoly is not enlarged by reason of the fact that it would be more convenient to the patentee to have it so; or because he cannot avail himself of its benefits within the limits of the grant.

---

[1] See *Leitch Manufacturing Company* v. *Barber Asphalt Company* (Supreme Court, 1938).
[2] *Barber Asphalt Company* v. *La Fera Grecco Contracting Company* (Third Circuit Court of Appeals, 1940).

The line of cases from *Motion Picture Patents* v. *Universal Film Manu-facturing* to *B.B. Chemical* v. *Ellis* is, to repeat, independent of the Clayton Act. But in one or two private actions dealing with similar practices the Clayton Act has been introduced into the argument. Thus in *Oxford Varnish Corporation* v. *Ault and Wiborg Corporation* (Sixth Circuit Court of Appeals, 1936) the defendant, Oxford, held process patents for applying a grained finish, like that of natural wood, to metal and other surfaces. It was found that some of its licence contracts under the patents required the user to purchase unpatented graining plates, varnishes, graining pastes and so forth from the patentee; in others a much higher royalty was imposed for practising the patent when the licensee used materials purchased from other suppliers. This was not an infringement suit, but one in which the plaintiff, Ault and Wiborg, which also produced suitable materials for use in the patented process, sought an injunction under the Clayton Act to bar the patentee's restrictive contracts.

In deciding for the plaintiff, the Court apparently came near to holding that any misuse of patents by means of tying clauses was a violation *per se* of the Clayton Act. After referring to the *Motion Picture Patents* and *Carbice* cases, Judge Simons observed: 'But that which the patent law does not authorize, the Clayton Act specifically forbids.' He went on to rule that the necessary effect on competition for an antitrust offence was present on the ground that the patents themselves defined a monopoly. 'If we may assume, as we do, that monopoly of a defined portion of an industry is equally subject to the condemnation of the antitrust laws as is a monopoly over an entire industry, then it requires in this case no statistical demonstration of monopolistic practices, for the patents themselves, which define the metes and bounds of the monopoly lawfully granted, likewise [to] define the metes and bounds of the monopoly here sought and achieved by the assailed contracts. No more was desired—no less was obtained.'

In fact, however, Oxford's business in paints and varnishes repre-sented less than $\frac{1}{2}\%$ of the national total, and it is an open question whether the tying clauses involved would have been found illegal under the Clayton Act,[1] had it not been assumed that a patent in itself defines a segment of commerce that can be monopolized and that misuse of a patent is an antitrust offence *per se*. These assumptions have been strongly criticized but, as will appear below, it is possible that they are still influential with some courts.[2]

---

[1] Indeed, they were also held to be unlawful monopolistic devices under the Sherman Act.

[2] The case might perhaps be brought under the rule of the *Klearflax Linen Looms* case (see above, Chapter V, pp. 131–2)—namely, that a clearly demonstrated purpose to monopolize serves of itself to establish that there is a market to monopolize. But the *Klearflax* case, decided in 1945, was not a precedent in 1936. In some cases dealing with perfumery—*United States* v. *Guerlain, United States* v. *Parfum Corday, United States* v. *Lanvin Parfum* (Southern

The Court's failure in this case to make any clear distinction between misuse of patents and violation of the Clayton Act was emulated in reverse by the Seventh Circuit Court of Appeals in *Morton Salt Company v. Suppiger* (Supreme Court, 1942). This was an infringement suit brought by a patentee who, like International Salt in a later case, hired out patented machines for depositing salt tablets in canned food on condition that the lessee should use its salt exclusively in operating the machine. The patentee sued another company for making and leasing machines that were alleged to infringe the patent. The Circuit Court of Appeals thought the patentee entitled to relief on the ground that the tying clauses in its leases did not sufficiently harm competition to constitute a violation of the Clayton Act.[1]

The Supreme Court in reversing this decision clearly re-established the distinction between a misuse of patents and a violation of the Clayton Act. 'The question we must decide is not necessarily whether respondent has violated the Clayton Act, but whether a court of equity will lend its aid to protect the patent monopoly when respondent is using it as the effective means of restraining competition with its sales of an unpatented article.' The case was therefore decided against the patentee on the authority of the previous misuse cases. Chief Justice Stone stated the rule of these cases in a particularly clear way: 'Where the patent is used as means of restraining competition with the patentee's sale of an unpatented product, the successful prosecution of an infringement suit even against one who is not a competitor in such sale is a powerful aid to the maintenance of the attempted monopoly of the unpatented article, and is thus a contributing factor in thwarting the public policy underlying the grant of the new patent.'[2] The fact that the defendant in the suit was not injured by the tying clause was held to be irrelevant and it was ruled that the patentee

District Court of New York, 1957), a trial Court actually held that it was illegal monopolization for sole importers of perfumes protected by trademarks to prevent other purchasers from competing in their sale by applying to the Customs authorities for their exclusion under the 1930 Tariff Act. In other words, a single trademarked brand of perfume was held to define a market that could be monopolized. When the defendants appealed to the Supreme Court, however, the Government did not fight the appeal but suggested that the Court should dismiss the cases (as was done) on the grounds that as a matter of policy it was inappropriate to deal with this problem by means of an antitrust suit, and that amending legislation would be preferable.

[1] It is noteworthy that this is the exact converse of the Court's argument in the *Oxford Varnish* case. In that case the Sixth Circuit Court said in effect that because the practice was misuse of patents, it also violated the Clayton Act. In the *Salt* case the Seventh Circuit Court said that because the practice did not violate the Clayton Act, it was not misuse. Neither Court preserved the distinction between the two rules.

[2] It is implied here that, beyond the strict limits of the patent grant, public policy favours competition. This policy may indeed go wider than the explicit coverage of the antitrust laws, thus explaining why patent misuse doctrines may bear more strictly on patentees exceeding the limits of the patent grant than does the antitrust law.

could seek equity relief against infringement only when it had abandoned its restrictive licences.

Despite this clarification the distinction between patent misuse and antitrust violation was again obscured in two important cases which also extended the misuse doctrine even further than the previous cases. These were *Mercoid Corporation* v. *Mid-Continent Investment Company* and *Mercoid Corporation* v. *Minneapolis-Honeywell Regulator Company* (Supreme Court, 1944). Their interest lies in the application of the misuse doctrine to combination patents.

Mid-Continent was the holder of a combination patent covering a domestic heating system comprising a mechanical stoker, a thermostat controlling the input of fuel, and a switch which ensured that the system was kept stoked when the thermostat did not call for any increase of heat over a long period. None of the elements was patented; the patent claims covered simply their combination and the only people who could be said strictly to practise the patent were the heating contractors who installed the system (i.e. *made* the combination) and the householders who used it. There was no practical way of enforcing the patent by licensing or collecting royalties from these people.

What the patentee did in this situation was to license Minneapolis-Honeywell exclusively to make, use and sell the combination with the right to sub-license others. Minneapolis-Honeywell did not make or sell the whole system but just the stoker switches, and royalties under its licence from Mid-Continent were calculated by reference to the number of switches sold. It was found that Minneapolis-Honeywell stated in advertisements that the right to practise the patent was granted only to those who used its switches. The Mercoid company, which also made stoker switches and sold them for use in the patented combination (it was said that they had no other use), was sued as a contributory infringer;[1] in its defence Mercoid pleaded that the arrangement was a misuse of the patent and also sought treble damages under a counterclaim that it violated the antitrust laws.

Although assuming that the patent was valid and that Mercoid 'did not act innocently', the Supreme Court (in *Mercoid* v. *Mid-Continent*) condemned the arrangement as a misuse of the patent: 'The patent is employed to protect the market for a device on which no patent has been granted.' This ruling is a high-water mark of the misuse doctrine, applying it to the enforcement of a patent against what appeared, on the face of it, to be deliberate contributory infringe-

---

[1] Contributory infringement is defined as assisting another person in an unlawful invasion of a patentee's rights. Thus, if a commodity is supplied which can only be used in a patented process or as part of a patented combination and the supplier knows that his customer has no licence under the patent, he is an accessory to the subsequent infringement. This was alleged of Mercoid.

ment. As Mr Justice Douglas put it: 'Where there is a collision between the principle of the Carbice case and the conventional rules governing either direct or contributory infringement, the former prevails.'

Yet despite this reliance upon and extension of the misuse doctrine, Mr Justice Douglas also made the point that 'but for the patent such restraint of trade would plainly run afoul of the antitrust laws'; and in the companion case he said expressly that 'the legality of any attempt to bring unpatented goods within the protection of the patent is measured by the antitrust laws and not by the patent law'. Nothing was said in this connexion about the substantiality of the effect on competition of the situation revealed in the *Mercoid* cases. Thus, although the clear distinction made in *Morton Salt* v. *Suppiger* remains perhaps the best legal authority on this topic, and although the subsequent cases have not on the whole relied on Mr Justice Douglas's equation of patent misuse with antitrust violation, his dicta in the *Mercoid* cases seem to the business world to leave open the risk that any patent infringement suit to which the misuse doctrine may apply could lead to swingeing counterclaims for treble damages under antitrust law.

The line of patent misuse cases culminating in the *Mercoid* decision has been included here because, despite the legal distinction between misuse and antitrust violation, they are deeply suffused with the antitrust philosophy. They show how vigilant the courts are to circumscribe the immunity granted by the patent from antitrust prosecution. In some circumstances, as has been seen, the rigid interpretation of the misuse doctrine renders the patent virtually unenforceable. This is the case particularly with process patents that are widely practised (such as *B.B. Chemical* v. *Ellis*) and with combination patents which may be practised only by the ultimate consumer. In the situation disclosed in the *Mercoid* cases, for example, it was simply not feasible for the patentee to obtain a reward for the invention by charging royalties to those who practised the patent. Yet this did not prevent the courts from condemning the method actually adopted as a means of protecting unpatented goods.

It was indeed widely supposed after the *Mercoid* cases that nothing remained of the right of action against contributory infringement. Mr Justice Douglas himself said in his opinion: 'The result of this decision, together with those which have preceded it, is to limit substantially the doctrine of contributory infringement. What residuum may be left we need not stop to consider.' It has since been suggested, however, that the patentee would still be entitled to sue the contributory infringer if licences were offered in some way that avoided tying the licence to the sale of the unpatented product. This might work where it was practicable to run a patent licensing scheme as a separate commercial operation. But it is difficult to see how it could be done in a situation, like that of the *Mercoid* case, in which a reward for the invention could be obtained in practice only by sales of an unpatented product. If the patentee in selling the unpatented component merely gave notice of the existence of the combination patent, offering perhaps to supply a licence for a nominal charge, he would certainly avoid expressly tying the licence to the purchase of the unpatented article. But unless he was prepared to issue licences on the same terms to those who purchased the unpatented component from other suppliers, he would probably still be caught under the rule of *Barber* v. *La Fera Grecco*.[1] It would in any case be a paradox if the right of action depended on not giving advance warning that the right would be exercised. The number of cases illustrating the Mercoid situation, however, may well be small, and companies whose primary business is promoting the sale of products (rather than patent revenues) may find it best to regard the patent as essentially a defensive weapon and not to enforce it positively.

The legal situation was still obscure on this topic when a legislative attempt was made in the Patent Act of 1952 to restore the patentee's remedy against contributory infringement. In section 271 (d) of that Act it is provided that no patentee shall be denied relief for infringement simply on the ground that he derives revenue (or licenses another to derive revenue) 'from acts which if performed by another without his consent would constitute contributory infringement of the patent', or that he seeks to enforce the patent against direct or contributory in-infringement. The courts have, however, since made it clear that they are still unwilling to depart from the rigid concept of misuse expressed in *Mercoid*, and that section 271 will be construed as narrowly as possible. The leading cases are two between the same parties, *The Aro Manufacturing Company* v. *Convertible Top Replacement Company*, decided by the Supreme Court in 1961 and 1964 respectively.[2] The background to the cases was that Convertible Top had obtained a patent for the combination of (*a*) a convertible car body with a special sealing strip adapted to fit against and seal the top fabric when the top was erected and (*b*) the top fabric shapes to receive the special sealing strips. It had, however, no patent rights over the fabric itself. Aro manufactured and sold a

[1] A plan on the lines suggested has indeed been tried unsuccessfully: see *National Foam System* v. *Urquhart* (Third Circuit Court of Appeals, 1953). The Court observed: 'While it is proper to grant licences and determine royalties through sales of unpatented materials used in connection with the patent, such method is interdicted as a patent misuse in instances where a licence can be obtained only by purchasing the unpatented materials from the person granting a licence, or, where given a choice of purchasing from that source or another, the royalty to be paid in the latter situation is so much higher that the would-be licensee is given Hobson's choice.'

[2] I must acknowledge my debt for this account of the complex *Aro* cases to Mr G. E. Frost, 'The Supreme Court and Patent Abuse', *A.B.A. Antitrust Section, Proceedings*, vol. 29, 1965, p. 122.

fabric which could be used by owners of cars produced by General Motors (who were licensees of Convertible Top for the manufacture of the convertible tops) in place of that made by Convertible Top, and was sued by Convertible Top on the ground that Aro's manufacture of the fabric was an infringement of the patented combination and not merely a repair. It was also claimed that Aro was guilty of contributory infringement in selling this fabric to car owners for use with the other elements of the combination. On this aspect of the case the Supreme Court held, on technical patent law grounds,[1] that Convertible Top's claim must fail. In reaching this decision, however, considerable emphasis was placed on the absence of any patent protection for the fabric by itself, and on the principle of the *Mercoid* cases that a combination patent covers only the totality of the elements in the claim and that no individual element is protected by the patent grant.

The second case was concerned with the supply by Aro of its own fabric to purchasers of cars manufactured by Ford, who, unlike General Motors, were not licensed to make use of Convertible Top's combination patent. A five to four majority of the Court held that, since Ford themselves had no authority to make the patented tops, purchasers of Ford cars were equally without authority to use them and even mere repair of the top structure would constitute an infringement. The question therefore arose of whether Aro had been guilty of contributory infringement, and again the Court by a five to four majority found that it had, by reason of the provisions of section 271 of the Patent Code. The minority would have held the section unconstitutional as having extended the rights of a patentee beyond those permitted by the constitution.[2]

Aro's argument was that its own sales were protected by the *Mercoid* decisions, and that Convertible Top was attempting to misuse its combination patent by attempting to protect an unpatented item (the fabric) from competition. Mr Justice Brennan for the majority disagreed, stating that Congress had enacted section 271 'for the express purpose of reinstating the doctrine of contributory infringement as it had been developed by decisions prior to *Mercoid* and of overruling any blanket invalidation of the doctrine that could be found in the *Mercoid* opinions'. The effect of the second *Aro* decision is, however, limited to situations where the original use of the combination is unlicensed, and it seems that, in the more usual situation where the original use is legitimate, the

---

[1] Namely that the use of Aro's fabric by car owners was a permissible 'repair' of the patented combination rather than a 'reconstruction'.

[2] Under Article 1, Section 8, of the United States Constitution, Congress has power 'to promote the Progress of Science and useful Arts by securing for limited times to Authors and Inventors the exclusive rights to their respective Writings and Discoveries'. The minority felt that to allow a suit for contributory infringement in respect of the non-patentable fabric was to allow too great an extension of the meaning of 'Discoveries'.

supplier of individual unpatented components (particularly if these are staple products) will normally still find the courts resistant, whenever possible, to attempts to declare him a contributory infringer. Thus the doctrine of misuse of patents still remains a potent reinforcement of antitrust.[1]

6. *Permissible conditions in patent licences: the* Transparent-Wrap *and* Hazeltine *cases. Combination patents:* Amalgamated Dental *v.* Getz, Dr Salsbury's Laboratories *v.* Russell Laboratories. *Non-use of patents*

One or two further rulings must be mentioned briefly to round off the subject. It is noteworthy that the misuse doctrine has not been applied with the full rigour of the *Mercoid* cases when the condition imposed by the patentee has been of a less restrictive kind that than of tying the licensee to the use of unpatented goods or stipulating the prices of such goods. Thus in *Transparent-Wrap Machine Corporation* v. *Stokes and Smith Company* (Supreme Court, 1947) the patents covered a packaging machine, and the patentee issued an exclusive licence to make and sell the machine subject to the condition that the licensee would assign to the patentee any patents it might obtain for improvements to the machine. When the licensee failed to abide by this condition, the patentee successfully brought an action to enforce it. Mr Justice Douglas said of this arrangement: 'One who uses one patent to acquire another is not extending his patent monopoly to articles governed by the general law and as respects which neither monopolies nor restraints of trade are sanctioned. He is indeed using one legalized monopoly to acquire another legalized monopoly.' Whereas logically the misuse doctrine might have been applied, the Court noted that the patent law authorized the assignment of patents and felt that no legal distinction could be drawn between buying the assignment for money and obtaining it in consideration of a licence under the basic patents.[2]

In 1950 in *Automatic Radio Manufacturing Company* v. *Hazeltine Research*, Hazeltine was the assignee of a pool of several hundred radio patents. It licensed these patents to all responsible radio manufacturers, deriving its income from the royalties. Automatic Radio was one of the licensees and under its licence was able to use all the Hazeltine patents it chose, paying as royalties a small percentage of its selling price of radio sets. Thus

---

[1] Two older but still excellent articles on the topics discussed in this section are 'The Tangle of Mercoid Case Implications' by Laurence I. Wood, *George Washington Law Review*, vol. 13, 1944, and 'Misuse of Patents in Relation to the Patent Code' by George E. Frost, in *Lectures on federal antitrust laws: 1953*, Michigan University Law School, 1953.

[2] There were other special factors in the case running against the conclusion that the patentee was getting any significant degree of extra-patent control: see Mr Frost's article, *loc. cit.* pp. 280–1. The Department of Justice subsequently announced that it would challenge such grant-back requirements in improvement patents in future.

the royalty payments were not tied to the use of any particular patents. The suit was brought to recover royalties which had not been paid.

Here again it could be contended in strict logic that the misuse doctrine should apply, for the patent owner was drawing royalties from a combination of patented and unpatented elements without regard to the use actually made of its patents. But the Supreme Court rejected this argument. It held that in the circumstances of the case the method of calculating royalties was convenient and reasonable; and it no doubt took into consideration the liberal licensing policy of the patent owner and the absence of restrictive tying or price conditions in the licences or of any showing that licensees could not have obtained licences, if they so desired, under fewer patents than were included in the pool.[1] Referring to the line of misuse cases, Mr Justice Minton said: 'The principle of these cases cannot be contorted to circumscribe the instant situation. This royalty provision does not create another monopoly: it creates no restraint of competition beyond the legitimate grant of the patent.' He also pointed out that the licensee had freely contracted to pay for the privilege of using the patent pool and could not complain about paying simply because it did not choose to exercise the privilege. He concluded: 'We hold that in licensing the use of patents to one engaged in a related enterprise, it is not *per se* a misuse of patents to measure the consideration by a percentage of the licensee's sales.'

The authority of the *Hazeltine* case must, however, be treated with some caution, for its scope has certainly been narrowed, though not completely curtailed, by the Supreme Court decision in *Brulotte* v. *Thys Co.* (1964). Thys owned certain patents covering the manufacture of hop picking machines. He could have exploited these patents either by selling these machines for a flat sum or at a price dependent on the use made of them (a form of royalty payment) or by a combination of the two elements. In the event the latter solution was adopted, so that Brulotte, a farmer in the State of Washington, was required to pay both a flat sum and a royalty based on the use of the machines, subject to a specified minimum. Unfortunately under the terms of the contract Thys was entitled to receive certain royalties after the expiration of the seventeen-year patent protection period. The Supreme Court held that royalties which accrued after the last of the patents covering the machine had expired could not be recovered since 'the use by a patentee of royalty agreements that project beyond the expiration date is unlawful *per se*'. The Court distinguished the *Hazeltine* case on two grounds. First, some of the Hazeltine patents had still been in force whereas all those

[1] It is of interest to compare block licensing with the form of 'block booking' which was declared illegal in the *Paramount* and *Loew's* cases; see above, Chapter VI, pp. 166 ff. and Chapter VIII, pp. 214–15 respectively.

of Thys had expired, and second, that the number of patents involved in the hop picking machine made by Thys were few in comparison with the several hundred patents involved in the Hazeltine pool.

There has, however, been a rather surprising sequel to the earlier *Hazeltine* case. In that earlier case one of the factors which influenced the Supreme Court to uphold the royalty arrangements was that licensees were not shown to have been prevented from obtaining, at no cost disadvantage, licences for a smaller number of patents than those comprised in the pool. But in *Hazeltine Research Inc.* v. *Zenith Radio Corporation* (Northern District Court of Illinois, 1965), Hazeltine brought an action against Zenith for infringement. This was rejected on the ground of patent misuse, and furthermore Zenith succeeded in their antitrust counterclaim in establishing that they had suffered damages (presumably to be trebled) totalling over $16 million. These damages were caused by Hazeltine's participation in foreign patent pools which had effectively prevented Zenith from exporting its products to those countries. The Court found that Hazeltine's policy (in sharp contrast to that set forth in the earlier case) was to license its patents only under a standard package licence, under which the licensee had to pay royalties for five years on its entire production regardless of whether any of the Hazeltine patents were actually practised.[1] Hazeltine argued that they had offered Zenith individual licences, but it was shown that, over a five-year license period, it would have cost Zenith over $500,000 more for a licence for ten patents for colour television alone than it would for the entire package covering over 500 patents and patent applications for both monochrome and colour television. In other words, the alternative offered to the licensee must be a genuine commercial alternative, and a 'Hobson's choice' is no choice at all. This is analogous to the rule established in the *La Fera Grecco* case (see p. 329 above) that the holder of a process patent is not entitled to offer the user of the process the 'alternative' of paying a royalty as part of the purchase price of the unpatented material or paying an exorbitant royalty on the actual use of that process.

It is, however, noteworthy that the courts do not eschew common-sense for an extreme pedantry in interpreting combination patents where this would be manifestly unjust to the patentee. Thus in an infringement suit—*Amalgamated Dental Company* v. *The William Getz Corporation* (District Court of Illinois, 1951)—the patent claims covered a dental-impression material made by dissolving certain chemicals in water.[2] In practice the firms licensed under the patent supplied the

---

[1] This was upheld by the Supreme Court in 1969, though with reduced damages due to a technicality.

[2] The patent was that concerned in *United States* v. *L.D. Caulk Company* (1954); see pp. 323–4.

chemicals in powder form and the dentist added the water before use. It could therefore be contended that the actual article of commerce was an unpatented mixture of chemicals. But the trial Court rejected this pedantry. 'It would seem to me to be absurd . . . to say that this plaintiff is misusing its patent because every time it sells a mixture of sodium alginate and sodium carbonate . . . it does not also sell a little water. I think that would be reducing the rule to an absurdity.'

Yet in *Dr Salsbury's Laboratories* v. *I. D. Russell Company Laboratories* (Eighth Circuit Court of Appeals, 1952) what might appear to be a similar 'absurdity' was committed by the Court. The plaintiff's patent again covered a mixture of chemicals in water—this time for a poultry medicine. Again the product was actually sold in powder or tablet form, leaving the user to add the water. But in this case the Court upheld the contention that, in seeking to extend the protection of the patent to the unpatented chemical, the plaintiff was guilty of misuse of the patent and not entitled to relief against one who knowingly supplied the same chemical to users who would clearly practise the patent.[1]

The vital difference in this case, as against the *Dental material* case, was the Court's finding that the chemical used in the poultry medicine was a staple commodity which it would be unduly restrictive to allow the patentee to protect. This finding points up in turn an important factor in all these cases—namely that the courts may be greatly influenced by the weight they attach to the importance of the invention. This influence probably explains much that is otherwise unclear about the different results of ostensibly similar cases. The American Patent Office has often been criticized for being unduly liberal in issuing patents for inventions that make a questionable advance in the art. When the validity of patents is challenged on this ground, it is common to find that the higher the court the stricter is the interpretation of what constitutes a patentable invention. And this stricter standard may well have a great deal to do with the results of infringement suits and the application of the misuse doctrine even when there is no express ruling as to the validity of the patent.

Mr Justice Jackson was expressing this kind of feeling in his dissent in one of the *Mercoid* cases. Though conceding that the validity of the patent was not in question he said: 'Undoubtedly the man who first devised a thermostat to control the flow of electric energy gave something to the world. But one who merely carried it to a new location, or

---

[1] It is noteworthy that the defendant's counterclaim for treble damages under the anti-trust laws also failed, the Court observing the correct distinction between patent misuse and antitrust violation. It is also of importance that the result of the case was confirmed by the Court of Appeals in 1954 against the contention that the suit for contributory infringement should succeed under the new Patent Act of 1952. The Court held that the new Act did not protect a patentee's sales of an unpatented staple commodity.

used two instead of one, or three instead of two, or used it to control current for a stoker motor rather than for a damper did not do much that I would not expect of a good mechanic familiar with the instrument, but that question of validity is not here. I assume that this patent confers some rights and ask what they are.'

Lastly the problem of the non-use of patents must be mentioned; for the allegation has often been made that large companies deliberately withhold new technical advances from productive use, and even buy up inventions and suppress them, in order to maintain the profitability of existing methods and equipment. It might be thought that both antitrust and the patent law would take a firm stand against any such practice; for example, that non-use of patents might lead the courts to deny relief against infringement as they do in cases of misuse.[1] But this is not a simple matter.

It is true, of course, that any agreement among competitors to withhold new techniques from use would fall foul of the Sherman Act.[2] If there were good evidence of the suppression of invention, this could also be a factor in a showing of illegal monopolization. But it is clear that the non-use of patents could not be *per se* an antitrust offence or a bar to relief against infringement: any such rule would be unworkable. This is because there are many good reasons for not practising particular patents. A provisional line of research may, for example, be overtaken by a more promising line and the non-use of the earlier patents can hardly be regarded as restrictive.

Even when an improved industrial method is discovered, it does not follow that it will be economically sensible, either for the patent holder or for the community at large, to scrap at once the capital invested in existing methods. The timing of investment in innovations is often a very difficult matter even for the most progressive of companies. It is hard to believe that the courts could determine the rights and wrongs of a business decision of this kind; and it is evident that crippling losses might be suffered by a firm which had invested heavily in research, if the lack of productive use of its patents at a particular moment were held to be sufficient reason for denying it relief against infringement.

There are in fact very few cases in which the non-use of patents has been the central issue and no modern cases in which the Supreme Court has squarely faced the question of whether non-use may be a ground for denying equitable relief to a patentee. Most commentators appear to agree that the rule of reason would have to be applied to

---

[1] It should again be noted that the American patent law contains no provisions like those in Britain and some other countries whereby patents which are not practised may in certain circumstances be compulsorily licensed.

[2] See *Blount Manufacturing Company* v. *Yale and Towne Manufacturing Company*, above, p. 314.

such cases, but incline to the view that relief against infringement might in practice be refused if it could be shown that the non-use was manifestly unreasonable or contrary to public policy.[1]

Criticism is often directed also at the type of non-use that occurs when large firms seek to patent numerous small improvements to or variants of their inventions or the inventions of rivals. There may be no intention of practising some of these patents. As respects improvements of a rival's product, the effect (and sometimes the intention) may be to 'block' his line of technical advance and force him into cross-licensing or pooling arrangements; improvements to a firm's own inventions may be merely an insurance against being 'blocked', or against having to pay royalties or making other concessions if the improvement or variant is subsequently discovered by a rival.

It is often said that these 'blocking' and 'fencing' uses of patents tend to discourage competitive research, and that where the patents are not practised they should be compulsorily licensed. But this again is a far from straightforward matter. How are the courts to distinguish between a genuine new line of research and one that merely 'blocks' a rival line? In some cases it might be highly inequitable to insist that an improvement patent be licensed to the holder of the basic patent without imposing any reciprocal obligation; in other cases it might be equally inequitable to require a reciprocal arrangement.

Thus the practical realities of business seem likely to inhibit the development of any 'non-use' doctrine that would be similar in scope and effect to the 'misuse' doctrine. The 'blocking' and 'fencing' practices may, however, have evidentiary significance in antitrust cases where they form part of a detailed record, which, like that in the *Gypsum* or *Hartford-Empire* cases, is used to establish a conspiracy to restrain trade or a purposive drive to dominate an industry.[2]

---

[1] In *Special Equipment Company* v. *Coe* (Supreme Court, 1945) the majority of the Court found it unnecessary to reach this question, but a minority of three led by Mr Justice Douglas advocated the denial of equity relief in a clear case of suppression. '. . . The Court sits as a court of equity. It should withhold its aid from a patentee who has employed or plans to employ the patent not to exploit the invention but to suppress it in order to protect another patent or otherwise. . . . If that purpose were clear, a patent should not issue in the first instance. If it has been used and not cancelled and the patent has been suppressed, any one should be permitted to use it at least on payment of reasonable royalties.' In the so-called *Paper bag* case (*Continental Paper Bag Company* v. *Eastern Paper Bag Company*) of 1908 the rule had been laid down that a patentee had the right not to make use of his patent, but the Supreme Court had indicated that this rule might not apply when the non-use was unreasonable or opposed to public policy.

[2] An admirable discussion of the difficulties involved in legal action to deal with non-use of patents may be found in another article by Mr G. E. Frost, 'Legal Incidents of Non-use of Patented Inventions Reconsidered', *George Washington Law Review*, vol. 14, 1946.

CHAPTER XII

INTERNATIONAL CARTELS AND ANTITRUST

1. The Sherman Act and 'trade with foreign nations'; the Webb-Pomerene Export Trade Act of 1918: the United States Alkali *case*

The general prohibition of contracts and conspiracies in restraint of trade in section 1 of the Sherman Act[1] applies not only to trade 'among the several States' but also to trade 'with foreign nations'.[2] A number of important antitrust cases have been concerned with trade with foreign nations—with restrictive agreements between American and foreign firms, with the operations of American companies and their local subsidiaries in foreign markets, with foreign companies run jointly by American firms and their international competitors, and so on. For the most part these cases do not contain much that will be new to the reader in the way of restrictive practices or of legal principles. They do, however, include some good examples of market sharing agreements, often based on cross-licensing of patents, which will serve to fill in gaps on this topic; and the position under antitrust of companies under the joint ownership of national or international competitors has interesting features.

But in any event the impact of antitrust on international trade warrants a separate chapter because of its peculiar interest to readers outside the United States. The case law under this head may directly affect British and other companies, particularly if their business involves making commercial agreements with American companies or if there is an important American stake in their ownership and control. Moreover, this case law gives rise to interesting questions about the extent of the jurisdiction claimed and exercised by the American courts over foreign concerns.

The operation of the Sherman Act in the field of foreign trade is qualified by the provisions of the Webb-Pomerene Export Trade Act

[1] The Clayton Act and Robinson-Patman Act are restricted in their language to restrictions or price discriminations in the sale of goods within the United States, and so have no application to export sales. It would appear, however, that section 7 of the Clayton Act does apply to a merger of a United States company and a foreign company which is, or might be, engaged in exporting to the United States (see *United States* v. *Jos. Schlitz Brewing Company* (Northern District of California, 1966)).

[2] The subject matter of this chapter is treated with the greatest thoroughness and authority by Kingman Brewster in *Antitrust and American Business Abroad*, McGraw-Hill, New York, 1958.

of 1918 which must be noted at the outset. Section 2 of this Act provides that nothing in the Sherman Act shall make illegal:

> ...an association entered into for the sole purpose of engaging in export trade, and actually engaged solely in such export trade, or an agreement made or act done in the course of export trade by such association, provided such association, agreement, or act is not in restraint of trade within the United States, and is not in restraint of the export trade of any domestic competitor of such association: *And provided further*, That such association does not, either in the United States or elsewhere, enter into any agreement, understanding, or conspiracy, or do any act which artificially or intentionally enhances or depresses prices within the United States of commodities of the class exported by such association, or which substantially lessens competition within the United States or otherwise restrains trade therein.

Other sections provide in detail for the supervision by the Federal Trade Commission of export trade associations operating under section 2 and for the prevention by the Commission of 'unfair methods of competition' in foreign trade, whether on the part of the export associations or others.

The effect of section 2 is to enable American exporters to make agreements among themselves, respecting foreign commerce only, that would otherwise violate the Sherman Act, for example, price fixing or market sharing agreements. These agreements, however, must not have restrictive effects on commerce in the United States and they must not be exclusionary or harmful as against American exporters who prefer to stay outside them. These conditions in themselves greatly restrict the scope of the exemption; but it has been held in any case that the Webb Act does not permit export associations to enter into restrictive arrangements with foreign competitors.[1]

This ruling was given in *United States* v. *United States Alkali Export Association* (Southern District Court of New York, 1949). The trial Court affirmed from the legislative history that the true purpose of the Act was 'to enable smaller producers and manufacturers in this country to form co-operative selling agencies in order to compete effectively with large foreign units abroad'. The idea that this objective entailed a complete withdrawal of foreign trade from the scope of the Sherman Act was sharply denied: 'Giving careful attention to the entire legislative history of its passage, the conclusion is irresistible that the Webb-Pomerene Act affords no right to export associations to engage on a world-wide scale in practices so antithetical to the American philosophy of free competition. The international agreements between defendants,

[1] The Webb Act has been held not to apply to foreign sales by American companies financed by American foreign aid—*Concentrated Phosphate Export Association* v. *United States* (1968). In the same year the Department of Justice testified before Congress that the Webb Act did more harm than good and should be repealed.

allocating exclusive markets, fixing prices on an international scale, and selling through joint agents are not those "agreements in the course of export trade" which the Webb Act places beyond the reach of the Sherman law.'[1]

2. *Agreements between United States companies relating to foreign markets:* Minnesota Mining and Manufacturing

The Webb Act is thus a very limited qualification of the Sherman Act, and the case law shows how strenuously the courts in recent years have applied the principles of the Sherman Act to international trade. The cases may conveniently be divided into two classes—those which deal mainly with agreements among American companies to work together in foreign markets and those which involve agreements between American and foreign companies. The former class, which best illustrates the strict limitations applying to what may be done under the Webb Act, will be taken first; and the best example is *United States* v. *Minnesota Mining and Manufacturing Company* (1950).

The defendants in this case, which was tried by Judge Wyzanski in Massachusetts, were four important manufacturers of coated abrasives in the United States together with the export company, Durex Abrasives Corporation (which they had formed under the Webb Act) and another jointly owned company, the Durex Corporation (which held their foreign patents and their investments in foreign concerns). The export company conducted a large foreign trade partly through American export houses, partly through foreign distributors and subsidiary distributing companies abroad. It met competition from both American manufacturers outside the group and foreign manufacturers.

The essence of the case lay in the fact that in certain countries—Britain, Canada and Germany—the group found that direct exports on a large scale from the United States were, as they said, 'economically impractical'; accordingly, in those countries they set up or bought interests in local manufacturers who were licensed through Durex to practise the group's foreign patents. It was found, as would be expected, that, where the group had foreign manufacturing subsidiaries, their exports from the United States dropped off virtually to nothing.

---

[1] In the *Alkali* case it was found in any case that the arrangements included an understanding that the United States market would be reserved to the American producers and thus restrained commerce in the United States; the scheme was also found to harm independent American exporters.

The case is also important for an earlier procedural decision by the Supreme Court (1945) that the supervisory powers given to the Federal Trade Commission under the Webb Act do not prevent the Department of Justice from bringing charges under the Sherman Act, whether or not the Commission is actively investigating an association.

For example, the British subsidiary's sales in Britain increased from just over $1½ million in 1938 to nearly $5½ million in 1948, while exports from the United States which were over $1 million in 1929 were less than $9 thousand in 1948.

The Department of Justice argued in effect that, at least in these countries, the export group, so far from promoting American exports, was acting to restrict them, and that their joint ownership of manufacturing subsidiaries was in these circumstances a violation of the Sherman Act. The defendants argued, on the other hand, that, owing to tariffs and other difficulties in the countries concerned, direct exports were impracticable and it was more sensible to supply those markets through subsidiary companies.

Judge Wyzanski rejected the defence case. 'More sensible' in his view merely meant 'more profitable'; there was no absolute legal ban on American exports but the local factories showed a much better return.

In short this Court finds as an ultimate fact that defendants' decline in exports to the United Kingdom is attributable less to import and currency restrictions of that nation and to the preferential treatment afforded to British goods by British customers than to defendants' desire to sell their British-made goods at a large profit rather than their American-made goods at a smaller profit and in a somewhat (but not drastically) reduced volume.

Thus the arrangement was an unlawful combination to restrict American exports to important markets. The existence of the jointly owned foreign factories also prejudiced the chances of other American exporters in these markets and this was one of the reasons why the scheme could not be saved by the Webb Act. The fact that the profitable foreign subsidiaries in the end brought more money to the United States than would direct exports was regarded as no excuse. 'It is irrelevant where the action is taken by a combination and the effect, while it may redound to the advantage of American finance, restricts American commerce. For Congress in the Sherman Act has condemned whatever unreasonably restrains American commerce regardless of how it fattens profits of certain stockholders.' This pointed to another reason why the Webb Act did not save the scheme; that Act was intended to help export trade, not foreign earnings. 'Nothing in the statute, nor in its legislative history, nor in the penumbra of its policy justifies or has any bearing upon the rights of defendants to join in establishing and financing factories in foreign lands. Export of capital is not export trade.'

Thus the case stands for the rule that American exporters may not enter upon combined operations in foreign markets which, though advantageous in other ways, have the effect of restricting exports.[1] Judge Wyzanski distinguished this activity from a number of practices which he regarded (in the absence of any 'special circumstances revealing their unfairness or oppressiveness in a particular setting') as legitimate for an export association under the Webb Act. These included 'the firm commitments of members to use the unit as their exclusive foreign outlet, the refusal of the unit to handle the exports of American competitors, the determination of what quotas and at what prices each member should supply products to the unit, the fixing of resale prices at which the unit's foreign distributors should sell and the limitation of distributors to handling products of the members'. He also stressed that his ruling applied only to combined ownership of foreign manufacturing subsidiaries. Unless there were danger of monopoly, an individual firm might legally run a foreign branch factory: indeed, several American firms might each have such factories and there would be no offence, in the absence of conspiracy, even though in total they had the same effect as the combination in reducing American exports. 'Nothing in this opinion can properly be read as a prohibition against an American manufacturer seeking to make large profits through the mere ownership and operation of a branch factory abroad which is not conducted as part of a combination, conspiracy or monopoly.'

3. *The* Timken *case*

The legal limitations applying to an individual firm's operations through foreign subsidiaries were one of the issues considered in the famous *Timken* case—*Timken Roller Bearing Company* v. *United States* (Supreme Court, 1951)—which forms a useful link between the cases dealing mainly with American commercial operations abroad (for example, the *Abrasives* case) and those dealing with agreements between American and foreign firms.

The Timken company is the leading manufacturer in the United States of tapered roller bearings, producing between 70% and 80% of American output with gross sales in 1947 worth over $77 million.[2]

---

[1] Judge Wyzanski hinted but did not decide that a combination of competitors to operate joint factories abroad might constitute an illegal restraint on American commerce even where it was established that foreign import restrictions imposed an absolute ban on American exports. His reason was: 'The intimate association of the principal American producers in day-to-day manufacturing operations, their exchange of patent licenses or industrial know-how, and their common experience in marketing and fixing prices may inevitably reduce their zeal for competition *inter sese* in the American market. . . . It may, therefore, be subject to condemnation regardless of the reasonableness of the manufacturers' conduct in the foreign countries.'

[2] This output amounted to only about 25% of all anti-friction bearings, but on familiar legal grounds the trial Court found that tapered roller bearings formed a separate and 'appreciable' segment of commerce.

Originally it had a strong patent position both in the United States and in foreign countries, and the evidence showed that as far back as 1909 it had commercial agreements with British and French companies in which territorial restrictions were based on patent licences. The trial Court indeed found: 'Those contracts were not merely patent licences for the manufacture of tapered roller bearings in limited areas, but they encompassed fields beyond the ambit of the existing patent rights . . . The territorial restrictions applied to markets where defendant had no patent rights. . . . They included future development and inventions in the industry.'

When the principal patents expired the foreign companies became potential competitors of American Timken. The evidence showed that in 1928 the first of a new series of restrictive agreements were made which became the central issue of the case. In 1927 American Timken had acquired a substantial interest in the stock of the British Timken company.[1] In 1928, in conjunction with the British owner of British Timken stock, they organized the French Timken company. Originally there were separate commercial agreements between the American and British companies and the British and French companies; later, in 1938, there was a 'tripartite contract' between all three which was to run until 1965.

According to the trial Court's findings the salient features of the agreements remained much the same throughout. Each company was given exclusive marketing areas in which the others agreed (with minor exceptions) not to sell. Broadly, the French company was to supply France and French dependencies (other than those in North and South America); the British company was to supply British Commonwealth countries (except Canada and other places in the American continents) and the rest of Europe; the American company retained the rest of the world. The British and French companies were licensed to use the trademark 'Timken' and agreed to manufacture and sell bearings only under that mark. They would thus build their goodwill on the Timken name and trademark but, by the terms of the agreements, they would lose the right to use the name and mark if the agreements came to an end. There were many ancillary conditions, including exclusive cross-licensing of present and future patents and undertakings to exchange all technical 'know-how' whether patented or not.

It was also found that the British and French companies entered into cartel agreements, involving price fixing and quota provisions, with

---

[1] At that time American Timken and a British businessman owned all the stock between them; later some stock was sold to the public, and at the time of the case American Timken held about 30% of the total and the principal British stockholder about 24%.

other European producers. The American company was not a party to these agreements but, according to the trial Court: 'They were the result of the understandings and co-operation of defendant with British and French Timken to bring them about. Defendant's territory was affected. It was the beneficiary of their operations. Its officials were in consultation with the officers of British and French Timken concerning them; they prompted and approved the agreements.'

One main question for the courts was whether American Timken's operations should come within the exception subsequently defined by Judge Wyzanski as 'the mere ownership and operation of a branch factory abroad which is not conducted as part of a combination, conspiracy or monopoly'. The defence laid great emphasis on the argument that their financial interests in the British and French companies made their operations a 'joint venture' or 'partnership'; and, as in the *Abrasives* case, it was contended that tariffs and currency and other restrictions abroad meant that the only practical way of going into foreign markets was through manufacturing subsidiaries.

The trial Court, sustained by a five to two majority in the Supreme Court, rejected these claims. It found that the British and French companies were throughout potential competitors of the American company. It attached importance to the fact that restrictive agreements between the American company and the predecessors of British and French Timken had been in existence long before the financial links were formed. The 1928 transactions were not a new departure: 'they merely extended the restrictive arrangements which had existed for almost twenty years between potential competitors'. The restrictive agreements did not arise out of American Timken's purchase of stock; on the contrary, the financial arrangements were made in order to carry on 'the combination to eliminate competition between the parties and to frustrate any competition of outsiders'.[1]

The argument that exports from the United States could not be commercially successful was also rejected. The trial Court accepted evidence to the effect that American Timken in fact received many inquiries from foreign purchasers and that 'small competitors of the defendant in the United States were able to make shipments on a relatively large scale'. Besides, as the Court shrewdly asked, if exports were really impossible, 'Why were the contracting parties . . . so

---

[1] Judge Freed in the trial Court stated the legal distinction as follows: 'If a joint venture or partnership is formed for the purpose of a lawful business enterprise and restraints result from the right to protect established business interests, no violation of the law occurs. But if the association is formed for the purpose of continuing a combination to allocate exclusive sales territories in the world, to fix prices and to eliminate competition both within and without the combination, it cannot hide from the effects of the law under the cloak of a joint venture or partnership.'

concerned about airtight agreements to keep each one within its own commercial domain?'

It was also pleaded that the territorial restrictions in the agreements were but reasonable conditions to attach to the exchange of technical 'know-how'. But, as the Court pointed out, a division of markets based on valid patents would be lawful only if the restrictions imposed were fully within the entitlement of the patent grant; thus it would be illegal to permit such restrictions to be based on exchanges of information about unpatented processes.

Much the same argument applied to the contention that the restrictions were reasonable conditions attached to licensing the use of the 'Timken' trademark. Apart from expressing doubt whether American Timken was in fact the legal owner of the mark in all the territories concerned, the Court observed that, in American law, a trademark is not a monopoly grant like a patent, but merely a distinguishing mark in which a proprietary interest is established by use. 'The owner of a trademark may not, like the proprietor of a patented invention, make a negative and merely prohibitive use of it as a monopoly.'

Under this ruling American Timken could, for example, legitimately prevent others, including the British and French Timken companies, from selling their products under its trademark without permission in the United States or anywhere else where it used the mark and established equitable ownership of it. But the fact that the courts will protect the owner and user of a trademark against 'passing off' does not mean that they will accord him any proprietary rights in countries where he specifically agrees not to use the mark. In any case the theory that the division of markets in the *Timken* case was merely incidental to licensing the trademark could not explain the obligation undertaken by the British and French companies not to sell any bearings without the trademark; this obligation prevented British Timken, for example, from selling bearings under a quite different trademark in the United States, even though such sales obviously could not harm the Timken mark or deceive the public.

For all these reasons the Timken arrangements were condemned by the Supreme Court as a conspiracy in restraint of foreign trade. This decision has been the subject of much criticism in the United States and it is important to be clear about what was and what was not decided. This has sometimes been obscured in American controversy, partly perhaps because of the terms in which Mr Justice Jackson couched a vigorous dissent. He said, for example:

I doubt that it should be regarded as an unreasonable restraint of trade for an American industrial concern to organize foreign subsidiaries, each limited to serving a particular market area. . . .

Timken did not sit down with competitors and divide an existing market between them. It has at all times, in all places, had powerful rivals. It was not effectively meeting their competition in foreign markets, and so it joined others in creating a British subsidiary to go after business best reachable through such a concern and a French one to exploit French markets. . . .

. . . I think a rule that it is restraint of trade to enter a foreign market through a separate subsidiary of limited scope is virtually to foreclose foreign commerce of many kinds. It is one thing for competitors . . . to divide the United States market which is an economic and legal unit; it is another for an industry to recognize that foreign markets consist of many legal and economic units and to go after each through separate means. I think this decision will restrain more trade than it sets free.

The form of these remarks might well have given the clue that the dispute between Mr Justice Jackson and the majority of the Court was a dispute as to the facts, not one about the law. For the majority, following the trial Court, simply did not see the situation as one in which the American company went after otherwise unattainable business by setting up subsidiary companies. To them what stood out was that British and French manufacturers of tapered roller bearings had existed all along; that when the main patents expired, these companies might have been expected to become important international competitors of American Timken; that it was precisely at this time that the set of related transactions took place by which the American company acquired a large measure of financial control over these potential competitors and entered into rigid, market sharing agreements with them. To the majority, in other words, the fact was that the investment was ancillary to and contributory to the restrictive scheme, not that the restrictions followed incidentally upon the investment.

Thus the case should not be taken as showing, as Mr Justice Jackson feared, that 'for an American industrial concern to organize foreign subsidiaries each limited to serving a particular market area' is in itself an unreasonable restraint of trade violating the Sherman Act. There are indeed many examples of manufacturing companies in Europe and elsewhere which are affiliates of American companies and which have not run into antitrust trouble. A foreign branch that was actually part of an American company, or even a wholly owned subsidiary, would incur practically no legal risk from the mere fact that it was directed exclusively to supplying its local market, for no restrictive agreements would be required in such a case.

Even where the affiliate is only partly owned by the American company and partly by local financial and commercial interests, it should not be assumed that the restriction of its selling effort to a particular market would be illegal *per se* in the absence of the type of evidence—of a long-term purpose to eliminate international competition—that impressed the courts in the *Timken* case. A territorial restriction might after all be a legitimate condition in licences under the American firm's foreign patents (assuming the absence of extensive cross-licensing or other complications) or it might be regarded as reasonably ancillary to the protection of an American investment which would not otherwise be made. As in other parts of the antitrust field, the 'ultimate fact' that is decisive is the intent and purpose of the parties. If the evidence is such as to convince the courts that this purpose is suppression of competition, particular excuses based on the need to protect patents, trademarks and other investments, or on the difficulty of exporting goods from the United States, are unlikely to succeed. But where there is no such evidence, the rule of reason may well operate to save arrangements which promote more trade than they restrain.

4. *Agreements between United States companies and foreign companies:*
National Lead. *Agreements arising out of exchanges of patents*
and 'know-how': Foundry Services v. Beneflux

Rightly or wrongly, the *Timken* case was treated as if it involved restrictive agreements between an American company and its international competitors. Most of the important 'cartel' cases of the post-war period have been concerned with agreements of this kind and the courts have applied to them all the usual rules and prescriptions of Sherman Act case law. Thus any price fixing agreement between American and foreign firms is illegal *per se*; and it has been held that the rule of the *Line Material* case—that minimum-price stipulations may not be included in licences issued under pooled or cross-licensed patents—is applicable in the field of foreign trade.[1]

Agreements to divide world markets, usually reserving to each participating firm its own national market, are, of course, the most convenient and consequently the commonest means by which competition in international trade is restrained. Often these agreements arise out of arrangements for licensing the practice of new technical innovations from one country to another. These arrangements may in themselves be highly desirable. There is no doubt, however, that agreements dividing markets among international competitors, given that they affect American exports or imports, are just as illegal as when the markets concerned and the participants are all within the United States. The best illustration is probably *United States* v. *National Lead Company* (Supreme Court, 1947). The rule of this case, as laid down by

[1] *United States* v. *General Electric Company* (the *Carboloy* case), 1948.

Judge Rifkind in the trial Court and sustained on appeal, was as follows: 'No citation of authority is any longer necessary to support the proposition that a combination of competitors which by agreement divides the world into exclusive trade areas, and suppresses all competition among the members of the combination, offends the Sherman Act.'[1]

The products involved were titanium pigments; it had been found in the First World War that certain compounds of this metal, in particular titanium dioxide, were greatly superior to any other material for the making of white paint and were valuable in other manufacturing processes. A new industry was founded on this discovery and there were three independent and competing patented processes that could be used in its development. One process was an American discovery and the patents for it were assigned to the Titanium Pigment Company in which the National Lead Company bought a substantial interest in 1920. Patents for another process, developed in Norway, were held by the Titan Co. A/S in that country. The National Lead Company negotiated an agreement, also in 1920, between Titanium Pigment and Titan A/S under which the former was to have exclusive rights under all existing and future patents of either party in North America and the latter in the rest of the world, except that the South American market was to be shared. The agreement had many other facets[2] and was summed up by Judge Rifkind in the trial Court as follows:

It is manifest that by the terms of this agreement the parties had divided the world into two trade areas or territories; that each party agreed not to trespass into the territory allotted to the other; and that all commerce between the two territories in titanium products was, as far as these parties were concerned, interdicted and could proceed only by the grace of their mutual consent. The suppression of this commerce was not limited to patented articles or to articles produced by patented processes but extended to all products within the 'licensed field'.

Over sixty subsequent agreements were introduced into the evidence in the case. In 1927 National Lead acquired 87% of the stock of Titan A/S and later organized Titan Company Ltd, which took over the rights and obligations of Titan A/S under the 1920 contract and became, as Judge Rifkind put it, 'National Lead's corporate pocket for the deposit of its holdings in foreign titanium enterprises'. First through Titan A/S and later through Titan Company Ltd, agreements were

---

[1] This rule was in fact applied as far back as 1911 in the *American Tobacco* case.

[2] The full story of the complex of agreements in this case may be found in Judge Rifkind's findings of fact, 63 Fed. Supp. 513. A useful summary is to be found in *Restrictive Business Practices: Analysis of Governmental Measures Relating to Restrictive Business Practices*, United Nations Economic and Social Council, (Official Records, 16th Session, Supplement 11A) New York, 1953, pp. 59–62.

made with French, German, British and other interests by which the original Titan share of the world market—that is, the rest of the world outside North and South America—was further subdivided, each new partner being 'brought within the orbit and subjected to the regulation of the principles of the 1920 contract'. For example, a new company, Titangesellschaft, owned jointly by I.G. Farben in Germany and Titan A/S, was formed in 1927 and was assigned a large area of central and eastern Europe, together with China and Japan, as its market. I.G. Farben agreed to assign all its existing and future patents to the jointly owned company and not to engage in the titanium business independently. Another jointly owned company was set up to cover the Canadian market.

Meanwhile assignees and licensees under the third patented process remained in the field as competitors and a new series of agreements was made, beginning in 1933, to regulate the commercial relations of these firms with the National Lead and Titan group; these agreements featured sales quotas, patent exchanges, market allocations, price stipulations and so on. In the United States the patents covering the third process had been acquired by a subsidiary of the du Pont company and in 1933 a cross-licensing agreement between the National Lead and du Pont subsidiaries was negotiated.

Such in brief was the picture which Judge Rifkind summed up as follows:

When the story is seen as a whole, there is no blinking the fact that there is no free commerce in titanium. Every pound of it is trammelled by privately imposed regulation. The channels of this commerce have not been formed by the winds and currents of competition. They are, in large measure, artificial canals privately constructed. The borders of the private domain in titanium are guarded by hundreds of patents, procured without opposition, and maintained without litigation . . . It was more difficult for the independent outsider to enter this business than for the camel to make its proverbial passage through the eye of a needle.

Since the effect of the agreements was to prevent any imports of titanium pigments into the United States except with National Lead's consent and to prevent any exports by National Lead outside the western hemisphere, Judge Rifkind had no doubt that they restrained the interstate and foreign commerce of the United States. Nor could they be justified as legitimate conditions attached to patent licences, for 'they applied to commerce beyond the scope of any patents, . . . extended to a time beyond the duration of any then-existing patent, . . . embraced acknowledgement of patent validity with respect to patents not yet issued nor applied for, and concerning inventions not yet conceived'.

It was argued in defence of the agreements that the economic performance of the industry had been on a high level throughout— prices had consistently fallen and output risen, while intensive research had improved the product. But, as always in the Sherman case law, the claim to assert the public interest above the philosophy of antitrust failed. Judge Rifkind's treatment of this point, strongly reminiscent of Mr Justice Stone's classic statement in the *Trenton Potteries* case, established that the rule of competition is no less applicable to foreign than to interstate trade.

Indeed, the major premise of the Sherman Act is that the suppression of competition in international trade is in and of itself a public injury; or, at any rate, that such suppression is a greater price than we want to pay for the benefits it sometimes secures. Nor does it necessarily follow that the advance of the art, the rise in production and the decline of prices are attributable to the effects of the combination. *Post hoc, propter hoc* is an invalid argument whether used by the plaintiff or the defendant. Anyone is free to speculate whether, in the absence of the arrangement, the stimulus of competition might not have produced far greater strides in these beneficial directions. The economic theory underlying the Sherman Act is that, in the long run, competition is a more effective prod to production and a more trustworthy regulator of prices than even an enlightened combination.

Similarly, the argument that American firms must join in cartel arrangements if they are to succeed in a cartelized section of world trade was rejected on the ground that only Congress could approve an exemption from antitrust. Judge Rifkind's findings of fact and law were sustained by the Supreme Court, and the case stands, therefore, as firm authority for the condemnation under antitrust of agreements between American and foreign competitors for allocating world markets and otherwise suppressing competition.

The *National Lead* case was the earliest to explore thoroughly this aspect of the law and it remains perhaps the best example because of the elaborate nature of the arrangements concerned. A number of subsequent cases have been broadly similar in their facts and legal results and need not be recounted in detail here.[1]

It may, however, be asked how international exchanges of new technical advances, which in themselves are plainly desirable, can be carried on unless the firms concerned are entitled to retain exclusive rights in their home territories. For manufacturers will surely not create a powerful source of competition for themselves by putting their foreign counterparts in possession of their technical secrets if they

---

[1] The trial Judges' opinions in *United States* v. *General Electric Company* (the *Carboloy* case), 80 Fed. Supp. 989; *United States* v. *General Electric Company* (the *Lamps* case), 82 Fed. Supp. 753; *United States* v. *Imperial Chemical Industries*, 100 Fed. Supp. 504, are the best sources for further study of the main cases.

cannot prevent the recipients from invading their domestic market. It is important to note that fears of this kind exaggerate the legal dangers arising out of the *National Lead* and similar cases.

Nothing in these cases prevents the individual patent owner from licensing his United States or foreign patents exclusively and laying down territorial restrictions in the licences. The rules applying to international patent licensing are no more and no less stringent than those applying within the United States outlined in the last chapter. Thus an American firm holding British or German patents for a new plastic material may choose to license a British or German firm exclusively under those patents (or even assign the patents outright) rather than attempt to export the material. A licence under a particular country's patent automatically confines the licensee to that country, and will convey to the recipient no immunity against legal action if it attempts to make or sell the patented product in the United States and so infringes the American firm's United States patents.[1] Equally the exclusive licensee under foreign patents will be legitimately protected by the licence against competition in his home market from the licensor or other American firms.

The fact that exclusive patent licensing, as such, creates no antitrust offence, especially when coupled with the fact that many difficulties protective tariffs, freight costs, the problem of setting up an adequate distributive organization in a foreign country—may beset the exporter, suggests that the impact of the Sherman Act in this field may be overrated. Indeed, to the outsider it sometimes seems that the agreements between American and foreign firms which have figured in the recorded cases have worked their own legal undoing by spelling out in great elaboration restrictive conditions which may not in practice add much to the protection of the parties. It is understandable that this should be so, since the businessmen and lawyers who represent the foreign companies in negotiating such agreements are usually unfamiliar with the need for hedging against Sherman Act risks and take it for virtue to protect their principals against contingencies.

Thus the extension of an agreement to cover the exchange of future patents in a wide industrial field, or to restrict trade in unpatented products which may be of relatively minor importance, is sure to court condemnation under the Sherman Act with the result that the court may well decree the abandonment of the agreement as a whole. Yet the absence of such extended provisions would in no way prevent the

[1] In the same way an agreement that a foreign firm shall use an American brand name or trademark in its domestic market, as in the *Timken* case, will convey no right to that firm to sell its product under that mark in the United States. The trouble arises, as was seen above, when the agreement requires the foreign firm to refrain from selling an unpatented product in the United States under any trademark.

parties from entering into fresh negotiations for exclusive licensing when new patented products appeared; nor would it mean that a brisk export trade in the unpatented items would necessarily take place. Many commercial facts of life might still give *de facto* protection. In this field it is important to recall Mr Justice Holmes' observation in the *Swift* case: 'The defendants cannot be ordered to compete, but they properly can be forbidden to give directions or to make arrangements not to compete.'

None of this is meant to imply, of course, that the Sherman Act is not a real barrier against many things that the parties to international business agreements sometimes want to achieve. Where their underlying purpose is to suppress all competition or jointly to monopolize an industry on a world-wide scale, they cannot expect to escape its impact.[1] Near the borderlines of Sherman Act case law dealing with patent licensing, it may be that apparently reasonable arrangements between American firms and their foreign rivals run serious legal risks. It is not clear from the recorded decisions whether, for example, the *Line Material* doctrine would be strictly applied to territorial restrictions included in licences under internationally cross-licensed or pooled patents. If it were, there would be grounds for fearing that antitrust might seriously inhibit exchanges of technology.[2]

It would, however, be dangerous to assume that the analogy would be mechanically applied. As in all antitrust case law, the courts would seek to establish the intent of the parties. What are they really doing? Simply promoting a fruitful interchange of techniques? Or aiming rather to extend unduly the proper bounds of their patent grants? From the fact that, rightly or wrongly, the Supreme Court regarded the second answer as correct in the *Line Material* situation, it by no means follows that the same conclusion would be reached in the

---

[1] It can hardly be gainsaid, on the record of the major cases which have come before the courts, that restriction has been not less the objective than technological exchanges, and it seems clear that, if patents were licensed piecemeal in the way suggested above, a more competitive pattern would have appeared than was actually disclosed in these cases.

[2] It is probably safest to regard the point as undecided. In *United States* v. *Imperial Chemical Industries* (1951), however, Judge Ryan, in a trial Court opinion, came near to saying that the *Line Material* rule would be applied: 'In view of our determination that the various agreements considered were part of an overall conspiracy to divide world territories, it becomes unnecessary to consider the *per se* validity of the individual agreements. It should be noted, however, that the Government has vigorously argued, primarily by analogy to *United States* v. *Line Material* . . . that the Patents and Processes Agreements were illegal on their face.' When he came to his opinion on relief one year later Judge Ryan went further still and, referring to the *Line Material* case, said: 'We have held that when patents are pooled to carry out a division of territories, it is equally as unlawful as when they are unified to effect price fixing.' But these dicta do not necessarily imply more than that division of territories is as much a *per se* violation of the Sherman Act as price fixing, whether or not it arises out of a patent pooling arrangement, and this is simply the rule of *Addyston Pipe* and *Standard Sanitary Manufacturing Company* (see above, Chapter II).

situation outlined above. The court would certainly compare, for example, the actual competitive situation with that which would be expected in the absence of the agreement. If, for example, the sole finding of fact in the *National Lead* case had been that National Lead's subsidiary was the exclusive licensee under the United States patents covering the Titan A/S process, and that Titan was the exclusive licensee under the various European patents covering the American process, it is at least open to doubt whether a conspiracy in restraint of foreign trade would have been established. Certainly the actual finding of conspiracy in that case was based on far more sweeping evidence.

More cases are needed to locate the borderlines accurately in this field because the evidence in the recorded cases has mostly been of the sledgehammer variety rather than the kind that requires delicate inferences. What emerges clearly from the decisions is that American and foreign companies, in making arrangements for exchanging patents and technical 'know-how', should make separate licensing agreements in respect of each patent or group of patents involved and avoid large general agreements covering a whole industrial field. The exclusiveness inherent in a sole licence issued under a particular country's patents should be relied on for protection and the lily should not be gilded by adding express restrictive covenants whereby each party agrees to stay out of the other's markets. The agreements should not stray outside the strict requirements of patent licensing or involve restrictions to trade in unpatented products or products made with the help of exchanges of unpatented 'know-how'. (As mentioned above, a restrictive covenant preventing such trade is in many cases not the only reason why such trade is unlikely to take place.) The agreements should not bind the parties to exchange all future patents over a wide field for a long period; after all, fresh negotiations can be undertaken when something new comes along.

These are not, of course, prescriptions for evasion; if the record showed that these techniques still concealed a broad anti-competitive purpose, they would probably fail. There is no prescription for evading the Sherman Act if what is desired and intended is the eradication of competition. Probably a large accumulation of exclusive patent licences granted reciprocally between firms which are dominant in their industries in their own countries will always carry heavy legal risks. Possibly the *Line Material* rule would after all apply before the accumulation had got very far. But it is not the case that exclusive patent licensing as such between international rivals violates the law.

One argument sometimes raised both by foreign companies and by United States companies engaged in foreign commerce is that the anti-competitive practices with which they have been charged are perfectly legitimate under the laws of the country in which they were made or to which they relate. Whilst this is a factor which might be taken into account in applying the rule of reason to any particular agreement, it is certainly not a blanket defence, as was made clear by the Southern District Court of New York in *United States* v. *Watchmakers of Switzerland Information Center* (1963). The facts here were that Swiss and United States manufacturers had entered into agreements in both countries to restrict the manufacture of watches in the United States. The agreements entered into in Switzerland were formulated primarily by the manufacturers but were 'recognized as facts of economic and industrial life' by the Swiss Government. It would have been a defence had the Swiss Government compelled the execution of these agreements under either administrative or statutory powers. Consent decrees are accordingly almost invariably phrased to take account of this.

Equally the involvement of a foreign Government in some of the actions upon which a charge under section 2 of the Sherman Act has been brought does not necessarily constitute a defence. In *Continental Ore Company* v. *Union Carbide & Carbon Corp.* (1962) the Supreme Court had to take account of the fact that one of the defendant's Canadian subsidiaries had, during the war, been under the direction of the Canadian Government,[1] and had in those circumstances refused to allow the plaintiff to supply vanadium to its existing Canadian customers. There was evidence that the exclusion of the plaintiff was the result of the exercise of the discretion of the directors of that subsidiary, and was not either required or specifically approved by the Canadian Government. Overruling the Ninth Circuit Court of Appeals, Mr Justice White for the majority said that any jury was perfectly entitled, in that situation, to decide the issue of whether the loss of Continental's Canadian business was caused by the defendant's activities or not, and the case was remanded to the District Court for them to make appropriate findings.

As a footnote to this section it is worthwhile mentioning a case which is on a much smaller scale than those discussed above and which shows that, where the scale is small and the parties of relatively minor importance in their industries, a restrictive covenant, even in an agreement for the use of unpatented processes, may not be regarded as illegal *per se*. This is *Foundry Services* v. *Beneflux Corporation* (Southern District Court of New York, 1953).

An English firm named Foundry Services Ltd had various secret processes and recipes for the production of fluxes used in metal casting. Its 'know-how' was not, however, protected by American patents. In 1934 it granted a firm called Foundry Services Inc. of New York an

---

[1] This was owing to the vital strategic use of vanadium, a metal employed as an alloy in the hardening of steel.

exclusive licence to manufacture its fluxes and sell them in the United States and Canada. The licence was to run initially for five years and it was agreed that the New York firm would supply the product only in the United States and Canada while the English firm would not enter those markets.

The agreement was extended by five-year periods and was still operative in 1951 when the English firm gave notice that it wished to terminate it, the reason given being that the American firm had sold an insignificant amount of the product ($4 worth) in Mexico. It was suggested to the Court that the real reason was the English firm's dissatisfaction with the New York firm's efforts to increase sales of the product, for in 1952 the English firm set up a subsidiary company —the Beneflux Corporation—in the United States to carry on business in the product.

Foundry Services Inc., the New York firm, applied to the Court for an injunction to restrain the Beneflux Corporation from competing with it in the sale of fluxes in breach of the exclusive licensing agreement. In resisting the application, Beneflux did not rely on the minor breach of the agreement caused by the sale in Mexico but contended that the agreement should be regarded as void as an illegal restrictive contract under the Sherman Act.

The case came before the Court on an application for a preliminary injunction pending a trial of the issues. In granting the application, the Court held that the contract was legal and enforceable. Judge McGohey pointed out that when the agreement began the English and New York companies were not competitors in any field. The English firm might have withheld its secret processes entirely from the American market. The fluxes made to the English recipes were not the only ones available or in use, and no new industry had been created by their discovery. He contrasted these facts with the situation in cases like *National Lead* and *Timken* where the courts had found conspiracy in restraint of trade between true competitors; in this case the New York firm was no more than an agent of the English firm and common justice required that the principal should not set up in opposition to his agent after contracting not to do so. On the legality of the restrictive covenant, Judge McGohey said:

It is still the law that restraints to be unlawful must be unreasonable. No case cited by the defendant declares unlawful, in itself, an isolated agreement of mutual restraint as to territory only between a single owner-licensor of a secret process and a single licensee not theretofore in competition with each other. There was no attempt to control the price of these fluxes or to control the distribution or price of products made through their use. . . . We have here only the usual covenant by an owner-licensor of a secret process not to compete with its single licensee in the assigned area and to be free from the latter's interference elsewhere. These restraints, clearly only ancillary to a valid primary purpose, are precisely of the kind consistently permitted at common law.

It would be dangerous to set too much store by this opinion. On the hearing for a preliminary injunction there was, of course, no full trial of the issues and the holding on the substantive point of law involved can hardly be decisive.[1] Nevertheless, this opinion at least shows that the courts do not close their minds to the rule of reason in this field.

5. *American jurisdiction over foreign companies in antitrust cases: Judge Hand's ruling in the* ALCOA *case; the* Banana *case; in personam jurisdiction; subpoenas served on foreign companies for discovery of documents; decrees directed against foreign companies—the* I.C.I. *case and the* General Electric (Lamps) *case*

To business people and others outside the United States one of the most interesting and important issues raised by the 'cartel' cases is that of the jurisdiction of the American courts over foreign firms. In what circumstances may British and other non-American firms find themselves answerable to American courts for antitrust offences? What penalties may be inflicted on them? What limits ought to be set to American jurisdiction and what limits are in practice acknowledged by the American courts themselves?

There can be no question, of course, of any weakening of the jurisdiction of American courts over American companies by virtue of agreements between those companies and foreign concerns. If such an agreement is found illegal, it is obviously no defence for the American company to urge that it could not help itself because it had undertaken obligations to a British or German concern or because the agreement was made in Milan or Zurich. That would be too easy. This point was made clearly by Judge Rifkind in the *National Lead* case:

The argument has been advanced that this Court cannot invalidate contracts with parties who are not within the Court's jurisdiction and amenable to its order.

---

[1] The Second Circuit Court of Appeals later held that Judge McGohey was wrong to grant a preliminary injunction. This decision was made on the ground that the plaintiff had not shown that he would suffer 'irreparable injury' unless the *status quo* was maintained pending trial of the suit. The Court of Appeals did not consider the legality of the restrictive contract. Judge Chase observed: '. . . we think it neither advisable nor necessary to decide at this time whether the contract is valid. It is enough to notice that there is a substantial doubt about that. . . .' Judge Learned Hand, however, hinted in a concurring opinion that the agreement might be illegal, and the case was settled out of court.

The absence of National Lead's foreign associates will, of course, place a practical limitation upon the scope of the Court's decree: it does not prevent the Court from finding a violation as the facts warrant and from restraining those within the reach of its mandate from continuing a conspiracy in defiance of the Sherman Act.

Equally there can be no doubt of the right of American courts to enforce American law against foreign companies carrying on business in the United States. Such companies must obviously conform to the law of the sovereign who gives hospitality to their commerce. A foreign company which imports and distributes large quantities of goods in the United States is no more entitled than an American company to make price fixing agreements in the American market. One who seeks the grant of United States patents for his inventions can clearly have no complaint if the grantor insists that the patentee abide by the terms of its statutes and be subject to the normal penalties for misuse of the grant. He may think the statutes unwise and the penalties draconian, but in that case his remedy is not to apply for or accept the grant.

The broad area within which the jurisdiction of the American courts is thus unchallengeable might be thought sufficient to accomplish the aims of antitrust in respect to American commerce with foreign nations. Where American firms, for example, so conduct their operations abroad as to restrict American exports, as in the *Abrasives* case, there is no problem over jurisdiction. Where an American firm makes an illegal agreement with a foreign firm, it can properly be ordered to abrogate it; and since it takes two to implement an agreement, this will be enough to stop it. Even where the agreement is between an American firm and a number of foreign concerns organized in a cartel, the power of the American courts to forbid the continued participation of the American firm may in practice be enough to make the cartel unworkable. When American companies are an important factor in international markets, their withdrawal from a cartel and hence the threat of their competition in markets formerly reserved to other participants may be a crippling blow to the cartel's success.[1] And if, despite the worrying absence of American participation, the benighted foreigners choose to carry on their cartel among themselves, what business is that of the American courts?

So it might be thought. But to those who administer antitrust and believe wholeheartedly in its beneficent influence, the unchallenged right of the courts to enforce American law against American companies and against foreign companies doing business in the United States has

---

[1] Though it must be remembered, of course, that antitrust cannot order businessmen to compete. An order to an American company that it must not agree not to compete in foreign markets would not invariably lead to its entry into those markets.

not always seemed sufficient. Sometimes it may be suspected that an American company has an understanding with foreign companies that they will not invade the North American market and it will not export to their markets, but no express agreement relating to the American side of the bargain can be found or proved.[1] Yet the foreign companies concerned may be quite open and explicit about their arrangements and obligations. It may seem very frustrating not to be able to bring before the court those who have agreed not to supply the American market, a course of action which rather clearly restrains competition in the United States.

It must also be tantalizing, in some cases, to the enforcement agencies to feel that the files of the non-American participants in a suspected cartel agreement are probably bursting with exhibits which would not only lay bare the workings of the restrictive scheme but would even record an uninhibited satisfaction at the suppression of competition envisaged and intended by the parties; whereas the files of the American company concerned, meticulously guided and reviewed by lawyers who have antitrust risks constantly in their thoughts, may yield but meagre or arcane indications of the true situation.

Finally it may seem that adequate remedial measures against proven antitrust offences will be possible only if injunctions and prohibitions can be directed against foreign companies. Particularly in the biggest cases of market allocation on a global scale, it may seem that to open up the United States market by cancelling the American partner's rights under the illegal compact and even by withdrawing its patent protection[2] will give an unfair and one-sided result, and that the foreign parties ought to be compelled to grant reciprocal immunities under their patents so that American firms may compete in their markets.

Thus for these three main reasons—to enforce the Sherman Act against conspiracies not to supply the United States market, to exploit for enforcement purposes the evidence obtainable from foreign companies and to secure adequate remedies—there has always been pressure on the courts from the enforcement agencies to take an expansive view of the scope of their jurisdiction. And in some important cases the courts have responded to this pressure in a way that has led foreign observers and even some leading American lawyers to believe that jurisdiction has been asserted to an extent which conflicts with accepted principles of international law.

---

[1] This, very roughly, was the picture in the *ALCOA* case which led Judge Learned Hand to the observations quoted below.

[2] The way in which patent protection may be withdrawn by the courts as a remedy against antitrust violations is explained below, Chapter XIV; the particular difficulty about applying that remedy in the case of international agreements unless jurisdiction can be exercised over foreign companies is illustrated by the *du Pont/I.C.I.* case later in this chapter.

In the famous *ALCOA* case, for example, Judge Learned Hand held that certain restrictive agreements between foreign companies violated section 1 of the Sherman Act, though they were made outside the United States and no American company was shown to be party to them. In this case, indeed, there was no express reference in the agreements to imports into the United States, but Judge Hand felt able to infer that 'they were intended to affect imports and did affect them'. He based his condemnation of the agreements on the proposition that: 'Any state may impose liabilities even upon persons not within its allegiance for conduct outside its borders that has consequences within its borders which the state reprehends.'

This dictum, in particular, has been widely criticized as contrary to accepted international law. It is true that there are certain contexts in which a state is regarded as competent to punish a foreigner for acts committed abroad which are directly connected with a crime within its territory. To take a crude example, if a man on an international frontier pulls a trigger in one country and shoots his enemy in another country, he is unlikely to escape retribution on jurisdictional grounds. But the principle underlying this type of example is usually regarded as applicable only to crimes which all civilized nations condemn. This is far from being true of the economic 'crimes' created by the Sherman Act, which reflect a specifically American policy. Moreover, the connexion between a commercial agreement made in Europe and an undue restraint of trade in the United States is less direct and obvious by any calculation than that between pressing the trigger in Mexico and the victim's dropping dead in California. To add the whole complex realm of Sherman Act case law with its subtle theology of 'conspiracy' and 'intent' to the rare contexts in which extra-territorial jurisdiction may be properly claimed would inevitably be unjust to the foreign businessmen, to whom this type of regulation is strange, and would set almost no limit in principle to jurisdictional claims.[1]

Finally the commentators have noted that Judge Hand's proposition conflicts with powerful authority from earlier American decisions.

---

[1] To be fair to Judge Hand, it should be noted that he qualified his proposition by important addenda which his critics do not always acknowledge. He noted that some agreements made outside the United States might actually affect American commerce, though not intended so to do. Because of the 'international complications likely to arise from an effort in this country to treat such agreements as unlawful', he thought that Congress could not have intended the Sherman Act to cover them. Also there might be agreements which, though intended to affect American imports, did not actually do so; and he was prepared to assume that these should not be covered. Thus he applied his rule only to agreements which were both intended to affect American commerce and shown actually to have had some effect. In practice this qualification might keep the situations covered by Judge Hand's view of American jurisdiction within relatively modest bounds. But even the assertion of jurisdiction over foreign activities abroad which purposely affect American imports clearly conflicts with the principle that a nation's laws should have sway only within its own territories.

Frequently quoted in this connexion is the view expressed by Mr Justice Holmes speaking for the Supreme Court in *American Banana Company* v. *United Fruit Company* (1909). This was a treble-damage action in which the plaintiff complained of the rough methods used by the defendant to maintain its dominant position in the ownership and control of fruit plantations in Panama.[1] The defendant in this case was an American company, but since the acts complained of took place in Central America, the Supreme Court held that no cause of action had been stated and Mr Justice Holmes dealt with the jurisdictional point as follows:

. . . The general and almost universal rule is that the character of an act as lawful or unlawful must be determined wholly by the law of the country where the act is done. . . . For another jurisdiction, if it should happen to lay hold of the actor, to treat him according to its own notions rather than those of the place where he did the acts, not only would be unjust, but would be an interference with the authority of another sovereign, contrary to the comity of nations, which the other state concerned justly might resent. . . .

The foregoing consideration would lead in case of doubt to a construction of any statute as confined in its operations and effect to the territorial limits over which the lawmaker has general and legitimate power. 'All legislation is prima facie territorial.'[2]

Nevertheless, Judge Hand's view of the matter has been influential in recent years and has been reflected in a number of actions and decrees of American courts. Some of these must now be examined. The proposition that foreign companies may rightfully be punished by American courts for activities abroad which are intended to affect and do affect American commerce unlawfully does not of itself mean, of course, that jurisdiction can always be exercised in practice. The companies concerned may not be within the reach of American authority at all. Where the companies do not carry on business in the United States and remain beyond the reach of the law, the claim to jurisdiction is only of academic interest—a bark without a bite.

[1] It should be noted, however, that the acts complained of were official acts of the sovereign Government of Costa Rica (which was alleged to have been influenced by the defendant).

[2] A clear statement of the view that Judge Hand's proposition conflicts with international law will be found in Mr G. W. Haight's article 'International Law and Extraterritorial Application of the Antitrust Laws', *Yale Law Journal*, vol. 63, 1954, p. 639. See also the immediately following article, 'Sources of Conflict between International Law and the Antitrust Laws' by Mr William D. Whitney, *loc. cit.* p. 655. For a cogent statement of the opposing view, see Sigmund Timberg, 'Extraterritorial Jurisdiction under the Sherman Act', *The Record of the Association of the Bar of the City of New York*, vol. 11, no. 3, March 1956. Mr Timberg contrasts Mr Justice Holmes' dicta above with his later statement, which closely anticipates Judge Hand's rule, in *Strassheim* v. *Daily*: 'Acts done outside a jurisdiction but intended to produce and producing detrimental effects within it, justify a state in punishing the cause of the harm as if he had been present at the effect, if the state should succeed in getting him within its power.' (This was a case of fraud involving extra-territorial jurisdiction as between different States of the Union.)

But the foreign companies are not always so fortunate. There have been instances in which the courts have asserted *in personam* jurisdiction over officers of foreign companies when they have appeared in the United States on business or personal visits. Where companies have had assets in the United States, writs threatening seizure have been used to compel their appearance in court. In this connexion the courts have been criticized for not maintaining a clear distinction between jurisdiction over the person and jurisdiction over the subject matter in a case. If, as the critics assert, it is contrary to international law for a state to claim jurisdiction over a foreign company in respect of activities outside its territory, then the fortuitous circumstance that persons or property belonging to the company are found within its territory should make no difference.[1]

There have been a number of instances in which Grand Jury subpoenas have been served on foreign companies, requiring the production in court of documents relating to antitrust indictments. It has been ruled that companies within the jurisdiction of the courts may not evade this type of summons simply on the ground that the documents required are abroad; control over the documents is decisive, not their location. Where jurisdiction is correctly asserted, as over American companies, this is reasonable. But where the documents are held by subsidiary companies which may be partly owned by foreign interests and which are under the jurisdiction of a foreign sovereign, considerations of international comity might be expected to cause restraint in thus extending legal processes beyond the borders of the United States. And where the companies concerned are wholly foreign—incorporated abroad, without any significant United States participation in their direction or control—and the documents required relate to activities carried on outside the United States, the serving of subpoenas seems very difficult to justify.[2]

It has indeed led more than once to a sharp reaction on the part of other Governments. When in 1947, for example, subpoenas were served on Canadian companies and individuals in the newsprint industry, the provincial legislatures of Ontario and Quebec both passed special enactments to prevent the removal of the documents from their provinces. The subpoenas were subsequently withdrawn.

Another incident of this kind, in connexion with the investigation

---

[1] See W. D. Whitney, *loc. cit.* p. 656.

[2] There have been a number of cases in which subpoenas have been served on foreign parent companies by being addressed to the offices of American subsidiaries, where the foreign companies carry on no business in the United States. It seems likely that English courts would not accept this procedure as proper service of subpoenas and would not enforce them. American courts do appear to accept it as proper service and this in itself is a point which might well be contested as a matter of international law.

by the Federal Maritime Commission of the freight rates charged by the member lines of certain transatlantic shipping conferences, occurred in the early 1960s. Demands by the Commission for documentary evidence within the possession of certain United Kingdom shipping companies led to considerable public protest in the United Kingdom and the enactment of a statute requiring persons within the United Kingdom to notify the Minister of Transport if they received demands for the production of documents in circumstances which might constitute a violation of United Kingdom jurisdiction, and entitling the Minister to prohibit their compliance with such orders.[1]

Again, when the Department of Justice set on foot a Grand Jury investigation into restrictive agreements affecting international trade in oil, subpoenas were served on the Anglo-Iranian Oil Company and other foreign companies, requiring the production of many hundreds of documents. The investigation was directed specifically and exclusively to operations outside the United States on the part of certain American and foreign oil companies. In this instance the British Government and the Governments of the Netherlands, France, Belgium, India and Pakistan all issued directives to companies under their jurisdiction that the subpoenas should not be complied with. The letter from the British Government to the Anglo-Iranian Oil Company said in part: 'Her Majesty's Government consider it contrary to international comity that you or your officers should be required in answer to a subpoena couched in the widest terms to produce documents which are not only not in the United States of America but which do not even relate to business in that country.'[2] Subsequently President Truman asked the Attorney General to bring to an end the criminal process against the companies and institute instead a civil suit. After the change of administration in January 1953 civil litigation was commenced, but only against the five American oil companies named in the original suit; the foreign companies were no longer joined in the case.

Probably the most serious jurisdictional issues arise over the decrees directed by the courts against foreign companies which are found in

---

[1] The Shipping Contracts and Commercial Documents Act, 1964. The statute also makes similar provisions with respect to orders for the production of commercial documents of any kind (not merely limited to shipping matters) in order to cover situations such as that referred to in connexion with the Anglo-Iranian Oil Company.

[2] It is of interest that when this action of the British Government came to the notice of the Court, Judge Kirkland excused the Anglo-Iranian Oil Company. But he did so on the ground that the British Government's substantial financial interest in the company made it in effect an arm of the Government and thus entitled to the immunity extended to a foreign sovereign. While this was no doubt a good ground for his action, it ignored the more important point at issue, namely that the jurisdiction of the Court had been wrongly asserted and that the subpoena was unacceptable even in the absence of any financial relation between the company and the foreign sovereign.

civil cases to have violated the Sherman Act. It appears that before the war the territorial principle of jurisdiction was respected, at least in consent decrees;[1] but in some post-war cases the injunctions and prohibitions which the courts have laid on foreign companies have at times involved far-reaching effects on the activities of those companies outside the United States and even on their obligations to third parties abroad.

The best illustration is the final decree in *United States* v. *Imperial Chemical Industries* (Southern District Court of New York, 1952). The trial had centred on the many agreements between I.C.I. in England and the du Pont company in the United States which provided for very elaborate exchanges of existing and future patents and technical information over a wide industrial field and which were held to involve a world-wide allocation of markets and other restrictions of competition between the companies. There could be no complaint in this case about the Court's jurisdiction over the subject matter in dispute or over the parties. If the Court's findings of fact were accepted, the agreements directly affected American exports and imports. The du Pont company was thus in clear violation of the Sherman Act and lay open, like any other antitrust defendant, to whatever measures of equity relief the Court had power to decree; I.C.I. was carrying on business in the United States at least to the extent that it maintained an office in New York and applied for and received a great many United States patents.

The Court's lavish view of its powers under its jurisdiction *in personam* over I.C.I. is, however, shown in many clauses of its decree. The Court's aim in the decree was to bring about a situation in which the two companies should not, simply by their own contrivance and agreement, be left without competition in world markets. So far as the United States market was concerned, there was no particular problem. The Court ordered that a vast range of United States patents held by du Pont and I.C.I. should be compulsorily licensed to any applicant against payment of reasonable royalties. Thus other American manufacturers would henceforth be able to make and sell the products covered by the illegal agreements and it would also be open to foreign companies, including I.C.I. itself, who made the products abroad under foreign patents, to sell them in the United States.

But the Court also wanted to open up the foreign markets which the illegal agreements had 'sewn up'. On the face of it this may seem not

---

[1] See Haight, *loc. cit.* p. 654, who quotes the following provision which was inserted in a number of decrees: '. . . nothing herein contained shall be construed to restrain or prohibit any defendant from doing any act or entering into any agreement which is entirely completed outside the United States and which does not require any act or thing to be done within the United States.'

unreasonable; given that du Pont and I.C.I. were more or less equally responsible for the illegal scheme, it would not seem fair that all protection should be removed from du Pont's home market while I.C.I. retained the exclusionary force of its patents in the markets previously reserved to it. It is at least understandable that the Court would be chary of favouring opportunities for foreign commerce in the United States while doing nothing to secure reciprocal opportunities for American exports.

Consequently the Court ordered both du Pont and I.C.I. to refrain from asserting any of their foreign patents against any American manufacturer who had made products under their United States patents. Thus I.C.I. would retain its exclusive manufacturing rights under, for example, its British patents, but was being ordered not to sue for infringement anybody who sold in Britain products made under the counterpart United States patents.

Judge Ryan clearly recognized that he was getting on to thin ice in this part of his decree. He justified it as 'merely directing I.C.I. to refrain from asserting rights which it may have in Britain, since the enforcement of those rights will serve to continue the effects of wrongful acts it has committed within the United States affecting the foreign trade of the United States'.

But he noted that, in taking power to give orders about foreign patents, he was relying purely on jurisdiction *in personam* over the two companies, and added: 'The effectiveness of the exercise of that power depends on the recognition which will be given to our judgment as a matter of comity by the courts of the foreign sovereign which has granted the patents in question.'

It had been pointed out to him that the grant of immunity against infringement action in favour of imported products might well be held to be against public policy in Britain and even expose the grantors to remedial action under British patent statutes. He said:

The grant of immunity under the British patents would be subject, of course, to the operation of these statutes and proscribed by such action as the comptroller of patents might take. This should not deter us from making directions we feel are required, even though the application of them be limited in operation by the possible action of an official of a foreign sovereign.[1]

He gave it as his own view, however, that by allowing I.C.I. to charge reasonable royalties wherever it granted immunity, he was giving 'full recognition . . . to the inherent property rights granted by the British

---

[1] It should be noted that there was a general saving clause in the decree which bears on this point. 'No provision of this judgment shall operate against I.C.I. for action taken in compliance with any law of the United States Government, or of any foreign Government or

patent to exclude from Great Britain merchandise covered by the patent'.

A rider to Judge Ryan's requirement that the companies grant immunity under their foreign patents prohibited them from so assigning or licensing the foreign patents that other people could prevent American imports into the countries concerned. This provision underlines the curious neglect in the Court's decree of the rights of third parties abroad who might already be licensed under I.C.I. or du Pont patents. This neglect led directly to a notable difference of view about jurisdiction between the American and British courts.

Du Pont's British patents covering various nylon products had been assigned outright to I.C.I. in 1947. (This took place after the American litigation began and in the view of the Court was a deliberate move to deprive the Court of jurisdiction and so evade the possible consequences of an adverse judgment.) In order that the part of his decree dealing with nylon products should be consistent with the provisions already outlined, Judge Ryan ordered that I.C.I. should reassign these patents to du Pont. It should then receive from du Pont an exclusive licence; but, as in the case of the other products concerned, I.C.I. should not assert this licence to prevent the sale in Britain of nylon products made by du Pont or its American licensees. I.C.I., however, had contracted to grant an exclusive licence under certain of the assigned patents to British Nylon Spinners, a company then owned jointly by I.C.I. and Courtaulds. If I.C.I. carried out the Court's order, B.N.S. clearly would not enjoy the exclusive right which it expected under its contract. So B.N.S., in order to be in a position to secure performance of the contract, applied to the High Court in England for an injunction to restrain I.C.I. from reassigning the patents. Mr Justice Upjohn granted the injunction and the matter came on appeal before the Master of the Rolls sitting with Lord Justices Denning and Romer.[1]

The Court of Appeal in sustaining Mr Justice Upjohn revealed that it disagreed markedly with the American Court on the jurisdictional issue. Whereas Judge Ryan, having addressed directions to I.C.I. *in personam* respecting its foreign patents, had then appealed to comity between nations as a factor which might lead foreign courts to recognize his decree, the English judges took the position that considerations of

instrumentality thereof, to which I.C.I. is at the time being subject, and concerning matters over which, under the law of the United States, such foreign Government or instrumentality thereof has jurisdiction.'

[1] *British Nylon Spinners* v. *Imperial Chemical Industries* (Supreme Court of Judicature—Court of Appeal, 1952). I.C.I. as the defendant was in the curious position of having to argue to the British Court the appropriateness of the American Court's claim to extra-territorial jurisdiction, and some American commentators do not hide their feeling that the arguments put forward lacked something of force and enthusiasm.

comity should have restrained the American Court from asserting extra-territorial jurisdiction in the first place. Or, as Lord Justice Denning put it very briefly: 'Those who expect comity should practise it.' And Judge Ryan's statement, that 'it is not an intrusion on the authority of a foreign sovereign for this Court to direct that steps be taken to remove the harmful effects on the trade of the United States', was referred to specifically by the Master of the Rolls as one which he could not accept.[1]

One year after Judge Ryan's decree against du Pont and I.C.I. came Judge Forman's decree in *United States* v. *General Electric Company*, a case which dealt, *inter alia*, with cartel arrangements in the electric lamp industry. It is of interest to compare the injunctions laid on the Philips Company of Holland in 1953 with those laid on I.C.I. in 1952. It is true that the *Lamps* case was largely concerned with the General Electric Company's alleged monopolization of the American market, and that its agreements with Philips and others were in a sense a subsidiary issue, whereas the *du Pont/I.C.I.* case dealt exclusively with international agreements. Nevertheless, the agreements between General Electric and Philips were found illegal on much the same grounds as the du Pont/I.C.I. agreements and they presented much the same problem when the Court was considering remedies.

As respects the United States market, the Court took the same type of action to induce competition, ordering that the United States patents of all the defendants, including Philips, should be made available to all who wished to use them.[2] But on this occasion the Court refused to order Philips to grant immunity from suit under its Dutch and other foreign patents in favour of American exports. In reaching this decision Judge Forman did not admit any limitation on his powers under the Court's *in personam* jurisdiction over Philips but argued it on the strictly practical ground that the Government had not shown the grant of immunity to be necessary to effective relief.

---

[1] The case again came before the American Court in 1954 when I.C.I. sought to enforce against du Pont the order that du Pont should grant immunity under its United States nylon patents in favour of imported nylon products made under the British patents. The products concerned were not those for which B.N.S. was licensed, but filaments, bristles, flakes and moulding powders. I.C.I. urged that it was able and willing to grant reciprocal immunities in Britain for these products and should therefore benefit from immunity in the United States. The Department of Justice supported I.C.I. But Judge Ryan held that I.C.I. could not pick and choose between products made under the same group of patents. Until I.C.I. could grant immunity to du Pont covering all nylon products, including those licensed to B.N.S., it would not require du Pont to grant immunity for a selection of the products.

[2] Indeed this part of the decree was even more draconian than the corresponding part of Judge Ryan's, for the lamp patents were ordered to be dedicated to the public, that is, any manufacturer could use them royalty-free. The question of the circumstances in which the courts may require the dedication of patents rather than compulsory licensing for reasonable royalties is discussed below, Chapter XIV.

He pointed out that Philips did not manufacture in the United States and would not benefit from the opening up of the American market by the dedication of patents. On the other hand, American manufacturers were unlikely in practice to have any great export potential in the markets protected by Philips's foreign patents. He concluded therefore:

It would hardly seem that any substantial contribution would be made to freeing competition in either domestic or foreign commerce by attempting in this judgment to compel Philips to place itself in the complicated situation of being required to grant immunity from suit on its foreign patents in so far as transactions in lamps outside the limits of the United States are concerned.

Judge Forman also noted:

Philips's activities are conducted in areas of the world where different standards of industrial behaviour prevail than are acceptable in this country. But it is only where such activities overflow their proper boundaries so as to affect domestic and foreign commerce of the United States that it becomes the concern of this country to suppress them.

Although Judge Forman conceded little in principle, the tone of this opinion and its practical restraint as respects the Philips Company's activities abroad may mark an ebb of the jurisdictional high tide. It is of value to have it recognized that directions concerning the exercise of foreign patent rights by a foreign company can lead to a 'complicated situation', and one may surmise that the judgment of the Court of Appeal in England in the *Nylon* case was not without influence on this point. Judge Forman's recognition of the fact that different standards of judgment are applied to problems of restraint of trade in different parts of the world is also a step in the right direction, for the next step is to recognize that the 'crimes' of antitrust, rightly or wrongly, are not universal crimes but arise out of a national policy which is not apt for extra-territorial legal application. This advance may well reflect the warnings given by the American bar after the I.C.I. decree and the subpoenas on the Anglo-Iranian and other oil companies; among other things, many lawyers had pointed to the danger of reciprocal claims to jurisdiction by the courts of other sovereigns whose commerce is closely affected by American action.

The world outside owes so much to American initiatives in economic as in other matters that it would be churlish to exaggerate the jurisdictional problem. It is bound to be difficult to administer domestic law concerning foreign trade without giving offence in some direction. Sometimes, indeed, there have been protests about exercises of jurisdiction which it is difficult to fault on technical grounds. In the *du Pont/ I.C.I.* case, for example, the Court ordered the termination of joint ownerships by the two companies of important foreign concerns. In the case of Canadian Industries Ltd. this order had particularly unfortunate effects, for I.C.I. and du Pont each held 42% of the stock of the Canadian company, while the balance of 16% was held by Canadians and the management of the company was mainly Canadian. Under this arrangement the Canadians were in a good strategic position to hold the balance between the major stockholders. The effect of the Court's decree was to require either I.C.I. or du Pont to dispose of their holdings but it did not prevent one or other from acquiring the whole 84%. The order might therefore profoundly affect Canadian interests in the concern. Yet so far as the Court's decree was a direction to du Pont, an American company, forbidding them to share a commanding interest in a foreign company with a co-conspirator, it is difficult to see it as an undue extension of jurisdiction.

It may be said in conclusion that there are indications that the American authorities are now more fully aware of the anxieties caused abroad by extreme claims to jurisdiction by the federal courts in anti-trust litigation, and that informal consultation procedures between the Department of Justice and the Department of State now apparently work more effectively than in former years.

CHAPTER XIII

THE ADMINISTRATION OF THE ANTITRUST LAWS

1. *Functions of the Antitrust Division of the Department of Justice and the Federal Trade Commission*

Antitrust is to a large extent enforced by the lawyers who advise business firms. Legal advisers tend to play a larger part in business administration in the United States than in Britain and many more corporations have their own legal staff. Once antitrust case law has developed firm lines of doctrine on a given topic, the legal advisers who must protect their employers or clients from expensive litigation will seek to keep business policies within these lines, and this undoubtedly prevents many infractions of the law.

But there must, of course, be public enforcement; otherwise, apart from private treble-damage actions, there would be no case law for the business lawyer to advise his client about. Moreover, it is the vigilance of public law enforcement which provides the drive towards conformity. In the United States two public authorities share the task of enforcing antitrust. These are the Antitrust Division of the Department of Justice and the Federal Trade Commission. As has already been noted, these two bodies have concurrent jurisdiction over a considerable part of the field. By court interpretation restrictive practices which might constitute offences against the Sherman Act may be attacked as unfair methods of competition under section 5 of the Federal Trade Commission Act. The Clayton Act itself provides for concurrent jurisdiction over the offences which it creates.

Broadly speaking the Department of Justice takes to itself the enforcement of the Sherman Act, in particular the prosecution of serious and significant infringements of that Act, and it also plays the major role in the enforcement of section 7 of the Clayton Act. It normally takes action under other sections of the Clayton Act only when charges under that Act are a factor in a broader picture of Sherman Act violation. The Federal Trade Commission, with its prophylactic and preventive role, enforces section 5 of the Federal Trade Commission Act and takes the main brunt of the work under the remaining sections of the Clayton Act. The Commission has no criminal jurisdiction. The procedures adopted by these two law enforcing agencies differ considerably and in this chapter the main lines along which each carries out its appointed task will be sketched out.[1]

The Department of Justice, alone having criminal jurisdiction, must naturally concern itself largely with flagrant offences against the criminal provisions of the Sherman Act, and it is convenient to begin with this activity. Under section 4 of the Sherman Act the Department of Justice also has the duty, however, of instituting civil proceedings to prevent and restrain any violations of the Act, and its procedures under this head will be considered below.

2. *The Antitrust Division; selection of cases for action*

Like any policeman the Antitrust Division of the Department of Justice must first detect crime before it can prosecute it. This is one of the most important of the difficulties of antitrust enforcement; one cannot catch a man monopolizing red-handed at a particular moment in time, like a man housebreaking or exceeding a speed limit. It is obviously impracticable to have a vast force of detectives hanging about in the corridors of industry waiting for the crimes of restraint of trade or monopolization to be committed under their noses. Detection in fact relies essentially on complaints which come from the public at large or, more often, from businessmen who are injured or threatened by restraint of trade or monopoly.

As well as detection, there must be selection, since a vast field of business activity has to be covered with limited resources. The direction of the Division's effort is bound to be guided by policy considerations. The Division keeps a staff of economists who advise about the critical spots in the economy which appear to require antitrust action. Many different types of policy are, of course, possible and many changes are made. It has been characteristic of the Department of Justice in recent years that the Antitrust Division has had a new Head every two or three years and this alone makes continuity difficult to obtain.

Sometimes particular industries or types of agreement become the subject of an antitrust campaign. For example, wartime revelations about alleged cartel agreements, particularly with German firms, as a result of which American productive power and technical progress were felt to have been retarded in some fields, drew the attention of the

---

[1] There is a system of exchanging notes between the two bodies about intended actions. Generally speaking, the Attorney General's National Committee to Study the Antitrust Laws seemed to be satisfied with the co-operation between the two and recommended only minor improvements: see chapter VIII of the Committee's *Report*, pp. 374–6. Chapter VIII of the *Report* (although by now somewhat out of date in matters of detail) should be consulted as an invaluable source on all matters of administration and will be referred to frequently in the following pages.

Department of Justice to such agreements.[1] After the war, with the great need for new housing for returning servicemen, restrictive practices in the building industries were for a time regarded as a particularly sensitive spot. Particular Heads of the Division will from time to time have strong feelings about some particular aspect of restrictive or monopolizing activities, perhaps about the restrictive effects of large aggregations of patents or about the prevalence of industrial mergers, and a line of cases will follow from the thrust of their initiative. All sorts of considerations, some political, some economic or social, may in this way determine the direction of special efforts by the Department of Justice in one section or other of the field. This, of course, is inevitable and by and large the 'campaigning' aspect of policy changes, though often criticized, reflects genuine public concern with one or other of the possible fields of antitrust action.

Meanwhile, of course, the daily bread of flagrant cases comes to notice all the time through complaints. The Department of Justice cannot ignore authenticated complaints any more than a police force can ignore murders or traffic offences simply on the ground that it is promoting a specially vigorous drive against racecourse frauds. The two things—day-by-day administration of justice as alleged offences come to notice, and taking the initiative with a special campaign in a particular field for reasons of policy—go on side by side. The placing of special emphasis on particular industries from time to time, in response to economic advice or public concern, is essentially a matter of the Department's resources. As a recent Head of the Antitrust Division put it: 'The resources in manpower and appropriations of the Antitrust Division do not permit us to survey all aspects of the United States' economy and to develop a program of continuing surveillance of all important industries.' Thus selection of fields for special effort is bound to occur. From time to time an attitude of consolidation comes into favour with the feeling that it is not the job of the Department to seek out particular areas for intensive enforcement but simply to prosecute the flagrant offences as they come to notice.

3. Detection of offences; methods of investigation; the Grand Jury subpoena

Complaints from the public may put the Department of Justice on the track of an offence, or the extensive general information which it acquires about industry may indicate that a particular situation is ripe for action. Information from these sources, however, is rarely complete

---

[1] See, for example, the monograph entitled *Economic and Political Aspects of International Cartels* submitted to the Sub-Committee on War Mobilization of the Senate Committee on Military Affairs, 1944.

or detailed enough for its lawyers to be able to prove a case in the courts. There is, therefore, a need for investigation.

This creates a serious difficulty. Most crimes are brought to book by the evidence of witnesses; when there has been a road accident or a murder direct witnesses are often to be found to throw light on the principal aspects of the situation. With antitrust offences all is different. The small businessman may find that the main suppliers of a commodity all send him notes saying that they are unable to fulfil his current orders. But this does not of itself prove the existence of a collective boycott. The Department's own investigators may find that prices in a given industry have been rigid over a long period; this does not prove a price fixing agreement. To get evidence of antitrust offences it is always necessary to search among the industry's own records and correspondence. But a businessman accused of an antitrust offence is not compelled any more than a suspected murderer or Communist to provide the evidence to condemn himself.[1]

The Department of Justice has three main lines of attack to get over this problem. First, under the 1962 Antitrust Civil Process Act it can serve on any company (or other legal entity other than an individual) a written demand for the production of documents in its custody or control which are relevant to some investigation which the Department is carrying out. The demand must state the nature of the antitrust violation under investigation, and describe the classes of documents to be produced with sufficient precision to enable them to be identified by the company. Again, as with any other crime, it may send a policeman to the suspect's premises to find out what he can. The Department of Justice uses for this purpose Federal Bureau of Investigation (F.B.I.) investigators or Antitrust Division attorneys who carry out the normal type of police inquiry into a suspected crime. They can go into a business firm and ask to see the files of correspondence bearing on the alleged offence. Sometimes, to avoid more trouble later on, companies give the F.B.I. agents access to their files and records and co-operate fully with them. The Department of Justice is always willing to work out a reasonable procedure with a co-operative company so as to avoid unnecessary interference with the company's work. Where good relations are established in this way and the suspected company allows the full facts to come to the notice of the Department, there is no difficulty about making the final decision on whether to bring a criminal prosecution, to proceed with a civil action or to close the case on the ground that no violation has been found. A company can always, however, refuse to allow the F.B.I. agents access to its critical files.

Alternatively, therefore, if the violations are of such a nature that

[1] But a corporation has no similar constitutional protection against self-incrimination.

criminal remedies seem appropriate, the Department of Justice's recourse is to seek an investigation by a Grand Jury. The Grand Jury is appointed to represent the Government and the People of the United States to inquire whether the evidence is enough to warrant prosecution.

The Grand Jury has a considerable degree of autonomy and once it has been called into being is not subject to direction by the law enforcing officers of the Government nor, to a considerable extent, by the court itself. As to the scope of its inquiry, it may call for any documents and subpoena any witness and is limited only by a duty not to impose an unreasonable and unnecessary burden upon the witness. A former Head of the Antitrust Division has said: 'It would appear from the reading of all the cases that it is the subject matter of the investigation being conducted by a Grand Jury which is the true basis for determining the reasonableness of the discovery demanded and not the inconvenience and detriment suffered by a corporate witness in complying with the *subpoena duces tecum* . . . All in all the cases seem to make it abundantly clear, as a matter of law, that a federal Jury in an antitrust matter possesses broad and sweeping powers to enquire into all aspects of possible violations of the antitrust laws.'

The use of the Grand Jury investigation in antitrust has often been criticized in the United States. To some extent the criticism is simply one form of the view that criminal procedures are inappropriate in a field of *mala prohibita* (as opposed to *mala in se*), where the people whose conduct comes under review are otherwise law abiding and respectable. It is part of this view that the vicissitudes of antitrust interpretation make the law too subtle and inconstant for the law abiding citizen to be sure of avoiding trouble.

The Grand Jury inquiry is an *ex parte* proceeding in which the company under suspicion has no opportunity to advance any form of defence or justification for its acts. Yet if it ends in an indictment, this will of itself carry a stigma of criminality, even though there may subsequently be an acquittal.[1] Even if there is no indictment, some stigma may be felt to remain and certainly the inquiry itself will be burdensome. For the further criticism is levied that the Department of Justice, which by hypothesis does not know a great deal in detail about the case when it resorts to Grand Jury investigation, is inclined to draw up subpoenas in unnecessarily broad and sweeping terms. One critic has written: 'As they sit conducting Grand Jury subpoenas free

---

[1] 'The stigma of the indictment tends to be the real punishment. The actual penalty comes at the beginning, rather than the end, of the trial. . . . The judgment emerges. . . from an *ex parte* process in which [the accused] is not heard in his own behalf; . . . and conviction comes as something of an anticlimax.' (Walton Hamilton and Irene Till, *Antitrust in Action* (United States Temporary National Economic Committee, Monograph 16), U.S. Government Printing Office, Washington, 1941, p. 80).

from any substantial restraint except that which they apply to themselves, they slip easily into an expansive mood. The result is a group of subpoenas which seek information covering most of the affairs of the principal companies in an industry during almost the whole of their corporate lives. The burden thus imposed on corporations subject to investigation is difficult to exaggerate. Compliance with such an antitrust subpoena may literally involve the expenditure of many man-years and hundreds of thousands of dollars in the search and examination of millions of documents.'[1]

The solidest line of criticism, however, is directed at the use by the Department of Justice of the Grand Jury investigation in cases in which it is by no means sure that criminal proceedings are warranted and it is alleged, even when it is not thinking in terms of criminal prosecution but wishes only to obtain sufficient evidence to form the basis of a civil complaint. In such circumstances the other criticisms are compounded, for both the burden and the tarnishing of the Grand Jury procedure are imposed where, it is claimed, there is no warrant for them. The enaction of the Antitrust Civil Process Act has, however, caused some reduction in the use of Grand Juries, as the companies under investigation can now be compelled to produce documents which previously only the Grand Jury procedure could extract, and internal Justice Department rules prevent the use of Grand Juries except in cases likely to result in criminal indictment.[2]

4. *The choice between criminal prosecution and civil action*

Once the Department of Justice is in possession of the information needed for making a case, it has to decide whether to proceed by criminal prosecution or by civil action. There are two aspects to this decision. The first is the question of what the action is to achieve.

The criminal case can do no more and no less than punish offenders for past offences. After the punishment has been exacted, the situation is exactly as it was before the case was brought. The punishment no doubt acts to some extent as a deterrent against further offences but this is all that has been achieved. The Department of Justice in most important cases wants also to regulate the industry so that its practices may conform with the law and with the policy lying behind antitrust.

The nature of some types of offence is such that punishment has

---

[1] Conversely, it is often believed that the best defence to an antitrust investigation is to flood the Government with more documents than the investigators can possibly digest.

[2] Once a civil complaint has been filed, the Department can obtain discovery of documents under the ordinary rules of Civil Procedure. The difficulty is its lack of investigatory powers at the stage when it is considering whether the issue of a complaint is warranted.

virtually no effect on the situation. If, for example, a monopoly has been illegally acquired in some important line of commerce, the mere imposition of a fine (unless the fine were of impossible severity) would leave the situation exactly where it was. The Department cannot regard the situation as improved unless the company concerned is no longer in a position to exercise monopoly power. In such a case, therefore, it wants to secure the dissolution or divestment of the monopoly concerned. If patents have been aggregated and misused by a company or group so as to secure a stranglehold on prices or conditions of entry into an industry, it wants to secure that the patents concerned may be freely used by other companies. Regulatory remedies of this kind may be obtained only as a result of civil proceedings in which the court acts as a chancellor dispensing equity. Most of the biggest cases in antitrust history have, therefore, been civil proceedings.

On the other hand, a flagrant example of one of the established *per se* offences cannot usefully be tackled by civil proceedings, for to secure from a court of equity an injunction against repeating the offence would merely be repeating in the injunction what is already contained in the statute. Such offences must therefore be prosecuted criminally so as to invoke the sanction of punishment.

Often, of course, the same situation encompasses both a flagrant breach of the law and the need for some remedy of a regulatory type. In such situations it is common for the Department of Justice to bring concurrent criminal and civil proceedings. Then the court in the criminal case may impose a penalty and later, sitting in the civil case, may hand down a decree containing injunctions regulating the industry for the future. The criminal proceeding can never affect the future; the civil proceeding can never affect the past. The one punishes past offences; the other lays down a model of conduct for the future.

The second aspect of the choice between criminal and civil proceedings is simply that of doing justice to those who are subject to antitrust discipline. The Congress of 1890 enacted—and no subsequent Congress has repealed—the criminal provisions of the Sherman Act and there would probably be no wide public support for any proposal to abandon them. On the other hand, it is widely felt that criminal proceedings are not appropriate in cases near the borderline of the law where there may be no precedents and no reasonable expectation on the part of business that a given line of conduct is actionable. Professors Kaysen and Turner[1] have suggested that those antitrust offences involving conduct which can be 'unambiguously denominated bad' should be listed in the antitrust statutes, and that these offences alone

[1] *Antitrust Policy*, p. 256.

should be treated as criminal. They would include cases involving specific attempts to indulge in bad conduct, and cases where the illegality is so well settled that it is reasonable to impute intent to the conduct itself, such as price fixing, boycotts, predatory practices, and attempts to monopolize. The Attorney General's National Committee, which sympathized with this view, put it that the criminal process 'should be used only where the law is clear and the facts reveal a flagrant offense and plain intent unreasonably to restrain trade'. The actual practice of the Department of Justice is not far removed from this prescription and the Committee felt able generally to endorse the Department's practice as expounded to it.

5. *Pleas of* nolo contendere; *consent settlements*

When the Department of Justice prosecutes criminal charges, the normal result is for the accused either to enter a defence or to plead *nolo contendere* rather than guilty. This Latin phrase means, broadly speaking, 'I am not going to dispute what you say'. It is thus in many respects equivalent to a plea of guilty in English courts. The American court will, on this plea, exact fines or other penances as if the case had been fought and lost by the defence.[1] A plea of *nolo contendere*, however, has the substantial advantage to the accused that it does not constitute an admission of any particular item of the Government's charges and no evidence is brought by the Government before the court. Thus the accused company is protected against the possibility that the Government's charges, having been found proved in detail and having become, in effect, the court's findings of fact, will be seized upon by private litigants, who consider themselves damaged by the offences concerned, as a basis for bringing a treble-damage action against the offender. Because of this the Government may refuse to accept the *nolo contendere* plea where the offences are flagrant.

The equivalent in a civil suit of pleading *nolo contendere* is to enter into negotiation with the Department of Justice for what is known as a consent decree. When the Department of Justice has stated a complaint to the court and asked for equity relief, it is open to the respondent companies to seek the Department's agreement to settle the case by means of a decree giving the Government the relief it considers necessary without going through the expensive process of trial.

This procedure has certain advantages and certain risks for both sides. Since most big trials can be spun out by one procedural device or another and appeals up to the Supreme Court are common, it is rare for the interval between the Government's original complaint and

---

[1] And in most courts the resulting disposition is listed as a judgment of conviction.

the court's final decree in a contested suit to be less than three years; often it is more than five. So the consent settlement gives the Government the advantage of achieving a quicker result. Both sides are often glad to avoid the expense of protracted litigation; companies have a duty to their shareholders to avoid unnecessary legal expense and the Department of Justice has a limited budget.[1] The industry side may have a further important advantage. As in the case of a *nolo contendere* plea in a criminal suit, a consent settlement avoids the deployment of all the evidence in a case in open court and the consent decree itself is not admissible as evidence in a private treble-damage suit. Consequently the consent decree may be a means of avoiding publicity and the risk of expensive private litigation after the Government's case is finished.

The risk for the Government is that it may not succeed in negotiation in obtaining the full relief that is regarded as necessary to bring the industry's practices into conformity with the law. As a law enforcing agency the Department of Justice cannot afford to pull its punches in its desire to obtain a quicker and cheaper result by a consent settlement. On the defence side the risk is the opposite one of giving up more by negotiation and committing itself to more stringent prohibitions for the future than the court would impose after a contested case. In view of the saving of the expense of litigation and in view of the protection against treble-damage suits which is obtained, there may be a temptation to consent to more drastic forms of relief than the courts would impose.

It is sometimes said, indeed, that the Government side plays on this factor to obtain unduly stringent terms. Both sides, however, have a good deal to lose if negotiations break down. At any stage either side can break off the parley and choose to go to trial with all that means in trouble and money. Usually there are precedents in the case law indicating the type of relief which the courts have given in similar circumstances in contested suits, and this provides a check against undue claims by the Government.

When the terms of a consent decree are agreed between the Department of Justice and the respondent parties, they are made public at least thirty days before they receive the formal approval of the court. This is to allow comment or criticism from interested parties who are not parties to the action. The terms thereafter become binding on the parties in the same way as a decree in a litigated case. The various

---

[1] In 1955 the Attorney General's National Committee *Report* (chapter VIII, p. 360) recorded that, since 1935, 72% of civil actions brought by the Government were terminated by consent settlement, and pointed the moral that the economy of the procedure made it essential to successful enforcement. Pp. 360–1 of the *Report* are a valuable amplification of this passage.

injunctions and prohibitions applying to the companies have the force of law and any infringement of them thereafter may be punished as contempt of the court which authorizes the decree. The court retains the right to modify a consent decree if either party can produce convincing proof that a change in circumstances makes modification necessary.

6. *Informal procedures of enforcement*

It is sometimes suggested that more could be done by the Department of Justice by way of informal procedures for enforcing the law. It has been suggested, for example, that businessmen and their lawyers should be able to apply to the Department of Justice for advice as to whether some proposed practice would be regarded by the Department as legal or illegal.

Although this type of informal, administrative adjudication has increased, there are of necessity severe limitations to what can be done in this way and the Department in fact has no authority to issue advisory opinions.

The Department has a public duty to prosecute offences against the laws, and the individual lawyer on the staff clearly could not commit himself, and still less the Department, to saying that a proposed scheme was lawful if he were in any doubt as to the full facts of the case or as to the competitive effects that the scheme would in practice produce. But, as has been seen, the facts are invariably complex; moreover, the facts known at any given time are not necessarily a safe guide to subsequent development. On the other hand, the businessman's own lawyer, if he is an expert in antitrust matters, should be able to give his client just as good advice about the general applications of the law as a government lawyer; and if the businessman and his lawyer believed that their scheme was in conformity with the law, they would probably not accept the view of an individual in the Department of Justice that it was illegal and ought not to be proceeded with.

The Department is, however, willing in suitable cases to examine a proposed course of action by a company or industry and has established a formal Business Review Procedure for this purpose. In particular it will state that it has no present intention to institute criminal proceedings in respect of the scheme. Such a decision is known as a 'railroad release'. The Department insists that full disclosure must be made of all the information needed to assess the lawfulness of the scheme and that it must be a prospective scheme and not one in actual operation. Even under this procedure the Department always reserves the right to institute civil proceedings if it subsequently wishes to test the legality of the practices concerned. Its waiver of the right to start a criminal case is also liable to be withdrawn if it comes to the notice of the Department that a full disclosure of the necessary facts has not been made or that the scheme when in operation goes beyond what has been laid before it.

Since the revision in 1950 of section 7 of the Clayton Act dealing with mergers, the Department has been willing on this particular topic to confer with companies proposing a particular merger and has been ready, under the Business Review Procedure, to indicate in writing to the parties whether or not it would take legal action against the proposed merger. This exception to the general rule presents the Department with no little difficulty and it reserves the right to take action if subsequent developments in the industry seem to require it.

7. The cost of enforcement: enforcing litigated and consent orders

Some indication should be given at this point of the cost of antitrust enforcement. The Antitrust Division itself employs a staff of about three hundred lawyers and operates on a budget, voted by Congress, which of recent years has been of the order of six million dollars a year. Apart from detecting offences, preparing and fighting cases and negotiating consent settlements, this staff and budget must also cover, of course, the enforcement of the many litigated and consent decrees which have been obtained in the past. This is a big job[1] and it seems probable that this is the weakest aspect of enforcement and that the Department's resources have permitted little more than investigation of complaints received from outside of non-compliance with decrees.[2] The cost of antitrust enforcement in terms of time spent by the courts is also considerable and there have been complaints from time to time of the undue burden placed on the courts by antitrust litigation. Judge Knox of the United States District Court for the Southern District of New York has revealed, for example, that big antitrust cases in that Court have occupied so much of the time of the judges that the whole administration of justice in the area has been jeopardized.

But the greatest burden of cost inevitably falls on business, and the legal expenditure incurred by corporations involved in antitrust litigation must be many times that incurred by the Government. As with criminal suits, the Department of Justice is, at the outset of a civil

[1] The Attorney General's National Committee reported in 1955 that there were then nearly 400 judgments to be enforced.

[2] It must be remembered, of course, that many injunctions in antitrust decrees vest an interest in third parties. If a court orders a firm to make available its patents to all applicants in return for reasonable royalties, applicants will certainly come forward and cannot be gainsaid. To this extent judgments can be self-enforcing.

case, imperfectly informed about the facts. Its initial complaint has, therefore, to be drawn in fairly broad terms and the discovery of documents which it demands is frequently sweeping.

A great deal of attention has been given in recent years by the lawyers concerned on both the government and defence sides to devising procedures for keeping the problem within bounds. Usually in the bigger cases there are pre-trial conferences between the lawyers of both sides and the judge taking the case. By a gradual process of give and take, the defence side seeks from the government side more and more detailed statements of the issues which the Government wishes to bring to trial. The documents to be produced may then be limited to some extent by reference to this statement of issues.[1] Nevertheless, nothing can make the process simple or short. In monopolization cases in particular, the rule of law by which the Government has to establish from a company's history and course of action a general intent to achieve or maintain a monopoly position means that long excursions into past history have to be made. The record in these large cases frequently runs into tens of thousands of closely printed pages of material. Judge Medina, who tried the *Investment bankers* case,[2] has recorded that 'altogether there have been printed in connexion with this litigation from start to finish approximately 100,000 pages of material'. The sheer extent and cost of the litigation involved are certainly factors to be borne in mind in assessing the pros and cons of a judicial system of anti-monopoly regulation such as antitrust.

8. *The Federal Trade Commission: structure and functions*

The Federal Trade Commission, unlike the Department of Justice, is not a body organized simply to prosecute crime or seek civil remedies; it is itself a tribunal dispensing judicial decisions, which are subject to review by the courts, but it is also an administrative agency of the Government. The Commission consists of five persons appointed by the President of the United States and it is laid down in the Federal Trade Commission Act that not more than three of the Commissioners shall be members of the same political party.

The staff of the Commission has several different functions which have to be kept separate. Some members of the legal staff, for example, advise the Commissioners about the state of the law in relation to the cases coming before them. These lawyers also represent the Commission

[1] The Attorney General's National Committee made a number of recommendations designed to meet the problems of the 'big case', in particular with regard to the means of limiting and particularizing the issues to be tried: see its *Report*, chapter VIII, pp. 362–6.

[2] *United States* v. *Morgan* (Southern District Court of New York, 1953).

in the appellate courts when the Commission's decisions come under review. Other Commission lawyers represent the Commission in a different sense in that they act, as it were, as a court of first instance, hearing cases on behalf of the Commission and handing down initial decisions which the Commission itself will review. Yet others among the Commission's lawyers are investigators and prosecutors, seeking out infringements in those fields of antitrust in which the Commission has jurisdiction and prosecuting these cases before the Commission itself or before those of its lawyers to whom the Commission delegates initial hearings. This seems at first sight a curious situation and gives colour to suggestions that are sometimes made that the Commission is at the same time prosecutor and judge in its own cases. Careful dispositions are made, however, so that the lawyers prosecuting cases are kept at arm's length from those initially hearing the cases and from those who advise the Commissioners when cases come before them for decision.

The Federal Trade Commission is a larger body than the Antitrust Division of the Department of Justice. It employs over 600 professionals but about half of this manpower is engaged on work outside the antitrust field as it is defined in this book. Section 5 of the Federal Trade Commission Act which makes unlawful 'unfair methods of competition in commerce' and 'unfair or deceptive practices in commerce' covers not only antitrust offences in the sense of restrictions or distortions of competition, but also a wide range of business activities which may be held to deceive or mislead the consumer. For example, false and misleading advertising comes under this head, and the Commission also has to administer legislation dealing with the correct labelling and description of certain types of goods. The administration of the law against misleading advertising, in particular, takes up a great deal of the time and effort of the Commission staff, so that only about half of its resources are devoted to antitrust.

Like the Department of Justice, the Federal Trade Commission in its antitrust work is dependent in the first place on complaints from the public and from the business world about infringements of the law. It also has as a division of its staff a Bureau of Industrial Economics whose job it is to maintain a vigilant watch over the American economy from the point of view of its competitiveness, its degree of concentration and so on. The investigations of this Bureau, like those of the economists in the Department of Justice, lead the Commission from time to time to concentrate as a matter of policy on particular aspects of the economic scene.

The Federal Trade Commission has separate statutory powers to obtain the information it needs to carry out its functions. Section 6 of the Federal Trade Commission Act vests in the Commission power:

(a) To gather and compile information concerning, and to investigate from time to time the organization, business conduct, practices and management of any corporation engaged in commerce, excepting banks and common carriers . . . and its relation to other corporations and to individuals, associations, and partnerships.

(b) To require . . . corporations engaged in commerce, except banks and common carriers . . . to file with the Commission in such form as the Commission may prescribe . . . reports or answers in writing to specific questions, furnishing to the Commission such information as it may require as to the organization, business conduct, practices, management, and relation to other corporations, partnerships, and individuals of the respective corporations filing such reports or answers in writing. Such reports and answers shall be made under oath or otherwise as the Commission may prescribe. . . .

Since 1960 the Commission has made very intensive use of section 6 (b), in order to effect a rapid industry-wide investigation without the necessity for its own personnel going through the files of the companies concerned. Under this Special Report Procedure, questionnaires are sent out by post simultaneously to a large number of companies in a particular industry, in order to enable the Commission to determine the relevant facts about practices in that industry, and whether these justify the issuing of formal complaints.

Subsection (c) permits the Commission on its own initiative to investigate the way in which any decree arising from a case brought by the Department of Justice under the antitrust Acts has been carried out and lays on it the duty to do so if so requested by the Attorney General. Subsection (d) adds power 'upon the direction of the President or either House of Congress to investigate and report the facts relating to any alleged violations of the antitrust Acts by any corporation'. Subsection (f) gives the Commission discretion to make public any information obtained under the foregoing powers, except trade secrets and names of customers, and subsection (h) empowers the Commission to investigate trade conditions in foreign countries where 'associations, combinations or practices of manufacturers, merchants or traders or other conditions may affect the foreign trade of the United States'.

Section 7 of the Federal Trade Commission Act enables the courts to refer civil actions brought by the Department of Justice to the Commission as a Master in Chancery to 'ascertain and report an appropriate form of decree therein'. Section 8 requires that, on the direction of the President of the United States, any other government department shall turn over to the Commission any records and information it may have about any company within the Commission's jurisdiction, and section 9 makes it clear that the Commission has the right, in connexion with all these powers, to obtain access to any company being investigated, to copy any of its documents and to subpoena witnesses as it thinks fit.

These very extensive powers of investigation leave the Commission with no similar problem to that facing the Department of Justice in obtaining information about suspected infringements of antitrust provisions. Indeed, on the face of it, the Commissioner's powers might be used to help fill the gap in the investigatory powers of the Department of Justice. That this has not happened may be due in part to the inconvenience and probable inefficiency that would be likely to result if investigations and prosecution were in different hands and in part to the feeling that the Federal Trade Commission, which has no criminal jurisdiction and is intended to help and advise business to conform to the policy of competition, should hold itself aloof from the criminal aspects of Sherman Act enforcement. Even sections 6(c) and 7 of the Federal Trade Commission Act which, respectively, give the Commission specific power to investigate breaches of antitrust decrees and allow the courts to refer to the Commission as a Master in Chancery for recommendations as to remedies in antitrust cases have not in practice been used.[1]

9. *Complaints; hearings; 'cease and desist' orders*

When as a result of complaints or after investigation it is believed that some breach of section 5 of the Federal Trade Commission Act or of the sections of the Clayton Act under the Commission's jurisdiction has occurred, the Commission may issue a formal complaint. Under section 5 of the Federal Trade Commission Act the Commission must not only have reason to believe that some unfair method of competition is being used, but also that 'a proceeding by it in respect thereto would be to the interest of the public'. Thus, unlike a police authority such as the Department of Justice, the Commission is not charged under the Federal Trade Commission Act with hauling every offender before it, but only when this can do good. (Under section 11 of the Clayton Act, however, the Commission has a duty to issue a complaint whenever it has reason to believe that a violation of that Act has occurred.)

The decision to issue a complaint is one for the Commission itself. The investigating part of the Commission's staff has to carry the Commissioners with it in showing cause for the issue of a formal complaint. Once the complaint has been issued, the various sections of the Commission's legal staff square off into their separate functions.

---

[1] The Attorney General's National Committee considered that action under section 6(c) would be 'frequently useful': *Report* of the Committee, chapter VII, p. 366.

The lawyers in the enforcement bureaus of the Commission have the task of preparing and presenting the case against the companies involved and the companies' own lawyers defend the suit. There are three enforcement bureaus, the Bureau of Restraint of Trade, the Bureau of Deceptive Practices and the Bureau of Textiles and Furs. For cases within its particular jurisdiction, each bureau has responsibility for the whole enforcement process from inception to completion. A Hearing Examiner tries the case and hands down an initial decision consisting of his findings as to the facts of the case, his conclusions of the relevant law and an appropriate 'cease and desist' order. This initial decision of the Hearing Examiner may dispose of the case altogether. But it is open to the defence side to appeal to the Commission itself against the decision of the Hearing Examiner, and it is open to the Commission, perhaps on the representations of its prosecuting lawyers, to review on its own account the Hearing Examiner's decision. Thus, if a breach of the law is found by the Hearing Examiner and the company concerned is content that this is a correct decision, the Hearing Examiner's 'cease and desist' order automatically becomes the Commission's order. If the Hearing Examiner does not find any breach, the case will be dropped unless the Commissioners themselves have reason to believe that the Hearing Examiner was wrong. If either the company concerned or the Commission disagrees with the Hearing Examiner's decision, the case will then be heard by the Commission itself.

The Commission's 'cease and desist' order corresponds to the decree which the court hands down at the conclusion of a civil antitrust suit. It consists, in effect, of a series of injunctions to the companies concerned to abandon for the future the practices which have been found to be unlawful methods of competition or to offend against one or other provision of the Clayton Act. These injunctions have the force of law. Under the Federal Trade Commission Act (as amended by the Wheeler-Lea Act of 1938) a 'cease and desist' order automatically becomes final when the time has run out for an appeal to the courts to be filed, or when such an appeal has been heard and the order affirmed. Once it is final, the order has the force of law and any violation is immediately subject to a fine. The maximum fine is $5,000 for each violation, and since 1950 the severe rider has been in force (but not used) that each day on which failure to respect the order continues shall be deemed a separate violation.

Until 1959 orders made by the Commission under the Clayton Act were not enforceable until reviewed by the appropriate Circuit Court of Appeals. This meant that the first breach of such an order by a defendant could not be punished, although the subsequent Court of Appeals order would make any further breaches contempt of court.

But under a statute passed in that year, orders of the Commission under the Clayton Act are now final when issued by the Commission in exactly the same way as those issued under the Federal Trade Commission Act.

10. *Review by appeal courts of Federal Trade Commission decisions and orders*

As has been noted, the Federal Trade Commission's findings of fact are by statute final and binding on the appeal courts so long as they are supported by testimony. The job of the appeal courts, therefore, is to review the Commission's decisions as matters of law. The precise scope of the courts' supervision of the Commission's interpretations of the law has been differently defined from time to time.

In the case of the *Federal Trade Commission* v. *Gratz* (Supreme Court, 1920), Mr Justice McReynolds held that 'it is for the courts, not the Commission, ultimately to determine as a matter of law what they include'. The 'they' in this quotation refers to unfair methods of competition. The Commission had found the practice of tying the sale of cotton bagging to that of the steel ties used with the bagging to be an unfair method of competition, whereas Mr Justice McReynolds thought of this as a practice 'never heretofore regarded as opposed to good morals because characterized by deception, bad faith, fraud or oppression . . .' Mr Justice Brandeis, in a famous dissent, held that the Act left the determination of what were unfair methods of competition to the Commission.

Instead of undertaking to define what practices should be deemed unfair, as had been done in earlier legislation, the Act left the determination to the Commission. Experience with existing laws had taught that definition, being necessarily rigid, would prove embarrassing, and if rigorously applied, might involve great hardship. Methods of competition which would be unfair in one industry, under certain circumstances, might, when adopted in another industry, or even in the same industry under different circumstances, be entirely unobjectionable. . . . Recognizing that the question whether a method of competitive practices was unfair would ordinarily depend upon special facts, Congress imposed upon the Commission the duty of finding the facts, and it declared that findings of fact so made (if duly supported by evidence) were to be taken as final.

Brandeis admitted that the question of whether a particular method of competition could on the facts be reasonably held to constitute an unfair method of competition was, as a question of law, open to review by the Court. He was arguing essentially that the Commission's expert knowledge and investigation should be given weight and should not be upset without substantial reason.

The matter has been discussed again in some more recent cases. The dissent of Mr Justice Jackson in *Federal Trade Commission* v. *Ruberoid Company* (Supreme Court, 1952) explained why the Federal Trade Commission must have a measure of discretion in interpreting the law under the Clayton Act. He noted that the Robinson-Patman Act involved investigations into grades and qualities of goods, the probable effect of discriminations, differences in cost, good faith in meeting competition and so on. On such a complex subject, he explained, Congress must legislate in general terms and 'delegate the final detailed choice to some authority with considerable latitude to conform its orders to administrative as well as legislative policies'. Congress indicates the general outline of the result it requires and sets out various matters 'about which the administrator must think when he is determining what within those confines the compulsion in a particular case is to be'. Statutes like the Robinson-Patman Act, says Jackson, are 'inchoate law'; an administrative body has to be interposed to formulate a complete expression of the law on a particular case. 'By the doctrine that it [the Federal Trade Commission] exercises legislative discretions as to policy in completing and perfecting the legislative process, it has escaped executive domination on the one hand and been exempted in large measure from judicial review on the other.'

The job of the courts on review, in Justice Jackson's view, is to examine the standards and criteria which the Commission has adopted to see whether its conclusions come within the prescribed terms of reference laid down by the statute and also to see whether the parties concerned have had the issue satisfactorily tried. It is to see, he says, 'whether the Commission has thought about—or at least has written about—all factors which Congress directed it to consider in translating unfinished legislation into a detailed set of guiding yardsticks that becomes law of the case for parties and courts'. It is not for the court of appeal to decide whether the result is the *only* correct one, for the result will include a policy making element which is not within the proper scope of the judicial function. 'Since it is difficult for a court to determine from the record where quasi-legislative policy making has stopped and quasi-judicial application of policy has begun, the entire process escapes very penetrating scrutiny.'

Mr Justice Frankfurter's dissent in *Federal Trade Commission* v. *Motion Picture Advertising Company* (Supreme Court, 1953) emphasized the other side of the coin; he insisted, like Mr Justice McReynolds, that the final determination of the scope of the prohibition of unfair methods of competition was a matter of law and hence one for the courts.

The creation of the Federal Trade Commission made available a continuous administrative process by which fruition of Sherman Act violations could be aborted. But it is another thing to suggest that anything in business activity that may, if unchecked, offend the particularizations of the Clayton Act may now be reached by the Federal Trade Commission Act. The curb on the Commission's power, as expressed by the series of cases beginning with the *Gratz* case, so as to leave to the courts rather than the Commission the final authority in determining what is an unfair method of competition, would be relaxed and unbridled intervention into business practices encouraged. The interpretation of the Acts by the agency which is constantly engaged in construing them should carry considerable weight with courts even in the solution of the legal puzzles these statutes raise. But he is no friend of administrative law who thinks that the Commission should be left at large.

These dicta of Justices Jackson and Frankfurter, though both taken from dissents and for all their difference of emphasis, contain the elements of a fair definition of the legal status of the Commission's work. Mr Justice Jackson was considering a Commission order which merely repeated in other words the general terms of the statute. In giving emphasis to the Commission's discretion he was also drawing attention to the Commission's responsibility for making it clear precisely what it was in a given situation that contravened the policy of the statute. The Commission's 'cease and desist' order should have been, in his view, a concrete prohibition of particular and defined offences; he wanted to return the case to the Commission to perform what should have been 'its most useful function in administrating an admittedly complicated Act'.

Mr Justice Frankfurter in his dissent was protesting at a Commission decision which might be right or wrong but did not seem to him to have been argued. 'If judicial review is to have a basis for functioning,' he said, 'the Commission must do more than pronounce a conclusion by way of a *fiat* and without explication.' It was for the Court to determine 'whether the Commission has correctly applied the proper standards and thus exhibited that familiarity with competitive problems which the Congress anticipated the Commission would achieve from its experience'.

There has been a good deal of criticism of the Commission in the past directed against its formulation of something like *per se* rules in the very field of antitrust where it was expected to exercise administrative discretion. The opinions of Justices Jackson and Frankfurter suggest the lines on which the Commission's work would avoid such strictures. The Commission has by virtue of its functions an inescapable margin of discretion; the courts have a final power of review as to matters of law; the scope of judicial review will be determined essentially by the care and clarity of the Commission's work as reflected in its written judgments. Where these judgments show, as Mr Justice Jackson

demanded, that the Commission has thought about the issues raised by
the legislation and has based its conclusion on a careful and conscien-
tious assessment of the relevant factors, then the court will give weight
to its expertise and will not upset its conclusion in the sense of inter-
posing its own view of the matter. If, however, there is evidence that
the Commission has been idle in reaching its conclusion or in specifying
in its orders what is to be prohibited, the court may well set aside the
Commission's work or return it to the Commission marked in effect
'Careless stuff; do the exercise again'.

11. *Non-litigated procedures: stipulations; trade practice conferences; advisory opinions*

Like the Department of Justice, the Federal Trade Commission has
procedures for settling cases without litigation. The equivalent of the
consent decree negotiated by the Department of Justice is the so-called
'consent order' which may be negotiated with the Federal Trade Commission. Consent Order Procedure has undergone significant changes.
Originally every complaint was assigned to a Hearing Examiner who,
at any time before his initial decision, could suspend the hearing to allow
negotiations for consent settlements. The Examiner accepted such a
consent agreement by making an initial decision, or rejected it by
issuing a notice. His rejection could be appealed to the Commission,
which could either accept the agreement or remand it for trial. This
procedure clogged the Hearing Examiner's timetable with cases which
were ultimately not tried at all or only partially tried, for in practice over
70% of all cases were settled by consent agreements. By allowing
settlement by consent right up to the moment of the Hearing Examiner's decision, both the Hearing Examiner and the other legal
staff of the Commission were burdened with much unnecessary litigation. Accordingly consent order proceedings have been transferred
from Hearing Examiners to a new and separate department dealing
solely with consent orders.

The rules governing adjudications do not now apply to the negotiation of agreements for consent settlements. The party against whom the
Commission issues a complaint will normally be notified and receive a
copy of the intended complaint and order. Within ten days after this
notice that party can tell the Commission whether it wishes to negotiate
a consent settlement or desires to contest the case. If the case is to be
contested, the complaint will be issued immediately. If, however, a
consent settlement is to be negotiated the negotiations must be completed
within thirty days, unless the Commission extends the time for some good
reason. When the Commission accepts a consent settlement agreement,

it thereupon simultaneously issues its complaint, its order and its decision. If no agreement can be reached on the terms of a consent settlement, the Commission proceeds to issue its complaint in the usual way and the matter goes for adjudication before the Hearing Examiner.

Another informal settlement procedure is that of so-called 'stipulations', which has long been used on the side of the Commission's work dealing with misleading advertising and other deceptive practices. The Commission has a Bureau of Industry Guidance within which there is a division dealing with stipulations. This division does not prosecute any cases but notifies companies of alleged contraventions of the law. Informal conferences are then held and the company is given an opportunity to enter into an agreement or 'stipulation' to discontinue such of its challenged practices as are agreed to be unlawful. The Commission may, of course, reject the stipulation on the ground that it does not cover the whole range of alleged infringements, or that the case is so serious that formal proceedings should be brought. Nevertheless, many cases dealing with advertising are settled by these stipulations which involve the firms concerned in making periodic reports showing that they are complying with the terms of the agreement.

In 1963 this procedure was expanded for use in connexion with all types of restraints of trade, whenever the Commission feels that an informal non-adjudicative approach is compatible with the public interest. The Commission in deciding whether to permit such a settlement pays attention, of course, to the nature and gravity of the offence, the party's previous record in the antitrust field, and the adequacy of assurances that the practices will not be resumed. The Chairman of the Commission has however stated that the Commission will still 'entertain a healthy scepticism towards reformations conceived after the policeman's hand is already on the shoulder'.

Another Federal Trade Commission procedure is that of the so-called 'Trade Practice Conference',[1] which is also the work of the Bureau of Industry Guidance. In a Trade Practice Conference the firms in an industry (both those within a trade association and those that stand outside it) confer with the Commission to formulate rules which define and proscribe marketing and business practices which are deceptive or otherwise unfair. The object of this procedure is to lay down for an industry in specific terms the type of business behaviour which will keep firms in conformity with the law. But, like the stipulation procedure, this procedure has in the main been used in the field of deceptive practices and 'fair competition'.

The rules are divided into two groups; the first are in a sense *per se* rules covering those practices which are considered clearly illegal under

---

[1] Sometimes also known as a 'Trade Regulation Rules Conference'.

various statutes. Breach of these rules will lead to the normal procedure of complaint and trial by the Commission. The second group of rules consists of voluntary and recommended practices as distinct from mandatory requirements. The fact that the Commission's staff have been concerned in formulating these rules gives them a certain authority and gives some assurance to the businessman that if he follows them he will not fall foul of the statutes. The Commission will not normally issue a complaint against a firm abiding by the voluntary rules without first letting it be known, if the facts so require, that it regards the particular rule as needing amendment. On the other hand, because of the nature of the second group of rules, it is not automatic that a breach of them will turn out to be an infringement of the statutes; but a firm infringes the 'group two' rules at its own risk. Normally efforts are made to secure voluntary compliance with the 'group two' rules before proceeding with any investigation or complaint.

As with the stipulation procedure, there have been indications in recent years of a readiness on the part of the Commission to apply the Trade Practice Conference technique more extensively to the anti-monopoly field. This had been done in the past—notably in the 1920s —but the general impression then was that it was too loose a procedure for securing effective compliance with the law. However, in the trade practice rules for the cosmetics industry, the complex requirements of sections 2(d) and 2(e) of the Robinson-Patman Act relating to the grant of advertising allowances or services to buyers of goods on 'proportionally equal terms' have been clarified in the form of rules. This was done because an investigation into the industry had suggested that violations of the law, as the Commission interpreted it, were widespread and it was hoped to bring the industry into line with the law without extensive litigation.[1] It is possible that more of this may be done, but the scope for it in the pure antitrust field is narrow. In the field, for example, of section 3 of the Clayton Act or the main provisions of the Robinson-Patman Act, it is clear that rules could only repeat the terms of the statute and the businessman's proper recourse must be to his lawyer and, through him, to the body of case law in question. As was noted in relation to the work of the Department of Justice, the scope for negotiation is narrow when business wishes to operate near the borderlines of the law on the more important antitrust topics, for it is one of the consequences of an adversary system of law on restraint of trade that, in important matters, the borderlines can be defined only by litigation.

---

[1] The Attorney General's National Committee approved 'of efforts thus to extend Conference rules through precise statements that may give effective guidance to particular industries': *Report*, chapter VIII, p. 370.

On the other hand, the Commission has, since the Celler-Kefauver Act, extended its Trade Regulation Rule procedures to the merger field. Under these the Commission will use its broad powers of investigation and inquiry to gather the facts relevant to the enforcement of section 7 of the Clayton Act in particular industries. Companies in those industries will themselves be able to participate in the consideration and analysis of these facts and to provide additional relevant data. The Commission will then issue a comprehensive report, setting forth both its findings on the salient facts and key criteria which should govern the application of section 7 in that industry. It is hoped that this will enable business and its legal advisers to predict with greater certainty whether proposed mergers will be challenged or not.

This new proposal stems from a widespread feeling that the case by case adjudication of mergers is too unpredictable and expensive. The Commission was of course originally founded partially from dissatisfaction with the adjudicative process for determining antitrust issues, to function as an agency for adjusting and correcting practices harmful to competition by a variety of alternative and supplemental methods.

A further innovation of the Commission that deserves mention is the issuing and publication of advisory opinions. Prior to 1961 it was possible to obtain from the staff of the Commission a tentative opinion as to the legality of a proposed course of action either newly to be undertaken or in the light of an existing 'cease and desist' order. Such an opinion, however, did not bind the Commission. In that year a new procedure was introduced therefore, under which an inquirer could be given an advisory opinion of the Commission that would protect him from formal challenge unless and until that opinion was rescinded. Even after rescission no proceedings would be taken in respect of any practices undertaken prior to that time in reliance on the Commission's opinion. The procedure has proved so helpful that it has become the practice to publish the details of the opinions rendered, omitting only the names of the parties and any details of trade secrets involved, and these are now regularly issued. An advisory opinion is not, however, given if the party requesting it is already under investigation by the Department of Justice or the Commission.

12. *Treble-damage actions: examples from the cinema and other industries*

There is one more important means of enforcing the antitrust laws. This is the private suit for damages. Section 7 of the Sherman Act declares: 'Any person who shall be injured in his business or property by any other person or corporation by reason of anything forbidden or declared to be unlawful by this Act may sue therefor . . .

and shall recover three-fold the damages by him sustained, and the cost of suit, including a reasonable attorney's fee.'

Section 4 of the Clayton Act applies the same provision to that Act. The Federal Trade Commission Act, which is not technically an antitrust statute, has no provision for private litigation.

The fear of treble-damage actions is one of the most potent influences in securing compliance with antitrust.[1] It is important, however, to understand the limitations of this type of action. The treble-damage action is not a means of enforcing the law by common informers. A member of the public or a businessman who sees what he regards as flagrant breaches of antitrust law going on may make a complaint to the Department of Justice, but he cannot bring an action on his own account unless he can show both that there was an offence and that he personally was damaged by it. On the other hand, it must also be understood that damage to a private person does not of itself constitute an antitrust offence. A businessman may suffer damage because a supplier refused to go on supplying him. Such a refusal may be part of an organized boycott or it may be a symptom of monopolization; but then again it may be a legitimate exercise of freedom of contract. To sustain a treble-damage action there must be an antitrust offence in the public sense—one which is a significant restraint of trade or which threatens substantially to injure competition in general—and the offence must have had the effect of damaging the plaintiff.

These limitations (and the broader considerations of expense and so forth, which limit private litigation in all fields) mean that treble-damage actions are not spread evenly over the antitrust field but tend to crop up in particular contexts. For example, it is theoretically possible that ordinary members of the public could bring actions against illegal monopolies or price rings on the ground that they had been forced to pay more for goods than would otherwise have been the case. In practice, of course, this never happens, because even three times the loss caused by overcharging to single individuals would not pay for expensive legal struggles with powerful corporations.[2] Treble-

---

[1] 'Private suits are becoming more of an important supplementary enforcement device. They may be the most effective way of policing the multitude of comparatively local and insignificant violations that will tend to escape the glance of federal enforcement authorities, or that even if noticed do not merit the expenditure of limited enforcement resources.' Kaysen and Turner, *Antitrust Policy*, p. 257.

[2] The Attorney General's National Committee endorsed a proposal that the United States should be entitled to sue for single damages when its own property rights (e.g. government purchases) had been damaged and this was enacted by Congress in 1955. Various States and municipalities have also taken an active role as plaintiffs in antitrust litigation against suppliers of such items as school textbooks and drugs. In addition, 'class actions', in which one purchaser institutes a suit on behalf of all similar purchasers, have become popular following a change in the rules of civil procedure.

damage actions, therefore, tend to arise in particular parts of the antitrust field, usually where government suits have established the illegality of practices which affect a number of small businesses.

Three fields in particular may be mentioned. When the Government won its cases against the cinema industry, showing that the collusive activities of the big producers and distributors and their agreements with large exhibitors systematically improved the terms of trade of their own cinemas or of the big circuits as against those of the small independent cinema owner, the way was clear for a spate of treble-damage actions by which small exhibitors sought compensation for the damage that had been done to them. Similarly the successful criminal and civil cases brought against General Electric, Westinghouse and others of the large electrical equipment manufacturers in the early 1960s unleashed an avalanche of treble-damage suits from companies and municipalities all over the country, who claimed to have paid prices for their equipment which had been artificially increased by the practices brought to light in these government cases. The Robinson-Patman Act is another favourite field for treble-damage actions. Once it had been shown, for example in the *Morton Salt* and subsequent cases, that injury to competition could be fairly easily established from the sheer fact of differences in buying price between competing distributors and that the cost justification defence for aggregate discount schedules was difficult and expensive to sustain, it became worth while for distributors to bring actions alleging that they had been discriminated against and damaged to the extent of the amounts that they had paid for goods over and above the amounts paid by their favoured competitors.

Another area in which treble-damage actions have been common is that of patent licensing. The Government having shown that many conditions imposed by patent holders on licensees were a misuse of the patent grant, it became possible for private firms not only to infringe these patents on the ground that the courts would not enforce the patentee's rights so long as he was misusing them, but also, if the patentee sued for infringement, to counterclaim for treble damages on the ground that the misuse of patents constituted restraint of trade.

The reason why prior antitrust action by the Government is important in relation to treble-damage suits is that, by virtue of section 5 of the Clayton Act, certain judgments and decrees in Government cases, civil or criminal, are admissible in private suits as prima facie proof of certain facts. Under the Sherman Act itself this was not so. It is recorded that between 1890 and 1914 only four plaintiffs in treble-damage suits won their cases out of forty-six who made the attempt, and only thirteen were successful up to 1940. The Attorney General's National Committee recorded that between 1947 and 1951 the number of private antitrust suits pending in the courts jumped from 118 to 367, and added that 'since 1951, growth has been even more rapid'.

Broadly speaking, the type of judgment which may be used by a plaintiff in a treble-damage action is one in which defendants have been found to violate the antitrust laws and which has become final in the sense that it is no longer subject to appeal. Such a judgment may be used as prima facie evidence in a private suit. This means that it is sufficient evidence of a violation by the defendant of the antitrust laws. But it is not complete evidence for the purposes of the plaintiff, for he must prove that the illegal conspiracy (or whatever offence it was) has operated directly against him. Even so, it is of considerable advantage to the plaintiff to be able to show in court that there is a proven history of the type of offence of which he is complaining. Moreover, as respects the issues on which the judgment in the government suit is prima facie evidence, the burden of proof is shifted to the defendant.

For example, in the Government's case against General Motors (the *Car finance* case discussed above, Chapter VI, pp. 156 ff.) the Government established a conspiracy to monopolize the financing of General Motors cars and the fact that coercive means had been adopted against dealers. In a subsequent private suit[1] the plaintiffs were therefore relieved of the necessity for proving the existence of such a conspiracy and coercion. They had to show only that the conspiracy had an impact on them—in other words, that the cancellation of their franchise arose out of this conspiracy—and that they suffered damage. There must be a real connexion between the government suit and the facts of which the plaintiff complains; he cannot simply bring in a previous government suit as a damaging and prejudicial innuendo.

Consent decrees in civil cases, which are entered into before any evidence is taken, are not judgments of the kind which may be used as prima facie evidence in treble-damage suits. Also criminal convictions based on a plea of *nolo contendere* do not count for this purpose. This is the incentive for making the *nolo contendere* plea or entering into a consent settlement.

Another matter of importance to those contemplating treble-damage actions is the attitude of the courts to the plaintiff's proof of damages. Common-law decisions in the law of damages, and indeed early decisions under the antitrust laws, maintained rigorous standards in this respect based on the proposition that the extent of damage should not be left to speculation or conjecture. Had the proof of damages in private antitrust suits remained a matter for rigorous proof, it is likely that few such suits could have succeeded and probably few would have been brought.

[1] *Emich Motors Corporation* v. *General Motors Corporation* (Supreme Court, 1951).

In the course of time, however, the attitude of the courts on this matter has been considerably liberalized. It has been calculated that up to 1940 plaintiffs succeeded in recovering damages in fewer than 10% of the actions brought, whereas since 1940 plaintiffs have won over 40% of the cases. It is supposed that liberalization of the rules of proof of damages is the most important factor in this development.

Among the judicial rulings which have worked this change is one that holds that, where the uncertainty about the amount of damage arises out of the very situation which has caused the damage, the defendant cannot complain when the damages are merely estimated. This rule comes from *Story Parchment Company* v. *Paterson Parchment Paper Company* (1931), where the plaintiff's claim was based on an attempt to exclude him from the trade by organized price cutting in his market. It was contended that the plaintiff then had to trade at unduly low prices and that he was damaged to the extent of the difference between these prices and the 'reasonable' prices which would have continued in the absence of the unlawful conspiracy. It could not, of course, be proved rigorously what the 'reasonable' prices in the trade would have been, but the Supreme Court held that since the defendants' conspiracy had upset normal price relationships in the industry, it was not for them to complain of any absence of rigour in the proof.

In many cases since this date fairly rough estimates of loss of profit during the period when illegal activities operated have been accepted as measuring damages in private antitrust actions. For example, in cases against the large motion picture companies, small exhibitors have successfully compared their profits before the period of alleged restraint with those during the period when they were unable to obtain first-run showings of popular pictures, or they have compared their profits during the period of restraint with the profits of allegedly similar theatres which did not suffer from the restrictions.

The Attorney General's National Committee summed up the state of the law as follows: '. . . once plaintiff shows any injury, juries may infer lost profits from plaintiff's past earnings or from current yields of similar enterprises; . . . monopoly increases in plaintiff's costs may be inferred from estimates of what market price might have been under competitive conditions.'[1] This is not, of course, to say that purely speculative estimates of damage will pass the courts: the rule, as laid down in *Bigelow* v. *R.K.O. Radio Pictures* (Supreme Court, 1946), is that there should be a 'just and reasonable estimate of the damage based on relevant data'.

Undoubtedly treble-damage actions are a substantial hazard to those whose antitrust infringements bear heavily on smaller competitors. It

---

[1] *Report*, chapter VIII, p. 379.

is noteworthy that the Attorney General's National Committee, while wishing to see private enforcement action continue,[1] appeared to feel that the balance had swung rather far against defendants in recent years and the majority recommended giving the courts discretion to award double or treble damages according to the seriousness of the case.

[1] 'Such proceedings have a vital role to play in aiding understaffed Government agencies to enforce antitrust prohibitions throughout the nation': *Report*, chapter VIII, p. 380.

CHAPTER XIV

ANTITRUST REMEDIES

1. *Criminal and civil remedies*

The last topic in this description of antitrust is that of remedies; the impact of these laws on business cannot be assessed without knowing what happens to those who break them. It has already been noted that the Government's choice between criminal and civil proceedings cannot be guided simply by the gravity of supposed offences and is to some extent artificial. The real guide is the expected end-result of the legal process. A flagrant, price fixing conspiracy must be made the subject of a criminal case. A civil proceeding ending in a set of injunctions for the future could do no more in such a case than repeat the injunctions of the statute itself. The only end-result worth having from the point of view of the authorities is the punishment of the wrongdoer.

On the other hand, a flagrant and cynical seizure of monopoly power by a single enterprise or by a conspiracy between a few large firms may involve an altogether more serious degree of restraint of trade. Punishment may be just as apt as in the former case and indeed criminal proceedings may be brought and fines imposed. But in such a case it would be highly unsatisfactory to the authorities if fines of a few thousand dollars ended the matter. The monopoly would still be in control and the fines might be regarded simply as a not unreasonable licence fee for monopoly power. In such a case, therefore, those who enforce the law must have recourse to civil proceedings in order to obtain control over the future behaviour of the monopolist and, if possible, to secure a decree of dissolution so that its power may be dispersed or diluted. Yet the decree in a civil proceeding is not in theory punitive.

All this is somewhat artificial. People who have built up a successful business will regard a decree breaking it up as punitive, whatever the legal textbooks may say. Even injunctive relief, when it is extensive and detailed, will be regarded as punitive, especially when activities are prohibited in a particular industry while in other industries, not yet in the toils of antitrust, similar activities may be carried on without let.[1] Injunctions requiring, for example, the compulsory licensing of patents to competitors are felt to be punitive in just this way.

[1] This argument is, of course, familiar in countries where there is no criminal law in the field of restraint of trade but where injunctions against the continuance of restrictive activities may, after inquiry, be imposed administratively. Such injunctions are not punitive by definition; they do not relate to past infringements of law, since there is no law to infringe. They may nevertheless appear inequitable by reference to other industries.

On the other hand, civil remedies do not carry the odium of criminal penalties, and for this reason, even when they are drastic in effect, do not touch the public sense of justice in the same way as severe criminal penalties. Criminal sanctions are notoriously difficult to administer when divorced from moral indignation. As already noted, antitrust offences are *mala prohibita*, not *mala in se*. There are, of course, other fields of criminal law in which offences do not carry any great degree of moral obloquy. Public opinion is notably less apt to applaud the punishment of parking offences or offences against obscure sections of finance acts than the punishment of thieves or blackmailers. Antitrust offences certainly come into the same category and those who commit them tend to be respectable persons not easy to associate with deliberate moral failing.

It is this fact which has largely prevented the imposition of jail sentences on antitrust offenders. The Sherman Act provides for sentences of imprisonment up to one year, but in practice such sentences are rarely imposed. The very few cases in which jail sentences have been imposed have mostly featured some special element of racketeering or fraud which aroused moral indignation.[1] From time to time the Government presses strongly for jail sentences in very flagrant cases of *per se* offences, in particular price fixing, and in a few post-war cases short sentences have been imposed on individual defendants.[2]

Section 6 of the Sherman Act actually authorizes the seizure and forfeiture to the United States of 'any property owned under any contract or by any combination or pursuant to any conspiracy (and being the subject thereof) . . . and being in the course of transportation from one State to another'. But this right of so-called libel of goods has hardly ever been used and is obviously full of administrative impracticalities. There is even a statute in the canon of antitrust which forbids vessels to pass through the Panama Canal if they are 'owned, chartered, operated, or controlled by any person or company which is doing business in violation of . . .' the Sherman Act. This again is a happily impractical provision. The ship would either have to be prevented from passing while an antitrust case was *sub judice*, in which event it would be claimed that no violation had been established; or it would have to be forbidden passage when the case was over, in which event the owner would claim that he had paid the penalty and was now no longer violating the law.

In practice the main criminal sanction in antitrust is the fine. Until 1955 the maximum fine for a violation of the criminal provisions of the

[1] In the early days, when the secondary boycott on the part of a labour union was regarded as repugnant to the Sherman Act, the union leaders were sometimes regarded as fair game for a jail sentence.

[2] Thus in the notorious price fixing cases in the electrical equipment industry, short prison sentences were imposed on seven executives of, *inter alia*, General Electric and Westinghouse.

antitrust laws was five thousand dollars. It is now fifty thousand dollars, as a result of legislation passed in that year. It has, of course, always been possible for a number of separate charges to be laid in the same case and fines imposed for each, so that the amounts may go up to three or four times the nominal maximum in practice. The most serious threat to the businessman arises when he is named as an independent defendant apart from his company. If antitrust offences can be brought home to his individual responsibility, large fines can be a serious punishment. (It has been held that fines may not count as a tax-deductable expense and that they may not be reimbursed by the company employing the offender.)

So far as companies are concerned, the old maximum rate of five thousand dollars was not likely to have any spectacular deterrent effect. Even twenty thousand dollars on four charges was not a vast amount for a large corporation to pay, particularly if the violations concerned had enhanced profits. The five thousand dollars maximum was written into the law in 1890 when the purchasing power of the dollar was substantially greater than at the present day. It was for this reason that many proposals were made over the years for increasing the maximum. Some people even argued in favour of having no maximum but leaving the fine to the discretion of the court.[1] The majority view of the Attorney General's National Committee was that the maximum should be increased to ten thousand dollars, but Congress adopted the minority view that fifty thousand dollars was more appropriate as a maximum, given the discretion of the courts to impose a lesser figure.

Even with the new maximum it is probable, however, that the real sanction of the criminal provisions of the antitrust laws will still lie not so much in the risk of financial penalty as in the sheer fact of criminal indictment as it affects businessmen who have a respected place in their communities. Criminal proceedings under the Sherman Act involve 'going quietly' with the policeman, having your fingerprints taken and all the other unattractive incidents of any crime, together, of course, with a considerable amount of unfavourable publicity and the heavy costs of defending the suit.

2. The equity powers of the courts in antitrust litigation: illustrated by the Paramount case

Much the more important category of antitrust remedies is that which stems from the equity powers of the courts in civil proceedings. These powers are practically unlimited. Once it has been decided that a

---

[1] The unlimited fine has been adopted in legislation in Canada, and courts there have imposed penalties running into hundreds of thousands of dollars.

company or group of companies has conducted its affairs in violation of the Sherman Act, the way is open for what amounts to a detailed piece of legislation directed to regulating the future conduct of the parties. In a sense the real purpose of all that goes before the court's decree—the complaint and trial—is to obtain jurisdiction over the parties for the purpose of regulating their business conduct. Professor Kenneth Carlston has put the point in the extreme form that 'the big subpoena, the trial of the case, are all a ritualistic prelude to the task of . . . setting forth the conduct which he must cease'. It is correct to call these equity decrees essentially legislative because they do more than define the equities between the litigating parties, that is, the Government on one side and the respondents on the other; they frequently create a whole prospectus of rights and duties affecting third parties. In this chapter some examples will be given of this process both from decrees in litigated cases and from consent decrees.

As has been noted, the more obvious classes of *per se* offence—for example, price fixing and boycotts—do not lend themselves to equity proceedings; they are usually dealt with criminally. But where price fixing is not a matter of express agreement but has been inferred from a course of conduct consisting of exchanges of information as to price and costs, civil proceedings may be brought; and in such a case the decree will regulate the whole range of conduct that has brought about the price fixing, even though some aspects of that conduct would not in isolation offend the law. Decrees were noted in Chapter I which, for example, prohibited the members of a trade association from collecting and disseminating among themselves any information or statistics relating to prices, discounts, terms or conditions of sale, or costs or elements of costs. It is accepted as a principle that activities of this kind which could be adopted innocently may be enjoined when they have once been used in pursuance of an illegal conspiracy.

In the more complicated cases the decree and the court's opinion accompanying it may constitute in effect an analysis of the whole state of an industry and a frankly legislative programme for bringing its operations into conformity with public policy. A good illustration of the way this process is carried on is provided by the *Paramount* case, in which the respondents were all the major producers and distributors of motion pictures.[1] Once collusion between these companies had been established to the satisfaction of the Court, the whole working of the industry became open to analysis and correction. Detailed rules were laid down to regulate the conditions under which the companies should make available the various runs of pictures and the clearances granted between various exhibitions. Pooling agreements by which a

---

[1] For an account of the case, see above, Chapter VI, pp. 166 ff.

number of theatres were operated as a unit and profits shared according to prearranged percentages had to be dissolved; joint ownership of theatres had to be terminated except where a particular firm's financial interest could be shown to be no more than an investment. Licensing agreements between the distributors and large exhibiting circuits, under which licence fees were calculated by reference to the total take of the circuit rather than by reference to individual theatres, were enjoined on the ground that they prejudiced the competitive opportunities of small individual competitors. Block booking of pictures, whereby a number of pictures were included in a package deal which had to be taken whole or not at all, was also forbidden.

The real problem in the industry, in the view of the courts, was to secure that each cinema, according to its size, location and pulling power, should have reasonably equal opportunities of showing popular pictures, regardless of whether it was a single, independently owned unit, or part of a large and powerful circuit, or a cinema directly owned by the big producing and distributing companies. The whole of the case really turned on the complaint that the arrangements in the industry systematically discriminated in favour of the powerful circuits or the major companies' own cinemas and against the small man. The argument about how this problem should be dealt with is very revealing in its indications of the breadth of the equity powers of the courts.

The District Court which had tried the case concluded that the various injunctions, already mentioned, against particular restrictive practices were not enough. Their decree would have required that all films should be licensed on a basis of competitive bidding so that each licence should in effect be auctioned to the highest bidder in each area. Mr Justice Douglas in the Supreme Court set aside this part of the District Court's decree. He pointed out the many practical difficulties which this kind of regulation would involve. Each bidder would have to state what run he wanted, how much he would be prepared to pay (whether a flat rate or a percentage of his takings) and various other matters, which would have made it difficult to compare one bid with another. In any case, cinemas differ in size, location, equipment and comfort; and exhibitors differ in integrity and responsibility. Mr Justice Douglas said: 'We mention these matters merely to indicate the character of the job of supervising such a competitive bidding system. It would involve the judiciary in the administration of intricate and detailed rules governing the priority, period of clearance, length of run, competition areas, reasonable return and the like. The system would be apt to require as close a supervision as a continuous receivership unless the defendants were to be entrusted with vast discretion. The judiciary is unsuited to affairs of business management; and control through the

power of contempt is crude and clumsy and lacking in the flexibility
necessary to make continuous and detailed supervision effective.' Mr
Justice Douglas went on to hold that the right kind of relief was a
substantial divestiture of the exhibiting interests of the major film
companies.

The District Court had noted that the five major companies producing
and distributing films controlled between them only about 17% of the
cinemas in the United States. It seemed to them that this was a
questionable ground for requiring any divorce of exhibiting interests
from the producing and distributing companies. Mr Justice Douglas,
however, held that the 'part of commerce' doctrine[1] should be applied
to the situation. The District Court had looked only to the exhibiting
interests of the major companies on a national scale. Mr Justice
Douglas looked first to that part of the market which dealt in first-run
pictures—the cream of the business—and then to the first-run market
in the largest cities of the United States. He found that 'in the ninety-
two cities of the country with populations over 100,000 at least 70 per
cent of all the first-run theaters are affiliated with one or more of the
five majors. Although in almost all these cities there was competition
against the major companies, this result was enough to show that the
conspiracy had gone far to achieve, by its restraints of trade, a monopoly
in a part of commerce. The problem under the Sherman Act is not
solved merely by measuring monopoly in terms of size or extent of
holdings, or by concluding that single ownerships were not obtained for
the purpose of achieving a national monopoly. It is the relationship of
the unreasonable restraint of trade to the position of the defendants in
the exhibition field (and more particularly in the first-run phase of that
business) that is of first importance in the divestiture phase of these
cases.'

The build-up of a dominating position in the best part of the exhibiting business—the first-run business in the cities with the largest
populations—might properly be regarded as the natural result of the
restrictive practices of the conspiracy, and if so would in itself be a
sufficient showing of a purpose on the part of the major companies to
achieve this position. The Supreme Court therefore sent the case back
to the District Court for the decree to be revised on the basis that divestiture would be justifiable on the facts of the case. The revised decree
did in fact require the major companies to divest themselves of ownership in large numbers of cinemas.

This result demonstrates two points very clearly. One is the great
breadth of the equity powers of the courts. There was no suggestion
in Mr Justice Douglas's opinion that the District Court went beyond

1 See the *Yellow Cab* and other cases described above, Chapter V.

their powers in ordering the licensing of films individually by auction, though this was in effect a piece of legislation which would have completely changed the industry's mode of doing business. It also shows, however, the strong sense of practicality among the courts in the job of finding suitable remedies. The competitive-bidding proposal would have involved comparing bids with too many variables to be correctly comparable and would probably have led to a mass of petty litigation between the parties. To avoid these practical difficulties the Supreme Court recommended the more straightforward remedy of divestiture.

3. Remedies ordered in cases of monopolization: the United Shoe Machinery and ALCOA cases

In the biggest cases of monopolization the finding of remedies is the central problem of the legal process. It is not too much to say that the possibility of finding suitable means of altering a monopoly situation influences the content of the law itself. For if there is no solution, what can be the meaning of finding violations of the law? Going a stage further back still, the final decree that is envisaged is bound to affect the choice of cases for prosecution. The lawyers in the Department of Justice are reluctant to start a case unless they can see with reasonable clarity what remedial measures can be achieved at the end so as to improve the situation. There is always, of course, a limit to the extent to which the tail can wag the dog in this way because the Department of Justice remains, after all, a body charged with the duty of enforcing the law: flagrant offences, once brought to the attention of the Department, must be prosecuted if public criticism is to be avoided. This is the answer to not infrequent criticisms that the Department does in fact start cases when there is little real expectation of any worthwhile result. The fact remains that it is not infrequently the remedy that starts the case and determines, within limits, its decision.

The courts have throughout the history of the Sherman Act kept a severely practical eye on the effects of their decrees. Judge Wyzanski put the judge's problem in this matter with great cogency in his opinion in *United States* v. *United Shoe Machinery Corporation* in 1953.[1] On the one hand, as he showed, the judge must frame the decree on the basis of the case law and underlying philosophy of the Sherman Act with its broad condemnation of monopoly power. Yet he has above all to be practical. As he put it:

Judges in prescribing remedies have known their own limitations. They do not *ex officio* have economic or political training. Their prophecies as to the economic future are not guided by unusually subtle judgment. They are

[1] For an account of the case, see above, Chapter IV, pp. 114 ff.

not so representative as other branches of the Government. . . . Judicial decrees must be fitted into the framework of what a busy, and none too expert, court can supervise. Above all, no matter with what authority he is invested, with what facts and information he is supplied, a trial judge is only one man, and should move with caution and humility.

That considerations of this type have always affected antitrust courts is plain from the history of the *Standard Oil*, *American Tobacco* and *ALCOA* cases. To many champions of the antitrust laws these cases indicate judicial timidity, economic innocence, lack of conviction, or paralysis of resolution. Yet there is another way of interpreting this judicial history. In the antitrust field the courts have been accorded, by common consent, an authority they have in no other branch of enacted law. . . . They would not have been given, or allowed to keep, such authority in the antitrust field, and they would not so freely have altered from time to time the interpretation of its substantive provisions, if courts were in the habit of proceeding with a surgical ruthlessness that might commend itself to those seeking absolute assurance that there will be workable competition, and to those aiming at immediate realization of the social, political, and economic advantages of dispersal of power.

Practising the caution which he preached, Judge Wyzanski rejected the Government's proposal that the corporation should be divided into three separate companies. He found that all the company's machines were manufactured at a single plant, so that there would be no practical way of dividing it into viable parts. He complained that the Government had not thought through its proposals and the consequential problems which they would entail. 'A petition of dissolution', he said, 'should reflect greater attention to practical problems and should involve supporting economic data and prophecies such as are presented in corporate reorganization and public utility dissolution cases.'

Judge Wyzanski contented himself with less radical relief measures. In a series of injunctions he required that the company's leases for shoe machinery should be purged of the restrictive features which he regarded as the chief evidence of their positive drive to retain monopoly power. He required that all their machines should be offered for sale, so that ultimately a second-hand market would be built up. He required that the company should not fix terms for leasing the machines which would make it substantially more advantageous for a shoe manufacturer to lease them rather than buy them. He ordered the divestiture of certain of United's subsidiary interests, for example, in the supply of nails, tacks and eyelets. Finally, he required that United patents should be compulsorily licensed on a reasonable royalty basis.[1]

---

[1] Recently the Justice Department claimed again, under the 'second-look' provision of the decree, that divestiture would be appropriate since workable competition had not been restored. A consent decree then negotiated by U.S.M. and the Government provided, *inter alia*, for divestiture by U.S.M. of sufficient machines to reduce its market share to 33 %.

A similar respect for the practicalities of industrial life is to be found in other court opinions on relief measures. The final result of the *ALCOA* case is of interest in this respect. It will be remembered that Judge Hand had found the Aluminum Company of America guilty of monopolization in 1945 on the basis of evidence going up to the beginning of the war. During the war, however, the Government had created new sources of aluminium in order to get sufficient expansion of production in a short time. Judge Hand had not proceeded with relief measures in 1945 because at the time the Government was in process of disposing of this new productive capacity. By the time it had done so the picture was markedly different from that which appeared in the trial. ALCOA had only just over 50% of primary aluminium capacity in the United States, albeit a vastly expanded capacity. Two other companies had entered the industry, the Reynolds Company with just over 30% of primary capacity and the Kaiser Company with the remaining 18%. The hearings on remedies thus took place in a largely modified situation.

The case was heard by Judge Knox in 1950. He had to decide whether there was still a need for imposing any remedial measures to establish competitive conditions and, if so, what these measures should be. Judge Knox saw his problem essentially as that of legislating for a state of 'effective competition' in the industry, so as to ensure 'lawful conditions throughout the foreseeable future'. He noted a change in the attitude of the courts to the need for and purpose of remedies in monopoly cases. During the 1920s attention had been focused on abuses of monopoly power, and even where a company (for example, the International Harvester Company) still retained substantial power, it was held that the abandonment of such abuses of power as predatory price cutting made remedial measures inappropriate. He continued: 'The latest remedy cases indicate two modifications of earlier judicial pronouncements, one practical, the other theoretical. On the practical side they show that courts are less likely than formerly to be impressed by evidence which tends to establish that defendants who have violated the Sherman Act in the past will not do so in the future. On the theoretical side, a rule has been formulated which, when applied, will serve to deprive defendants of the fruits of their wrongdoing. This, no doubt, is an outgrowth of an awareness that strong measures are required to restrain a tendency to recidivisim.'

In the various motion picture industry cases, divestiture of cinema ownership had been ordered on the ground that otherwise defendants would retain the dividends of unlawful monopolistic conduct. This principle, Judge Knox showed, was an addition to the purposes of remedies as originally defined by Chief Justice White in the *Standard Oil*

case of 1911. White's principles had been: 'First: to forbid the doing
in the future of acts like those which we have found to have been done
in the past which would be violative of the Statute. Second: the
exertion of such a measure of relief as will effectively dissolve the
combination found to exist in violation of the Statute, and thus
neutralize the extension and continual operating force which the possession of the power unlawfully obtained has brought and will continue
to bring about.'

In considering the position of ALCOA, given that it had been found
in 1945 to be in possession of unlawful monopoly power, Judge Knox
had to provide 'against the reasonable expectation of the resumption
of future unlawful conditions' and had to ensure that the company's
monopoly power was neutralized. This meant that the standard for
assessing the need for remedies was different from that by which illegality
was determined in the first place. Although the creation of Reynolds and
Kaiser as competitive companies had reduced ALCOA's dominance in
the field, its previous proclivity to build up monopoly power must be
taken into consideration: 'As an example, if it can now be said that
Alcoa shall have monopoly thrust upon it under reasonably predictable
market developments because of the economic collapse of a competitor
or competitors, remedial action is appropriate.'

He found in fact that ALCOA had lost its former exclusive control
of the market. ALCOA was still supreme as a supplier of primary
aluminium to independent fabricators, but Reynolds and Kaiser, using
their own primary aluminium, were substantial competitors in the
sheet market and had consistently enlarged their shares. Although
ALCOA was still the price leader, the extent to which prices could be
raised was limited by the potential competition of the two other primary
producers. He found too that, in the new situation, ALCOA's dominant
ownership of patents in the industry did not constitute a serious threat
to effective competition.

He then considered the position of the Canadian company, Aluminium Limited, which originally had been under common ownership
with ALCOA; some degree of common ownership still existed and there
were family ties between the two companies. In the earlier hearings
it had been held that there was no improper relationship between the
two companies. But Alted (the Canadian company) had become the
largest producer of primary aluminium in the world and a substantial
supplier to the United States market. Most of its supplies went to
ALCOA. Judge Knox did not find that ALCOA enjoyed more
favourable terms from Alted than other companies but held, nevertheless, 'that in order properly to safeguard the public interest bespoken
by the Sherman Act it is highly expedient that there be no restraint

whatever on the competitive potential which now exists from Canadian production'.

He thought it 'too much to expect that the competition between Alcoa and Limited . . . will be as keen and comprehensive as the Sherman Act demands'. The development of Reynolds and Kaiser as effective competitors would be a chancy business; there might be strikes or breakdowns in supplies of raw material or waterpower from time to time. If, when difficulties of these kinds faced the industry, Reynolds and Kaiser had to meet them from their own resources while ALCOA was in a position to draw supplies of primary aluminium from the Canadian company because of the intimate relationship of the past, the survival of the small companies might be jeopardized. 'One must indulge the conviction that the control which may be exercised over Aluminium Limited by the controlling stockholders of Alcoa is a resource of enormous importance. No matter how lawful the relations with Limited may have been in the past, were I now to ignore the potential power which resides in the nexus above described, my duties in this proceeding as I understand them would not be adequately discharged.'

Judge Knox noted that the chances of any more newcomers finding the huge investment needed to enter such an integrated field of production were remote. So great were the resources needed to survive in the industry that even companies created by dissolving ALCOA into separate parts might well not be viable. Here one sees the overriding practicality of the Court's approach to the problem of remedies. The aluminium industry is vital to both the prosperity and national security of the United States. Only integrated production is viable. Thus, in Judge Knox's view, the economic and technical framework of the problem imposed a minimum effective size on firms in the industry. Big business was inevitable in this framework. For all its huge size and resources ALCOA had only two plants for producing primary alumina and one of these would be too weak to survive in independence. So Judge Knox was not prepared to take the social, economic and security risks of disturbing the physical organization of ALCOA's properties. He contented himself with ordering that the common control of ALCOA and Alted should be eliminated; the shareholders of ALCOA were required to dispose of stock interests in the Canadian company. He also decreed that provisions in the agreements setting up Reynolds and Kaiser, by which their use of ALCOA patents had been made conditional on their granting to ALCOA the right to use any improvement patent discovered by them, should be unenforceable. The object of this order was to stimulate effective competition among the three American companies in research and development.

The whole of this opinion is of the greatest value for understanding the ways of antitrust. It will be noted that there is hardly any direct connexion between the activities that created the illegality and the remedial measures which Judge Knox decreed. No court of law had found that the relationship between ALCOA and the Canadian company was of itself illegal under the Sherman Act. Yet the connexion between the two companies was ordered to be dissolved. No suggestion was made that the grant-back provisions in the patent licences under which Reynolds and Kaiser operated were in any way illegal. Indeed, Judge Knox noted that, in the wartime negotiations setting up the two new companies, ALCOA had been markedly generous in making its patents available free of royalties. The grant-back was in effect its only return. On the other hand, ALCOA had been found, rightly or wrongly, to have built up monopoly power in the industry by unlawful means. Traditionally this was a sufficient ground for ordering the dissolution of the company, just as Standard Oil and American Tobacco had been dissolved in 1911. Yet this was not done because the practicalities of industrial organization in the twentieth century, at least in this particular industry, seemed to attach to it a disproportionate national risk. Thus, the upshot of the story is that ALCOA's previous illegality was taken to confer on the Court jurisdiction to legislate for the future of the aluminium industry in whatever way seemed most apt to bring about a state described as 'effective competition'. Finally, as is now common practice in these cases, Judge Knox retained jurisdiction of the case for a further five years so that the Government might petition for further and more complete relief if conditions appeared to warrant it. This provision is very much analogous to legislation in which a rule making power by subordinate legislation is retained.

4. *Practical limitations in the use of dissolution or divestiture decrees: the* American Tobacco *case. Divestiture in merger cases: the* du Pont/General Motors *case*

A strong sense of practicality has in fact been manifested throughout the case law dealing with monopolizing under section 2 of the Sherman Act. In the early cases—dealing with the 'trusts' which were broken up in the years following the *Standard Oil* and *American Tobacco* cases of 1911—physical dissolution did not on the whole present insuperable practical problems. Standard Oil and American Tobacco themselves, as well as organizations like the Dupont Explosives Trust, consisted of large numbers of producing plants knit together by financial control. In the same way the early railway cases involved the financial control by large holding companies of two or more physically complete and separable railway systems. The courts, therefore, were able to decree in straightforward terms that the holding companies in each case should be dissolved, so as to restore autonomy to the separate parts of the organization, and that substantial stockholders should not extend their interests over more than one component part of the organization.

As we have seen, the next serious assault by the Government on entrenched monopoly positions—that of the series of cases decided after 1945—presented more difficult practical problems. Neither in the *ALCOA* case nor in that of the *United Shoe Machinery Company* would the courts initially accept, as a practical matter, the physical dissolution of the organizations concerned. The fact that the United Shoe Machinery Company manufactured all its machines in one plant and the fact that ALCOA had only two plants to produce alumina, one of which was not economically viable, overrode the case for dissolution, and the aim of the decree imposed in each case was essentially to permit competitors of the big organizations to survive and flourish. Practices, like the conditions attaching to the United Shoe Machinery Company's leases, which tended to tie customers or suppliers exclusively to the monopoly, were prohibited. Even loose arrangements like the nexus between ALCOA and the Canadian, Aluminium Limited, by which the dominant firm in the American industry might have been more fully insured against industrial risks than its rivals, were enjoined.

In some cases the practical difficulties of dissolution seem to have frustrated the search for effective remedies altogether. For example, the second *American Tobacco* case—the criminal case of conspiracy to monopolize the industry which the Government won in 1946 against the three major cigarette manufacturers—did not result in any civil proceedings from which relief measures might have been obtained. Fines were imposed upon the three companies, but there the matter rests to this day. It seems likely that this is owing to the difficulty which the government lawyers would have found in considering what relief measures to ask for. Cigarettes are made in quite small plants with relatively light and cheap machinery. To have ordered the three big companies to sell off certain existing plants to smaller rivals would have been useless; they could quickly have constructed new plants to replace the lost capacity. The real assets of the major companies are huge stocks of tobacco and, more especially, the brand names of their cigarettes. Possibly the only effective form of dissolution would have been to put such brand names as 'Lucky Strike', 'Camel' and 'Chesterfield' into the public domain; to have allowed other producers, in effect, to use these names and the associated designs of the major companies' packaging without fear of legal action. Yet even this very radical course might not have changed the structure of the industry significantly in the long run, since the resources of the major firms might well enable them to build up new brand names by heavy advertising within a relatively short time.

In other cases the practicalities of the matter may point to some form of dissolution as a comparatively convenient solution. The divestiture of cinema holdings from the major film producers and distributors has been mentioned above. In general, where the size and power of a business organization rests to a large extent on the vertical integration of easily separable activities, dissolution may appear practicable and expedient. In the *Pullman* case, for example, the court ordered the separation of the manufacture of Pullman cars from their operation.[1] Convenience and expediency may in a sense exert a discriminatory force on the cases, so that types of industry structure which are readily dissoluble may from that very fact suffer dissolution, even though the activities that went to the monopolization may be no more heinous, and possibly less so, than those which have led to situations not amenable in practice to a similar remedy.

Divestiture is in any case a more likely remedy in cases where the antitrust violation is a completed merger which has been held invalid under section 1 of the Sherman Act or section 7 of the Clayton Act. In such cases, as opposed to those brought under section 2 of the Sherman Act, the 'unscrambling' procedure is usually more straightforward because either the merger is of a comparatively recent date or because a court order forbidding the commingling of assets pending determination of the case has been issued. Even if the unscrambling is not easy, it is still likely to be required in such a case, for the wording of section 7 in particular suggests that the natural remedy for its violation is the undoing of the prohibited acquisition, and commonsense would indicate that normally this is the only appropriate remedy.

The issue of divestiture in merger cases came before the Supreme Court when the *du Pont/General Motors* case came before it for a second time[2] in 1961, on this occasion purely on the issue of remedy. Following the Court's ruling that section 7 of the Clayton Act had been violated by the large du Pont holdings in General Motors, both the Government and du Pont put forward proposals for remedying the situation. Du Pont's plan was that all its voting rights in General Motors stock should be passed to the shareholders in du Pont (other than the du Pont family) in proportion to their holdings in du Pont itself, while du Pont would retain all other attributes of ownership in the General

---

[1] *United States* v. *Pullman Company* (District Court of Pennsylvania, 1943).
[2] For an account of the Supreme Court's decision on the substantive issues of the case see Chapter VI, pp. 172–3.

Motors stock including the right to receive dividends and to a share of assets on liquidation. The Government on the other hand had proposed that du Pont should divest itself completely of its 63 million General Motors shares over a ten-year period, by having about two-thirds distributed to du Pont's shareholders in the form of a dividend, and the other one-third (which would otherwise have gone to the du Pont family) gradually sold by a court appointed trustee.[1]

Largely influenced by the unfavourable tax consequences for du Pont shareholders, and the probability that the market value of both companies' stock would be severely reduced, the District Court approved a decree very similar to that put forward by du Pont. The Supreme Court, however, by four to three, reversed this decision and accepted the Government's plan of relief. Mr Justice Brennan, who wrote the majority decision, pointed out that, although the District Court had the responsibility for initially fashioning the remedy, the responsibility for an effective remedy must ultimately lie with the Supreme Court.

'The proper disposition of antitrust cases', he continued, 'is obviously of great public importance, and their remedial phase more often than not crucial. For the suit has been a futile exercise if the Government prove the violation but fail to secure a remedy adequate to redress it.' If, therefore, the only remedy effective in eliminating the anti-competitive results of the du Pont stockholding in General Motors was divestiture, then this must be ordered, regardless of any economic hardship on third parties. After pointing out the factors which would render du Pont's proposed plan ineffective, including the dubious point that it would be in the interest of the du Pont shareholders (who, under du Pont's plan, would become shareholders in General Motors) to vote in such a way as to induce General Motors to favour du Pont, the majority concluded that complete divestiture of all the stock must be ordered.[2]

5. *Remedies in patent cases:* Hartford-Empire; National Lead; General Instrument; *the* General Electric (Lamps) *case*

Remedies in those cases which depend on the market power arising from aggregations of patents have a special interest. In the *Hartford-Empire* case a conspiracy was found to monopolize the glassmaking industry by means of patents covering the manufacture of glass-

[1] There were other restrictions in the plan of relief approved by the District Court with which the Supreme Court agreed. These included prohibitions on preferential or discriminatory trade relations between the companies and on any interlocking officers or directors.

[2] The minority's eloquent dissent written by Mr Justice Frankfurter stressed the principle that the Supreme Court should not sit to draft antitrust decrees *de novo* and argued that the findings of the lower Court should not be reversed except in cases where its discretion had been abused.

making machinery. On practical grounds the Court was unwilling to accept the Government's claim that the Hartford-Empire Company should be broken up. As a research organization it seemed important to the technical strength of the glass industry. The problem was, therefore, to frame a decree which would preclude in some other way the resumption of unlawful practices. The District Court had in fact ordered that the company should license compulsorily and without royalty or any other charge any of its existing patents to any applicant; and, furthermore, it enjoined the company for all time to license any future patents it might acquire to any applicant at a reasonable royalty (to be fixed in case of dispute by the Court). The Supreme Court thought that these provisions went beyond what was needed to prevent unlawful conduct in the future. Since the company had come by the patents legally and they were valid, the Supreme Court felt that it was going too far to dedicate them to the public. Indeed, the majority opinion of Mr Justice Roberts appeared to find difficulties of principle in ordering dedication (or confiscation) of patents as a remedy in a civil suit. The decree was therefore altered to require only that Hartford-Empire should license its patents for major types of machinery to any applicant on the basis of reasonable royalties.

Mr Justice Black dissented from the majority view on the ground that antitrust remedies should, among other things, involve giving up the fruits of the previous illegality. Mr Justice Rutledge, who agreed with the dissent, showed in his opinion how difficult it is in practice to draw a sharp line between punishment for past misconduct (which the majority felt they should avoid) and prevention of future misconduct. In his view it was wrong 'that men who have misused their property and acquired much of it violating the Sherman Act are free for the future to continue using it as are other owners who have committed no such offence'.

He went on to say: 'When the patent holder so far overreaches his privilege as to intrude upon the rights of others and the public protected by the antitrust legislation, and does this in such a way that he cannot further exercise the privilege without also trespassing upon the rights thus protected, either his right or the other person's, and the public right, must give way. It is wholly incongruous in such circumstances to say that the privilege of the trespasser shall be preserved and the rights of all others that he has transgressed shall continue to give way to the consequences of his wrongdoing.'

These dissenting opinions are of importance because the view which they embody tended later to become dominant in the courts. The next case of importance in this line was *United States* v. *National Lead Company* (Supreme Court, 1947). In this case it had been found that the National

Lead Company and du Pont together controlled some 90% of American production of titanium pigments and had conspired with foreign companies to divide world markets. Once again the dominance of the companies rested on patents. The District Court, under the authority of the *Hartford-Empire* case, had ordered compulsory licensing of patents for reasonable royalties and the Government appealed to the Supreme Court on the ground that the patents should be dedicated in order to secure an adequate remedy. Mr Justice Burton, speaking for the majority of the Supreme Court, noted that National Lead and du Pont were vigorous competitors. Since this was a civil case it would be wrong to look upon the misuse of patent rights as a matter for punishment. It seemed that adequate assurance against further restraints would be obtained by compulsory licensing for reasonable royalties and the Court found that dedication of patents had not been shown to be necessary. But Mr Justice Burton made it clear on this occasion that he was not holding that dedication would never be justified.

This case is also of interest because the Government claimed that both National Lead and du Pont, each of which operated two large titanium pigments plants, should be required to divest themselves of their second plants so as to create four main competitors instead of two in the industry. This claim was rejected not on the ground that dissolution would be impracticable but on the ground that it had not been shown to be necessary. Du Pont and National Lead had not acquired their plants illegally and, given the other forms of relief awarded in the decree, the smaller competitors of both companies should now be in a better position to compete. 'It is not for the courts to realign and redirect effective and lawful competition where it already exists and needs only to be released from restraints that violate the antitrust laws. To separate the operating units of going concerns without more supporting evidence than has been presented here to establish either the need for, or the feasibility of, such separation will amount to an abuse of discretion.'

The compulsory licensing of patents for reasonable royalties has now become to all intents and purposes a routine measure of relief in cases of monopolization where the company concerned has built up its position largely through patent holdings. Mr Justice Reed's opinion in the *Gypsum* case[1] contains a particularly clear statement of the grounds on which such action is taken:

A trial court upon a finding of a conspiracy in restraint of trade and of monopoly has the duty to compel action by the conspirators that will, so far as practicable, cure the ill effects of the illegal conduct and assure the public freedom from its continuance. Such action is not limited to prohibition of

[1] See above, Chapter XI, pp. 310-11.

the proven means by which the evil was accomplished but may range broadly through practices connected with acts actually found to be illegal. Acts entirely proper when viewed alone may be prohibited. The conspirators should, so far as practicable, be denied future benefits from their forbidden conduct.

An opinion of Mr Justice Jackson in the *International Salt* case[1] throws further light on the same point:

A district court is not obliged to assume, contrary to common experience, that a violator of the antitrust laws will relinquish the fruits of his violation more completely than the court requires him to do. And advantages already in hand may be held by methods more subtle and informed and more difficult to prove than those which, in the first place, win a market. When the purpose to restrain trade appears from a clear violation of the law, it is not necessary that all of the untravelled roads to that end be left open and that only the worn one be closed. The usual ways to the prohibited goal may be blocked against the proven transgressor and the burden put upon him to bring any proper claims for relief to the court's attention. . . . In an equity suit, the end to be served is not the punishment of past transgressions nor is it merely to end specific illegal practices. The public interest served by such civil suits is that they pry open to competition a market that has been closed by defendants' illegal restraints. If this decree accomplishes less than that, the Government has won a law suit and lost a cause.

Thus the compulsory licensing of patents—even valid patents lawfully acquired through the research efforts of the company's own employees —is intended not as punishment but as a way in which rival companies may be brought into the market with some hope of making it a competitive one. Not only the whole folio of a company's existing patents may be compulsorily licensed but also all its improvement patents for a period in the future and even all its new patents in particular fields. The courts apply a rule of reason to determine what is required to obtain an effective state of competition without going so far as to be punitive.

In the *du Pont/I.C.I.* case of 1952, for example, Judge Ryan, still basing himself on the *Hartford-Empire* decision, held that to order the compulsory licensing of all the American patents held by the two companies in all fields would be punitive and destructive of the necessary incentive for them to maintain their huge research efforts. Accordingly he ordered the compulsory licensing of their existing patents in the fields to which their restrictive agreements applied, and of improvement patents but not new patents in these fields. In this case an auxiliary remedy was awarded which has become common in recent

[1] See above, Chapter XI, p. 327.

years. Both I.C.I. and du Pont were ordered to provide applicants, at a reasonable charge, with technical manuals which would show in detail how the patents were practised.

Although the Supreme Court in the *National Lead* case did not rule out the dedication of a company's patents (that is, ordering them to be compulsorily licensed free of royalties), it was widely believed at that time that this remedy could hardly fail to be punitive and even that it ought not to be applied without specific legislative authority. Subsequently, however, dedication of patents has been ordered in both litigated and consent decrees. The arguments relating to this form of relief were set out by Judge Forman in two opinions in 1953. In *United States* v. *General Instrument Corporation* (District Court of New Jersey), the Judge rejected the Government's claim that patents should be dedicated. (The company had claimed that dedication was not a permissible requirement under the existing law.)

Judge Forman noted that the legality of ordering the dedication of patents had been left open by the Supreme Court's decision in the *National Lead* case; the dictum in the *Hartford-Empire* case that dedication was confiscatory had been, as he put it, 'substantially diluted'. He continued: 'Under the present circumstances, however, I do not believe that dedication of patents is required in order to free competition from the fetters fashioned by the defendant's illegal activities. This is not a situation where one enormous firm in the industry, overshadowing all competitors, owns a huge bundle of patents with which it maintained its dominance in violation of the antitrust laws and with which, even were it compelled to license them to competitors at reasonable royalties, it could preserve a competitive edge by virtue of the drag such royalties would have on the success of these competitors.'

As in the *National Lead* case, the ending of the conspiracy between the main firms in the industry was expected to result in competition between them. This being so, it was held that the compulsory licensing of patents for reasonable non-discriminatory royalties, together with the compulsory licensing of future patents for five years, would be enough to restore competition.

A few weeks later the same judge issued his decree in *United States* v. *General Electric Company* which dealt with that company's monopoly position in the electric lamp field. In this case he did in fact order the dedication of the company's patents for lamps and lamp parts. He explained this decision by the following argument:

I have held that General Electric's attempt to maintain control over the lamp industry has been largely by way of extending its basic patents on lamps and lamp parts. To compel the completely free use of these patents is not to impose upon General Electric and other defendants penalties for misuse of patents and violation of the antitrust laws, but rather to check the intrusion of advantages thereby gained into the mechanics of competition in the lamp industry.

Where the profit margin on the production of lamps is as narrow as it is at the present time any licensing fees may prove an important factor in limiting or inhibiting the growth of competition. In view of the fact that General Electric achieved its dominant position in the industry and maintained it in great measure by its extension of patent control, the requirement that it contribute its existing patents to the public is only a justified dilution of that control made necessary in the interest of free competition in the industry. . . .

General Electric and other defendants are mounted upon an arsenal of a huge body of patents that can easily overwhelm and defeat competition by small firms desiring to stay in or gain a foothold in the industry. These operators may well be unequipped to engage in litigation on the validity of one patent after another at what could be incalculable expense. In order to avoid it they could be required to shoulder royalties which could prove to be the very factor that would push them out of the competitive circle of the market.

In circumstances such as these it would appear that royalty-free licensing of patents on lamps and lamp parts is an essential remedy as a preventive against a continuance of monopoly in this industry. It would appear to be no more objectionable as confiscatory than where compulsory licensing is ordered. In the latter case the owner admittedly is permitted to receive a royalty but he nevertheless loses a monopoly inherent in his ownership of the patent, and the royalty he is forced to accept at times is not one that he fixes. Royalty-free licensing and dedication are but an extension of the same principle, not to be directed indiscriminately, of course, but well within the therapeutic measures to be administered under circumstances such as were made to appear in this case.

Judge Forman in this order did not decree the physical dissolution of the General Electric Company nor even the divestiture of its holdings in foreign companies. The opinion shows once again the pragmatic nature of the decisions of the courts on remedies. All is judged by the expected end-result. If the payments of royalties will constitute a factor that in practice prevents effective competition from growing up, then the outright confiscation of patents is justified. If it is not necessary, it is not ordered. The decision rests not on the manner or severity of the monopolization, nor on how the patents were obtained or used, but solely on the result to be achieved.

6. *Remedies ordered in consent decrees: illustrated by the* ASCAP *case*

The decisions of the courts on remedies naturally set limits to what the Government can obtain in consent decrees. A defendant is unlikely to accept by consent measures which would not be awarded by the courts in litigated cases. Nevertheless, the advantages which defendants may obtain from consent settlements are such that the measures obtained by the Government in consent decrees often press hard against these limits. Sometimes they have even seemed to anticipate rather than follow the edicts of the courts and some of the most remarkable and comprehensive examples of judicial legislation are to be found among negotiated consent decrees.

It is well worth considering in this respect the case of *United States* v. *The American Society of Composers, Authors and Publishers* (Southern District Court of New York, 1950), usually known as ASCAP. ASCAP is a performing-rights society. It licenses and collects royalties for rights of public performance for profit of copyrighted musical compositions, other than as part of a dramatic performance such as an opera. (These performing rights must be distinguished from the copyright of the printed score and the recording rights under which record and motion picture companies make records and sound-tracks.) Organizations like ASCAP are found in several countries, and their justification is that individual composers would find it quite impossible to pursue their rights or detect infringements in all the thousands of places where their music (or records of their music) may be played for profit.

A performing-rights society of this kind would be of little value either to the composers or to the performers of their music unless it were in a position of monopoly or near-monopoly. It would be an intolerable nuisance if there were a host of competing societies, so that bandleaders and broadcasting companies had to make several separate agreements every time they gave a concert or recital. In point of fact it is reckoned that ASCAP controls the performing rights of from 85 to 90% of all copyrighted music in the United States. In addition, foreign performing societies have agreements with ASCAP covering the licensing and collection of royalties for their members. The ASCAP repertory is therefore almost as wide as the musical repertory itself (it is guessed at a million compositions) and the user who obtains a licence from ASCAP can be pretty sure that he will run no risk of action for copyright infringement by any other party.

Apart from the practical necessity of ASCAP's having a near-monopoly position in the field, it is also a practical necessity for it to grant only blanket licences for the use of its entire repertory by performers. The licensing of individual pieces on individual occasions

would be a hopeless task. The composers would suspect discrimination
if this were done and the users would be put to intolerable inconvenience. As a commentator has put it: 'The disc jockey's itchy fingers
and the bandleader's restive baton, it is said, cannot wait for contracts
to be drawn with ASCAP's individual publisher members, much less
for the formal acquiescence of a characteristically unavailable composer or author, or—heaven forfend the legal ramifications!—the
manifold unascertainable, unlocated heirs, assigns or other legal
representatives of the composer or author. A blanket licence covering
ASCAP's total repertory is the price of avoiding industrial palsy in the
entertainment world, says ASCAP, and thus far no important commercial user of ASCAP's music has contradicted this assertion for any
length of time.'[1]

By analogy with the doctrines of antitrust in relation to the aggregation and blanket licensing of patents—that is, imposing a condition
that a would-be licensee of a particular patent must take licences for
many others—it is clear that ASCAP practices raise antitrust issues.
Indeed, in a treble-damage suit brought in 1948 by cinema exhibitors,
it was held that ASCAP was an illegal monopoly and was illegally
restraining trade in violation of the Sherman Act.[2] Even earlier the
Government had taken action in respect of the radio industry's
grievances against ASCAP and a consent decree had been entered into
in 1941. As a result of the litigation with the cinema people and because
of complaints from broadcasting stations and also from members of
ASCAP itself, the Department of Justice negotiated the complete
revision of the 1941 consent decree and an amended decree was
approved in 1950. It is of interest to note the various types of complaint
made against ASCAP's practices and what was done about them in
this consent decree.

The complaint of the cinema exhibitors was that, since ASCAP had
monopoly power, they were worried about the level of the charges they
had to pay ASCAP for the right to perform the music coming into the
sound-track of the films they showed. In the end they got no damages
because they could not show that ASCAP's royalties were unreasonable.
But an ASCAP rule, which prevented its members from assigning to
film producers, at the time the film was made, the right to 'perform' the
sound-track, had been held in the private suit to be a restraint of trade.
Also, the film producers, who had strong ownership and contractual
interests in many of the music publisher members of ASCAP, insisted

---

[1] Sigmund Timberg, 'Antitrust Aspects of Merchandising Modern Music: the ASCAP
Judgment of 1950', *Law and Contemporary Problems*, Spring 1954 (Duke University School of
Law, Durham, North Carolina). I am indebted to Mr Timberg's article for much of the
material in this section.

[2] *Alden-Rochelle* v. *ASCAP* (Southern District Court of New York, 1948).

on a rule that they would license their films for exhibition only to exhibitors with ASCAP licences, and this too was held to be a conspiracy in restraint of trade.

In the consent decree the attempt was made to legislate for a reasonable resolution of the conflicting interests and rights of the members of ASCAP, both publishers and composers, and the film producers and cinema owners. It was decreed that the cinema owner, who after all had no control over the music that appeared on the sound-track of films that he showed, should not in future have to pay for performing rights for this music and should not be liable to any infringement suit by ASCAP. So far as films are concerned, ASCAP now has to grant a once-for-all performance licence to the producer of the picture and the cost of this licence becomes part of the cost of making the film. It was further decreed that no member of ASCAP should grant a recording right to a film producer unless he or ASCAP granted corresponding performance rights at the same time. The decree also dealt with various consequential problems relating to alleged infringements prior to the date of the judgment.

In order to prevent the financial and contractual links between film producers and music publishing houses from influencing the terms of bargains undesirably, another section of the consent decree provides that no member of ASCAP who has at the time some pecuniary interest in a film company shall vote or participate in negotiations about the licensing of music for films.

The revised consent decree also contains many injunctions regulating transactions between ASCAP and broadcasting stations. The big radio networks are, of course, powerful enough to look after themselves in negotiating with their suppliers and they have waged a prolonged feud with ASCAP. Indeed, before the 1941 consent decree, the radio industry had managed to go for a whole year without using any ASCAP music—a form of buyers' strike calculated to obtain better terms. The revised consent decree lays down various rules governing the prices, terms and conditions under which radio stations are to be licensed to use ASCAP music, and indeed directs ASCAP to issue licences on request to radio stations and networks on these terms. In the case of disputes about reasonable licensing fees, the parties in conflict may apply to the Court to determine a reasonable fee. These provisions apply to the use of ASCAP's repertory not only by radio stations but by other users as well. Other injunctions provide for licensing ASCAP's music at the source (that is, the recording or transcribing point), instead of to individual small stations. This is similar to the provision that individual cinema owners should not require separate licences.

A number of the injunctions in the consent decree are quite general. One, for example, is a broad provision against vertical integration so that ASCAP is prevented from acquiring the other forms of copyright in addition to the performance right. Another prohibits discrimination in fees or other terms between licensees similarly situated. Another prevents any member of ASCAP from participating in its negotiations while being at the same time financially interested in a prospective licensee. The conditions under which different forms of licences may be issued are also regulated.

Finally the consent decree of 1950 regulates the internal relations of the members of ASCAP. The general rule of ASCAP has been that the publishers of the music and the authors and composers share control of ASCAP and its revenues on a fifty-fifty basis. The fact that blanket licences for the entire ASCAP repertory are issued means that the breakdown of ASCAP's revenue between the individual members is readily capable of generating disputes. The Society's comprehensive scope and economic power must mean that any inability on the part of a composer to join ASCAP or to get 'fair play' in comparison with older-established members would represent a severe economic sanction against him. (This problem is somewhat akin to that which the courts probed in the *Associated Press* case described above in Chapter II.)

Accordingly, the consent decree required ASCAP to admit to membership any composer who has had work published and any commercial publisher. (It is interesting to note that the decree, however, gives ASCAP power to keep out so-called 'song shark' publishers, who secure contracts with composers by promises to exploit work which they are not equipped to fulfil.) Another section protects the right of any member to withdraw from ASCAP and remove his performing rights from its control on giving proper notice. Others require that its transactions, in particular its methods of classifying members for purposes of distributing revenue, shall be made public to the membership, and that the ASCAP repertory shall be made known to all users and prospective users so that there will be no danger of infringement suits relating to compositions which are not in the repertory at all.

Other sections regulate the voting procedures of ASCAP so that different groups and interests within the Society may secure proper representation. Yet other sections formulate standards for the equitable distribution of ASCAP's revenue, providing for full publicity for what is done, reliance on reasonably objective criteria and impartial arbitration of disputes. In practice the revenues of ASCAP are divided into three funds. One-fifth of the revenue is distributed on the basis of the number of current performances of a work. Three-fifths are distributed on the basis of a five-year average of performances. The final fifth is distributed on the basis of the length of time the writer has been a member, together with his rating in the 'Society Performance Fund'. The general objective of this plan of distribution is to obtain a reasonable stability of income for the composer and prevent his income from suffering the wide fluctuations that would occur if current performances were the only standard.

The consent decree was itself modified in 1960, following complaints by some of its members that the purpose of the 1950 decree was not being fulfilled. In particular it was claimed that the rules for the distribution of income gave too great an advantage to the older members, and accordingly certain alterations have been made to the methods of calculation so that members now have the option to receive royalties either on the basis of the current performances of their works or under the multifund system already described. Members are also now to have the right to vote on future alterations to these methods of calculation. Among other changes introduced are the making of voting rights dependent on performance credits rather than on actual income received through ASCAP, and the right of all members to appeal to an impartial arbitration board against classification of their compositions. Finally, ASCAP is required to grant membership to all qualified applicants without regard to their prior ASCAP performances, and to make public the necessary qualification for such membership.

There are a great many more detailed rules in this consent decree, only the most important having been outlined; what is of such great interest for a student of antitrust is to see how the original finding, that some aspects of ASCAP's structure and practices are in violation of the Sherman Act, blossoms out into a highly detailed piece of technical legislation regulating almost every aspect of the conduct of its affairs. Many of its activities and procedures which would not, taken alone, be open to attack as restraints of trade or acts of monopolization are now regulated by law. In some cases activities which could probably be attacked under the Sherman Act are specifically allowed to continue or even positively required. The process thus becomes separated from the actual content of the law, which is taken as the occasion or warrant for subjecting the organization to the Court's jurisdiction. This jurisdiction is then applied through extensive negotiations between the various parties having interests in the matter. The conclusions they reach about what is fair to all concerned and what the Department of Justice lawyers regard as proper in the public interest are brought within the decree and then become enforceable by the Court. Arrangements are made for the Court to retain jurisdiction of the issue so that any of the parties who find the decree bearing too harshly on them may apply to the Court for modifications.

The scope of the consent decree has been illustrated by the ASCAP case because it is a comprehensive example, showing clearly the extent to which future legislation for the industry may be undertaken almost independently of the antitrust offences which confer jurisdiction.[1] But it is in no sense unique. There are many consent decrees similar in scope. As the rules of law laid down in the bigger cases, particularly those dealing with monopolization in the line of the *ALCOA, American Tobacco, Paramount* cases, etc., have become more firmly established, so it has become worthwhile for even the most powerful defendants to avoid expensive litigation and negotiate a comprehensive consent settlement.

[1] Also because it illustrates the antitrust treatment of copyright matters which is not elsewhere described.

PART II

ANTITRUST ASSESSED

CHAPTER XV

ANTITRUST AS AN AMERICAN POLICY

1. *The motivation of antitrust: radical and 'small business' motives;*
economic objectives; the provision of legal checks to the exercise
of economic power as the mainspring of antitrust

People outside the United States want to know what lessons the
antitrust system has for them. Before this question is reached, however,
it is necessary to consider, on the basis of the case law, how far antitrust
should be accounted a success on its own home ground and by reference
to the assumptions and motives which sustain it as a public policy in
the United States; for the extent to which antitrust is a response to
specifically American conditions and concerns has to be taken into
account in the process of judging whether it may have general application as an answer to the problem of monopolies and restrictive practices,
and whether it is the kind of growth that will 'take' if transplanted to
other countries with different historical and social backgrounds and
different political and administrative arrangements. Thus the first
question of all is what the Americans are trying to achieve with
antitrust.

A number of different motive factors go to make up the driving power
of the antitrust policy in the United States. It would not have consistently attracted so broad a range of political support without the
essential quality of having something for everybody (or nearly everybody). Thus there is no single yardstick of its achievement; different
groups of people in the United States look to antitrust for different
things and account it a success or a disappointment by different standards.
But some motives and assumptions have deeper roots than others; some
are relatively sectional in their appeal or intermittent in their influence.

One important factor of the sectional and intermittent type, for
example, is political radicalism. It has been noted that the Sherman
Act owed its origin largely to political pressures of an agrarian and
radical flavour; and there is little doubt that in more recent times
antitrust has been an outlet for powerful currents of 'anti-big business'
radicalism growing out of the years of depression. Because of the many

historical and other circumstances which have stood in the way of a viable political labour movement in the United States, 'trust busting' has been for many a radical programme of action and a focus of enthusiasm, in much the same way as, for example, nationalization in Britain; and not a few of those employed in the enforcement agencies have probably worked with a greater relish for the feeling that their task has been something of a crusade.

Another sectional cause has been that of 'small business'. This cause may be seen in action in the hard-headed lobby pressures which have helped to secure the virtual exemption from the Sherman Act of resale price maintenance and which have fashioned the intricacies of the Robinson-Patman (price discrimination) statute. But it may also be seen, in terms of social theory, as hardly distinguishable from the element of radicalism. We may recall, for example, Judge Hand's dictum in the *ALCOA* case: 'It is possible, because of its indirect social and moral effect, to prefer a system of small producers, each depending for his success on his own skill and character, to one in which the great mass of those engaged must accept the direction of the few.'[1]

But, though these radical and 'small business' elements in the motivation of antitrust are important, they are clearly not determinative, for the vitality of the antitrust policy seems to be not greatly impaired when their influence wanes. At times, for example, the *Zeitgeist* has taken an anti-radical turn and with sustained prosperity 'big business' has regained public favour.[2] It is noteworthy that the Attorney General's National Committee to Study the Antitrust Laws was set up by the Republican Administration in 1953 and was not, on balance, representative of radical currents of thought or 'anti-big business' sentiments; yet it reported in 1955, with impressive unanimity, in favour not only of the fundamentals of antitrust policy but also of the general state of existing case law. Despite the fact that many of the post-war decisions had been widely regarded as unduly radical, the modifications suggested by the Committee to the statutes themselves and to their construction were of quite minor importance when compared with the vast body of law that it found acceptable.[3] 'The basic philosophy of the Sherman Act', the Committee averred,

---

[1] Compare the parallel dictum of Justice Douglas in his *Columbia Steel* dissent: 'Industrial power should be decentralized, it should be scattered into many hands so that the fortunes of the people will not be dependent on the whims and caprice, the political prejudices, the emotional stability of a few self-appointed men.'

[2] Some post-war literature, for example, has glorified 'big business' in terms hardly less romantic than those in which it was but lately denigrated. See Mr David E. Lilienthal's book, *Big Business: a New Era*, Harper, New York, 1953.

[3] It is significant, however, that among the modifications it proposed were the repeal of the federal legislation which exempts resale price maintenance from the discipline of antitrust,

'today remains above partisan controversy as a "charter of freedom", a constitution governing the economy of the United States.'

An important contribution to the assumptions and motives underlying antitrust is undoubtedly made by economics and economists, and it is tempting (and common) to regard the antitrust policy simply as a kind of economic engineering project. On this theory the success of antitrust is bound up with the efficiency of the economic system. Economists are believed to have shown that competition (in some sense) between firms makes for efficiency (in some sense), and that antitrust is simply a means of enforcing competition as the legal rule of business life. As the first sentence of the *Report of the Attorney General's National Committee* put it: 'The general objective of the antitrust laws is promotion of competition in open markets.'[1]

It is true that many Americans broadly accept the assumptions implicit in this view of antitrust. To say that American public opinion supports the antitrust policy is very much the same thing as to say that it favours a competitive, private-enterprise economy. Moreover, it seems characteristic of the American cast of mind to conceive of pieces of economic or social legislation as a type of engineering project designed to bring about specified results. But even the economic springs of the policy cannot be regarded as determinative. Antitrust has a broader base than the findings of economists as to the conditions required for optimum economic performance. It is indeed highly doubtful whether economists offer an agreed body of doctrine on which policy could be based.[2] Certainly, confidence in the practical relevance of orthodox theoretical models of competitive behaviour has declined, and many economists would concede nowadays that it is a far from straightforward matter to determine whether this or that departure from the models aids or hinders economic progress. Current economic doctrine on the monopoly problem is in too unsettled a state for antitrust to stand or fall by virtue of its validity as a political application of economic knowledge. And, as the cases show, the predictions of

and the amendment of certain provisions of the Robinson-Patman Act, such as the 'brokerage' clause, to which 'small business' attached importance.

Radical criticism of the Committee was directed rather at some of its recommendations on administration (e.g. those in favour of greater use of pre-trial consultative procedures), which the critics regarded as likely to weaken enforcement, than at its conclusions about the state of the law.

[1] It will be noted that the Committee reflected here the modern 'maintaining competition' view of antitrust (see above, Introduction, p. 17). A little later in the report the Sherman Act was construed, in the light of the *Standard Oil* opinion of 1911, as embodying 'a flexible public policy directed against all undue limitations of competition'. It may be doubted whether Chief Justice White would have approved the conceptual jump from this policy to one of 'promoting' competition.

[2] The contribution of economic teaching to the policy issues presented by monopoly problems is considered below, Chapter XVI.

economists about the effect of restrictive practices on efficiency are not decisive in law. In short, the 'competition' which antitrust seeks to promote (or at least to prevent from being unduly obstructed) is 'competition' in some rough-and-ready popular sense which leaves plenty of room for changes in the currents of economic opinion as to the technical requirements of a competitive system.

It seems likely that American distrust of all sources of unchecked power is a more deep-rooted and persistent motive behind the antitrust policy than any economic belief or any radical political trend. This distrust may be seen in many spheres of American life; it affects public power no less than private and underlies many of the political and constitutional arrangements of the United States. It is expressed in the theories of 'checks and balances' and of 'separation of powers'. In the United States the fact that some men possess power over the activities and fortunes of others is sometimes recognized as inevitable but never accepted as satisfactory. It is always hoped that any particular holder of power, whether political or economic, will be subject to the threat of encroachment by other authorities (for example, the executive by the legislative and judicial arms of Government) and at the same time that any authority which seeks to encroach on another's power will be strenuously resisted and held in check.

In large part antitrust is the projection of these traditional American beliefs into the economic sphere.[1] An economy made up of independent, competing business units fulfils the condition that economic decision making should be dispersed and renders the holders of economic power liable to mutual encroachment. It is important to this conception that the individual's right to engage in business activities of his own choice shall be preserved and that no single economic unit, whether in the form of monopoly or combination, shall be able to exclude rivals at its own behest and so render its own power immune from invasion. The pursuit of these objectives is the true function of antitrust policy and constitutes its broadest appeal.

At one with this basic motivation of antitrust is its reliance on legal process and judicial remedy rather than on administrative regulation. The famous prescription of the Massachusetts Bill of Rights—'to the end it may be a government of laws and not of men'—is a favourite American quotation and an essential one for understanding antitrust. Without this factor it would be impossible to explain the degree of acceptance—so astonishing to those outside the United States—that is accorded to the antitrust policy by those interests, especially big-

---

[1] This point is illustrated by the many references that are made to the Sherman Act as a 'constitution' for the United States economy. The very word 'constitution' in the United States has come to stand, above all, for the existence of legal checks to the exercise of power.

business interests, which are frequently and expensively subject to its discipline. Big business is certainly not a negligible source of pressure on government in the United States; yet antitrust thrives and the Attorney General's National Committee, with the legal advisers of big business well represented, unanimously declared that the Sherman Act stood above partisan controversy. No doubt there is an element in all this of lip service to a political 'winner', but this service would not long be paid if antitrust were a system of administrative regulation carried on by politicians and economic experts. Antitrust, as a 'government of laws', is even recognized by business interests as a protection against the government of men which might otherwise descend on them in such forms as price controls, state regulation and ultimately public ownership.

In American eyes, in short, the success of antitrust is closely bound up with the avoidance of situations in which industrial or commercial power is free from the threat of encroachment. But although this basic concern accounts for the breadth and persistence of the public favour enjoyed by antitrust, the support of those with narrower sectional causes to promote is still needed and freely drawn upon. These special interests are not always reconcilable either with one another or with the requirements, which Professor Brewster has summarized under the heads of 'fairness' and 'feasibility' (or 'compliability'), of a rule of law.[1] Hence some of the paradoxes and apparent inconsistencies of the antitrust system.

The economists, for example, who think that the courts should decide cases solely by reference to the cause of economic progress, not only run into legal difficulties but are bound to clash with the proponents of 'small business', who sometimes seem to regard the preservation of small firms as anti-monopolistic *per se*. Those who want the most competition are often at odds with those who want the most competitors. Radicals often see no need for legal qualms about measures that promise to impede the growth of businesses which in their view are already big enough. Meanwhile the business men themselves, large and small, though they may, by and large, accept antitrust as a fact of life, are not above an effort here and there to mitigate the efficacy of its scourging and are under no obligation to be silent about those aspects of the law which seem to impose undue constraints on their own freedom of decision.

Thus there are always controversies in progress as the different groups seek to persuade the legislature or the courts that the letter of

[1] See 'Enforceable Competition: Unruly Reason or Reasonable Rules?' by Kingman Brewster, Jr., in *American Economic Review*, vol. 46, no. 2, May 1956, p. 482. This article is a valuable and persuasive statement of the legal requirements of antitrust policy.

the law or its interpretation should be amended in this direction or that. Antitrust is a running compromise, in which distrust of power and the need for 'compliable' law usually have the largest say, but in which the voices of economist and businessman, social reformer and lobbyist are heard in varying strengths at different times. In the remainder of this chapter the areas of agreement and of controversy in the various fields of antitrust law will be marked out as a means of showing which parts of the policy secure general consent and which raise the largest doubts in American opinion. From this discussion there should emerge an assessment of the extent to which antitrust in action succeeds in fulfilling the expectations of its wide range of supporters with their many different and more or less deep-rooted concerns.[1]

2. The effectiveness of antitrust in relation to restrictive agreements between competitors: price fixing, exclusive-dealing, boycott and other agreements; the meaning of the rule of reason; per se rules

Most Americans would point first to the success of antitrust in effectively putting a stop to a wide range of restrictive agreements between competitors. There is little doubt that detection and enforcement are reasonably effective in this field; and it must be stressed again that whereas most of the cases quoted in expounding the law deal with difficult borderline issues, these are outnumbered many times by straightforward cases dealing with clear violations of section 1 of the Sherman Act. The relatively large probability that offences in this category will be prosecuted and punished, with the full backing of public opinion, is a potent influence on business conduct.

Price fixing agreements come first in importance among these offences and nobody in the United States now expects to get away with overt price agreements or any of the obvious variants such as agreements for level tendering, formula pricing and so on. Moreover, the courts, as shown above (Chapter I), have developed sharp senses for detecting price agreements which are camouflaged, for example as price filing arrangements, or which consist in a common understanding to follow a price leader.

In some contexts agreements between competitors to divide up markets, allocating specified areas or customers or types of product to particular participants, may be more convenient and workable than price fixing as a means of avoiding competition; and agreements of this kind are no less clearly barred. Sometimes the maintenance of the

[1] The antitrust literature is not strong on the effects and effectiveness of the enforcement of antitrust decisions. *Antitrust Policies*, by Simon N. Whitney (Twentieth Century Fund, New York, 1958) has useful material on this topic.

price level may entail the restriction of output below capacity; and again, any agreement allotting production quotas among competitors so as to regulate their output is a clear violation of the law.

Hardly less important than agreements directly affecting prices are the many types of agreement which aim at barring the way to new entrants into industry or at reserving preferential terms of trade to a favoured group. Thus another class of flagrant offences includes exclusive-dealing agreements between groups of established suppliers and distributors. There are many varieties of such agreements—sometimes the members of one group will deal only with the other group's 'approved list' of firms, sometimes special rebates or other concessions are confined to the participants—but all operate to make it difficult for the outsider or newcomer to break into the trade and all offend against the Sherman Act. In this class too come agreements for reserving the control of scarce facilities to the participating group, as illustrated by the *Associated Press* and other cases described above (Chapter II). Lastly, all measures of collective boycott come within the ban, whether directed against new entrants as such or against those whose trade practices incur the displeasure of the majority.[1]

The prohibition of this whole range of agreements between competitors is undoubtedly the aspect of antitrust which commands the widest measure of popular support. Moreover, on this topic the different factions among antitrust supporters speak virtually with one voice. Making this prohibition effective is seen as a necessary task which is on the whole well done. Even those critics of antitrust administration who urge the enforcement agencies not to take the law to theoretical extremes, but to concentrate on flagrant violations, would usually concede that the types of restrictive agreement outlined above properly count as flagrant offences. It is worth noting in this connexion that if antitrust consisted of nothing else but this prohibition, it would still be by far the most rigorous anti-monopoly law in the world.[2]

The reasoning underlying this broad consensus of American opinion is that to allow competitors to combine in their market operations creates an arbitrary power and that the objections to such power are

[1] This list of flagrant offences is not, of course, exhaustive. Agreements between competitors to eliminate forms of competition other than price competition should also be mentioned, though they give rise to relatively few cases. An agreement, for example, to suppress or defer the introduction of a new type of product would certainly fall foul of the Sherman Act. As was shown above (Chapter XI), many types of agreement between competitors relating to the licensing and enforcement of patents are clearly illegal.

[2] It is of interest to note that the range of agreements between competitors which constitute flagrant violation of section 1 of the Sherman Act is quite close to the range of agreements against which the presumption of being against the public interest operates in the British Restrictive Trade Practices Act, 1956.

not met by showing that the power is reasonably used at any particular time. Mr Justice Stone gave classic expression to this argument in the *Trenton Potteries* case: 'The power to fix prices, whether reasonably exercised or not, involves power to control the market and to fix arbitrary and unreasonable prices. The reasonable price fixed today may through economic and business changes become the unreasonable price of tomorrow.' To most Americans this argument is conclusive. If the case for regulating prices or entry into the market can be established for any industry, it ought to be exercised under some form of public supervision approved by the legislature. This is done, for example, in the field of public utilities, where the case for regulating rates and other forms of competition has been accepted. But the power to regulate prices or entry is not to be entrusted without check to private persons who have obvious incentives to abuse it.

It will be noted that this is not an economic argument but one about the use of power: as such it partakes of the basic appeal of antitrust and with most Americans it would prevail even in a case where it could be shown that the public would gain some definite economic advantage from a restrictive agreement.[1] That it has so prevailed in antitrust generally is shown by the current state of doctrine about the rule of reason and *per se* offences.

Business people have often claimed that, whatever might be the general undesirability of private restraints of competition, their particular agreement was wholly necessary to combat some greater evil such as ruinous price competition or an indefensibly piratical trade practice.[2] Some economists have lent support to the view that the law should not ignore evidence to the effect that a given agreement might be of long-term economic advantage. Those who advance views of these types often direct their argument to the proper scope of the rule of reason which should, they contend, entail full consideration of the context and consequences of each restrictive agreement, so that where the restraint is not unreasonable in its context or effect it may escape legal penalty. This, of course, is a familiar idea outside the United States, where it is often a matter for surprise that under antitrust the mere existence of a price fixing agreement or collective boycott is an offence against the law, and where it is natural to assume that the rule of reason, to which

---

[1] It is fair to add that most Americans—especially American economists—would hold that the conflict postulated here, between the wish to secure maximum economic advantage and the wish to check the power of business combinations, would in practice occur very rarely. They would expect, in any normal case, that where combination was proscribed and competition maintained, no economic disadvantages would ensue.

[2] See the *Fashion Originators Guild* case (above, Chapter II), in which design piracy by garment manufacturers was regarded in the trade but not in law as justifying a boycott of retailers who dealt in the pirated designs.

the American courts so frequently refer, requires a consideration of economic consequences.

But the rule of reason in modern antitrust does not require any economic analysis of this kind: on the contrary, the range of restrictive agreements under consideration in this section covers just those anti-trust offences which are described as being illegal *per se* and in respect to which, in consequence, no evidence of economic justification is admissible. This situation is simply another reflection of the primacy of the political over the economic motivation of antitrust; agreements between competitors create economic power which may be abused, and this is thought undesirable even if it should also yield economic advantages. But it also reflects the fact that the courts themselves have always opposed the idea that they should attempt to assess the economic balance of advantage. Economic argument, even of the simplest kind, tends to be seen as a slippery slope on which the firm footing needed for a properly justiciable issue cannot be obtained. Once any such argument is admitted (for example, that an agreement is justified as a defence measure against excessive competition), there will be nothing to prevent the introduction of more and more subtle economic arguments. The strongest judicial tradition in antitrust is that which disclaims any competence in weighing these arguments and denies that any case by case assessment of the public interest in the light of them is or ought to be required by the law.[1]

The classic statement of this tradition was that of Judge Taft in the *Addyston Pipe* case:

It is true that there are some cases in which the courts, mistaking, as we conceive, the proper limits of the relaxation of the rules for determining the unreasonableness of restraints of trade, have set sail on a sea of doubt and have assumed the power to say, in response to contracts which have no other purpose and no other consideration on either side than the mutual restraint of the parties, how much restraint of competition is in the public interest and how much is not.

The manifest danger in the administration of justice according to so shifting, vague and indeterminate a standard, would seem to be a strong reason against adopting it.[2]

[1] See Brewster, *American Economic Review*, vol. 46, pp. 484 ff. The following passage (pp. 486–7) in particular hits off this tradition: 'The essence of the judicial message is that if you give this job to the courts in the form of criminal or public tort adjudication, you must expect the courts to act like courts. And, so it seems to me, they should. For the values served by not having courts act like legislative bodies are just as important to the society as are the values which might be served by having every case decided by economically rational but essentially *ad hoc* determinations of the public economic interest. The net goodness or badness of effects is not a proper subject of judicial determination.'

[2] The following dictum of Mr Justice Stone in the *Trenton Potteries* case makes much the same point in relation to arguments about prices: 'Moreover, in the absence of express legislation

The evident fear of the courts that the balancing of economic considerations will take them outside the sphere of properly justiciable issues weighs heavily against the case for a broader rule of reason; for, as has been noted, one of the fundamentals of antitrust is its reliance on judicial processes of enforcement. This consideration powerfully influences professional legal opinion in the United States. Shortly before the Attorney General's National Committee to Study the Antitrust Laws was set up, Professor S. C. Oppenheim, who became a co-chairman of the Committee, ventilated the theory that, even in the case of restrictive agreements between competitors, the concept of illegality *per se* should be discarded and these agreements should instead be regarded as prima facie illegal. According to this theory the prosecutor's onus of proof would be confined, as now, to showing the existence of the price fixing or other agreement, but the defendants would be entitled to accept the onus of proving positive economic justification for the agreement.[1] It is noteworthy that this view was not endorsed by the Committee and presumably did not survive analysis and discussion by the Committee's many eminent lawyers. This is particularly interesting because it won applause from influential sections of business opinion, and many Committee members probably had some initial sympathy with its aims.[2]

There can be no doubt that *per se* violations are now a permanent feature of the antitrust system and that all those who favour effective enforcement of the law approve of this. By confining the evidence to facts and excluding consideration of economic consequences, *per se* rules greatly simplify and speed up the process of prosecution. It is clear that the bread-and-butter cases under antitrust could not be so effectively handled on any other terms. Even business opinion, while not unwilling to see the impact of antitrust weakened, does not speak with one voice on this issue. On the one hand, the broader type of rule of reason offers the attraction of an infinite number of possible defences

requiring it, we should hesitate to adopt a construction making the difference between legal and illegal conduct in the field of business relations depend upon so uncertain a test as whether prices are reasonable—a determination which can be satisfactorily made only after a complete survey of our economic organization and a choice between rival philosophies.'

Justice Frankfurter was expressing the same tradition in the *Standard Stations* case when he held that to require predictions of the economic consequences of requirements contracts 'would be a standard of proof, if not virtually impossible to meet, at least most ill suited for ascertainment by courts'.

[1] 'Federal Antitrust Legislation: Guideposts to a Revised National Antitrust Policy', *Michigan Law Review*, vol. 50, 1952, p. 1139. The similarity between this proposal and the policy embodied in the Restrictive Trade Practices Acts, 1956 and 1968, in Britain, is interesting. Professor Oppenheim advocated the use of concepts of 'workable' or 'effective' competition as tests of economic justification. This topic is considered further in Chapter XVI below.

[2] See, for example, *Effective Competition*, U.S. Government Printing Office, Washington, 1953.

to a charge. But on the other hand, one of the perennial business complaints about the Sherman Act has been of its uncertainty and of the difficulty of knowing what is and what is not illegal. To this latter complaint the *per se* rules provide an answer.[1]

It is sometimes thought that *per se* rules give effect to empirical generalizations based on observation of economic effects: that, for example, price fixing is illegal *per se* because many instances of the practice have shown over the years that it always (or nearly always) does economic harm. But this is a mistaken view. (No doubt antitrust reflects, *inter alia*, a general consensus in the United States that price fixing and other restrictive practices are, on balance, economically harmful: but the legal rule that price fixing is illegal *per se* would be in no way upset by the occurrence of cases in which fixed prices could be shown to be beneficial.) What is clear and unmistakable in a *per se* offence is not its economic effect but its restrictive intent.

Sometimes evidence of effects must be considered in order to throw light on intent. In the *Price filing* cases described above (Chapter I),[2] for example, the courts had to decide whether the participating firms were simply swapping statistics and other information or whether what they were really up to was price fixing; and it was helpful to know whether prices were in fact uniform over a period, whether the course of prices ran differently in relation to raw-material prices once the agreement was made, and so on. Where the necessary effects of an agreement are restrictive, this is enough to establish the illegal intent, for 'he who wills the means, wills the end'.[3] But where the intent is clear—where, for example, an agreement to fix prices or restrict entry is written down in black and white—then no evidence of effects is needed.

Apart from being clearly restrictive in intent, an agreement that is condemned as illegal *per se* will normally be shown to exert effective power in the market. But, as the *Socony-Vacuum* case showed, no specific measure of market power is required in law and, in the case of a price fixing agreement, it is certainly not decisive that the parties may be

[1] Business people being human like the rest of us, it is not uncommon to find their spokesmen demanding a broader use of the rule of reason and a greater measure of clarity and certainty in antitrust at the same time. Probably big-business opinion, which is chiefly concerned with the vitality of the rule of reason in relation to cases of monopolizing and which is not so concerned about the expense of lengthening the processes of litigation, is the strongest voice in favour in a broader rule of reason.

[2] Above, pp. 40 ff., dealing with the *Lumber, Linseed Oil, Maple Flooring* and *Sugar* cases.

[3] See above, Chapter IV, p. 94. This is not to say that economic effects are enough in themselves to establish an antitrust offence; for there may be no agreement. In some of the movie cases, for example, individual distributors were able to show sound commercial reasons for refusing 'first runs' to exhibitors. The latter were certainly damaged by the refusals, but the damage obviously did not in itself prove that the refusals were collusive.

unable to set the price at any level they choose.[1] Intent may usually be taken as the indicator of power. It is no doubt possible to conceive of an agreement for common prices in which the parties would have no possibility of affecting price levels—the hypothetical example of an agreement between two small bakers in London and Edinburgh has already been mentioned—and such an agreement would hardly be condemned. But some power to affect the market will almost invariably be shown by the very fact that an agreement is made, for in real life competing firms do not go to the trouble of negotiating an agreement unless they expect and intend it to make some difference to trading conditions. That is why it is said of *per se* offences that the amount of commerce affected by them is immaterial. This means not that a powerless and pointless agreement would still be illegal, but that as a matter of common experience a pointless agreement would not be made.

This summary of the nature of *per se* offences points in turn to the nature of the rule of reason as it is revealed by a study of the cases. If *per se* offences are those in which the restrictive intent is clear and unmistakable, so the rule of reason in modern antitrust is the requirement that by rational inquiry the courts shall establish the true character or intent of what is done when that intent is not at first sight clear. This examination of intent is not an advanced psychological study of the motives of the parties but simply a commonsense inquiry into what they are really doing.[2] Were the defendants in the price filing cases simply exchanging legitimate information or were they really arranging for common prices? Was this particular film distributor's refusal to allot a first run to this exhibitor a sound commercial decision or really part of a systematic discriminatory plan? These questions are ultimately questions of fact—familiar questions such as all courts have to tackle. Does the evidence about the road accident indicate the offence of

[1] Above, Chapter I, pp. 35 ff. Equally in cases dealing with 'bottleneck' facilities, for example, *Associated Press* (Chapter II, pp. 67 ff.), it is not decisive that the facility in question is not indispensable to a competitor.

[2] See Dirlam and Kahn, *Fair Competition*, p. 50. 'Intent' in this legal context is a less subjective term than 'purpose' or 'intention'. The view that the modern rule of reason has departed somewhat from the rule defined by Chief Justice White in 1911 (see above, Introduction, pp. 24 ff.) largely rests on this distinction. When White spoke of an 'intent to do wrong to the general public', he was surely thinking of a consciously formulated exploitative purpose. Given no evidence of such a predatory purpose (and given no necessary effects harmful to the public interest), he might find a restrictive agreement justifiable, as in the *Railway* cases in which he dissented from the majority view in the Supreme Court. Nowadays the test is not so much that of predatory purpose—White's 'intent to do wrong to the general public'—as of intent to restrict competition to a significant degree; there is a presumption that any significant impairment of competition is against the public interest, and any agreement which does as a matter of fact have significantly restrictive effects is tainted with illegal intent under the rule that 'he who wills the means, wills the end'. As a rule of thumb, one might say that White's rule of reason took account of intention; the modern version takes account only of intent.

manslaughter or only that of careless driving or no offence at all? Courts must always determine the true character—which is, broadly speaking, what lawyers have called the 'intent'—of acts alleged to be unlawful. The rule of reason is not after all so very special as a judicial technique.

In the field of restrictive agreements between competitors there is usually no need to inquire into intent because the content of the agreement, often indeed its very existence, makes palpable the intent of the parties.[1] Hence the prevalence of *per se* rules in this sector of antitrust and the relatively minor role of the rule of reason. There are cases, however, in which the impairment of competition is insignificant in scope and effect and which may be dismissed by the rule of *de minimis*; there are cases (for example, some of the *Price filing* cases) in which the existence of an agreement of some sort is established but there is doubt whether it is an agreement to fix prices or otherwise impair competition; there are cases in which typical effects of a restrictive agreement are found (for example, prices are 'sticky' or a particular cinema is refused first runs by several distributors), but there is doubt whether an agreement actually exists and some alternative explanation of the facts seems possible; there are still cases in which a restrictive clause may be found to be merely ancillary to a legitimate form of contract.[2] In all these cases, besides inquiry into the existence of an agreement there must be reasoned inquiry into the nature of what is agreed, so as to determine whether in truth its inevitable effect or its evident purpose is significantly anti-competitive. This inquiry has succeeded to the title of Chief Justice White's rule of reason, whether or not it is possessed of all the properties which he originally meant to bestow upon it. Once any factual doubt is cleared up, however, and the existence of a significantly anti-competitive contract or agreement is established, that contract or agreement is illegal *per se*. The concept of *per se* illegality is not at odds with the rule of reason but arises out of it.

To sum up this section: in the field of restrictive agreements between competitors American opinion has come down in favour of outright prohibition with no exceptions for special circumstances or hard cases. This choice is based first and foremost on American reluctance to see any form of power exerted without check. It reflects, secondly, the fact that Americans want the market power created by restrictive

---

[1] Compare Judge Taft's description of agreements which 'have no other purpose and no other consideration on either side than the mutual restraint of the parties'.

[2] The limits of valid ancillary restraints of trade are among the less well charted antitrust boundaries, and the rule of reason may perhaps have more sway in this sphere than elsewhere. Compare the possible use of the concept in connexion with international transactions, above, Chapter XII, p. 350. As the law stands, however, a restraint that is significantly anti-competitive in itself will not be exonerated by virtue of being ancillary to some wider plan.

agreements to be checked by law and not by administrative action; and the courts have shown that they can get at the facts of agreement and restrictive intent but cannot find a truly justiciable issue in the choice between rival economic predictions. Thus cases are not decided by an assessment of economic advantage, though most Americans would probably hold that instances in which positive economic harm is done by banning restrictive agreements are extremely rare and far outweighed by the general economic benefits of the policy. Since the restrictive intent of agreements between competitors is usually self-evident, they constitute the main *per se* offences. The rule of reason stands for the need to inquire into intent in those instances where it is not self-evident and, as will be seen in the following sections, it has a greater importance in the field of monopolies and monopolistic practices.

3. *The effectiveness of antitrust in relation to monopolizing: legal criticisms of court decisions under section 2 of the Sherman Act; the importance of 'intent' in these decisions; economic criticisms of the decisions*

In this field we must first consider the success of antitrust in dealing with the extreme or limiting case of monopolistic activity by a single concern—the comparatively rare instances of full-scale 'monopolizing'. Because they mostly deal with firms whose names are household words, the relatively few cases of this kind tend to create more interest and controversy than the many dealing with restrictive agreements; but the legal argument is not at bottom much different or more complex. Just as with agreements between competitors, the hallmark of illegal monopolizing is the intent to restrict competition and consolidate or exploit a position of power in the market. With restrictive agreements, as has been shown, both the power and the intent to restrict competition are most often given by (or at least implicit in) the sheer facts of the case; the very fact that a price fixing or boycott agreement exists is sufficient witness to the intent to restrict competition. But the fact that a single firm is in a position of power in the market may not be sufficient, for the power may have been 'thrust upon it' or have accrued to it willy-nilly by unalloyed commercial success. Restrictive intent can hardly be self-evident in the case of a single firm, however powerful. This is the important difference between sections 1 and 2 of the Sherman Act. Monopolizing is not simply dominating an industry but meaning to dominate an industry. Hence the courts have to determine whether the methods used by the concern in building up its power, or the use made of its power, bear witness to an illegal element of positive drive or deliberateness.

As the cases described above (Chapter IV) reveal, however, the inquiry still remains ultimately factual—an inquiry into what the concern was 'really up to'. Were the United Shoe Machinery company's leases no more than a means of conducting the business efficiently or were they, in part at least, a means of excluding competition? Once again the question is legally very similar to that which has to be decided when in a road accident case the prosecution alleges that the motorist's speed approaching the junction amounted to dangerous driving while the defence urges that it was a normal way of carrying on the journey. The true character of particular acts is often revealed through a course of conduct. What the courts do not have to decide is whether the monopolizing firm's economic performance is progressive, whether its profits are reasonable, whether the ambitious programmes of research which its financial strength allows may not, in the long run, benefit the industry and the consumer more than would a more competitive and less profitable structure.

It seems probable that what has been done by the courts under section 2 of the Sherman Act has reflected public opinion in the United States pretty accurately. Given that there is genuine support for an effective anti-monopoly law, it is hard to see how concerns like the Aluminum Company of America (ALCOA) and the United Shoe Machinery Corporation (U.S.M.) could expect to escape its impact. As with the courts' findings of collusion in price fixing and other cases, it is probably fair to say that their findings of monopolistic intent have on the whole been soundly and shrewdly based. Yet there has, of course, been criticism of these decisions from various legal, economic and other points of view.

The basis of one line of legal criticism, which comes chiefly from influential sources of business opinion, is that the law, as it has developed, leaves too little room for vigorous competition which happens to succeed. On this view the mistake liable to be made by the courts is to misinterpret bona fide competitive activity—'honestly industrial' and progressive measures—as deliberate attempts to exclude rivals. Since it would be foolish and improvident for an organization like ALCOA not to secure in advance its sources of bauxite or water-power against the expectation of expansion, it must surely be unjust to interpret the measures it takes for these purposes as evidence of an intent to exclude competitors. For all that Judge Hand in the *ALCOA* case conceded that 'the successful competitor, having been urged to compete, must not be turned upon when he wins', it is urged that this case and others of recent years have sold the pass to the view that monopoly power (and even great size) is illegal *per se*. It is said that the courts have accepted such tenuous evidence of intent to dominate that the large concern is no longer legally safe in competing vigorously. On this view a single firm which behaves in a no more predatory way than, for example, U.S.M. with its leasing practices should not be held to have illegally monopolized its industry;[1] only 'unreasonably' restrictive behaviour in acquiring or exploiting monopoly power should constitute an offence under section 2.[2] It is in line with this view that economic tests of performance are put forward as the appropriate criteria by which cases should be judged.

Basically this is the same argument as that for a broader rule of reason which was analysed in the foregoing section in relation to restrictive agreements; and the weight of American opinion again rejects it in relation to monopolizing for much the same reasons. The Sherman Act is meant to curb private economic power, and the fact that power is exercised responsibly at any particular time is not of itself a sufficient protection. The responsibility of today may become the irresponsibility and exploitation of tomorrow. Besides, economists have not provided agreed and objective tests of economic performance and the courts cannot deal with rival economic predictions; they are simply not fitted to tell whether the state of prices or the rate of innovation in an industry is better or worse as a result of monopoly power. They must deal ultimately with facts, and where the fact is that a concern shows itself to be intent on market dominance, this is proof enough of violation of the Sherman Act, whether or not that dominance has already resulted in unduly high prices or bankrupt competitors.

There is one important respect, however, in which considerations of economic performance tend to be given more weight in cases under section 2 than under section 1. This is in relation to remedies. When a restrictive contract or agreement is found illegal under section 1, the law requires (leaving aside the penalties that may be imposed in a criminal case) simply that it be brought to an end.[3] The firms concerned may carry on business in all other respects as usual. But when a firm is found to have monopolized its industry under section 2, the only effective relief may be some form of divestiture or even dissolution which radically changes the structure of the firm itself. For a court to order this kind of remedy takes it inescapably into the realm of economic legislation.

In practice there is a notable tendency for the courts to shy away from imposing drastic changes in industrial structure and to rely whenever possible on injunctions directed to the conduct of the firm.

---

[1] See the account of the case in Chapter IV, above, pp. 114 ff.

[2] It is often, but wrongly, claimed that only this view is consistent with Chief Justice White's statement of the law in the *Oil* and *Tobacco* cases: see above, Chapter IV, pp. 97 ff.

[3] In a civil case there may, of course, be court injunctions dealing with matters related to the illegal agreement: see above, Chapter I, p. 49, n. 2.

In this sense it might be said that a broad rule of reason has come to govern the choice of remedies in monopoly cases; Judge Knox in his opinion on remedies in the *ALCOA* case spoke expressly of 'effective competition' as his guide. But it is interesting and important to note that this emphasis on business conduct rather than structure in the matter of *remedies* does not represent a concession to the view that the *decisions* in the cases should turn on economic consequences: on the contrary, it arises precisely because of the traditional reluctance of the courts to engage in economic predictions. Just because the effects of breaking up an organization like ALCOA or U.S.M. into two or three separate parts are so little predictable (certainly by a judge, but probably by an economic expert too), the courts will not incur the responsibility of ordering dissolution if they see a chance of creating reasonably 'workable' competition by means of injunctions.[1]

It seems probable that what Judge Wyzanski called the 'caution and humility' of the courts in this respect commend themselves to public opinion generally in the United States, for Americans often tend to take a romantic view of the achievements and efficiency of large industrial organizations even while they take a suspicious view of their power. To have the power condemned in the courts as illegal, and its exercise beset by complex injunctions, while the organization itself remains intact, is a solution which reflects this ambivalence of attitude pretty closely.

The restraint of the courts in ordering dissolutions, however, is one target of another powerful current of legal criticism which contends that the enforcement of section 2 of the Sherman Act has not gone far enough. Critics who take this line point to the post-war record of the courts as evidence of feebleness: neither ALCOA nor U.S.M. broken up after successful government actions under section 2; the 'big three' cigarette companies found guilty of joint monopolization in a criminal case but no civil suit for relief begun by the Government; National Lead and du Pont found to dominate the production of titanium pigments but the Supreme Court refusing divestiture because there 'is no showing that four major competing units would be preferable to two. . . . Likewise, there is no showing of the necessity for this divestiture of plant or of its practicality and fairness.' Apart from some divorcement of vertically integrated concerns, as in the *Pullman* and *Paramount* cases, the recent case law, however radical its decisions are believed to be, has resulted in no major structural changes in

[1] Judge Wyzanski's observations—quoted above, Chapter XIV, pp. 407–8—brilliantly interpret the prevailing mood of the courts on this issue. The almost invariable practice of the courts in recent cases of retaining jurisdiction for a period (usually of five or ten years) is another sign of reluctance to use radical remedies whose effects are unpredictable, while remaining willing to be shown if the lesser remedies prove inadequate.

American industry, and this record, which has been wittily described as one of 'disillusion instead of dissolution', is contrasted unfavourably with the period of 1911.[1]

This line of criticism—in contrast to the other line sketched above, which comes, on the whole, from the 'right' and sees economic performance as the crucial test—is broadly radical in origin and emphasizes the importance of economic structure. The 'structuralist' holds that uncompetitive market structures should be amenable to antitrust action without too much regard to the conduct that produces them. This idea is based in turn on the proposition that the power of the largest concerns is of itself destructive of competition; in short, that monopoly power should be illegal *per se*. The argument for this view derives from the rule that 'he who wills the means, wills the end', so that performance normally establishes intent. Thus, if the structure of an industry, through the concentration of power in one or few hands, of itself chokes off competition and impedes new entry, the firm or firms whose course of conduct maintains that structure can properly have imputed to them an 'objective' intent to exclude competitors; and this intent is the hallmark of illegal monopolizing. Would it not then be an improvement to deal in the wholly objective terms of market structure instead of continuing to worry about 'intent' with its inescapably subjective overtones?[2]

But although Judge Learned Hand in his *ALCOA* opinion came near to this position, with his insistence that even 'honestly industrial' activities, if they have exclusionary effects, can disclose an intent to monopolize, the law does not pursue 'structuralist' logic so far. An intent to monopolize need not be purely subjective but it must be active. The rule that a man is held to intend the natural consequences of his acts still requires, as a basis for legal responsibility, positive acts whose natural consequences can be readily apprehended by the ordinary reasonable man. When a business firm forms part of a concentrated industry, its mere participation, without anything more, cannot be made illegal by a showing on economic grounds that the industrial structure is anti-competitive. To have it so would render the law 'non-compliable', in Professor Brewster's word: those who wanted to conform to the policy of the law would not know how to be sure of

---

[1] G. Stigler stated, in 'Report on Antitrust Policy—Discussion', *American Economic Review*, vol. 46, no. 2, May 1956, p. 507: 'Those of us who wish to see greater use made of what is often the only real remedy are not reckless innovators; we are simply traditionalists who wish to regain the 1911 level of use of the remedy of dissolution.' A footnote to p. 354 of the *Report of the Attorney General's National Committee to Study the Antitrust Laws* contains a useful list of the twenty-four cases (up to 1954) in which decrees of divorcement, divestiture or dissolution had been entered.

[2] Compare the view of Kaysen and Turner quoted on p. 186, above.

doing so. And this offends against the sense of fairness that all law should satisfy.

The opposing criticisms of the case law under section 2 point to a real dilemma that any anti-monopoly law must needs solve. On the one hand it seems good sense to judge the monopolist by his works. If his record as an innovator is good, if his prices and profits are reasonable, if the productivity and rewards of the labour he employs are high—are not the various social ends of industry being achieved? If in addition there are no complaints of predatory conduct or exploitation, why should society worry? The difficulty with this solution is that there are not—and probably cannot be—satisfactory performance tests to apply. As Chief Justice Stone put it, any judgment of performance requires 'a complete survey of our economic organization and a choice between rival philosophies'. Even if we can say that a monopolist is technically advanced or low-cost at the moment, how do we know that he would not be more so if he had to compete, and how do we know where he will stand in five years' time? Economics provides no rules of thumb by which questions of this kind can be answered in the consistent way required by a rule of law. In any case, economic performance tests cannot take account of the social and political factors that may underlie an anti-monopoly policy.

On the other hand, it might seem feasible simply to crack down on monopoly as it appears and stamp it out like a disease. But this solution, as we have seen, is incompatible with a fair and 'compliable' rule of law, because the mere acquisition of a monopoly position may be blameless; it may be, for example, the temporary result of successful innovation or the outcome of just that type of efficient competitiveness that an anti-monopoly policy is designed to encourage.[1]

Antitrust has avoided the horns of this dilemma by taking 'intent to monopolize' as its touchstone. Monopoly power as such is no offence; but it is no guarantee of legal immunity that monopoly power is not (at any given time) exploited to drive prices up or competitors out, nor even that it is economically progressive. The offence is either to exploit monopoly power, or to build or maintain it by collusion or exclusionary devices; in short, the offence lies in conduct which reveals that the firm likes to have and means to keep its power.[2] This solution commands assent in the United States just because it succeeds, not perfectly but

---

[1] '. . . . market power, as distinguished from conduct, is a non-compliable standard even if it could be made definite and certain. The sense of fairness rebels at visiting penalties without having afforded the opportunity to avoid them.' (Brewster, *American Economic Review*, vol. 46, p. 487.)

[2] There is no better account of the difficulties of both 'behavioural' and 'structural' tests of monopoly and the consequential importance of intent in the law than Chapter 2 of Dirlam and Kahn, *Fair Competition*.

better than any alternative, in making the issues justiciable and the offence recognizable and avoidable.

It is open to two opposing lines of economic criticism which correspond closely to the legal criticisms already noted. On the one hand, the businessman in a leading position in a concentrated industry may feel that almost any vigorous competitiveness on his part will be regarded by the Department of Justice and the courts as an effort to monopolize. If this type of feeling were common in American industry, the effect could conceivably be regressive and stagnating. Some commentators have suggested that certain firms already 'pull their punches' and are afraid to go all out to get as much of the market as they could. There is some evidence that here and there American business executives do in fact hesitate about exerting their full competitive power, even by legitimate means.[1]

If the full rigour of the structuralist case were accepted, there might well be a danger of serious adverse effects on business initiative in this way; it might be decided, for example, to set an upper limit to the size of businesses (whether absolute size or size relative to the industry), and businesses approaching the critical size would then have no incentive to improve efficiency.[2] But, as the law stands, it is difficult to believe that fear of prosecution as a monopolist is often a positive disincentive to efficiency. Very few companies are in a position like that, say, of General Motors in the automobile industry in which they hover on the brink of monopoly: in the light of the courts' distaste for ordering dissolutions, fewer still can really suppose that legitimate means of improving efficiency will involve a legal risk of life-or-death dimensions. As Dirlam and Kahn suggest, the burden must lie on the critics to show that types of conduct inhibited by the law are necessary for efficient performance—and 'this is something that for the most part they have failed to do'.[3]

The attack from the other flank is perhaps, in terms of the objectives of antitrust, more plausible: the radical critics insist that American industry is still organized in units too large and powerful to be com-

[1] There was in 1956 a case study of the General Motors Corporation by the staff of the Senate Antitrust Sub-Committee: in this study it was suggested that the company's return on investment was high (relative to industry in general) and that it might therefore reduce the price of its product. One can imagine that the heads of the firm had to consider carefully what the legal dangers might be, if, by taking this advice, they made things still more difficult for their few remaining competitors. (*Bigness and Concentration of Economic Power: a Case-study of the General Motors Corporation*, U.S. Government Printing Office, Washington, 1956.)

[2] The possibility of raising a presumption of illegality against any firm producing more than 10 to 15% of a product in any given market is ventilated, for example, by Ward Bowman, Jr., in 'Toward Less Monopoly', *University of Pennsylvania Law Review*, vol. 101, no. 5, March 1953, p. 577.

[3] Dirlam and Kahn, *Fair Competition*, p. 41.

patible with the competitive system that antitrust is supposed to promote.[1] Since there are inescapable economic and technological factors in the way of small-scale enterprise in many industries, it must surely be wrong to ignore the extent to which business concentration acts as an extra and unnecessary barrier to competition. Yet the refusal of the courts to condemn mere size or even market power, as such, seems to put many gratuitously uncompetitive situations out of reach of the law. If that view is right which holds that the main cause of monopoly is competition,[2] then the 'better mousetrap' situation is a common one and a good deal of monopoly may persist unchecked. Economists who hold that even inescapable monopoly is likely to be or become unprogressive dislike this position.

But this line of attack can also be carried too far. Some of the very large firms in the United States are very large because of the great size of the market for which they cater and their size does not give them control of the market or freedom from competition. In many cases the market power of large concerns is at best a shared power in an oligopolistic market from which competitiveness is by no means excluded. Situations of this kind must be examined more closely below. But so far as 'pure' monopoly is concerned, the legal loophole is probably narrower than it seems: few of the firms with a really significant degree of market control seem to have escaped altogether the attentions of the Department of Justice.[3] It seems doubtful whether a pure 'better mousetrap' situation is more than an exotic rarity in practice; given the courts' pragmatic sliding scale, by which the greater the market power of the firm, the less obtrusive need be the indications of its unlawful intent, few monopolists will be found to owe their position to 'pure' competitive skills with no admixture of power seeking stratagem. The main cause of monopoly may be competition but is not very often that 'fair' competition which antitrust demands. Apart from the first *United Shoe Machinery* case in 1918 and the *Cellophane* case in 1953, it is difficult to think of cases under section 2 in which the 'better mousetrap' defence has been successful. Nowadays even patented mousetraps are but

[1] Corwin D. Edwards' book *Maintaining Competition*, McGraw-Hill, New York, 1949, reviews the economic and other implications of 'big business': see especially chapter 4.

Professor Edwards has gone further than other economists in drawing attention to strategic advantages of large size in business as distinct from market control—advantages, for example, in litigation, politics, public relations and finance. See also his article, 'Conglomerate Bigness as a Source of Power', in *Business Concentration and Price Policy* (National Bureau of Economic Research, Special Conference Series, 5), Princeton University Press, 1955, pp. 331–59.

[2] See Professor Joan Robinson's article, 'The Impossibility of Competition', in *Monopoly and Competition and their Regulation* (ed. E. H. Chamberlin), Macmillan, London, 1954, pp. 245–54.

[3] They have not always been charged with monopolizing under section 2 of the Sherman Act: the question of how far Clayton (and Robinson-Patman) Act cases against powerful companies affect business conduct is examined below.

rarely 'better mousetraps' in the strict sense, as the cases outlined above (Chapter XI) will testify.

The upshot is that most of the (quite few) firms left in the United States which could justly be called monopolies are markedly affected in their conduct by section 2 of the Sherman Act. Though it is true, as already noted, that not all those convicted under section 2 have been dissolved, many of them have to conduct their business in accord with elaborate court injunctions arising out of past antitrust litigation. Even those others which have managed to avoid antitrust trouble in the past almost certainly look over their shoulder towards the Department of Justice when determining major policies. Far from shouldering aside the new entrant or the inconvenient small rival, they must often show an unnatural solicitude for his survival; their legal advisers will want to scrutinize, as possible evidence of intent to monopolize, any conceivably suspect proposal such as to acquire another business, whether horizontally or vertically linked to the main firm, to buy the patents of a rival process, to secure raw-material supplies by long-term contracts, to undertake to supply the full requirements over a period of important customers, to buy or sell at discriminatory prices, and so forth.

Although it may not satisfy the radicals and the structuralists, this genuine impact of section 2 on business conduct probably counts as a success in most American eyes. The enforced sensitiveness of the dominant (or nearly dominant) firm to what is 'fair' competition is of value to the new or small firm which has a new process or some other means of winning a larger share of the market, even if other less tractable obstacles still beset its path. If monopoly power as such cannot be avoided, at least its exercise is beset with legal checks, and this is a large part of what is expected of antitrust as a 'constitution' for the economy. It is true that the extreme remedy of dissolution is used with restraint,[1] but the cautious empiricism of the courts in this respect reflects a wider public reluctance to take risks with institutions which on the face of it perform their functions very successfully. It would take a new initiative by Congress to turn the antitrust policy towards a more radical revision of industrial structures than it now produces; and there is little present sign of the requisite measure of public support for this. It may well be that the great inequalities of size and power that remain in American industry will be tackled, if indeed public opinion wants them tackled, by institutional and policy changes in other fields, such as taxation and research, before any more radical twist is given to antitrust.[2]

[1] The virtual confiscation of patents is, of course, a form of divestiture that has been lavishly used in recent cases; see above, Chapter XIV.

[2] See Dirlam and Kahn, *Fair Competition*, pp. 34–5.

4. *The effectiveness of antitrust
in relation to oligopoly: limitations of the legal
concept of conspiracy*

Most of the firms which spring to mind as typifying 'big business' in the United States are not monopolies: in many important industries there is no single colossus but a small number of giant firms (of greater or lesser degree) which together account for almost the total output of the industry. The names of General Motors, Ford and Chrysler stand out in the automobile industry; United States Steel with Bethlehem and Republic in steel; the 'big three' cigarette manufacturers are well known, as are the 'big five' producers and distributors of motion pictures.[1] The oil industry in the United States is so vast that its major companies run well into double figures, the smallest of them counting as a giant by the standards of any other industry or country. Certain industrial giants—du Pont is an obvious example—have a substantial stake in a number of different industrial fields but with important competitors in each.[2]

In short, the typical market structure in which 'big business' operates is oligopoly rather than monopoly. Accordingly, both the radical and the economic streams of thought that nourish antitrust policy have long been concerned about the 'problem' of oligopoly. 'The final problem of antitrust policy . . . is its inability to make satisfactory contact with oligopoly.'[3] So wrote Professor J. K. Galbraith in 1948; and Professor Jesse W. Markham wrote in 1956 of the 'most important and elusive problem of antitrust policy—oligopoly'.[4] The radical view, as already noted, is that the strategic advantages of great size in business—advantages on the financial and political fringes of the market as well as in the market itself—tend to increase and consolidate the degree of concentration of power in industry; hence their effect is inherently anti-competitive and, in view of the democratic ideal of dispersed decision making, anti-social as well. Meanwhile economists have developed the theory—to use Professor Markham's summary—'that with small numbers of independent sellers the equilibrium price and output in a given market may without actual collusion approach that which would result from collusion, and overt conspiracy may take

[1] See the *Tobacco* and *Paramount* cases, above, Chapter VI.
[2] This has been called 'conglomerate bigness': see Corwin D. Edwards, 'Conglomerate Bigness as a Source of Power', *loc. cit.*
[3] J. K. Galbraith, 'Monopoly and the Concentration of Economic Power', in *A Survey of Contemporary Economics* (ed. H. S. Ellis), Blakiston, Philadelphia, for the American Economic Association, 1948, pp. 99–128.
[4] J. W. Markham, 'The Report of the Attorney General's Committee on Antitrust Laws', *Quarterly Journal of Economics*, vol. 70, no. 2, May 1956, p. 193.

place without leaving in its wake tangible evidence'.[1] Both views lead to the proposition that antitrust should 'do something' about oligopoly.

In order to come within the scope of the statutes oligopoly must be seen either as some form of (possibly tacit) agreement between competitors, albeit few competitors, or as something akin to monopolizing, albeit by more than one firm. As the cases described above (Chapters III and VI) show, however, there are legal limitations affecting what can be done along these lines. Speaking broadly, there must be real proof either of collusion (under section 1) or of exclusion[2] (under section 2) before the Sherman Act can be brought to bear; and such proof is not always easy to get. Nevertheless, it would be wrong to rush to the opposite extreme and assume that nothing ever is or can be done; in fact the legal successes of the authorities against oligopoly industries are by no means negligible and many of the well known giants in those industries have had their full share of antitrust trouble.

In the *Tobacco* case of 1946, for example, collusion among the 'big three' was successfully established by evidence so wholly circumstantial that some economists were misled into thinking that the case was decided by reference to their theories.[3] In the *Car finance* case the target was exclusion, and the devices by which General Motors brought pressure to bear on dealers in order to pre-empt the financing business for its subsidiary company were found to violate the Sherman Act. The key to this situation was coercion; given that coercive devices were used against the dealers, the Court needed no convincing of restrictive purpose.[4] Subsequently the prohibition of these devices by detailed decree was extended to all of the big three in the industry, thus showing that where coercive measures are used to foreclose a market to competition, a number of leading firms in an oligopolistic industry may all be brought within the ban on them, even though they are not adopted collusively. In short, the offence of monopolizing under section 2 need not involve monopoly in the strict sense where

[1] J. W. Markham, *loc. cit.* Compare the 'convention' described by Professor Galbraith in his book *American Capitalism: the Concept of Countervailing Power*, Houghton Mifflin, Boston, 1952, which 'simply outlaws the use of price as a competitive weapon'.

[2] 'Exclusion' is here used as shorthand for 'intent to exclude' and the various exclusionary devices and tactics which may reveal such an intent.

[3] See the account of the case in Chapter VI, above, pp. 162 ff. As that account shows, the case went no further than many others in using circumstantial evidence to prove collusion and did not lay down any rule that price similarities in oligopoly conditions could be deemed collusive without evidence of a 'meeting of the minds'.

[4] The *General Motors* case is a good example of the fact that coercion is the best of all evidence of illegal intent, besides being very unpopular with the courts in itself. If a large company is prepared to bully its dealers to take financial services (or anything else) only from its subsidiary, it is idle to argue that there is no separate market to monopolize and no 'intent' to monopolize it.

there is coercion. This principle became even clearer in the *Motion Picture Advertising* case.[1]

In the *Paramount* case evidence of both collusion and exclusion was presented.[2] The evidence of collusion in fixing admission prices and clearances was slender and circumstantial; there was, however, a great volume of evidence to the effect that each of the major companies used a variety of exclusionary devices and tactics to foreclose an appreciable part of the market for movies. The effect of the story as a whole was to convince the courts that the major companies were involved in a plan to maintain and strengthen their dominant hold in an important sector of the exhibition field, and all were subsequently divested of some cinema ownership besides being placed under the constraint of detailed injunctions.

These three examples—the cigarette, car and movie industries—are by no means the only oligopolies to come up against the law. There has, for example, been much litigation against major oil companies, directed especially to their distribution policies, and some of the patent and cartel cases outlined above (Chapters XI and XII) deal with industries dominated by a few large firms rather than by one colossus.[3] As with most monopolies in the strict sense, so with a large number of the giant firms making up the important oligopolies, the conduct of 'big business' is either already regulated by detailed court decrees arising from past litigation or at least is closely guided by legal advisers whose duty it is to ward off litigation in the future. Yet the fact remains that the structure of these industries is obstinately different from the conventional picture of competitive free enterprise that many antitrust supporters—particularly of the 'radical' and 'small business' schools—have in mind. There is therefore a constant pressure for more to be done about oligopoly.

One common idea is that the legal definition of collusion or conspiracy should be broadened so as to embrace the type of uncompetitive conduct resulting from mutual awareness that is supposed to be typical of oligopolies. As was shown above (Chapter III), various attempts have actually been made by the enforcement authorities to broaden the meaning of 'conspiracy' in this way and some have even appeared successful for a time. The Federal Trade Commission got as far as enunciating the principle that 'where a number of enterprises

---

[1] The account of this case is in Chapter VI, above, pp. 159 ff.   [2] Above, pp. 166 ff.

[3] The *A. & P.* case (see above, Chapter V, pp. 133 ff.) may also be regarded as one dealing with an oligopoly. There is no reason in law why others of the main food 'chains' in the United States, even though smaller than A. & P., should not be equally open to Sherman Act charges if their business conduct were equally vulnerable. Indeed, by a consent decree in December 1957, Safeway Stores became subject to injunctions similar to those imposed on A. & P.

follow a parallel course of action *in the knowledge and contemplation of the fact* [emphasis supplied] that all are acting alike, they have in effect formed an agreement'; and the Supreme Court at least did not dissent from the proposition in the *Triangle Conduit* case that 'conscious parallelism of action' on the part of the individual firm could be an unfair method of competition.[1] The semantics of this topic are subtle and the words 'in the knowledge and contemplation . . .' above may or may not convey to the reader a necessary inference of agreement in the sense of a 'meeting of the minds'. There is little doubt that in a modern antitrust suit evidence of price uniformity (especially of uniform conduct in making price changes) coupled, in a situation of oligopoly or price leadership, with quite slight (though distinct) indications of an 'agreement to agree' would be enough to establish illegal collusion. Just as the courts tend to work to a pragmatic sliding scale whereby the greater the power of a monopoly (or combination) the less obtrusive need be its illegal intent, so too it is probably the case in practice that the greater the *de facto* restrictiveness of a situation (for example, the 'stickier' in prices), the less difficulty there will be in convincing the courts of collusion. But, as the *Theatre Enterprises* cases showed, agreement remains something rather more than 'knowledge and contemplation' of similarity; there must be a true nexus, not simply a congruence of views,[2] and, as a consequence, there are inevitably some cases of avoiding price competition which escape the legal net.

Another version of the same basic urge to broaden the notion of conspiracy is that which seizes upon the words 'combination in the form of trust or otherwise' in section 1 of the Sherman Act and asks in effect why any group of firms whose existence and conduct present a *de facto* barrier to competition should not be regarded as an 'otherwise form of combination' and thus vulnerable under that section.[3] This theory is, of course particularly applicable to oligopoly situations; for there is little doubt that, in an industry with important economies of scale, the existence of three or four entrenched giants with vast assets in well articulated plant, with skilled technicians and managers, with patent protection covering key points of technique, with the goodwill of well advertised brand names, with relatively easy access to new finance, is bound of itself to make 'freedom of entry' a largely meaningless concept. If the courts were prepared to construe the word 'combination' as meaning little or no more than 'aggregation' in this context, then indeed a case would lie against the leading firms in any industry where the concentration of power in a few hands seriously impairs in practice the competitive chances of small firms and new entrants. But

[1] See above, Chapter III, pp. 89–91.   [2] Chapter III, pp. 87–8.
[3] See Chapter VI, pp. 174–5.

once again this theory takes a semantic liberty that the courts do not endorse. It is clear enough from the legislative history that 'combination' in section 1 was always intended to involve a calculated merging of previously separate concerns by means of a trust, holding company or other device; there must be a true nexus, not merely an aggregation.

Yet another way in which more oligopoly situations might become susceptible to legal action is through the extension of the principle underlying the *Automobile finance* and *M.P.A.* cases. Given that, as in those cases, each of the main participants in an oligopoly can be charged simultaneously (but with no suggestion of collusion) with using coercive anti-competitive devices, such as tying clauses, exclusive-dealing provisions and so forth, why not bring charges in the same way if each shows by its course of conduct an 'intent to oligopolize'? On the analogy of 'intent to monopolize', this would extend the conduct that might open the oligopoly firm to legal attack beyond such flagrantly coercive exclusionary devices as those mentioned above to 'honestly industrial' behaviour which, nevertheless, when taken together with similar behaviour by others, would be exclusionary in effect—behaviour such as the U.S.M. leases or even ALCOA's practice of 'embracing each new opportunity as it opened'. This indeed seems the most likely theory on which an extension of existing law might be based in the event of antitrust's taking a further radical turn.[1]

But for all that the law as it stands may leave some anti-competitive structures and some tacit collusion unscathed, it is doubtful if American public opinion will support action going much beyond the limits of existing law—the law, say, of the *Paramount* case. Chiefly this is because the requirements of fair and 'compliable' law are hard to reconcile with the various means that have been suggested for broadening the legal doctrines. This is what has worried people, for example, about the concept of 'conscious parallelism of action'. In certain situations of price leadership (and oligopoly) a particular firm may set its price at the level initiated by another and this 'parallelism' may well occur 'in the knowledge and contemplation of the fact' that others are also likely to follow this price. Yet this may happen entirely without collusion, and, indeed, the consequence of setting any other price may appear so unattractive to the firm that to require non-parallel action would be a mockery. Similarly, if a mere aggregation of business power in few hands, albeit restrictive in its effects, could count as an illegal combination under the Sherman Act, how could any large firm in a concentrated industry be sure of complying with the law?

This last point also runs against the idea of developing the concept of 'intent to oligopolize'. It is probably rare, as has been noted, for

[1] See above, Chapter VI, p. 177.

true monopoly power to be 'thrust upon' its possessor; genuine 'better mousetrap' monopolies seem few and far between. But it must on the face of it be more common for that degree of market power, if it be power, which comes from being one of the firms in an oligopoly, to accrue to its possessor willy-nilly or purely by dint of competitive skills. 'No monopolist monopolizes unconscious of what he is doing' is a dictum that becomes less plausible when translated into terms of oligopoly. Indeed, the conditions of efficient production or distribution in some industries may be such that oligopoly is inevitable: a Chrysler or a Warner Brothers may be in the position of having either to maintain a place in the oligopoly market or perish. In these circumstances it would be a palpably unfair and 'non-compliable' law which condemned a firm on the ground that its course of conduct was directed to maintaining the oligopoly structure.

There are economic as well as legal reasons for public reluctance to see the law pushed much further. 'Big business' has always been admired as well as suspected in the United States: the degrees in which these emotions are felt vary over time and it is not perhaps surprising that admiration should come uppermost in a period of prosperity. It seems obvious that many of the great achievements of the economy are owed to large-scale business units. However this may be, there seems to be little public support at present for radical experiments in breaking up oligopoly structures in American industry. Moreover, economic opinion generally, as has been noted, is much less confident than formerly that the way to progress lies in approaching as nearly as possible to 'pure' competition. An influential segment of opinion among economists is following up the clue left by Schumpeter to the effect that the real dynamic of modern capitalism lies in a larger scale (and longer term) of investment than is likely to be realized without substantial concentration of business power.[1] Other economists—often those with the widest knowledge of actual business operations—are disposed to doubt whether 'pure' oligopoly (in which, according to the theory, quasi-collusive pricing will develop) occurs very often in practice; vigorous competitiveness, though not necessarily in price, is observed among oligopolists. Professor Heflebower, for example takes a fairly optimistic view of real-world situations: 'What actually happens stems from impure oligopolies operating under conditions of uncertainty. . . . Altogether, surprisingly "perfect" results emerge from the imperfect functioning of imperfect markets.'[2]

---

[1] See A. D. H. Kaplan, *Big Enterprise in a Competitive System*, Brookings Institution, Washington, 1954. This subject will be considered more fully in the next chapter.

[2] R. B. Heflebower, 'Monopoly and Competition in the United States of America', in *Monopoly and Competition and their Regulation* (ed. Chamberlin), pp. 110–40.

In the absence of a more fully persuasive and unanimous theoretical basis for breaking up oligopolies, and given the real legal difficulties involved and the public's evident satisfaction by and large with the performance of America's concentrated industries in recent years, there is in short no strong impetus to more radical law. Meanwhile the evidence that 'pure' oligopoly is rare in practice supports the view that existing law covers the ground more or less adequately by preventing coercion and collusion; for if the oligopolists of the real world typically operate in conditions of uncertainty, they will probably not be able to exert a serious degree of market control without giving rise to evidence of collusion at least as strong as that in *American Tobacco* or *Paramount*.[1] And if they severally seek to maintain their position against smaller rivals by any form of exclusive-dealing or tying device, the rule of the *Automobile finance* or *M.P.A.* cases will soon catch up with them. In practice the big firms in oligopoly industries are probably as much influenced in their conduct by the shadow of the Department of Justice and the Federal Trade Commission as are those in a position of monopoly, and no less conscious of the requirements of 'fair' competition.

5. The effectiveness of the Clayton Act provisions: mergers and acquisitions

One of the problems raised by oligopoly situations is that some forms of competition continue, even seem to thrive, in them while other forms are clearly inhibited. This makes it difficult to be as single-minded about them as about blatant price fixing agreements or boycotts—especially when the obstructive effects on competition cannot be ascribed to collusion or coercion in such a way that a ban on them would be properly 'compliable'. But the dilemma posed by business conduct that lessens competition in one way but is consistent with its continuing (sometimes even with added vigour) in other ways is seen most clearly in that sector of antitrust law—broadly speaking the law of the Clayton Act—which deals with anti-competitive practices on the part of individual firms. One such branch of the law, which connects closely with the problem of oligopoly, is that dealing with mergers: for acquisitions are one of the means (though not the only one) by which oligopoly structures may be built up. Hence the Clayton Act ban on mergers and acquisitions is often seen as a way of 'doing something' about oligopoly.

---

[1] This is not to say that extremes of price competition may not be avoided by the operation of what Professor Galbraith calls 'the convention against price competition'. But as Galbraith observes (in *American Capitalism*, pp. 48–9), this convention need not preclude all flexibility of pricing.

Mergers and acquisitions by which companies take over or amalgamate with other companies are going on all the time, but in some periods the numbers of them are enough above the average to receive public attention as a 'merger movement'. Successive merger movements draw attention in turn to the degree of concentration of American industry, that is the extent to which the assets (or output or labour force or some other suitable measure of size) in each industry (and over industry in general) are in the hands of a few large firms. Lively arguments go on in the United States as to whether concentration is increasing and to what extent any increase should be attributed to mergers.[1] There is certainly a widespread belief that concentration 'has increased, is increasing and ought to be diminished'.

Yet whatever refinements may be brought to the study of *changes* in the level of concentration, the layman is still likely to be impressed by figures indicating what the actual level is (for example, the often quoted Federal Trade Commission report showing that in 1947 a little over 100 manufacturing companies in the United States owned very nearly half of the physical assets used in manufacturing) and the 'concentration ratios' showing that there are many industries in which the three or four largest companies own sixty, seventy or even higher percentages of the assets.[2] And whatever statisticians may say of the overall effect of mergers on concentration, it seems only commonsense that any substantial merger immediately increases concentration of ownership in some meaningful sense and that to disallow such mergers would tend to slow down the trend to oligopoly.

Hence it is easy to see why various of the streams of thought supporting antitrust favour drastic action against mergers. Small business pressures, the basic preference for dispersed decision making, the advice of those economists who predict restrictive pricing and output policies from oligopolist firms—all these influences tend to be ranged somewhat automatically on the side of enforcing section 7 of the Clayton Act as rigorously as possible. This approach may well be sustained by the feeling that no great economic harm is likely to result from such action. Where growth is economically justified, it will no doubt take place within the framework of the single corporation; and this will have the advantage of adding resources on the supply side of

---

[1] Professor J. W. Markham's article 'Survey of the Evidence and Findings on Mergers', in *Business Concentration and Price Policy*, National Bureau of Economic Research, pp. 141–212, is an admirable short review of the history and literature of the subject, and something of the spirit of the controversy can be seen in the appended comments on the article by Professors Walter Adams and George W. Stocking.

[2] See the *Report on the Concentration of Productive Facilities, 1947*, Federal Trade Commission, 1949. Comparable figures for British industry appear in R. Evely and I. M. D. Little, *Concentration in British Industry*, Cambridge University Press, 1960.

the market instead of subtracting a competitor, as happens when firms expand by acquisition. Why not then ban mergers more or less *per se* whenever the amount of trade done by the companies involved is substantial enough to overcome a finding of *de minimis*? A quantitative standard would, after all, be readily 'compliable'.

It seems clear that many of the supporters of the Celler-Kefauver Act of 1950 which amended section 7 of the Clayton Act were thinking along these lines. The Senate Report on the Bill stated explicitly that it was meant to 'cope with monopolistic tendencies in their incipiency and *well before* [emphasis supplied] they have attained such effects as would justify a Sherman Act proceeding'. Professor Walter Adams and others in a dissenting note in the *Report of the Attorney General's National Committee to Study the Antitrust Laws* claim that 'the test is whether the amount of competition *lost* is substantial'.[1]

It may be doubted whether in practice a purely quantitative test of this kind could accommodate all kinds of mergers and acquisitions. Not all acquisitions aim at market power; many simply mark the fact that a lot of businesses disappear from the scene by being sold rather than wound up. Some mergers undoubtedly make for real economies of scale, for example where two firms are both below the optimum size or where it is essential for up-to-date methods of production to combine different types of 'know-how'. Within this category are mergers aimed at providing more effective competition with the largest firms in an existing oligopoly industry. Other mergers and acquisitions are undertaken to secure fiscal or financial advantages. It would seem inescapable that some analysis of the motivation or intent of mergers, or alternatively of their probable economic consequences, is needed in applying section 7 to a wide variety of circumstances.

Before any cases reached the courts, there was indeed much discussion of the economic tests that should be applied. When the first case reached the Federal Trade Commission in 1951, the Chairman of the Commission defined the task as bringing the Commission's expertise in business and economic conditions to bear on the problem of applying the general prescriptions laid down by Congress to particular cases. 'There must be a case by case examination of all relevant factors in order to ascertain the probable economic consequences.' In a speech at about the same time the Attorney General indicated that the Department of Justice too would apply economic analysis in order to determine how the character of competition in the markets concerned would be affected by a

---

[1] It is of interest to note that a kind of 'quantity theory of competition' underlies this view: it is assumed that a fixed quota of competition exists in the economy and that to lose any of it is 'a bad thing'. The note of dissent says: 'Once we accept the notion that small companies may merge to compete more effectively with the large ones . . . we are in fact inviting the proliferation of oligopoly.'

merger.[1] The Attorney General's National Committee also produced in its *Report* in 1955 a list of points to be considered covering more than two pages.[2]

The decided cases, however, as described in Chapter VII above, show that the courts have exhibited their traditional reluctance to be drawn into economic argument. In the *Philadelphia National Bank* case, for example, the banks concerned argued the need in their area for a bank of sufficient strength to compete in industrial lending with the big banks of New York City. But the Supreme Court specifically rejected any argument based 'on some ultimate reckoning of social or economic debits and credits' and declared that 'a value choice of such magnitude is beyond the ordinary limits of judicial competence'. Thus even under the Clayton Act, with its apparent reliance on the analysis and prediction of economic effects, the courts have tried hard not to 'set sail on a sea of doubt' as Mr Justice Taft put it, in relation to restraint of trade, over sixty years before.

This feeling of judicial incompetence in face of complex economic argument, together with the needs of compliable law, has led the courts wherever possible to concentrate their attention on specific anti-competitive effects which they could assume it was the intention of Congress to prevent when section 7 was amended. Thus the foreclosure to competition of a substantial amount of trade was picked out as the important anti-competitive effect of the vertical integration in the 1962 *Brown Shoe* case, even though the retail outlets of the smaller company involved accounted for less than 2% of total shoe sales. Similarly in the conglomerate merger cases much emphasis has been placed on the restrictive effect of encouraging 'reciprocal trading' which might foreclose not insubstantial markets to competitors. There has also been great emphasis on the protection of viable small businesses, on the assumption that where small companies are able and willing to continue

---

[1] Attorney General Brownell mentioned eleven points that would need to be considered. These were: '(1) The location, physical and financial size, past acquisitions, products, and activities of the merging companies, individually and in combination. (2) The structure and size of the industry in terms of production and capacity. (3) The relative position in the industry of the two companies individually and combined. (4) The ease by which new competitors may enter the industry. (5) The number of companies active in the industry, their respective size and relative standing in sales and total assets. (6) Sales, relative standing and like factors of the two companies and their competitors in definable market areas, if relevant. (7) The nature of the industry—that is, whether infant, dynamic or declining. (8) The effect the proposed merger may have on sources of raw materials and methods and patterns of distribution. (9) Whether the acquisition may result in a significant reduction in competition. (10) Whether the acquisition may increase the relative size of the purchasing company in such a fashion as to give it a substantial advantage over its competitors. (11) Whether the relationships between the purchaser and other companies that may be brought about by the merger might result in a lessening of competition.'

[2] *Report of the Attorney General's National Committee to Study the Antitrust Laws*, pp. 125–7.

trading independently, it was part of the congressional intention that they should be able to do so, even though the survival of particular firms may be only remotely connected with the effectiveness of competition in an industry in an economic sense.

Yet it is still perhaps open to doubt whether these evasions by the courts of the pitfalls of economic analysis can provide a satisfactory basis for a rule of law on mergers generally. This doubt is reflected in the powerful dissents of Mr Justice Harlan. He made it clear, particularly in the *Von's Grocery* case, that in his view a more thorough-going economic analysis of the markets concerned would have been required to reach a judgment based on the market power produced by the merger. His concurring opinion in the *Procter and Gamble* case suggests that a substantial increase in market power is the appropriate test for a prima facie case under section 7, but also explicitly provides that merging companies should be able to adduce countervailing economics as a defence. This line of thought would come much nearer to the type of analysis that would be regarded as necessary in Britain or most other countries before a merger could reasonably be forbidden.

Will the courts in practice come round to applying economic tests of this kind? This may depend on the nature and content of the cases coming before them. It is noteworthy that the decided cases have had to do largely with retail trade or banking, or with vertical and conglomerate mergers in which foreclosure of competition through the vertical link or through reciprocal trading could be identified as an issue. Horizontal mergers which might be defended on the ground that smaller companies may need to merge in order to compete more effectively with the giants in an oligopoly industry have not figured so prominently in the case law. This may be because, as suggested in Chapter VII above, large sectors of manufacturing industry in the United States were already highly concentrated in oligopolistic structures before the 1950 Act was passed. It is true that the Southern District Court of New York condemned a merger between the United States and Bethlehem steel companies as early as 1958 and this decision was not appealed; but, as these were respectively the second and sixth largest producers in the United States, a defence on economic grounds was perhaps unlikely to be convincing. On the other hand the Department of Justice did not proceed against a number of mergers in the early 1950s between smaller automobile manufacturers (Kaiser and Willys, Hudson and Nash, Studebaker and Packard) which might have tested this aspect of the law.

Thus in principle there should be many mergers where adjudication under the Clayton Act requires a sophisticated balancing of economic considerations. In practice the significance of section 7 may be seen, in the light of the decided cases, as a severe constraint on the growth of powerful firms by acquisition; this constraint operates through the readiness of the courts to condemn mergers whenever they produce disabilities for competitors, for example by pre-empting markets through vertical links or reciprocal arrangements affecting a significant volume of trade. This may not be sophisticated economics but it tends to be acceptable to American opinion on the basis that no serious economic harm is likely to be done in such a large and rich market as the United States by requiring firms which already have the strategic advantages of considerable size to rely for growth essentially on internal expansion rather than on acquisition.

6. *Exclusive dealing: analysis of the* Standard Stations *and* Richfield *cases*

The case law under section 3 on exclusive dealing illustrates even more clearly the constraints imposed on business conduct by the Clayton Act. A typical situation with which this section deals is one in which a number of firms enter (independently) into exclusive-dealing contracts or requirements contracts with distributors. Although they operate in conditions of oligopoly, there may be no doubt about the genuine vigour of their competition for sales and these contracts may be a means by which they compete.[1] On the other hand, the effect of tying a large number of distributors to particular suppliers may well be adverse to the competition of smaller suppliers or new entrants. How should antitrust handle this problem?

Once again believers in a quantity theory of competition advocate what amounts to a *per se* rule by which all such contracts covering a substantial volume of trade should be condemned. And the courts have in fact come near to applying such a rule in the section 3 cases. As shown above (Chapter VIII),[2] cases like *Dictograph* (exclusive dealing) and *Standard Stations* and *Richfield* (requirements contracts) apparently apply a mainly quantitative test of illegality and Mr Justice Frankfurter's dicta in particular seem expressly designed to avoid economic prediction.

Some commentaries, it is true, have been at pains to discount the purely quantitative element in these decisions. The Attorney

---

[1] The economic basis for exclusive dealing may differ from that for requirements contracts. Exclusive-dealing or 'sole agency' agreements tend to be used where the supplier attaches importance to associating the distributor solely with his particular brand and where after-sales service may be important—for example, in consumer durables such as automobiles. Requirements contracts are more used for homogeneous goods, such as petrol, where the important consideration for the supplier is probably that these contracts enable him to plan a steady flow of output.   [2] See above, pp. 205 ff.

General's National Committee, for example, distilled from the cases a doctrine which holds that actual foreclosure of competitors from a substantial volume of trade is enough to establish a Clayton Act offence, but that exclusive contracts covering a large volume of trade do not necessarily foreclose competition. 'Under some circumstances rivals may easily cultivate their own channels of distribution, especially where the essential capital investment is relatively low. . . . The heart of the matter is the ease with which rival suppliers can practicably secure consumer access in alternative ways.'[1] On this theory the courts should determine by economic analysis 'whether a system of challenged exclusive arrangements in fact "forecloses" competitors from a substantial market', and the fault of Mr Justice Frankfurter's opinion in *Standard Stations* was that he assumed this but did not prove it.

In general the Committee's efforts to maintain the position that economic prediction is involved in Clayton Act enforcement and that the test of 'probable economic effect' is a middle way between the Sherman Act test of intent to exclude (or actual exclusion) and a purely quantitative test seem to lack support in the cases. The interesting paradox is that in the very case in which Mr Justice Frankfurter eschewed economic prediction and appeared to endorse a quantitative measure of injury to competition, Judge Yankwich (as also in *Richfield*) had found that the requirements contracts pointed to an intent to exclude competition and therefore violated the Sherman Act. The two extreme tests, in short, produced the same result.

It is indeed more difficult in this area than with acquisitions to define clearly the new ground covered by the Clayton Act that is not already implicit in Sherman Act decisions. It has been noted above that the case law under the Sherman Act itself has gone a long way (considerably further than with acquisitions) to bring within the general prohibition of restraint of trade a wide range of exclusive-dealing arrangements. These cases have shown that important firms in an industry, even though they may be competing quite vigorously one against the other in some respects, may not legally tie dealers and distributors to themselves where, on the evidence, the intent or effect is to produce a serious handicap to competing units which would otherwise be viable. In assessing the evidence of intent or effect the courts may look (as in the *Car finance* and *Motion Picture Advertising* cases) to the cumulative effect of similar practices by a number of leading firms on smaller competitors.

---

[1] See the Committee's *Report*, p. 147. Compare also Dirlam and Kahn, *Fair Competition*, p. 100, who conclude that 'what was forbidden in *Standard of California* and *Richfield* was a dominant company's using its market power to impose full requirements contracts, as a condition of sale, on dealers lacking reasonable alternatives to do business on a non-exclusive basis, where also competitors were seriously handicapped as a result'.

It is perhaps not surprising that the case law under the Clayton Act, even with the courts' recourse to simplified quantitative tests, can hardly go much further than the case law under the Sherman Act. In practice the inquiries by which the courts examine whether a company's exclusive contracts will probably result in substantial harm to competition are very like those by which they decide whether these contracts are meant to do harm to competition—inquiries into such questions as whether the company is powerful enough to affect competition, whether the exclusive contracts are voluntarily accepted (perhaps even initiated) by the distributors or whether they are forced on them, and so forth. If the Federal Trade Commission, jealous of the expertise imputed to it by the legislative history and the textbooks, likes to call these inquiries economic analysis, there is no harm in it. The courts will probably prefer, in cases brought under the Sherman Act, to speak of 'intent' as a concept better suited to compliable law and will as ever be unhappy about relying on economic predictions. Where cases are brought under the Clayton Act they will tend, as with mergers and acquisitions, to concentrate on the evidence of specific anti-competitive effects together with some relatively simple tests of quantitative significance.[1]

The fact that the courts like to rely on intent rather than probable economic effect came out clearly in Mr Justice Frankfurter's opinion in *Standard Stations* when he was discussing the relative degrees of restrictiveness of requirements contracts and tying contracts. The latter, he said, '*serve hardly any purpose* beyond the suppression of competition'. No doubt because of this clarity of intent the courts have not hesitated about condemning arrangements of the *International Salt* type in which a dominant company seeks to exploit its power over a tying product by forcing customers to take the tied product with it.[2] Thus in the regulation of exclusive-dealing arrangements, including requirements contracts and tying contracts, the distinction between the Sherman and

[1] It is of interest that the Attorney General's Committee (*Report*, pp. 148–9) insists that the criterion chosen for section 3 should be the same whether the Federal Trade Commission or the courts hear the cases. The Committee believes that its test of 'actual foreclosure' meets this need. But 'actual foreclosure' means that the exclusiveness of the contracts really bites against competition; in other words, it discloses an intent to exclude. Thus the Committee's own test for the Clayton Act will meet Sherman Act requirements.

[2] See the *Report* of the Attorney General's Committee, pp. 144–5. The Committee agreed that a 'relatively narrow inquiry' should be enough to test the legality of tying arrangements that '*wield monopolistic leverage*'. Without such leverage it is not clear that any antitrust offence arises, for the buyer can go elsewhere for both tying and tied products, and a tying clause, if accepted at all, will be accepted voluntarily. With the 'leverage' (which is simply another name for monopoly power) a tying contract is inherently coercive *vis-à-vis* the buyer and almost inevitably reveals an intent to exclude competition from the market for the tied product; hence it is an offence against the Sherman Act. See also Dirlam and Kahn, *Fair Competition*, p. 116.

Clayton Acts is less important than their joint effect of imposing a general constraint against the use, at least by substantial companies, of contractual ties as a competitive weapon. Under either statute the necessary showing of illegality can be derived from less and less spectacular economic effects, the more the challenged arrangement is a coercive restraint on the trade of third parties.

This point may be best explained by an example. Thus a large metal smelter or oil refiner may see advantages in branching out into fabrication or distribution respectively. If it does this by expanding within the framework of the single corporation, it may well be able to amass a substantial share of the market in the new field without incurring a charge of monopolizing.[1] If it were to seek to secure a like share (with similar economic effects) by buying an existing fabricating (or distributing) business, the legal risk would be markedly greater. But if the metal smelter (or oil refiner) seeks to tie up a share of the market by binding independent fabricators (or distributors) contractually to deal with no other supplier, or by insisting on supplying their full requirements over a substantial period, then antitrust trouble is even more likely to ensue, although the share foreclosed is relatively small. Equally, if the distributor is forced to take the integrated company's subsidiary lines as a condition of getting the main line in which it has a dominant position, this will be almost automatically condemned.

There are many reasons for this apparent subordination of the economic substance of the matter to the form of restrictive arrangement. The best is that, as a matter of fact, an intent to exclude is quite likely to manifest itself at an earlier stage in the process of monopolizing, when the would-be monopolist relies on coercive devices, than when he builds up his position gradually by more orthodox forms of competition. The firm that concentrates on making the mousetrap better may well get a very large share of the business before it can be fairly inferred (if it ever can) that it is out for monopoly power; whereas the firm that buys up competitors or ties up customers in a web of exclusive

---

[1] It is noteworthy, however, that it will be exposed to much greater legal risks by operating in two related fields rather than one. It must take care, for example, not to deny supplies to a previously regular customer in favour of its own activity in the customer's market (compare the *Eastman Kodak* case, above, Chapter V); the reader will recall many other examples— the various discriminatory devices of the *Paramount* case, the operations of ACCO in the *A. & P.* case, the 'squeeze' between ingot and fabricated metal prices in *ALCOA*, etc.— in which the use of power in one market to forward the integrated company's interests in another has provided evidence of intent to monopolize. Compare also the Attorney General's Committee's conclusion that the notion of conspiracy between affiliated companies makes sense when the conduct complained of is a burden on the trade of strangers (for example, the *Car finance* cases), but not when it is simply a mutual restraint like intra-group price fixing.

arrangements soon shows what sort of game it is playing. The Clayton Act obviously requires the enforcement agencies to be alert for early indications of monopolistic purpose.

Some of the other reasons are of a more pragmatic flavour. It seems clear, for example, that the courts are the readier to condemn restrictive conduct on the part of individual companies, the easier (and the less economically hazardous) it is to enforce the ban.[1] Thus there is real difficulty and risk about dissolving a concern like U.S.M. into two or three parts (see Judge Wyzanski's testimony on this issue in Chapter XIV, above); it is rather less of a responsibility to divest an integrated company of one of its business activities, as in the *Pullman* case; it is relatively straightforward to decree that a recent merger should be undone, and no problem at all arises about ordering firms to cease and desist from enforcing exclusive-dealing contracts.

A closely connected point is that the courts look at the question of whether challenged practices 'serve any purpose . . . beyond the suppression of competition'. Where they do—where, for example, some sort of requirements contract or franchise arrangement serves legitimate interests of the buyer as well as of the supplier—the fact is always noted and may indeed constitute a valid defence under either statute.[2] But when the restriction is (at best) gratuitous from the buyer's standpoint— as Mr Justice Frankfurter pointed out in *Standard Stations*, the ending of the restriction would not prevent buyers who so wished from obtaining their full requirements from Standard—the courts are fairly easily persuaded to condemn it. And when the restriction is (at worst) coercively imposed on an unwilling buyer, no persuasion is needed; for the very fact of coercion tends to establish both dominance and illegal intent in the minds of the courts without further inquiry.

Thus another of the expedient and pragmatic sliding scales of anti-trust[3] is at work in the Clayton Act field—that is, the more the restriction is gratuitous (and especially if it is coercive) and easily remediable, the less the need for evidence of its economic effects. Probably this type of shrewd, pragmatic judgment attunes fairly well with American public opinion, which is inclined to ask what harm it can possibly do to large oil companies such as Standard of California and Richfield to canvass for business like everybody else instead of using their bargaining

---

[1] This is not an unfamiliar idea in other branches of law. It became very difficult to get juries to convict in England at a time when quite minor thefts were visited with capital punishment.

[2] Compare the *J. I. Case* decision (above, Chapter VIII, p. 210), in which there was evidence that many dealers who distributed Case farming implements exclusively did so of their own volition: also the *American Can* decree, in which one-year requirements contracts were specifically permitted as of benefit to both sides.

[3] See above, p. 447 (the greater the power, the less need be the evidence of intent; the greater the restraint, the less need be the evidence of collusion).

power to tie customers exclusively to them. Any application of anti-trust which tends to level up the competitive power of the giants and the others can count on applause. There is an element of pure 'under-doggery' in the law; an element of throwing the weight of the enforce-ment authorities into the scale on the side of the weaker parties, which has little to do with the economic control of monopoly.

Indeed, the views of economists about Clayton Act enforcement are divided. Some share the popular view that any action which tends to level out differences in business power and size must somehow be 'reducing oligopoly' and consequently be beneficial—or at least not harmful. Others have asked what the justification is for ascribing any significant power to restrain trade to some of the firms that have been in trouble because of exclusive-dealing and suchlike arrangements. If the *Richfield* case is taken as an example, it may well be asked what power or 'dominance' such a company possesses—one of seven 'majors' in the Pacific area with a share of perhaps 7 or 8% of retail sales of petrol in the area—to impose exclusive arrangements on distributors. In a meaningful sense the independent distributor's relations with such a company must be voluntary even when he accepts an obligation to deal exclusively; for if he does not like Richfield's proposal, he has the alternative of dealing with one of the other majors: and if he dislikes all exclusive arrangements with large companies, he will still have no difficulty in obtaining petrol to sell from smaller companies on non-exclusive terms.[1] (Similar questions may be asked about some of the mergers which the courts have condemned in industries where there are numerous strong competitors.)

It may be said that exclusive contracts by major suppliers are never-theless harmful to competition because they seal off part of the channels of distribution from smaller suppliers. As has been noted, the courts look in practice to the cumulative foreclosing effect of all such contracts made by major suppliers even though they are not made collusively. But those who are opposed to this trend in the decisions can then ask what the justification is for this cumulative view and why the law should concern itself exclusively with the competition of small suppliers. Detailed studies of oligopoly industries suggest that competition between major suppliers may be by no means ineffective; their several arrange-ments with distributors may well be one of the ways in which they compete for sales volume. Richfield's contracts, according to this line of thought, are not aimed at smashing the competition of the small man;

[1] The independent filling station owner can usually get substantial advantages out of signing up exclusively with one of the 'majors'—contributions to the maintenance of the station and suchlike. The bargain is a free one, for the choice facing him is not, 'Sign on the dotted line or you will have *no* petrol to sell', but merely, 'Sign exclusively with us or you cannot sell *our* petrol'.

they *are* the competition faced by Standard of California and the other big suppliers.

It is certainly surprising to observers outside the United States that in this area of antitrust law the courts have no ears for arguments based on the strength or effectiveness of the major competitors themselves. No 'ultimate reckoning of economic debits and credits' can overcome evidence of specific anti-competitive effect. Both in relation to mergers and acquisitions and in relation to contractual tying arrangements, this lack of interest in the competitive strength and efficiency of the large firm is in marked contrast to the attitude taken by European administrators and tribunals. It is of interest, for example, to compare the British Monopolies Commission's report on the merger between Thorn Electrical Industries Ltd and Radio Rentals Ltd, which involved the horizontal and vertical integration of concerns together having over 30 % of both the manufacture and the renting trade for television sets in the United Kingdom. The Monopolies Commission found neither the horizontal nor the vertical aspects of the merger to operate or to be expected in future to operate against the public interest; and part of the reasoning leading to this conclusion rested on concern for the major manufacturer's strength in competition with its large European and Japanese rivals. This difference no doubt reflects the wide disparity between the United States market and the market in any individual European country, and also the fact that for the United Kingdom, as for other European countries, the share of international trade in total trade is vastly greater than in the United States.

It cannot be said that this aspect of antitrust enjoys the virtually unanimous approval that is accorded to the prohibition of price fixing agreements or boycotts. Economic thought, as we have noted, is divided on the issue, and to many it is far from clear that the quality of competition is related to the numbers taking part or that some of the devices of 'monopolistic competition' which the law impedes are not just as legitimate as those which it freely permits.[1] Much business opinion, naturally enough, takes a similar view. Nevertheless, the chances are that the radical and 'small business' elements which applaud the trend of decisions will continue to secure the acquiescence of enough uncommitted opinion to their side, so long as they can successfully challenge their opponents to show that business conduct inhibited by the law is positively necessary in the context of the United States market for efficient performance.[2] Given all the factors that tend

[1] Compare, for example, the recruitment of a tied body of competent dealers whose premises are decked in the livery of the manufacturer with other forms of advertising display.
[2] See Dirlam and Kahn, *Fair Competition*, p. 41.

towards greater concentration and more oligopoly, can it seriously be contended—so runs the challenge—that requiring giant companies to eschew gratuitous exclusive measures will lose any significant advantages of large-scale organization? Meanwhile, it may do something to preserve a number of choices—the small supplier's choice of trader, the dealer's option to change his supplier when he likes, the consumer's supposed wish for the greatest possible range of alternatives —which would otherwise be extinguished. And until economists can show that serious losses are being incurred, is this not justification enough?

7. *Price discrimination: analysis of Robinson-Patman Act decisions*

An element of 'underdoggery' has been noted in the enforcement of the Clayton Act prohibitions. The way in which the courts pay less heed to economic effects once there is proof of coercion, the way in which they focus on the competitive viability of small firms rather than on the competition between large ones—all this points to a tendency in antitrust administration to extend the sway of the policy to the correction of apparent hardship and 'unfairness' in private commercial relations, rather than to confine it to the control of monopoly power in the public interest. This same tendency gives rise to the jibe that in some respects antitrust shows more concern for competitors than for competition.

No branch of the law is more open to this type of criticism than that dealing with price discrimination under section 2 of the Clayton Act as amended by the Robinson-Patman Act. The origins of the latter measure, as shown above (Chapter IX), witness to its essential concern with small distributors as against the chain stores. Its elaborate drafting is in marked contrast to the breadth and flexibility of the Sherman Act and even to the generality of the other substantive sections of the Clayton Act. Thus, instead of simply declaring price discrimination unlawful, subject only to the usual qualification that a tendency to monopoly or to a substantial lessening of competition must be shown, the Robinson-Patman Act attempts to prescribe in detail the economic conditions of an offence. Discrimination occurs when goods of like quality are sold at different prices: the difference may not, after all, be discriminatory if it is due to cost savings arising from sales in bulk: but it becomes discriminatory again unless it makes 'only due allowance' for the cost savings:[1] it may be saved again if it is simply a competitive response to some other supplier's low price: but only if

[1] Unless again the Federal Trade Commission has established a quantity limit, in which case even a price difference making only due allowance for cost savings may be unlawful; see above, Chapter IX, pp. 258–9.

16

this response is 'in good faith'. All this detailed specification of the offence in economic terms might be thought to add to the clarity and hence to the 'compliability' of the law's requirements: but, as the cases described above (Chapter IX) show, the truth is quite otherwise and each point in the specification engenders its own controversy. No statute better demonstrates the legislative folly of trying to define 'sin' in detail.

Moreover, the lawmakers elaborated the Clayton Act test of injury to competition by adding after the usual words '. . . where the effect . . . may be substantially to lessen competition or tend to create a monopoly' the extra passage '. . . or to injure, destroy or prevent competition with any person who either grants or knowingly receives the benefit of such discrimination, or with customers of either of them'. Although this wording does not imply that any injury to competitors of the discriminating supplier or of his favoured customer makes discrimination illegal,[1] it does focus attention on the evidentiary value of injury to particular competitors; and since this kind of evidence is often the best (even the only kind) available, it is not perhaps surprising that in practice the harassed enforcement officer tends to blur the distinction between injury to competitors and injury to competition. (Indeed, in the absence of some test of monopolistic intent, this distinction is not an easy one to maintain, for in a quite literal sense injury to competing firms presumably will lessen the impact of the competition attributable to them.)

Of all the branches of antitrust law, in short, the Robinson-Patman Act relies the most on economic inquiry and the least on indications of intent to monopolize or to restrain trade. It is interesting that its case law is the richest in muddle and anomaly. Without rehearsing the cases here, we may recall, for example, how the mere acceptance of the going price in a distant market may constitute prima facie discrimination under the Act and expose a firm to litigation depending on the vagaries of the 'good faith' defence;[2] or how a supplier selling to vertically integrated distributors is prevented from granting them the normal wholesaler's discount on all their purchases, thus denying in effect that such a distributor can perform the wholesaling function on goods which he resells by retail; or how a supplier selling to both wholesalers and retailers is bound, because of the wording of the Act, to concern himself with the 'fairness' of competition between his

---

[1] Nor have the courts, despite some of the dicta, applied any such rule.

[2] See, above, the supplementary note to Chapter IX, pp. 264–5: the prosecution must, of course, show that competition stands to be injured or lessened; but this has been successfully done simply on the basis that different prices to users in different locations may injure competition between them.

'direct' and 'indirect' retailers and hence with the resale prices of his wholesalers—although he may legally sell at the same price to both wholesalers and retailers whatever the subsequent effects on different retailers.

These complexities, which seem remote from anti-monopoly policy as such, are largely due to over-elaboration in the drafting of the statute. So, too, although the lawmakers admit that some selective price reductions may be warranted by cost savings, they have made the proviso to section 2(a) on this topic restrictive and inflexible in operation by attempting to define in detail the sources of cost savings which they regard as legitimate and, by the same token, to prevent evasion through discriminatory allocations of overhead costs.[1] The equally cautious wording in the proviso to section 2(b) on the 'good faith' defence again makes for inflexibility; for, in order that this proviso should not work unduly in the favour of large buyers, it was so drafted as to confine competition between suppliers, where price discrimination is involved, to meeting but not beating a low price already set by a rival.

The last point leads to one of real substance. It seems clear that selective (and often secret) price concessions constitute one of the ways in which oligopolists compete. Exclusive-dealing and requirements contracts, as has been noted, may similarly be a means of competition for sales, so that some economists are far from clear about the justification for a rigorous interpretation of the Clayton Act ban on them. But this point may be answered by challenging the economists to show what harm is done by the alternative. Does it really hurt American Can to take orders for only a year's supplies at a time? And this reply, with its suggestion that exclusive-dealing restrictions in contracts are often gratuitous, at least draws a good deal of the sting from the attack. But when an analogous economic criticism is made of the law on price discrimination, it cannot be met so satisfactorily by challenging the critic to show what harm comes of the alternative. For in conditions of oligopoly the alternative to selective price concessions may well be no effective price competition at all.

Indeed, a whole line of antitrust cases rests on the notion that for competitors to bring all their prices out into the open—to file all price changes with a central agency, to agree on an 'open competition' plan, and so on—is only too likely to be a means of evading the prohibition of price fixing agreements.[2] In the *Sugar* case the offence was found specifically to consist in mutual undertakings not to depart secretly

---

[1] One of the difficulties on this topic is that no allocation of overhead costs between different classes of customer can be 'correct' in any strict sense: the many variables are simply not calculable to the nearest cent, and it is a matter for decision, not for arithmetic, to arrive at a broadly reasonable allocation.

[2] See above, Chapter I, pp. 40 ff.—the *Price filing* cases.

from announced prices. When competitors are numerous, the chances are, as these cases show, that an attempt to prevent or mitigate price competition will not succeed without giving rise to evidence of collusion. But in an oligopoly, where competitors are few, it is not impossible that some tacit avoidance of price competition may go unchecked. To the critic of the Robinson-Patman Act this seems just the result that is likely to follow from preventing selective price concessions, and it seems curious to him that the Act should virtually require the type of 'open competition' that the *Sugar* decision condemned. Thus the line of economic criticism of the law, based on a realistic view of oligopoly markets, is more forceful as applied to the Robinson-Patman Act than to other branches of antitrust.[1] In view of this and given the anomalies and complexities already mentioned, it is not surprising that this is the most controversial branch of antitrust and the one for which public support is least unanimous.

The convinced supporter of antitrust, it is true, cannot escape the need for some action against price discrimination, which may manifestly be a means of monopolizing or injuring competition. But so far as a policy against price discrimination is strictly an anti-monopoly policy, it might surely be embodied in broader and more flexible legislative provisions. Indeed, one might suppose that, if no Robinson-Patman Act had been passed and if modern trends in antitrust case law had been applied to the price discrimination problem either under the Sherman Act or under the original section 2 of the Clayton Act, a more flexible body of law would in fact have been built up. There is no reason to suppose that the courts would not have devised workable distinctions between, for example, cost justified price differences and unjustified discrimination, even if the lawmakers had not considered the point; similarly with the distinctions needed in considering any discriminatory aspect of functional discounts or delivered prices.

If the courts were indeed working to a general directive they would chiefly rely, as has been seen in so much of the other case law, on forming from the evidence a sound impression of the intent of the parties and they would condemn price discrimination when the intent was to monopolize or significantly to lessen competition. There is, of course, a special difficulty about judging price discrimination by reference to intent, namely, that the monopolistic intent often lies with the distributor who induces and receives the price concession rather than with the supplier who grants it. Since, for obvious reasons of enforceability, the law must be directed mainly against the supplier,

---

[1] Economic critics are not, of course, concerned only with the effect of the statute on competition between suppliers: many believe that it works against efficiency in distribution because some of its provisions positively discriminate against efficient, integrated units.

this is no doubt part of the reason why the lawmakers have eschewed the test of intent in this field and have sought to specify the commercial symptoms and effects of an offence in detail.

There is, too, a real dilemma between encouraging competition between suppliers, even in the form of selective price concessions which must inevitably confer advantages on the buyers who receive them, and holding the ring between buyers so that all start fair in the competition in distribution. The difficulty with any process of weighing the advantages of one kind of competition against the disadvantages of the other in each new context is the old one that different judges (even economic experts) would often reach different conclusions as to where the balance of advantage lay; hence consistent and compliable case law would be hard to build up. Nevertheless, it would not seem impossible to bring a general prohibition of price discrimination to bear against the discriminating supplier either if he himself seeks to monopolize or if he furthers the monopolistic intent of a favoured customer: and general provisions might be more effective than section 2(f) of the Clayton Act in dealing with the customer who, with such intent, induces or bullies the supplier to grant him concessions. Indeed, this last proposition is to some extent borne out by the treatment of inducing concessions in the *A. & P.* case under the Sherman Act as compared with that in *Automatic Canteen* under section 2(f).[1]

Those whose concern is with anti-monopoly policy would probably be content with a broader statute on these lines.[2] Its present elaboration, though it may in part be due to the difficulties mentioned above, mainly results from the fact that in the Robinson-Patman Act a piece of special-interest legislation was superimposed on the original policy— legislation designed to secure the survival of small independent retailers, especially in the grocery field, against the competition of the large chains.[3] Hence the inflexibilities and complexities that tend to give

---

[1] The *A. & P.* case is described above, Chapter V, pp. 133 ff., and *Automatic Canteen* in Chapter IX, pp. 243 ff. It is interesting to note that the Federal Trade Commission has also proceeded against retailers who were said to have induced concessions under section 5 of the Federal Trade Commission Act.

[2] See the discussion of the Robinson-Patman Act, in the *Report of the Attorney General's National Committee to Study the Antitrust Laws*, pp. 155 ff. Although the Committee proposed relatively little by way of amendments to the statute, it is notable that it advocated greater 'flexibility' of interpretation and enforcement at almost every point—for example, in assessing 'cost justification', 'good faith' in meeting competition, and so on—and that it stressed the distinction between injury to competitors and injury to competition. It is hard to see what basis there can be for flexibility other than reference to intent. It is interesting to note that the Committee, in summing up its recommendation on 'good faith', wrote as follows: 'In practice this will disqualify the seller to whom meeting of competition is only an incidental byproduct of a *scheme to monopolize or other objective inimical to overall antitrust policy*' [emphasis added].

[3] It also aimed at securing the survival of independent brokers in the food trades; see above, Chapter IX, p. 260.

the benefit of any doubt to a policy of denying selective price concessions to large buyers, even where there is warrant for them. Legislation of this kind, once on the statute book, is often highly resistant to change: it is likely, after all, to retain substantial 'small business' and radical support which other supporters of antitrust may feel must be humoured in the interests of the general policy. Thus, as the emphasis changes in the running compromise that constitutes antitrust, it is perhaps more likely that greater flexibility will be obtained by interpretation than that radical alterations will be made in the legislation.

It seems likely that there will always be strong pressures in favour of special protective measures for small distributors. The State and federal measures which enable resale price contracts to be enforced in the courts (above, Chapter X) are also, of course, measures of this kind; the inspiration for them comes indeed from much the same sources as those underlying the special-interest features of the Robinson-Patman Act. State laws directed against sales below cost also come within this complex. This really is a different subject from that under consideration here, although the fact that such special-interest legislation can be passed testifies, of course, to the strength of the 'small business' voice in antitrust policy proper.

8. *Summing up of the effectiveness of antitrust*

The conclusion that emerges from this review of the various branches of the law is the unexciting one that, by and large, the operation of antitrust reflects pretty well the balance of opinion in the United States. This indeed is as it should be in a democracy. As we have seen, the antitrust policy stems from two basic propositions: first, that private, unaccountable persons should not wield significant amounts of economic power; secondly, that should they seek to do so, they should be checked by a rule of law.

The first proposition is linked with the assumption that in the absence of monopoly (whether of a single firm or a combination) economic decisions (for example, pricing decisions) will be imposed on firms by competition, and not as matters of individual or collective discretion. Hence the policy aims to prevent the suppression of competition and the growth of monopoly. The second proposition requires that the obligations laid on individuals in pursuance of this aim shall be fair and compliable legal rules and that issues brought to trial as a result of alleged breaches of these rules shall be properly justiciable.

In accordance with these considerations the heart of antitrust is an absolute prohibition of restrictive agreements between competitors and of courses of conduct on the part of individual firms which demonstrate an intent to monopolize. This prohibition is enforced firmly but with an eye to practicalities; it is subject to sensible *de minimis* rulings and, as the cases have shown, to shrewd, pragmatic conventions whereby the evidentiary requirements for proving collusion tend to be shaded when restrictive effects on competition are particularly obvious, and those for proving monopolistic intent tend likewise to be shaded when the possession of monopoly power is least deniable. The heart of the enforcement process is the inquiry into intent (by the rule of reason); since this inquiry is ultimately factual, given the rule that men are held in law to intend the natural consequences of their acts, it has been found the best means of producing justiciable issues and, by the same token, a compliable rule of law.

The basic prohibition, so enforced, covers most of the ground expected of an anti-monopoly policy and the argument up to this point carries with it virtually the whole range of opinion that supports antitrust—not only the basic sentiment in favour of opposing legal checks to the possession of private economic power, but also the radical and 'small business' sectors of opinion which for various reasons dislike the concentration of business in large units, and the main body of economic opinion.

There is nothing in the form of the basic Sherman Act prohibition or its enforcement to ensure that it operates to produce optimum economic results. On the contrary, the courts have consistently refused to take economic consequences as the criterion of antitrust right and wrong. First-class economic performance is no defence once an intent to monopolize is established: conversely, the prohibition of collusive restraint of trade would be strictly enforced even in a case in which economic harm seemed sure to follow from breaking up an agreement.[1] Nevertheless, a substantial majority of orthodox economists would probably be found to say that, in general, the maintenance of competition makes for greater industrial efficiency;[2] and very few would cavil at the more sophisticated proposition (as cited previously from Dirlam and Kahn) that antitrust enforcement, as it stands, cannot be shown, save quite exceptionally, to obstruct or inhibit business activity directed to improving efficiency.

Highly concentrated industrial structures—oligopolies—may be built up without collusion and without any single company's displaying an intent to exclude others sufficient to lead to its conviction and

---

[1] If the threatened harm were on a large enough scale and of long enough duration, it would be regarded as up to Congress to find a legislative remedy. Compare, for example, the bituminous coal legislation of 1933. To the extent that such legislation exempted restrictive practices from antitrust, it would be expected to subject the industry to some form of public regulation.

[2] The discussion of this proposition and its limitations will be found in the next chapter.

dissolution under the Sherman Act. The requirement that the law should be fair and compliable means that these structures (in the absence of collusion or exclusion) are often not vulnerable to legal attack, even though they may in practice abridge or impede some forms of competition. This is the main reason why businesses of great size and influence persist and flourish in the United States in a way that is superficially inconsistent with the antitrust policy; they are not, for the most part, monopolies in the strict sense, though their strategic position in the market is unquestioned and their influence—political, financial, social—is pervasive beyond it.

Those who would place the major emphasis on the first basic proposition of antitrust—the denial of economic power to private organizations—do indeed find the disparities of power in modern industry at odds with the purposes of the policy. The 'limitist' view is advanced that business size ought to be kept within bounds and that there ought to be as many firms in each industry as are consistent with demonstrable economies of scale or other legitimate economic needs, such as research. But the actual working of the policy has to keep a proper balance between the two bases of the policy: the denial of power and the rule of law to enforce it. Arbitrary changes in industrial structure—changes imposed without reference to predictably illegal conduct—would be inconsistent with this second basic concept of antitrust and so beyond the scope of fair enforcement. The 'limitist' view would require new and separate legislative sanction and it is improbable that enough public support could be obtained for it to persuade Congress to any such enactment.

It seems likely that oligopolist firms which are prevented by law from resorting to overt collusion or coercive exclusionary devices are by no means always or easily able to suppress competition between them. '. . . . Surprisingly "perfect" results emerge from the imperfect functioning of imperfect markets.' Nevertheless, it would be a mistake to fall into an easy optimism about the effectiveness of antitrust in this respect and to suggest that when oligopoly is legally unassailable it is invariably innocuous, and when it is significantly restrictive it always gives rise in practice to evidence of collusion or coercion. Of course there is avoidance of price competition in the United States in some industries some of the time: of course the concentrated structure of many industries is a barrier to new entrants—or at least reinforces the inevitable barrier presented by the magnitude of the minimum capital and technological requirements of so much modern industry. Of course, too, enforcement is far from perfect; evidence of collusion, for example, is often hard to come by in close-knit industries. Moreover, in this type of law (that of *mala prohibita* as opposed to *mala in se*), in which no serious moral obloquy attaches to offences, self-enforcement is not always intensive and, except when the case law is very clear, business-men are inclined to go ahead as they think best, and argue about the law if and when the need arises.

Thus, in the wide borderland between, on the one side, overt agree-ments between competitors and outright monopolization, with which the law can get to grips fairly effectively, and, on the other side, a state of adequate competition[1]—the borderland, in short, of oligopoly—the policy makes only an approximation to its aims. Fair law is not at all points compatible with the prevention of uncompetitive structures. But this state of things probably corresponds quite closely with a state of public opinion which is impressed with the achievements of large business organizations, far from sure that oligopoly is always a bad thing, and full of doubts as to just what conditions are required for adequate competition and how to recognize them.

The prevention of undue concentrations of private power is no longer seen, for example, as a simple matter of eliminating monopoly and promoting all possible competition. It has become orthodox doctrine that in the real world of 'monopolistic competition' the individual firm normally has some measure of discretion ('monopoly') in deciding on prices and outputs, even though the exercise of this discretion for a firm that wishes to survive and prosper is usually, of course, kept within close limits by competitive considerations. Few economists would now see any welfare advantage in eliminating the element of monopoly in this degree of discretion.[2] All the signs are that the public like to have a choice between differentiated products, which enjoy an element of 'monopoly' in this sense. Moreover, the activity that businessmen call competition usually consists in finding means further to differentiate the product so as to preserve and if possible widen the element of discretion.[3]

This is what makes the Clayton Act sector of antitrust so difficult and controversial. The practices made illegal in that Act (subject, of course, to their tending to create monopoly or a substantial lessening of competition) are used as weapons of competition between oligopolists. The smaller participants in an oligopoly may need to combine in a merger in order to survive in the company of the larger: they may like-wise want exclusive outlets in order to maintain steady sales of their

---

[1] The question begging word 'adequate' is used here precisely to avoid begging the question—for discussion in the next chapter—of whether 'pure' or 'workable' or 'effective' competition ought to be the aim of an anti-monopoly policy. 'Adequate' here really means 'adequate to prevent the accumulation of undue amounts of private economic power'—this being the basic aim of antitrust in the United States.

[2] Professor Chamberlin himself has frequently defended the welfare advantages of monopolistic competition. 'Not only the real world but also the welfare ideal is a complex of monopoly and competition.' See his article, 'Measuring the Degree of Monopoly and Competition', in *Monopoly and Competition and their Regulation* (ed. Chamberlin), pp. 255–67.

[3] See below, Chapter XVI, section 2.

product in competition with integrated rivals who have their own outlets: they may make secret price concessions to get the business of important customers, knowing that an open price cut across the board (which in any case they might well be unable to afford) would at best be met and at worst be capped by a retaliatory cut which would ruin them. Yet all these practices may also, of course, harm the prospects of still smaller firms or, in the case of discrimination, distort the competition between their customers. Where, as in these conditions, one type of competition is harmed but another type continues (and possibly would not continue without the very practice that harms the former type), which type should antitrust policy promote? Given that real-world competition often involves seeking elements of monopoly (in the strict sense), why are some of the devices used condemned and not others? What is the rationale of the line taken in these dilemmas?

It is evident that in this field antitrust policy looks on the whole to the viability of small business units rather than to the quality of competition between the large. Possibly because it is seen to be inevitable that, even under antitrust, much of industry will continue to consist of huge businesses organized in oligopoly structures, the tendency is to see no harm in, even positively to applaud, legal measures which act as restraints on the operation of these firms. Thus the concept of illegal intent in this field becomes attenuated in practice by a number of considerations which are only loosely connected with the policy of preventing monopoly.

Even under the Clayton Act, as has been noted above, illegal 'intent' in some sense tends still to be taken as the earmark of an offence (by the courts, if not by the Federal Trade Commission) because it is more susceptible than economic prediction to testing by the type of evidence that courts are used to. But this is no longer 'intent to monopolize' or the 'intent' that is inherent in a restrictive agreement between competitors. It is no more than intent (as shown, usually, by actual foreclosing effects) to operate in a way that presents some significant barrier to smaller competitors; and this intent no longer implies the possession of dominant power in the industry, but only a share of the market which, when aggregated with the shares of other oligopolists, will render the practice in question exclusionary as against those outside the oligopoly.[1]

The considerations which have led to this result have been outlined above—the feeling that legal restraints which no more than incon-

---

[1] As has been noted above, this attenuated concept of 'intent' which might very well have developed as the distinctive feature of Clayton Act enforcement appears, on the evidence of such cases as *Richfield*, to be used also in Sherman Act cases which are concerned with individual conduct of the same kind as that covered by the Clayton Act.

venience the large oligopoly firms may mean life or death to small firms, an associated element of pure 'underdoggery', a tendency to be against coercive business dealings *per se*, a pragmatic convention whereby restrictions are the more readily condemned (and on less elaborate evidence of intent and effect) if they are gratuitous, coercive and easy to put a stop to. Evidently these factors are not necessary parts of an anti-monopoly policy; they testify to the strength of radical and 'small business' elements in the support for antitrust, and even more, perhaps, to the negative point that no important elements in that support have had enough at stake to counteract them. Finally, in certain parts of the Robinson-Patman Act case law the concept of 'intent to monopolize' becomes attenuated virtually to the point of extinction; the offence is defined in terms purely of commercial effects. In this field (and even more in the legislation on resale price maintenance) anti-monopoly policy tails off into special-interest legislation designed to protect small shopkeepers.

CHAPTER XVI

ANTITRUST FOR EXPORT?

1. Political and institutional differences between the United States and Britain and their effect on the objectives of anti-monopoly policy

Political aims and concerns are bound to differ from country to country. While the United States and Britain both recognize a problem of monopoly and restrictive practices, it is by no means the same problem in the two countries. As we have seen, the basic concern in the United States is with the sheer possession of economic power; so much so that restrictive agreements and deliberate monopolizing are illegal *per se* even though it might be established in particular instances that they produce economic advantages. Rightly or wrongly, it seems unlikely that in Britain the cause of dispersing economic decision making would of itself attract decisive public support; it would be widely believed that, if need be, economic power could be 'controlled' or dealt with in some other way, and an anti-monopoly policy would tend to be advocated mainly on other grounds.

One of the profoundest institutional differences between the two countries is the absence in the United States of anything corresponding to the amorphous but recognizable assemblage of public bodies and personages that we know in Britain as 'the Establishment';[1] and this has much to do, as both cause and effect, with American distrust of authority *per se*. In general the possession of power by established authorities arouses a much lesser degree of anxiety or resentment in Britain, where the emphasis is much more on the use of power.

Whereas American institutions often appear to be designed to hamper the exercise of power, ours are designed on the whole to facilitate it, though great importance is attached to protecting minorities against its abuse and elaborate safeguards are adopted to this end. This general attitude to power extends beyond the Establishment proper, to a wide range of wielders of power who are 'established' only in the broader sense that the persons concerned are linked by well

[1] 'The Establishment' provides a continuity of authority which may overlie dramatic changes. Not only do its component institutions change markedly over time—consider the functions and powers of the Crown itself in 1550, 1750 and 1950—but new institutions are constantly being brought within it or into well understood relationships with it—consider the M.C.C., B.B.C. or T.U.C. Very radical policies may be adopted in Britain if they are presented as the next logical step after Magna Carta. In the United States, on the other hand, continuity tends to have to be disguised as change. The same policies have constantly to be presented in a new light—consider the many different initials, E.C.A., M.S.A., F.O.A., A.I.D., etc., etc., which have denoted the agency administering American foreign aid.

understood ties with those within the Establishment proper. Thus, even where power is not subject to any form of public accountability, for example the economic power of private business units and associations, the normal course is to let it ride unless and until there is substantial evidence of abuses: then some form of inquiry may be set on foot in which those who exercise power are expected to justify their use of it, and regulative legislation (which may involve the supervision of the power by some public body or even, in extreme cases, the outright transfer of power to the public domain) may follow if they are unable to do so.

It is in line with the same general attitude to power that, if regulation is required, British opinion tends to be more open-minded than American about the choice between judicial enforcement of rules of law and some form of administrative supervision. It is, of course, often difficult under any system to judge whether issues have crystallized sufficiently to be the subject of firm, justiciable rules or whether their fluidity is still such that *ad hoc* administrative decisions must be made, guided perhaps by the recommendations of a committee of inquiry. In the United States administrative decisions (the 'government of men') tend to be unpopular as such, and the search is always for a 'government of laws'. In Britain the choice is more open; administrative acts, as such, are not so suspect; a government of men subject to law is desired but not a 'government of laws' in the American sense.[1]

In short, the two basic considerations underlying antitrust—the wish to disperse economic power and the wish to rely on judicial processes to do so—though no doubt present to British opinion, have a lesser impact here than in the United States. And, when these considerations are removed (or at least weakened), it follows that much more hangs on the economic pros and cons of the matter.[2] Since it is less concerned about the mere existence of private economic power, British opinion tends to focus on the way in which the power of monopolies and restrictive associations is exercised; and this is essentially an economic matter.

[1] The British tend to be allergic to government by lawyers—towards which a 'government of laws' may sometimes lean.

[2] Radical and 'small business' pressures for vigorous anti-monopoly policies are less in evidence in Britain than in the United States. Radical opinion mostly opposes private monopoly, but in Britain it has many other irons in the fire besides 'trust busting'. 'Small business' opinion is organized to some extent in Britain as a lobby in favour of resale price maintenance, but hardly at all as an 'anti-big business' or anti-monopoly pressure.

2. *The economics of the monopoly problem: the inadequacy of the conventional models of 'perfect' or 'pure' competition and of the theories of monopolistic competition and oligopoly; absence of information about business decisions*

There is, however, great difficulty about the application of economic principles to the problem of market power in real industrial situations. This is mainly because the diversity of situations in the real world appears to defy generalization of the comprehensive kind needed for model building and hence for prediction and useful rules of thumb for regulation. It is clear, for example, that the model of 'perfect competition', however useful it may be as an elementary teaching aid, has little or no relevance to modern industrial economics. According to this model, the existence of a large number of competing suppliers, each of whose contributions to the total supply of a commodity is so small that its withdrawal cannot affect price, ensures that consumers will get their demand for the commodity satisfied at the lowest price (highest efficiency) possible in a given state of the arts. Any lowering of costs by improvements in the organization of production will be passed on to the consumer because those that make them will expand at the expense of any who fail to follow them. Other ways can be shown in which the efficiency of the system is maximized on this model—changes in the pattern of demand, for example, finding an immediate response in appropriate switching of resources from one use to another.[1]

The assumptions made for the purpose of constructing this model are, however, wildly at variance with the conditions which nowadays govern the markets in most industrial products in the real world. We may perhaps ignore the unreality of the assumption that there is complete and instantaneous knowledge by all buyers and sellers of the transactions taking place in the market and a correspondingly complete and rapid mobility of labour and other resources; this assumption merely facilitates the mathematical development of the 'perfect' model.[2]

But other assumptions of the model are in important ways unrealistic in substance. Whereas the model treats of dealings in homo-

---

[1] Chapter 2, pp. 14 ff., of Professor J. K. Galbraith's *American Capitalism* contains an admirably concise summary of the competitive model.

[2] 'Pure' competition is usually understood as relaxing the rigorous assumption of completely 'frictionless' operation which characterizes the model of 'perfect' competition. But the model of 'pure' competition in fact makes little of the practical implications of friction and it retains the other assumptions discussed here. (See Clair Wilcox, *Competition and Monopoly in American Industry*.) Marshall's sensible and realistic concept of 'normal' competition relaxed the assumption that the commodity being sold was so perfectly homogeneous that buyers would have no reason at all to prefer one supplier to another; that is, it allowed for such 'monopoly' elements as arise from goodwill and regular customers. This concept thus went some way to anticipate Chamberlin's 'monopolistic competition', but the 'monopoly' elements in 'normal' competition were not thought of as powerful enough to affect price.

geneous commodities, the great bulk of the products of modern industry are heterogeneous in that the various makers go to much trouble to differentiate their particular brand from others. Whereas the model requires enough sellers so that none can individually affect price by varying output, it is obvious that economies of scale are so marked in many modern industries—for example, motor cars, electric lamps—that the largest markets, sometimes even the world market, can be completely satisfied by only a few suppliers of optimum size. Finally, the model takes as given the existing state of the arts. But Schumpeter has pointed out[1] that major advances in wealth arise from wholly new techniques rather than from detailed improvements within a given technological framework; hence an economic system encouraging to technical development but imperfect in day-to-day operation may well outstrip one which operates perfectly in a given state of the arts but does little to see that the state of the arts advances. And technical development requires strong firms with substantial accumulated resources.[2]

All these points have been made many times before. It has been pointed out, notably by Professor J. M. Clark in the famous article which introduced the concept of 'workable competition',[3] that if any necessary condition of 'perfect' (or 'pure') competition is not present, it no longer follows that the pursuit of the other requisite conditions will in practice be beneficial: it may be positively detrimental. Certainly it is not the case, as the words 'perfect' and 'pure' in this context might misleadingly suggest, that in the real world any situation in which there are 'imperfections' in the market can automatically be improved by governmental or other action designed to make actual industrial behaviour more like the 'perfect' model. It is essential to remember that the words 'perfect' and 'pure' characterize the model, not the reality. Moreover, the word 'competition' itself in this technical sense has a quite different meaning from that which it is given in everyday use in real industrial situations. Under the 'perfect' or 'pure' competition of the models, for example, the individual entrepreneur is faced with a given price. In technical language the demand curve facing him is horizontal: at the going price he can sell all that he can produce but no effort of his in any direction will alter the price. This position,

[1] Joseph A. Schumpeter, *Capitalism, Socialism and Democracy* (3rd ed.), Allen and Unwin, London, 1950, chapter 8. See also E. S. Mason's article, 'Schumpeter on Monopoly and the Large Firm,' in the *Review of Economics and Statistics*, vol. 33, no. 2, May 1951, p. 139.

[2] The 'perfect competition' model in fact makes no provision for such long-term costs of production as investment in research and development: price equals marginal cost in the given state of the arts and no entrepreneur can be recompensed for avoidable long-run costs; the financing of innovation is thus assumed to be external to the operation of industry.

[3] J. M. Clark, 'Toward a Concept of Workable Competition', *American Economic Review*, vol. 30, no. 2, part 1, June 1940, p. 241.

however, would not be thought of as one of *competition* at all by the average businessman, to whom competition cannot of its nature be passive.[1] To him 'competing' is conceived in terms of improving his product relatively to rival products, showing and advertising it attractively, getting a well trained sales force to push it, judging just the right price at which to offer it. Yet all these exertions are regarded by the textbook as signs of monopoly elements in the market, at best of 'monopolistic competition'. In technical language again, the demand curve facing the firm is downward sloping: to some degree the firm can select its own price. Its competitive activities are designed to maintain and increase the degree of its discretion (the 'monopoly element', in economic language) in pricing policy.[2]

The real industrial scene against which policy must be formulated is commonly one in which a relatively small number of suppliers (sometimes very few indeed) sell differentiated (though often closely substitutable) products in highly imperfect markets to smallish numbers of (usually professional) buyers. The distorting effects of restrictive agreements and outright attempts to monopolize should be measured against this sort of 'normality'. But the attempts that have been made to provide a theory of this type of economic activity are of but little greater applicability to the diverse reality of modern industry than the old classical model of the 'perfect' market.

Thus the theory of 'monopolistic competition'[3] considers the behaviour of the firm which differentiates its product but still faces the competition of close substitutes. As formulated by Professor Chamberlin this theory showed how, given certain assumptions, price under 'monopolistic competition' would be higher than under 'perfect competition' and how excess capacity would emerge in the industry. The assumptions on which these conclusions were based were, in brief, that each firm would seek to maximize profits and would know enough about demand conditions and the structure of costs to follow the prescription (from monopoly theory) of equating marginal cost and marginal revenue; and that the interaction of different firms' decisions could be ignored.

---

[1] The point may be illustrated by the type of economic activity that comes nearest to the classical model—for example, sales of grain by farmers in a grain exchange. No single farmer can affect the price by withholding his supply, and the going price has to be accepted passively by all. If it is a good price, all the farmers selling in that market on that occasion do well, and if it is a bad price, they all do badly. They would not regard themselves, nor would they be regarded in ordinary language, as 'competing' one against the other, for this concept among laymen implies that some competitors do well while others do badly on the same occasion.

[2] Professor Galbraith deals trenchantly with this point in *American Capitalism*, pp. 15–16.

[3] E. H. Chamberlin, *The Theory of Monopolistic Competition* (Harvard Economic Studies, 38), Harvard University Press, 1932.

Other economists have subsequently challenged the realism of these assumptions. In particular, it has seemed more likely, given free entry, that firms would foresee (and forestall) the danger of inducing new entry by high profits, than that they would foresee the very complex and uncertain pattern of demand and costs accurately enough to achieve the theoretical maximum of revenue. On different assumptions prices may not be set above the competitive level and excess capacity may not appear.[1]

Because it ignores the interaction of firms' decisions, the theory of monopolistic competition as such does not cover oligopolistic situations, but theories intended to deal with these situations have similarly depended on the choice made among rather narrow and arbitrary assumptions. Cournot's formal solution of the duopoly position, for example, according to which the equilibrium price will be above that under competition but below that under monopoly (output being smaller than under competition and greater than under monopoly), assumes that each duopolist proceeds as if his rival will not vary his existing output. Once again, other economists (Bertrand, Edgeworth, Fellner) reach other solutions based on other (as they believe, more realistic) assumptions.

Modern theory starts from the point that each firm in an oligopoly will do best if the total profit of the industry is maximized.[2] The demand for the product of an industry will often be relatively inelastic while the demand for a particular firm's product is highly elastic. People will soon switch from Blogg's paint to Mugg's if there is a price differential, but if all paint goes up, they may accept this as a fact of life and buy much the same amount. It is argued that in these conditions business-men will recognize the folly of competing and tend towards an agreement, overt or tacit, which enables a monopoly price to be charged.

But it is recognized that this proposition rests on very rigid assumptions of short-term profit maximization on the part of sellers with rather static expectations. Even among small groups of suppliers it often happens in practice that some expect to improve their position relatively to others and will not sacrifice their freedom of action for the greater security of agreement. Once again, there are in practice many

[1] See R. F. Harrod, 'Doctrines of Imperfect Competition' and 'Theory of Imperfect Competition Revised', in *Economic Essays*, Macmillan, London, 1952, pp. 111–38 and 139–87; also N. Kaldor, 'Market Imperfection and Excess Capacity', *Economica* (New Series), vol. 2, no. 5, February 1935, p. 33. It should be noted that even if excess capacity were proved to be an *inevitable* concomitant of product differentiation, this would not necessarily be a 'bad thing' economically. As Professor Chamberlin has pointed out, the cost of the excess capacity might be no more than the price willingly paid by the public for the amenity of diversity of products.

[2] See W. Fellner, *Competition Among the Few: Oligopoly and Similar Market Structures*, Alfred A. Knopf, New York, 1949.

uncertainties in the way of correctly assessing marginal revenue and marginal cost so as to maximize joint profits, and errors that pitch prices too high are usually more costly even in the short term than those of overcaution. Moreover, short-term maximization policies often have unhappy long-term consequences, such as encouraging potential competitors, stimulating the development of 'countervailing power' among buyers or in the labour market, holding back the growth of consumption, and so forth. 'Get rich quick' policies are usually held in low repute among businessmen. On balance the supposed tendency for price/output equilibrium under oligopoly to approach that of monopoly probably stops well short of the goal, but there is no saying on theoretical grounds how far short.[1]

Indeed, the difficulty about developing any satisfactory theory to cover the more complex situations of differentiated product competition and oligopoly is that quite vital facts about the making of business decisions in these situations are simply not known, and in consequence realistic assumptions cannot be framed as the basis for theoretical models. Most model solutions, for example, assume that businessmen seek to maximize profits; but do they? Almost certainly not in any short-term sense that would enable the theoretician to find a determinate solution for price/output equilibrium. It may be said that businessmen in fact seek to maximize the long-run profit prospects of their companies (that is, the future net value of the enterprise discounted back to the present). But, if so, the quantities in question are certainly not simple functions of current prices; they are compounded of all manner of 'hunches' about external matters such as the trend of demand, of technical developments, of interest rates and so forth, and as such are useless as tools for the model builder.

It is all part of the same problem that economists are very uncertain about the way in which businessmen decide how much to charge. It can readily be proved that in order to make the most profit the businessman should aim to equate marginal cost and marginal revenue; the calculations necessary to this end involve knowing what the marginal cost of increments to output is, and also what are the demand conditions facing the firm. In practice it is probably rare for businessmen to know these quantities accurately. The well known English empiric study of the 1930s revealed that many businessmen regard it as 'normal' to set their prices so as to cover their full costs and yield a 'fair' margin

---

[1] As is too common in economics, the theory is directed almost exclusively to analysing the effect of oligopoly on price, ignoring other aspects of competition. Even if it were accepted that price under oligopoly approaches that under monopoly, the fact that firms in an oligopoly often compete vigorously in research, in developing new and improved products, in sales methods and so forth would be an important ground for preferring oligopoly to monopoly.

of profit.[1] This so-called 'full cost' principle implies that businessmen take no notice of demand conditions at all in deciding their prices. Further empiric work since the war has suggested modifications of the 'full cost' principle in its pure form; in particular that demand conditions and other factors may enter into the computation of the profit margin or mark-up that the firm can obtain. Other empiric work has shifted the emphasis from the initial determination of prices to the conditions in which firms depart from going prices.[2]

There are many other respects in which vital information about business decisions is lacking. In particular, economists are very much in the dark about the making of investment decisions. Do firms tend to be overcautious about expanding output? Do they tend to plough back profits into their normal line of business even when there might be good prospects of a higher rate of return in some other field? A plausible case could no doubt be made for answering both questions in the affirmative, though two such answers would be plainly incompatible.[3]

These uncertainties about such central matters of business decision as prices and investment illustrate the need for more empiric study of the strategy and operation of modern business. Walton Hamilton has pointed to the influence on economics of the analogy of Newtonian mechanics, whereby the task of economic analysis has been seen as one of constructing models in which opposing 'forces' are shown resolved in equilibrium.[4] As a human and social science, economics would be

---

[1] R. L. Hall and C. J. Hitch, 'Price Theory and Business Behaviour', *Oxford Economic Papers*, no. 2, May 1939, p. 12. Reprinted in T. Wilson and P. W. S. Andrews (eds.), *Oxford Studies in the Price Mechanism*, Clarendon Press, Oxford, 1951, pp. 107–38.

[2] The whole debate is splendidly surveyed in Professor Richard B. Heflebower's article, 'Full Cost, Cost Changes, and Prices', in *Business Concentration and Price Policy*, National Bureau of Economic Research, pp. 361–96. There is, of course, a vast literature on price determination which cannot be cited here: the interested reader will find references to the main sources in the footnotes to Professor Heflebower's article.

[3] See 'Various Views on the Monopoly Problem' by E. S. Mason and others, in *Review of Economics and Statistics*, vol. 31, no. 2, 1949, p. 104, where Professor Carl Kaysen, in developing the theme that the continued stable existence of the firm is the true aim of business policy rather than profit maximization, affirms that in investment decisions loss probabilities tend to be overvalued and profit probabilities undervalued; and Professor Mason, on the other hand, suggests that, while this may be true of decisions about output for which investment is planned, nevertheless firms probably reinvest profits more than to the extent justified by objective analysis of internal and external investment opportunities.

[4] Walton Hamilton wrote: 'The economists were captivated by the Newtonian physics and they set about creating the mechanics of competitive business. To this end they employed a bit of observation, a goodly amount of abstraction and a bountiful measure of the most rigorous logic of the day.' The troubles which have arisen from basing classical economics on mechanics are not dissimilar to those which have arisen from basing traditional logic on Greek geometry. The reader of chapter 4 of Mr Stephen Toulmin's book *The Uses of Argument*, Cambridge University Press, 1958, can hardly fail to be struck by this analogy. Mr Toulmin remarks at one point in his critique of traditional logic: 'This is not to say that

better based on the analogy of anthropology: the study of Polynesian marriage rites would have advanced little without careful observation of Polynesians, and the analysis of industrial markets requires close observation of business operations rather than abstract calculation.

All this has been recognized and in recent years a vast amount of empiric work has been organized and carried out both in the United States and in Britain and elsewhere.[1] The effect of this body of work, however, is more to underline the diversity of real industrial situations and behaviour than to provide a basis for sounder generalization or more sophisticated models. A theory of the firm which would enable predictions to be made about rational investment or pricing behaviour requires a *ceteris paribus* clause of such dimensions as to embrace most of what is interesting about decision making in any particular case. The business strategy of the powerful company in the real world will differ according to the technological state of its industry and, with the increasing importance of 'conglomerate' firms, that of other industries in which it may see investment opportunities; its strategy will be greatly affected by international competition, taking account of existing tariffs and prospective tariff changes, of the chances of joining customs unions and of threats of dumping; it will have to assess innovation and market risks in the light of what is known or guessed about the plans of powerful foreign competitors; its own plans will be affected by domestic (and often foreign) taxation and by guesses about changes in taxation, by its estimate of the course of labour relations and many other external factors.

The combination of all these external circumstances will be specific to the particular industry and often unique to the particular firm. Where it is desired, therefore, to supervise or regulate the exercise of market power on national economic grounds, as distinct from the social and political grounds which underlie antitrust in the United States, it is necessary not only to have an adequate theory or model of industrial behaviour but to undertake very detailed investigations of particular situations in order, first, to understand fully how the powerful company takes its decisions in its private interest, and, secondly, to consider whether the social and national interest requires any change in its behaviour. These are formidable tasks.

the elaborate mathematical systems which constitute "symbolic logic" must now be thrown away; but only that people with intellectual capital invested in them should retain no illusions about the extent of their relevance to practical arguments.' We have only to substitute 'economic theory' for 'symbolic logic' in this quotation to have a pregnant suggestion for economists.

[1] For an empiric study of investment decisions, for example, see J. R. Meyer and E. Kuh, *The Investment Decision* (Harvard Economic Studies, 102), Harvard University Press, 1957.

3. *The concept of workable competition and anti-monopoly policy*

In the United States the problem presented by the diversity of real industrial situations has given rise to the concept of workable competition which has been developed out of a conscious desire by economists to contribute helpfully to antitrust policy.[1] Economists investigating this concept have, for example, seen good sense in some of the pricing policies which the Robinson-Patman Act, on the basis of 'orthodox' price theories, condemns as price discrimination and have noted various long-run factors which mitigate the supposed price raising influence of oligopoly.

But workable competition turns out to be a highly variable and subjective concept. Some economists have adopted it while making only the minimum concessions to realism in their assumptions. Thus Professor Stigler presents as his requirements for workable competition: (i) a considerable number of firms selling closely substitutable products in each market, (ii) no collusion between these firms and (iii) that the long-run average-cost curve for a new entrant is not materially higher than for an established firm.[2] It is clear that many industry patterns in the real world—even in the United States under antitrust—would fail to pass muster by these tests, especially if collusion were read widely to embrace price leadership and 'conscious parallelism'.

Other economists have used the concept of workable competition in contexts which might more accurately be described as workable monopoly. Thus Professor J. W. Markham, though admitting that price stability—due to oligopolistic price leadership among other things—has been a notable feature of the rayon industry, nevertheless concludes that 'no clearly indicated changes effected by public policy would result in greater social gains than social losses'.[3] But this conclusion clearly arises from a value judgment about the facts of the particular case and not because the rayon industry could be brought within previously agreed criteria for workable competition.

To the economic analyst a more fruitful approach might be by way of negative criteria or tests of 'non-workable' competition. Professor Bain, for example, has listed as signs of defective industrial structure: (i) a profit rate consistently higher than the normal return on investment, (ii) many firms in the industry of a scale outside the optimal range, (iii) chronic excess capacity, (iv) selling costs bearing

[1] J. M. Clark, 'Toward a Concept of Workable Competition', *American Economic Review*, vol. 30, no. 2, part 1, June 1940, p. 241.

[2] G. J. Stigler, 'The Extent and Bases of Monopoly', *American Economic Review*, vol. 32, no. 2, part 2, June 1942, p. 1.

[3] J. W. Markham, 'An Alternative Approach to the Concept of Workable Competition', *American Economic Review*, vol. 40, no. 3, June 1950, p. 349.

an abnormally high proportion to total costs, (v) slow response to technical changes.[1] Some of these tests, of course, depend on assumptions about normality—for example in profit rates or selling costs—which could lead to endless argument about the norm for different sets of circumstances. Moreover, even where some of these indications of faulty performance were found in an industry, it might still make sense to assert of it that 'no clearly indicated changes effected by public policy would result in greater social gains than social losses'.

The investigation of the concept of workable competition has been of real value in directing attention to the inadequacies of the conventional models of competition. With particular reference to antitrust, it may also have been helpful in restraining the enforcement agencies from pursuing the type of legal attack on oligopoly as such which at one time seemed likely.[2] The competition-at-any-price school of thought is brought up against a new climate of opinion by these findings of economists of authority: when J. M. Clark, for example, suggests that the best results in terms of industrial efficiency may arise from a moderate number of large, strong and growing concerns with a fringe of smaller specialist manufacturers,[3] or when J. S. Bain suggests that, in an oligopoly pattern, moderately difficult entry into an industry may produce lower prices than easy entry.[4]

But in general it cannot be said that the concept of workable competition has had any great effect on antitrust policy in the United States. The difficulty about any subtle economic diagnosis of the Bain type is that it cannot be applied in a system of 'fair and feasible' law. Bain's criteria of non-workable competition are in effect performance tests, and, as we have seen above, the courts cannot make decisions by reference to economic performance which of its nature may vary over time. The courts have to deal with concepts which can be reduced ultimately to matters of fact—concepts such as intent to monopolize or conspiracy to restrict competition—and cannot base their judgments on such arguable considerations as whether the scale of firms is outside the optimum range or whether their selling costs constitute an excessive proportion of total costs.

Moreover, there has on the whole been little need to introduce arguments about workable competition into the antitrust cases because the decisions of the courts have not seriously attacked the types of industrial structure and behaviour that the theory of workable com-

[1] J. S. Bain, 'Workable Competition in Oligopoly: Theoretical Considerations and Some Empirical Evidence', *American Economic Review*, vol. 40, no. 2, May 1950, p. 35.
[2] See above, Chapter VI, pp. 176–7.
[3] J. M. Clark, 'The Orientation of Antitrust Policy', *American Economic Review*, vol. 40, no. 2, May 1950, p. 93.   [4] J. S. Bain, *loc. cit.*

petition might justify. A great deal of American industry is oligopolistic, but, in the absence of overt collusion,[1] the law has not found means to attack the oligopoly structure of industry as such, even where some restraining effects on price competition, for example through price leadership or mutual canniness, have been indicated.

But the main reason why the doubts thrown by economists like Bain and Clark on simple models of competitive behaviour do not have a large impact on antitrust is that, as has been seen, the rationale of antitrust is essentially a desire to provide legal checks to restrain economic power and is not a pursuit of economic efficiency as such. Consequently, the question asked is not whether antitrust decisions lead to the greatest economic efficiency but whether it can be said, given the non-economic reasons for antitrust policy, that these decisions do any serious economic harm. And since the economic advantages of oligopoly are not on the whole impeded by antitrust decisions, this cannot fairly be said.

4. *Anti-monopoly policy in Britain: Restrictive Trade Practices Act of 1956 and subsequent amendments; the Monopolies Commission*

Outside the United States, and particularly perhaps in Britain, anti-monopoly policy is seen not so much as a matter of placing economic power under legal restraint or as an exercise in checks and balances, but essentially as a means of promoting economic efficiency and the best use of resources. In a relatively small economy highly dependent on international trade (especially where, as in Britain, anxiety about the balance of trade and of payments is unceasing), effectiveness in international competition is likely to loom larger in the minds of policy makers than the effectiveness of competition in the domestic market itself. Moreover the ever present worry about increasing imports in almost every field of manufactured goods, given a liberal system of international trade, makes it seem unlikely that domestic manufacturers will lack whatever stimulus is attributed to the existence of powerful competitors. Against this background the concept of workable competition may appear to be a less useful tool than a realization that, in some situations, the pursuit of competition may conflict with the pursuit of innovation and productivity.

It is outside the scope of this book to analyse at length the economic and industrial evidence that would illustrate this conflict. There is now an extensive literature, both from the academic world and from the official reports of bodies like the Restrictive Practices Court, the Monopolies Commission and the National Board for Prices and Incomes, in which

---

[1] And leaving aside in this context the Clayton Act aspect of antitrust.

actual examples can be studied. But it is important not to take this too far. From the proposition that the economic evidence offers little ground for a blind pursuit of competition *per se*, it by no means follows that industrial markets and business behaviour, as they stand, represent the best of all possible worlds and can safely be left completely unregulated. Competition remains an important means towards a necessary mobility of resources, and private restrictions of competition may still have predatory or protective rather than constructive objectives. In industries where protective tariff barriers are still high, international competition may not be a complete answer to the need for some external stimulus that keeps managements alert to possible reductions in costs and responsive to changing patterns of demand. The problem is essentially one of balance, so that the day-to-day advantages of a competitive environment in challenging the effectiveness of managements are weighed against the advantages for constructive investment and innovation policies of a certain strategic and financial strength and a sufficient security for far-sighted planning.

It is not surprising, therefore, that the forms of anti-monopoly policy and of government regulation of private industry in Britain and other European countries differ markedly from those of antitrust. In Britain in the field of restrictive trade practices—broadly the area covered by section 1 of the Sherman Act—the compromise embodied in the Restrictive Trade Practices Act of 1956 was to introduce a presumption that collusive restrictions operated against the public interest, but to provide that particular collusive agreements could be successfully defended on certain specified economic grounds, provided that the evidence of economic benefit appeared to the court to outweigh the detrimental effect of the restrictions on the public interest. This system has in practice resulted in the abandonment over the years since 1956 of a very large number of those agreements which would have been judged unlawful *per se* under section 1 of the Sherman Act.[1]

One undoubted difficulty about these arrangements is that they have required the Restrictive Practices Court in Britain to assess rival economic arguments and claims in precisely the way that the American courts under antitrust have always sought to avoid. In consequence it is doubtful whether the comparatively few cases in which the Court has found restrictive agreements acceptable in the public interest can be said to exhibit a coherent body of economic doctrine or, more narrowly, to offer practising lawyers a sound basis for advising their clients about kinds of restrictive agreements that may in general be expected to

---

[1] Following the passage of further legislation in 1964 a similar system of a general presumption coupled with possible defences on economic grounds has resulted in the virtual abandonment in the United Kingdom of resale price maintenance for the bulk of consumer goods.

survive the Court's scrutiny. This makes difficult the building up of a 'compliable' body of law in the American sense.

The resulting uncertainty, together with the considerable costs in time and effort of defending agreements before the Court, has led to pressure for some alternative means of permitting restrictive agreements which appear to serve accepted government policies for promoting industrial efficiency and rationalization. The 1956 Act has therefore been amended in the Restrictive Trade Practices Act, 1968, so as to give the Government administrative discretion to withhold from registration (and hence from the jurisdiction of the Court) for a limited period new restrictive agreements which are deemed to serve these national interests.[1] Judgment will have to await experience of the use made in practice of this new power.

The rebuttable presumption (of being contrary to the public interest) in the 1956 Act applies only to collusive restrictive arrangements affecting the supply of goods. In Britain the law is neutral as regards other kinds of exercise of monopoly or market power, but the Government has a discretionary power to refer situations involving monopolistic power (and also collusive restrictive agreements in service industries) to an administrative tribunal, the Monopolies Commission, for investigation and report.[2] Where such a report finds that the monopoly situation, or industrial conduct arising out of it, operates against the public interest, the Government has certain powers to secure remedies.

In this field, too, the problem is seen in Britain as essentially one of striking a balance between conflicting national interests. The possibilities of harm arising from market power are not neglected. Indeed British industrial history is not without examples of powerful firms whose entrenched position in the market has appeared to lead to unadventurous management and policies. It is recognized that market power may be exercised in predatory ways to impede the development of inconvenient but possibly lively and efficient competitors, or simply in ways which protect an entrenched position. On the other hand in a domestic market so much smaller than that of the United States, a

---

[1] This new legislation also strengthened the existing law in some respects, notably by giving the Government discretion to call for the registration (and hence liability to court proceedings) of classes of information agreement. This followed from a belief that some agreements of this kind may have been intended to take the place of price fixing agreements abandoned as a result of the 1956 Act.

[2] Under the Monopolies and Mergers Act, 1965, the Government also has discretion to refer for investigation mergers or acquisitions which may create monopoly situations, and these can be disallowed if the Monopolies Commission finds that the merger or acquisition may be expected to operate against the public interest. These powers have been used sparingly. At the same time the Government has sought, through the Industrial Reorganization Corporation, to promote rationalization and restructuring of British industry where the strength of existing firms has appeared to be inadequate for effective competition in world markets.

substantial concentration of power in the national market may appear to be necessary and inevitable if British firms are to compete effectively in the big international league, and the problem comes to be seen as one of finding appropriate means for checking that the managements invested with substantial power use it constructively for innovation and for improving industrial efficiency.

Ideally—and to a creditable degree in practice—the reports of a body such as the Monopolies Commission should enable the Government to hold a balance between the need to have, in many industries, firms of sufficient size and strength to make the huge investments and development expenditures required for effective international competition, and the desire to avoid predatory or protective conduct which may impede the advance of livelier managements in smaller firms while leading in time to a loss of dynamism in the dominant ones.

As mentioned earlier, however, the difficulty of distilling an acceptable body of economic theory from the vast diversity of actual industrial situations, and the consequent need to investigate and analyse in great detail the full circumstances of each particular situation, make this a formidable task, and present Governments in turn with the near-impossible one of measuring the costs and benefits of intervention. Moreover, the balance between the dangers and advantages of market power may well change over time—large organizations often appear to reach a peak of achievement and then go 'over the hump'—and may depend crucially on non-economic factors such as the abilities (and availability) of particular individuals to continue to lead and organize firms successfully through changes in external circumstances.

In addition to analysing British experience in this field, the student will no doubt wish to compare other approaches to the problems, for example, the post-war developments of German cartel law, and such case law as emerges under the Treaty of Rome's provisions concerning the 'dominant firm'.[1] It may well be—and many American observers would hold—that in Europe the belief in the superior efficiency of larger industrial organizations is overdone and that, even on narrow economic grounds, a regime more favourable to competition would be likely to produce livelier managements and a higher rate of growth of productivity. The subject is peculiarly liable to swings of fashion, and it will take time to see whether some of the new conglomerate giants prove themselves by their industrial performance over a period.

Perhaps the principal lesson of a study of American antitrust is that the attempt to base government regulation of industry on a sophisticated

---

[1] A convenient and valuable summary of national laws and administration in (broadly) the OECD countries up to about 1964 is provided by Corwin D. Edwards, *Trade Regulation Overseas*, Oceana Publications, New York, 1966.

economic analysis of particular situations, given the immense diversity of the industrial scene in an advanced economy, is incompatible with the antitrust ideal of a system of 'fair and feasible' law. The characteristic feature of the Sherman Act is its reliance on definite prohibitions—in effect on *per se* rules which the courts have distilled over the years from the generalized form of prohibitions in the Act itself. No exceptions are admitted to these prohibitions and they can be established by evidence of fact without requiring any assessment of economic advantage. The impressive tradition of the American courts after nearly eighty years' experience with the Sherman Act is against the admission of economic argument in the cases. So strong and unanimous is this tradition that, if enforcement of any law on restraint of trade is sought through the courts, it can be ignored only at peril. The American judges have had good reason for their view that the confrontation of economic experts on both sides of the case would not lead to clear and easily applicable decisions. Hence they have restricted themselves to facts about the existence of collusion and of restrictive intent, and have left it at that.

There are two great, perhaps decisive, advantages about clear, exceptionless prohibitions of restrictive arrangements, that is, of *per se* rules on the model of antitrust. The first is that they secure that the law will be enforced by the lawyers advising businessmen, and the bulk of the enforcement problem is overcome in this way. The second is that clear and easily understood prohibitions are fair to the business community, which knows where it stands and what are the limits which must not be overstepped. No administrative tribunal or economic inquiry can be expected to provide a basis for general rules of this kind.

The other side of the coin is that antitrust rests on a commitment to competition which, as has been suggested above, is in large part non-economic in origin and motivation, but which it is hard to show has in practice produced economic damage in the American context. In other countries with smaller domestic markets and a far greater dependence on international trade, a rule of law based on this commitment may well be inconsistent with the need to make the best use of economic resources. But this means that forms of government regulation have to be found which rest on something other than clear and compliable law.

MERGER GUIDELINES

issued by the United States Department of Justice

1. *Purpose.* The purpose of these guidelines is to acquaint the business community, the legal profession, and other interested groups and individuals with the standards currently being applied by the Department of Justice in determining whether to challenge corporate acquisitions and mergers under section 7 of the Clayton Act. (Although mergers or acquisitions may also be challenged under the Sherman Act, commonly the challenge will be made under section 7 of the Clayton Act and, accordingly, it is to this provision of law that the guidelines are directed.) The responsibilities of the Department of Justice under section 7 are those of an enforcement agency, and these guidelines are announced solely as a statement of current Department policy, subject to change at any time without prior notice, for whatever assistance such statement may be in enabling interested persons to anticipate in a general way Department enforcement action under section 7. Because the statements of enforcement policy contained in these guidelines must necessarily be framed in rather general terms, and because the critical factors in any particular guideline formulation may be evaluated differently by the Department than by the parties, the guidelines should not be treated as a substitute for the Department's business review procedures, which make available statements of the Department's present enforcement intentions with regard to particular proposed mergers or acquisitions.

2. *General Enforcement Policy.* Within the overall scheme of the Department's antitrust enforcement activity, the primary role of section 7 enforcement is to preserve and promote market structures conducive to competition. Market structure is the focus of the Department's merger policy chiefly because the conduct of the individual firms in a market tends to be controlled by the structure of that market, i.e. by those market conditions which are fairly permanent or subject only to slow change (such as, principally, the number of substantial firms selling in the market, the relative sizes of their respective market shares, and the substantiality of barriers to the entry of new firms into the market). Thus, for example, a concentrated market structure, where a few firms account for a large share of the sales, tends to discourage vigorous price competition by the firms in the market and to encourage other kinds of conduct, such as use of inefficient methods of production or excessive promotional expenditures, of an economically undesirable nature. Moreover, not only does emphasis on market structure generally produce economic predictions that are fully adequate for the purposes of a statute that requires only a showing that the effect of a merger 'may be substantially to lessen competition, or to tend to create a monopoly,' but an enforcement policy

emphasizing a limited number of structural factors also facilitates both enforcement decision-making and business planning which involves anticipation of the Department's enforcement intent. Accordingly, the Department's enforcement activity under section 7 is directed primarily toward the identification and prevention of those mergers which alter market structure in ways likely now or eventually to encourage or permit non-competitive conduct.

In certain exceptional circumstances, however, the structural factors used in these guidelines will not alone be conclusive, and the Department's enforcement activity will necessarily be based on a more complex and inclusive evaluation. This is sometimes the case, for example, where basic technological changes are creating new industries, or are significantly transforming older industries, in such fashion as to make current market boundaries and market structure of uncertain significance. In such unusual transitional situations application of the normal guideline standards may be inappropriate; and on assessing probable future developments, the Department may not sue despite nominal application of a particular guideline, or it may sue even though the guidelines, as normally applied, do not require the Department to challenge the merger. Similarly, in the area of conglomerate merger activity, the present incomplete state of knowledge concerning structure-conduct relationships may preclude sole reliance on the structural criteria used in these guidelines, as explained in paragraphs 17 and 20 below.

3. *Market Definition.* A rational appraisal of the probable competitive effects of a merger normally requires definition of one or more relevant markets. A market is any grouping of sales (or other commercial transactions) in which each of the firms whose sales are included enjoys some advantage in competing with those firms whose sales are not included. The advantage need not be great, for so long as it is significant it defines an area of effective competition among the included sellers in which the competition of the excluded sellers is, *ex hypothesi*, less effective. The process of market definition may result in identification of several appropriate markets in which to test the probable competitive effects of a particular merger.

A market is defined both in terms of its product dimension ('line of commerce') and its geographic dimension ('section of the country').

(i) *Line of commerce.* The sales of any product or service which is distinguishable as a matter of commercial practice from other products or services will ordinarily constitute a relevant product market, even though, from the standpoint of most purchasers, other products may be reasonably, but not perfectly, interchangeable with it in terms of price, quality, and use. On the other hand, the sales of two distinct products to a particular group of purchasers can also appropriately be grouped into a single market where the two products are reasonably interchangeable for that group in terms of price, quality, and use. In this latter case, however, it may be necessary also to include in that market the sales of one or more other products which are equally interchangeable with the two products in terms of price, quality, and use from the standpoint of that group of purchasers for whom the two products are interchangeable.

The reasons for employing the foregoing definitions may be stated as follows. In enforcing section 7 the Department seeks primarily to prevent mergers which change market structure in a direction likely to create a power to behave non-competitively in the production and sale of any particular product, even though that power will ultimately be limited, though not nullified, by the presence of other similar products that, while reasonably interchangeable, are less than perfect substitutes. It is in no way inconsistent with this effort also to pursue a policy designed to prohibit mergers between firms selling distinct products where the result of the merger may be to create or enhance the companies' market power due to the fact that the products, though not perfectly substitutable by purchasers, are significant enough alternatives to constitute substantial competitive influences on the production, development or sale of each.

(ii) *Section of the country.* The total sales of a product or service in any commercially significant section of the country (even as small as a single community), or aggregate of such sections, will ordinarily constitute a geographic market if firms engaged in selling the product make significant sales of the product to purchasers in the section or sections. The market need not be enlarged beyond any section meeting the foregoing test unless it clearly appears that there is no economic barrier (e.g. significant transportation costs, lack of distribution facilities, customer inconvenience, or established consumer preference for existing products) that hinders the sale from outside the section to purchasers within the section; nor need the market be contracted to exclude some portion of the product sales made inside any section meeting the foregoing test unless it clearly appears that the portion of sales in question is made to a group of purchasers separated by a substantial economic barrier from the purchasers to whom the rest of the sales are made.

Because data limitations or other intrinsic difficulties will often make precise delineation of geographic markets impossible, there may often be two or more groupings of sales which may reasonably be treated as constituting a relevant geographic market. In such circumstances, the Department believes it to be ordinarily most consistent with the purposes of section 7 to challenge any merger which appears to be illegal in any reasonable geographic market, even though in another reasonable market it would not appear to be illegal.

The market is ordinarily measured primarily by the dollar value of the sales or other transactions (e.g. shipments, leases) for the most recent twelve month period for which the necessary figures for the merging firms and their competitors are generally available. Where such figures are clearly unrepresentative, a different period will be used. In some markets, such as commercial banking, it is more appropriate to measure the market by other indicia, such as total deposits.

I. HORIZONTAL MERGERS

4. *Enforcement Policy.* With respect to mergers between direct competitors (i.e. horizontal mergers), the Department's enforcement activity under section 7 of the Clayton Act has the following interrelated purposes: (i) preventing elimination as an independent business entity of any company likely to have been a substantial competitive influence in a market; (ii) preventing any company or small group of companies from obtaining a position of dominance in a market; (iii) preventing significant increases in concentration in a market; and (iv) preserving significant possibilities for eventual deconcentration in a concentrated market.

In enforcing section 7 against horizontal mergers, the Department accords primary significance to the size of the market share held by both the acquiring and the acquired firms. ('Acquiring firm' and 'acquired firm' are used herein, in the case of horizontal mergers, simply as convenient designations of the firm with the larger market share and the firm with the smaller share, respectively, and do not refer to the legal form of the merger transaction.) The larger the market share held by the acquired firm, the more likely it is that the firm has been a substantial competitive influence in the market or that concentration in the market will be significantly increased. The larger the market share held by the acquiring firm, the more likely it is that an acquisition will move it toward, or further entrench it in, a position of dominance or of shared market power. Accordingly, the standards most often applied by the Department in determining whether to challenge horizontal mergers can be stated in terms of the sizes of the merging firms' market shares.

5. *Market Highly Concentrated.* In a market in which the shares of the four largest firms amount to approximately 75 % or more, the Department will ordinarily challenge mergers between firms accounting for, approximately, the following percentages of the market:

Acquiring firm	Acquired firm
4 %	4 % or more
10 %	2 % or more
15 % or more	1 % or more

(Percentages not shown in the above table should be interpolated proportionately to the percentages that are shown.)

6. *Market Less Highly Concentrated.* In a market in which the shares of the four largest firms amount to less than approximately 75 %, the Department will ordinarily challenge mergers between firms accounting for, approximately, the following percentages of the market:

Acquiring firm	Acquired firm
5%	5% or more
10%	4% or more
15%	3% or more
20%	2% or more
25% or more	1% or more

(Percentages not shown in the above table should be interpolated proportionately to the percentages that are shown.)

7. *Market With Trend Toward Concentration.* The Department applies an additional, stricter standard in determining whether to challenge mergers occuring in any market, not wholly unconcentrated, in which there is a significant trend toward increased concentration. Such a trend is considered to be present when the aggregate market share of any grouping of the largest firms in the market from the two largest to the eight largest has increased by approximately 7% or more of the market over a period of time extending from any base year 5–10 years prior to the merger (excluding any year in which some abnormal fluctuation in market shares occurred) up to the time of the merger. The Department will ordinarily challenge any acquisition, by any firm in a grouping of such largest firms showing the requisite increase in market share, of any firm whose market share amounts to approximately 2% or more.

8. *Non-Market Share Standards.* Although in enforcing section 7 against horizontal mergers the Department attaches primary importance to the market shares of the merging firms, achievement of the purposes of section 7 occasionally requires the Department to challenge mergers which would not be challenged under the market share standards of paragraphs 5, 6 and 7. The following are the two most common instances of this kind in which a challenge by the Department can ordinarily be anticipated:

(a) acquisition of a competitor which is a particularly 'disturbing', 'disruptive', or otherwise unusually competitive factor in the market; and

(b) a merger involving a substantial firm and a firm which, despite an insubstantial market share, possesses an unusual competitive potential or has an asset that confers an unusual competitive advantage (for example, the acquisition by a leading firm of a newcomer having a patent on a significantly improved product or production process).

There may also be certain horizontal mergers between makers of distinct products regarded as in the same line of commerce for reasons expressed in paragraph 3 (i) where some modification in the minimum market shares subject to challenge may be appropriate to reflect the imperfect substitutability of the two products.

9. *Failing Company.* A merger which the Department would otherwise challenge will ordinarily not be challenged if: (i) the resources of one of the merging firms are so depleted and its prospects for rehabilitation so remote that the firm faces the clear probability of a business failure, and (ii) good faith efforts by the failing firm have failed to elicit a reasonable offer of acquisition more consistent with the purposes of section 7 by a firm which intends to keep the failing firm in the market. The Department regards as failing only those firms with no reasonable prospect of remaining viable; it does not regard a firm as failing merely because the firm has been unprofitable for a period of time, has lost market position or failed to maintain its competitive position in some other respect, has poor management, or has not fully explored the possibility of overcoming its difficulties through self-help.

In determining the applicability of the above standard to the acquisition of a failing division of a multi-market company, such factors as the difficulty in assessing the viability of a portion of a company, the possibility of arbitrary accounting practices, and the likelihood that an otherwise healthy company can rehabilitate one of its parts, will lead the Department to apply this standard only in the clearest of circumstances.

10. *Economies.* Unless there are exceptional circumstances, the Department will not accept as a justification for an acquisition normally subject to challenge under its horizontal merger standards the claim that the merger will produce economies (i.e. improvements in efficiency) because, among other reasons: (i) the Department's adherence to the standards will usually result in no challenge being made to mergers of the kind most likely to involve companies operating significantly below the size necessary to achieve significant economies of scale; (ii) where substantial economies are potentially available to a firm, they can normally be realized through internal expansion; and (iii) there usually are severe difficulties in accurately establishing the existence and magnitude of economies claimed for a merger.

II. VERTICAL MERGERS

11. *Enforcement Policy.* With respect to vertical mergers (i.e. acquisitions 'backward' into a supplying market or 'forward' into a purchasing market), the Department's enforcement activity under section 7 of the Clayton Act, as in the merger field generally, is intended to prevent changes in market structure that are likely to lead over the course of time to significant anti-competitive consequences. In general, the Department believes that such consequences can be expected to occur whenever a particular vertical acquisition, or series of acquisitions, by one or more of the firms in a supplying or purchasing market, tends significantly to raise barriers to entry in either market or to disadvantage existing non-integrated or partly integrated firms in either market in ways unrelated to economic efficiency. (Barriers to entry are relatively stable market conditions which tend to increase the difficulty of potential competitors' entering the market as new sellers and which thus

tend to limit the effectiveness of the potential competitors both as a restraint upon the behavior of firms in the market and as a source of additional actual competition.)

Barriers to entry resting on such factors as economies of scale in production and distribution are not questionable as such. But vertical mergers tend to raise barriers to entry in undesirable ways, particularly the following: (i) by foreclosing equal access to potential customers, thus reducing the ability of non-integrated firms to capture competitively the market share needed to achieve an efficient level of production, or imposing the burden of entry on an integrated basis (i.e. at both the supplying and purchasing levels) even though entry at a single level would permit efficient operation; (ii) by foreclosing equal access to potential suppliers, thus either increasing the risk of a price or supply squeeze on the new entrant or imposing the additional burden of entry as an integrated firm; or (iii) by facilitating promotional product differentiation, when the merger involves a manufacturing firm's acquisition of firms at the retail level. Besides impeding the entry of new sellers, the foregoing consequences of vertical mergers, if present, also artificially inhibit the expansion of presently competing sellers by conferring on the merged firm competitive advantages, unrelated to real economies of production or distribution, over non-integrated or partly integrated firms. While it is true that in some instances vertical integration may raise barriers to entry or disadvantage existing competitors only as the result of the achievement of significant economies of production or distribution (as, for example, where the increase in barriers is due to achievement of economies of integrated production through an alteration of the structure of the plant as well as of the firm), integration accomplished by a large vertical merger will usually raise entry barriers or disadvantage competitors to an extent not accounted for by, and wholly disproportionate to, such economies as may result from the merger.

It is, of course, difficult to identify with precision all circumstances in which vertical mergers are likely to have adverse effects on market structure of the kinds indicated in the previous paragraph. The Department believes, however, that the most important aims of its enforcement policy on vertical mergers can be satisfactorily stated by guidelines framed primarily in terms of the market shares of the merging firms and the conditions of entry which already exist in the relevant markets. These factors will ordinarily serve to identify most of the situations in which any of the various possible adverse effects of vertical mergers may occur and be of substantial competitive significance. With all vertical mergers it is necessary to consider the probable competitive consequences of the merger in both the market in which the supplying firm sells and the market in which the purchasing firm sells, although a significant adverse effect in either market will ordinarily result in a challenge by the Department. ('Supplying firm' and 'purchasing firm', as used herein, refer to the two parties to the vertical merger transaction, the former of which sells a product in a market in which the latter buys that product.)

12. *Supplying Firm's Market.* In determining whether to challenge a vertical merger on the ground that it may significantly lessen existing or potential competition in the supplying firm's market, the Department attaches primary significance to (i) the market share of the supplying firm, (ii) the market share of the purchasing firm or firms, and (iii) the conditions of entry in the purchasing firm's market. Accordingly, the Department will ordinarily challenge a merger or series of mergers between a supplying firm, accounting for approximately 10 % or more of the sales in its market, and one or more purchasing firms, accounting *in toto* for approximately 6 % or more of the total purchases in that market, unless it clearly appears that there are no significant barriers to entry into the business of the purchasing firm or firms.

13. *Purchasing Firm's Market.* Although the standard of paragraph 12 is designed to identify vertical mergers having likely anticompetitive effects in the supplying firm's market, adherence by the Department to that standard will also normally result in challenges being made to most of the vertical mergers which may have adverse effects in the purchasing firm's market (i.e. that market comprised of the purchasing firm and its competitors engaged in resale of the supplying firm's product or in the sale of a product whose manufacture requires the supplying firm's product) since adverse effects in the purchasing firm's market will normally occur only as a result of significant vertical mergers involving supplying firms with market shares in excess of 10 %. There remain, however, some important situations in which vertical mergers which are not subject to challenge under paragraph 12 (ordinarily because the purchasing firm accounts for less than 6 % of the purchases in the supplying firm's market) will nonetheless be challenged by the Department on the ground that they raise entry barriers in the purchasing firm's market, or disadvantage the purchasing firm's competitors, by conferring upon the purchasing firm a significant supply advantage over unintegrated or partly integrated existing competitors or over potential competitors. The following paragraph sets forth the enforcement standard governing the most common of these situations.

If the product sold by the supplying firm and its competitors is either a complex one in which innovating changes by the various suppliers have been taking place, or is a scarce raw material or other product whose supply cannot be readily expanded to meet increased demand, the merged firm may have the power to use any temporary superiority, or any shortage, in the product of the supplying firm to put competitors of the purchasing firm at a disadvantage by refusing to sell the product to them (supply squeeze) or by narrowing the margin between the price at which it sells the product to the purchasing firm's competitors and the price at which the end-product is sold by the purchasing firm (price squeeze). Even where the merged firm has sufficient market power to impose a squeeze, it may well not always be economically rational for it actually to do so; but the Department believes that the increase in barriers to entry in the purchasing firm's market arising simply from the increased risk of a possible squeeze is sufficient to warrant prohibition of any merger between a supplier possessing significant market power and a substantial purchaser of any product meeting the above description. Accordingly, where such a product is a significant feature or ingredient of the end-product manufactured by the purchasing firm and its competitors, the Department will ordinarily challenge a merger or series of mergers between a supplying firm, accounting for approximately 20 % or more of the sales in its market, and a purchasing firm or firms, accounting *in toto* for approximately 10 % or more of the sales in the market in which it sells the product whose manufacture requires the supplying firm's product.

14. *Non-Market Share Standards*

(a) Although in enforcing section 7 against vertical mergers the Department attaches primary importance to the market shares of the merging firms and the conditions of entry in the relevant markets, achievement of the purposes of section 7 occasionally requires the Department to challenge mergers which would not be challenged under the market share standards of paragraphs 12 and 13. Clearly the most common instances in which challenge by the Department can ordinarily be anticipated are acquisitions of suppliers or customers by major firms in an industry in which: (i) there has been, or is developing, a significant trend toward vertical integration by merger such that the trend, if unchallenged, would probably raise barriers to entry or impose a competitive disadvantage on unintegrated or partly integrated firms, and (ii) it does not clearly appear that the particular acquisition will result in significant economies of production or distribution unrelated to advertising or other promotional economies.

(b) A less common special situation in which a challenge by the Department can ordinarily be anticipated is the acquisition by a firm of a customer or supplier for the purpose of increasing the difficulty of potential competitors in entering the market of either the acquiring or acquired firm, or for the purpose of putting competitors of either the acquiring or acquired firm at an unwarranted disadvantage.

15. *Failing Company.* The standards set forth in paragraph 9 are applied by the Department in determining whether to challenge a vertical merger.

16. *Economies.* Unless there are exceptional circumstances, and except as noted in paragraph 14(a), the Department will not accept as a justification for an acquisition normally subject to challenge under its vertical merger standards the claim that the merger will produce economies, because, among other reasons: (i) where substantial economies of vertical integration are potentially available to a firm, they can normally be realized through internal expansion into the supplying or purchasing market; and (ii) where barriers prevent entry into the supplying or purchasing market by internal expansion, the Department's adherence to the vertical merger standards will in any event usually result in no challenge being made to the acquisition of a firm or firms of sufficient size to overcome or adequately minimize the barriers to entry.

III. CONGLOMERATE MERGERS

17. *Enforcement Policy.* Conglomerate mergers are mergers that are neither horizontal nor vertical as those terms are used in sections I and II, respectively, of these guidelines. (It should be noted that a market extension merger, i.e. one involving two firms selling the same product, but in different geographic markets, is classified as a conglomerate merger.) As with other kinds of mergers, the purpose of the Department's enforcement activity regarding conglomerate mergers is to prevent changes in market structure that appear likely over the course of time to cause a substantial lessening of the competition that would otherwise exist or to create a tendency toward monopoly.

At the present time, the Department regards two categories of conglomerate mergers as having sufficiently identifiable anticompetitive effects as to be the subject of relatively specific structural guidelines: mergers involving potential entrants (paragraph 18) and mergers creating a danger of reciprocal buying (paragraph 19).

Another important category of conglomerate mergers that will frequently be the subject of enforcement action—mergers which for one or more of several reasons threaten to entrench or enhance the market power of the acquired firm—is described generally in paragraph 20.

As paragraph 20 makes clear, enforcement action will also be taken against still other types of conglomerate mergers that on specific analysis appear anticompetitive. The fact that, as yet, the Department does not believe it useful to describe such other types of mergers in terms of a few major elements of market structure should in no sense be regarded as indicating that enforcement action will not be taken. Nor is it to be assumed that mergers of the type described in paragraphs 18 and 19, but not covered by the specific rules thereof, may not be the subject of enforcement action if specific analysis indicates that they appear anticompetitive.

18. *Mergers Involving Potential Entrants*

(a) Since potential competition (i.e. the threat of entry, either through internal expansion or through acquisition and expansion of a small firm, by firms not already or only marginally in the market) may often be the most significant competitive limitation on the exercise of market power by leading firms, as well as the most likely source of additional actual competition, the Department will ordinarily challenge any merger between one of the most likely entrants into the market and (i) any firm with approximately 25 % or more of the market; (ii) one of the two largest firms in a market in which the shares of the two largest firms amount to approximately 50 % or more; (iii) one of the four largest firms in a market in which the shares of the eight largest firms amount to approximately 75 % or more, provided the merging firm's share of the market amounts to approximately 10 % or more; or (iv) one of the eight largest firms in a market in which the shares of these firms amount to approximately 75 % or more, provided either (A) the merging firm's share of the market is not insubstantial and there are no more than one or two likely entrants into the market, or (B) the merging firm is a rapidly growing firm.

In determining whether a firm is one of the most likely potential entrants into a market, the Department accords primary significance to the firm's capability of entering on a competitively significant scale relative to the capability of other firms (i.e. the technological and financial resources available to it) and to the firm's economic incentive to enter (evidenced by, for example, the general attractiveness of the market in terms of risk and profit; or any special relationship of the firm to the market; or the firm's manifested interest in entry; or the natural expansion pattern of the firm; or the like).

(*b*) The Department will also ordinarily challenge a merger between an existing competitor in a market and a likely entrant, undertaken for the purpose of preventing the competitive 'disturbance' or 'disruption' that such entry might create.

(*c*) Unless there are exceptional circumstances, the Department will not accept as a justification for a merger inconsistent with the standards of this paragraph 18 the claim that the merger will produce economies, because, among other reasons, the Department believes that equivalent economies can be normally achieved either through internal expansion or through a small firm acquisition or other acquisition not inconsistent with the standards herein.

19. *Mergers Creating Danger of Reciprocal Buying.*

(*a*) Since reciprocal buying (i.e. favoring one's customer when making purchases of a product which is sold by the customer) is an economically unjustified business practice which confers a competitive advantage on the favored firm unrelated to the merits of its product, the Department will ordinarily challenge any merger which creates a significant danger of reciprocal buying. Unless it clearly appears that some special market factor makes remote the possibility that reciprocal buying behavior will actually occur, the Department considers that a significant danger of reciprocal buying is present whenever approximately 15 % or more of the total purchases in a market in which one of the merging firms ('the selling firm') sells are accounted for by firms which also make substantial sales in markets where the other merging firm ('the buying firm') is both a substantial buyer and a more substantial buyer than all or most of the competitors of the selling firm.

(*b*) The Department will also ordinarily challenge: (i) any merger undertaken for the purpose of facilitating the creation of reciprocal buying arrangements, and (ii) any merger creating the possibility of any substantial reciprocal buying where one (or both) of the merging firms has within the recent past, or the merged firm has after consummation of the merger, actually engaged in reciprocal buying, or attempted directly or indirectly to induce firms with which it deals to engage in reciprocal buying, in the product markets in which the possibility of reciprocal buying has been created.

(*c*) Unless there are exceptional circumstances, the Department will not

accept as a justification for a merger creating a significant danger of reciprocal buying the claim that the merger will produce economies, because,
among other reasons, the Department believes that in general equivalent
economies can be achieved by the firms involved through other mergers not
inconsistent with the standards of this paragraph 19.

20. *Mergers Which Entrench Market Power and Other Conglomerate Mergers.* The
Department will ordinarily investigate the possibility of anticompetitive
consequences, and may in particular circumstances bring suit, where an
acquisition of a leading firm in a relatively concentrated or rapidly concen-
trating market may serve to entrench or increase the market power of that
firm or raise barriers to entry in that market. Examples of this type of merger
include: (i) a merger which produces a very large disparity in absolute
size between the merged firm and the largest remaining firms in the relevant
markets; (ii) a merger of firms producing related products which may induce
purchasers, concerned about the merged firm's possible use of leverage, to
buy products of the merged firm rather than those of competitors; and (iii) a
merger which may enhance the ability of the merged firm to increase product
differentiation in the relevant markets.

Generally speaking, the conglomerate merger area involves novel problems that have not yet been subjected to as extensive or sustained analysis
as those presented by horizontal and vertical mergers. It is for this reason
that the Department's enforcement policy regarding the foregoing category
of conglomerate mergers cannot be set forth with greater specificity. Moreover, the conglomerate merger field as a whole is one in which the Department considers it necessary, to a greater extent than with horizontal and
vertical mergers, to carry on a continuous analysis and study of the ways in
which mergers may have significant anticompetitive consequences in circumstances beyond those covered by these guidelines. For example, the Department has used section 7 to prevent mergers which may diminish long-run
possibilities of enhanced competition resulting from technological developments that may increase interproduct competition between industries whose
products are presently relatively imperfect substitutes. Other areas where
enforcement action will be deemed appropriate may also be identified on a
case-by-case basis; and as a result of continuous analysis and study the
Department may identify other categories of mergers that can be the subject
of specific guidelines.

21. *Failing Company.* The standards set forth in paragraph 9 are normally
applied by the Department in determining whether to challenge a conglomerate merger, except that in marginal cases involving the application of
paragraph 18(*a*) (iii) and (iv) the Department may deem it inappropriate
to sue under section 7 even though the acquired firm is not 'failing' in the
strict sense.

LIST OF WORKS CITED

I. BOOKS, ARTICLES AND SERIAL PUBLICATIONS

Adelman, M. A. 'The A. & P. Case: a Study in Applied Economic Theory', *Quarterly Journal of Economics*, vol. 63, no. 2, May 1949, p. 238.
   'Integration and Antitrust Policy', *Harvard Law Review*, vol. 63, part I, 1949, p. 27.
American Bar Association. *Proceedings of the Antitrust Section of the American Bar Association* (*A.B.A. Antitrust Section, Proceedings*) (now *Antitrust Law Journal*) *passim*.
   'Symposium on State Antitrust Laws', *A.B.A. Antitrust Section, Proceedings*, vol. 29, 1965, p. 255.
Anon. 'Eine kleine juristische Schlummergeschichte', *Harvard Law Review*, vol. 79, 1965, p. 921.
Bain, J. S. 'Workable Competition in Oligopoly: Theoretical Considerations and Some Empirical Evidence', *American Economic Review*, vol. 40, no. 2, May 1950, p. 35.
Bok, D. C. 'Section 7 of the Clayton Act and the Merging of Law and Economics', *Harvard Law Review*, vol. 74, 1960, p. 226.
   'The Tampa Electric Case and the problem of exclusive arrangements under the Clayton Act', *Supreme Court Review 1961* (University of Chicago), p. 267.
Bowman, Ward, Jr. 'Toward Less Monopoly', *University of Pennsylvania Law Review*, vol. 101, no. 5, March 1953, p. 577.
Brandeis, L. D. *The Curse of Bigness* (New York: Viking Press), 1934.
Brewster, Kingman, Jr. *Antitrust and American Business Abroad* (New York: McGraw-Hill), 1958.
   'Enforceable Competition: Unruly Reason or Reasonable Rules?', *American Economic Review*, vol. 46, no. 2, May 1956, p. 482.
Brown, H. Templeton. 'Monopoly—the 1953 Model' in *Lectures on federal antitrust laws: 1953*, Michigan University Law School, q.v.
Buck, S. J. *The Granger Movement* (Cambridge, Mass.: Harvard University Press), 1913.
Chamberlin, E. H. (ed.) *Monopoly and Competition and their Regulation* (London: Macmillan), 1954, *passim*.
Chamberlin, E. H. 'Measuring the Degree of Monopoly and Competition' in *Monopoly and Competition and their Regulation*, Chamberlin, E. H. (ed.), q.v.
   The Theory of Monopolistic Competition, Harvard Economic Studies, 38, 1st ed. (Cambridge, Mass.: Harvard University Press), 1932.
Clark, J. M. 'Toward a Concept of Workable Competition', *American Economic Review*, vol. 30, no. 2, part 1, June 1940, p. 241.
   'The Orientation of Antitrust Policy', *American Economic Review*, vol. 40, no. 2, May 1950, p. 93.

Commerce Clearing House, Chicago, see Index of Cases, p. 511 below.

Dirlam, J. B. and Kahn, A. E. *Fair Competition: the Law and Economics of Antitrust Policy* (Ithaca, N.Y.: Cornell University Press), 1954.

Edwards, C. D. 'The Effect of Recent Basing Point Decisions upon Business Practices', *American Economic Review*, vol. 38, no. 5, December 1948, p. 828.

Maintaining Competition (New York: McGraw-Hill), 1949.

'Conglomerate Bigness as a Source of Power' in *Business Concentration and Price Policy*, National Bureau of Economic Research, q.v.

The Price Discrimination Law (Washington, D.C.: Brookings Institution) 1959.

Trade Regulation Overseas (New York: Oceana Publications), 1966.

Edwards, C. D. and others. 'Comments and Discussion' in *Robinson–Patman Act Symposium for 1947*, New York State Bar Association (q.v.), pp. 57–8.

Evely, R. and Little, I. M. D. *Concentration in British Industry*, NIESR Economic and Social Studies XVI (Cambridge: University Press), 1960.

Fellner, W. *Competition among the Few: Oligopoly and Similar Market Structures* (New York: Alfred A. Knopf), 1949.

Fetter, F. A. 'Exit Basing Point Pricing', *American Economic Review*, vol. 38, no. 5, December 1948, p. 815.

Frost, G. E. 'Legal Incidents of Non-use of Patented Inventions Reconsidered', *George Washington Law Review*, vol. 14, 1946.

'Misuse of Patents in Relation to the Patent Code' in *Lectures on federal antitrust laws: 1953*, Michigan University Law School, q.v.

'The Supreme Court and Patent Abuse', *A.B.A. Antitrust Section, Proceedings* (q.v.), vol. 29, 1965, p. 122.

Galbraith, J. K. 'Monopoly and the Concentration of Economic Power' in *A Survey of Contemporary Economics*, Ellis, H. S. (ed.) (Philadelphia: Blakiston), 1948.

American Capitalism: the Concept of Countervailing Power (Boston: Houghton Mifflin), 1952.

Haight, G. W. 'International Law and Extraterritorial Application of the Antitrust Laws', *Yale Law Journal*, vol. 63, 1954, p. 639.

Hall, R. L. and Hitch, C. J. 'Price Theory and Business Behaviour', *Oxford Economic Papers*, no. 2, May 1939, p. 12, reprinted in *Oxford Studies in the Price Mechanism*, Wilson, T. and Andrews, P. W. S. (eds.) (Oxford: Clarendon Press), 1951.

Handler, M. 'Contract, Combination and Conspiracy', *A.B.A. Antitrust Section, Proceedings* (q.v.), vol. 3, 1953, p. 38.

Harrod, R. F. 'Doctrines of Imperfect Competition' and 'Theory of Imperfect Competition Revised' in *Economic Essays* (London: Macmillan), 1952.

Heflebower, R. B. 'Monopoly and Competition in the United States of America' in *Monopoly and Competition and their Regulation*, Chamberlin, E. H. (ed.), q.v.

'Full Cost, Cost Changes and Prices' in *Business Concentration and Price Policy*, National Bureau of Economic Research, q.v.

Hollabaugh, M. A. 'Recent Antitrust Developments Affecting Patents' in *Lectures on federal antitrust laws: 1953*, Michigan University Law School, q.v.

Kaldor, N. 'Market Imperfection and Excess Capacity', *Economica* (New Series), vol. 2, no. 5, February 1935, p. 33.

Kaplan, A. D. H. *Big Enterprise in a Competitive System* (Washington, D.C.: Brookings Institution), 1954.

Kaysen, C. 'Basing Point Pricing and Public Policy', *Quarterly Journal of Economics*, vol. 63, no. 3, August 1949, p. 289.

United States v. *United Shoe Machinery Corporation*, Harvard Economic Studies, 99 (Cambridge, Mass.: Harvard University Press), 1956.

Kaysen, C. and Turner, D. F. *Antitrust Policy*, Series on Competition in American Industry, 7 (Cambridge, Mass.: Harvard University Press), 1959.

Laughlin, J. T. in discussion on 'Trade Regulation, Rules and Mergers', Bodner, J., Jr. (Chairman), *A.B.A. Antitrust Section, Proceedings* (q.v.), vol. 27, 1965, p. 115.

Letwin, W. L. 'Early History of the Sherman Act', paper read to University of Chicago Law School Antitrust Seminar, 1953.

'The English Common Law Concerning Monopolies', *University of Chicago Law Review*, vol. 21, no. 3, Spring 1954, p. 355.

'Congress and the Sherman Antitrust Law: 1887–1890', *University of Chicago Law Review*, vol. 23, no. 2, Winter 1956, p. 221.

Lilienthal, D. E. *Big Business: a New Era* (New York: Harper), 1953.

McAllister, B. P. 'Where the Effect May be to Substantially Lessen Competition or Tend to Create a Monopoly', *A.B.A. Antitrust Section, Proceedings* (q.v.), vol. 3, 1953, p. 124.

Markham, J. W. 'An Alternative Approach to the Concept of Workable Competition', *American Economic Review*, vol. 40, no. 3, June 1950, p. 349.

'Survey of the Evidence and Findings on Mergers' in *Business Concentration and Price Policy*, National Bureau of Economic Research, q.v.

'The Report of the Attorney General's Committee on Antitrust Laws', *Quarterly Journal of Economics*, vol. 70, no. 2, May 1956, p. 193.

Mason, E. S. 'Schumpeter on Monopoly and the Large Firm', *Review of Economics and Statistics*, vol. 33, no. 2, May 1951, p. 139.

Mason, E. S. and others. 'Various Views on the Monopoly Problem', *Review of Economics and Statistics*, vol. 31, no. 2, May 1949, p. 104.

Massel, M. S. *Competition and Monopoly* (Washington, D.C.: Brookings Institution), 1962.

Meyer, J. R. and Kuh, E. *The Investment Decision*, Harvard Economic Studies, 102 (Cambridge, Mass.: Harvard University Press), 1957.

Michigan University Law School. *Lectures on federal antitrust laws: 1953* (Ann Arbor: Michigan University Law School), 1953, *passim*.

National Bureau of Economic Research. *Business Concentration and Price Policy*, Special Conference Series, 5 (Princeton: University Press), 1955, *passim*.

New York State Bar Association. *Robinson-Patman Act Symposium for 1947* (Chicago: Commerce Clearing House), 1947, *passim*.

Nicholls, W. H. 'The Tobacco Case of 1946', *American Economic Review*, vol. 39, no. 3, May 1949, p. 284.

Nowell-Smith, P. H. *Ethics* (Harmondsworth, Middlesex: Penguin Books), 1954.

Oppenheim, S. C. 'Federal Antitrust Legislation: Guideposts to a Revised National Antitrust Policy', *Michigan Law Review*, vol. 50, 1952, p. 1139.

Rahl, J. A. 'The Demise of Vertical Price Fixing through Consignment Arrangements: the Simpson Case', *A.B.A. Antitrust Section, Proceedings* (q.v.), vol. 29, 1965, p. 216.

Robinson, Joan. 'The Impossibility of Competition' in *Monopoly and Competition and their Regulation*, Chamberlin, E. H. (ed.), q.v.

Schumpeter, J. A. *Capitalism, Socialism and Democracy*, 3rd ed. (London: Allen and Unwin), 1950.

Stigler, G. J. 'The Extent and Bases of Monopoly', *American Economic Review*, vol. 32, no. 2, part 2, June 1942, p. 1.

In 'Report on Antitrust Policy—Discussion', *American Economic Review*, vol. 46, no. 2, May 1956, p. 504.

Stocking, G. W. and Watkins, M. W. *Monopoly and Free Enterprise* (New York: Twentieth Century Fund), 1951.

Thorelli, H. B. *The Federal Antitrust Policy* (Stockholm: Norstedt; London: Allen and Unwin), 1954.

Timberg, S. 'Antitrust Aspects of Merchandising Modern Music: the ASCAP Judgment of 1950', *Law and Contemporary Problems*, Spring 1954 (Duke University School of Law).

'Extraterritorial Jurisdiction under the Sherman Act', *The Record of the Association of the Bar of the City of New York*, vol. 11, no. 3, March 1956.

'Territorial Exclusives', *A.B.A. Antitrust Section, Proceedings* (q.v.), vol. 29, 1965, p. 233.

Toulmin, S. E. *The Uses of Argument* (Cambridge: University Press), 1958.

Turner, D. F. 'The Validity of Tying Arrangements under the Antitrust Laws', *Harvard Law Review*, vol. 72, 1958, p. 50.

'Conglomerate Mergers and Section 7 of the Clayton Act', *Harvard Law Review*, vol. 78, 1965, p. 1313.

Whitney, S. N. *Antitrust Policies* (New York: Twentieth Century Fund), 1958.

Whitney, W. D. 'Sources of Conflict between International Law and the Antitrust Laws', *Yale Law Journal*, vol. 63, 1954, p. 655.

Wood, L. I. 'The Tangle of Mercoid Case Implications', *George Washington Law Review*, vol. 13, 1944.

'Recent Antitrust Developments Affecting Patents' in *Lectures on federal antitrust laws: 1953*, Michigan University Law School, q.v.

Wooden, W. In 'Comments and Discussion' in *Robinson-Patman Act Symposium for 1947*, New York State Bar Association (q.v.), p. 53.

Wright, R. L. 'Conspiracy and Conspire— What do these Words Mean in Sherman Act Decisions?' paper read to University of Chicago Law School Antitrust Seminar, 1953.

2. OFFICIAL PUBLICATIONS

(a) United States of America

Department of Commerce. *Effective Competition*, report by the Business Advisory Council (Washington, D.C.: U.S. Government Printing Office), 1953.

Federal Trade Commission. *Statement of Federal Trade Commission Policy towards Geographic Pricing Practices for Staff Information and Guidance*, issued 12 October 1948.

Report on the Concentration of Productive Facilities, 1947 (Washington, D.C.: U.S. Government Printing Office), 1949.

Department of Justice. *Report of the Attorney General's National Committee to Study the Antitrust Laws* (Washington, D.C.: U.S. Government Printing Office), 1955.

91st Congress, 1st Session. *Congressional Record* (Washington, D.C.: U.S. Government Printing Office), 1969.

Senate Committe on Judiciary, Sub-Committee on Antitrust and Monopoly. *Bigness and Concentration of Economic Power: a Case-Study of the General Motors Corporation* (Washington, D.C.: U.S. Government Printing Office), 1956.

Senate Committee on Military Affairs, Sub-Committee on War Mobilization. *Economic and Political Aspects of International Cartels* (Washington, D.C.: U.S. Government Printing Office), 1944.

Temporary National Economic Committee. Monograph 16, *Antitrust in Action* by Walton Hamilton and Irene Till (Washington, D.C.: U.S. Government Printing Office), 1941.

Monograph 21, *Competition and Monopoly in American Industry* by Clair Wilcox (Washington, D.C.: U.S. Government Printing Office), 1941.

Monograph 38, *A Study of the Construction and Enforcement of the Federal Antitrust Laws* by M. Handler (Washington, D.C.: U.S. Government Printing Office), 1941.

(b) United Kingdom

Monopolies and Restrictive Practices Commission. *Report on the Supply of Cast Iron Rainwater Goods* (London: H.M. Stationery Office), 1951.

Ministry of Works. *Report of the Committee on Cement Costs.* (London: H.M. Stationery Office), 1947.

(c) United Nations

Economic and Social Council, Official Records, 16th Session, Supplement 11 A. *Restrictive Business Practices: Analysis of Governmental Measures Relating to Restrictive Business Practices* (New York: United Nations), 1953.

INDEX OF CASES

Introductory Note

A word about sources may be useful to introduce this index. The fullest record of American cases is, of course, to be found in the official or national law reports, and the practising lawyer or law student will have these reports available. As this book is not designed primarily for professional lawyers, it has not been thought necessary to give the official or national reporter citations for the cases. Armed with the name of the case, the court and the date from the index below (as well as the secondary sources given below), the serious student will in any case have no great difficulty in tracing the citations.

The reader who simply wishes to study the court opinions quoted in this book in more detail will probably find the secondary sources more convenient. For a general conspectus of the subject and a convenient source of the older cases, he will want a good legal textbook. There are several excellent ones; the latest editions of those most used in the writing and updating of this book being:

> S. C. Oppenheim, *Federal Antitrust Laws*, American Casebook Series (West Publishing Co., St Paul, Minn., 1968);[1] M. Handler, *Cases and other Materials on Trade Regulation*, University Casebook Series (Foundation Press, New York, 1967); Fox & Fox, *Corporate Acquisition and Mergers* (Matthew Bender, New York, 1968).

Those who compile textbooks suffer, as has the present author, from the impossibility of being completely up-to-date. The indispensable source for the recent cases is the series of volumes of *Trade Cases*, published annually by the Commerce Clearing House, Chicago, and the means of keeping up-to-date is to consult these volumes and the same company's current *Trade Regulation Reporter*.

In addition many commentaries give lavish citations of cases. Perhaps the most useful is *The Report of the Attorney General's National Committee to Study the Antitrust Laws* (Washington, 1955), and a supplement to the Report, *Antitrust Developments, 1955–1968*, prepared by the Antitrust Section of the American Bar Association. It may be helpful to mention also the annual *Symposia* of the Section on Antitrust Law of the New York State Bar Association published by the Commerce Clearing House, and in particular the volume entitled *How to Comply with the Antitrust Laws* (Commerce Clearing House, Chicago, 1954) which incorporates the Symposium for 1954.

In the index which follows, cases in which the United States or the Federal Trade Commision was the plaintiff are listed only under the name of the other party.

Abbreviations

Cir.	Circuit Court of Appeals (preceded by figure indicating the circuit concerned or D.C. for District of Columbia)
D.	Federal District Court (followed by the abbreviation for the State concerned)
F.T.C.	Federal Trade Commission
S.C.	Supreme Court
U.K.	United Kingdom Courts

[1] Oppenheim has written a companion volume, *Unfair Trading Practices*, which deals, among other things, with the cases on resale price maintenance and price discrimination. (American Casebook Series, West Publishing Company, St Paul, Minn., 1965).

Page numbers in **bold** type indicate the main discussion of the cases

INDEX

References to companies involved in antitrust litigation are indexed here under the relevant industries. The names of the companies will be found in the Index of Cases on pp. 512–20.

Adams, Professor Walter, 456 n., 457
Adelman, Professor Morris, 136 n.
advertising
  earnings from, 128–30
  price cutting as a form of, 273, 280
advertising allowances, 260–1, 394
advertising expenditure, 193
agriculture (including marketing), 7, 21–2, 35 n., 43, 79 n., 94–5, 127–8, 182 n., 200, 204, 228 n., 232–3, 235–7, 241, 261–2, 356, 364
airlines, *see* shipping
Alabama, fair trade laws, 291
Alaska, fair trade laws, 291
aluminium industry, 100, 105–12, 120–1, 123, 146 n., 187–8, 362 n., 363, 409–13, 441, 443
Antitrust Civil Process Act (1962), 376, 378
Arnold, Thurman, 17
Attorney General's National Committee to Study the Antitrust Laws, 8 n., 241, 374 n., 380 ff., 428, 431, 436, 458 ff.
  Report of, 5 n., 7 n., 27 n., 157 n., 228 n., 381 n., 429, 444 n., 457, 471 n.
Automobile Dealers' Franchise Act (1956), 219
automobile industry (including parts), 64 n., 73–4, 144–7, 156–9, 171–3, 177, 218, 221, 246–7, 256–8, 290, 295–6, 334–6, 398, 414–15, 446 n., 449, 450, 459
see also rubber, tyres

Bain, Professor J. S., 487–9
Bank Mergers Act (1960), 142
banking, insurance and investment, 7–8, 142–3, 185–7, 196, 201, 384, 458
basing-point pricing, 51 ff., 263–6, 268, 311
Belgium, reaction to antitrust subpoenas, 366
'better mousetrap', 92, 99, 102, 106, 116, 119, 123, 322–3, 447–8
'big business', 124, 411, 428, 430–1, 443, 447 n., 449, 454
bituminous coal legislation, 38 n., 473 n.
  see also mining and minerals
Black, Justice Hugo L., 61–2, 72–3, 188–9, 214, 221, 230–2, 234, 268, 416
block booking, 168, 214–15, 337 n., 405
Bok, Dean D.C., 190 n., 209–11

bottleneck facilities, 66–70, 433, 438 n.
  and patents, 315
bottleneck monopolies, 127–31
Bowman, Ward, Jr., 446 n.
boycotts, 5–6, 131–3, 136
  collective, 28, 70–5, 275 n., 297, 319–21, 433, 434
Brandeis, Justice Louis D., 21–2, 42–3, 48, 213, 276, 315–16, 329, 389
Brennan, Justice William J., 223, 335, 415
brewing, *see* distilling
Brewster, Professor Kingman, 342 n., 431, 435 n., 444–5
brokerage, 134–5, 137, 259–60
Brown, H. Templeton, 121 n.
Brownell, Attorney General, 457–8
Bryan, Judge, 201–2
Buck, Solon J., 12 n.
building materials
  abrasives, 344–5, 361
  cement and concrete blocks, 43 n., 54 n., 61–2, 247–8, 357, 268–9, 319
  gypsum products and hardboard, 308–13, 417–18
  roofing materials, 252–3, 329 n., 390
  see also glassware, pottery and tiles; lumber industry
Burton, Justice Harold H., 112, 163–6, 239, 249, 305 n., 315, 417
Business Review Procedure, 382–3

California, Fair Trade Act, 283–5
Canada, affected by antitrust, 365, 372, 410–12
Cannella, Judge, 192
Capper-Volstead Act (1922), 7
Carlston, Professor Kenneth, 404
cartels
  German, 374–5, 492
  international, 9, 76–7, 107, 315, 343 ff.
'cease and desist' orders, 4, 182, 242, 255, 270, 388–9, 391, 464
Celler-Kefauver Act (1950), 3, 142, 182, 190, 457
Chamberlin, Professor E. H., 475 n., 480 n., 482, 483 n.
Chase, Judge, 360 n.
chemical industry, 183 n., 192, 198–9, 202,

[521]

PUBLICATIONS OF THE
NATIONAL INSTITUTE OF ECONOMIC
AND SOCIAL RESEARCH

published by

THE CAMBRIDGE UNIVERSITY PRESS

Books published for the Institute by the Cambridge University Press are available through the ordinary booksellers. They appear in the four series below.

ECONOMIC & SOCIAL STUDIES

*I *Studies in the National Income, 1924–1938*
Edited by A. L. BOWLEY. Reprinted with corrections, 1944. pp. 256. 15s. net.

*II *The Burden of British Taxation*
By G. FINDLAY SHIRRAS and L. ROSTAS. 1942. pp. 140. 17s. 6d. net.

*III *Trade Regulations and Commercial Policy of the United Kingdom*
By THE RESEARCH STAFF OF THE NATIONAL INSTITUTE OF ECONOMIC AND SOCIAL RESEARCH. 1943. pp. 275. 17s. 6d. net.

*IV *National Health Insurance: A Critical Study*
By HERMANN LEVY. 1944. pp. 356. 21s. net.

*V *The Development of the Soviet Economic System: An Essay on the Experience of Planning in the U.S.S.R.*
By ALEXANDER BAYKOV. 1946. pp. 530. 45s. net.

*VI *Studies in Financial Organization*
By T. BALOGH. 1948. pp. 328. 40s. net.

*VII *Investment, Location, and Size of Plant: A Realistic Inquiry into the Structure of British and American Industries*
By P. SARGANT FLORENCE, assisted by W. BALDAMUS. 1948. pp. 230. 21s. net.

VIII *A Statistical Analysis of Advertising Expenditure and of the Revenue of the Press*
By NICHOLAS KALDOR and RODNEY SILVERMAN. 1948. pp. 200. 25s. net.

*IX *The Distribution of Consumer Goods*
By JAMES B. JEFFERYS, assisted by MARGARET MACCOLL and G. L. LEVETT 1950. pp. 430. 50s. net.

*X *Lessons of the British War Economy*
Edited by D. N. CHESTER. 1951. pp. 260. 30s. net.

*XI *Colonial Social Accounting*
By PHYLLIS DEANE. 1953. pp. 360. 60s. net.

*XII *Migration and Economic Growth*
By BRINLEY THOMAS. 1954. pp. 384. 50s. net.

*XIII *Retail Trading in Britain, 1850–1950*
By JAMES B. JEFFERYS. 1954. pp. 490. 60s. net.

*XIV *British Economic Statistics*
By CHARLES CARTER and A. D. ROY. 1954. pp. 192. 30s. net.

XV *The Structure of British Industry: A Symposium*
Edited by DUNCAN BURN. 1958. Vol. I. pp. 403. 55s. net. Vol. II. pp. 499. 63s. net.

*XVI *Concentration in British Industry*
By RICHARD EVELY and I. M. D. LITTLE. 1960. pp. 357. 63s. net.

*XVII *Studies in Company Finance*
Edited by BRIAN TEW and R. F. HENDERSON. 1959. pp. 301. 40s. net.

XVIII *British Industrialists: Steel and Hosiery, 1850–1950*
By CHARLOTTE ERICKSON. 1959. pp. 276. 45s. net.

XIX *The Antitrust Laws of the U.S.A.: A Study of Competition Enforced by Law*
By A. D. NEALE. 1st ed. 1960. pp. 516. 55s. net.

XX *A Study of United Kingdom Imports*
By M. FG. SCOTT. 1963. pp. 270. 60s. net.

* At present out of print.

OCCASIONAL PAPERS

* At present out of print.

STUDIES IN THE NATIONAL INCOME AND EXPENDITURE OF THE UNITED KINGDOM

Published under the joint auspices of the National Institute and the Department of Applied Economics, Cambridge.

NIESR STUDENTS' EDITION

THE NATIONAL INSTITUTE OF ECONOMIC AND SOCIAL RESEARCH

publishes regularly

THE NATIONAL INSTITUTE ECONOMIC REVIEW

A quarterly Review of the economic situation and prospects.
Annual subscription £3. 10s.; single issues £1. each.
The Review is available directly from N.I.E.S.R.
2 Dean Trench St., Smith Square, London S.W. 1

The Institute has also published

Factory Location and Industrial Movement
By W. F. LUTTRELL. 1962. Vols. I and II. pp. 1080. £5. 5s. net.
The IVth French Plan
By FRANCOIS PERROUX, translated by BRUNO LEBLANC. 1965. pp. 72. 10s. net.

These too are available directly from the Institute.